The Psychoanalytic Study of the Child

VOLUME FORTY

The
Psychoanalytic
Study
of the Child

VOLUME FORTY

New Haven
Yale University Press
1985

Designed by Sally Harris
and set in Baskerville type.
Printed in the United States of America by
Vail-Ballou Press, Inc., Binghamton, N.Y.

Library of Congress catalog card number: 45–11304
International standard book number: 0–300–03503–9
10   9   8   7   6   5   4   3   2   1

Contents

APPLIED ANALYSIS

In Memoriam
Muriel M. Gardiner, M.D.
(1901-85)

SAMUEL A. GUTTMAN, M.D.

MURIEL MORRIS GARDINER (MRS. JOSEPH BUTTINGER) WAS BORN IN Chicago on November 23, 1901. She died of cancer in Princeton, New Jersey, on February 6, 1985. Dr. Gardiner was a selfless, most devoted person who had a rigorous conscience and a rare intellect. At least from adolescence she fought for ideals as they relate to the helpless, the weak, the disenfranchised, and the oppressed. Always well traveled, exquisitely educated, and with it all possessing a sense of humor, she had no pretense and a humility.

Actually Muriel Gardiner wanted to be a teacher. She attended Wellesley from which she graduated in June, 1922. She recalled that before the national election in 1912, when she was not yet 11 years old, she led a quite serious parade of schoolchildren for women's suffrage. At the very proper Faulkner School for girls, she was active on the debating team, editor of the yearbook, class president, and captain of the basketball team. Her family did not mind her debating, but they probably did not know of her socialist leanings. At Wellesley this interest continued—it was really a socialist attitude similar to that of the

Formerly Professor of Psychiatry and Human Behavior (Psychoanalysis), Jefferson Medical College of Thomas Jefferson University, Philadelphia, Pennsylvania (currently Honorary). Training and Supervising Analyst, Institute of the Philadelphia Association for Psychoanalysis. Director, Center for Advanced Psychoanalytic Studies (CAPS), Princeton, New Jersey, and Psychoanalytic Studies at Aspen (PSA), Aspen, Colorado.

1

Social Democrats of Austria—although Muriel Gardiner at that time was not able to label her political convictions. In her last two years at Wellesley she was a Durant scholar. This was the highest academic honor awarded to Wellesley students. In her senior year she was head of the Wellesley Student Forum. As speakers there were Norman Thomas, Roger Baldwin, Harry Laidler, Scott Nearing, and others. With several girls from Wellesley and Radcliffe and several Harvard undergraduates and law students, she helped to found and was the first president of a student organization called "The Intercollegiate Liberal League." Then, because the word "liberal" in England was applied to a party, the name was changed to "The National Student Forum." This was perhaps the first intercollegiate liberal organization in America.

Muriel Gardiner lived in Europe most of the time from 1922 until after the beginning of World War II. She spent a year in Italy and then went on to Oxford for graduate work and a study of Mary Shelley. In defending her thesis before two Oxford dons who were clergymen and one woman don, she was examined more on ethical, moral, and religious questions than on anything that had to do with scholarship or literature. Although part of this thesis was accepted by the prestigious literary journal *The London Mercury,* the dons did not accept the thesis and said there was no sense in further editing or submitting it again. This was Muriel Gardiner's only "failure" in a very distinguished academic career. In the oral examinations she did not condemn suicide or Shelley's having been married and then falling in love with another woman, and still wanting to be friends with his wife, in fact, still loving her. One remark Muriel Gardiner recalls was probably held very much against her. She said that scholars writing about Shelley found it hard to understand this attitude of his, but that it seemed to her that people living in a polygamous society can understand it easily. This did not go over at all well with the dons at Oxford in 1925. At this time Muriel Gardiner made an unhappy marriage and then went to Vienna for personal psychoanalysis. Freud referred her to Ruth Mack Brunswick, and over the course of some years there were two periods of psychoanalysis. She married again, and in 1931 a daughter, Constance, was born. Then Muriel Gardiner decided to become a psychoanalyst, though never for the sole purpose of doing psychoanalytic treatment but rather to apply psychoanalytic understanding to education and educators. However, she was convinced that this could be done only after she had a full psychoanalytic educational experience and a rich clinical background. Her convictions were such that she went on to medical school in Vienna and graduated in 1938. Her sister Ruth had already graduated from Cornell University Medical School. It was Muriel Gardiner's original intention to come back to the States and continue her medical education. She had been uninvolved politically for some years and was to leave Vienna in the summer of 1934. However, during this time she saw the Fascists beat down and kill Social Democrats in Vienna—yes, literally kill with machine guns stationed on street corners. She became most involved and decided to remain in Vienna. She could not get her apartment back, but, in spite of the housing shortage in Vienna at that time, she managed to get something for herself, her daughter, and Gerda, a young teacher and governess for Constance. She attended psychoanalytic seminars in Vienna and was fortunate enough to have preceptorial work with Robert Waelder for a couple of hours twice a week from 1931 to 1933. Also, she attended seminars conducted by Aichhorn and Bernfeld during this time. Some of her classmates included Edith Jackson, Edith Entenman, and Helen Ross.

Dr. Gardiner has always made available a very considerable portion of her annual income to literally hundreds of people and a large number of organizations. Always, this was done after deliberation, with great humility, and very often anonymously. Since the age of 11, Dr. Gardiner has had to contend with a special problem of how to spend with wisdom and judgment income from her inheritance from her father, which, in particular because of the acumen of her brothers Nelson and Edward, appreciated considerably. What Dr. Gardiner has done was to use her "business sense" most wisely in order to benefit many people and educational and humanitarian organizations. A strict conscience such as hers is a relentless life companion, but I know that Muriel Gardiner has over the years enjoyed, of course silently, the obvious achievements of many persons and organizations. The beauty is that most beneficiaries, unaware of her actions, cannot feel beholden in any way. This is the quintessence of a charitable character.

World War II disrupted Europe. The Buttingers could no longer remain there, so with Connie they reestablished themselves in Pennington, had an apartment in Manhattan, and must have often thought of the little weekend house in that very special place in the Wienerwald near Sulz. (This survived the Nazis and Russians.) Muriel Gardiner pursued her professional goal, which necessitated a rotating internship and a residency in psychiatry. She associated herself with the Philadelphia Association for Psychoanalysis and its Institute, and there she furthered her clinical experiences in psychoanalysis. After about six years of an active psychoanalytic practice, she accepted no new patients but continued with those she had for another few years. She taught for a brief period at the Institute of the Philadelphia Association for Psychoanalysis, and then at the Trenton State Hospital. Dr. Gardiner was an Adjunct Professor in the School of Social Work at Rutgers University from 1955 to 1959. From 1957 to 1962 she was Chief Psychiatric Consultant to the public schools of Bucks County, Pennsylvania. And from 1960 to 1971 she was Chief Psychiatric Consultant to the New Jersey State Department of Education, Office of Special Education. Muriel Gardiner was appointed a training and supervising analyst for the Institute of the Philadelphia Association for Psychoanalysis in 1955, but she never accepted any candidates. In the 1960s she was busily engaged in consultation work with educators. She had an excellent working relationship with school guidance personnel, teachers, and superintendents, as well as children and parents. This work she loved, but she had to retire from it at the age of 70.

Muriel Gardiner for some years was a most valuable member of the editorial board of the *Bulletin of the Philadelphia Association for Psychoanalysis*. For 10 years we worked together on this venture. After much encouragement, she agreed that the Wolf-Man papers be translated and published. Eventually they were published as a book. I have never had an opportunity to express publicly my indebtedness to her for her always being most forthright, completely dependable, and sensible. Nearly all of Muriel Gardiner's psychoanalytic papers appeared in the *Bulletin of the Philadelphia Association*. Perhaps, in a measure, out of a sense of loyalty, she submitted these to our small publication instead of first, at least, submitting them to the better established, more prestigious journals. The *Bulletin of the Philadelphia Association* contains seventeen of her papers.

The Wolf-Man was published in 1971. This was a very successful publication, with the royalties going to the Wolf-Man. For the first time since he lost his fortune—now over 50 years ago—he was free of financial worries with enough money for the remainder of his days.

She wrote the introduction to *Art as Therapy with Children,* by Edith Kramer, published in 1971. This is a very valuable and unusual book. In 1976 *The Deadly Innocents* was published. These portraits of children who kill is a remarkable document. When she finished that book, she told me that if she were 20 years younger, she would obtain a full-time job in some prison and work there so she could study the prisoners and see what could be done.

In 1983 *Code Name "Mary"* appeared. Here we read about a most remarkable woman of greatest conviction and courage— probably the model for Lillian Hellman's story of "Julia."

Muriel Gardiner's contributions were primarily in the area of application of psychoanalytic understanding to children in school, their parents, and teachers. She taught educators, social workers, psychologists, and psychiatrists. She wanted to teach, loved to teach, and was a very effective teacher. Five-day-a-week psychoanalysis as a treatment method seemed less to her interests and liking. Perhaps she felt too confined and constricted in this atmosphere. However, she was an enthusiastic and very knowledgeable supporter of those who elected to engage in this arduous task.

Muriel Gardiner gave much of herself in all ways to very many individuals. She also donated funds, often anonymously, to various causes. Much funding went through the New-Land Foundation which she founded. She was a most generous supporter of the Hampstead Clinic, The Sigmund Freud Archives, and the Center for Advanced Psychoanalytic Studies (CAPS) in Princeton, and Psychoanalytic Studies at Aspen (PSA). Here she was mainly concerned with extending and deepening psychoanalytic understanding. Shortly before her death she was occupied with the creation of The Freud Museum in London, and very recently donated Brookdale Farm in Pennington to The Stonybrook-Millstone Watershed Association.

Some of Muriel Gardiner's organizational interests included

the International Rescue Committee, YM-YWHA of Greater New York, the Democratic Socialists of America, and many others. She was a Life Member of the Philadelphia Association for Psychoanalysis, The American and International Psychoanalytic Associations, and an Honorary Trustee of The Center for Advanced Psychoanalytic Studies (CAPS) Princeton, and Psychoanalytic Studies at Aspen (PSA).

Muriel Gardiner's husband, Joseph, is not able to comprehend her death, but she will be sorely missed by her only daughter, Constance, her son-in-law, Harold Harvey, her sister, Dr. Ruth Bakwin, her grandchildren, Joan, Ann, Joseph and his wife Kelly, Hal, Mark and Muriel Harvey, and her very many friends.

BIBLIOGRAPHY

GARDINER, M. (1952). Squirrels' dreams. *Bull. Phila. Assn. Psychoanal.*, 2:16.
———— (1952). Meetings with the Wolf-Man. *Bull. Phila. Assn. Psychoanal.*, 2:36–44.
———— (1953). The "Life Self" and the "Death Self." *Bull. Phila. Assn. Psychoanal.*, 3:82–84.
———— (1953). A letter from the Wolf-Man. *Bull. Phila. Assn. Psychoanal.*, 3:79–80.
———— (1953). Meetings with the Wolf-Man. *Bull. Menninger Clin.*, 10:38–46.
———— (1954). A fleeting phobia in a girl of three. *Bull. Phila. Assn. Psychoanal.*, 4:30–31.
———— (1954). "Make good the damage done." *Bull. Phila. Assn. Psychoanal.*, 4:17–18.
———— (1955). Feminine masochism and passivity. *Bull. Phila. Assn. Psychoanal.*, 5:74–79.
———— (1958). Introduction to "How I came into analysis with Freud" by the Wolf-Man. *J. Amer. Psychoanal. Assn.*, 6:348.
———— (1960). A note on accreditation. *Bull. Phila. Assn. Psychoanal.*, 10:56–58.
———— (1961). Introduction to memoirs of the Wolf-Man, 1914-1919. *Bull. Phila. Assn. Psychoanal.*, 11:1–5.
————, Ed. (1961). Memoirs, 1914-1919. *Bull. Phila. Assn. Psychoanal.*, 11:6–31.
———— (1962). The seven years of dearth. *Bull. Phila. Assn. Psychoanal.*, 12:168–170.
———— (1963). A snowfall memory. *Bull. Phila. Assn. Psychoanal.*, 13:28–31.
———— (1964). Introduction to memoirs of the Wolf-Man, 1905-1908. *Bull. Phila. Assn. Psychoanal.*, 14:77–79.

_____ (1967). Introduction to memoirs of the Wolf-Man, 1908, Part 1. *Bull. Phila. Assn. Psychoanal.*, 17:185.

_____ (1967). Discussion of A. J. Lubin, "The influence of the Russian Orthodox Church on Freud's Wolf-Man." *Psychoanal. Forum*, 2:163–65.

_____ (1970). Introduction to memoirs of the Wolf-Man, 1938. *Bull. Phila. Assn. Psychoanal.*, 20:87–104.

_____, Ed. (1971). *The Wolf-Man.* New York: Basic Books.

_____ (1972). Feminine masochism and passivity. *Bull. Phila. Assn. Psychoanal.*, 22:131–138.

_____ (1972). A contribution to the psychology of femininity. *Bull. Phila. Assn. Psychoanal.*, 22:139–142.

_____ (1976). *The Deadly Innocents.* New York: Basic Books.

_____ (1983). *Code Name "Mary."* New Haven & London: Yale Univ. Press.

_____ (1983). The Wolf-Man's last years. *J. Amer. Psychoanal. Assn.*, 31:867–97.

_____ (1985). *The Deadly Innocents.* New Haven & London: Yale Univ. Press.

DEVELOPMENT

Internalization and Psychological Development Throughout the Life Cycle

REBECCA SMITH BEHRENDS, Ph.D. AND
SIDNEY J. BLATT, Ph.D.

ALTHOUGH THE CONCEPT OF INTERNALIZATION IS FUNDAMENTAL
to theories of child development, cognitive development, and
therapeutic action, the term itself has been used to cover multiple, and oftentimes contradictory, meanings and processes.
Theorists refer to internalization as though its meaning were
universally shared and agreed upon. In point of fact, however,
internalization has no single, precise definition.

Both the lack of a clear definition and the multiple uses of the
term are, in part, a function of the fact that the underlying
mechanisms of the internalization process have never been
clearly specified. Historically, incorporation, introjection, and
identification have been considered mechanisms of internalization. These terms, however, were actually derived from earlier

Rebecca Behrends is Chief Psychologist, Yale Psychiatric Institute; Assistant
Professor of Psychology in the Department of Psychiatry, Yale University
School of Medicine, New Haven, Ct.; research candidate, Western New England Institute for Psychoanalysis; Sidney J. Blatt is Professor of Psychology in
the Departments of Psychiatry and Psychology at Yale University; and Chief of
the Psychology Section in Psychiatry, Yale University School of Medicine; faculty, Western New England Institute for Psychoanalysis.
The authors wish to thank Drs. Hans Loewald, Charles Gardner, and Ira
Levine for their constructive comments on an earlier draft of this paper.

periods in the history of Freud's development of psychoanalytic theory, and he himself tended to use them synonymously at times. Subsequently, there have been numerous attempts to separate out these modes of internalization and to define them clearly. No single position has ever been generally accepted, however, and the result has only been even greater complexity and confusion. The existing literature on internalization is replete with instances of different terms referring to the same process, the same term referring to altogether different processes, and various combinations of them being employed interchangeably (see, for example, Meissner, 1981, for a review of this literature). At present, the usage of any of these concepts tends to be idiosyncratic and arbitrary, depending upon the preference of a given author.

Still another problem, historically, has been the tendency to equate internalization with symbol formation (Klein, 1950), in which case the concept would be inapplicable as an explanatory construct for psychological development in the presymbolic infant. Although Schafer (1968) originally made important contributions in clarifying the concept of internalization, he has since gone so far as to propose that we abandon it altogether, because of its misleading spatial connotations and the danger of anthropomorphizing and reifying dynamic processes (Schafer, 1972).

This paper is an attempt to clarify some of the theoretical complexities which now encumber our understanding of the internalization process. It is possible to define internalization in a way that neither equates it with symbol formation, nor confuses it with spatial connotations, reification, and anthropomorphism. The importance of establishing such theoretical clarity derives from our view that internalization is the primary vehicle whereby psychological growth is accomplished. Throughout the life cycle, psychological development occurs through progressive internalizations of aspects of relationships with significant others.

Our formulations of internalization are guided by a single fundamental assumption: The mechanisms which instigate growth at one level of personality functioning are precisely those which insure it at any other level—from birth through senescence, even though individuals grow in their complexity and change with regard to their social-psychological context. By examining the mother-infant matrix, we attempt to identify the essential dimensions of the internalization process in normative development. We then seek to demonstrate the manner in which these same basic dimensions serve as the mechanisms for psychological growth, at all developmental levels.

EARLY PSYCHOLOGICAL DEVELOPMENT

In contrast to most other mammals, which are born both neurologically mature and with sufficiently developed muscular coordination to ensure fairly rapid adjustment to life outside the womb, human infants are biologically unprepared to sustain life on their own. If life is to be maintained, infants need a mothering person throughout their prolonged period of absolute dependence.

This dependency of infants in no way implies that they are merely passive recipients of the mother's ministrations. All available evidence indicates that the neonate is a highly organized entity, with perceptual and memory systems intact, with learning and communicating faculties available, and thus with interpersonal capabilities operative shortly after birth (e.g., Wolff, 1959; Fantz, 1961; Caplan, 1973; Sander, 1977; Beebe and Stern, 1977). For example, DeCasper (1979) demonstrated that infants 24 to 36 hours old could repeat a pattern associated with the sound of the mother's voice, which they were able to distinguish from the voices of other people.

Additional evidence indicates that despite the general immaturity of the infant's musculo-skeletal system, the mimetic musculature of the face is highly developed. These facial muscles, under the control of the involuntary nervous system, enable newborns to signal whether or not they are optimally stimulated (Tomkins, 1963). Reviewing these findings, Basch (1975) concluded that the success of the mother-infant relationship is due not only to the mother's activity, but also to this ability in the newborn to form a system of communication with the mother, enabling her to discern the infant's needs.

The needs of the infant include not only the gratification of basic physiological needs for food, water, warmth, etc., but also the equally crucial need for an optimal level of stimulation which can be provided only through the relationship with a mothering person. For example, as demonstrated by Spitz (1946), Provence and Lipton (1962), and others, infants in orphanages whose basic physical needs were well met, but who did not have the benefit of a loving mother's caressing and heartbeat, cooing, singing, and talking simply failed to thrive. Unless the stimulation was provided in sufficient time to avert their decline, these infants grew increasingly irritable, withdrawn, and apathetic, with motor retardation and facial expressions bearing close resemblance to depressed adults (see also Engel and Reichsmann, 1956). These findings suggest that the human infant's needs go beyond a simple basic organismic need for homeostasis or satiety. Far from being satisfied with passive quiescence, during periods of wakefulness, the infant continuously and actively seeks interaction with the environment and with people in it.

The research findings which indicate that the newborn is capable of complex functioning have led many theorists to reject traditional concepts such as an "objectless period" or an "undifferentiated phase" in infancy (e.g., Peterfreund, 1978; Pine, 1981). It is important to note, however, that the evidence obtained thus far points only to differentiation in the *biological* sense of the term—"differentiation" that refers to specificity and complexity of particular functions and actions of the organism. The evidence does not pertain to *psychological* differentiation, that is, the infant's capacity to conceptualize self and object as separable entities.

The communicative signals which the infant conveys through various facial expressions attest only to the specificity of the facial musculature in response to the infant's *physiological* condition. The presymbolic infant is not yet capable of conceptualizing affective states until the onset of symbolic functioning (Church, 1961; Vygotsky, 1962; Piaget and Inhelder, 1969; Gaensbauer, 1982). Consequently, infants' early communications with their mothers are of a particular kind, corresponding to the ability to evidence nonreflective, involuntary responses to stimulation or lack of it. The infant's activity, alertness, and responsiveness should not be confused with psychological awareness. For example, the evidence regarding the infant's ability to discriminate the mother's voice from the voices of others should not be taken to indicate that the infant has a concept of "mother" or even of an "other" person.

These formulations are consistent with the ethological findings of Lorenz (1937), Tinbergen (1951), and others, which indicate that certain species-specific, instinctual capabilities are pre-programmed and inherent in the basic equipment of the organism. From this standpoint, the complex behaviors found shortly after birth can be understood as highly specific, inborn characteristics, inherent in the biological equipment of the human species. They offer no more evidence of psychological awareness or self-object differentiation than reflexive responses such as eye blinking, startle reactions, or the imprinting behaviors observed in other species.

In classical psychoanalytic terms, it may still be assumed that, in early infancy, neither id nor ego has emerged, nor can distinctions between conscious and unconscious be made. The newborn is as yet incapable of making symbolically meaningful discriminations among things in the environment, or between self and environment. Consequently, the primary psychological task of infancy is separation-individuation—the emergence of self and object differentiation which becomes increasingly organized within the mother-infant matrix.

A comprehensive understanding of psychological development within the mother-infant matrix also requires an examination of the mother's role in the process. In order to determine the appropriate kind and intensity of caretaking required, it is necessary for the mother to attune herself to her infant's signals. Winnicott (1960) eloquently portrayed the essence of the maternal function when he described the mother as feeling herself into her infant's place in order to meet the infant's needs. An essential aspect of this task is the mother's ability to invest the infant symbolically with her own needs and interests. The infant's signals in the form of crying, cooing, grimacing, or smiling arouse the mother's empathic identification, enabling her to attribute to the infant the distress, pleasure, discomfort, or delight she would be feeling if she herself were to act in these ways (Basch, 1975). This system which mother and infant together form and maintain can accurately be characterized in terms of a "dual unity" (Benedek, 1938; Mahler, 1968), given that the infant has not yet developed boundaries which differentiate self and other, and the mother must temporarily blur her own boundaries in order to intuit her infant's needs.

Such an appreciation of the origins of psychological life leads both Mahler (1963) and Winnicott (1953) to conclude that the good-enough mother-infant relationship is essential to subsequent psychological growth and development. We propose that the establishment of this mother-infant unity represents the first developmental prerequisite for internalization and that it in fact contains in rudimentary form the essential operative components for all subsequent internalizations throughout the life cycle.

If the initial phase of the internalization process is the formation of the mother-infant unity, the next developmental step can only be some disruption of that near-perfect union. As Mahler (1963) observed, with increasing maturation, it is simply less possible to comfort and hold the larger, more active, alert infant than to cradle the newborn. In addition, she hypothesized that the normal human infant is endowed with an "innate given," which prompts separation from the mother, thus furthering individuation. With the advent of locomotion, no mother, however attentive, can fully keep pace with a normally energetic toddler. Furthermore, the mother herself actively begins to foster the child's separation, due to her own growing sense that the previous level of total involvement is no longer warranted or desirable for either of them. With these considerations in mind, Mahler concludes that separation from the good-enough mother entails inevitable, progressive minute losses of the original mother-infant relationship.

We would argue that disruptions of the mother-infant relationship not only are *inevitable,* they are *required* as a necessary precondition for all psychological development. We propose that the second developmental prerequisite for internalization in infancy, following the establishment of the mother-infant unity, is the disruption of that relationship in its original form. Provided that such disruptions are not too great and do not exceed the adaptive capacity of the child, the normal child is innately endowed with the ability to manage the minute losses of the mother-infant relationship through the process of internalization. Consistent with this view, Loewald (1962) describes identification as a process "whereby the child reaches out to take back from the environment what has been removed from him in an ever-increasing degree since his birth" (p. 496). In a similar vein, Tolpin (1971) specifically links each step in the separation-individuation process to internalization: "When a 'tolerable' phase-appropriate loss of some discrete function that the object carried out for the child is experienced . . . , the psyche does not resign itself to the loss; instead, it preserves the function of the object by internalization" (p. 317).

It is crucial to note that the infant's early internalizations are represented on a sensorimotor level.[1] According to Piaget (1945), from birth to about 18 months, action sequences evolve into increasingly complex sensorimotor schema through "interiorization," a process analogous to internalization.

In the mother's absence, the infant forms sensorimotor patterns which eventually enable recognition and later recall of the sensory qualities of the mother's activity and her appearance associatively linked with gratification, comfort, and stimulation. The mother repeatedly reestablishes these activities in response to the infant's distress signals, and these repeated experiences result in the establishment of schemas of certain crucial aspects of the mother-infant relationship. The schemas for first recognizing and later enactively recalling the sensory experiences with the mother reflect the beginnings of psychological organization and individuation, as brought about through the process of internalization. In this manner, the original biological functions of the infant are modified and augmented (Hartmann, 1939). This rudimentary psychological organization, which begins at a sensorimotor level, then proceeds to preoperational and operational levels (Piaget, 1937), as the child continues to internalize aspects of significant relationships.

LATER PSYCHOLOGICAL DEVELOPMENT

We have so far identified the first two steps in the course of development which we believe to be the initial precursors to

---

1. Piaget viewed the sensorimotor stage as *pre*representational. In contrast, we view representations as occurring in a number of different modalities, including sensorimotor, imagistic, and lexical forms (e.g., Bruner, 1964).

internalization in infancy and early childhood. Numerous theorists, using terminology somewhat different from our own, have drawn similar conclusions about the steps leading to separation-individuation in the early phase of life (e.g., Winnicott, 1953; Loewald, 1960; Jacobson, 1964; Balint, 1968).

Our own work, however, is premised on the assumption that the mechanisms which instigate psychological growth at one level of development are precisely those which insure it at all subsequent levels. Thus, the establishment of the mother-infant unity and the inevitable disruptions that follow provide a template for all developmental sequences leading to internalization throughout the life cycle. With these assumptions in mind we turn to identifying the fundamental mechanisms of internalization.

What is the essence of the mother-infant relationship, which is common to all subsequent significant object relationships and which, if disrupted, prompts internalization as a means of recovering what has been lost? We fall prey to reductionism if we assume that a longing for symbiosis or fusion is the basis for all internalizations. Although some dedifferentiation of boundaries occurs in any significant object relationship in which individuals empathize with and depend upon each other, the notion of an unconscious longing for symbiosis or fusion is far too literal and primitive to be broadly applicable to higher developmental levels.

It is equally problematic to assume that internalization seeks to recapture such states as a sense of security, love, basic trust, or confident expectation. Whereas older children and adults might conceptualize their relationships in such terms, it is adultomorphic and erroneous to presume any of these experiences for the presymbolic infant, for whom such mental processes do not yet even exist.

Recognizing the pitfalls of adultomorphizing and falsely presuming infant mental states, Basch (1975) saw the essential function of the mother-infant unity as the provision of order, harmony, or organization. Prenatally, the rhythm of the intrauterine environment, as it reverberates to the mother's heartbeat, is the paradigm for this ordering. Birth disorganizes this rhythm and, according to Basch, leaves a permanent, neurologically encoded trace which serves as the prototype for all later anxiety, the essence of which is the threat of impending disorder. Viewed in this manner, what the mother-infant relationship provides is the reestablishment of this fundamental order. By empathically and reliably attuning herself to her infant's signals, the mother conveys an ordering rhythmicity which somewhat replicates the predictable rhythmicity of the womb.

Using different terminology, but in a similar vein, George Klein (1976) proposed that the primary developmental objective is the maintenance of identity, unity, coherence, and overall integrity of the self schema. Internalization and psychic structuralization occur as a consequence of various crises of integration. The primary subjective event which signals the dissolution of self-integration is anxiety and helplessness. The fundamental prototype is the infantile experience of helplessness (see also Bibring, 1949), resulting from loss of a source of gratification. The development of psychic structures which guide thought and action originates in the inherent organismic tendency to resolve such breaches of integration.

Although approaching the matter from somewhat different vantage points, both Basch and Klein make the fundamental assumption that the optimal state which the developing child seeks to maintain or restore is one of order, coherence, and integrity. This position is certainly consistent with our own. Where we differ from both Basch and Klein, however, is in our conviction that the maintenance of such optimal integration is possible only through continued relationship with others, upon whom we depend to help us sustain our coherence and stability. As Tarachow (1963) put it, "The search for objects and the absolute necessity for objects remain with us for life" (p. 12).

With these considerations in mind, we have chosen a term to capture the basic human experience, common to all significant object relationships, which internalization seeks to recapture. At any level of psychological development the first step in the internalization process is the establishment of a *gratifying involvement* with another human being. The word "gratifying" conveys the assumption that only when the relationship meets certain fundamental needs is there the impetus to internalize the need-gratifying functions of the relationship when they are disrupted. We have intentionally chosen not to explicate what these needs are, or the manner in which the relationship functions to meet them, because this would depend entirely upon the developmental level of the participants and upon their unique personal histories. In general, with increasing development, both the individual's needs and the manner in which relationships meet them change in form and complexity. As individuals grow in psychological complexity, they become capable of establishing different types of relationships which are gratifying in many different ways.

By the term gratification we do not mean homeostasis. Just as the infant requires an optimal level of stimulation and activity from the mother, the adult has comparable requirements. The most gratifying involvement of adulthood might occur in the context of those relationships which not only offer closeness and intimacy, but which also encourage one's efforts at individuation and autonomy. Nor does gratifying involvement mean a simple indulgence of the individual's every need, impulse, and whim. It implies that gratification is provided in an appropriate form and at an appropriate developmental level, enabling the person to function with a degree of coherence and integrity that would not otherwise be possible.

The inevitable disruption of the mother-infant unity is the prototype of the second step in the internalization process. In attempting to find a term which adequately conveys what is fundamental to such disruptions, it is again essential to guard the hazards of reductionism and adultomorphism. We have borrowed a term which originated with George Klein (1976), who held that breaches in self integrity prompt resolution in the form of cognitive-emotional schema which frame subsequent perceptions and actions. The result is a newly formed psychological structure which alters the direction of motivations and aims. He referred to such crises of integration as *experienced incompatibilities*. These can take any number of forms, including object loss, deprivation of function, intrapsychic conflict, conflict between one's own wishes and the demands and limitations of the environment, and maturational crises which occur when the "structures of self identity" (p. 209) at one developmental stage are confronted by both internal and environmental events which usher in the next stage.

The concept of experienced incompatibility broadens our understanding of the notion originally proposed by Freud in conceptualizing the formation of the superego; namely, that it is the threat of object loss which precipitates recovery or restitution through identification with, or internalization of, the lost object. Freud (1938) said, "A portion of the external world has, at least partially, been abandoned as an object and has instead, by identification, been taken into the ego and thus become an integral part of the internal world. This new psychical agency continues to carry on the functions which have hitherto been performed by the people [the abandoned objects] in the external world" (p. 205). This conceptualization of internalization has been extended beyond superego formation to include all processes in which interactions in the environment are transformed into inner regulators and are taken on as characteristics of the self (Hartmann, 1939; Loewald, 1962, 1973; Sandler and Rosenblatt, 1962; Schafer, 1968). The internalization of aspects of object relations provides a primary basis for the development of intrapsychic structures.[2] The concept of experienced incompatibility, because it does not restrict the definition of the disruption to object loss alone, provides an expanded conceptualization of the various cleavages, rifts, and discontinuities in interpersonal relations that can instigate the process of internalization.

Incompatibility signifies, for us, that the previously established relationship no longer meets the needs of at least one of the participants. This emphasis on relational incompatibility stands in contrast to Klein's emphasis on the phenomenological experience of *intrapsychic* incompatibility. In our view, although the incompatibility is certainly felt intrapsychically, and may be experienced either unconsciously or consciously, presymbolically or symbolically, the breach of integration resides pri-

2. To cite only a few references, see Fenichel, 1945; A. Freud, 1952; Hartmann, 1950; Hartmann et al., 1949; Hoffer, 1952; Décarie, 1965; Kernberg, 1966, 1972.

marily in the experience of relationship. When the structure and function of gratifying involvements are disrupted by experienced incompatibilities, the individual attempts to preserve the psychologically significant aspects of the relationship through internalization. If the disruption in the relationship is premature or is too sudden or severe, however, the individual may not be capable of internalization and consequently will be forced to resort to other less successful means of adaptation; e.g., the experience of anxiety and the formation of symptoms or the development of some form of pathological mourning.

Previous authors have stressed the importance of such disruptions as precursors to internalization, emphasizing the importance of optimal timing and dosage of frustration (Kris, 1951). The concept of optimal frustration has been utilized to describe a situation in which the parent deprives, frustrates, or even fails the child in some way, prompting the child to recover the loss through internalization. In this case, the disruption is conceptualized from an external perspective; i.e., what the parent is or is not doing in relation to the child. Rather than conceptualizing the experience from the parent's perspective or from the perspective of an outside observer, we place the emphasis on the *subjective experience* of the *internalizing object,* in this case the child. Many instances of experienced incompatibility may, in fact, be instigated by the child, who grows to feel less satisfied when the relationship in its current form no longer fully meets his or her emerging needs—needs which the parent may not yet realize. The child is an active, constructive, experiencing agent in the process, not merely a passive recipient of the parent's activities.

Having identified and conceptualized the essential mechanisms of the internalization process, we are now prepared to offer a definition of internalization which reflects the dynamic issues that underlie it: Internalization refers to those processes whereby individuals recover lost or disrupted, regulatory, gratifying interactions with others, which may have been either real or fantasied, by appropriating those interactions, transforming them into their own, enduring, self-generated functions and characteristics.

In this definition of internalization, the emphasis is upon the representation of aspects of *relationships,* not upon a conception of a representational world populated by fantasied objects or part objects which are replicas of people in the external world. Rather, what is internalized are functions and experiences, significant aspects of relationships, which must become part of oneself if the individual is to progress to the subsequent levels of development. This definition of internalization is therefore not restricted to symbolic processes, but reflects internalizations that occur in a variety of modes such as sensorimotor or enactive, imagistic, lexical, or symbolic (see Piaget, 1937; Bruner, 1964; Horowitz, 1972; Blatt, 1974). At different developmental levels, the forms of gratifying involvement, experienced incompatibility, and internalization vary in content, structure, and complexity. Psychological growth occurs as these elemental steps are repeated, again and again, over the course of the entire life cycle, taking the form of a "hierarchical spirality" (Werner, 1948). Although subsequent internalizations prompt greater psychological differentiation and higher levels of organization, the underlying mechanisms remain the same.

MODES OF INTERNALIZATION

Several thoughtful and comprehensive reviews of the concept of internalization have already appeared in the literature (e.g., Knight, 1940; Greenson, 1967; Schafer, 1968a; Meissner, 1981). We will restrict our attention to what we consider to be two fundamental issues raised by prior contributions: the distinction between primary and secondary internalization, and Meissner's recent efforts at differentiating the processes of incorporation, introjection, and identification. These formulations are crucial to address, because they have very different theoretical implications from our own. The primary difference is that we view internalization as the same fundamental process throughout the life cycle.

It was Freud (1917) who originally suggested that the earliest internalizations, which he termed "primary identifications," are immediate and direct, rather than the result of attempts to recover relinquished object cathexes. Loewald (1962) views these primary internalizations not as defenses but as boundary-setting processes, because defense against object loss through internalization presumes a degree of self-object differentiation which is not initially present. He regards these primary internalizations as obscure in their basic nature and altogether different from later forms of internalization (see also Sandler, 1960; Jacobson, 1964). Secondary internalizations take place only *after* the self-other boundary is established, and refer to a process whereby something which was previously external becomes internal.

In Meissner's (1981) rendering of the intricacies of internalization, he ultimately concludes that, not one, but *three* different and distinct mechanisms underlie the internalization process; i.e., one for primary identification, another for incorporation and introjection, and still another, altogether different one for identification. Meissner maintains that incorporation and introjection, both forms of secondary internalization, are instinctually derived, defensive measures for dealing with the threat of object loss. In both incorporation and introjection, boundaries are dedifferentiated, as something is "taken in" from the object, although the manner in which this occurs differs for each. Meissner contrasts the processes of incorporation and introjection with the highest level of internalization, identification, which he considers to express the inner dynamic tendencies of the ego toward differentiation and integration (see also Hartmann, 1939; Axelrad and Maury, 1951; Jacobson, 1954; Hartmann, 1964; Schafer, 1968). Identification is a "modeling and self-organizing process" (p. 53), which operates in relative autonomy from instinctual pressures as the motivating sources. At this level, therefore, relationships become need-free. Mature love relationships are marked by mutual identifications in which positive attachments lead each member to model his or her behavior and internal dispositions according to what each sees, admires, and values in the other (Meissner, 1979).

In contrast to these formulations, we propose that the essential mechanisms of internalization are the same at every level of development. From this standpoint, the distinction between primary and secondary internalizations obscures an appreciation of the continuity of the growth process. Although the earliest internalizations are not experienced symbolically by the infant as a response to loss of the object, there is no reason to assume that the mechanisms are different from later forms in which object loss is recognized. As Loewald (1970) has cogently argued, it is not objects which are internalized, but *relationships*. Certainly the mother-infant unity constitutes a complex relationship, however undifferentiated the infant may still be psychologically. The rifts which occur in that relationship clearly constitute separations from a former state of well-being and integrity, and thereby present a loss of gratifying involvement at a presymbolic level.

The substrate of any internalization is always the relationship, however differentiated or not its participants may be. Occasions of experienced incompatibility in the relational matrix prompt its participants to recover aspects of what may have been lost, for each, in the process. As a consequence, representations of both self and other are modified and the participants are able to relate to each other in new ways, thus providing a richer, more complex substrate for subsequent internalizations.

We propose, in contrast to Meissner, that every significant relationship, however mature, meets fundamental needs. Consistent with this view, Loewald (1971) has stated, "The higher forms into which instinctual motivations become transformed, and the more highly organized instinctual energy conformations which we call higher psychic structures, assume dominance—to a greater or lesser degree—within the developing individual. But instincts as the original motive forces never become extinct, nor do the structures corresponding more closely to these primitive forces" (p. 102).

Two primary avenues exist whereby individuals seek to restore a sense of gratifying involvement. One is object relationship, and the other is internalization. According to Joffe and Sandler (1965), "Object love, like the whole development of the ego, can be seen as a roundabout way of attempting to restore the ideal primary narcissistic state" (p. 398). Yet, no object relationship, however satisfying, can fully recapture the total involvement of those early weeks of life. We are inevitably and rudely disillusioned; and so we internalize, beginning the struggle to do for ourselves what others cannot or will no longer do for us. With each internalization, we grow in our capability and our independence. Just as no object relationship can fully meet our needs, however, neither can any amount of internalization. On the contrary, no matter how mature we become, there always lingers a deep longing to be fully taken care of again and to achieve a basic and fundamental sense of well-being. And so we continue to relate to objects partly out of that need, even though we grow more realistic in our expectations of them.

What takes place in adulthood is certainly different in form and degree from the total union of symbiosis in infancy. Increased maturity brings a growing capacity for intimacy. Mature love relationships, in which the partners are able to relinquish controls temporarily and achieve emotional and sexual union, without permanent loss of identity, are prototypic of this highest form of human development. So, too, is empathy, which necessitates a blurring of boundaries in order to "feel with" the experience of another person, but which also, at the highest level of "generative empathy," is accomplished while maintaining individuality and perspective (Schafer, 1959).

These formulations differ markedly from Meissner's position that the highest form of internalization is merely a process of modeling and self organization. On the contrary, quite different from modeling, internalization always continues to build psychic structure as aspects of significant interpersonal relationships are transformed into increasingly differentiated, complex psychological processes.

Although we believe the underlying mechanisms of internalization to be the same at all developmental levels, internalizations are characterized by vast gradations in differentiation and complexity, not only at different levels of development, but even within any given level. For this reason, it is probably insufficient to restrict ourselves to three categories of internalization, as manifest in incorporation, introjection, and identification. Moreover, although incorporation, introjection, and identification may be modes in which internalization takes place, they should not be considered *causal mechanisms*.

It is likely that further investigation will reveal a greater richness and subtlety of the developmental gradient of internalization, perhaps resulting in more fully articulated and expanded concepts which will better account for the tremendous differences in which internalizations are manifest and experienced with increasing psychological development. For example, Loewald (1962) proposed the concept of degrees of internalization, which implies shifting distances of what is internalized with reference to the ego core, as well as shifting distances within the ego-superego system. Schafer (1968b) reformulated this concept in terms of activity and passivity. With high degrees of internalization, the person's subjective experience is characterized by activity and intentionality. In the case of lower degrees of internalization, subjective experience is marked by a sense of passivity. As Schafer (1968a) stated, "it must always be borne in mind that internalization is a matter of degree: the degree to which external regulations have been taken over by the subject and stamped with his self representations; the degree of influence exerted by the internalizations; and the degree of stability of the internalizations, that is, their resistiveness to being regressively abandoned and restored to the environment or lost altogether in the systemic dedifferentiations that involve primitive mergings of self and object representations" (p. 14). Additional considerations include (a) the forms or sensory modalities in which internalized representations are embodied at different developmental levels (see Blatt et al., 1979; Geller et al., 1981); (b) the degree of structuralization of the representation; (c) the degree to which the representation is conscious or unconscious; (d) the functional significance of the representation (Stolorow and Lachmann, 1978); (e) the particular aspects of the relationships which have been internalized; e.g., a mother's soothing, a father's empathic listening, a sibling's competitiveness, a teacher's criticalness or guidance, or the playfulness of one's own child. Throughout these variations in which internalization is manifest and subjectively experienced, the basic mechanisms that prompt the internalization process remain the same.

Another important issue to consider is whether *both* gratifying involvement *and* experienced incompatibility are, in fact, necessary for all instances of internalization, or whether internalizations can occur either without loss or without intimate involvement. If such internalizations are possible, another crucial question is whether they would be manifest or experienced differently when prompted by only one of the mechanisms.

From a theoretical standpoint, it is difficult for us to imagine that internalization could possibly occur without gratifying involvement. Even the most hostile introject represents the internalization of a parent who, however punitive, met certain fundamental needs for the child. Although the child may have been painfully victimized, the parent was needed by the child for his very survival. This too, then, constitutes a gratifying involvement. The word "gratifying" indicates only that the relationship meets fundamental needs, and does not imply that it is necessarily healthy, pleasurable, or satisfying. If the relationship were not need-gratifying, the child, the adolescent, and later the adult would have no reason to recover the loss through internalization.

Our definition of internalization indicates that the relationship in which the gratifying involvement occurs may be either real or imagined (see also Schafer, 1968a). The gratifying involvement may not even be apparent to an outside observer, but at least one of the parties in the relationship must experience, consciously or unconsciously, that contact with the other person or thinking about the other person is gratifying. We are attempting to develop a *psychological* theory which deals with personal meanings. The *experience* of relatedness is the issue, not necessarily direct behavior or actual observable events. Certainly, the gratifying involvements of early childhood are, of necessity, rooted directly in the relationship with the mothering person, because at that level of development, the child's needs call for certain specific activities of the mother. With increasing development, as earlier relationships become internalized, gratifying involvements need not necessarily be current and ongoing. People can, and very often do, experience gratifying involvements with persons whom they have never even met, projecting onto them meanings out of the past which provide psychological gratification in the present. Likewise, experienced incompatibility is also a phenomenological event defined by personal meaning, which may or may not have obvious or immediate behavioral referents. From this standpoint, at higher developmental levels, internalizations can come about when the elements of gratifying involvement and experienced incompatibility are both present at a purely phenomenological level, without any overt behaviors or activities which would be apparent to an outside observer.[3]

3. We also believe that the resolution of intrapsychic conflict leading to

Having articulated our argument for the necessity of gratifying involvement in the internalization process, we ask the converse question: Can internalizations occur without an experienced incompatibility? Loewald,[4] for example, maintains that certain identifications are based not on some experienced loss or disruption, but on an intimacy by which processes or feelings in one person are "continued" or resonating in the other person without any sense of disruption. The primitive equivalent would be found under favorable conditions in the mother-infant relationship. With later development, these primary identifications involving no loss or disruption would be blended with "secondary internalizations" which do involve loss (see Loewald, 1976).

We would agree with Loewald that the experience of resonance and shared feeling in a relationship is crucially important. In our view, however, the internalization process only begins with the establishment of such gratifying involvements. With a fully available object (which is difficult to imagine in and of itself) a person needs only to maintain the affectional tie, not to convert it to psychic structure which would enable the individual to provide for his or her own needs. Internalization becomes necessary only when there is some disruption of the gratifying involvement. Part of the difficulty in thinking about these issues may be Loewald's use of the word "identification," a term which he uses to denote a shared experience of empathic bonding while others use identification to signify the highest level of internalization. We would advocate reserving the term identification for the more mature level of the internalization process, whereby increased psychological structuralization occurs, rather than for the gratifying involvement which sets the process in motion.

The question of whether both components which we have singled out are always necessary in every instance of internalization will ultimately not be resolved through theory and

---

psychological growth must involve the two primary elements of gratifying involvement and experienced incompatibility. In subsequent formulations we shall attempt to reconceptualize the complexities of the resolution of intrapsychic conflict in these terms.

4. Personal communication.

logic alone. In the final analysis, these questions can be answered only through systematic clinical and empirical investigation of the developmental process, of which the therapeutic process is one example. We are currently engaged in such an investigation.

INTERNALIZATION IN OEDIPAL AND POSTOEDIPAL DEVELOPMENT

A major implication of our formulations is that the end of the separation-individuation phase as defined by Mahler (1965) in no way heralds the end of the separation-individuation process. Mahler has identified important behavioral and psychological processes which emerge out of the relationship between mother and child in the first three years of the child's life. In our view, however, these processes are the consequence of internalization, a concept which Mahler herself does not use. Moreover, Mahler has described only the beginning stages of a lifelong process. The shift to internal regulation requires a lifetime—psychological individuation is in fact never fully achieved. Consequently, we would argue that it is both arbitrary and inaccurate to dichotomize developmental theory into mutually exclusive, preoedipal and oedipal categories, assuming that issues of separation-individuation occur primarily only in the former. Internalization, leading to increased separation-individuation, represents a developmental resolution of the polarity between longing for intimate union and striving for autonomy and mastery. Internalization and separation-individuation constitute the very essence of the growth process.

The oedipal period, for example, may be conceptualized as a highly significant manifestation of the basic issues of internalization leading to increased separation-individuation. Based upon Freud's (1923) assumption of universal bisexuality, mother and father are each experienced by the child as both a love object and an object of rivalry for the affections of the other parent. As Freud (1923) noted, "a boy has not merely an ambivalent attitude towards his father and an affectionate object choice towards his mother, but at the same time he also behaves like a girl and displays an affectionate feminine attitude to his father and a corresponding jealousy and hostility towards his mother" (p. 33). Thus, in relation to each parent, the oedipal phase introduces new forms of gratifying involvement (sexual wishes) and experienced incompatibility (rivalry, death wishes, fear of castration, penis envy, and the incest taboo), prompting new internalizations.

Identification does not occur solely with the same-sexed parent. Our emphasis on the relational matrix suggests that identification must occur in relation to both parents in order for the child to consolidate a firm gender identity and sexual orientation. For example, the boy does not identify merely with his father's masculinity; i.e., internalizing those aspects of the father-son relationship in which the father makes it clear to his son that they are alike as males. The boy, in addition, internalizes a sense of his mother's relating to him as a person of the opposite sex. He also internalizes other unique aspects of their relationship which prompt him to seek a female peer as a love object for himself in the future. To the extent that the child internalizes the incest taboo, communicated by *both* parents, he is able to give up incestuous object ties. As Loewald (1962) described it, "oedipal objects . . . are relinquished as external objects, even as fantasy objects, and are set up in the ego. . . . This is a process of desexualization in which an internal relationship is substituted for an external one" (p. 483f.).

Given that the oedipal phase occurs in the context of a triadic matrix, in contrast to the dyadic structure of preoedipal relationships, the child internalizes not only aspects of his relationship with each parent, but also the triadic structure of the parental/marital system in relation to him. As Laplanche and Pontalis (1973) stated, "in concentrating on the triangular relationship itself, we are led to assign an essential role . . . to the other poles of this relationship—the unconscious desires of both parents, seduction, and the relations between the parents—as well as to the subject and his instincts. . . . It is the different types of relation between the three points of the triangle which . . . are destined to be internalised and to survive in the structure of the personality" (p. 286).

This process of internalization leads from primarily enactive modes of representation to more abstract, conceptual forms of symbol formation. As a consequence of the shift from the inter-

nalization of dyadic to triadic relationships in the oedipal period, the child achieves a greater capacity for delay and a newfound ability for complex cognitive transformations. Thought
is no longer restricted solely to immediate, direct, and literal
form. Rather, part properties and features can be varied and
reconstructed in new, complex interrelationships. Thinking is
no longer strictly reproductive and based directly on concrete
past experiences. In addition to earlier, more literal forms of
thought, the child can begin to anticipate and plan for activities
and events never before experienced directly. A full sense of
time and the future begins to emerge during the oedipal period, as well as the recognition that one is a unique person among
all other people, with a different and unique perspective. Increasingly, the child not only recognizes his own point of view,
but can also begin to appreciate the perspective of others. Concomitantly, affects increasingly assume meaningful signal properties, rather than primarily having a discharge function (Blatt,
1984).

The birth of a sibling adds further complexity to the family
structure as a matrix for internalization. Freud (1916–17, p.
333f.) stated, "When other children appear on the scene the
Oedipus complex is enlarged into a family complex.
This . . . gives grounds for receiving the new brothers or sisters
with repugnance and for unhesitatingly getting rid of them by
a wish." Colonna and Newman (1983), in a review of the psychoanalytic literature on siblings, pointed out that siblings are
traditionally viewed as stand-ins for parents—as objects in relation to whom both negative and positive feelings are displaced
and transferred. From our perspective, siblings offer the potential for both gratifying involvement and experienced incompatibility in their own right, as well as being objects of transference from relationships with parents. These relationships
provide new opportunities for additional internalizations which
are likely to influence both subsequent friendship patterns and
choices of a love object.

The period of adolescence has been discussed by Blos (1967)
as "the second individuation process," the first having been
completed in early childhood with the attainment of object constancy. In both the first and second individuation phase pro-

found changes in psychic structure occur in response to a rapid maturational surge. Blos conceptualizes these two periods as operating in reverse of each other. In early childhood, the child gains independence through *internalization* of the mother's ministrations and emotional attunement. In contrast to childhood, the adolescent achieves individuation by *disengagement* from internalized familial objects, thus opening the way for replacement with extrafamilial object relationships. We would disagree with this formulation, arguing instead that separation-individuation occurs in adolescence in the same manner as it did in childhood. The adolescent can separate from familial objects, seek new relationships and redefine old ones, only because significant aspects of these familial relationships have been internalized. Once again, in these new relationships, the adolescent seeks more mature and refined forms of gratifying involvement through attachments to peers, ideologies, and idealized others. In the inevitable disillusionments that follow, new internalizations take place, leading to further maturation. Adult psychological functioning comes about not merely as a result of the disengagement from or externalization of previously internalized familial objects, but from a consolidation of new internalizations at a higher developmental level.

Even adult development can be viewed as proceeding according to precisely the same paradigm of gratifying involvement, experienced incompatibility, and internalization, resulting in further individuation. Development, far from ending with the onset of adulthood, evolves according to a lawful process throughout the life cycle (Erikson, 1963; Gould, 1978; Levinson et al., 1978; Vaillant, 1977). For example, in adulthood unresolved oedipal issues are often stimulated by the transition to parenthood (Benedek, 1959), only to be reawakened once again in subsequent interactions with oedipal-age, adolescent, and young adult offspring (Rangell, 1953). Parents react to the emerging sexuality of their children with at least occasional overrestriction or seductiveness. In addition, parents' recognition of their older child's abundant future as the child attempts to separate from home may evoke unconscious jealousy and even retaliation (Pearson, 1958). Thus, the various changes which children introduce as they grow often bring experienced incompatibilities for their parents, who are then prompted to rework previously unresolved issues of their own through the internalization of aspects of the parent-child relationship.

The psychological growth of adulthood is not only stimulated by one's children, however, but also emerges out of relationships with one's spouse, one's aging parents, one's mentors, and one's friends. These relationships are all affected by the adult's growing recognition of the finiteness of time and the inevitability of personal death. Colarusso and Nemiroff (1981) identify four major factors which contribute to this awareness: (1) physical signs of aging—grey hair, wrinkles, modulation of sexual drive, menopause, and male climacteric; (2) death of parents, friends, and contemporaries; (3) maturation of one's own children into adulthood; (4) the realization that not all one's life's ambitions and goals will be realized.

Thus, the gratifying involvements of adult life are repeatedly disrupted by various experienced incompatibilities. Bibring (1959) wrote, "between one phase and the next . . . decisive changes deprive former central needs and modes of living of their significance, forcing the acceptance of highly charged new goals and functions" (p. 119). The acceptance of these changes comes about through the internalization of significant dimensions of prior relationships, enabling the individual to consider new options which are more viable at that phase of adulthood. This process continues over and over again, until the ultimate separation in death (Blatt, 1974). Thus, the anticipation of death and dying is the final experienced incompatibility, and the ultimate internalizations hopefully allow one to die in peace.

SUMMARY

Our formulations of internalization are based on a single fundamental assumption: The mechanisms which instigate psychological growth at one level of functioning are precisely those which ensure it at any other level—from birth through senescence. The individual's major existential task throughout the life cycle is one of continued separation-individuation, which is accomplished through progressive internalizations of need-gratifying aspects of relationships with significant others. We extracted from various theories of normative development what we believe to be the underlying mechanisms of the internalization process: the establishment of a gratifying involvement, the experience of incompatibility in the relationship, and internalization resulting in increased psychological differentiation and individuation. Psychological growth continues as these elemental steps occur, in hierarchical spirality, over and over again throughout the course of the entire life cycle.

Having applied this paradigm to all levels of internalization and to illustrative developmental periods, we conclude that the concept of internalization is still a highly useful tool for understanding psychological development. The confusion which has resulted from differential usage of the term as well as the dangers of anthropomorphism and reification are in no way inherent in the concept. The concept of internalization, as we have defined it, and the mechanisms which underlie it can be useful in understanding not only normal development, but psychopathology and the psychotherapeutic process as well.

BIBLIOGRAPHY

Axelrad, S. & Maury, L. M. (1951). Identification as a mechanism of adaptation. In *Psychoanalysis and Culture,* ed. G. B. Wilbur & W. Muensterberger. New York: Int. Univ. Press, pp. 168–184.

Balint, M. (1968). *The Basic Fault.* London: Tavistock.

Basch, M. F. (1975). Toward a theory that encompasses depression. In *Depression and Human Existence,* ed. E. J. Anthony & T. Benedek. Boston: Little, Brown, pp. 485–534.

Beebe, B. & Stern, D. (1977). Engagement-disengagement and early object experiences. In *Communicative Structures and Psychic Structures,* ed. N. Freedman & S. Grand. New York: Plenum Press, pp. 35–55.

Benedek, T. (1938). Adaptation to reality in early infancy. *Psychoanal. Q.,* 7:200–215.

——— (1959). Parenthood as a developmental phase. *J. Amer. Psychoanal. Assn.,* 7:389–417.

Bibring, G. L. (1959). Some considerations of the psychological processes in pregnancy. *Psychoanal. Study Child,* 14:113–121.

Blatt, S. J. (1974). Levels of object representation in anaclitic and introjective depression. *Psychoanal. Study Child,* 29:107–157.

——— (1984). Narcissism and egocentrism as concepts in individual and cultural development. *Psychoanal. & Contemp. Thought,* 6:291–303.

_____ WEIN, S. J., CHEVRON, E., & QUINLAN, D. M. (1979). Parental representations and depression in normal young adults. *J. Abnorm. Psychol.*, 88:388–397.

BLOS, P. (1967). The second individuation process of adolescence. *Psychoanal. Study Child*, 22:162–186.

BRUNER, J. S. (1964). The course of cognitive growth. *Amer. Psychologist*, 19:1–15.

CAPLAN, F. (1973). *The First Twelve Months of Life*. New York: Grosset & Dunlap.

CHURCH, J. (1961). *Language and the Discovery of Reality*. New York: Random House.

COLARUSSO, C. A. & NEMIROFF, R. A. (1981). *Adult Development*. New York: Plenum Press.

COLONNA, A. B. & NEWMAN, L. M. (1983). The psychoanalytic literature on siblings. *Psychoanal. Study Child*, 38:285–309.

DÉCARIE, T. G. (1965). *Intelligence and Affectivity in Early Childhood*. New York: Int. Univ. Press.

DECASPER, A. J. (1979). "The mommy tapes." *Science News*, 115(4):56.

ENGEL, G. L. & REICHSMANN, F. (1956). Spontaneous and experimentally induced depressions in an infant with a gastric fistula. *J. Amer. Psychoanal. Assn.*, 4:428–452.

ERIKSON, E. H. (1963). *Childhood and Society*, 2nd ed. New York: Norton.

FANTZ, R. L. (1961). The origin of form perception. *Sci. American*, 204:66–72.

FENICHEL, O. (1945). *The Psychoanalytic Theory of Neurosis*. New York: Norton.

FERENCZI, S. (1909). Introjection and transference. In *Sex in Psychoanalysis*. New York: Basic Books, 1950, pp. 35–93.

FREUD, A. (1952). The mutual influences in the development of ego and id. *W.*, 4:230–244.

FREUD, S. (1915). Instincts and their vicissitudes. *S.E.*, 14:109–140.

_____ (1916–17). Introductory lectures on psycho-analysis. *S.E.*, 15 & 16.

_____ (1917). Mourning and melancholia. *S.E.*, 14:237–258.

_____ (1923). The ego and the id. *S.E.*, 19:1–66.

_____ (1938). An outline of psycho-analysis. *S.E.*, 23:141–207.

GAENSBAUER, T. J. (1982). The differentiation of discrete affects. *Psychoanal. Study Child*, 37:29–66.

GELLER, J. D., COOLEY, R. S., & HARTLEY, D. (1981). Images of the psychotherapist. *Imagination, Cognition, and Personality*, 1:123–146.

GOULD, R. L. (1978). *Transformations*. New York: Simon & Schuster.

GREENSON, R. R. (1967). *The Technique and Practice of Psychoanalysis*. New York: Int. Univ. Press.

HARTMANN, H. (1939). *Ego Psychology and the Problem of Adaptation*. New York: Int. Univ. Press, 1958.

_____ (1950). Comments on the psychoanalytic theory of the ego. In *Essays on Ego Psychology*. New York: Int. Univ. Press, 1964, pp. 113–141.

_____ (1964). *Essays on Ego Psychology*. New York: Int. Univ. Press.

_____ KRIS, E., & LOEWENSTEIN, R. M. (1949). Notes on the theory of aggression. *Psychoanal. Study Child,* 3/4:9–36.

HOFFER, W. (1952). The mutual influences in the development of ego and id. *Psychoanal. Study Child,* 7:31–41.

HOROWITZ, M. J. (1972). Modes of representation of thought. *J. Amer. Psychoanal. Assn.,* 20:793–819.

JACOBSON, E. (1954). Contribution to the metapsychology of psychotic identifications. *J. Amer. Psychoanal. Assn.,* 2:239–262.

_____ (1964). *The Self and the Object World.* New York: Int. Univ. Press.

JOFFE, W. G. & SANDLER, J. (1965). Notes on pain, depression, and individuation. *Psychoanal. Study Child,* 20:394–424.

KERNBERG, O. F. (1966). Structural derivatives of object relationships. *Int. J. Psychoanal.,* 47:236–253.

_____ (1972). Early ego integration and object relations. *Ann. N.Y. Acad. Sci.,* 193:233–247.

KLEIN, G. S. (1976). The resolution of experienced incompatibility in psychological development. In *Psychoanalytic Theory,* ed. M. M. Gill & L. Goldberger. New York: Int. Univ. Press, pp. 163–209.

KLEIN, M. (1950). *Contributions to Psycho-Analysis.* London: Hogarth Press.

KNIGHT, R. P. (1940). Introjection, projection, and identification. *Psychoanal. Q.,* 9:334–341.

KRIS, E. (1951). Some comments and observations on early autoerotic activities. *Psychoanal. Study Child,* 6:95–116.

LAPLANCHE, J. & PONTALIS, J.-B. (1973). *The Language of Psychoanalysis.* New York: Norton.

LEVINSON, D. J., DARROW, C. N., KLEIN, E. B., LEVINSON, M. H., & McKEE, B. (1978). *The Seasons of a Man's Life.* New York: Knopf.

LOEWALD, H. W. (1960). On the therapeutic action of psychoanalysis. *Int. J. Psychoanal.,* 41:16–33.

_____ (1962). Internalization, separation, mourning, and the superego. *Psychoanal. Q.,* 31:483–504.

_____ (1970). Psychoanalytic theory and the psychoanalytic process. *Psychoanal. Study Child,* 25:45–68.

_____ (1971). On motivation and instinct theory. *Psychoanal. Study Child,* 26:91–128.

_____ (1973). On internalization. *Int. J. Psychoanal.,* 54:9–17.

_____ (1976). Perspectives on memory. In *Papers on Psychoanalysis.* New Haven & London: Yale Univ. Press, 1980, pp. 148–173.

LORENZ, K. (1937). *Studies in Animal and Human Behavior.* London: Methuen, 1970.

MAHLER, M. S. (1963). Thoughts about development and individuation. *Psychoanal. Study Child,* 18:307–324.

_____ (1965). On the significance of the normal separation-individuation phase. In *Drives, Affects, Behavior,* ed. M. Schur. New York: Int. Univ. Press, 2:161–169.

_____ (1968). *On Human Symbiosis and the Vicissitudes of Individuation.* New York: Int. Univ. Press.

MEISSNER, W. W. (1979). Internalization and object relations. *J. Amer. Psychoanal. Assn.*, 27:345–360.

_____ (1981). *Internalization in Psychoanalysis.* New York: Int. Univ. Press.

PEARSON, G. (1958). *Adolescence and the Conflict of Generations.* New York: Norton.

PETERFREUND, E. (1978). Some critical comments on psychoanalytic conceptualizations of infancy. *Int. J. Psychoanal.*, 59:427–431.

PIAGET, J. (1937). *The Construction of Reality in the Child.* New York: Basic Books, 1954.

_____ (1945). *Play, Dreams, and Imitation in Childhood.* New York: Norton, 1951.

_____ & INHELDER, B. (1969). *The Psychology of the Child.* New York: Basic Books.

PINE, F. (1981). In the beginning. *Int. Rev. Psychoanal.*, 8:15–33.

PROVENCE, S. & LIPTON, R. C. (1962). *Infants in Institutions.* New York: Int. Univ. Press.

RANGELL, L. (1953). The role of the parent in the oedipus complex. *Bull. Menninger Clin.*, 19:9.

SANDER, L. W. (1977). Regulation of exchange in the infant caretaker system. In *Communicative Structures and Psychic Structures*, ed. N. Freedman & S. Grand. New York: Plenum Press, pp. 13–34.

SANDLER, J. (1960). On the concept of the superego. *Psychoanal. Study Child*, 18:139–158.

_____ & ROSENBLATT, B. (1962). The concept of the representational world. *Psychoanal. Study Child*, 17:128–145.

SCHAFER, R. (1959). Generative empathy in the treatment situation. *Psychoanal. Q.*, 20:342–372.

_____ (1968a). *Aspects of Internalization.* New York: Int. Univ. Press.

_____ (1968b). On the theoretical and technical conceptualization of activity and passivity. *Psychoanal. Q.*, 37:173–198.

_____ (1972). Internalization. *Psychoanal. Study Child*, 27:411–436.

SPITZ, R. A. (1946). Anaclitic depression. *Psychoanal. Study Child*, 2:313–342.

STOLOROW, R. & LACHMANN, F. (1978). The developmental prestages of defenses. *Psychoanal. Q.*, 47:73–102.

TARACHOW, S. (1963). *An Introduction to Psychotherapy.* New York: Int. Univ. Press.

TINBERGEN, N. (1951). *The Study of Instinct.* London: Oxford Univ. Press.

TOLPIN, M. (1971). On the beginnings of a cohesive self. *Psychoanal. Study Child*, 26:316–352.

TOMKINS, S. S. (1963). *Affect, Imagery, Consciousness.* New York: Springer.

VAILLANT, G. (1977). *Adaptation to Life.* Boston: Little, Brown.

VYGOTSKY, L. S. (1962). *Thought and Language.* Cambridge, Mass.: M.I.T. Press.

WERNER, H. (1948). *Comparative Psychology of Mental Development.* New York: Int. Univ. Press, 1957.

WINNICOTT, D. W. (1953). Transitional objects and transitional phenomena. *Int. J. Psychoanal.,* 34:89–97.

―――― (1960). The theory of the parent-infant relationship. *Int. J. Psychoanal.,* 41:585–595.

WOLFF, P. H. (1959). Observations on newborn infants. *Psychosom. Med.,* 21:110–118.

Intergenerational Separation-Individuation

Treating the Mother-Infant Pair
PETER BLOS, JR., M.D.

MAHLER AND HER COLLEAGUES THROUGH THEIR LONG, EXCITING and diligent observational work with normal infants and toddlers have provided us with a particularly interesting and useful concept: separation-individuation. As we all know, separation refers to the psychological process of differentiation, the setting apart of one being from another. Individuation refers to the complementary and intimately related process of consolidation and integration within the newly differentiated being.

Mahler's research, and much of the subsequent work with this concept and its many derivatives, has centered upon the infant/toddler's experience of object and self, psychic structure formation, and the vicissitudes of the child's further development. Although the emphasis has been on delineating the psychic development of the young child, the parental and interactional aspects of these processes have been clearly acknowledged. For example, Mahler (1963) stated, "The Leitmotifs of . . . maternal vicissitudes are reflected in their children's individuation" (p. 310). She further said that since her studies were of mother-toddler pairs in nontherapeutic situations, i.e., an

Training and Supervising psychoanalyst at the Michigan Psychoanalytic Institute and Lecturer, Department of Psychiatry, University of Michigan.

This paper in its original form was presented at the Margaret S. Mahler Symposium, Philadelphia, Pennsylvania, May 12, 1984.

observational nursery, only limited inferences about the dynamics of the mothers' psychic state were permitted.

By 1975, Mahler et al. were ready to state more broadly that, "Like any intrapsychic process [separation-individuation] reverberates throughout the life cycle. It is never finished; it remains always active; new phases of the life cycle see new derivatives of the earliest process still at work" (p. 3). We are, of course, familiar with the idea that a child's phase-specific conflictual struggles reawaken the parents' unresolved early libidinal conflicts. It has been difficult, however, to be attentive to both parts of this interacting and actively differentiating system and most observations have focused on the child. In this paper I present some clinical data from mother-infant psychotherapy to illustrate the maternal side of the individuation process. The fathers, although playing important and contributing roles in their families, will not be discussed.

Mother-infant psychotherapy refers to a particular interventive technique developed at the now closed Child Development Project (CDP) under the leadership of Selma Fraiberg at the University of Michigan. It is a form of psychotherapeutic intervention which requires that the mother and her infant/toddler are both present in the office. Data obtained in this situation differ significantly from those obtained when the infants are not present. Perhaps the actuality of the baby heightens the contrast between what is said and felt. Perhaps it is that the infant's sensitivity to subtle parental affect leads to observable reactions. Perhaps *seeing* the actual behavioral interactions, or conversely the very lack thereof, makes the therapist aware of things which the mother is unable to verbalize.

The case material I shall present is about two preverbal infants. I should note that this unique situation changes as the toddler acquires speech and begins to develop a capacity to sustain a significant relationship with a person who is only seen once a week.

Fraiberg and her colleagues have described this treatment method in a series of papers (1980). In "Ghosts in the Nursery" (1975), they tell vividly how unresolved and forgotten trauma, pain, and conflict that occurred between the mother when *she* was small and *her* mother are unwittingly reenacted in the next generation by the child, now become the mother, and her current infant. The baby becomes the object upon which the mother unconsciously displaces, projects, externalizes, and acts out her strong and conflicted feelings. The ghost in Fraiberg's nursery is formed of the shadowy remains of forgotten but still affectively charged memories which are now evident only in action.

Appropriately enough, mother-infant psychotherapy allows the language of action, the acting out, to be understood in words. Thereby the intense but ego-dystonic affect is reunited with the recovered memory of the original event. The maternal neurosis, which threatened to engulf the baby and distort development, once again is placed where it belongs—to the mother and her past. This frees the healthy maternal ego to recognize and minister to the legitimate needs of the current infant/toddler and, in addition, permits conflict-free education of the toddler's demands within a developmentally suitable range.

CASE ILLUSTRATIONS

In both cases, the mothers' difficulties with their babies are, to a certain and useful degree, highlighted by the fact that both mothers had progressed well in other areas of their own development.

CASE 1

Mr. and Mrs. H. were a professional couple in their early 30s who had been married for 6 years.[1] Both were currently employed and busy, active people. Mrs. H. and her husband consulted the CDP in the eighth month of her first and planned pregnancy. She was experiencing considerable unrelieved anxiety and unexpected negative feelings about this much desired baby. Perplexed and fearing that these feelings would interfere with her abilities as a mother, Mrs. H. had begun to be afraid that motherhood was incompatible with a career. She did not know

1. This case was treated by Dr. Alicia Lieberman and supervised by me at the CDP. A detailed case report entitled "Make Way for Abby" has been published (Lieberman and Blos, 1980). Only one episode in the 9-month treatment of mother, father, and Abby will be described here.

how to think about this conflict, let alone resolve it. Mr. H. repeatedly tried to reassure his wife by telling her everything
would be all right and they would resolve whatever problems
occurred as they went along. Mrs. H. perceived these reassurances as a rejection of her premonition that terrible troubles
lay ahead.

Shortly after therapy was begun, Abby was born, a lovely girl
without any problems. Breast-feeding on a demand schedule
seemed to go well. Many anxieties about Abby came and receded
during the early months of treatment and, in the meantime,
Abby was developing nicely. Memories and isolated affects from
Mrs. H.'s childhood gradually emerged and illuminated the current relationship with Abby. I have chosen one to relate here.

When Abby was 5½ months old, solid food was begun. Although for several weeks she ate pureed fruits well and happily,
she would turn her head away when cereal was introduced. Mrs.
H., with a sense of pressure and urgency, felt impelled to force
the spoonful of cereal into Abby's mouth. It was only a matter of
days before Abby rejected all solids. When the mother felt driv-
en to feed Abby forcibly, the baby would spit up. Clearly, a battle
was under way, and food was the battleground.

Reassurance and advice from the pediatrician were to no avail.
Mrs. H. *understood* that her fears of malnutrition were unwar-
ranted, but the intensity of her fears and the compulsion to
force-feed Abby were untouched. If anything, Mrs. H. felt confused by the strength of her feelings and ridiculous about her
incapacity to control them. Only in talking with Dr. Lieberman
could Mrs. H. acknowledge her utter helplessness in the face of
her daughter's resistance *and* the mounting fury which this resistance stimulated in her.

The theme of being forced and forcing were both experienced by Abby's mother. She felt helplessly forced by Abby's
apparent intransigence as well as by her own intense compulsion
to force-feed Abby. Mrs. H.'s fears worked to justify the compulsion, and the intensity and apparent irrationality of these feelings frightened her. With the help of Dr. Lieberman, the issues,
which I shall condense here, were traced out.

When Abby refused the cereal, it made Mrs. H. worry about
illnesses such as anemia. In order to avert this potential harm,

she tried to coax her baby to eat the cereal; but Abby only cried and struggled. Mrs. H. perceived this as Abby's accusation that she was not giving Abby what the child wanted and needed. Mrs. H. recalled that a strong urge to please and an anxious feeling that she was not successful also had been present at work. She did not want to impose anything on her baby for fear of distorting Abby's development. Almost in mid-sentence she switched subjects and spoke of how arbitrary her mother's rules had been when she was little. As a child she had been obedient, but in adolescence she became furious. When Dr. Lieberman asked her about this sudden switch, Mrs. H. remembered having been physically restrained, and reacting with rage, at the age of 3. She went on to say that "The most infuriating part of my childhood was that I had no choice. I was forced to do things I did not want to do. I was also forced to pretend that I had no feelings about it." A little later, she added, "It was so sad because my mother tried so hard. She had the best intentions and yet she failed in so many things. That is what worries me. We also have very good intentions."

The first fear, as we began to understand, was: I will become a mother like my mother was. The second: Abby will become just as angry with me as I was with my mother so many years ago. The third and most poignant fear was that of being sadly estranged from each other.

Simultaneously Mrs. H. became aware that her retaliatory fury at Abby stemmed from her (mis)perception that Abby was thwarting her desire and that this had its roots in long-ago fights with her mother. Now she could realize that Abby's turning her head away indicated nothing more than a dislike of cereal. Abby was neither critical, disappointed, nor angry at her; nor was she purposefully and deliberately thwarting her mother. As Mrs. H.'s worries disappeared, the eating problem subsided. The benefits were twofold. The initial and gratifying mother-infant relationship reappeared; and in the treatment situation Mrs. H. could explore the now conscious, conflicted feelings about her own mother.

In this brief vignette, we could almost see the tide of the mother's rising neurotic experience as it engulfed the baby with developmentally distorting reactions. As timely interpretations and rather quickly perceived insights caused the neurosis to recede, the baby emerged, apparently unharmed, and development resumed. This particularly striking episode occurred over a two- to three-week period.

Mrs. A. was a 31-year-old, middle-class woman.[2] At the age of 19 she married a businessman 10 years her senior and shortly afterward became pregnant. She resented the pregnancy, had a terrible time with her infant, and felt she was not a good mother. As she put it, "Max didn't fit in so well."

About 3½ years before consulting us, Mrs. A. had begun psychotherapy because of marital difficulties and problems in separating from her parents. Her symptoms included depression, fatigue, crying, intermittent weight gain and loss, and sleep disturbances. Excessive use of alcohol, amphetamines, barbiturates, and Valium had ended 5 years previously. Mrs. A. reported that her treatment had been of great help to her and had allowed her to develop to the point where she felt she now knew how to raise a child. The second pregnancy was planned and, as Mrs. A. said later, "Maxine is my second chance to be a good mother." (I should note that our use of the names Max and Maxine reflects the parents' actual choice of masculine and feminine forms of the same name.)

By the time Maxine was 14 months old it was clear that the hoped-for successful and confirming motherhood was not working out. The family was referred for infant treatment by Mrs. A.'s therapist since the baby seemed to be in jeopardy. At this point Mrs. A. described her young daughter as very demanding, irritable, unhappy, and temperamental. Concerned about their relationship she added, "I really love her, you know, but sometimes I can't stand her. I try to do everything right and I never seem to satisfy her. When I can't make her happy, I feel frustrated. When she doesn't respond to me, I get angry with

2. Mrs. A. and her 14-month-old daughter, Maxine, were treated under my supervision by Dr. Susan Theut, a Fellow in Child Psychiatry at the University of Michigan.

her. She makes things so difficult for me that I'm always irritable and it makes real difficulties in my marriage."

Although Mrs. A. had tried to achieve technical training, marriage, parenthood, and emancipation from her parents, she thought she had never successfully reached any of these goals. She still felt dependent upon the outside world and vividly experienced the barriers to maturity, an integral sense of comfort, a coherence and self-adequacy as lying outside herself. Maxine, whom the mother described as dominating, intrusive, and insatiable, proved to be an agile, healthy, attractive little girl. It was clear that her mother saw in Maxine only the latest object who had denied her her due of being appreciated.

I shall trace selectively the vicissitudes of the maternal side of the separation-individuation process through the first 15 weekly sessions.

During the third assessment meeting Mr. and Mrs. A. and Maxine were present. Maxine had had a cold, then chickenpox, and been very fussy. The mother described how Maxine had been twisting in her highchair, didn't want to be held, didn't want to be on the floor, and had been crying frantically. Dr. Theut asked Mrs. A., "If Maxine could talk, what do you think she would be trying to say to you?"

Without hesitation Mrs. A. replied, "I'm totally miserable and frustrated." She paused and said with some surprise and reflection, "But that's exactly how *I* felt!" This was a striking indication that under duress Mrs. A. could not distinguish between Maxine's feelings and her own and therefore could not be helpful to her daughter. Frequently, we began to learn, they seemed like two children caught up in a contagion of frantic anxiety in search of an adult caretaker to soothe and comfort them.

In the second treatment session we heard the first associative link with past events. Mrs. A. reported with distress and fatigue about an awful week filled with incessant demands. Dr. Theut could see that Maxine was indeed very restless and that her mother seemed less in tune with Maxine than ever. Mrs. A. finally said, "You know, I try to do right with them, the kids that is, so nothing will happen to them."

Dr. Theut asked what she felt might happen. I quote her reply from the record:

Mrs. A. began telling me how it had been for her as a child. How she sees her parents as very strict, very cold, and how they have provided everything for her as far as food, shelter, and care had been concerned. But she did not feel they cared about her emotionally and helped her in that way. She said it was "so hard to grow up like that and I don't want this to happen to my own kids. . . . My parents were so strict that I tried to be just the opposite with my kids and maybe I've gone the other way. Maybe I'm too lenient with them. My family thinks I'm too much into the emotional components and that psychological stuff doesn't matter that much, but I think it does."

Toward the end of the hour Maxine became more and more fussy; part of it, I believe, was due to the fact that Mrs. A. was so involved in talking to me that she lost her attentiveness to Maxine. Mrs. A. says that when Maxine becomes like this, she doesn't know what to do with her, but in fact, [Dr. Theut observed] she doesn't do anything with her. [When] Mrs. A. finally picked Maxine up, she was not easily comforted. Mrs. A. commented with a smile, "Now she gets to see what you're really like, Maxine."

The story was beginning to unfold. As Mrs. A. became more distressed and agitated, she began to experience Dr. Theut in the transference as the emotionally withdrawn mother and helplessly longed for help from her therapist. Maxine perceived her mother's regression and withdrawal and responded with expressions of separation anxiety—greater restlessness, agitation, and bids for attention. Mrs. A. did not just talk of her childhood experience of parental unavailability, strictness, and premature expectations of autonomy—we could see it happening before our very eyes!

Because the mother at that very moment *was* that needy, anxious little girl, she was demonstrably unable to respond to Maxine. Nor, in her splitting and regression, could she become aware of the anxiety implicit in her daughter's behavioral response to her own emotional preoccupation and withdrawal.

The next treatment session brought further clarification.

Mother reports that Maxine had been given a set of bowls by her grandmother. She has them about the house with dry cereal in them. Periodically Maxine will go to the cereal cabinet, getting her mother to go with her. But then she just stands there. Mrs.

A. understands that she is supposed to take the correct cereal box out and give it to Maxine. However, if she selects the wrong one, Maxine screams and becomes angry. Sometimes Mother has to go through six or seven different boxes before she figures out which one Maxine wants. I ask about Maxine's reaction and wonder if she thought Maxine was accusing her. She said, "Yes, she is saying to me, 'You can't do anything right.'" I said to feel that must really be difficult when you're trying so hard to please her. Mrs. A. replied, "Yes, that's exactly how it feels." I ask her if this reminds her of a feeling that she has had at some other time. Mrs. A. recalls, "It reminds me of what it was like for me with my mother. No one was around for me when I needed some emotional help. I don't want Maxine to feel that I don't understand or care about her." [Dr. Theut comments] "But then it also makes it difficult to set limits with her because you so much want to please her."

This interchange enabled us to catch Mrs. A.'s sense of failure both in the past and present and provided us with evidence of considerable intergenerational confusion. We began to see that Mrs. A.'s need to please Maxine was motivated by a deep desire to avoid awakening her own repressed fury which she felt as a little girl toward her own unappreciative and ungiving mother. Reexperiencing her own sense of despair, neediness, and neglect, Mrs. A. felt Maxine as unappreciative of her efforts ("You can't do anything right") and, thereby, Maxine now became the object of the old fury which was originally aimed at the ungiving mother of her youth. At the same time the old desire to please the object in order to be beloved was also evident. But another element must also be recognized, namely, that as an adult and mother Mrs. A. truly wanted to spare her little daughter the pain and suffering of having an uncaring and disinterested mother.

Two weeks later, in the fifth session, Mrs. A. again talked about what a horrible week it had been. She was furious with her husband because he did not help with Maxine. "Well, he did help some," she conceded, "but I don't want just physical help with her. I want him to understand me." Dr. Theut said, "It's hard to care for Maxine when you don't feel cared for yourself." Mrs. A. agreed and, for the first time, revealed that they had some worrisome financial problems at home and that she might have to go to work. Exploring further the feelings of being uncared for, Mrs. A. recalled how angry she felt when she realized that she cared for Maxine in ways she herself had never been cared for. Apparently Mrs. A. now perceived the child as the mother who did not care for her as well as the rival who received what she wanted.

Mrs. A. expressed disappointment with her husband who made her angry and furious. Dr. Theut wondered about times in the past when Mrs. A. had asked for help and been disappointed. Mrs. A. replied, "My mother had five kids and, you know, you couldn't ask for help because you wouldn't get it. Occasionally I would ask my father for help with homework, but I was always scared because if I didn't get it the first few times, he would really get angry."

Mrs. A. began the thirteenth session by saying that Maxine had been a real monster in the past few days. She then mentioned that her parents were having a resurgence of intense marital problems and that she felt caught in the struggle. In talking about this, Mrs. A. recalled that when she was a child, her mother had decided to raise dogs and became so totally involved with them that the little girl felt ignored. At that time her mother also confided in her about marital difficulties. Now her mother demanded that she keep divorce plans a secret from her father. "My mother always took care of her needs," Mrs. A. said emotionally, "but what about *my* needs?" She continued, "I often get angry when I'm giving to Maxine, when I didn't get what she's getting." At another point in the hour she threw some toys to Maxine, saying, "Here, go and get them." This seemed remarkably like a trainer's command to a puppy and suggested that at times Maxine represented, for her mother, the hated rival dogs.

By the fifteenth session Mrs. A. looked better, said she was happy, and felt things were going more smoothly with Maxine. She discovered that her mood became worse whenever she was around her mother. She noticed that she said little to her mother, but then displaced her fury onto her husband, Max, and Maxine. But this week had been better because "I told my mother to keep me out of her marriage problems." She added, "This is the first time I can say anything like this without being angry."

Mrs. A. said she no longer expected her needs to be met by her mother. When Dr. Theut asked, "Needs?" Mrs. A. replied,

"Well, there really aren't any, are there!" While this discussion revealed that she was still angry about those unmet needs of long ago, she nevertheless was better able to interact with her child. As Maxine pointed to objects, saying, "This! This!" Mrs. A. smiled and named the object. Both obviously enjoyed the interaction, and Mrs. A. could convey her pleasure and excitement in the youngster's curiosity and language learning.

As the mother-infant treatment continued, we could watch the ebb and flow of Mrs. A.'s unresolved separation from the infantile parental psychic representations and, at the same time, the individuation process as Mrs. A. achieved firmer psychic consolidation. She gained evident satisfaction from using her understanding of Maxine to provide for her age-appropriate needs. Mrs. A., the unappreciated child, was becoming the valued mother.

DISCUSSION

The clinical data were obtained from two cases in which mother-infant psychotherapy was the interventive technique. My focus has been on the unfinished developmental work of the mother which I consider to be a counterpoint to the infant and toddler separation-individuation; hence the title of my paper: Intergenerational Separation-Individuation.

The privilege of treatment, as we have seen, provides an entry into a mother's own childhood memories, thoughts, and affects, which are stimulated by her infant's moving through the corresponding developmental phase. Normally the maternal side of this action and reaction is silent or kept private, but we then suppose that a similar reworking is taking place.

We have often wondered what accounts for the relatively quick change in how these mothers perceive and respond to their babies? And we have been struck by the dramatic rapidity with which the mothers respond to interpretations in mother-infant psychotherapy. This quick uptake and the subsequent improvement are the more surprising because they do not correspond to our experience in adult psychotherapy. We have also noted that if, later on, the same mothers perceive the need for, and enter into, traditional psychotherapy, the course then follows conventional lines in both time and structure.

Earlier, I speculated on the significance of the baby's actual presence in the therapy room. While this surely is a contributing factor, it cannot by itself account for the particular flexibility in the maternal psychic structure which we repeatedly observe during our work with mothers and their infants. Crisis as the creator of this heightened capacity for psychic change also seems too simplistic as an explanation.

In order to develop a more adequate answer to this problem it is necessary to approach the matter from a different vantage point. The physiological and psychic tasks which pregnancy brings, and the physical and mental changes which occur during pregnancy are well known. In 1959, Grete Bibring, in her study of pregnant mothers in an obstetrical clinic, was startled to find that an extraordinarily high number of patients were diagnosed as "borderline." Deciding finally that this diagnosis was not plausible, she entertained the idea that the observations more accurately reflected the changing state of the maternal psychic structure during pregnancy. Scarcely two years later Solnit and Stark (1961), citing Helene Deutsch (1945) and Therese Benedek (1959) among others, stated quite matter-of-factly, "The study of pregnancy . . . reveals a loosening up of defenses in the more direct, and at times more threatening, access to unconscious representations, wishes, and scars (fixations). In a normal pregnancy, labor, and delivery, there are psychological rearrangements and achievements necessary for the developmental advances leading to early motherhood" (p. 524).

Thus with each pregnancy and birth, especially the first, but not limited to it, there is an ego-syntonic regression which is an essential, normal, and necessary part of motherhood as a developmental phase. This regression in both drive and ego contributes to the flexibility of the psychic structures, the heightened capacity to rework old conflicts, and, eventually, the psychic growth of mother and infant. Our clinical data suggest that the heightened capacity for regression, greater access to childhood memories, unconscious wishes, conflicts, and fixations, and loosening of defenses outlasts the physical and endocrinological changes of biological pregnancy and the postpartum period.

This psychic openness is sustained for many months and begins to attenuate only during the middle of the young toddler's second year. Normally and gradually, it seems, this period of psychic flexibility is brought to a close by the toddler's increasing awareness of his or her own psychological separateness and the mother's recognition that this has occurred. Many mothers experience this step with some sadness; for others, such as those for whom the "oneness" was not pleasurable, it is a relief.[3]

I suggest that this period of psychic parturition may either be an opportunity to rework unfinished psychological individuation from primary objects, *or* be an extremely hazardous time in which the regression is poorly tolerated and the residual infantile ambivalence is acted out on the baby as the object.

When the maternal psychic defensiveness resists change, the infant may be at risk because of the mother's potential for acting out. This often becomes evident in the attribution of malevolent purpose to the baby, with the risk of child abuse, or in an aloof, depressive withdrawal with the risk of child neglect. We have often found that this neglect is a defensive protection of the baby from feared abuse. In these infant-at-risk situations mother-infant psychotherapy seems to be particularly useful because it can be effective so rapidly. It is important to underscore, however, that we have often found conventional psychotherapy to be necessary to consolidate and integrate the gains achieved.

Is this postulation of a mental state which far outlasts its physical stimulus without precedent? I think not. Our well-accepted conceptualizations of adolescence are based upon just such a biphasic psychophysiological development. After all, the biological changes of puberty occur rather quickly. But the psychic impact, plasticity, restructuring, and consolidation go on for a number of years. As is well known, this circumstance entails both risks and opportunities.

In 1967, Peter Blos, Sr., proposed a second individuation process in adolescence. He suggested that one of the overarching tasks of adolescence is the psychic relinquishment of the primacy of the parents; or, as he puts it, the "disengagement from infan-

3. See also Coleman et al. (1953), who traced similar "variations of parental attitudes" in response to the infant's developmental progress.

tile internalized objects" (p. 164). The end of adolescence then
offers a consolidation of one's sense of individuality, psychic
autonomy, responsibility, and purpose in life. Beyond this there
is a capacity for mature reciprocity in responding to others. One
of the sources of pathology, he went on, is the evasion of this
closure and the prolongation of adolescence with its dreams of
achievement and a defensive stance against awareness of the
unmodified psychic primacy of the parents. Incomplete adolescent individuation can, I think, be demonstrated in many of our
mother-infant cases and may be reflected in their commonly
reported, competitive, and comparative feelings: "I'm going to
be a *better* mother than my mother was; *I* will not make the same
mistakes as she did." Unspoken is the sentiment: "And for which
I hate her."

I would further suggest that the more the adolescent transition has been sidestepped, postponed, and avoided by the young
woman, the more potential difficulties lie ahead when parenthood arrives. Of course, even when successful adolescent
closure has been achieved, early motherhood will, and must,
bring further challenges and reworking of these central issues.

In the first case, although adolescence had in many respects
been brought to suitable closure, it had not achieved the needed
closure vis-à-vis her mother and, for this reason, interfered with
Mrs. H.'s becoming and *being* a mother. Specifically: when she
became pregnant and faced motherhood, her unconscious and
unresolved hostility and libidinal attachment to her mother returned with tremendous, unexpected, and disruptive power,
but now her ambivalence took her own baby as its object. In this
case the flaw revealed by approaching motherhood was power-
fully ego-dystonic.

For Mrs. H., and others like her, so long as career and other
strivings are the dominant issues, to be a woman *unlike* her mother can be successfully lived out with little evidence of pathology
or discomfort. However, becoming a mother necessarily brings
up maternal identifications and, in part, rekindles the individuation issues of the past. We are not surprised to find that when the
mental representatives of the ambivalently perceived parent
have not been sufficiently revised and decathected, they remain
highly influential, although dormant. Often the daughter feels
that she wants to be a mother "but not like *my* mother"; she is

then anguished, humiliated, ashamed, and depressed to find that she has maternal traits just like the ambivalently hated mother's. It is as though the planned grand escape failed, and the daughter is caught again. Now the combined figure of judge and jailer in this small, stern system—the one who requires postponement of gratification and a high frustration tolerance—is no longer the parent as viewed by the adolescent but is the present infant. The baby is thus experienced as the agent of the mother's disillusionment and the cause of her despair.

Mrs. A. had a much more disturbed adolescence than Mrs. H. In the mother-infant treatment we observed the consequences of her failure to differentiate her own feelings and need states from those of her infant daughter. As the distinctions became clearer, we could trace the emergence of her more realistic appreciation of Maxine. This development was accompanied by her painful, but liberating awareness of the lifelong battle between her wishes for appreciation by, and emancipation from, her own and powerful mother.

I believe that we are now better able to account for the relatively quick change which occurs in these mothers in mother-infant psychotherapy. From our work we can suggest that the attendant psychic plasticity which we know accompanies pregnancy, labor, and delivery outlasts the physiological changes and persists until the toddler is about 18 months of age. Thus early intervention rides the tail wind of a normative potential for psychic restructuring.

If further investigation supports these observations, the importance of early intervention will be underscored. When a mother cannot respond adequately and positively to support her baby's growth and development, the early months will be shown to be the most expeditious period for intervention. The rewards will enhance the life prospects of both members of the dyad; for one, an opportunity to rework old but interfering conflicts; for the other, a more felicitous developmental opportunity with less risk of experiencing the conflicts of the previous generation.

BIBLIOGRAPHY

BENEDEK, T. (1959). Parenthood as a developmental phase. *J. Amer. Psychoanal. Assn.*, 7:389–417.

BIBRING, G. L. (1959). Some considerations of the psychological processes in pregnancy. *Psychoanal. Study Child,* 14:113–121.

BLOS, P., SR. (1967). A second individuation process of adolescence. *Psychoanal. Study Child,* 22:162–186.

COLEMAN, R. W., KRIS, E., & PROVENCE, S. (1953). The study of variations of early parental attitudes. *Psychoanal. Study Child,* 8:20–47.

DEUTSCH, H. (1945). *The Psychology of Women,* 2. New York: Grune & Stratton.

FRAIBERG, S., ed. (1980). *Clinical Studies in Infant Mental Health.* New York: Basic Books.

———— ADELSON, E., & SHAPIRO, V. (1975). Ghosts in the nursery. *J. Amer. Acad. Child Psychiat.,* 14:387–421.

LIEBERMAN, A. F. & BLOS, P., JR. (1980). Make way for Abby. In Fraiberg (1980), pp. 242–269.

MAHLER, M. S. (1963). Thoughts about development and individuation. *Psychoanal. Study Child,* 18:307–324.

———— PINE, F., & BERGMAN, A. (1975). *The Psychological Birth of the Human Infant.* New York: Basic Books.

SOLNIT, A. J. & STARK, M. H. (1961). Mourning and the birth of a defective child. *Psychoanal. Study Child,* 16:523–537.

Narcissism and Object Love

The Metapsychology of Experience

H. SHMUEL ERLICH, Ph.D. and
SIDNEY J. BLATT, Ph.D.

THE DEVELOPMENT OF PSYCHOANALYTIC THEORY CAN BE CHARAC-
terized by three major periods, each dominated by a particular
construct or concept, coloring both the clinical and the theoretical advances of the period. These periods can be defined as
the instinctual; the structural; and object relations. The first
yielded the topographic and economic models; the second elaborated issues of intrapsychic conflict, particularly in terms of the
development of superego and the defenses; the third, still very
much with us, has had impact on our entire theoretical
superstructure.

The main issue we try to explore in this paper is one which is
not easily definable, nor readily allows for an intuitive understanding. It calls for a closer look into the dimensions of experiencing the object—the significant other related to in an object
relation, in an instinctual wish, and in an intrapsychic conflict.
Difficulty in discussing dimensions of experiencing an object is

H. Shmuel Erlich is Senior Lecturer in Clinical Psychology, Hebrew Uni-
versity; Member, Israel Psychoanalytic Association; Faculty, Israel Institute of
Psychoanalysis. Sidney J. Blatt is Professor of Psychology, Departments of
Psychiatry and Psychology at Yale University; Chief, Psychology Section in
Psychiatry, Yale University School of Medicine; Faculty, Western New En-
gland Institute for Psychoanalysis.
An earlier version of this paper was presented at the 31st International
Psychoanalytical Congress, July 29–August 3, 1979, New York, N.Y.; Israel
Psychoanalytic Society, January 11, 1985.

largely due to the fact, so we have come to understand and believe, that we are not trained to think about or even to consider these matters. We believe, however, that this point of view can have great organizing and structuring power, allowing both for some resolution of existing contradictions in our theoretical constructions, and at the same time for a better intuitive and comprehensive grasp of clinical phenomena, both in the treatment situation and in its etiological counterparts and correlatives, i.e., the study of normal and psychopathological development.

This paper thus represents an initial exploration into dimensions of *experience* in an attempt to *articulate a phenomenological point of view* not yet fully studied and conceptualized in the various metapsychological perspectives. We shall attempt to identify underlying, generic dimensions in the experience of self and object by and within the synthesizing ego. In this paper we define and attempt to describe two primary experiential dimensions—one of *being*, the other of *doing*. We trace in some detail the derivation of these dimensions from Freud's most seminal and significant work on the subject (1914), largely to underscore our belief that these concepts are not at all inimical to traditional psychoanalytic theorizing, and indeed they intermesh well with it. We then elaborate some of the theoretical and clinical implications that such an experiential view affords us. We are aware that the dimensions we propose for the study of experience, *being* and *doing*, have been discussed at length in philosophy and some social sciences, though hardly at all in psychoanalysis. The task we set ourselves in this paper, however, is to consider these basic dimensions from a psychoanalytic perspective, leaving the integration of the psychoanalytic and the philosophical conceptualizations for subsequent work.

Controversy and progress in psychoanalytic theory construction over recent decades have brought some of the major underpinnings of metapsychology into sharper relief, frequently also exposing them to serious reexamination and scrutiny. As one of the consequences of these theoretical conflicts, the concept of the self appears to be an area around which many of the divergent themes seem to converge. This seems to be the case on both the clinical and the conceptual levels. Developmentally, we now possess more comprehensive and enriched models of the early differentiation and consolidation of the self in its interaction with psychic and physical reality, as well as its role in the early formation of psychic structure (e.g., Blatt, 1974, 1975; Jacobson, 1964; Kernberg, 1966, 1972; Kohut, 1971). The exceedingly important area of transitional phenomena (Winnicott, 1953) as well as the intricate unfolding of early object relations leading to separation-individuation and autonomy (Mahler, 1968) are widely accepted. On another level, more precise formulations about the development of the self and ego ideal have greatly enriched traditional conceptualizations of the superego (Sandler et al., 1963; Kohut, 1966).

In its pursuit of scientific recognition and legitimacy, psychoanalysis seems to have widened its own internal split between phenomenological and metapsychological considerations. This is clearly reflected in the dichotomy that prevails between the metapsychological point of view and the more clinically and experientially oriented conceptualizations (Klein, 1976). Bridging the gap between the metapsychological and the phenomenological may require serious reconsideration of the philosophical underpinnings of much of our theorizing (Saperstein and Gaines, 1973). Some sensitive attempts have been made to capture the uniqueness and the recessed and private experience of the self, without, however, sufficient recourse to metapsychological considerations and grounding (e.g., Guntrip, 1969; Khan, 1974). Others have apparently chosen to ignore this area, staying firmly within the structural conflict model. Still others, such as Kohut, have linked the understanding of the self exclusively with the vicissitudes of narcissism.

One of the first to deal with the concept of the self in both metapsychological and experiential terms was Federn (1953), who emphasized the role of "ego experience," or *Erlebnis*, and attempted to study it in its dynamic, economic, and topographic aspects. Some of Federn's specific contributions are highly relevant to our own work and consonant with it: (1) the necessary span in the study of the ego experience from normality through pathology; (2) the emphasis upon the ego as an *experience*, subjectively available and unified to varying extents; and (3) the conception of the ego as constituted of different modes and attitudes, in addition to functions, and involving such dimensions as activity-passivity, subject-object, neutrality or objectlessness, each with its specific experiential components. While stressing this experiential aspect of the ego, Federn also accepted this experience in itself as a given, almost irreducible and unaccountable characteristic of psychic life. Bibring (1953), in his milestone treatment of depression, clearly delineates a "simple depression," exemplified by grief reactions, which results from disappointment by a narcissistically chosen object. After this reformulation of Freud's concepts, he goes on to redefine the basic mechanism of depression as the ego's experience of helplessness regarding its aspirations. Though he never elaborates the experiential dimension in itself, he clearly makes it a central determinant of psychic economy and adaptation. He elaborates the helplessness experienced by the ego in infancy as well as in its later regressive reactivation. In essence he sees helplessness as a narcissistic event of loss and diminution which takes place primarily within the sphere of the ego and which influences its experiential state. The particular ego experience is that of helplessness and extreme limitation. In terms of our discussion, this carries two implications: (1) vicissitudes of narcissism are a dimension encompassing all ego states or experiences; and (2) a clear distinction can be made between the ego's experiences of itself in some sense and its experiences in the realm of object libido.

Any exploration of the self in ego psychological and metapsychological terms must return to Freud's (1914) original and seminal work on the subject, and thus also come to grips with the question of narcissism. It is, of course, true that in this work Freud deals with this issue against the backdrop of a particular stage in the development of his theory, preceding both the dual instincts and the structural hypotheses. In "On Narcissism" he still envisioned intrapsychic conflict as arising from tensions between self-preservative "ego drives" and sexual or libidinal object-directed drives. He insisted for a long time on the separate nature of these energic sources, and his position in this work is among other things also a "polemic against Jung's 'monistic' concept of the libido."[1] While it is true that Freud later eschewed

1. See Edoardo Weiss's Introduction to Federn (1953).

this position in favor of the structural theory and the life and death instincts (1921), the concepts of primary and secondary narcissism with all the attendant issues they raise are still very much with us, despite various criticisms leveled at them from a number of quarters. Perhaps Balint (1958, 1960) has joined this issue most poignantly by demonstrating the pitfalls of the concept of primary narcissism, and especially the apparent contradictions between autoerotism, primary narcissism, and primary object love.

A rereading of the problems Freud was struggling with (1914) and which led to the formulation of the concept of narcissism points up the nature of the issues that are essentially with us today. In postulating the two forms of energic investment, Freud had to account in some way for the distinctive or mutative source of each. He does so in a tautological way, as we shall see, by defining and tracing the development of each within the experiential, interpersonal matrix. In the famous analogy or metaphor of the amoeba, he locates originally all the libido in the ego (primary narcissism) and then, as it is sent out to cathect objects, it becomes transformed, as it were, into object libido. Freud (1914) recognized, however, that it was also possible, indeed necessary from a developmental and substantively experiential point of view, to allow for the possibility of objects being cathected in a different way, i.e., in a way that has more to do with the originally narcissistic character of the charge. He speaks of secondary narcissistic object choices. He states it as a general axiom that (secondary?) narcissism is developmentally the necessary first step and that the libidinal choice is grafted onto, as it were, or differentiated out of this original narcissistic investment: "The first autoerotic sexual satisfactions are experienced in connection with vital functions which serve the purpose of self-preservation. The sexual instincts are at the outset attached to the satisfaction of the ego-instincts; only later do they become independent of these" (p. 87). Freud chose to call this type of object choice "anaclitic" and stated that therein lies the root of the observation that "the persons who are concerned with the child's feeding, care, and protection become his earliest sexual objects: that is to say, in the first instance his mother or a substitute for her" (p. 87). In contrast to this developmental treatment of the libidinally cathected, anaclitic object relation, he then turns to the other kind of object choice, the narcissistic one, and argues that in perverts and homosexuals one can observe that "they have taken as a model not their mother but their own selves. They are plainly seeking *themselves* as a love-object, and are exhibiting a type of object-choice which must be termed 'narcissistic'" (p. 88). One issue left obscure in this description is the nature of the process that occurs, and that results in the former case in the remodeling of the libido into an object relation that involves libido, and in the latter into an object relation involving narcissism. To this question, Balint's conception of secondary narcissism as an intermediate stage between auto-erotism and object love, while possibly correct, still provides no explanation.

Let us point out two further characteristics of the interrelationship between narcissistic and object libido highlighted by Freud. In the first place, he saw them as extremely different in terms of their *visibility*: "All that we noticed were the emanations of this libido—the object-cathexes" (p. 76). And further on, "we are led to the conclusion that to begin with, during the state of narcissism, they exist together and that our analysis is too coarse to distinguish between them; not until there is object-cathexis is it possible to discriminate a sexual energy—the libido—from an energy of the ego-instincts" (p. 76). The two energic forces thus differ greatly in terms of their availability to observation and study, even under the analytic microscope. The second distinction Freud introduced regarded their *reciprocity*: "We see also . . . an antithesis between ego-libido and object-libido. The more of the one is employed, the more the other becomes depleted" (p. 76). It seems entirely possible that these two dimensions, of visibility and reciprocity, may be interdependent, or two ways of describing accessibility to observation, rather than independent, orthogonal factors.

What then determines the vicissitudes of the development of the libido? Stated differently, what are the forces that shape and determine the extent and nature of the transformation of primary narcissism into either (secondary) narcissistic or object libido?

If we read what Freud outlined in this work, it is apparent that we are dealing with a seemingly circular definition: What determines the type of object choice in the final analysis is—the object choice itself! "A person may love," Freud (1914, p. 90) tells us, "according to the narcissistic type: (*a*) what he himself *is* . . . , (*b*) what he himself *was*, (*c*) what he himself would like *to be*, (*d*) someone who *was* once part of himself" (italics added). Whereas a person (the same?) may love, according to the anaclitic type: "(*a*) the woman who *feeds* him, (*b*) the man who *protects* him, and/or their substitutes" (p. 90; our italics).

Is there circularity in this reasoning? Not if we take into account that the above two categories of loving or relating to objects, narcissistically and anaclitically, suggest fields of forces, or relationships, in which the very nature of relating to and with the object defines the nature of the cathexis involved. Support for this assumption comes from the work of Loewald (1970) who defines the hypercathexes as a function of the "supraindividual psychic field" within which they arise. This approach is highly consistent with Freud's definition of the nature of narcissistic and anaclitic ties as determined by the particular object choice involved.

What exactly is the difference in experience between the narcissistic and the libidinal object choices, and how is this experiential difference related to a change in the nature of the energy involved? Although Freud does not elaborate, we may search for clues in what he writes. Looking over the definitions he suggests for the two types of choices, we are struck by the emergence of two distinct dimensions that characterize the nature of the *experience* of the object by the ego. In the narcissistic object choice, the object is experienced by the ego as in some state of *being*—in terms of what it "was," "is," "could be," or "would like to be." In the anaclitic object choice, on the other hand, the object is experienced as in some relation of *doing* to the ego: "tending" or "protecting."

This point is central to our thesis and bears some further explication. The psychological events and inner transformations to which an individual is subject and which he gradually begins to author from the earliest stages of life can be described from an objective or external vantage point as dealing with neutralized, libidinal, aggressive, or narcissistic energies or cathexes. From a subjective, internal point of view, however, such energic events are perceived or experienced, to the extent or on the occasions that they are at all perceived, as experiences taking place within some relational context. The context may involve self and other, or be entirely contained within oneself, or be at some point on a gradient between internal and external, real and imagined. To the extent that a psychological *event* has transpired, it implies a psychological *experience* of some sort.

Psychoanalysis has taught us that this experience may take place at different levels of consciousness, or that consciousness is not a *sine qua non* of human experience. Experiential dimensions, however, do not necessarily tally with metapsychological concepts. In his discussion of the subjective experience of activity-passivity, for instance, Rapaport (1953) suggests that this internal phenomenon, often assessed better from an external point of view, is in the final analysis the psychological product of the ego's experience vis-à-vis the drives, and not merely the result of the mode of discharge of the drive in question. Loewald's point, in this context, is thus very valuable. It states in effect that what determines the *nature* of the energic or cathectic investment under scrutiny is the *field* in which it takes place. To this we add that the field, first and foremost, is the relational field, or the experience of the object by the subject, i.e., the self, through its psychological means of experiencing, i.e., the ego. In Winnicott's terms (1971), this refers to the experiencing of the subjective object by the objective subject.

In any attempt to describe or define an object relation, there are at least three sets of variables that may enter the description, either explicitly or implicitly. These variables are formed of the polarities of self-object, internal-external, and subjective-objective. Thus it should be very clearly stated who is the self and who is the object, whether the description or statement refers to the internal or external level of the relation, and whether it is undertaken from an objective or subjective point of view. Any number of combinations of these variables is of course possible. In introducing the dimensions of *being* and *doing* we are adding a fourth polarity to these dimensions of treating an object relation. In order to at least minimize the confusion that may ensue, let us clarify the level of experience and observation we are now dealing with. The experience of the object by the ego as *being* is intended as the fully subjective experience by the experiencing self of the subjective object—mediated entirely through the internal representations of self and object—as in a state of *being* with it, i.e., with the ego. Similarly and correspondingly, the experience of the object as *doing* refers to the ego's subjective experiencing of the objective object as essentially *doing* to, with, or for the self.[2]

Let us examine once again the questions around narcissism and object love as they are shaped by this experiential vantage point. It seems that Freud has already hinted at the fact that the object, so necessary for psychological growth, could be experienced along two basic, irreducible and immutable dimensions: as *being* and *doing*. The intrapsychic impact, and hence also the manner and method of transmission, encoding and decoding, and resulting structural and energic modifications of the internalization of the object would depend on and vary with not only the "what" of the internalization but also the "how." If we conceive of the ego as experiencing the object in one of these two basic, fundamental modes, then the resulting experiences must give rise to different qualities of ego organization and function, and also to different economic, genetic, and even topographic configurations. In other words, we postulate these basic experiential modalities not merely as contents of the psychic apparatus, though they are that too, but as dimensions that contribute to or co-determine the formation of aspects of structure, the nature and quality of object relations, thought and cognition, and psychopathological configurations. *Being* and *doing* contribute to the formation of the concept of the self as well as to the concept of the object. There is an intrinsic dialectic relationship between

2. Psychoanalysis obviously deals almost entirely with experience at the clinical level (e.g., transference, resistance, and feelings). On the metapsychological level, however, experience has been transformed into and primarily dealt with as a series of dissected ego functions (e.g., affect, cognition, defense) (Klein, 1976). The concept of the synthetic function of the ego (Nunberg, 1931) was a major theoretical attempt to get beyond this metapsychological dissection and to capture the unity inherent within experience. The concept of the synthetic function of the ego, however, has not been explored and utilized to its full potential.

the development of the concept of the self and the concept of the other (Blatt and Shichman, 1983). Self and object are essentially cognitive constructs that emanate from experiences of both *being* and *doing*. These experiences crystallize into external and internal frames of reference.

What are the differences between these two experiential modes? We may descriptively define the experiential dimension of *being* as encompassing sensation, perception, and crude cognitions of *one's own self and of others* as in a state of "being," seemingly ongoing and endless while it lasts, of suspension in time, and disregard for place and other boundaries or qualifications. It may be tinged or colored with some affect or with a quality of pleasure-unpleasure. Since the essence of this experience is the state itself, or the quality of "being," it is relatively impervious, for its duration, to other impingements. Events, to the extent that they occur contiguously with the series of *being* and do not disrupt it, become woven into the same experiential matrix. Experiences of timelessness and oceanic feelings as well as alogical thinking that disregards cause and effect sequences are all characteristic of mental contents and operations typical of this state. Clinically, this is very similar to the self-object, narcissistic object relation described by Kohut (1966).

In the experiential dimension of *doing*, on the other hand, the experience is of some action or functional sequence. One experiences *oneself and others* as interacting, acting upon, or being acted upon. Sequence and causality are intrinsically involved no matter how crudely, because in action—and in the experience of action—there is always some kind of sequence and definition of activity-passivity, subject-object, before-after, and so on. The experience of others and of contiguous events is once again assimilated to form a part of the action or doing-centered experiential schemata. In the infant or young child, such an experience may seem crude or undifferentiated from the observing adult's point of view. Nonetheless, it is one in which the self and the object are experienced essentially as in a state of doing or being done to, with affects and pleasure-unpleasure associated with it. Clinically, this is always associated with the vicissitudes of drives and instinctual derivatives, both sexual and aggressive.

To repeat: *being* and *doing* are here thought of as two fundamental, independent dimensions along which self and object are experienced from the very beginning of life. These are the superordinate, generic categories in which the human ego apparatus deals with (processes, registers, transmits) the experiential field which consists of self and object, beginning with the most archaic self and object configurations and proceeding through all subsequent representations, with increasing levels of differentiation and elaboration. Self and object, both archaically and more maturely, are experienced as existing (or functioning) psychically in either the one or the other mode. In certain states it is possible to have admixtures of both experiential modes, but if examined minutely, the one or the other mode will dominate at any given moment.

Let us now address the issue of the *encounter,* or what happens to the experiencing ego under the impact of the impingement of the object. The approach or query of the other person, addressing himself to the experiencing ego or inquiring, verbally or otherwise, into the nature of its experience, is itself typically couched in one of the two experiential modes. The analyst, for instance, attempts to understand or intuit what goes on in his patient. He might approach the patient with his own frame of mind, dominated by the mode of *doing.* He would then wonder what the patient is bent on *doing* to himself, or to the analyst, and comprehending it essentially in terms of *doing*—of an action sequence of some kind, with a sequential course, with intended or unintended outcomes, results, or impacts. This comprehension will then be phrased, expressed, and interpreted—if we continue to observe the analytic situation as an example—in terms of conflict and defense, involving internal or external (interpersonal) events and objects, and the feelings associated with them. If the analyst's focus happens to be in the mode of *being,* however, the same analytic effort will center on an intuitive understanding of "what" and "where" the patient *is,* within himself and in relation to the analyst—not on what he wishes to *do* to him, but on how he *is* with him, whether the analyst is perceived as being with or for him, what is sensed as good and satisfying in this relatedness, or what in it is missing, frustrating, bad, or impossible. Clearly, when couched and experienced in the experiential mode of *being,* the analyst's understanding of the patient's experience and efforts will be much closer to what is often referred to as the "empathic" mode, and will quickly tend to center on narcissistic contents and issues.

We may return here to the question of the interaction between two persons, or the experience of "goodness of fit" between them referred to briefly above. We must take it for granted that, analogously to the experiencing subject, the other person (object) is himself primarily engaged in an experiential mode of his own. The effect of the encounter on the subject's ego would depend very much on the "goodness of fit" between the experiences of the two. If they happen to find themselves in the same mode, whether *being* or *doing,* the experience will essentially be one of pleasure, harmony, and well-being. If, however, there is a "poor fit," i.e., the object's ego is in a different mode than the subject's, there are essentially three courses available to the individual: (1) He may fail to respond altogether, employing any one of a gradient of defensive maneuvers designed to shun the object and remove the source of disharmonious experience. These efforts may consist of motor activity, such as picking oneself up and leaving or simply turning one's back; or of any kind of internal defensive moves—from denial and avoidance to dissociation and even to psychotic regression. (2) He may respond with frustration or rage, making either an inappropriate, meaningless, or inadequate response, or what is more often an unsuccessful effort to change the experiential mode of the object to fit with his own. (3) Finally, depending mostly on how susceptible he is to the object, and this is usually the measure of the anxiety the object is capable of generating in the ego, he may switch from the prevailing experiential mode to that "imposed" by the object. This is usually accomplished as an anxiety-allaying tactic, and at great cost in terms of self-denial and resentment, as well as more lasting structural alterations (a probable extreme example would be the development of a "false self" or an "as if" personality). It becomes quite clear why sensitivity to variations in the patient's experiential mode and the capacity to maintain congruence with its variations and fluctuations become a cornerstone for the capacity to facilitate exploration and inquiry within the analytic process. In a highly similar and parallel way, we may see in this capacity the *sine qua non* of the mothering and, later on, parenting function, at least as a definition of what constitutes their "good enough" performance.

It is extremely difficult to conceive of "true amalgams" of the two experiential modes. Yet it is possible that one such amalgamation, or an instance in which we encounter a confluence of the two modes (perhaps in a somewhat idealized way), is to be found in the developmental tasks and crises as conceptualized by Erikson (1950, 1959). The developmental crises of Identity and Intimacy, to name only the two more obvious ones, cannot be conceived of as taking place exclusively in one experience mode or the other. Indeed, it is certain that any one-sided resolution in terms of either *being* or *doing* would reflect or result in a severe skewing of intrapsychic balance, and possibly even indicate some psychopathology. It may therefore be stated that at certain points in the course of normal development a synthesis takes place of the two experiential modes, or that greater synthesis becomes a pressing, mandatory developmental requirement, in the service of ego integration or synthesis. At such junctures, or developmental crises, the synthesis of the two modes of experience becomes a more visible and problematic issue. It is also possible, however, that such amalgamation or synthesis is the specific task of adolescence and postadolescent development. Earlier points in the developmental continuum may represent imbalances, in which shifts of emphasis and excessive weighting of the one mode at the expense of the other are still called for. This may, of course, be related to the varying phases and rates of maturation of the different components of the psychic and physical apparatus of the ego. Thus, the stage of Basic Trust, for instance, seems to call for the dominance of *being* as an experiential mode (perhaps this may be further subdivided into the substages of the oral phase). The stage of industry during latency, on the other hand, involves a (defensive?) refocusing on *doing*. In other stages shifting balances and varying combinations of emphasis on the two modes seem more characteristic. Be that as it may, however, the crucial point is that these dimensions of ego experience are fundamentals of ego organization which become more differentiated with time. They constitute organizing principles or schemata around which aspects of ego-id-superego as well as self and object representations are anchored. Stated differently, any aspect of psychic life, from the most primitive and archaic to the most elaborate, differentiated, and sublimated, exists and can be experienced along the dimension of *being* and/or of *doing*. Intrapsychically, this would include aspects of drive, cathexes, and structure, and extrapsychically it will find expression in and influence behavior.

It is apparent that there are real intrinsic differences between the two experiential dimensions under discussion. There is, however, also an important distinction in their respective accessibility, or perhaps in what Freud referred to as "visibility." The experience of *being* is much more private, has fewer external references and manifestations, and is less amenable to elaboration. The most poignant expression of this fact is in the dearth of expressions in our language capable of depicting or communicating it. Our language is predominantly an instrumental one, developed in and subservient to the dimension of *doing*. When language is employed to capture the experience of *being*, it quickly becomes highly metaphoric, filled with allusion and imagery, less precise, and much more personal. In short, it begins to approach poetic language. This, incidentally, may not be universally true. We observe here a powerful confluence of the intrapsychic world and the forces that shape it, and the extrapsychic environment enshrined in culture and civilization. Our language, reflective as it is of our Western culture, a culture heavily involved in, reliant on, and exponential of *doing*, is much richer in the terminology of that mode. Oriental cultures that are closer to, more in tune with, and also more respectful of the dimension of *being* are also richer in language development pertinent to it. Indeed, our own psychoanalytic science's efforts at constructing a model of mind and psyche without recourse to the experiential dimension, borrowing heavily from physical and biological sciences, as psychoanalysis has traditionally done, are another illustration of the disrepute and disuse (if not misuse) of the experiential mode of *being*. Recent attempts to cast psychoanalysis in terms of action alone (e.g., Schafer, 1976) in a sense continue in the same vein, regarding all of psychic life in terms of *doing*, whether captured through language or other aspects of behavior.

Although a full application is clearly beyond the limits of this paper, some of the implications and possible gains in using the experience dimension metapsychologically must be enumerated, however briefly. First and most significant, as well as possibly most controversial, is the restructuring of psychoanalytic metapsychology as a quasi-open system. The dimension of experience opens up to a certain extent the relatively closed system of intrapsychic structure, drive, and economy. It allows for the criss-crossing flow of external and internal events between self and object and for its processing by the ego within an organizing schema of experiential dimensions (Saperstein and Gaines, 1973). The bimodality of these dimensions implies a selective, articulated, and well-organized understanding of experience, not one that is consonant with amorphousness and idealized or romantic notions of the concept. Perhaps Winnicott's (1953) concepts of the transitional object and transitional phenomena are closest to this notion of quasi-openness and to the sphere of phenomena here described. A further advantage of this conceptualization of experience is the fact that in no way need it replace or diminish the power of structural or economic models; it is rather an attempt to complement and enrich such models, and perhaps provide a better bridge to phenomenological, clinical, as well as existential observations.

A related metapsychological issue deals with the understanding and status of narcissism. One cannot avoid the impression that over the years narcissism has come to be pejoratively understood and regarded; indeed, this point is increasingly articulated in the recent literature. As the other side of this coin, libidinal object relations have tended to be fashionably and positively regarded. This distinction, though crudely stated, cannot be anything but misleading. In expanding the understanding of narcissism and object love in terms of the experiential modes of *being* as well as the complementary or reciprocal development of *doing*, we open up the realm of object choices, psychic economy, and structural configurations for further study. The elaboration of the experiential modes of *being* and *doing* can greatly enrich our understanding of the subjective bases for the development of object choice and allow for a fuller integration of a subjective and objective perspective in the study of object choice. Normal and pathological narcissism and object relations can be understood as related to the vicissitudes of *being* and *doing* in a wide variety of ways: deprivation as against overstimulation; the privacy of the self as against the transactional self; and richness, endowment, or talent as against paucity and emptiness. The important thing is that narcissism and object relations can be regarded developmentally and positively, as well as antidevelopmentally and negatively, once we view it through these experiential dimensions and ask the pertinent questions.

The most relevant and controversial current demonstration of the differences in analytic theory and conceptualization related to this may be expressed by the divergent approaches of Kohut and Kernberg. Kernberg's contributions are primarily within the area of object love or anaclitic object relations. They are couched in and directed toward the world of *doing* and action, internal and external, and its contributions to the development of psychological structures. Kohut appears to be seeking a balance between the areas of object love and narcissism, between *doing* and *being,* between the building of psychological structures and the nature of personal experience. The divergence in approach is most clearly reflected in whether or not we assume different, parallel developmental tracts for narcissism and anaclitic relations. We may view the development of narcissistic transformations as following an essentially normative pattern of their own, from early, immature forms to later, more mature adult transformations, as Kohut (1966) has suggested. We may, however, prefer to view pathological narcissism with Kernberg (1974, p. 219) and others as "the result of vicissitudes of aggressive as well as libidinal drives and defenses (that) differs from the 'ordinary adult narcissism and from fixation at or regression to normal infantile narcissism'" (Moore, 1975, p. 270). The dimensions of *being* and *doing,* characterizing as they do the experience of the object from the very start, support the position of parallel developmental lines. Yet it is immediately apparent that the one and same event, act, or situation contains the seeds of both dimensions, and the pertinent question is thus never a monistic but a dualistic one; namely, we must ask ourselves what and how in the experience under discussion relates to the sphere of being-experience, and what and how in it relates to the sphere of doing-experience. The same act of caring ministration by the mother, for example, is therefore seen as containing *both* experiences: we may be able to tease out of it those elements that relate to *doing* (e.g., stimulation and satisfaction of drive and drive derivatives) as well as those that are experienced by the infant as *being* (e.g., sense of oneness, fusion, and omnipotence with object as confirmation or of adoration, reflected beauty, importance, or centrality).

Although the descriptions and examples given thus far have a basically positive cast, experiences in both experiential tracts can, of course, be negatively coded as well. We know much more, however, about the vicissitudes of what goes wrong within the experience of *doing* and its consequences. There seems to be a difference in kind, as it were, between *being* and *doing* here, which may mislead us to posit *being* as the more fundamental of the two, yet we feel it would be a mistake to assign primariness of origin to the one over the other. Thus when the child's experience of *being* is a thwarted one, the main consequences would be, and might be sought, in the impact this will have on his sense of self. Yet one very common outcome, frequently observed in children of overprotective, overly anxious mothers, is that for many practical outcomes the child's ego will be strengthened in many spheres, giving the quite correct impression of a good capacity for functioning and coping. This is so since the deficient or partly atrophied sense of *being* found compensatory outlets in an increased and expanded emphasis on *doing*. Treatment may then focus on various disorders related to *doing* (e.g., sexual perversions, obsessive-compulsive, hysterical, and/or paranoid symptomatologies). What may be overlooked, if not carefully attended to, in such a clinical picture is that underneath this symptomatology there is a deficient, thwarted, or conflicted experience of *being* cloaking itself in these various symptom pictures. This situation obviously bears heavily on the origin and development of the false self (Winnicott, 1979) and similar pathologies of the self and the narcissistic economy of the ego.

Sandler (1960) describes a "background feeling within the ego, a feeling that can be referred to as one of safety, or perhaps of security," which he assumes to be the polar antithesis to anxiety, much as satisfaction or contentment is related to instinctual tension: "It is a feeling of well-being, a sort of ego-tone . . . and reflects . . . some fundamental quality of living matter which distinguishes it from the inanimate. . . . These safety-signals are related to . . . the awareness of being protected; for example, by the reassuring presence of the mother" (p. 353f.). He concludes that this "safety-feeling" is "not necessarily identical with the libidinal cathexis of objects . . . though it may often be difficult in practice to discriminate the one from the other" (p. 355). In distinguishing this ego quality, Sandler goes a long way toward describing the sense of well-being that is aroused when the *being* experience of the object proceeds along largely normative, positive lines. It is, indeed, the opposite of anxiety, but only of the kind of anxiety that is aroused by a functional threat to or flaw in the maintenance of an adequate sense of ego integration and the continuous sense of self necessary for survival. We may term it "annihilation anxiety" or the sense of nonbeing. This should be differentiated very clearly from the anxiety aroused by failure, thwarting, or conflict around *doing*, which in itself is shaped in terms of *doing*, e.g., "If I do this, I shall be done to such and such" (e.g., be punished). The clearest examples of this kind of anxiety are the various anxieties the ego experiences vis-à-vis the superego, particularly castration anxiety. In practice, as has already been noted, it may not always be easy to differentiate the two. Yet such differentiation is crucial for the correct discernment of the transference and resistance involved in the clinical material and for the correct handling of levels of interpretation. This, of course, is also where the object relation between analyst and analysand is most crucially and severely tested. Importantly this becomes a reflection of the distance, referred to earlier, between the analyst's experience mode and that experienced by the patient.

The modes of *being* and *doing* have been briefly alluded to in the literature. It would appear that analysts of the British school have been particularly open or sensitive to this issue. Sandler's notion of the place and role of the experience of well-being in the ego has already been mentioned. Yet Sandler's discussion is couched in another ego function, i.e., perception, and not in object relations.

Winnicott (1971) has treated the subject most cogently and clearly. Similarly to our position, he couches his discussion of *being* and *doing* entirely in the earliest roots of object relations, and regards *doing* to be the mode in which instinctual life unfolds, while *being* is related to the earliest mother-infant experiences of "being a oneness" (primary identity): "*the baby becoming the breast (or mother), in the sense that the object is the subject.* I can see no instinct drive in this" (p. 93). These concepts are further elaborated by Guntrip (1969). Two important distinctions exist, however, between Winnicott's notions of *being* and *doing* and ours. First, he marks *being* as the primary phase in the developmental sequence and as a necessary condition for the subsequent emergence of *doing*. Second, he links them to bisexuality, identifying *being* with femaleness and *doing* with maleness. From this he makes some further deductions concerning the *maternal* quality of *being*, a notion much expanded by Guntrip. Our definition of *being* and *doing* posits these as fundamental, coeval dimensions of experiencing the object inherent in the ego from the start of life, though usually differing in their visibility. Furthermore, we see no advantage to linking these to specific gender or sexual-role dimensions. Both femaleness and maleness involve with equal prepotence the dimensions of *being* and *doing*, as well as the capacity to shift and flow from one to the other. This also prevents us from making somewhat romantic or quasi-mystical statements, such as: "Technique is what the analyst is 'doing', how he is operating his protocol for interpretations . . . but the therapeutic factor lies in what the therapist 'is', what he is 'doing' unselfconsciously in relation to the patient" (Guntrip, 1969, p. 312). We rather see good technique as the application of the analyst's fullest understanding of the clinical situation the patient and his material present him with. In that sense, it would depend equally on his capacity to "be" and to "do" in relation to whether and what the patient is "being" or "doing" with him. Indeed, anything that contributes to the splitting of the two modes from one another, in real life as much as in the treatment situation, is in that sense bound to have detrimental connotations and outcomes.

Before proceeding, we would like to comment on a footnote in which Winnicott (1971, p. 89) says: "Giving clinical examples here involves me in a risk of distracting the reader's attention from my main theme; also, if my ideas are true and universal, then each reader will have personal cases illustrating" them. Likewise, and for the same reason, we have refrained from giving many clinical examples in this presentation. The universality and essential correctness of these ideas, however, is perhaps best illustrated by the fact that the earlier version of our paper was written without knowledge of Winnicott's important and seminal contributions on the subject, and proceeded from a different starting point.

Although we have refrained from elaborate clinical examples, we would like to elucidate the important implication our model has for the phenomena variously grouped together as regression. It is well-known but not readily explainable that certain experiences, though labeled regressive by the usual standards for the functioning of the psychic apparatus, are not necessarily "regressive" at all. We refer to experiences of great joy or sorrow, of losing oneself in a movie or book, in vigorous dance, exciting sports, etc. One important element in such regressions is the suspension of time consciousness, and sometimes also of danger, physical pain, and pressures. We suggest that such experiences may not be regressive at all, but occurring in the experience mode of *being* rather than *doing*. Our definitions and gradients for regression, usually cast and anchored in the framework of *doing*, seriously distort and disregard the true meaning the experience may have for the subject in the sphere of *being*.

This brings us to the final consideration to be undertaken here, namely, the implications our model may have for a psychoanalytic theory of thinking, including imagery and dream life. In the experience of the object as *being*, it is never clearly distinct from one's own self. The object is experienced as part of one's self and associated with what is then described as oceanic feelings, feelings of diffuse boundaries or lack of boundaries, as well as hallucinatory, omnipotent, and wish-fulfilling thoughts and experience, since the power of the object is incorporated into the ego. In brief, it is the kind of thinking referred to as primary process. In *The Interpretation of Dreams* (1900), Freud speaks of primary process as following a regression model, in which the perceptual end of the psychic apparatus, later the ego, is recathected, giving rise to hallucinatory or dream imagery. In terms of his later work (1914), such a regression is essentially a narcissistic one, as it involves the reinvestment of the ego with its own energy. The experience is typified in psychotic regressions as well as in dreams, and is one of lack of boundaries and poor distinction between self and object. It is timeless, as Freud suggested. Thinking based on this dimension of *being* has little regard for the independent external existence of objects. The experience of action, whether it is the action of the self or the object, is incidental to the process, and consequences of action are either disregarded or not carefully evaluated in the light of the reality principle.

In the experience of the object as *doing*, on the other hand, the object is placed in some kind of functional relationship to the self. Thinking that develops on the basis of this experiential mode is clearly more attuned to reality considerations. It relies on sequence, cause and effect, time and body boundaries. Logical patterns of expectations and contingencies play an important role, and on the whole it reflects more faithfully the structure and events of external reality. Hence, it is the kind of thinking usually referred to as secondary process. Some writers on dreams and primary and secondary process (Holt, 1967; Noy, 1969, 1973) have already suggested that these two models of thinking represent essentially parallel and independent modes of thinking, and perhaps also of central nervous system functioning, present in the organism from the start (Blatt and Shichman, 1983).

In his most recent work on the psychoanalytic theory of cognition (1979), Noy delineates two cognitive modes as well as a model of the mind that parallels ours in two crucial aspects: he sees two cognitive dimensions operating in the mind in parallel fashion, one intrinsically associated with the self, the other in tune with (external) reality. Although he does not elaborate the possible antecedents in and connections with developing object relations and experiential factors, it seems to us the two discussions essentially complement one another.

In addition, it seems that the classical model of the development of thinking as based upon the hallucinatory wish-fulfilling image (Freud, 1900; Rapaport, 1950) is an essential aspect of the dimension of *being*. In contrast, the model put forth by Piaget (1937), in which action schemata precede internalization and thought, is congruent with the experiential mode of *doing*.

In conclusion, our hypothesis of a bimodal registering and

experiencing of the object by the ego is linked to two distinct and fundamental ego-experiential states and hence also levels of ego organization. The experiential modes of *being* and *doing* pertain to configurations of both object and self. In turn, these experiential modes develop into specific differentiations and patterns of object relations, cognitive levels, types of organization, and characterological and psychopathological typologies. Above all, however, they give rise to the subjective ego experiences that are an intrinsic determinant, as well as resultant quality, of what we encounter and describe both clinically and metapsychologically as narcissism and object love. Such a conceptualization enables us to advance and integrate some conflicting and controversial issues in psychoanalytic theory construction.

BIBLIOGRAPHY

BALINT, M. (1958). The three areas of the mind. *Int. J. Psychoanal.*, 39:328–340.
_____ (1960). Primary narcissism and primary love. *Psychoanal. Q.*, 29:6–43.
BIBRING, E. (1953). The mechanism of depression. In *Affective Disorders*, ed. P. Greenacre. New York: Int. Univ. Press, pp. 13–48.
BLATT, S. J. (1974). Levels of object representation in anaclitic and introjective depression. *Psychoanal. Study Child*, 29:107–157.
_____ & SHICHMAN, S. (1983). Two primary configurations of psychopathology. *Psychoanal. & Contemp. Thought*, 6:187–254.
_____ WILD, C. M., & RITZLER, B. A. (1975). Disturbances of object representations in schizophrenia. *Psychoanal. & Contemp. Sci.*, 4:235–288.
ERIKSON, E. H. (1950). *Childhood and Society*. New York: Norton.
_____ (1959). Identity and the life cycle. *Psychol. Issues*, 1.
FEDERN, P. (1953). *Ego Psychology and the Psychoses*. London: Imago.
FREUD, S. (1900). The interpretation of dreams. *S.E.*, 4 & 5.
_____ (1914). On narcissism. *S.E.*, 14:67–102.
_____ (1921). Beyond the pleasure principle. *S.E.*, 18:3–64.
GUNTRIP, H. (1969). *Schizoid Phenomena, Object-Relations and the Self*. New York: Int. Univ. Press.
HOLT, R. R. (1967). The development of the primary processes. In *Motive and Thoughts. Psychol. Issues*, 18/19:344–383.
JACOBSON, E. (1964). *The Self and the Object World*. New York: Int. Univ. Press.
KERNBERG, O. F. (1966). Structural derivatives of object relationships. *Int. J. Psychoanal.*, 47:236–253.
_____ (1972). Early ego integration and object relations. *Ann. N.Y. Acad. Sci.*, 193:233–247.
_____ (1974). Further contributions to the treatment of narcissistic personalities. *Int. J. Psychoanal.*, 55:215–240.

KHAN, M. M. R. (1974). *The Privacy of the Self*. New York: Int. Univ. Press.

KLEIN, G. S. (1976). *Psychoanalytic Theory*. New York: Int. Univ. Press.

KOHUT, H. (1966). Forms and transformations of narcissism. *J. Amer. Psychoanal. Assn.*, 14:243–272.

——— (1971). *The Analysis of the Self*. New York: Int. Univ. Press.

LOEWALD, H. W. (1970). Psychoanalytic theory and the psychoanalytic process. *Psychoanal. Study Child*, 25:45–68.

MAHLER, M. S. (1968). *On Human Symbiosis and the Vicissitudes of Individuation*. New York: Int. Univ. Press.

MOORE, B. E. (1975). Toward a clarification of the concept of narcissism. *Psychoanal. Study Child*, 30:243–276.

NOY, P. (1969). A revision of the psychoanalytic theory of the primary process. *Int. J. Psychoanal.*, 50:155–178.

——— (1973). Symbolism and mental representation. *Ann. Psychoanal.*, 1:125–158.

——— (1979). The psychoanalytic theory of cognitive development. *Psychoanal. Study Child*, 34:169–216.

NUNBERG, H. (1931). The synthetic function of the ego. In *Practice and Theory of Psychoanalysis*. New York: Int. Univ. Press, 1948, pp. 120–136.

PIAGET, J. (1937). *The Construction of Reality in the Child*. New York: Basic Books, 1954.

RAPAPORT, D. (1950). On the psychoanalytic theory of thinking. In *The Collected Papers of David Rapaport*, ed. M. M. Gill. New York: Basic Books, 1967, pp. 313–328.

——— (1953). Some metapsychological considerations concerning activity and passivity. In *The Collected Papers of David Rapaport*, ed. M. M. Gill. New York: Basic Books, 1967, pp. 530–568.

SANDLER, J. (1960). The background of safety. *Int. J. Psychoanal.*, 41:352–356.

——— HOLDER, A., & MEERS, D. (1963). The ego ideal and the ideal self. *Psychoanal. Study Child*, 18:139–158.

SAPERSTEIN, J. L. & GAINES, J. (1973). Metapsychological considerations on the self. *Int. J. Psychoanal.*, 54:415–424.

SCHAFER, R. (1976). *A New Language for Psychoanalysis*. New Haven & London: Yale Univ. Press.

WINNICOTT, D. W. (1953). Transitional objects and transitional phenomena. In *Collected Papers*. New York: Basic Books, 1958.

——— (1971). *Playing and Reality*. London: Tavistock.

——— (1979). *The Maturational Processes and the Facilitating Environment*. London: Hogarth Press.

On Fusion, Integration, and Feeling Good

ERNA FURMAN

The Initial Clinical Findings and Technical Problems

OVER MANY YEARS MY CHILD ANALYTIC WORK HAS PRESENTED ME with special difficulties and challenges in helping patients who manifested a diminished capacity for feeling good. This deficiency, the obstacles it posed to these patients' maturation and improvement, and my analytic efforts to help them with it led me to investigate the nature of feeling good, what promotes and impedes its development, and how it relates to other aspects of the personality makeup. I further endeavored to understand these clinical phenomena theoretically and to develop technical means of working with patients who cannot feel good.

Feeling good is hard to describe and to define, but is readily recognized. It is characterized by pleasure in living, is often accompanied by a heightened sense of bodily and mental well-being, by an ability to extend oneself to others and to initiate and enjoy harmonious interactions with them, by an ease and comfort in giving to and taking from life what it has to offer, and by being creative in thought, word, or deed, however humble a form it may take. Feeling good is usually experienced in more

From the Cleveland Center for Research in Child Development, the Hanna Perkins Therapeutic Nursery School and Kindergarten, and the Department of Psychiatry, Case Western Reserve School of Medicine.

An earlier version of this paper was presented at the scientific meeting of The Cleveland Psychoanalytic Society, January, 1982.

simple or complex ways at all levels of development and differs as early as in the second half of the first year from instinctual pleasure and from mere quiescence. It is a treasured feeling, sorely missed when absent. Even infants and toddlers protect it, protest interference with it, and seek to regain it; for example, older babies and toddlers show this in protesting discomfort, avoiding inflicting pain on themselves, and seeking and accepting comfort ("kiss it better"). In older children and adults, feeling good is linked to their enjoyment of activities and mental harmony; and, if inner strife interferes with this feeling, the wish to experience it again forms an important part of their incentive to resolve conflicts through their analytic work. Although my patients suffered a chronic lack of feeling good, bodily and/or mentally, they did not miss feeling good, could not sustain feeling good when they achieved it temporarily, and did not try to work toward it in their treatment.

These patients, though different in other respects, had certain personality characteristics in common: (1) They showed a marked impairment of the synthetic function. Its deficiency sometimes manifested itself pervasively in all areas, sometimes was especially marked in some areas, such as in the integration of the body image, or of different ego functions, or of the personality structure. Superego integration in early latency was especially difficult. (2) There was an inability to achieve phase-appropriate drive fusion—with severe effects on their attitudes to themselves and to others. The patients had a measure of libidinal investment in self and objects, but could not maintain modulated positive and considerate feelings. Their love could never bind the aggression effectively and was often swept away by the onslaught of rage, leaving the patient and his world hopelessly devastated. In relation to themselves, unmitigated aggression lowered their self-love and self-esteem and found expression in extremely harsh superego demands and punishments. With people, some patients were very touchy and suspiciously shied away from close contact; in others, excited instinctual pleasure often alternated with indiscriminate, raw aggressive impulses or primitively fused them in sadomasochistic manifestations. Heightened ambivalence and lack of adequate drive fusion interfered in self-investment and relationships to such an extent that these children could not progress to a viable oedipal phase. Some entered latency essentially from the phallic-narcissistic position (R. A. Furman, 1980). (3) They manifested a difficulty in neutralizing instinctual energy in the service of the ego. In spite of good, even superior, intelligence, the children's neutral investment of ego functions, activities, interests, and skills was impaired. They lacked creativity and could not adequately develop or maintain sublimations.

These characteristics also posed serious therapeutic problems. The patients' impaired synthetic function often included a difficulty in integrating interpretations, even clarifications, to the point of not hearing me or not allowing me to say anything. Even when they were able to work with me, they often could not utilize insight and understanding. This was especially striking in the area of drive fusion and modification. When they were helped to become aware of their aggression and could link it to significant contexts and experiences in their lives, including the transference, they still could not fuse, neutralize, modify, or channel constructively the expression of their aggression against self and others. Similarly, interpretations and understanding of pregenital contents did not facilitate the subordination of the component impulses to a more mature genital organization; nor did they aid in the related development of considerate relationships with love objects. The analytic work had only limited effect on achieving inner peace and attenuated pleasure, on the harmonious structural integration of the personality, on developing neutral interests and activities, and on improving the patients' capacity for feeling good.

Among the patients who shared these pathological features were obsessional neurotics (E. Furman, 1975); children with self-hurting and suicidal tendencies (E. Furman, 1984c); children who had been raped, seduced, aggressively abused, and/or suffered chronic overstimulation of both drives in chaotic homes (A. Katan, 1973; E. Furman, 1982b); youngsters traumatized by accidents, illness, and medical/surgical interventions (E. Furman, 1964); some young atypical children (E. Furman, 1956; R. Hall, 1982, 1983, 1984) and some who, since their infancy or toddler years, had lived in one-parent families (E. Furman, 1974, 1981c; R. A. Furman, 1980, 1983).

In comparing the data from these cases, some initial findings emerged: Their difficulties with feeling good, with integration, with drive fusion and neutralization were interdependent within their personalities. This pathological syndrome, however, did not seem to stem from identical primary causes, although there was some overlap; the primary cause in some cases could be seen to operate as a subsidiary cause in others. With the raped, abused, and traumatized children, drive defusion and interference with integration were mainly linked with their overwhelming experiences. The obsessional children showed various early deficiencies and interferences in the mother-child relationship. Other patients suffered chronic overstimulation of both drives in chaotic home environments. In the children from one-parent families, the absence of one parent appeared to have diminished their opportunity to love and be loved and increased their aggression so as to produce an imbalance of the drives. In this respect, though not in others, they resembled the emotionally deprived juvenile delinquents described by A. Freud (1949). The young atypical children had, as a rule, experienced most of these interferences. Variations in instinctual endowment (Alpert et al., 1956) may have constituted another primary or subsidiary cause in any or all of the cases, but this could not be ascertained clearly in their treatments.

Most of the patients mentioned thus far were in five-times weekly psychoanalysis, and some were treated via the parent and observed long-term while attending the Hanna Perkins Therapeutic School (R. A. Furman and A. Katan, 1969). I found, however, very similar manifestations in a very different group of children of all ages. My contact with them came through psychotherapy and through my ongoing consultative work with the child life workers from several pediatric hospitals in the Cleveland area (E. Furman, 1981a). The children in this group suffered from advanced stages of debilitating diseases and most were actually dying. Nothing "felt good" to them. They were irritable and hostile when approached, withdrawn and miserable when alone, disinterested in and dissatisfied with whatever was offered to them. They ceased to interact with peers and became extremely ambivalent, rejecting and/or demanding, with their parents, and they lost interest in the world around them and in previously pleasurable activities. Every minor change in routine or environment and every access of stimuli were experienced as overwhelming upsets, beyond their power of mastery and integration. They also resisted and resented the prescribed treatment programs. This last symptom usually singled them out for concern and referral. Their professional caretakers and parents had known them as functioning individuals, enjoying what could be enjoyed and essentially allied with the adults in combating or "curing" their illness by cooperating even with difficult regimes and therapies. The adults usually denied the fatal turn of events, ascribed the change in the children's mood and behavior to stubbornness, laziness, or neurotic conflict, and intensified their active efforts to fight off the illness and to overcome the child's "resistance." Closer study revealed that these children, although not told about it or necessarily knowing it consciously, sensed their dying through their diminishing pleasure in the functions of living and decreased zest in striving for it. Alone with their burden, they focused only on avoiding pain and protecting themselves against excess stimulation from within and without to achieve a minimal inner equlibrium of relative peace. The active intrusions of their would-be helpers intensified their discomfort and anger and further contributed to the imbalance in their drives and disintegration of their personalities which, in their case, were consequences of the fatal diseases.

Further findings emerged when, in time, I adapted my techniques to work with these patients more effectively. I shall briefly describe this in relation to the analytic and dying patients.

With the help of empathy, trial and error, and with what I learned from my patients, I found ways of working with my analysands which made it easier for them to integrate and utilize interpretations. Throughout, however, I limited myself to analytic measures and avoided parameters. For example, I became more sensitive to these patients' tenuous capacity for integration and learned to limit the frequency, length, and content of what I said, and I took care to speak softly and to move slowly. I also worded interpretations tentatively, such as "It feels to me that perhaps . . . ," or "Is it possible that this could have to do with. . . ." With some patients I could only state my wish to interpret but left the timing up to them; for instance, I would say,

"There is something I have thought about. I would like to share it with you. Please let me know when you want me to tell you." Whereas many patients could then quickly ready themselves and integrate what I told them, one 8-year-old boy would respond with up to 40 minutes of total silence, after which he would blurt out, "Now." Until we could understand better how his difficulty related to earlier periods of being force-fed, it simply took him that long to prepare himself to listen and to take in what he heard. Another patient, a little girl of 5, would often, even after preparation, interrupt my sentence with an urgent "Stop, stop," which I heeded at once and apologized for making her uncomfortable, because I sensed that any excess of stimuli threatened her personality with loss of ego functions and overwhelming anxiety. It was a long time before she could integrate stimuli sufficiently to work on this difficulty and could uncover that it related to having been tickled and genitally stimulated to the point of overwhelming in spite of her repeated requests that her seducer "stop." Rudolph (1981), reporting on the analysis of a similarly disturbed boy, adapted his approach along the same lines.

I also developed a better feel for these children's failure in coping with their aggression, sensing that it obliterated their love and made it unavailable to them. With an obsessional 6-year-old girl who gave vent to her aggression and sadistic fantasies when she learned that her mother had to leave her to undergo an operation, I commented, "I guess it's hard right now to remember how much you also love Mommy, how much you will want her when she is away, and how much you wish that she'll come home safely." Although she at first protested my reminder of her love, she could, tearfully, go on to make a little gift for her mother to take along. On a later occasion, preceding a brief vacation from the analysis, she herself was already able to call on her positive feelings by offering me a candy to remember her with, and could then work on some of the origins of her aggression and achieve better drive fusion and mastery. Similarly, when a young patient hurt himself, deliberately or through carelessness, I found myself saying, "I am so sorry this happened. I wonder what got in the way of your being kind to yourself?" I stressed the absence of his libidinal self-cathexis rather than the presence of aggression and, through my tone of voice and words, showed that *I* still kept in mind his caring concern for himself. This would help him to summon enough self-investment to explore the symptomatic act analytically and to bind some of the underlying aggression (see also Winnicott, 1963).

Time and again I noted that steps in integration were accompanied by steps in drive fusion, and vice versa. Also, work on these aspects seemed to promote progress in other areas of concern: neutral interests developed, activities were newly pursued with zest and perseverance, and "feeling good" was increasingly experienced. The very fact that the children could welcome this kind of pleasure and make it a part of themselves indicated an inner change. Some youngsters were very aware of it and commented on it with spontaneous joy. One 7-year-old told me, "It was so *nice* at school today. We did a lot of sums and *that* was fun. And then just before recess I knew I felt so *good*. I was just *me* and it was wonderful." I am not suggesting easy miracles; rather, there were definite but slow strides which required a lot of time and working through to achieve a measure of stability.

With the dying children the task was of course different but relatively simpler. Most of them had experienced feeling good when they were still less ill and even during their terminal phase they still wanted to feel good. Their withdrawal, irritability, and "contrariness" aimed at warding off activities that would intensify pain and aggression, in part actually served to husband their waning life instinct and to protect a remaining measure of drive balance and personality cohesiveness. The question was how could their loved ones and caretakers best assist their efforts. Some parents could do so intuitively, and others could be helped to do so, especially when the professional staff supported them and their child and worked along the same lines. The adults helped primarily in two ways: one is to acknowledge and accept the child's dying status and his sense of it and, in doing so, to relieve him of some of his lonely burden by sharing it. Although nothing about death may be said in words, the children at once feel and appreciate the adults' attitude of awareness and understanding. The mutual tension and hassle cease and a calm, contained togetherness takes its place: "We know what this is all about. We face it together and we will make the best of it." This in

itself facilitates a shift in favor of "good feelings." The second
way of helping is to reduce the imposed irritants and to support
the children's striving for pleasures of *their* choosing, so that they
can utilize their remaining libidinal energy for optimal enjoyment or, at least, some sense of well-being. This implies limiting
procedures to the truly essential minimum and carrying them
out at a time and in a manner that best suits the child, even if that
means that hospital routines and schedules have to be adjusted
accordingly. It also implies eliciting the child's ideas as to what he
would like and fulfilling them as best as possible; for example,
giving him food *he* considers good, even if it deviates from the
prescribed diet, or serving it where, when, and with whom he
wants to eat. It is surprising how well children tolerate food they
really want, in contrast to what is supposed to be "good" for
them, and how much they enjoy it, even if it is only a taste, or how
much pleasure it gives them to eat with the parent or to eat in the
lounge.

These approaches usually produce dramatic changes. They
not only renew the child's capacity for feeling good, or at least
for feeling more inner peace, and enable him to interact again
with others in a harmonious, mutually rewarding manner, but
they frequently also lead to a resumption of interests and a surge
of creative activities. Depending on the child and his age, some
of these activities are highly sophisticated, like writing poetry,
others are more mundane, like dressing up a doll in a new outfit,
but all are pursued with amazing zest and investment. We sometimes see dying children overcome major hurdles of fatigue and
disability to accomplish their goals and to glow in their enjoyment of them (E. Furman, 1981a).

Questions began to crystallize as I examined the ways in which
I approached the clinical problems with my analytic patients and
compared these with what I had learned from my work with
dying children: What enables us to "feel good?" How does it
relate to drive fusion, integration, and neutralization? What is
the relationship between drive fusion and the synthetic function? What accounts for the close clinical concomitance between
them so that impairment or improvement in one is paralleled in
the other? Which factors facilitate drive fusion, and which contribute to the unfolding of the synthetic function in normal de-

velopment? What happens in pathology? And what are the implications of all this for analytic work and for the task of parents, educators, and health professionals?

A detailed account of the paths of inquiry I followed, laboriously linking data, theory, and application, would far exceed the reader's capacity for integration. However, I shall outline some of the answers to my queries.

CLARIFICATION OF CONCEPTS

The concept of fusion is inextricably linked to Freud's dual instinct theory and appears for the first time in *Beyond the Pleasure Principle* (1920). He notes there that sexual libido, the life instinct, binds and neutralizes the death instinct by blending with it and by subordinating it to its services, sadism being a prime example. In the subsequent "Encyclopaedia Article" (1923b) and *The Ego and the Id* (1923a), he adds the concept of defusion and establishes the now clinically verified and generally accepted concept that maturational instinctual progression is associated with increased drive fusion, drive regression with drive defusion: "we might conjecture that the essence of a regression of libido (e.g. from the genital to the sadistic-anal phase) lies in a defusion of instincts, just as, conversely, the advance from the earlier phase to the definitive genital one would be conditioned by an accession of erotic components. The question also arises whether ordinary ambivalence, which is so often unusually strong in the constitutional disposition to neurosis, should not be regarded as the product of a defusion; ambivalence, however, is such a fundamental phenomenon that it more probably represents an instinctual fusion that has not been completed" (p. 42).

A. Freud (1949) discussed fusion in the same terms. She noted that if "the erotic, emotional development . . . has been held up" or there is a "deficiency of emotional development, . . . the aggressive urges are not brought into fusion and thereby bound and partially neutralized, but remain free and seek expression in life in the form of pure, unadulterated, independent destructiveness" (p. 496f.).

As to whether fusion occurs within the ego or the id, Freud (1920) and A. Freud (1949) relate it to the id. Freud (1923a) writes explicitly that desexualized libido can no longer bind the destructiveness that was combined with it (p. 54). Nunberg (1930), by contrast, attributes fusion to the synthetic function of the ego. It "reconciles the conflicting elements in the autonomous instincts within the id and allies them one with another" (p. 121) and "when it fuses two opposites into a unity, it performs only one piece of work—that of fusion—instead of pouring out energy in various directions in a conflict of ambivalence" (p. 125).

I define fusion in Freud's and A. Freud's terms, but use "neutralize" according to Hartmann (1955) instead of in their earlier sense which connoted render harmless, modify, tame. I do not ascribe fusion solely to the id or to the synthetic function of the ego. Rather, my clinical data suggest that fusion is, at least during the years of personality development, the outcome of close interdependence between id and ego, an idea I shall take up later.

The subordination of pregenital impulses within a genital organization also seems to me to be related to drive fusion, because the material of the cases studied shows that this process is impeded when drive fusion fails to progress and is facilitated when drive fusion increases. Freud and A. Freud do not directly address this topic, although it is perhaps implied in their maturational concept. Nunberg (1930) attributes it to the synthetic function.

I now turn to the concept of integration and its relation to libido. Freud (1923a) introduced the concept of a neutral energy or desexualized, sublimated libido, which retains "the main purpose of Eros—that of uniting and binding—in so far as it helps towards establishing the unity, or tendency to unity, which is particularly characteristic of the ego" (p. 45). In 1926 he described its role in the epinosic gain from illness and in making neurotic symptoms ego-syntonic by fitting them into the personality.

According to Nunberg (1930), it is the synthetic function of the ego which unites and binds and brings coherence to the personality and its functioning. It harmonizes external, internal, and structural conflicts and plays a major role in reasoning and creativity. Neurotic symptoms too are the outcome, though pathological, of the tendency to bring about compromise between conflicting mental forces. And "analysis is, properly speaking, a 'synthesis'" (p. 136). "For running parallel to the process of recollection in analysis is the discovery of connection—the uniting and reconciling of the repressed ideational elements and . . . the assimilation of the repressed" (p. 134). Pointing to many analogies between libido and the synthetic function, Nunberg suggests that the ego in fact assumes a function of Eros, albeit desexualized "through the transition from one psychic system to the other" (p. 124). Developmentally, Nunberg views the synthetic function as progressing in strength and effectiveness. Although he sees the need for causality as a derivative and heir to the infantile sexual researches, and the primitive initial unity between ego and id as an origin of synthesis, to him the earliest manifestations of the synthetic function are the harmonization of the conflicting elements within the oedipus complex, the formation of the superego, and its integration into the personality.

Hartmann (1939) utilizes Nunberg's concept of the synthetic function within his larger framework of adaptational processes. He equates synthesis with integration (p. 53) and, although not quite consistent in his terminology, describes it, in the psychological realm, as a form of fitting together, the latter being a more basic adaptational process. He connects "the synthetic function of the ego with the libido" (p. 54) and relates differentiation to destruction, stressing the essential interaction between them. In fact, he later (1950) defines integration and differentiation as comprising the organizing function. Hartmann postulates a range of synthetic factors operating in different ways within the mental structure, "some of them belong to the superego, most of them to the ego, and some of these belong partly to the conflict-free regulative functions of the ego" (1939, p. 75). Taking into account his later work on neutralization (1955), I believe it correct to assume that some aspects of the synthetic function are initially libidinized and gradually invested with desexualized energy. Developmentally, Hartmann, like Nunberg, thinks of a progression from more primitive forms of synthetic regulation, such as in the oedipus complex, its resolution and superego formation, to more advanced, sophisticated forms, such as its role in analytic therapy.

Frankl (1961) speaks of integration "as a tendency inherent in
the ego to unify all the elements at its disposal [from within and
without]. . . . In this process the ego exercises a function which
we refer to as the synthetic function" (p. 147). She, as well as
Hoffer (1949), trace the first manifestations of the synthetic
function to the earliest differentiation between id and ego in the
first year of life. Frankl stresses the difficulty as well as importance of describing and assessing the development of the synthetic function in early childhood, prior to the oedipal period,
because its early impairment, arrest, or lags, due to internal or
external causes, can increasingly complicate and jeopardize the
later chances of harmonious development.

Hartmann's (1950) definition comes closest to my way of
thinking, i.e., the coordinating or integrating tendencies of the
ego are the synthetic function which, together with differentiation, comprises the concept of an organizing function. I also
follow Hartmann (1950, p. 77) in equating the terms "synthetic"
and "integrating" function, but I am not altogether comfortable
with the term "function" in this connection. Clinically, the synthetic function is not linked to any specific ego apparatus, unlike
the other ego functions, but affects all of them and operates in a
much more pervasive form within the entire personality. Perhaps neurological research, with which I am not familiar, can aid
us in pinpointing the relationship between the synthetic function and the apparatus of the central nervous system; perhaps
there is a more helpful psychoanalytic term than I am aware of.
For the present I can only stress that the synthetic function
represents, to me, something that stands hierarchically above as
well as apart from the other ego functions.

I do, however, follow other authors in assuming that (1) the
synthetic function operates in a variety of ways within the ego
and in relation to the other parts of the personality and the
external world; (2) it is, at least in part, invested with desexualized energy, following a developmentally earlier libidinization which has been gradually neutralized; (3) it progresses developmentally from the very beginnings of mental life to more
advanced forms, becomes stronger and more effective, and increasingly encompasses most areas of personality functioning;
(4) each successful step in its development underlies the next,

and each arrest or impairment jeopardizes progression; and (5) its development is facilitated as well as impaired by internal and external factors.

Last, some consideration of feeling good. I could not find any discussion of it in the literature, but Freud's thinking on the relationship between libido and pleasure points a way toward understanding. He states (1920) that the pleasure principle can come into operation only after the energy, the excitatory processes, have been bound. His use of the term "binding" in this context means changing freely flowing energy into a quiescent state. In a footnote dating from 1925, he adds that since pleasure and unpleasure are conscious feelings, they are attached to the ego (p. 11). This as well as his exposition of how the repetition compulsion attempts to lead to binding and to reestablishing the dominance of the pleasure principle following traumatic disruption suggest that the ego is active in the process. Binding in this sense thus means mastery or integration of stimuli.

Returning to the relationship between the excitatory processes of instinctual energy and feelings of pleasure and unpleasure, Freud (1920) questions whether bound as well as unbound energy can make us feel pleasure and unpleasure. He suggests on the one hand that "the unbound or primary processes [which prevail at the beginning of mental life] give rise to far more intense feelings in both directions than the bound or secondary ones" which are experienced in later times when the dominance of the pleasure principle is more secure. On the other hand, he wonders whether the difference between bound and unbound processes of energy is reflected in the difference between the ordinary feelings of pleasure and unpleasure and those that relate to a "peculiar tension" within, or whether these latter feelings derive from changes "in the magnitude of the cathexis *within a given unit* of time" (p. 63). Although no definite conclusion is reached, it seems that the less intense forms of pleasure and unpleasure are always related to bound energy, perhaps to quantitative factors, and that the ego and the id play a part. Since feeling good is a more or less attenuated affect, I shall, following Freud, relate it to bound energy and consider ego and id factors in the processes underlying it.

Tentative Conclusions

Except for a few brief but significant statements, especially by Anna Freud, I was unable to find in the literature any clarification of, or answers to, the questions I had asked myself about drive fusion, integration, and feeling good. I therefore had to venture into largely uncharted territory, relying mainly on clinical data to guide me. I did not aim to arrive at hard and fast conclusions but to proceed along a path of thinking which would prove helpful in approaching the understanding and handling of puzzling clinical phenomena.

THE RELATIONSHIP BETWEEN FUSION, INTEGRATION AND FEELING GOOD

Drive fusion occurs only under certain conditions. Several authors point out that a sufficient quantity of libido has to be present for fusion to take place. By "sufficient" I mean relative to the death instinct or destructive instinctual drive. A relative preponderance of aggression impedes fusion altogether or allows only developmentally primitive forms of fusion to occur, as in sadomasochism. Freud (1923a, p. 42) viewed the maturational increase in fusion from earlier phases to the genital one as "conditioned by an accession of erotic components." A. Freud (1949, 1965) related pathological aggressiveness in children to a deficiency of libidinal development. In 1966, she drew attention to this in relation to obsessional neurosis. She regretted the lack of scientific contributions toward an understanding of the important economic factor in terms of "relative quantity in the instinctual endowment" (p. 254) and pointed out the need to consider "*intrasystemic contradictions* within the id" (p. 246). She also noted that failure of fusion and synthesis "above all . . . determines the occurrence of an obsessional neurosis . . . when excessive amounts of aggression are turned inward against the self, the individual becomes torn within himself and develops a preference for inner strife as opposed to striving for inner harmony. This increases normal ambivalence, and ambivalent strivings are used for the purpose of perpetuating inner conflicts" (p. 246f.). Rosenfeld and Sprince (1963) address this question in their discussion of borderline children. Noting lack of fusion, integration, and neutralization among the main characteristics of these disturbances, they point to "excessive aggression characteristic of the prephallic stages" (p. 618) as one of the factors which make for the heightened ambivalence. McDevitt (1983), discussing youngsters' relative success or failure in coping with aggression, concludes, "Libido outweighs aggression, and the toddler achieves some degree of object and self-constancy" (p. 296). He finds that an excess of aggression compared to libido interferes with separation-individuation during the third and fourth subphases and contributes to difficulty in coping with oedipal conflicts.

Some of the patients I studied showed a similar quantitative disproportion between libido and aggression, although the reasons for their instinctual imbalance differed. This applied to children with obsessional neuroses, children with self-hurting tendencies, aggressively abused children, some atypical or borderline disturbances, a number of children from one-parent families, and dying children.

My Cleveland colleagues and I, however, also worked with many children whose drive fusion was inadequate, although they did not appear libidinally underendowed, nor were they libidinally deprived or depleted. Some had indeed experienced an excess of sexual stimulation at early levels of development, for example, the sexually overstimulated and seduced children. It seems therefore that fusion depends not only on the quantity of available libido, but also on its quality. By this I mean that the libido has to be bound, so that it has come securely under the sway of the pleasure principle, and is capable of being absorbed and contained by the available ego. When the excitatory processes cannot be bound and mastered, they lead to traumatic overwhelming or to very intense, uncontrollable, sexual excitement. Under these conditions, fusion does not seem to take place or only to a much lesser extent, such as in the form of primitive sadomasochism.

I assume that the capacity to bind or master excitatory processes is largely, if not exclusively, a function of integration; in this sense, integration participates in fusion. The requisite quantitative aspects of libido, relative to aggression, are the id's contribution to fusion; the requisite of libidinal energy being bound (mastered, ego-integrated) is the ego's contribution, exercised through its synthetic function. Whereas the child with an unfavorable drive balance cannot fuse adequately because of libidinal deficiency, the overstimulated or traumatized child experiences difficulty with fusion because his or her integrative capacity cannot bind the excess of stimuli and/or, in the case of traumatic overwhelming, because the synthetic function is damaged.

Integration, however, not only contributes to fusion by binding stimuli, but seems also to depend on the capacity to achieve fusion because the ego utilizes fused energy. The relationship between integration and fusion is reciprocal—one of the many instances of the mutual influences in the development of ego and id (A. Freud, 1952; Hartmann, 1952). An increase in fusion leads to an increase in the capacity for integration, and an ego with a more stable and effective synthetic function is more adept at coping with increases in stimuli from within and from without and of harmonizing conflictual demands.

Integration and drive fusion are also interrelated with neutralization. The ego's investment of functions with neutralized energy is only a gradual maturational achievement (Hartmann, 1950, 1952, 1955). During the earliest phases of personality development, the ego is only minimally differentiated from the id and utilizes instinctual or partially neutralized energy. We may assume that the ego draws only on the amount of instinctual energy it can bind. Fusion thus helps to provide a source of energy which the ego can neutralize and use for the increasing investment of all functions. This explains why patients' improvement in fusion and integration is paralleled by an increase in available neutral energy which also furthers the development of sublimations.

How does feeling good relate to these processes? The libidinal contribution seems self-evident, in that feeling good is always pleasurable. A relative deficiency of libido as compared to aggression inevitably lowers the potential for pleasure. A. Freud (1966) spoke of the inner strife which results from excessive aggression being turned inward in obsessional neurosis, and my own paper (1982b) showed how a similar imbalance of the drives adversely affected some one-parent children's personality development and their capacity for feeling good. However, a large quantity of libidinal excitatory processes also does not make a child feel good. The intensely excited child may like and enjoy what he feels up to a point, but he never really feels good. For libido to be experienced as pleasurable in a sufficiently attenuated form—and this is a hallmark of feeling good—it has to be available in a sufficient amount relative to aggression and it has to be bound, integrated by the ego, and filtered through it, as is the case with all modulated affective states. The more effectively integration works within the ego and vis-à-vis the libido, the better it contributes to the maintenance of feeling good. Thus feeling good arises from and accompanies the interaction of fusion and integration. The synthetic function at work in this process may range from very primitive to very advanced forms, and the libidinal contribution too may vary from direct bodily or drive gratifications to highly sophisticated derivatives, the latter including many neutralized or partially neutralized functions and activities. Feeling good presupposes a small measure of developmental fusion and integration and, at that level, may be experienced by the older infant during a good feeding or, at a much later time and in a more complex psychic setting, by the adult who enjoys a concert.

THE DEVELOPMENTALLY FACILITATING FACTORS

How do fusion, integration, and feeling good get under way? What facilitates their mutual maturational unfolding and progression? On the one hand we have to take into account an individual's id and ego endowment. I include here such factors as innate variations in the strength of the drives and intactness of the ego apparatus (Alpert et al., 1956; Weil, 1970). Whereas variations in id endowment are very difficult to ascertain, the effects of impairment of the ego apparatus have been widely documented. Analytic studies of blind children (Burlingham, 1972; Wills, 1979), of children with gastrointestinal anomalies (Dowling, 1977) and other handicaps, have shown how much such defects may diminish a child's opportunity for pleasurable experiences and how much they interfere with the development

of integration. On the other side are the facilitating and imped-
ing external factors, the environment and accidental life experiences. Illness or injury and their attendant treatments can seriously affect the drive balance, significantly increase
stimulation of both drives, and, at the same time, damage the
synthetic function. This is especially true with children who have
actually experienced traumatic overwhelming from whatever
cause. Most importantly and with all children, however, the environment includes the personal factors, the role of caring
adults, especially the mothering person, a relationship that plays
a particularly crucial part during the earliest years.

The importance of the mother-child relationship in this regard is referred to by McDevitt (1983). He states that object and
self constancy, which presuppose drive fusion, can be achieved
in the latter phases of separation-individuation if "the child's
libidinal investment in the mother outweighs his aggressive
cathexis of her in each subphase" (p. 297). This concept of overall sufficient love and loving is, however, too general to help us
understand just how the mother-child relationship affects these
specific processes. Freud (1905) pointed to the mother's particular role of stimulating libido by ministering to the erotogenic
zones. A. Freud discussed two further aspects of the maternal
role, the mother as auxiliary ego and as mediator between her
infant's id and ego. Her thinking on this topic is briefly summarized by Rosenfeld and Sprince (1965): "Anna Freud, in a recent
discussion on a borderline child, . . . drew attention to the fact
that growth and development of the normal child center around
pleasurable experiences. This has an immediate bearing upon
both instinctual and ego development. We have always accepted
the mother's role as an auxiliary ego, but we have not sufficiently
spelled out her function in offering herself as a mediator between instinct development and ego development. The normal
child is able to make use of the object, thereby strengthening his
capacity for object cathexis and further ego integration. Deprivation of such early pleasurable experiences interferes with
these processes" (p. 498). The emphasis on pleasurable experiences not merely refers to libidinal stimulation and gratification,
but further implies the mother's role of shielding the child from
excesses of libidinal and aggressive stimulation so that he or she

can integrate stimuli arising from an appropriate drive balance and experience pleasure in attenuated form, i.e., feel good. I think this is what Winnicott (1960a, 1960b, 1962, 1963b) means when he stresses that a mother has to meet her child's needs in an empathic manner. When he adds that the mother needs to provide a secure and consistent holding environment, he refers to her concomitant function of assisting her infant in integrating stimuli from within and without.

Fusion, integration, and feeling good in the mother and in her relationship to her child play an important part. A mother can function as an effective auxiliary ego only when the instinctual trends are adequately fused in her own personality and in her investment of her child. This also enables her to withstand the child's aggression to her (E. Furman, 1982a). Given this investment, the mother's ability to integrate then enables her to do so for the infant and to gauge his integrative capacity. A mother's difficulty with fusion and integration in her own personality and in her cathexis of her baby presents an interference in her role as his auxiliary ego, as would a discontinuity in the relationship due to physical separation or emotional unavailability (E. Furman, 1984a; R. A. Furman and E. Furman, 1984). Most important, the mother herself has to be able to feel good, value and like feeling good, and one of the things that has to make her feel good is her child's feeling good. This conscious or preconscious feeling contact between mother and child motivates her to adapt her handling so as to help him feel good because this also makes her feel good.

The mother's effective role as auxiliary ego and id-ego mediator is only the first step. The subsequent steps in her task are to transfer her function to the child. This is as crucial as her initial role and again depends greatly on whether it makes the mother feel good to help her child toward making himself feel good. With most ego functions, the mother initially does them for the child but, at the same time, begins to effect the "transfer" by providing opportunities for him to exercise them and by supporting and encouraging their development in his own personality. Her appreciation of and pleasure in the infant's beginning independent efforts and successes help him to enjoy (libidinize) each function, prompt him to practice it and use it fully. Gradually he takes over, identifies with mother's ways of functioning, and makes the function a positively invested part of himself. Experience with infants and toddlers (E. Furman, 1984a) has shown that their capacity to progress from intense pleasure/unpleasure sensations to experiencing and sustaining a variety of modulated feelings occurs along similar lines within the context of the mother-child relationship. At first the mother interprets the infant's sensations and contains them as feelings within herself and for him; then she shares them with him and supports his developing ability to feel affects in lieu of merely experiencing sensations. As with ego functions, the mother has to value and appreciate feelings in herself and in her child, so that he will make them a liked and valued part of himself. This applies to feeling good. When, with the mother's help, the child wants to make himself feel good, feeling good begins to be a motivating force to create inner and outer situations which facilitate the intrapsychic processes which result in feeling good.

DEVELOPMENTAL ASPECTS OF INTEGRATION

In stating that the same internal and external factors affect the development of fusion and integration, I have treated the synthetic function as an entity, setting aside the many different ways in which it manifests itself and the fact that, within the individual personality, some areas of its functioning may be more or less efficient than others. For example, some patients experience special difficulty in the integration of their body image, or in structural integration, or in the integration of various functions within the ego, or in their thought processes, or in their capacity to cope with new experiences. With many children their impaired synthesis manifests itself especially in learning problems, often including their inability to "learn" in their analyses. In the atypical children we often see the most widespread failure of integration. In the neurotic, developmental, and characterological disturbances we tend to see one or another area of special impairment. I have omitted discussion of the various aspects of the synthetic function because clinical data suggest that the same factors facilitate or impede it, regardless of whether they affect all aspects equally or some aspects more specifically.

What then accounts for the variation? It appears that disturbances in one or another aspect of integration relate to the timing of the internal and external interferences during the course
of development and to their involvement of specific areas. The
earlier and the more severe the interferences are, the more do
they seem to affect all aspects of integration, along with fusion.
However, even in such cases some areas may be more affected
than others; for example, partially immobilizing orthopedic leg
casts used during the first year of life, coupled with the mother's
difficulty in accepting (liking and integrating) the child's bodily
defect, may interfere more with the integration of the body
image than with other developing functions (Fiedler, 1965).
Hartmann (1939) has long since pointed out that precocious
development of ego functions is related to retarded development of synthesis. Material from the analyses of atypical children and young obsessional children often traces splinter skills
and uneven id and ego development to interferences in integration during the second and third years of life. Obviously this
topic deserves full exploration, but that would far exceed the
scope of this discussion.

Let me now return to the questions I initially posed and summarize my
tentative answers: I see the relationship between drive fusion and
the synthetic function as one of mutual dependence. Both are
related to factors in the id as well as in the ego. Drive fusion can
take place when there is a sufficient quantity of libido in relation
to aggression and when it is sufficiently bound to be securely
under the sway of the pleasure principle. Integration is active in
the process of binding stimuli and, at the same time, draws on
the bound libido to fuel its own functioning. As these processes
get under way, every step in the achievement of fusion aids
integration and increased capacity for integration aids fusion.
The mutual dependence of fusion and integration accounts for
the close clinical concomitance between them, i.e., the fact that
improvement and impairment in one are paralleled in the other.

Mutual dependence of id and ego is seen also in other maturational processes. Its close and ongoing nature is, however, so
basic in regard to fusion and integration that it may represent an
area in which ego-id differentiation remains minimal, at least

during the developmental years. This allows the synthetic function continually to draw on and to affect libidinal energy from the id.

The ongoing processes of fusing and integrating serve to increase the availability of partially neutralized energy. This allows for the ego-syntonic development of neutral interests, activities, and creativity, usually observed when progressive steps in fusion and integration are achieved. Similarly, improvement in fusion and integration helps the personality to deal with pregenital impulses (partly neutralizing them, partly subordinating them within the framework of genitality), and this frees the path for phase-appropriate personality maturation.

Feeling good is experienced as an attenuated pleasure, harmoniously encompassed within the personality. This would seem to presuppose a state of bound libido and sufficiently fused and/or neutralized aggression, with the synthetic function adequate to integrate the drive impulses. However, it does not appear that feeling good is generated by the mere static coexistence of these preconditions. The invigorating aspect of feeling good points to an ongoing economic process between them. I therefore suggest that feeling good arises from and accompanies the interaction of integration with bound libido which has sufficiently fused aggression. Clinical data suggest that a sufficient opportunity to experience feeling good is one of the crucial facilitating factors in the development and maintenance of fusion and integration. Whereas feeling good requires a minimal developmental capacity for binding libido, fusing aggression, and synthesizing, the feeling experience is a state in which these mental processes are "practiced," and when, through repeated feeling good, this state comes to be "liked" (libidinally invested), the personality strives to maintain it and/or to reexperience it. Feeling good varies greatly in the extent of conscious awareness and in degree of pleasurable intensity. It may be experienced as exhilarating, or mild, or merely as a relative improvement on unpleasure and distress, depending on the circumstances; for example, the pleasurable feeling may be very intense when libidinal impulses are stimulated and gratified as in a baby's "good feed," but a mere comfortable maintenance of feeling good may accompany the avoidance of frustration which, through minimizing aggression, helps to keep or restore the necessary balance between the drives.

The factors which foster feeling good are the very factors which facilitate fusion and integration. They include innate id and ego potentials, such as quantitative variations in drive strength and intactness of the ego apparatus, and environmental factors, the individual's many life experiences. Throughout the developmental years, the external factor of special importance is the role of the parenting persons. They assist the child first as an auxiliary ego and mediator between id and ego. They stimulate and gratify libidinal strivings and reduce stimulation of aggressive impulses, thus aiding appropriate drive balance. They protect the child against an excess of stimulation from without and within, and help with integration. They like feeling good as parents, and like to make their child feel good. In time they transfer their functioning to the child and help him to make himself feel good. They support, encourage, and appreciate his efforts, value and enjoy his successes in this regard. This furthers his investment of the functions and related feeling good as well as his internalization of their ways and attitudes, till he gradually makes them a part of his own personality.

In pathology any one or all of the facilitating factors fail. This may be due to innate deficits in ego and/or id endowment, or due to the inadequacy or unhelpfulness of external factors, or it may result from a combination of these factors.

These tentative answers obviously leave many open ends at best, and the answer to my last question about practical applicability also lacks conclusiveness. I shall only highlight some areas.

CLINICAL APPLICATIONS

In child analytic work it has proved helpful to apply the concepts about drive fusion, integration, and feeling good to understand better some of our cases and to further the therapeutic process. This does not mean that the analyst uses different analytic measures, much less such parameters as literally holding and comforting his patients or providing pleasurable experiences for them.

Erna Furman

In regard to integration, the technical application includes a heightened awareness of the patient's capacity for synthesis within the analytic setting and, as I initially illustrated, adapting the interpretive work accordingly. The time-honored analytic emphasis on respect, tact and timing of interpretations recognizes the need to take into account the patient's integrative function. When there is special difficulty with synthesis, the facilitating role initially becomes the analyst's task: wording interpretations in an integratable manner, gauging carefully the amount and intensity of stimuli the patient can master in terms of emerging conflictual material, assisting him with integration, in part through the analyst's own ability to integrate the material and to make meaningful ego-syntonic connections, in part by supporting the patient's capacity for doing so and giving it scope within the joint analytic work. The analytic setting inherently places the analyst in this role; it is just a question of using it as fully as possible and with conscious intent. However, adapting to the patient's lowered capacity for integration is not an end in itself. A parallel effort is devoted to observing the ways in which the patient's integration manifests itself in all areas of his functioning and in assisting him to observe these areas himself. Not an easy task. Self-observation involves both aspects of the organizing function, differentiation as well as synthesis, and is therefore often quite impaired in disturbances with special difficulties with integration. Nevertheless, it requires the patient's and analyst's joint efforts to address the main analytic task of tracing the genetic origins which contributed to the interferences in the development of synthesis and of enabling the patient to integrate what he discovers.

In regard to fusion I want to stress that the techniques I suggest are not used instead of, but in addition to, the usual analytic work on aggressive impulses. It is only when the patient's difficulty with fusion makes it impossible for him to utilize and channel his aggression within his personality (fuse, neutralize, modify expression) that further measures are indicated. The analyst's task then varies with the nature of the child's disturbance and developmental phase. As I attempted to illustrate, initially such patients have to be helped to mobilize their own libidinal resources as an aid in fusing aggressive impulses. Young atypical children often feel overwhelmed and deeply distressed by the aggressive destruction of their libidinal self and object investment (E. Furman, 1981b). Some patients seemingly altogether withdraw from love objects in order to protect them from their rage. One 6-year-old girl, whose treatment by B. Griffin I supervised, complained bitterly that she wanted a "pure Mommy." Asked to clarify, she explained, "It's a Mommy I can remember"—a mother whose mental representation is not killed when she is physically absent. The therapist helped this girl at times of primitive rage by reminding her repeatedly of her love for her mother, of positive experiences with her. As the child achieved a minimal measure of drive fusion, she herself began to recall periods of feeling good from the middle of her second year. It came in bits of baby-talk phrases (subsequently confirmed by the mother), in facial expressions and posture, and helped her to recapture an early healthier base which she could then use to explore the experiences that had contributed to the imbalance of her drives. Bornstein (1953) utilized these techniques with her young obsessional patient and noted the helpful effect on the girl's drive fusion and maturational progression in object relations. Brenman (1982) pointed out the clinical usefulness of assisting adult patients in recapturing their positive relations and feelings to achieve drive fusion and thereby the capacity to cope with separations.

Whereas the most severely disturbed children welcome the therapist's reminder of the unavailable loving feelings, less ill youngsters with pronounced difficulty with drive fusion often resist them strenuously. This indicates that they use the lack of drive fusion for defensive purposes. For example, not loving and not remembering being loved may serve to justify aggression and allow it to be discharged without restraint or guilt against self and loved ones. Also, children whose drives are minimally fused in the form of sadomasochism may regressively derive excited satisfaction from their aggressive verbalizations, behavior, and fantasies. Work on these defenses makes libidinal investments more available and aids fusion. With latency-aged children work on fusion proceeds largely via superego analysis. Their superego usually cannot be integrated harmoniously because of its harsh unfused aggression, and the

patient is reduced to raging at the world as his superego rages
at him. Here too it helps to point out not only the externalization but areas of loving investment in self and others and to
make them more consciously available. This facilitates the patient's capacity for exploring the sadistic masturbation fantasies
which augment the self-condemnation and for tracing the origins of the introjects.

The implications for educational handling pertain especially to
working with babies, toddlers, and young preschoolers in treatment via the parent or in a consultative capacity. On these early
developmental levels, the direct facilitating role of the parents is
still most effective. For example, treatment via the parent for
Jason began when he was 16 months old. He was physically well
developed and healthy, very active, and quite talkative. During
his first year pleasurable experiences had been interfered with
by a persistent rash inside his mouth and by his mother's difficulty in consistent loving investment of him. As a toddler he was
overstimulated libidinally and aggressively and, due to stress in
the family, his mother was often unexpectedly absent physically
or emotionally, while sitters cared for him. Jason was demonstrative in his affection, but also extremely aggressive and quite
impervious to pain. He often invited or exposed himself to attack, failed to learn to protect himself from common dangers,
and never complained of pain or sought comfort and, when it
was offered, did not accept it from parents or caretakers. His
mother was convinced that he was endowed with a pain threshold which organically differed from the norm and, although
concerned, she also took some pride in his stoicism. In time we
learned more about the mother's difficulty in helping Jason to be
kind to himself. She never calmly alerted Jason to approaching
danger. Instead, she either failed to notice what he was up to or
into, or she would suddenly shriek warnings at him, along with
dramatic descriptions of the terrors that could befall him. When
she found that he had been hurt, she either dismissed it with
"That's nothing," or frantically proclaimed how dreadful and
possibly irreparable the injury was. Moreover, she often used
painful tinctures to treat minor hurts so that her cure inflicted
more pain than the injury. The mother's own difficulty with
fusion and integration is obvious and had, no doubt, bearing on
the child's troubles. In part his denial of pain actually served to

protect him from his mother's onslaught, in part he perhaps identified with aspects of her handling. When the mother could be helped to recognize how unhelpful she was, she altered her approach considerably and Jason responded. His self-protectiveness improved and he began to seek and accept comfort—a first step toward improved drive fusion in Jason's self-investment and in the mother-child relationship.

Observation and work with toddlers in daycare (E. Furman, 1984a) shows that they easily lose their capacity to protest pain and to seek comfort during the mother's absence when the relationship with the mother-substitute is still tenuous and/or when the separation interferes with the mother's investment of her child so that she cannot continue adequately to fulfill her role of helping him to feel good. In these situations, libidinal depletion seems to affect the toddler's drive balance. At the same time, the discontinuity in the relationship with the mother and the transition to double or multiple mothering interfere with the development of the synthetic function. Lessening the periods of physical separation and assisting mother and child in maintaining their libidinal tie with each other during their separation help to restore drive balance, to support the development of integration, and to maintain the ability to feel.

With ill and dying children I have already described how the caring adults can assist them. In less extreme situations, when the child is ill at home, most mothers make up for the libidinal depletion and help their children to feel better, if not good, by providing extra tender loving care, special treats, and favorite dishes. They also try to minimize the irritants of therapeutic procedures. When parents and professionals disregard this need in the sick child or fear that "pampering will spoil him," they augment the psychological effects of illness and endanger the child's capacity for feeling good. In these ways the caring adults function as auxiliary ego and id-ego mediators with the ill or dying child much as the mothering person functions with the infant and toddler in normal development.

I hope that these theoretical and clinical points will suffice to introduce my thinking, will draw renewed attention to the importance of the economic aspects for psychoanalytic understanding, and will stimulate further investigation to correct, confirm, or extend these formulations and findings.

BIBLIOGRAPHY

ALPERT, A., NEUBAUER, P. B., & WEIL, A. P. (1956). Unusual variations in drive endowment. *Psychoanal. Study Child,* 11:125–163.

BORNSTEIN, B. (1953). Fragment of an analysis of an obsessional child. *Psychoanal. Study Child,* 8:313–332.

BRENMAN, E. (1982). Separation. *Int. J. Psychoanal.,* 63:303–310.

BURLINGHAM, D. T. (1972). *Psychoanalytic Studies of the Sighted and the Blind.* New York: Int. Univ. Press.

DOWLING, S. (1977). Seven infants with esophageal atresia. *Psychoanal. Study Child,* 32:215–256.

FIEDLER, E. (1965). Excerpts from the analysis of a boy with congenital club feet. *Bull. Phila. Assn. Psychoanal.,* 15:137–159.

FRANKL, L. (1961). Some observations on the development and disturbances of integration in childhood. *Psychoanal. Study Child,* 16:146–163.

FREUD, A. (1949). Aggression in relation to emotional development. *W.,* 4:489–497.

———— (1952). The mutual influences in the development of ego and id. *W.,* 4:230–244.

———— (1965). Normality and pathology in childhood. *W.,* 6.

———— (1966). Obsessional neurosis. *W.,* 5:242–261.

FREUD, S. (1905). Three essays on the theory of sexuality. *S.E.,* 7:125–243.

———— (1920). Beyond the pleasure principle. *S.E.,* 18:7–66.

———— (1923a). The ego and the id. *S.E.,* 19:12–68.

———— (1923b). Two encyclopaedia articles. *S.E.,* 18:255–262.

———— (1926). Inhibitions, symptoms and anxiety. *S.E.,* 20:77–178.

FURMAN, E. (1956). An ego disturbance in a young child. *Psychoanal. Study Child,* 11:312–335.

———— (1964). Observations on a toddler's near-fatal accident. *Bull. Phila. Assn. Psychoanal.,* 14(3):138–148.

———— (1974). *A Child's Parent Dies.* New Haven & London: Yale Univ. Press.

———— (1975). Some aspects of a young boy's masturbation conflict. In *Masturbation from Infancy to Senescence,* ed. I. M. Marcus & J. J. Francis. New York: Int. Univ. Press, pp. 185–204.

———— (1981a). Helping children cope with dying. *J. Child Psychother.,* 10:151–157.

———— (1981b). Some questions about fusion and integration and their application to the understanding and treatment of atypical children. Read at Dr. A. Katan's Monday Night Child Analysis Seminar, Cleveland.

———— (1981c). Treatment-via-the-parent. *J. Child Psychother.,* 7:89–102.

———— (1982a). Mothers have to be there to be left. *Psychoanal. Study Child,* 37:15–28.

———— (1982b). Something is better than nothing. Summary in *Bull. Hampstead Clin.,* 6:168–171, 1983.

———— (1984a). Mothers, toddlers and care. Pamphlet Series of the Cleveland

Center for Research in Child Development. Read at the Special Workshop of the Cleveland Center for Research in Child Development.

———— (1984b). On trauma. Read at the Scientific Meetings of the Association for Child Psychoanalysis, London.

———— (1984c). Some difficulties in assessing depression and suicide in childhood. In *Suicide in the Young*, ed. H. S. Sudak, A. B. Ford, & N. B. Rushforth. Boston: John Wright, pp. 245–258.

FURMAN, R. A. (1980). Some vicissitudes of the transition into latency. In *The Course of Life*, ed. S. I. Greenspan & G. H. Pollock. Washington, DC: NIMH, U.S. Dept. of Health and Human Services, pp. 33–43.

———— (1983). The father-child relationship. Pamphlet Series of the Cleveland Center for Research in Child Development. Read at the Annual Workshop of the Cleveland Center for Research in Child Development, Cleveland.

———— & FURMAN, E. (1984). Intermittent decathexis. *Int. J. Psychoanal.*, 65:423–433.

———— & KATAN, A. (1969). *The Therapeutic Nursery School.* New York: Int. Univ. Press.

HALL, R. (1982). A boy with elective mutism. Read at the Scientific Meeting of the Assn. for Child Psychoanal., Denver.

———— (1983). Follow-up on a boy with elective mutism. Read at the Scientific Meeting of the Assn. for Child Psychoanal., Princeton.

———— (1984). A boy with a claw defect of the hand. Read at the Scientific Meeting of the Assn. for Child Psychoanal., Chicago.

HARTMANN, H. (1939). *Ego Psychology and the Problem of Adaptation.* New York: Int. Univ. Press, 1958.

———— (1950). Comments on the psychoanalytic theory of the ego. *Psychoanal. Study Child*, 5:74–96.

———— (1952). The mutual influences in the development of ego and id. *Psychoanal. Study Child*, 7:9–30.

———— (1955). Notes on the theory of sublimation. *Psychoanal. Study Child*, 10:9–29.

———— (1956). Notes on the reality principle. *Psychoanal. Study Child*, 11:31–53.

HOFFER, W. (1949). Mouth, hand and ego-integration. *Psychoanal. Study Child*, 3/4:49–56.

KATAN, A. (1973). Children who were raped. *Psychoanal. Study Child*, 28:208–224.

McDEVITT, J. B. (1983). The emergence of hostile aggression and its defensive and adaptive modifications during the separation-individuation process. *J. Amer. Psychoanal. Assn., Suppl.*, 31:273–300.

NUNBERG, H. (1930). The synthetic function of the ego. In *Practice and Theory of Psychoanalysis.* New York: Int. Univ. Press, 1948, 1:120–135.

ROSENFELD, S. K. & SPRINCE, M. P. (1963). An attempt to formulate the meaning of the concept "borderline." *Psychoanal. Study Child*, 18:603–635.

———— (1965). Some thoughts on the technical handling of borderline children. *Psychoanal. Study Child*, 20:495–517.

RUDOLPH, J. (1981). Aggression in the service of the ego and the self. *J. Amer. Psychoanal. Assn.*, 29:559–580.

WEIL, A. P. (1970). The basic core. *Psychoanal. Study Child*, 25:442–460.

WILLS, D. M. (1979). "The ordinary devoted mother" and her blind baby. *Psychoanal. Study Child*, 34:31–50.

WINNICOTT, D. W. (1960a). The theory of the parent-infant relationship. In *The Maturational Processes and the Facilitating Environment*. New York: Int. Univ. Press, 1965, pp. 37–55.

———— (1960b). Ego distortion in terms of true and false self. *Ibid.*, pp. 140–152.

———— (1962). Ego integration in child development. *Ibid.*, pp. 56–63.

———— (1963a). The development of the capacity for concern. *Ibid.*, pp. 73–82.

———— (1963b). From dependence towards independence in the development of the individual. *Ibid.*, pp. 83–92.

The Influence of an Older Sibling on the Separation-Individuation Process

MARTIN LEICHTMAN, Ph.D.

IN CONSIDERING THE INFLUENCE OF SIBLINGS ON PERSONALITY DE-
velopment, psychoanalysts have traditionally focused on three
sets of issues (Colonna and Newman, 1983). First, the role of
siblings as rivals for parental (largely maternal) attention has
long been recognized, with conflicts around the birth of new
siblings being singled out for particular emphasis (Levy, 1937).
Second, psychoanalysts have always been sensitive to the manner
in which traumatic experiences with siblings in childhood (e.g.,
sexual incidents, intense hostility, or the death of siblings) may
be major determinants of later pathology. Third, from the earliest days of psychoanalysis, siblings have been included among
the members of the supporting cast in oedipal dramas, playing
such roles as fantasized offspring, parent surrogates, additional
rivals, or alternative objects. In general, classical psychoanalytic
accounts of sibling relationships have concentrated on their
problematic aspects and pathological consequences, considered
these relationships chiefly in terms of their effects on the resolution of oedipal conflicts, and implied that the significance of
such relationships derives largely from children's primary relationships with their parents.

Director of Psychology in the Children's Division of the Menninger
Foundation.

The author is indebted to Drs. Dorothy Fuller, Joseph Kovach, and Maria
Luisa Leichtman for their thoughtful critical reviews of this paper.

Until recently, the influence of siblings on identity formation and object relationships in the first years of life has received little attention, with the notable exceptions of clinical studies of such atypical or pathological phenomena as relationships between twins (Joseph and Tabor, 1961; Leonard, 1961), "twinning reactions" among nontwin siblings (Erikson, 1953; Shopper, 1974), and sustaining mutual identifications among children raised without parents in concentration camps (A. Freud and Dann, 1951). To be sure, Mahler and Jacobson, the two psychoanalysts whose theories of early development have contributed most to efforts to integrate object relations theory into ego psychology, have recognized that siblings can affect the separation-individuation process in significant ways. The clinical cases Mahler et al. (1975) present make it clear that relationships with siblings bear on the timing of separation from the mother and the handling of rapprochement crises. Jacobson (1964) states emphatically that identifications and ambivalent relationships with fathers and siblings are among the most important influences on "the child's discovery of his identity" in the period roughly corresponding to Mahler's rapprochement subphase. However, these insights were not elaborated. The theoretical sections of Mahler's work consider only mother-child relationships, while Jacobson's treatment of the issue of "rivals" is so brief and schematic that the roles of fathers and siblings are not differentiated. Nonetheless, these limited considerations of sibling influences on early development represented a departure from the tendency of most psychoanalysts and other students of the first years of life to focus almost exclusively on dyadic relationships with mothers.

The last several years have witnessed the beginning of a striking shift in this regard. A number of child analysts have argued persuasively for recognition of "the importance of the sibling experience" in early life and consideration of the "development-promoting" aspects of that experience (Colonna and Newman, 1983; Kris and Ritvo, 1983; Neubauer, 1982, 1983; Provence and Solnit, 1983; Solnit, 1983). These trends in psychoanalysis parallel those in a variety of other fields, as clinical and developmental psychologists, clinicians, personality theorists, and students of nonhuman primates have all begun to investigate the role of relationships with older siblings in early development (Bank and Kahn, 1982; Lamb and Sutton-Smith, 1982).

This paper will explore the influence of older siblings on the separation-individuation process in normal children. The first section will present a case highlighting the manner in which a girl's relationship with an older brother shaped her emerging identity and object relationships in the course of her first 3½ years. The second section will draw on this case and recent research on behavior with siblings to offer a series of hypotheses about the potential impact of the presence of older siblings at each stage of the separation-individuation process. In particular, I shall argue (1) that siblings, in their own right, are significant figures in children's lives during infancy; (2) that their influence grows in the course of the second year and often has major effects on the handling of rapprochement crises; (3) that older siblings have a critical influence on the consolidation of identity during the third year of life; and (4) that "separating" and "individuating" from older siblings constitutes an important developmental task in the preschool years.

On the Vicissitudes of Being a Younger Sister

EARLY DEVELOPMENT

Jennifer was the second of two children of professional parents. Through most of her infancy, her mother worked two and a half days a week, leaving the children in the care of a grandmotherly woman who came to the house. Jennifer's brother, John, who was 22 months older, remained with her while their mother was away. Because there were few other children in the neighborhood, the two siblings were unusually close companions throughout Jennifer's first 3 years.

A competent infant with a strong, seemingly innate striving toward individuation, Jennifer negotiated her first 16 months with few problems. In contrast to her brother, who was highstrung and, even at 3, required considerable parental help in regulating his activity level and moods, Jennifer was an even-tempered baby who was far less subject to mood swings, easily comforted, and, in general, easy to manage. For example, after her fourth month, when upset, she typically popped her thumb in her mouth and quickly calmed herself. She handled developmental challenges with little evidence of strain. At 7 months, to her mother's regret, Jennifer weaned herself, in part because she was more interested in play and exploration. She reached major developmental milestones early. Her gross and fine motor coordination were excellent; she walked by 10 months; she talked at 11 months; and, by the middle of her second year, she had a formidable vocabulary and occasionally spoke in sentences of 10 words. The extent of her precocious development could be gauged best shortly after her second birthday when she entered a Montessori preschool. Although almost a year younger than any of the children in her class, because of her size, coordination, fluency, and concentration, she was able to negotiate the cognitive, emotional, and social tasks expected of children at the school and fit with the group comfortably.

Well before the end of her first year, it was clear that Jennifer's brother was a major figure in her life. For Jennifer, as for many infants, little beings her own size or not too much larger held a particular fascination. Even in her fourth month, when a group of people were present, she was most curious about and devoted most of her attention to observing children in preference to adults. Her brother was an object of special interest and, by her sixth month, a source of endless amusement to her. A photo taken when she was 7 months old captures the quality of their relationship. Jennifer can be seen sitting in a little walker, gazing up at John who is eating in his highchair. She is beaming at him with what appears to be admiration and affection, unaware that the antics by which she is being entertained consist of his giving her raspberries and other expressions of contempt that 2½-year-olds are all too ready to visit on their younger sisters.

By the end of her first year, John was a favorite playmate and teacher. His influence on her was readily apparent, for example, in her choice of a transitional object. John was attached to a blanket and had a favorite corner which he called "the Louise part" because it contained a label by the woman who had made it. By her first birthday, not only was Jennifer deeply attached to a blanket of her own, but she was already calling a preferred corner, one distinguished only by some fraying and extra stitching, "part." While it is perhaps only likely that her brother had provided a major spur to her walking and talking early, after her first birthday there could be no doubt about his profound influence on her activities, as she tried constantly to play with his toys, imitate his activities, and engage, as best she could, in play similar to his.

In characterizing Jennifer's relationship with her brother during her first 16 months, three points stand out. First, John was clearly a major presence in Jennifer's life by her sixth month. When she was in need or in distress, her attention was focused exclusively on her mother; at other times, indeed through most of her waking day, her brother was often an object of considerable interest. Second, John's influence on her was most apparent, and probably greatest, in those aspects of development involved in the early individuation process. Her observation of him and efforts to imitate him were undoubtedly a significant spur to her precocious perceptual-motor and cognitive development well before her first birthday. Third, through much of this period, her relationship with her brother was a remarkably benign one on her part. While her interest in and attachment to him were unmistakable, signs of anger or jealousy were rare and fleeting or, at least, difficult to detect.

THE RAPPROCHEMENT PERIOD

A rapid and striking shift in Jennifer's behavior occurred around her 16th month. Whereas earlier, she had been an even-tempered, easily managed, albeit determined and independent youngster, now she became moody and demanding. She shadowed her mother and was underfoot constantly. Her relationship with her parents, especially her mother, seemed to consist chiefly of an incessant battle of wills and involved those rapid oscillations between clinging and assertions of autonomy and between expressions of love and hate characteristic of youngsters during this developmental phase. John and Jennifer now exhibited a touching concern for each other. Jennifer seemed especially empathic when her brother was hurt and, when she was upset, John might try to comfort her by bringing her favorite blanket, a favor his sister returned when she was a bit older.

But, above all, Jennifer's relationship with her brother seemed fraught with conflict. Whereas earlier she had been content to imitate her brother and accept happily whatever he was doing, she now wanted desperately to have what he had and to do what he did. In contrast to her brother, who almost from birth directed aggression inward and tied himself in knots when upset, Jennifer was combative. She had few compunctions about taking what she wanted when she wanted it and, by 18 months, was ready to assault playmates with blunt objects if need be to obtain her ends. Similarly, whereas she had slept through the night since early childhood, now, and sporadically over the next year and a half, she awoke in the early hours of the morning. Not surprisingly, she occasionally reported nightmares the content of which consisted of monsters attacking her or her brother in ways reminiscent of her assaults on him earlier in the day.

Jennifer's relationship with her brother affected her negotiation of the "rapprochement crisis" in two ways. First, although she had to struggle with this "crisis" in many of the same intense, conflicted ways as other children, the separation aspects of the process may have been eased for her. Certainly, she appeared to have less difficulty with the issue than her brother. For example, her response to those comparatively brief separations when her parents left for work or went out for an evening on a weekend were far less intense not only than her brother's reactions at a similar age, but than his current responses. Although John could still be quite demanding and cry as his parents left, Jennifer was more subdued, retreated to her blanket, and at least overtly accepted, however reluctantly, their going. While probably related to temperamental and characterological differences, her response also reflected the fact that, because John remained with her, separations were not as complete as they had been for him.

Second, and even more significant, Jennifer's relationship with her brother was now a potent influence on the individuation process. She still exhibited considerable affection for John and treated him as an admired model whom she was eager to imitate. Yet envy of and competition with him, which had emerged with startling rapidity at this time, became central themes in her life. To be sure, John contributed to the undercurrent of envy and rivalry that was present in all their activities together. For John, Jennifer had long been a competitor for parental attention, particularly in the evenings when he wanted it most, and this competition grew as she became an increasingly competent and assertive toddler. Although he seldom attacked her directly, he was not above setting her up to get into trouble. However, John's envy of the regressive prerogatives allowed his younger sister was far less than her envy of what he was able to accomplish. By and large, he was pleased to be the older child, while she constantly wished to be able to do what he could do and felt driven to compete with him in what was forever an unequal contest of skills. Consequently, whereas until her 16th month, Jennifer was content simply to imitate John in whatever he was doing, after her 18th month this was never enough. Whether in displaying motor skills, working on puzzles, doing early academic tasks, or simply being able to go to school, she was acutely aware of how much he could do and she could not. While these attitudes were no doubt fed by the high value her parents placed on accomplishments and by the recognition they gave her brother for his skills, her attitudes were so deeply ingrained that her parents found there was little they could do to modify them. No amount of recognition for her impressive and often quite extraordinary achievements seemed to help her to feel at ease and no intervention her parents could think of diminished her pain at not being able to compete with her brother on equal terms.

Jennifer's determination to emulate and equal her brother in his accomplishments was now a central aspect of her character, one that shaped her negotiation of basic developmental tasks. For example, at a year and a half, she tried to toilet train herself because her brother had done so. At first this task was too hard for her and she let it go briefly. Two months later she tried again and succeeded rapidly. Her parents put no pressure on her (her brother did not train himself until he was about 3) and they did little more than offer praise and recognition for her accomplishment of a process with which she seemed to need little help. Similarly, whether pedaling a tricycle, swinging on swings, riding a large rocking horse, drawing, or doing puzzles, Jennifer strove to master a host of new skills chiefly because her brother had done so. Indeed, with some reluctance, her parents were persuaded to allow her to go to her brother's preschool shortly after she was 2, a half year younger than the school typically accepted children. During the preceding 6 months, they had to witness Jennifer's unhappiness each morning as her brother left for school and during the summer they struggled with her even more marked upsets at the fact that John was able to go to day camp and returned excitedly each day with drawings, craft projects, coloring books, and stories of all he had done during the day. Their reluctance and concerns about Jennifer's age were overcome when she spent the last weeks of the summer putting various odd possessions in paper bags and insisting she was taking them to school for Show-and-Tell.

Significantly, in spite of her age, she adjusted to preschool with relative ease. She showed no concerns about separation from her mother when she was left at school nor did she need to seek to remain close to her brother while there. When older girls in the class flocked around wishing to play little mother to her, she shooed them off, insisting that she "had work to do." Like other youngsters at the school, she was able to spend a considerable amount of time on independent projects. In fact, it was especially important to her that she do such projects so that she would have "work" to bring home with her. She became quite upset if she had been so involved with puzzles, games, or other activities at school that she forgot to complete a project to take with her. While she enjoyed her parents' praise, that praise did not appear to be a central factor in her wish to bring work home. Nor did an identification with her working parents appear important at this point. Rather, she was preoccupied with playing the role her brother had played a year earlier and continued to play, that of "someone who brought work home from school." In this respect, as in many others, her wish to be like and compete with her brother played a central role in her emerging sense of identity in this period.

JENNIFER'S THIRD YEAR

Jennifer's identification and competition with her brother exerted a profound influence on the crystallization of her identity during her third year. Because of her capacity for increasingly differentiated self representations during this year and the significance of sex-role issues, the influence of the sibling relationship in shaping her sexual identity was especially striking.

A core gender identity based chiefly on Jennifer's relationship with her mother was already firmly established by the time she was 2. For example, shortly after her first birthday she would spend extended periods of time imitating her mother, pretending to cook on a toy stove in the kitchen as her mother prepared meals. Throughout the latter part of her second and even more during her third year, one of her favorite activities in the evening was "playing baby." In this play, she would pretend to be a mother ministering to the needs of a baby, a role played by her mother or father. She would delight in treating her "babies" with that mixture of nurturance and bossiness she felt she had experienced during the day. At 2, she had no doubts that she was a little girl, although her relationship with her brother had a major impact on the kind of little girl she felt herself to be and her attitudes toward that sex role.

Her knowledge of anatomical differences between the sexes, at least as they pertained to her, was probably more heavily influenced by observations of John than anything else. It was John whom she had seen undressed often and it was with his body that she most often compared her own. Her awareness of the differences between them was apparent at 18 months when, chiefly as a result of having seen him go to the potty, she spent an extended period of time on several occasions standing in front of the toilet with her shirt pulled up, struggling to urinate through her bellybutton, a sight as much poignant as humorous because of the intensity of her wish. It was her curiosity about differences between her body and his that led her to question her parents about male and female anatomy. At 20 months, she was quite interested in exploring her "pagina," a concept that seemed to link those parts of her body she liked to explore during her bath with the pajamas she wore soon afterwards. Shortly after she was 2, she gave clear expression to what might aptly be called "penis envy." Having mastered toilet training, she now on several occasions insisted on trying to urinate standing up as she had seen her brother do. On one occasion, after yet another explanation

from her parents about the anatomical differences between the
sexes and the likely consequences of her efforts (namely, that she
would wet her pants and the floor), she persisted—with the
predicted results. Her parents' concern about sparing her shame
and embarrassment around the incident proved quite unnecessary. As she was being changed, she explained that, although she
had not been successful this time, she was going to have a penis
some day. Asked how, she replied with her characteristic mixture of brashness and determination: "Superpowers! Superpowers!! I'm going to get my superpower gun."

Even this emergent interest in "superheroes," which increased through her third year, reflected the interests of her
brother, who was addicted to Saturday morning cartoons. Jennifer was quite ready to accept the concept of female superheroes, and she spent most of her third year wearing underwear
with designs of female superheroes on them. In coping with
night fears, she frequently mixed different superhero tops and
bottoms to give herself special combinations of powers. However, it was always the masculine quality of these figures that was
most important to her. For example, on Halloween, when she
was 28 months, she vetoed her parents' suggestion that she be a
princess or even Supergirl, and insisted that she would be Superman like her brother. Over the winter and spring that followed,
she often wore her Superman cape from Halloween while playing. In the spring, when her parents bought her Superman pajamas, she wore them nightly through the next months, agreeing
only with greatest reluctance to wear other pajamas on nights
when they were being washed.

Jennifer's obsession with being like her brother left its imprint
on her dress, activities, interests, and fantasies throughout the
course of her third year. She preferred wearing pants and shirts,
often hand-me-downs from her brother and, before her Superman pajamas, she wore John's old pajamas instead of the attractive new nightgowns her parents bought for her. Although she
sporadically showed an interest in playing with dolls, she much
preferred toys like her brother's. For example, by the end of her
third year she, too, had a large collection of Matchbox cars. His
interests, such as lawn mowing or watching garbage men, be-

came her interests, although he engaged in the activities for their own sake, whereas she was interested chiefly in emulating John and doing things with him. Her brother's influence was most striking in her choice of TV shows and the fantasies she played out. She was particularly attracted by another favorite show of his about highway patrolmen, a show that consisted of scenes of car chases and sanitized crashes alternating with ones of the two policemen being helpful to people. Like her brother, Jennifer identified with the two main male leads. She acquired a toy motorcycle like theirs and, in her play, she pretended to be a patrolman as she rode her tricycle. While her interests were heavily influenced by her brother, she was far too assertive and independent a young lady to be content simply to imitate him and she came to give those interests her own distinctive stamp. For example, she made parts of the highway patrol show her own. For the better part of her third year, at the beginning and end of the show, all activity in the house had to cease while she danced to the theme music with the rest of the family serving as her audience.

As Jennifer approached her third birthday, her relationship with her brother began to change in ways characteristic of youngsters as they get older. While still usually following his lead, she now tried to set rules for their games and even made up games for John to play. As the older brother, he decided which games to go along with and which to laugh off. Jennifer now always managed to tag along with John and his playmates and horn in on their play. Often the boys allowed her to be part of their activities, but equally frequently they were so absorbed with each other that they ignored or deliberately excluded her. With a pugnaciousness and humor that could be quite charming, Jennifer would try to get John and his friends to accept her either because they felt what she was doing was genuinely funny or they simply enjoyed having her look silly. If these efforts did not succeed in winning her entree into their activities, she might either hit them or withdraw, crying and nursing her hurt feelings. At the end of her third year, even though she now showed more individuality in her interactions, she had great difficulty separating from her brother and needed to be with, imitate, compete with, and surpass him in all of the activities and tasks he set for himself.

JENNIFER AT 3

In the weeks prior to her third birthday, Jennifer began to exhibit new interests that suggested concerns about femininity and the presence of early oedipal issues. For example, having seen TV commercials for dolls, she decided that she wanted Barbie on one side of her birthday cake and Supergirl on the other. In contrast to wishing only for masculine toys such as motorcycles as she had a month earlier, she now decided that she also wanted some children's cosmetics among her birthday gifts. Although dismayed, her parents acceded to the latter request because it seemed to herald an identity more independent of her brother, because it contained softer and more "feminine" elements, and because it offered some hope of cutting down on the level of domestic violence Jennifer was still prepared to wreak. However, her earlier preoccupations were also much in evidence. Jennifer still wished to receive toys like those of her brother and, at the time of her birthday, she was particularly pleased to help her father cut out and paint a large cardboard box decorated to represent Superman's "Fortress of Solitude." On her birthday itself, this mixture of old and new themes was exemplified both in her delight in receiving a dainty purse as a gift from a favorite aunt and in the fact that the purse had been broken by the end of the day because she had used it as a weapon on her brother.

In the two months following her birthday, Jennifer started to express oedipal wishes openly. She talked about marrying her father when she grew up, remaining undecided about whether or not her mother would continue to live with them. In the late summer, she spent the better part of the week trying to keep herself from going to sleep after getting up late one night to discover her parents having an infrequent candlelight dinner. When asked why she stayed up, she asserted that she would not go to sleep because she felt her parents would have another such dinner and she "never got invited to them!" Discussions of the differences in age between parents and children, of parents having rights and interests of their own, and of children's need for sleep proved quite fruitless in the face of her insistence that there were now three adults in the house. The issue was resolved only by a show of force, with her parents insisting that she stay in bed at night or they would turn off the night light and music she used to help her go to sleep. Although her father was usually the disciplinarian in such matters, she was most oppositional with her mother and was generally much more malleable with him.

Jennifer's relationship with her brother was more relaxed during this period. Both her growing maturity and the fact that one of John's close neighborhood friends had moved away made her more of a playmate for him than ever before. Also, Jennifer grew less resentful as she was able to engage in more activities with him. For example, in the course of the summer, she attended two different day camps with him, ones from which she had been excluded the preceding year because of her age. As she started camp, she amazed her family with vivid, detailed memories of all of the camp activities John had described and all of the projects he had brought home a year earlier. She now engaged in these activities with relish, demonstrating to herself and others that she could do the same things her brother could.

At the same time, throughout these same two summer months, the prospect of an impending separation and disengagement from her brother in the fall when he would begin kindergarten was very much on the minds of Jennifer and her parents. John had eagerly anticipated starting school since a preenrollment meeting the preceding spring. During the spring, the children had daily reminders that school lay ahead for him as they watched the school bus go past their house each morning. Over the summer, John frequently shared his excitement about beginning school, particularly when the family drove by the building on errands. Jennifer responded to this threat by asserting that she too was going to kindergarten. When others in the family explained that she had to be 5 years old to attend public school, she insisted that one only had to be 3 and, if this argument was not convincing, she would repeat it more emphatically, holding up 3 fingers as if this settled the point. The vigor with which she insisted that she was going to kindergarten and her refusal to consider any other possibility for the fall gave her family fair warning of trouble ahead at the end of the summer.

THE "CRISIS"

As anticipated, two months after her third birthday, when John began school, Jennifer experienced a crisis that involved facing both separation from him and coming to terms with the differences in age and status between them. On the Friday John started kindergarten, Jennifer showed little overt reaction, although she was more irritable than usual. However, the following day, while shopping for school bags for her and her brother, she had a tantrum in the department store far more intense and prolonged than any she had had in her life, a tantrum precipitated by her parents' refusal to get her *two* book bags instead of merely one. In discussing her feelings later, she acknowledged readily that she was mad because her brother could go to school and she could not. The reality of the transformation in her and her brother's lives confronted her continually during the next week. Each morning she accompanied John to the bus stop and watched him leave for school; each afternoon, she witnessed his exuberant return with stories about friends and activities as well as papers displaying his work at school; and, as if fate were determined to underline differences between them, that very week John attended two birthday parties to which she had not been invited.

After her weekend tantrum, Jennifer's reaction to the situation was characterized chiefly by a mixture of moodiness, unhappiness, and regression. Whereas in the past she was generally cheerful and, when upset, ready to direct aggression outward, she now appeared depressed. For a week she had little interest in food, was distracted and listless, and spent long periods of time holding her blanket and sucking her thumb. Although she had been toilet trained for over a year, she began having frequent accidents during the day. She also had problems around separation at bedtime. As she had a year earlier, she pleaded with her parents to stay with her at night because she was "frightened." Only after two weeks of her parents' allowing her considerable leeway for regression and providing her with a great deal of support did her spirits begin to improve.

Over the next weeks, Jennifer struggled to come to terms with the narcissistic blows she had experienced and the change in her relationship with John. One aspect of this struggle lay simply in mastering the immediate experience of separating from her brother each morning as she and her parents accompanied him to the bus stop. By the end of the first week, she created a ritual in which she left her own distinct imprint on that process. Before the family left the house each morning, she carefully packed her blanket, papers, and markers in her book bag, which, like her brother, she wore to the bus stop. When she reached the street corner, she spread out her blanket, took out her papers, and began working on a project until she heard the bus coming. At that time, she leapt to her feet and used a marker to hit a street sign, making a ringing sound that was to signal the family that the bus was about to arrive. She then stationed herself by the back of the bus where she could wave to a group of older children as the bus left. Within a day or two, she had established for herself a coterie of sixth grade girls who gathered on her side of the bus to wave to and otherwise entertain her. She then repacked all of her possessions and insisted on being carried home by her parents as if she were a younger child.

Almost as soon as her brother began school, marked shifts in Jennifer's behavior and relationships were apparent. The most significant of these changes lay in her relationship with both of her parents, but especially her mother. Over the preceding year, her mother had been troubled by a distance between the two of them that seemed to reflect Jennifer's efforts to handle separation from and anger at her mother through a kind of premature individuation and a subtle reliance on her brother and father for dealing with dependency issues. As soon as John began school, Jennifer abandoned her preoccupation with budding oedipal wishes, drew close to her mother, and sought to renegotiate rapprochement issues she had handled far differently a year earlier. She now became more eager to have her mother with her in the evenings than her father. When she awoke at night with nightmares, she sought comfort from her mother rather than her father. In the week after the beginning of school, Jennifer exhibited many highly regressive behaviors with her mother rarely seen in the last year. She talked baby talk, sucked her thumb, and particularly enjoyed it when her mother, allowing and responding to her regression, treated her like a baby. When Jennifer's own preschool began a week later, she had moderate separation problems, voicing wishes not to go to school immediately before leaving home and clinging and crying at the point she was left by her mother. Such behavior was short-lived—the moment her mother left, she turned happily to familiar activities—and the behavior was influenced by the fact that there were many new, young children at the school whose marked problems around separation could have been contagious. However, the appearance of such problems at all was striking since Jennifer had exhibited none of them a year earlier at the same school and, during the summer, had negotiated several far more challenging separations for day camp experiences with larger numbers of older children. In addition to becoming more dependent and concerned about separations, during this same period Jennifer began wetting herself provocatively during the day and having problems around bowel movements as well, stimulating conflicts around toilet training that had been remarkable by their absence over the preceding year and a half. Along with such regressive behaviors and conflicts, however, Jennifer was also far more affectionate with her mother in mature ways and enjoyed their activities together when her brother was away at school. The independence, stubbornness, and even roughness she had exhibited with both parents over the preceding year were now toned down considerably and she seemed far softer and more affectionate. Hence, as an almost immediate consequence of the separation from her brother as he began school, Jennifer seemed to reopen and renegotiate with her mother a host of earlier issues, particularly ones relating to separation.

A second major development in this period centered on Jennifer's efforts to establish an identity of her own apart from her brother. The most striking manifestation of this process occurred during her bedtime routine when one of her parents would read her several books shortly before she was to go to sleep. The week after John started school, Jennifer insisted that she wanted to look at a photograph album of pictures from the time of her birth instead of one of her books. The album began with several pictures of her mother noticeably pregnant and her brother engaged in various 2-year-old activities, but also clearly curious about his mother's pregnancy; there followed a series of pictures from the delivery room that included her mother beaming at the new baby and her father's pleasure at the birth; next came evidence of friends' recognition of the event such as a large banner across the house welcoming Jennifer home and her new crib filled with stuffed animals contributed by people she now knew well; the album concluded with pictures showing her parents and brother caring for her. On the first evening she reviewed the pictures, Jennifer approached them with a mixture of interest and apprehension that seemed related to the mysteries of birth, seeing her parents in the delivery room in puzzling costumes, and the regressive pull of seeing herself as an infant. However, within a few days, it was difficult to find a trace of anxiety as she converted the album into an epic with herself as the heroine. The story, as she experienced it, was one of the family eagerly awaiting her arrival; her parents' intense pleasure at having a girl; her family and friends celebrating her arrival; and her embarkation on a new life—a story that, for all of her embellishments, was not far from the truth. While clearly a means of dealing with the narcissistic injuries coming in the wake of her brother attending kindergarten, this preoccupation with her early history also appeared to be a way to accept and come to terms with a recognition that she and her brother were separate and to establish a sense of her own individuality and worth.

A third set of developments that followed in the wake of this separation from her brother consisted of her rapid consolidation of a feminine identity. Such a change could be seen in her clothes and appearance. Earlier she preferred to wear pants and shirts that had belonged to her brother and resisted new clothes, especially dresses, strenuously; a week after her brother began school, she expressed an interest in wearing a pretty dress to surprise her mother. Earlier she insisted on wearing pajamas at night; now, as her fall clothes were unpacked, she discovered two frilly nightgowns that she was eager to try on and show off and that she wore nightly from this time on. She no longer resisted when her parents combed or brushed her hair and even began doing so herself. Earlier she had preferred books about owls, frogs, and toads engaged in silly and amusing activities for her evening reading; now she insisted on having a long version of Cinderella read nightly. So intently did she listen to the story that, despite its length, her parents learned to read with great care lest they miss an adjective and be reproved sternly for departing from the text. Earlier she had not been a particularly demonstrative child; now, at least sporadically, she was interested in giving her father hugs and kisses and took great pride in her skill in this matter.

Perhaps most significant, beginning in the third week after her brother began school and increasingly in the months to come, the idea of having babies and of being someone who could have babies became a major preoccupation. Over the preceding year, Jennifer had occasionally spoken about having babies and undoubtedly had had passing fantasies about where they came from. Yet this subject was only one of many in which she was interested and was never pursued in a sustained fashion. Moreover, usually her interest in having babies centered on a wish to occupy a role like that of her parents, either being a nurturant figure caring for an infant or being an authority who could dictate to others how they should behave. Now, she was fascinated by the birth process itself and by the thought of having babies. She occupied herself with such questions as whether she would have 10, 15, or 100 children!

After a week of reviewing the album of photographs of herself as an infant, she developed an intense and persistent curiosity about how babies develop in their mothers and pressed her father into giving an explanation of the matter. She wanted to know exactly where the vagina and uterus were located and had her father draw crude simplified diagrams along with his explanations. She listened intently as he told her how girls were born with tiny eggs in a special place in their bodies, how when they grew up the eggs were released and moved toward the uterus, how when girls were ready to be mommies the eggs were fertilized and implanted in the uterus, and how the baby grew in the uterus and the mommy became "fatter" as the baby grew. Jennifer was especially interested in drawings of the baby getting bigger and the mother's shape changing. A very determined youngster, she seemed to know exactly what she was interested in, asking extensive and detailed questions in these areas and quickly moving her father off topics that didn't capture her attention. To his relief, she showed little curiosity at this time about the role of the male in the birth process and focused all of her questions on matters such as what the egg was like, how the baby grew, and how the vagina stretched when the baby came out.

Two days later, the manner in which she assimilated this information became clear. Engaging in her favorite evening activity, "playing baby," she assumed her usual role as the mother and ordered her father not to be simply a baby, but "a little boy baby." After waking her father-baby and changing, dressing, and feeding him as usual, she insisted that he ask to have a baby. When he said he wanted to have one when he grew up, she informed him in an authoritative way, and with considerable glee, that he could not, that he was a boy who merely had a penis and that you had to be a girl with a uterus in order to have a baby. When he insisted that, nonetheless, he wanted to have a baby very badly, she told him that he didn't have a vagina either which, she felt, settled the matter. She then proceeded to give him a detailed and surprisingly accurate version of the lecture she had heard two nights earlier, explaining that girls were born with eggs that descended into the uterus and grew there.

After the lecture, the father-baby asked if daddies had any role in babies being produced, a topic that had been covered with only the most passing reference to fertilization previously. Jennifer thought for a while and offered her own explanation, one that pleased her sufficiently that she repeated it on a number of occasions over the next weeks. The father's role, she decided, occurred at the end of the pregnancy and was confined chiefly to getting the baby out of the mother by cracking the egg. He did this by shaking the mother vigorously which broke the shell of the egg and allowed the baby to come out. Delivering babies was a special variation of making an omelet.

A number of influences appear to have been significant in the formation of this fantasy. First, an obvious source was her interest in the photographs from the time of her birth, especially those showing her father in the delivery room. Second, an equally obvious influence was her father's "lecture" of two nights earlier. Although he tried to make clear the difference between human eggs and those of chickens, she understood the former in terms of what she knew best. Third, over the preceding months,

she had often enjoyed cooking breakfast with her father, her
favorite task being that of cracking and scrambling eggs. Fourth,
a few weeks earlier, she had been deeply impressed by an episode of her favorite show about highway patrolmen in which a
woman at a discotheque had gone into labor while dancing and
had had her baby delivered by the ever-present, ever-helpful
heroes of the show. In the weeks following this show, she insisted
that her parents recount the plot on numerous occasions. The
connection between dancing and having babies may have had
special meaning for her because of the importance she had long
attributed to the family watching her while she danced to the
theme music of the program. Finally, the fantasy had clear
oedipal meanings, although she placed all of the sexual excitement at the wrong end of the process of conception and delivery.

Although oedipal issues would assume increasing importance
for Jennifer over the next year, what appeared to be the central,
overriding influence on this play and fantasy was Jennifer's
effort to consolidate a feminine identity, an effort motivated,
above all else, by the need to establish an identity distinct from
that of her brother. This influence was clear in the form of her
play. For the first time, she wished to assume the role of an
authoritative mother in relation to a baby boy rather than an
infant whose sex did not matter, suggesting both a closer identification with her mother and a wish to reverse a relationship in
which she had been hurt by being subordinate to and deserted
by her brother. The content of her fantasy highlighted this issue
even more clearly. Her concerns with the female anatomy and
having babies were not at this time chiefly efforts to cope with
"penis envy," but rather a reflection of her determination to find
means of establishing her difference from, not to mention supe-
riority to, her brother. Her anxiety around the birth process,
and men cracking eggs, may well have reflected both fears of
being assaulted for her wish to use sexual differences to triumph
over her brother and reassurance that the men with whom he so
strongly identified, the highway patrolmen, would be benign
and helpful. In sum, both the fantasies and the form in which
they were played out speak to a far clearer and stronger identification with her mother and a recognition and accentuation of
the distinctness of being a girl, events initiated in no small mea-

sure because of efforts to separate and individuate from her brother.

This "crisis" and Jennifer's early attempts to negotiate it had a major impact on her development. The trends present at this time could be seen clearly several months later when Jennifer was 3½. As is characteristic of the development of children, earlier emotional issues and behavior patterns did not simply disappear, but rather continued to be exhibited periodically. However, they occurred less frequently and were subordinate to new issues. In particular, at 3½, the shifts in Jennifer's relationship to her brother and her parents and the shifts in sexual identity present at the time of the "crisis" were now more pronounced.

She had taken significant new steps toward separating and individuating from her brother. He remained a favorite playmate; she still often imitated what he was doing; and their rivalry continued to be much in evidence. Yet their relationship had a far different quality than earlier. Jennifer was more mature and ready to engage in games and play on a more equal footing. Earlier, in their activities, she needed either to imitate what John was doing or try to coerce him into doing exactly what she was doing. Now there was much more reciprocity, negotiation, and rule following. She was no longer obsessively concerned with being with her brother, doing what he did, or having exactly what he had. She did not need to intrude on all of his activities and could often play by herself when he was doing something in which she was not especially interested. When he had other playmates his own age or when he went to a friend's house, she no longer sought frantically to join him, nor was she preoccupied with what he was doing while he was away. She was often content to engage in games or activities with her parents at those times, deriving considerable enjoyment from them. In short, she could now tolerate separations from her brother and was better able to pursue interests of her own.

Jennifer's efforts to renegotiate earlier developmental issues with her parents continued as well. On the one hand, although she remained an assertive, relatively independent little being, she continued to be more affectionate with her parents, especially in the evenings. She clung to her mother more and often sought her out to minister to dependency needs when she was hurt or lonely. Her teachers at preschool noticed similar changes. Although she had lost little of her independence or ability to carry through on projects, without her brother present, she sought out teachers much more often to help with her work, show off her accomplishments, or simply maintain a relationship. On the other hand, conflicts around compliance and defiance were prominent as well. Indeed, in the midst of stubborn and provocative battles, Jennifer might wet herself or become deeply conflicted around having bowel movements. To their surprise, long after the period of regression when her brother began school, her parents found themselves struggling with the kinds of conflicts around toilet training that had been expected, but were not present when she was 2.

Finally, although Jennifer had not lost her rambunctiousness or daring, she now gave abundant evidence of a solidified feminine identification. She continued to be interested in wearing dresses as well as slacks, preferred nightgowns to pajamas in the evening, and went through a period in which she delighted in painting her nails with magic markers, an activity that had to be watched closely because she was quite ready to further adorn her arms and legs with colorful designs that did not wash off easily. Her interest in babies remained intense. However, as the issue of oedipal rivalry with her mother became far more prominent and concerns with differentiation from her brother less pressing, she had mixed feelings about pregnancy because of fears of the dangers involved. She now occasionally expressed the wish to be a boy, although this wish appeared to be an outgrowth of oedipal anxieties and a new kind of ambivalent relationship with her mother rather than an effort to deal with her relationship with her brother as it was earlier.

Neither Jennifer's strong attachment to her brother nor her rivalry with him ceased when she was 3½. Both characteristics were much in evidence a year later and, to the extent that her development remained "normal," would probably be present in one form or another throughout the course of her life (Bank and

Kahn, 1982; Lamb and Sutton-Smith, 1982). Yet as Jennifer grew older, these issues did not have the same impact on her. Her brother remained important to her, but she made friends of her own and her attachment to him did not preempt or overshadow relationships with other playmates. Jennifer's rivalry with John—and his with her—were still woven into the fabric of their family life, but that rivalry was no longer as direct or all-encompassing as it had been earlier. In her pursuit of attention and recognition, Jennifer was now free to follow her own interests and develop her own talents. For example, John taught himself to read early and displayed a flair for tasks involving verbal reasoning. While often jealous as he displayed such skills, Jennifer no longer sought to imitate him or compete with him on his terms. Instead, she devoted herself to art, to developing skills in mathematical areas, and to swimming, in which she felt she was "better than John." Perhaps most important, whereas in the course of Jennifer's third year her relationship with her brother exerted a profound influence on her emerging identity, by 3½ this relationship moved off center stage, as her efforts to negotiate oedipal relationships with both of her parents became the preeminent issue in her life.

Siblings and the Separation-Individuation Process

Jennifer's case and recent research on the behavior of young children with older siblings have significant implications for psychoanalytic theories of early identity formation and object relationships, theories that have focused almost exclusively on the mother-child dyad. One way to appreciate the significance of this research is to consider it in relation to the most influential current psychoanalytic view of how children develop a sense of themselves as separate and distinct from their mothers and establish a sense of their own unique identities, Mahler's theory of the separation-individuation process. Each of the sections that follow will (1) summarize main features of particular stages described by Mahler; (2) note the most salient features of normal children's interactions with older siblings during these periods; and (3) on the basis of these observations, offer a number of hypotheses regarding the influence of sibling relationships on the process of separation and individuation. Although for the purpose of exposition, reference will simply be made to "children" and "older siblings," it should be stressed that the ideas advanced concern the development of "normal" children in intact, reasonably healthy families in which there is an age span of approximately 1½ to 3½ years between siblings.

THE NEONATAL PERIOD

There is little reason to believe that siblings have any significant direct effect on infants during the first four to six weeks of life. As children struggle to adapt to extrauterine existence, to regulate bodily systems and stimulation from their environment, the chief task facing them is "to achieve a homeostatic equilibrium by predominantly physiological means" (Mahler and McDevitt, 1982, p. 396). Because inborn behavior patterns play a major role in neonates' interactions with their environments and because long periods of time are spent asleep or only half-awake, the attunement of newborns to the outside world is limited and such attunement as they display centers on establishing contact with and facilitating the ministrations of caretaking figures who are at best only dimly perceived. In such circumstances, the only influence siblings are likely to have on neonates is indirect, as the demands of older children affect maternal attitudes and the time, attention, and energy mothers can devote to new babies.

THE "NORMAL SYMBIOTIC" PHASE

By the end of the second month, with the further maturation of the central nervous system, there is a decisive shift in infants' psychological organization and social relationships. Attentional patterns shift as patterns of sleep and wakefulness become more distinct and children become more attuned to the outside world; perceptual organization changes as a primary orientation toward proprioceptive-interoceptive stimulation gives way to an increasing investment in external stimulation; and the smiling response appears and serves as a regulator not only of infants' behavior, but also of the social systems around them. By any measure of time, intensity, or significance, infants' relationships with their mothers are now so important that they almost eclipse all other relationships. It is mothers who meet infants' needs for nurturance and contact, relief from distress, and help in regulating external stimulation and internal tension states. Moreover, on a moment-by-moment basis, infants and their mothers enter into complex affective-communicative systems involving cyclical patterns of attention and withdrawal of attention, excitement and recovery, and engagement and disengagement in which an affective synchrony between the pairs is established (Brazelton and Als, 1979). Because of developments of these kinds, Mahler designates the period from approximately 6 weeks to 5 months of life as the "symbiotic phase" and hypothesizes that during this time infants gradually build up primitive, labile, diffuse, affective-cognitive schemata in which the "I" and "not I" are undifferentiated, but slowly emerging poles of experience.

In these months, infants already exhibit a significant amount of behavior toward siblings of two kinds. Smiles are not reserved for mothers alone, and siblings, who often view babies as a cross between pets, dolls, and animated toys, delight in eliciting them. Observing this phenomenon, Brazelton (1969, p. 76) asserts: "The positive reinforcement of the infant's smiles which comes from older children shows why second and third children are likely to be gayer than first children. Although parents are just as delighted with an infant's smiles, their reactions are not as free or spontaneous as are those of children. Here we have just one more instance of how much a baby gets from his siblings!" In addition, in those periods of "alert inactivity" during which Mahler suggests babies learn most about the world around them, infants show a particular interest in watching other children. As was the case with Jennifer, who was fascinated by her brother by her fourth month, most children of this age love to look at other children and "given a choice, they will often choose a child to observe rather than an adult" (Brazelton, 1969, p. 99).

In assessing the significance of such behavior with siblings, it is important to consider the conditions in which it occurs. First, interactions between infants and siblings usually take place with mothers present. For example, when John played with Jennifer, she was often seated on her mother's lap, held by her mother, or in a highchair or crib with her mother in close proximity. Hence, infants' experiences of siblings at this time include the presence of mothers at least in the background. Second, mothers typically regulate contacts between infants and siblings. For example, Jennifer's mother allowed interactions between the children when Jennifer was in a relatively good mood; permitted the interactions to continue only while they were relatively playful and benign; sought to modify John's behavior as it became too rough or overstimulating for Jennifer; and terminated the interactions and enveloped Jennifer at points when she became upset. Finally, lest the importance of sibling relationships in this period be overemphasized, it should be stressed that they in no way compare with the significance of relationships with mothers. The time infants spend with siblings is only a fraction of that spent with mothers; contacts with mothers are regular and relatively constant, whereas those with siblings are sporadic; mothers satisfy basic drives, alleviate distress, and regulate stimulation and activity levels, whereas siblings at best play minor roles in these regards; and infants' experiences with mothers occur across all psychological states, while those with siblings occur chiefly during periods of calm and well-being.

Such observations of infants' interactions with siblings between their second and fifth months have two implications for Mahler's theory of the development of early object relations:

1. *While clearly subordinate to relationships with their mothers, infants' experiences with siblings are conducive to the establishment of a modest form of the healthy "symbiosis" that arises with mothers at this time.* Extensive interactions around smiling, interest in siblings as perceptual objects, experiences occurring during periods of "alert inactivity" and relative well-being, and experiences occurring in the presence of mothers and taking on the affective coloration of maternal relationships are precisely the kinds of experiences that contribute to the formation of attachments and the building up of schemata in which siblings are included within the symbiotic orbit. Support for this inference can be found in subsequent stages of development when infants begin to show attachment behaviors to siblings similar to, though less intense than, those found with mothers and when the presence of siblings mitigates separation reactions when mothers are absent (see p. 145f.).

2. *Early experiences with siblings facilitate a differentiation process that may well begin in the later part of the "symbiotic phase."* Infants'

curiosity about, careful observation of, and distinctive patterns of interaction with a variety of familiar figures in the home provide a basis for recognizing their mothers' uniqueness and differences from other people. On the basis of microanalyses of infants' differing patterns of engagement and disengagement with mothers and fathers, Brazelton et al. (1979) note that introducing a third party into formerly dyadic homeostatic-interactional systems results in disruptions and resynchronizations of those systems that "allows for separation, differentiation, and individuation for each member of the triad" (p. 41). Since infants' contacts with siblings during the day are often more extensive than those with fathers and since their patterns of interactions with siblings are likely to differ even more markedly from those with mothers than the patterns exhibited with fathers, the same argument can be advanced with regard to the influence of siblings on the early differentiation process.

THE DIFFERENTIATION SUBPHASE

Between 5 and 9 months, there are striking transformations of infants' psychological organization and their relationship to their world. At the outset of this period, children exhibit "a new look of alertness, persistence, and goal-directedness" that Mahler and McDevitt (1982, p. 401) see as behavioral manifestations of "a more permanently alert sensorium" and "a more consistent sensory investment in the outside world." With their growing control over muscular systems, infants are able to assume and maintain a sitting position so that they orient themselves toward their world from an upright position; with their growing coordination of visual and motor systems, infants are able to manipulate and explore the world within their reach; and with advances in cognitive development that make possible Piaget's secondary circular reactions, "the focus of activity shifts from body action to the effect which this action has on the outside world" (Wolff, 1960, p. 86). Accompanying these perceptual, motor, and cognitive developments, there are far-reaching changes in children's object relationships. Early in this period, the social smile has become increasingly specific as it is directed toward mothers and other familiar figures as opposed to strangers; powerful

"attachment behaviors" toward mothers—i.e., seeking proximity with them and protesting their departure—become prominent (Schaffer and Emerson, 1964); stranger reactions and
stranger anxiety appear as children recognize differences between their mothers and others (Spitz, 1964; Bowlby, 1969; Mahler et al., 1975); and infants are now able to engage in increasingly complex interactive, object-related games with their
mothers that both provide pleasurable interactions and increase
mastery of their environments. Mahler and McDevitt (1982) interpret these developments as forming the basis for a differentiation process in which children begin to establish distinct
body images and recognize differences between their mothers
and others. They view such differentiation as a first step in an
extended developmental sequence in which children become
able to disengage from their mothers and achieve intrapsychic
autonomy and distinctive identities, processes that "culminate in
internalized self-representations, as distinct from internal object
representations" (p. 402).

There are significant changes in infants' behavior with siblings
in these months as well. As children become more alert and more
invested in observing the world around them, their interest and
pleasure in watching siblings increase. For example, at 7 months,
Jennifer, like most infants of her age, found her brother enormously entertaining and, when not upset or anxious, often preferred observing him to other family members. The reasons for
this phenomenon are not hard to appreciate. To infants, the
antics of active, playful, bubbly preschoolers are often far more
varied, exciting, and interesting than the activities of most
adults. With infants' growing motor skills and cognitive capacities, sibling pairs also engage in frequent and surprisingly sophisticated interactive sequences (Dunn and Kendrick, 1979).
Although typically older siblings initiate such games, often by
imitating behavior of younger children, infants are eager to interact, become active participants in the play, and, indeed, often
wish to prolong such play far longer than older siblings care to
(Brazelton, 1969). Moreover, by 8 months, infants are already
beginning to initiate this interactive play (Dunn and Kendrick,
1979). These sequences, including simple games such as Peek-a-
Boo, are precisely the behaviors Mahler suggests are especially

important for the differentiation process when they occur with mothers.

Most important, all of the major behavioral indices of specific, differentiated social attachments that begin to be displayed toward the mother at this time start to appear with siblings shortly thereafter. For example, the specific social smile with which Jennifer favored her mother by 5 months was also awarded to her brother and father at about the same time. Schaffer and Emerson (1964) note that "attachment behavior" may begin to appear toward siblings as early as a month after it is displayed toward mothers. Stranger reactions have been reported in relation to siblings as well. For example, Mahler et al. (1975, p. 171) describe manifestations of stranger anxiety in an 8-month-old boy as he recognized that a child he was looking at was not his brother. Offering a charming example of the kind of sibling attachments emerging in this period, Provence and Solnit (1983, p. 341) describe a 2-year-old boy's discovery that he could make his 6-month-old sister "smile, laugh, chortle, and act excited," that he was "an object of fascination to her," and that "by his actions, he could turn her tears into smiles." They make the interesting observation that such behavior on the part of infants may well be an important factor in helping older siblings come to terms with conflicts around rivalry and develop loving feelings toward their younger brothers and sisters. All of these social behaviors and indices of attachment appear far less frequently and in less intense forms with siblings than with mothers, and all appear subordinate to primary relationships with mothers. Nonetheless, they clearly point to the emergence of significant, distinct object relationships.

Such behavior with siblings has a number of implications for theories about the separation-individuation process during the differentiation subphase:

1. *The influence that sibling relationships already exerted on the development of a differentiated sense of self and significant others at the end of the symbiotic phase increases* (see p. 136f). The behavior now evident with siblings—the careful observation, the beginnings of imitation, and the signs of deepening attachment—are all behaviors that, when they occur with mothers, have been taken to be manifestations of the differentiation process.

2. *The life circumstances of children with older siblings provide both an impetus toward and support for separation from mothers.* Because mothers are often not only primary caretakers for, but also sole companions of, firstborn and only children, parents and children are thrown into especially intense relationships in which intimate contact alternates with periods during which children are left more or less alone as mothers tend to household chores or other pursuits. In contrast, 7-month-old infants with older siblings typically receive less attention from their mothers because the needs of other children must be met as well. At the same time, these infants are alone less than only children because other family members are around to entertain them, play with them, soothe them, or simply keep them company when mothers are occupied. For example, Brazelton (1969, p. 186) notes that already by 8 months the presence of siblings significantly eases brief separations from mothers for infants. Consequently, all other things being equal, infants with older siblings may experience less intense early attachments to their mothers than infants who are only children, but also wider attachments to other family members.

3. *Insofar as older siblings serve as models and teachers of the motor and cognitive skills infants develop during this period, they begin to leave an imprint on the ego functions that provide the foundations for an emerging sense of identity.* Because of the level of infants' cognitive development and their still limited motor capacities and because of the absence of fine-grained analyses of infants' behavior with siblings during the differentiation subphase, it is still difficult to demonstrate the extent of this influence. However, the fact that some clear-cut imitation of siblings' behavior can be found with infants by 8 months and the extensive imitation of siblings' speech, motor behavior, and play in the months that follow make it difficult to believe that such behaviors do not have their roots in this earlier period.

THE PRACTICING SUBPHASE

During the period from 8 to 15 months, Mahler's "practicing subphase," the accelerating development of infants' perceptual, motor, and cognitive skills is manifested in two of the most distinctive human achievements—mastery of locomotion and the utterance of children's first words. Of these two achievements, Mahler emphasizes the former because these perceptual-motor skills, combined with children's curiosity, cognitive development, and growing autonomy and initiative, make possible exploration and mastery of the immediate physical environment. In "practicing" such newfound skills, it is hypothesized, children begin to move away from their mothers, although, because of their "love affair with the world" and their lack of cognitive sophistication, they do not experience this movement as leading toward actual separations. Moreover, in "practicing" the full array of cognitive and motor skills emerging in this period, children gain a growing awareness of their bodies and capacities and, as these skills are used for imitation and to express early identifications, nascent identities begin to take shape.

In these months, quantitative and qualitative changes in children's behavior leave no doubt about the influence of older siblings on the actions and personality of toddlers. Quantitative changes include a marked increase in the amount of sibling interaction (Dunn and Kendrick, 1979) and in the number of children displaying "attachment behavior" toward siblings (Schaffer and Emerson, 1964). Among qualitative changes, three are especially noteworthy.

First, toddlers now imitate the behavior of older siblings in direct and unambiguous ways. For example, well before her first birthday, Jennifer's choice of toys, her play, and even her selection of a transitional object reflected the clear and unmistakable influence of her brother. Brazelton (1969) describes extensive imitation of motor behavior of older siblings as common with infants by 9 months and suggests such imitation is a major spur to motor and language development by 11 months. Similarly, on the basis of experimental studies of children of 12 and 14 months, Dunn and Kendrick (1979) and Lamb (1978b) suggest that older siblings serve as models who can play important roles in facilitating younger children's mastery of their physical environments. It is not hard to appreciate why siblings function in this way. Because their interests, talents, and play are relatively close to those of toddlers, siblings are more readily chosen as models for the development of basic ego skills than adults for many of the same reasons that high school freshmen pattern their behavior on that of seniors far more than on that of teachers and principals.

Second, whereas in the preceding subphases, interactions between siblings were initiated chiefly by older siblings, early toddlers assume a more active role in starting such interactions (Dunn and Kendrick, 1979) and, even at 9 months, modify their behavior in an effort to keep older siblings interested in playing with them (Brazelton, 1969).

Third, relationships between siblings now become fraught with significantly more conflict and aggression, but of an asymmetrical kind. That is to say, conflict and aggression are typically experienced and initiated by older siblings, while younger siblings are less affected by, and even oblivious to, them. At this time, older brothers and sisters encounter what Brazelton (1969) describes as "the second hump of sibling rivalry." While they had resented new babies as intruders into their families and envied the regressive prerogatives allowed them, now feelings of rivalry intensify and assume new forms as younger siblings become toddlers who are recognizable social beings and who receive adulation from parents for each new skill or trick they display. In addition, older siblings find their lives intruded upon constantly as the curiosity and mobility of toddlers lead them to take over toys, interfere with play, or spoil projects. As a consequence, in addition to positive feelings toward younger siblings, older children experience heightened competition and jealousy that is often expressed in hostile actions (Brazelton, 1969, 1974). For toddlers, however, relationships with older siblings often remain remarkably benign. Toddlers' actions that lead to conflicts with brothers and sisters are rarely motivated by envy or hostility. Rather, toddlers are like "calves in a china shop," wreaking havoc on their environments out of curiosity, high spirits, and sheer clumsiness rather than power or malevolence. Moreover, while aware of older children's hostility and "sensitive to their darker moods" (Brazelton, 1969, p. 226), toddlers' pain and unhappiness around conflicts may be relatively short-lived. For example, when upset in her interactions with John, Jennifer was easily comforted by adults at this time. Because of her short attention span and the nature of her interests, if toys were taken

away, she readily accepted substitutes. Like other young toddlers, she was often oblivious of the extent to which she had been
rejected or excluded by her brother. If John was playing with
others, she was often content to sit and watch from a distance or
accept a role on the fringe of the group. In short, early toddlers'
"love affairs with the world" may well extend to relationships
with siblings and carry them over difficult times.

The increasing amount, frequency, variety, and richness of
interactions with older siblings during the practicing subphase
suggest that at least two inferences are warranted with regard to
separation and individuation issues:

1. *Because toddlers manifest a growing attachment to siblings and an
investment in being with them, sibling relationships increase the physical
and psychological distances toddlers move away from their mothers.* Recognizing this phenomenon, Bank and Kahn (1982) suggest that
older siblings serve as "transitional objects" in this period. This
analogy does not hold up well, however, because rather than
being passive mediums upon which toddlers impose their own
meanings, older siblings are active, forceful beings who exercise
a strong influence on their brothers and sisters. A better metaphor may be that of a gravitational field in which older siblings
are seen as objects whose powerful attraction expands the orbits
in which toddlers move around their mothers. Human beings
may well be similar in this regard to groups of nonhuman primates in which young animals leave their mothers earlier and
expand their behavior repertoire more rapidly when reared
with siblings than when reared alone (Suomi, 1982).

2. *Because toddlers readily copy and perhaps even identify with older
siblings, siblings exert an increasing influence on the individuation
process during the practicing subphase.* As has been noted, siblings
serve as primary models for developing the kinds of skills toddlers are most interested in "practicing" and, consequently, extensive imitation of older children shapes the unfolding "autonomous ego functions" at the core of young toddlers' emerging
identities. Moreover, because toddlers may well have some capacity to empathize with the feelings of older siblings (Brazelton,
1969; Dunn and Kendrick, 1979), they may already exhibit genuine identifications with their brothers and sisters (Mahler et al.,
1975, p. 173f.). While questions can be raised about whether this

imitation of siblings reflects the kind of "internal processes" usually taken to be the mark of "true identifications," such arguments may be largely academic. To the extent that the basic cognitive modes of toddlers are sensorimotor in nature, their identities, such as they are, will be inherent in what they do and extensive imitation of siblings represents at the very least the *Anlage* of what will later be potent identifications.

RAPPROCHEMENT

In the period from approximately 16 to 24 months, children's relationships with their mothers, their sense of themselves, and their orientation toward their worlds undergo extraordinary transformations. At the root of these changes is the emergence of representational thought that makes it possible for children to recognize and have a continuing sense of the existence of an "I" and "others." With this recognition of a true sense of "separateness," children come to engage in progressively more complex social interactions with their mothers and experience intense anxiety in the face of separation and fears of separation. Mahler and McDevitt (1982, p. 404) note the child's "former obliviousness to the mother's presence is now replaced by an active approach behavior—a wish to share his new skills and experiences with her, a need for her love, and a constant concern for her whereabouts . . . he is no longer as impervious as he was previously to knocks and falls, and he can be 'upset' even by a sudden realization of his separateness." At the same time, children's heightened sense of themselves lead to constant internal and interpersonal struggles around self-assertion, the maintenance of autonomy, the handling of possessiveness, and the management of ambivalence, hostility, and anxiety.

During the rapprochement period, sibling relationships evolve and change. Earlier trends continue: more toddlers exhibit "attachment behavior" toward siblings (Schaffer and Emerson, 1964); the amount of imitation of older siblings increases (Abramovitch et al., 1982; Lamb, 1978a, 1978b); and the influence of older siblings as models, teachers, and audiences becomes even more pronounced. For example, Brazelton (1974) notes that it is common for younger siblings such as Jennifer to

toilet train themselves earlier than firstborn children by modeling themselves on and seeking to impress older siblings. More
important, with the rapprochement subphase, toddlers experience intense rivalry with older siblings that colors and utterly
transforms earlier relationships. Whereas in the preceding subphase, conflict and aggression in sibling relationships were initiated almost exclusively by older children and younger ones were
chiefly victims, now toddlers become full participants in these
battles, although older siblings are still most likely to be the
aggressors (Abramovitch et al., 1982). As has been seen with
Jennifer, by 16 months she was already engaging in battles for
possessions with her brother, trying to take toys away from him,
and reacting with fury when he took her possessions. Soon after,
she wanted to have whatever he had, do whatever he did, and be
whatever he was. The "penis envy" she exhibited at this time was
not a distinct, isolated experience; it was a special case of a far
more general phenomenon. She envied everything John had or
did. In short, the cognitive and representational capacities that
lead to a recognition of separateness from the mother and the
emergence of a sense of self also lead to an appreciation of
differences between the self and others that makes envy and
rivalry central aspects of human existence from this time
forward.

In the rapprochement subphase, the influence of siblings on
the separation and individuation processes becomes increasingly significant and increasingly complex:

1. *The presence of siblings can ease the process of separating from
mothers by helping toddlers move away from mothers and by reducing the
intensity of reactions when they are left.* Older siblings exert an attraction that encourages toddlers to move away from their mothers
during their play. In addition, because younger siblings are likely to remain with some familiar figures to whom they are attached as mothers leave for brief separations, they are less likely
to feel as abandoned as firstborn children had and their separation reactions are likely to be more muted. For example, although Jennifer was clearly troubled by her mother's departures
during these months, her reactions were far less intense than
those of her brother had been. Likewise, she was comfortable
going to nursery school as early as the age of 2, showing little

anxiety when leaving her mother because her brother was with her. Similar phenomena have been noted by others in far more striking circumstances. For example, Brazelton (1974, p. 126f.) describes a depressed 2-year-old making use of attachments to older siblings when her withdrawn and overwhelmed mother was unavailable to her; Meyendorf (1971) reports a serious depression occurring in a 19-month-old girl, not when she was placed in an aunt's home with two older siblings during her mother's hospitalization, but, rather, a week later when she was separated from her siblings; and Heinicke and Westheimer (1965) and Bowlby (1973) observe that the intense separation reactions of 13- to 32-month-old children placed in a residential nursery while their mothers were hospitalized were significantly mitigated by the presence of older siblings.

2. *The presence of siblings can complicate and interfere with negotiation of the rapprochement crisis.* For example, because a surrogate attachment figure was available, Jennifer was able to achieve a kind of premature independence from her mother, one perhaps expressing her anger at her mother for leaving for work. As noted, her mother was unhappy about the distance Jennifer seemed to maintain between them throughout Jennifer's third year. The shift in Jennifer's relationship with her mother at the time of separation from John at the age of 3, in particular her efforts to renegotiate issues characteristic of the rapprochement subphase with her mother, suggest that the presence of her brother left Jennifer with "unfinished business" from this earlier developmental period. Also, for Jennifer and other children, the feelings of hatred and envy aroused by having to share their mothers with siblings may make the negotiation of rapprochement issues more difficult in a wide variety of ways.

3. *Siblings may have a potent influence on the individuation process in the rapprochement subphase as crystallizing identities are shaped heavily by identifications now fueled by powerful rivalries.* As has been seen, Jennifer exhibited a strong identification with her brother at this time. Her intense envy of and competition with him pervaded all aspects of her life, leaving their imprint on everything from her choice of clothes to her play and interests. Indeed, this rivalry overrode any traditional conflicts with her parents around toilet training toward which this strong-willed child might have been inclined as she trained herself in a rapid and

determined manner in an effort to keep up with John. Far from being limited to Jennifer, the same phenomenon has been noted with children in general. For example, Brazelton (1974, p. 69) contends that the desire of children of this age to keep up with and please older siblings is "out of proportion to any other kind of motivation I know."

Among psychoanalytic theorists, the role of siblings in the individuation process has been recognized most clearly by Jacobson (1964). Stressing the influence of ambivalent relations and partial identifications with fathers and siblings in the second year of life, she asserts: "I have emphasized the child's earlier delineation from the hated rivals, which soon promotes the development of his sense of identity more than does his closeness to the mother" (p. 64). Because Jacobson's discussion of the issue of "rivals" is brief and condensed, however, a number of clarifications of the points she makes appear warranted.

First, Jacobson lumps fathers and siblings together in the category of rivals, yet with Jennifer and with most normal children, relationships with parents and siblings are fundamentally different. While toddlers may perceive fathers as rivals for maternal attention at times, fathers are typically seen as parenting figures with whom children play out many of the same rapprochement struggles they experience with mothers, albeit in less conflicted ways because these relationships do not involve the same intensity or contain the same threats of fusion (Brazelton, 1974). In contrast, siblings are likely to be perceived constantly as rivals because they are, in fact, similar to toddlers and because they compete directly for the kind of parental attention, nurturance, praise, and recognition that toddlers seek.

Second, it is essential to recognize that the rivalry with siblings that emerges in this period is not the first significant relationship children have with older siblings; this rivalry is superimposed on long-standing, largely positive attachments to and identifications with older siblings. Competition, envy, and hatred are introduced into relationships already characterized by idealization, admiration, and positive feelings. It is the latter qualities that provide the foundations for healthy selective identifications and contribute to the truly ambivalent relations with siblings that arise at this time.

Finally, rivalry with siblings during the rapprochement subphase involves not only competition for parental attention, but also significant narcissistic components. While children's wishes for parental love and attention are pronounced, the symbolic capacities responsible for recognition of self make narcissism, in the true sense of the word, possible. Children now become preoccupied with what "I" have, what "I" do, and what "I" achieve. No longer content to simply imitate or model themselves on siblings, toddlers wish to possess the attributes of older brothers and sisters and they compare themselves constantly with their competitors. Much of the competition they experience is related to a striving for self-enhancement that makes that rivalry in many respects independent of the search for parental attention and approval. For example, after she was 18 months old, Jennifer often seemed oblivious to her parents' reactions in her competition with John. Their recognition of and genuine admiration for her accomplishments often had little meaning for her in the face of her sense that what she did did not measure up to her brother's achievements. For example, her toilet training and her wish to bring projects home from nursery school seemed to have less to do with the praise or affection that she might receive from her parents than with her need to feel herself equal to her brother.

Such qualifications, it should be stressed, do not call into question Jacobson's main thesis. Rather, they serve to reinforce the contention that during the rapprochement period competition and selective identifications with rivals, especially sibling rivals, are potent influences on identity formation.

IDENTITY CONSOLIDATION AND THE MOVEMENT TOWARD OBJECT CONSTANCY

Mahler and her colleagues view the third year of life as a period of consolidation of identity and movement toward object constancy. In important respects, these developments are an extension of trends begun during the rapprochement subphase. However, with their rapidly expanding capacity for representational thought, their increasingly rich fantasy life, and their growing sophistication in social interactions, children now become better able to separate from their mothers, establish new and less dependent relationships with them, and develop more differentiated identities based on selective identifications with others. Mahler and Jacobson emphasize the role of the discovery of sexual identity in the individuation process at this stage, treating it as a central organizer of personal identity as a whole.

During this period, children's interactions with siblings become more extensive, varied, and sophisticated. In a longitudinal study of children of 18 and 36 months, Abramovitch et al. (1982) note that the amount of social interaction with older siblings increases with age, that there is a rich mixture of "prosocial" and "agonistic" (libidinal and aggressive?) interchanges at both ages, and that younger siblings become "more equal partners" in relationships over time. Provence and Solnit (1983) give vivid examples of the multifaceted, oscillating quality of such interactions between a normal 2½- and 4-year-old sibling pair. In addition to the increasing range and depth of sibling interactions, there are also significant changes in the social context within which they occur. As children gain a degree of independence from their mothers, more and more interactions with siblings occur outside of the immediate purview of adults and 2-year-olds become parts of quasi-independent systems of siblings and peers. Mothers are often sensitive to such changes as their concerns about providing close supervision, support, and companionship for toddlers during the day begin to give way to concerns about facilitating children's independent play with siblings and peers, controlling the excesses in this play, and adjudicating disputes between youngsters.

While success in the negotiation of the separation process and movement toward object constancy depend most heavily on children's abilities to manage ambivalence and mothers' capacities to respond sensitively to children's needs to merge, to gain distance, and to assert autonomy, sibling relationships contribute to the separation process in two significant respects during Mahler's fourth subphase:

1. *Because of 2-year-olds' investments in exercising their growing abilities to play and interact with other children, older siblings exert a powerful attraction that encourages children to initiate repeated brief separations from their mothers.* Separation is not simply a matter of moving *away from* mothers; it is one of moving *toward* others. It is

not only a process of disengagement from a primary relationship; it is also one of engagement in other relationships. As 2- and 3-year-olds achieve a degree of autonomy from their mothers, they are typically eager to join in activities with older siblings and their friends. The lure of these groups pulls them out of the house into the yard and, later, the surrounding neighborhood. Mothers remain home base, to which children return frequently in the face of rebuffs and injuries at the hands of siblings, but the attraction and at least sporadic support of sibling and peer systems foster moving farther and farther from that base for longer and longer periods of time. In Jennifer's case, her wish to be with her brother and his friends frequently led her to leave her mother; her wishes to emulate and be with John made her eager for such major separation experiences as preschool and day camp; and, in part because these separations were ones Jennifer sought and because they involved actively taking leave of her mother in order to be with others, such potentially difficult experiences were manageable ones for her. In effect, as a consequence of sibling relationships, many of the actual separations 2-year-olds such as Jennifer experience are ones they initiate, control, and even welcome rather than painful passive ones in which they must struggle with having been left.

2. *The presence and support of older siblings help 2-year-olds tolerate feelings of abandonment and loss they experience in the face of separations.* As was the case during the preceding subphase, Jennifer's separation reactions in her third year were far less marked than those of her older brother. Similarly, the far more serious separation reactions of 2-year-olds placed in residential nurseries for extended periods are eased by the presence of older siblings (Heinicke and Westheimer, 1965). It is likely that the major factors in mitigating such reactions are simply the presence of familiar attachment figures. Although mothers may leave, children with older siblings usually remain with family members and do not experience as complete a sense of "abandonment" as an only child. In addition, although there are undoubtedly enormous individual variations, older siblings may provide tangible support that helps their younger siblings deal with the experience of separation. Among the most extraordinary characteristics of siblings in the preschool years is that youngsters

whose jealousy, envy, and rivalry often leave them unable to witness a brother's or sister's happiness without needing to spoil it can respond to the same sibling's suffering with touching efforts to comfort them. While these characteristics of sibling interactions were present during the preceding stage, because of their ego development, the growth in their capacity for a range of object relationships, and the diminution in their actual dependency on their mothers, children are now able to make far greater use of siblings to deal with separation experiences. Support from siblings may be especially important at this time, for many 2-year-olds must deal with the painful experiences of abandonment and rivalry that arise in the wake of the arrival of new babies in the family.

Relationships with siblings may have an even greater influence on the individuation process in the third year of life. Three aspects of this influence are especially noteworthy:

1. *There is a marked increase in the extent and specificity of the influence of sibling relationships on 2-year-olds' identities in general.* It has been suggested that competition and selective identifications with siblings are already major factors in identity formation by the end of the second year. In the next year, as children gain greater independence from their mothers, spend more time with siblings alone, and seek places for themselves within sibling and peer subsystems, the influence of such factors grows markedly. Moreover, with the cognitive development characteristic of this year, especially with the expanding capacity for play and fantasy, children become capable of increasingly refined identifications. In Jennifer's case, for example, the impact of her identification with her brother could now be seen in her dress, her play, her fantasies, her activities, and, indeed, all aspects of her life. At the same time, rather than simply imitating her brother, she became more selective in what she took over from him and began to shape fantasies and interests such as those of superheroes and highway patrolmen to serve her own ends.

2. *Siblings now play an important role in determining aspects of children's identities related to sex roles.* There is no reason to question Stoller's (1980) contention that gender identity, the sense of whether one is a boy or a girl, is established in an earlier period and that relationships with mothers are central to the process.

However, in the third year, sibling relationships weigh heavily in children's struggles with the issues of what kinds of boys and girls they are and their attitudes toward their gender. For example, at this time Jennifer had no doubt she was a girl, but her dress, activities, play, fantasies, and interests left little doubt that, as a consequence of her rivalry and identification with her brother, she was a very "masculine" little girl. Empirical studies relating sibling constellations to personality characteristics later in life suggest that Jennifer is not alone in this regard. In two-child families, the younger of sisters are likely to be described as the "most feminine" of girls (Edington and Wilson, 1979), while younger sisters of older brothers tend to display "tomboyish" qualities in childhood (Koch, 1955) and relatively "masculine" characteristics as young adults (Kammeyer, 1966; Sutton-Smith and Rosenberg, 1970). In a similar vein, younger brothers of older sisters have been characterized as the "most sissyish" of boys (Koch, 1955) and rank highest among boys on measures of "femininity" (Sutton-Smith and Rosenberg, 1970). To be sure, research in the area is still limited and subject to a variety of, at times, conflicting interpretations (Edington and Wilson, 1979). Moreover, strong arguments have been advanced that focusing on fixed character traits leads to an oversimplified and distorted picture of sibling effects on personality because it neglects the range and complexity of influences present at each stage in the life cycle (Rosenberg, 1982). However, at the least, cases such as that of Jennifer suggest that, to the extent that relationships between sibling constellations and sex roles are found, developments in the third year of life constitute a major source of these patterns.

3. *Identifications with older siblings and, even more, the necessity of establishing a place for themselves within family systems and sibling subsystems are central determinants of social aspects of children's identities.* The observation Erikson (1956) makes about the importance of communal confirmation of identity in adolescence is no less true of early periods of identity consolidation. As their cognitive development enables 2-year-olds to appreciate the nature of social relationships within their families and as their striving for individuation leads children to seek their own distinctive position in their families, identities cannot but be shaped by the

expectations, statuses, opportunities, and problems associated with being an older or younger sibling and a brother or sister. As identities crystallize, sibling positions within families appear to become incorporated into fundamental attitudes toward oneself and others and into outlooks on life (Toman, 1976). Such attitudes and outlooks may well be manifested later in differences in readiness to assume responsibility and leadership, attitudes toward authority, and a host of other issues bearing on interpersonal relationships and group membership (Edington and Wilson, 1979).

These attitudes and outlooks are also influenced by sibling relationships outside the immediate context of the family. In seeking to become true, equal participants in the activities of older siblings and their friends, children have their first experience of negotiating entrance into a social system of peers. For younger siblings, this experience involves becoming part of established systems in which power and authority lie with older and more sophisticated children and in which there are significant constraints on the roles open to new members. There are undoubtedly enormous variations in how children cope with this situation, variations influenced by age differences between children, sex of siblings, and a plethora of intrapsychic and interpersonal considerations. For the present purposes, what is most important to note is that the ways in which 2-year-olds come to terms with this situation, both in their relationships with others and in their fantasies, are likely to have a significant influence on the sense of the social order they develop and their attitudes toward it.

For example, by her third year Jennifer was aware that John was part of a broader social world beyond the family, a world of preschool and friends; she was eager not only to be his playmate, but also to become part of that world; and she expended great effort and considerable ingenuity in doing so. She worked hard to get her parents to enroll her in preschool early and, once there, strove to enact roles she had seen John play. As a 2-year-old, she wanted desperately to play with John and his friends, but had to struggle with a situation in which it was they who knew and set the rules for their group and decided whether and how to let her be part of activities. In her interactions with them, she responded with alternating mixtures of aggression, competition, acquiescence, and withdrawal. While one can only speculate about the intrapsychic effects of this situation, it is likely that Jennifer's preoccupation with fantasies of being a superhero throughout this period was in part determined by a need to deal with her sense of powerlessness in these relationships. Later in childhood younger sisters of older brothers have been described as more quarrelsome, tenacious, resourceful, and competitive than other girls (Koch, 1955). With Jennifer, it is not difficult to see how such characteristics would be rooted in identifications and relationships with her brother during this period of early identity consolidation.

"SEPARATION" AND "INDIVIDUATION" FROM SIBLINGS

If the preceding analysis of the influence of siblings on the separation-individuation process is correct, an important step remains to be taken in the consolidation of identity. In the course of separating from their mothers and developing a sense of identity in the first 3 years of life, it has been argued, children establish strong attachments that may lead them to feel driven to be with their brothers and sisters and they imitate, emulate, and identify closely with siblings. While these developments contribute to children's emancipation from symbiotic relationships with their mothers, as Brazelton (1974, p. 65f.) has anticipated, such relationships also create a problem, that of "separating" and "individuating" from siblings.

The terms "separation" and "individuation" are used hesitantly in this context, and only because none better come to mind. The processes involved bear enough resemblance to what occurs between children and their mothers so that the terms are not altogether out of place, yet the two sets of processes differ significantly as well. The separation-individuation process with mothers is more intense, prolonged, and important than what occurs with siblings. Moreover, the central issues with which children struggle in relation to their mothers are conflicts around wishes for and fears of fusion and around autonomy and control. In contrast, the problems children experience in relation to siblings are likely to be affected most by conflicts around envy, rivalry, and jealousy.

Instead of focusing on labels, however, it is more productive to concentrate on the phenomena to which they are applied. At the end of the third year, children frequently insist on being with older siblings, on being part of siblings' activities, or on siblings being part of their own activities. They seem caught in a reflexive competition with older brothers and sisters on grounds determined by the siblings' interests and talents. Their identities are often shaped by powerful wishes to be like siblings and surpass them at their own pursuits. If children are to move toward true autonomy, in the preschool years they must begin to disengage from their siblings, recognize and accept differences between themselves and their rivals, and feel free to pursue their interests and talents in their own ways.

Jennifer's case provides a dramatic example of the kind of process described. At 3, through much of the day, Jennifer wanted to be with John and do whatever he was doing. She lost interest in even her favorite activities with her parents if she saw John leave the house to join a friend. Her dress, interests, and fantasies attested to her close identification with him. When John began school, she was forced to deal with separation from him and with a recognition that they were fundamentally different. The event produced a crisis in her life, a transformation in her personality, and a change in her relationships with others that were second only to those encountered in the rapprochement period. Faced with a recognition of that separateness, Jennifer became depressed, underwent significant regression, and returned to negotiate separation issues with her mother that had been delayed or prematurely foreclosed 1½ years earlier because of the availability of her brother. Equally important, there was a significant shift in the individuation process as Jennifer struggled to come to terms with the narcissistic blow entailed in recognizing differences between herself and John; life circumstances simply did not permit her to compete with him on exactly the same terms or maintain an illusion that they were the same. As has been seen, in struggling with this blow, she reexamined her history in the form of pictures from her birth, adopted a strikingly new attitude toward femininity, and formed a new alliance and identified more strongly with her mother. Her concern with being a girl and having babies at this time, while no doubt reflecting early oedipal issues, represented, above all, a way of grappling with the narcissistic insult suffered in relation to John and provided a means of consolidating a sexual identity that she could view as distinct from and superior to that of her brother. These issues were not settled once and for all at this time. They continued to be reworked over the months and, indeed, year that followed. However, the nature of this initial crisis highlights the kind of developmental task with which she grappled.

It is unlikely that most children face a "crisis" as they separate and individuate from siblings. Jennifer's struggle with these issues was undoubtedly heightened because she was close to John in age, because she was sufficiently precocious that competition between them was intensified, because of the differences in their sexes, and because of a family situation that threw them closely together in their early years. With a greater difference in age between siblings, children of the same sex, and/or differing life circumstances, such conflicts are probably less intense. Nonetheless, these conflicts are likely to be present because of a number of factors inherent in children's development during their fourth year. In this period, children achieve a sufficient degree of autonomy from their mothers to permit concerns about negotiating autonomy from other family members. Their increasingly differentiated sense of identity permits differences from siblings to be appreciated more fully. Growth in "reality testing" makes the hopelessness of direct competition with siblings clearer, particularly where that competition is with a sibling of the opposite sex. In addition, "reality" often intervenes in ways that necessitate separation and individuation from older siblings. By the time children enter their fourth year, older brothers and sisters have typically entered elementary school, become increasingly concerned with early latency age pursuits, and begun engaging in more mature peer relationships that often forcefully exclude "little kids." Consequently, *to the extent that older siblings have played a significant role in the separation-individuation process, preschool children face a developmental task that involves recognizing differences from siblings, coming to terms with separations from them, and forging identities distinct from them.*

Conclusion

The theory that has been advanced in the preceding sections can be summarized briefly. Its central tenet is that older siblings play a major role in early identity formation and object relationships, a role that, while affected by relationships with parents, is also, in important respects, independent of those relationships. Its main features include the assertions: (1) sibling influences are discernible at the outset of the separation-individuation process and increase in variety and intensity with each new subphase; (2) while the specific effects of sibling relationships on the process are determined by the nature of children's ego development and the salient developmental issues confronting them at each stage, the general effects across stages with normal children are those of providing encouragement and support for separation from mothers and influencing identity formation on the basis of increasingly ambivalent identifications with older brothers and sisters; (3) by the third year of life, the extent of sibling influences grows to the point where they are major factors in the consolidation of social and sexual aspects of identity; and (4) as a consequence of this process, "separating" and "individuating" from siblings may well constitute a critical developmental task for many youngsters in the preschool years.

Even the most sympathetic reader is likely to entertain a number of reservations about this theory and the manner in which it has been developed. In concluding, it is important to acknowledge these reservations and address three sets of issues that warrant particular attention.

First, generalizations based on a single case should be viewed cautiously. Often the very features that make it possible for a case to exemplify particular principles also make the case "unrepresentative." For example, the potential impact of an older brother on a younger sister's development can be seen clearly in Jennifer's case in part because of her intelligence, precocity, and aggressive self-assertion and in part because her family situation contributed to an unusually close relationship with John. The same characteristics make the case atypical in precisely these respects. Even when the case is supplemented with other findings in the clinical and developmental literature, the empirical base for the theory remains limited. Clearly, further clinical studies and empirical research are needed to test its assertions.

Second, while the position outlined may be correct in its main features, insofar as it emphasizes general characteristics of the influence of older siblings on identity formation, it tends to over-simplify a complex process. No single case could possibly be representative of the manner in which relationships with older siblings bear on normal development because of the range of variables involved. One would anticipate that the nature and extent of the influence of siblings will vary with differences in parental attitudes and relationships to their children, birth order, number of siblings, age between children, gender of children and their siblings, culture and child-rearing patterns, and a host of other considerations. While this paper, at best, has touched on only a few of these issues in a rather cursory fashion, all of them call for thorough investigation.

Finally, the theory has been organized around that most hypothetical of constructs, "normal development." The ideas advanced concern the development of healthy, intact children growing up with a "good-enough mother" in an "average expectable environment." While there are many such children, children are also born and grow up with a host of vulnerabilities; they are raised by parents whose own conflicts interfere with child-rearing in diverse ways; they live in single parent families or families that otherwise depart from theoretical norms; and they have siblings whose conflicts and pathology significantly affect relationships with younger brothers and sisters. All of these variables require careful consideration and, as they are introduced, the task of understanding the impact of siblings on early development becomes still more complex.

While such reservations are justified, it should be stressed that they support rather than call into question the main thesis of the paper. For the most part, the specific questions raised presuppose that siblings have major effects on identity formation and object relationships in the early years of life. More significant, the questions may be seen to constitute a series of empirical and theoretical problems that lend themselves to investigation. In the early stages of the exploration of any new area of research, the refinement and, indeed, the correctness of a particular theory may well be less important than its capacity to generate such problems, problems whose solution will lead to the comprehensive theories the phenomena warrant. In this sense, the very range of questions raised by this theory may be a measure of the value of the perspective it provides.

BIBLIOGRAPHY

ABRAMOVITCH, R. W., CORTER, C., & LANDO, B. (1979). Sibling interaction in the home. *Child Develpm.,* 50:997–1003.

———— PEPLER, D., & CORTER, C. (1982). Patterns of sibling interaction among preschool-age children. In *Sibling Relationships,* ed. M. E. Lamb & B. Sutton-Smith. Hillsdale, N.J.: Lawrence Erlbaum, pp. 61–86.

BANK, S. P. & KAHN, M. D. (1982). *The Sibling Bond.* New York: Basic Books.

BOWLBY, J. (1969). *Attachment.* New York: Basic Books.

———— (1973). *Separation.* New York: Basic Books.

BRAZELTON, T. B. (1969). *Infants and Mothers.* New York: Delta Books.

———— (1974). *Toddlers and Parents.* New York: Delacorte Press.

———— & ALS, H. (1979). Four early stages in the development of mother-infant interaction. *Psychoanal. Study Child,* 34:349–370.

———— YOSMAN, M. W., ALS, H., & TRONICK, E. (1979). The infant as a focus for family reciprocity. In *The Child and Its Family,* ed. M. Lewis & L. A. Rosenblum. New York: Plenum, pp. 29–44.

COLONNA, A. B. & NEWMAN, L. M. (1983). The psychoanalytic literature on siblings. *Psychoanal. Study Child,* 38:285–310.

DUNN, J. & KENDRICK, C. (1979). Interaction between young siblings in the context of family relationships. In *The Child and Its Family,* ed. M. Lewis & L. A. Rosenblum. New York: Plenum, pp. 143–168.

EDINGTON, G. & WILSON, B. (1979). Children of different positions. In *Basic Handbook of Child Psychiatry,* ed. J. D. Noshpitz. New York: Basic Books, 1:397–406.

ERIKSON, E. H. (1956). The problem of ego identity. *J. Amer. Psychoanal. Assn.,* 4:56–121.

FREUD, A. & DANN, S. (1951). An experiment in group upbringing. *Psychoanal. Study Child,* 6:127–168.

HEINICKE, C. M. & WESTHEIMER, I. J. (1965). *Brief Separations.* New York: Int. Univ. Press.

JACOBSON, E. (1964). *The Self and the Object World.* New York:Int. Univ. Press.

JOSEPH, E. D. & TABOR, J. H. (1961). The simultaneous analysis of a pair of identical twins and the twinning reaction. *Psychoanal. Study Child,* 16:275–299.

KAMMEYER, K. (1966). Birth order and the feminine sex role among college women. *Amer. Sociol. Rev.,* 31:508–515.

Koch, H. L. (1955). Some personality correlates of sex, sibling position, and sex of sibling among five- and six-year-old children. *Genet. Psychol. Monogr.*, 52:3–50.

Kris, M. & Ritvo, S. (1983). Parents and siblings. *Psychoanal. Study Child*, 38:311–324.

Lamb, M. E. (1978a). Interactions between eighteen-month-olds and their pre-school-aged siblings. *Child Develpm.*, 49:51–59.

—— (1978b). The development of sibling relationships in infancy. *Child Develpm.*, 49:1189–1196.

—— & Sutton-Smith, B., eds. (1982). *Sibling Relationships*. Hillsdale, N.J.: Lawrence Erlbaum.

Leonard, M. R. (1961). Problems in identification and ego development in twins. *Psychoanal. Study Child*, 16:300–320.

Levy, D. M. (1937). *Studies in Sibling Rivalry*. New York: American Orthopsychiatric Association.

Mahler, M. S. & McDevitt, J. B. (1980). The separation-individuation process and identity formation. In *The Course of Life*, ed. S. I. Greenspan & G. H. Pollock. Washington: DHHS Publication No. (ADM) 80-786, 1:397–406.

—— Pine, F., & Bergman, A. (1975). *The Psychological Birth of the Human Infant*. New York: Basic Books.

McDevitt, J. B. & Mahler, M. S. (1980). Object constancy, individuality, and internalization. In *The Course of Life*, ed. S. I. Greenspan & G. H. Pollock. Washington: DHHS Publication No. (ADM) 80-786, 1:407–423.

Meyendorf, R. (1971). Infant depression due to separation from siblings. *Psychiat. Clin.*, 4:321–335.

Neubauer, P. B. (1982). Rivalry, envy, and jealousy. *Psychoanal. Study Child*, 37:121–142.

—— (1983). The importance of the sibling experience. *Psychoanal. Study Child*, 38:325–336.

Provence, S. & Solnit, A. J. (1983). Development-promoting aspects of the sibling experience. *Psychoanal. Study Child*, 38:337–352.

Rosenberg, B. (1982). Life span personality stability in sibling status. In *Sibling Relationships*, ed. M. E. Lamb & B. Sutton-Smith. Hillsdale, N.J.: Lawrence Erlbaum, pp. 167–224.

Schaffer, H. R. & Emerson, P. E. (1964). The development of social attachments in infancy. *Monogr. Soc. Res. Child Develpm.*, 29(3):1–77.

Shopper, M. (1974). Twinning reaction in nontwin siblings. *J. Amer. Acad. Child Psychiat.*, 13:300–318.

Solnit, A. J. (1983). The sibling experience. *Psychoanal. Study Child*, 38:281–284.

Spitz, R. A. (1965). *The First Year of Life*. New York: Int. Univ. Press.

Stoller, R. J. (1980). A different view of oedipal conflict. In *The Course of Life*, ed. S. I. Greenspan & G. H. Pollock. Washington: DHHS Publication No. (ADM) 80-786, 1:589–602.

Suomi, S. J. (1982). Sibling relationships in nonhuman primates. In *Sibling*

Relationships, ed. M. E. Lamb & B. Sutton-Smith. Hillsdale, N.J.: Lawrence Erlbaum, pp. 329–356.

SUTTON-SMITH, B. (1982). Birth order and sibling status effects. In *Sibling Relationships,* ed. M. E. Lamb & B. Sutton-Smith. Hillsdale, N.J.: Lawrence Erlbaum, pp. 153–166.

———— & ROSENBERG, B. G. (1970). *The Sibling.* New York: Holt, Rinehart, & Winston.

TOMAN, W. (1976). *Family Constellation,* 3rd ed. New York: Springer.

WOLFF, P. H. (1960). The developmental psychologies of Jean Piaget and psychoanalysis. *Psychol. Issues,* 2:1–181.

Preoedipal Objects and Object Primacy

PETER B. NEUBAUER, M.D.

THE PSYCHOANALYTIC THEORY OF DEVELOPMENT AS WELL AS clinical theory work with the assumption that development proceeds from the early dyadic relationship of mother and child to the oedipal triadic interaction. This implies that the child's preoedipal object relation is primarily a one-to-one relationship with mother; accordingly, the preoedipal pathology is viewed in the context of the mother-child interaction. I shall examine this proposition in the belief that it may constitute a simplification which does not do justice to the young child's ability to explore his environment and to extract from it what he needs, and which therefore leads to clinical reductionism, particularly as it relates to genetic reconstruction.

Object relations theory implies that all other relationships only mirror the child's relationship with mother, are substitutions for mother until the phallic-oedipal phase. It is not surprising that these assumptions have endured for so long, because indeed early infant studies have until recently supported the exclusive role of the mother-child dyadic relationship and the clinical data from analyses have consistently reconfirmed the primary role of this parental constellation.

It is the aim of this presentation to review new findings which

---

Clinical Professor of Psychiatry at the Psychoanalytic Institute, New York University; Chairman Emeritus at the Columbia University Psychoanalytic Center.

Based on the Freud Anniversary Lecture presented to the Psychoanalytic Association of New York, on May 21, 1984.

expand these developmental schemas and to present data which demand a widening of our developmental propositions.

Freud's early outline of the psychosexual libidinal phases emphasizes the role of the mother in the oral-anal period and establishes the significance of the primary object. It implies that there must be continuity of sensorimotor affective stimulation and what could be termed a psychological presence, that there is regularity, and that the child's development is safeguarded by the strength of the tie to the primary object. Thus, interruptions and dissonances in this relationship introduced by the vicissitudes of life constitute hazards leading to pathological development. Those analysts who study early self-object differentiation again point to the mother-child system within which imitation, incorporation, and identification contribute to psychic structure formation in the infant. The evolvement of object constancy is seen as a result of this dyadic process, the self-object differentiation, and as a basic step in the formation of structure. We only need to remind ourselves of the work of Melanie Klein, Jacobson, Mahler, Kohut, Kernberg, and many others.

Yet, we have become increasingly aware of a preoedipal triangularity involving child, mother, and father. Furthermore, the study of the role of siblings in early development permits us to observe the child's rivalry with his sibling for mother's affection, and this too constitutes a preoedipal triangularity. The sibling as a new object allows for new islands of identification, for significant new interactions, and for sexual explorations that give these experiences a singular significance.

From birth on the infant clearly reacts to mother; between them there is a finely tuned orchestration in which the sensory modalities, the affective interchanges, and cognitive development participate. The observer is impressed by the infant's early capacity to extract from the mother what he needs and to stimulate the environment to respond to his demands. Thus, we assume that the environment, as embodied by the mother's care, does not stimulate random drive expressions, but that she has to tune into the child's existing organization—i.e., the organization that precedes id-ego differentiation—and that the infant influences the mother's reactions in turn. The child's maturational sequences continuously demand new levels of interactions. As early as 1962, Sander went so far as to suggest that we study the infant-mother interaction as a unit and develop new measures for evaluating this system.

As I have mentioned before, one of the psychoanalytic tenets which guides our theory and practice is the requirement for the continuity of relationship. The child, from infancy onward, needs the continuity of stimulation in perception, sensorimotor function, cognition, and the affect as the drives reach for the object. This continuity then provides the necessary experience for the anticipation of events; it allows for the hallucinatory, that is, early cognitive, expectations; and it channels need and drive orientation. Furthermore, the mother's capacity to stimulate in accord with her child's condition evokes those ego functions which lead to inner organization—the synthesizing, integrative, and, we must add, the organizing functions of the developing ego.

The infant, from birth on, strives for a "selective environment," is able to choose from the external world what suits him and to exclude that which is either too intense or insufficiently stimulating. His inborn curiosity, derivative of aggressive and sexual drive tensions, leads him to explore the environment and respond to those stimuli which are relatively new but not too distant or alien to previous experiences. This principle of continuity, therefore, further highlights the role of the mother as the primary object and the detrimental consequences when the relationship between mother and child is disturbed. On the other hand, research data reveal a surprising ability on the part of the child to complement and compensate for defects in this unity. Fraiberg (1977) found that blind babies can establish object primacy with only a 6-month delay. Obviously, other sensory modalities can lead to a unified object representation and object constancy. Other studies demonstrate that even limbless thalidomide babies under normal conditions show no deficit of ego development and object relatedness despite their inability to explore their mothers' bodies and their own by physical, tactile contact (Décarie, 1969). These findings indicate that even in handicapped infants we have to focus on the child's capacity for integration and his faculty for evolving maturational and developmental sequences, in spite of his deficits. We can assume that the visual, auditory, tactile, and olfactory mother becomes slowly unified, as object and self become slowly differentiated. As the internal representational world emerges, the external world is seen as concomitant with and independent from actions, i.e., from sensorimotor schemas. These harmonious interactions emphasize the libidinal tie. Often these formulations do not include the role of aggressive strivings.

Thus, we must question the assumption that the synchronicity with the primary object alone leads to object-self differentiation as a linear consequence solely of their mutual interaction. The representational self emerges at about 15 months. We know that the infant is able to distinguish others by gender, age, and familiarity long before the oedipal period. Continuity of relationships can be seen either as the uninterrupted libidinal availability of one primary object or from the vantage point of how the child constructs his representational world. The latter perspective includes the effect of separation and separateness. It is the basis of Mahler's separation-individuation process. The response to loss, to delay of immediate gratification, contributes to incorporation and identification. Sandler and Rosenblatt (1962) distinguish between identification as a modification of the self representation and introjection. Introjection involves a particular kind of hypercathexis of the object representation by which it is vested with "the authority and power of the real parents" (p. 138). These formulations place the object-self differentiation within the matrix of the mother-child dyadic constellation. In addition to the libidinal tie to mother, we usually stress multiple steps in the process of differentiation. It is important to note that in this process we can recognize the role of different objects, of different relationships, all of which contribute to the process of object-self differentiation. The other objects that affect early development are father, siblings, and various caregivers.

Over the years, attention has been paid to the early father-child relationship, due to the increasing participation of fathers in the care of their children. The place of the father in early development must be studied in reference to (1) father as the sole or primary caregiver; (2) the absent father; and (3) father as a participant in providing care. Lamb (1980), an important contributor to the study of the father-child relationship, differs from many other observers because he positioned himself in the natural environment of the child: he observed children at the age of 8 to 9 months in their homes and studied their reactions to father *and* mother. He too studied attachment processes, and thus had to rely on behavioral responses and to infer the internal representational world. This does not diminish the significance of his finding that the child's search for protection and comfort was directed equally to mother and father when both were present. The father is not just a good caregiver because he carries out mother's role or is a substitute for her. Lamb was impressed with the differences between the infant's interaction with each parent. The infants seemed to turn more often to the mothers for protection, while the fathers stimulated a more intense interaction with more individualized interplay and with a different repertoire than the mothers offered. The mothers held the babies more frequently to comfort them—the fathers to play with them and to stimulate their explorations. It will depend on the infants' disposition which of these experiences they prefer or which they will seek at different times during the day and at different stages of development. The *early differences* may contribute to gender development, as early as 18 months of life. And, to repeat, differentiation is proof of the child's ability to form and benefit from multiple relationships.

Moreover, studies of parental roles when both parents are caregivers (Carlson, 1984) indicate that no differences were found in the development of the infants as to paternal involvement. The stereotyping of the maternal role was not confirmed. He concluded, "It is possible that what is most salient to the child is the father's *increased* responsibility for the child care and housekeeping roles . . . rather than the mother's *decreased* participation" (p. 133). Furthermore, he assumed that the paternal nurturance reflects "changes in paternal behavior that result from the demands of the child care role, rather than from preexisting differences in father behavior" (p. 133).

We see here again, in the absence of other evidence, that the child's innate processes accept early triangularity with differentiated objects. When in 1960 I studied the oedipal child specifically where the fathers were absent, it was surprising to see the powerful effect of the fantasied father on the child's further development. Among other factors, I related the child's relationship to the fantasied father to the mother's ability to convey to her child her own oedipal-heterosexual strivings complemented by the innate triadic assertion of the child.

In a study group (1979–83) that explored the effect of siblings on development,[1] we arrived at the following formulation: Intense rivalry in the second year of life already is a reflection of the preoedipal triangularity between the child, his or her sibling, and their relationship to mother and/or father. The relationship to the sibling is more than a repetition of the primary relationship to the parent. Each child forms his or her own particular relationship to the parent; children also form their own different relationships to each other. This opened the question as to the definition of multiple primary objects in early life. Furthermore, we stressed the child's reaction to the parents' relationship with each other and his rivalry before the oedipal phase. Many of Freud's early case histories describe the effect of several objects on the life history of his patients. Similarly, Freud explored, in his own early life, the impact of the death of his brother, Julius, before he was 2 years old. In his study of "The Prototype of Preoedipal Reconstruction," Blum (1984) examined Freud's reaction to the death of his brother: "It is significant that Freud, having analyzed his fainting, 'expressed the opinion that all his attacks could be traced to the effect on him of his young brother's death'" (p. 774).

When we review the preoedipal mother-child relationship, the *necessity* of early attunement, the establishment of object constancy, the structuring of the self, is it then not surprising that the child gives equal status to the father during the phallic-oedipal phase? In the past and at present most fathers have not been the nurturing objects, satisfying the infants' needs, nor, after the "hatching" period, have they been available for that necessary continuity of care. Well-to-do parents employed governesses for their children, the poor depended on older siblings or other members of the extended family to take care of the children. The fathers were not part of early child care. How then

---

1. Preliminary findings were reported by Colonna and Newman (1983), Kris and Ritvo (1983), Neubauer (1983), Provence and Solnit (1983).

do we understand the significance fathers achieve in the development of children? Is it not surprising that this question has not stimulated us to search for answers? We can assume that when the father is continuously present, and the mother is absent, the child would accord him a comparable need-satisfying role. Similar questions arise out of observations of children in extended families or in kibbutzim where there are at least three primary caregivers.

Theoretical considerations suggest that the infant needs only *one* continuous object at first, and that the mother then endows the father with whatever meaning he achieves for the child. This triangularity then leads to the triadic oedipal constellation. But today, there is much evidence of the father's earlier influence on the child. Greenacre (1966) and Mahler and Gosliner (1955)[2] speak of the father as a "less contaminated object," implying that the child's relationship to the mother (the symbolic attachment) and his need to separate from her and reach individuation are conflictual experiences. The father rescues the child from it by providing an alternative coexistence. Exploring the role of the father, Abelin (in Panel, 1978) too speaks about the uncontaminated symbolic father image that excludes the intense ambivalence to mother. He introduced the notion of a "father thirst" observed in children deprived of contact with fathers. This corresponds to Herzog's (1980) concept of "father hunger." Abelin speaks about the pathological consequences when the early triangularity cannot be attained. The maternal dominance may lead to passivity in boys and a feminine core gender identity. He refers to a built-in maturational blueprint leading boys toward a triangular identification with the father around 18 months. As I have mentioned before, these formulations focus only on the father in reference to a maturational-developmental pull which demands triangular completion. We still retain a dyadic model if we merely extend our studies of mother-child interactions to father-child or sibling interactions. In contrast, I wish to stress the impact of multiple relationships on the child's development.

---

2. Who, however, attribute the "uncontaminated father" to Ernst Kris (see Mahler and Gosliner, p. 310, n.).

Hartmann (1939), examining the interaction between the bio-
logical-maturational and the environmental processes, confirmed the influence of the maturational blueprint: "The processes of adaptation are influenced both by constitution and
external environment, and more directly determined by the on-
togenetic phase of the organism" (p. 30). Hartmann assumes not
only that the environment influences adaptation, but that basically the organism forms itself by adaptation. Furthermore,
Hartmann indicates that from the beginning of life, the ego
apparatus performs an additional function of adaptation.

Erikson (1940) continued this proposition: "the child merely
obeys and on the whole can be trusted to obey inner laws of
development, namely, those laws which in the prenatal period
had formed one organ after another, and now (as these organs
search out reality) create one behavior item after another." This
is, as we know, Erikson's maturational-epigenetic conception.
Freud introduced an additional factor by ascribing to the ego a
tendency to unite and to become united, i.e., its coherent
organization.

If we take the position that by incorporation, introjection, and
identification, the child establishes the beginning of object constancy at age 3—with the capacity to be separated from the
object for short periods of time and with the achievement of
object and self differentiation—then we must pursue this process into the phallic-oedipal phase and explore those new characteristics of the object representation which are specific for the
succeeding stages. Therefore, the notion of object constancy
refers to the earliest stability in the psychic structure and its
unfolding functions, but object constancy does not refer to the
changing quality of object representation.

I have referred to the early role of the father and the significance of siblings in establishing new modes of relationships, and
now turn to the influence of other adult caregivers on early
object relations. While I shall present vignettes from disturbed
mother-child interactions, they nevertheless allow us to draw
some conclusions about normal infant development.

Among the programs of the Child Development Center is a
mental health daycare center for children in their first 3 years of
life and various services for parents. Most of the infants are at

risk due to emotional and social conditions. Most of the mothers are teenagers, unmarried and unready to supply minimal nurturing for their children. In these circumstances we can study the child's evolving object relations—his response to the caregivers and their influence on his relationship to his mother and father. We have undertaken a study to investigate whether daycare programs divert the establishment of primary object relations or whether they substitute for or complement it. I have chosen three variations of infant-mother interactions. The first infant was neglected by his mother and showed all the signs of the resulting developmental deficiencies. In the second case, the mother-child relationship was unreliable and discontinuous. The third child received appropriate mothering from a mother who relied on daycare for assistance.

CASE 1

Martin came to our clinic when he was a few months old because Ms. M., his mother, planned to continue her own education. She was the oldest of 5 children; her father left the family when she was 1 year old and from then on she had only rare contacts with him. Her own mother remarried when Ms. M. was about 10 years old. She idealized her absent father and later her stepfather. She would say, "I kissed the ground he stepped on." During her second marriage Ms. M.'s mother gave birth to two more children. Since Ms. M. could never find acceptance from her mother, who preferred the younger sons, she felt abandoned; as she repressed her resentments, she became depressed.

When Ms. M. became pregnant, she projected the old fantasies to be rescued by her own father and stepfather onto the father of her baby. When she entered Martin in the daycare center, she was depressed. She experienced him as a source of much gratification, but she responded to any autonomous action or demand on his part as a rejection and a disappointment. When Martin showed friendliness to other members of her family (they lived together), she felt betrayed once more.

Martin appeared inactive, unexplorative; he neither molded to the body of other adults, nor did he resist physical contact.

There was only minimal mutual eye gaze. The caregiver whom he seemed to prefer planned to foster a close relationship with him. At the beginning, the dosing of her stimulation had to be carefully orchestrated to his capacity to absorb it, but soon enough his innate need revealed itself by an increasing longing and reaching out for holding and comforting. By 7 months he had developed a strong tie with her; he clung to her and, during her one-week vacation, searched for her. He was able to accept other caregivers, except when he was upset. This emerging capacity for an interacting close relationship to the caregiver was transferred by Martin to his mother, from whom he now expected similar responses. It is important to note that he did not give up reaching out for a better contact. Martin became more curious, exploratory, and more rivalrous with other children.

When Martin was 15 months old, his mother, in spite of her pride in her son's use of language, began to respond to his increasing demands and autonomous strivings with ambivalence. At that time his father, who had never lived with him because he found another woman, saw him less often. When Martin had a new caregiver assigned to him, he became depressed. Faced with this combination of circumstances, he regressed to earlier modes and ego restraints and needed more help, lest he become restless and unable to maintain his activities. This was followed by an increasingly aggressive attitude toward other children, whose toys he took away without wanting them for his own use. Once again, however, he established a more intense relationship with his new caregiver; his mother took a job and began a new relationship with a man. This then lessened her ambivalent feelings toward Martin and enabled her to maintain a more positive attitude to him.

Later, Ms. M. joined a vocational training program and took an evening job. It is characteristic of many of the mothers at the Center that they can maintain their contact with their children only when they follow their own developmental progress. Martin became appropriately angry at his mother and tugged on her, demanding attention from her and his caregivers, with an increased rivalry for their attention. He could not tolerate it when they spoke to other adults and was possessive about toys.

Martin's development indicates his special "facility" for finding in the various caregivers, first, need-gratifying responses and, later, differentiated interactions by selecting his preferred person, taking what he needed from those consistently available. In no way did this situation lessen his longing for an increasingly close relationship with his mother. The more his development progressed, the more did he expect to have mother's special attention. Her uneven availability burdened him, but it did not discourage him from responding to substitute objects. The maturational and developmental pull was reflected in his increasing search for the primary object. His attachment to the caregivers increased his maturational and developmental progression, which in turn he could carry over to his relationship to his mother.

CASE 2

Fred came to the Center when he was 2 months old. His 21-year-old mother, Ms. F., lived with her mother and three younger siblings; her father had left when she was 4 years old and from then on she saw him rarely. Her mother had remarried and given birth to two younger siblings, one of whom was in psychiatric care for a serious illness. Fred's father did not live with them and disappeared often. Ms. F.'s own mother refused to take care of Fred, "except," she said, "to study and to further her own future." While Fred's grandmother did not pay special attention to her grandson, Ms. F.'s sister played with Fred and sat with him in the afternoon.

From the beginning we observed that Fred made eye-to-eye contact, was curious, and watched the caregivers intensely; but there was an absence of appropriate stranger reactions and exploratory vigor. Later, we observed body rigidity in new situations, uncertain motor-visual actions, and poor visual tracking. The Scales of Infant Development at age 6 months put him within the normal range. When his mother was absent, he showed no separation reactions and with much interest turned to the caregivers. It soon became clear that the mother needed to be cared for as much as Fred. She considered the Center to be her new home, expecting the social worker to be totally available to *her* while other staff members took care of her son. She needed mothering to become a mother. Thus, during the early months of Fred's life, there was an absence of maternal care. This deprivation manifested itself in Fred's subdued affect and in inappropriate object interactions. His mother could not accept his demands for her attention, and was rivalrous with him for the attention of the staff. When Fred became more assertive and angry, his mother would turn away from him even more. During the following year, the degree of attachment to one caregiver was tested when he lost her. It had the effect of reducing his exploratory impetus. Later, he formed a relationship to a new caregiver. We learned from this the obvious: that certainly for our group of deprived children, the caregiver should remain with the child over the years and not be changed when the child advances to the next group.

Fred's history reveals that his mother's inability to provide primary care had its usual consequences; but Fred's resilience and the availability of a full daycare program stimulated his responsiveness and his capacity to form significant relationships to people other than his mother. This, in turn, led him to demand similar interactions with her.

Case 3

David came to the Infant Care Center when he was 6 months old. Ms. D., his mother, who lived in the same building that houses our services, asked for daycare because she wanted to pursue her education. She was a guarded person, isolated from her own feelings and from the other parents and the staff. Still, David had a close tie to her. The mother was protective of him, and stayed with him during the first interviews. She enjoyed cuddling him and resented his becoming more independent—a frequent finding in our adolescent mothers. She replicated the relationship with her own mother. Ms. D.'s open longing was always for her father, who had left when she was 5 years old. She had longed for a child; David fulfilled her underlying longing for closeness. It is not surprising that there was a strong bond between mother and child. David's development proceeded appropriately, except for affective restraint and some somberness of mood. During the first months at the Center, he did not always seek the caregivers' affection or stimulation, but he did respond when they were given. Slowly, he made an attachment to one staff member, while he continued his intense preference for and his tie to his mother. He had the expected stranger reactions. Later, he was able to enjoy both caregivers, turning from one to the other, but always choosing his mother when she was present. His recovery time during separations from her was longer than that seen in other infants. We interpreted this to be a sign of greater attachment. While these changes were not without stress for David, he proceeded to develop appropriately, became more expressive in his demands for attention, more possessive of toys, and more rivalrous with other children. He was more "alive and energetic." Spontaneously, he would turn to his mother and hold on to her when she was ready to leave him and would cuddle for a time in her arms. When he was 1½ years old, his mother returned to work; she brought him to the Center much earlier and did not stay with him. He responded to this by again being more restricted in his affect and in his exploration and assertiveness. The three Hunt-Nzigiris subtests showed good overall development, but the area of his weakness seemed to be the anticipation of an object's trajectory and the understanding of in-out relationships. A few weeks after the mother began to work, he recovered enough to show much improvement.

David maintained continuous attachment to his mother and father in spite of many inconsistencies in their relationship to him. Multiple caregivers had not diverted David from the primary object. They gave him more security, supported his development, and helped to maintain an emotional relationship to his mother, minimizing his reaction to her absence.

Discussion

I shall not focus on the infants' pathology and the consequences of abnormal mother-infant relationships. Rather, I shall extract from these vignettes what seems to me to be relevant to *normal* development, taking into account those aspects which safeguard continuity of care and appropriate stimulation in a mental health daycare setting:

1. In the presence of multiple caregivers the search for the mother is maintained or, when she previously was absent, can begin to assert itself.
2. The infant with a normal endowment explores the available human environment to extract the needed stimulation and gratification.
3. Continuity of care does not necessarily imply the exclusive continuity of care by one person. What is important is the continuity of relationships.
4. The infants' individual dispositions to form relationships vary greatly, dependent on drive and ego characteristics. Some infants actively engage in interactions, while others only react to environmental stimulation. Thus the "reading" of the infant, the dosing of the stimulation, becomes an essential part of the attempt to repair the deficiency syndrome resulting from the unevenness of stimulation so that the child's tendency to form object relations is set in motion once again.
5. The matching of the caregivers' capacities and the infant's needs is most important. The child's selection of the person, when there is a choice, gives us important clues about the infant's needs and his special requirements.
6. Since mothers are not always able to match all their children's demands equally, the availability of others gains significance, not only as a choice but as a complement to eliciting the full potential of the various dispositions of different children.
7. While in our group of children it was difficult to decide who, at various times, was the primary caregiver for an infant, we nevertheless can say that the mother maintained or gained an increasingly important position.

The construction of the inner representational world and the meaning of the object can at best be inferred, and thus the emergence of the primary object can only be deduced. Meissner (1979) refers to this issue by suggesting that we should use the term "object relatedness" when we describe external interaction with objects, and the term "object relations" for intrapsychic experience. In order to avoid polarization between external and internal reality and to give recognition to the interplay of reality and fantasy objects, we can follow Hartmann (1956) who explains that the reality principle "indicates a tendency to take into account in an adaptive way, in perception, thinking, and action, whatever we consider the 'real' features of an object or a situation" (p. 244). Hartmann also assumes that the ego apparatus from early infancy allows a preadaptedness to the environment. Through perception, memory, and action the person's sense of reality comes into being as his ego matures and expands in interaction with the environment and drive impulses. The restraint on the immediate need for discharge is an additional requirement for the construction of reality. Thus, the child's inner representations of parent will become clearer as the ego evolves its functions. This formulation differs significantly from those which are drive-oriented and assigns to the parents the libidinal supply which allows the ego to regulate itself, to establish constancy of object representation and self. Or, as Arlow (1969) put it, "There is . . . a reciprocal interplay between reality and fantasy, selective perception on one side, cathectic intensification on the other" (p. 41). This recognition of the reality aspects of the objects must contribute to the awareness of the differences in object relationships.

We are interested in the timetable according to which the primary objects are established. The process of internalization includes the real as well as the fantasied object, which then leads to secondary internalization. Freud (1938) said that under the pressure of separation and loss, a "portion of the external world has, at least partially, been abandoned as an object and has instead, by identification, been taken into the ego and thus become an integral part of the internal world. This new psychical agency continues to carry on the functions which have hitherto been performed by the people [the abandoned objects] in the external world" (p. 205). This ascribes to identification a defensive function, i.e., to cope with loss, with separation. Identification assists the normal processes of separation from the early object. In later development, identification of the boy with the father also is understood to be a defensive maneuver against hostility toward him. Freud (1921) also referred to identification as "the earliest and original form of an emotional tie . . . with an object" (p. 107). Thus, we would assume that identification with early ob-

jects—parents, siblings, and others—precedes the later identifications that come about in a conflictual context. This assumption
refers to separation as a contributing factor. Separation and
individuation continue through childhood into adulthood to
foster development and growth. Blos (1967) refers to the second
individuation process in adolescence as represented by a detach-
ment from the internalized primary objects. Yet I would not
assume that all internalization takes place only as a defensive
maneuver to restore loss.

These considerations may be extended to include Loewald's
(1970) proposition that what becomes internal is the representation of the relationships. He refers to the earliest imprints of
interactions which become patterned until the time when the
ego asserts itself by evolving object representations. It is certain
that none of these conceptualizations sufficiently emphasizes the
processes of differentiation—not only of object and self, but also
between the objects, and, in Loewald's terms, between object
relationships. On each level of developmental organization the
mental representation changes. This must be based on the continuous differentiation of objects in areas of perception, affective response, and cognition in each succeeding stage.

I wish to make a short reference to the function of the transitional objects. Tolpin (1971) does not accept Winnicott's (1953)
idea that the blanket is no longer necessary when the child proceeds to self-regulation; Tolpin rather suggests that the mother,
since she is increasingly perceived as the real object, is unable to
bring about appropriate relief. Therefore, the infant relies on
the blanket—the blanket as self and as object. This formulation
again brings us to intersectional or relationship processes.
Bowlby (1969) assumes that the blanket is a substitute for the
mother, but this assumption does not explain why children with
adequate mothering use a transitional object, whereas few institutionalized children do (Provence and Lipton, 1962). Unable
to achieve a more complete separation from the mother, the
child finds substitute inanimate objects. We can assume that
other persons in the child's life perform similar "transitional"
functions—that is, as long as they fulfill basic needs; and
Provence and Lipton made it clear that these basic needs include

the affective interchange between caregivers and infant and not merely the satisfaction of bodily needs.

Today we have a better understanding of the "layering" of the representational world, the complexities in the interplay between drive and ego motivations. Each is in search of the object—the drive with the aim of obtaining discharge, the ego by taming of the drive influences, and by assigning reality to the objects. Thus the secondary process will increasingly lead to identification with new aspects of the external objects, and thereby to the achievement of internal differentiation.

It may be self-evident that if we pursue this line of thought, we recognize that the primary object world emerges continuously and that object primacy can truly occur only during the phallic-oedipal level of psychic differentiation. In usual circumstances, when the parents are the primary objects, they achieve primacy. Under certain conditions others besides mother may for a time become the primary object, or there may be various objects that simultaneously exert a primary influence. We would agree that object primacy during the phallic-oedipal period is exclusively assigned to both parents.

Parents have traditionally employed caregivers to participate in or take over childcare, when they could afford it, or they have relied on older siblings, grandparents, and others to help with child rearing. Now, more than 50 percent of mothers have full-time jobs; the number is rapidly increasing, and they will rely more and more on community services for daycare for infants and young children. We need not warn society that changes in the nuclear family, brought on by the introduction of childcare help which modifies the exclusive dyadic relationship between mother and child, inevitably must lead to harmful effects on child development. What is harmful are the inappropriate caregivers and services which exist and come into being. At the time when the family shrank to the "nuclear" family, the presence of the mother was indeed crucial, because there existed no substitute for her. Infant observation cannot capture the full developmental experiences when it focuses only on the mother-child relationship. Our data will have to come from visits to homes where the full range of interactions is available for observation.

Our literature often ascribes to the mother-child interaction a position which appears to be too rigid, measured against the child's capacity to extend, elaborate, and adapt to various simultaneous relationships, and to benefit from them.

Under normal conditions of mother-child relationships, the simultaneous relationship to other adults and siblings during the first years of life does not dilute or divert the quality of the relationship to mother and father, but rather contributes to the shaping of primary objects and the primacy of the oedipal objects. Throughout I have implied a difference between the *primary* objects during the pregenital phase and the *object primacy* that is achieved only during the phallic-oedipal phase. One can support the classical notion that the object primacy during the phallic-oedipal phase is exclusively assigned to both parents. New findings have markedly increased our knowledge of the preoedipal world; infant studies are in the foreground of new frontiers of knowledge. From a developmental point of view, we can surely accept the notion that we must pursue early development to understand its impact on later progression. Similarly, we must study the effect of later development on the reorganization of earlier structures.

The search for the preoedipal objects refers to the *analyst's* requirement to search for the various early objects that contribute to early multiple relationships, and the subtlety of personality shaping, in order to avoid the reduction to and reconstruction of an exclusive early dyadic relationship. In addition, it also refers to the young child's search for early objects. Furthermore, we must examine the steps which lead the child to create the internal representational world from the primary objects to object primacy.

BIBLIOGRAPHY

ARLOW, J. A. (1969). Fantasy, memory and reality testing. *Psychoanal. Q.*, 38:28–51.

BLOS, P. (1967). The second individuation process of adolescence. *Psychoanal. Study Child*, 22:162–186.

BLUM, H. P. (1977). The prototype of preoedipal reconstruction. *J. Amer. Psychoanal. Assn.*, 25:757–786.

BOWLBY, J. (1969). *Attachment and Loss.* New York: Basic Books.

CARLSON, B. E. (1984). The father's contribution to child care. *Amer. J. Ortho-psychiat.*, 54:123–136.

COLONNA, A. B. & NEWMAN, L. M. (1983). The psychoanalytic literature on siblings. *Psychoanal. Study Child*, 38:285–310.

DÉCARIE, T. (1969). A study of mental and emotional development of the thalidomide child. In *Determinants of Infant Behaviour*, 4:167–187. London: Methuen.

ERIKSON, E. H. (1940). Problems of infancy and early childhood. In *Cyclopedia of Medicine*. Philadelphia: Davis, pp. 714–730.

FRAIBERG, S. (1977). The development of human attachments. In *Insights from the Blind*. New York: Basic Books, pp. 113–146.

FREUD, S. (1913). Totem and taboo. *S.E.*, 13:1–161.

——— (1921). Group psychology and the analysis of the ego. *S.E.*, 18:67–143.

——— (1923). The ego and the id. *S.E.*, 19:3–66.

——— (1938). An outline of psychoanalysis. *S.E.*, 23:141–207.

GREENACRE, P. (1966). Problems of overidealization of the analyst and of analysis. In *Emotional Growth*, 2:743–761. New York: Int. Univ. Press, 1971.

HARTMANN, H. (1939). *Ego Psychology and the Problem of Adaptation*. New York: Int. Univ. Press, 1958.

——— (1956). Notes on the reality principle. In *Essays on Ego Psychology*. New York: Int. Univ. Press, 1964, pp. 241–267.

HERZOG, J. M. (1980). Sleep disturbance and father hunger in 18- to 28-month-old boys. *Psychoanal. Study Child*, 35:219–233.

JOFFE, G. W. & SANDLER, J. (1965). Notes on pain, depression, and individuation. *Psychoanal. Study Child*, 20:394–424.

KERNBERG, O. F. (1976). *Object Relations Theory and Clinical Psychoanalysis*. New York: Aronson.

KRIS, M. & RITVO, S. (1983). Parents and siblings. *Psychoanal. Study Child*, 38:311–324.

LAMB, M. E. (1980). The role of the father in early childhood. *Aufbau und Störungen frühkindlicher Beziehungen zu Mutter und Vater*, p. 138.

LOEWALD, H. W. (1970). Psychoanalytic theory and the psychoanalytic process. *Psychoanal. Study Child*, 25:45–68.

MAHLER, M. S. & GOSLINER, B. J. (1955). On symbiotic child psychosis. *Psychoanal. Study Child*, 10:195–212.

MEISSNER, W. W. (1979). Internalization and object relations. *J. Amer. Psychoanal. Assn.*, 27:345–360.

NEUBAUER, P. B. (1960). The one-parent child and his oedipal development. *Psychoanal. Study Child*, 15:286–309.

——— (1983). The importance of the sibling experience. *Psychoanal. Study Child*, 38:325–336.

PANEL (1978). The role of the father in the preoedipal years. R. C. Prall, reporter. *J. Amer. Psychoanal. Assn.*, 26:143–162.

PROVENCE, S. & LIPTON, R. C. (1982). *Infants in Institutions*. New York: Int. Univ. Press.

———— & SOLNIT, A. J. (1983). Development-promoting aspects of the sibling experience. *Psychoanal. Study Child,* 38:337–351.

SANDER, L. W. (1962). Issues in early mother-child interaction. *J. Amer. Acad. Child Psychiat.,* 1:141–166.

SANDLER, J. & ROSENBLATT, B. (1962). The concept of the representational world. *Psychoanal. Study Child,* 17:128–145.

TOLPIN, M. (1971). On the beginnings of a cohesive self. *Psychoanal. Study Child,* 26:316–352.

WINNICOTT, D. W. (1953). Transitional objects and transitional phenomena. *Int. J. Psychoanal.,* 34:38–97.

On Mirror-Image Anxiety

An Observational Study
BEATRICE PRIEL, Ph.D.

> When I look I am seen, so I exist.
> —WINNICOTT (1967)

THE CHILD'S RECOGNITION AND UNDERSTANDING OF THE IDENTITY of the mirror image imply a capacity for self representation as well as a concept of the self as visible to others, just as others are visible to the child. In our culture children are exposed at a very early age to their own and their caretakers' reflections; observational studies have yielded clear evidence of self recognition at the end of the second year. Does familiarity with one's own and others' reflections play a role in a child's ability to identify the image as his or her own? Is this familiarity relevant to the emergence or construction of a representation of the body? What happens in this respect to those children who do not have mirrors in their environments?

Self recognition in the mirror is in fact a privileged technique used by those who study how the representation of the body develops during the first years of life, but, like any other technique, it introduces its own limitations: the specular image's characteristics—tridimensionality, synchronicity of movement, lack of path—confront the child with a series of problems. The systematic observation of children's reactions to the first discovery of their specular images permits clarification of some aspects

Senior Clinical Psychologist, Psychiatric Division, Medical Center and Behavioral Sciences Department, Ben Gurion University, Beer Sheva, Israel.

of the problems the child confronts and of the solutions he or she finds to the mirror self-image enigma.

The first studies of self recognition in the mirror can be found in Darwin's (1877) and Preyer's (1881) writings. Systematic and detailed material on this subject was included in the Gesell and Ames Scales of Development (1947), as well as in other development scales. In the last 15 years we have witnessed a proliferation of systematic research on mirror self recognition in the first 2 to 3 years of life (Amsterdam, 1972; Amsterdam and Levitt, 1980; Berthental and Fisher, 1978; Brooks and Lewis, 1976; Gallup, 1970, 1977; Décarie, 1983; Lewis and Brooks, 1975, 1978; Papousek and Papousek, 1974; Schulman and Kaplowitz, 1977; Zazzo, 1975, 1981).

The existing body of knowledge now permits us to delineate the developmental process of self recognition in the mirror: from "social" joyful reactions directed to the image (4 to 5 months), to concentration on comparisons between body parts and their reflection (about 8 to 10 months), to withdrawal and concern reactions (about 15 to 18 months), and to self recognition according to objective criteria (20 to 22 months).

Two criteria of self recognition generally have been used: verbal self recognition and, in the preverbal stage, "mark manipulation" (Amsterdam, 1972) which consists in painting a mark on the child's face, unknown to him, and observing his subsequent behavior in front of a mirror. Intentional mark manipulation in front of the mirror is considered to imply self recognition.

A study of the discovery of the specular image's identity was carried out on 60 children aged 6 to 26 months old, who were systematically observed while they were confronted for the first time with their mirror image. The children studied were nomadic Bedouins dwelling in tents in the Negev desert remote from any populated area. The 60 children who had no previous experience with mirrors fell into 3 age groups: (1) 6 to 12 months; (2) 13 to 19 months; and (3) 20 to 26 months. Each of the three age groups consisted of 10 boys and 10 girls. The reactions of the children who saw their mirror images for the first time were compared with those of a control group consisting of 60 Jewish city dwellers similar in age distribution and sex representation; these children had the usual Western familiarity with mirrors. No significant sex differences were registered regarding the reactions to the mirror image in the two groups.

The observations were made in three distinct phases: in the first, the child was exposed to a mirror for 5 minutes; in the second, the child saw a toy reflected in the mirror for 2½ minutes. Later, during a break, a colored mark was put on the child's forehead unknown to him. In the third phase, the marked child was exposed to the mirror for 2½ minutes. During the entire procedure the children's behaviors were recorded every 10 seconds.

The children's mothers were present throughout the observation period, but they were not reflected in the mirror. At our request, they did not initiate any interaction with the child until the end of the observation period. Afterward the Bedouin mothers generally stayed for a while, playing with the children and the mirror.

The observed reactions to the specular image among the children familiar with mirrors corroborate the findings of most of the previous research on this subject. In comparison with these children, our Bedouin subjects showed the following characteristic behaviors:

1. The 6- to 12-month-old children who were unfamiliar with the mirror showed significantly less active exploration of the image (such as looking at a reflected moving part of the body) and less social behavior (smiling at the image, playing with it), but they spent a considerable amount of time looking attentively, without any action, at the image. This prolonged eye-to-eye contact with the image was much less frequent among the children who were used to mirrors. In addition, the Bedouin children showed withdrawal reactions (turning away from the mirror) as early as 8 months of age. The 6- to 12-month-old children who had had experiences with mirrors showed no withdrawal reactions, nor was such behavior at this age reported elsewhere in the literature.

2. The Bedouin children in the second age group (13 to 19 months) still looked passively (in a behavioral sense only, probably) at the image more frequently than the children familiar with mirrors in the same age group. The Bedouin children explored the image less actively, but the differences between the two

groups (familiar and unfamiliar with mirrors) were smaller. In each of the groups we observed manipulation of the mark on their faces in among 4 to 5 of the children. Withdrawal reactions occurred in both groups, but were more frequent among the Bedouin children. In the group of Jewish children (who were familiar with mirrors) we observed withdrawal reactions from 15 months on.

3. Among the 20- to 26-month-old children we found no significant differences related to self recognition. Nevertheless, the children unfamiliar with mirrors explored their specular images less frequently and showed considerably more concern and withdrawal reactions.

In summary, the Bedouin children reacted to the specular image with a generally less active approach, with less social behavior, and with considerably more eye-to-eye contact; moreover, they showed more frequent and earlier withdrawal reactions. There were no significant differences in regard to self recognition (according to the mark-manipulation criterion) in the two groups of children.

The results concerning self recognition in the mirror indirectly corroborate our theoretical understanding of self representation and early object relations; in this sense, self recognition among the Bedouin children I studied corroborates, on an observational level, Winnicott's statement (1967) that "in individual emotional development, the precursor of the mirror is the mother's face" (p. 26). Among the children who grew up without mirrors in their environment, withdrawal reactions appeared at a much earlier age—at 8 instead of 15 months—and were significantly more frequent than among the children who were familiar with mirrors. The unexpected difference in the reactions of concern and withdrawal offer valuable clues to the interpretation of these well-documented but puzzling reactions in front of the mirror (Preyer, 1881; Gesell and Ames, 1947; Amsterdam, 1972; Dickie and Strader, 1974; Lewis and Brooks, 1975, 1978; Zazzo, 1975, 1981; Amsterdam and Levitt, 1980).

The withdrawal reactions are a kind of mirror-image anxiety: the child who was happily playing with the mirror suddenly becomes preoccupied, fearful, retreats, looks away, and sometimes looks askance and cries.[1] Different tentative interpretations have been offered for this phenomenon: it has been considered as evidence of self consciousness (Lewis and Brooks, 1978; Amsterdam and Levitt, 1980), self recognition (Dixon, 1957), and as a stage preceding self recognition (Schulman and Kaplowitz, 1977). None of these interpretations, however, explains the precocity and the high frequency of withdrawal reactions in children unfamiliar with mirrors. These explanations are even less satisfactory if we consider the fact that I found no differences in these children's capacity to identify their specular images.

I suggest that familiarity with mirrors disguises the cues that indicate mirror-image anxiety. In children familiar with mirrors, anxiety reactions appear only when the specific identification of the mirror image emerges (according to the self recognition criteria utilized); until then the habitual experiences with mirrors disguise the images' uncanniness. Conversely, children unfamiliar with mirrors display mirror-image anxiety from 8 months on. What in the mirror frightens the child?

One way of conceptualizing the self-image anxiety would be to consider it as a special case of stranger anxiety. This formulation would imply that the child reacts to the image as if it were another child; but stranger anxiety reactions are rare in relation to other children, even if they are strangers (Lewis and Brooks, 1975). Nevertheless, one may still be inclined to the stranger anxiety hypothesis because of the very idiosyncratic characteristics of the interactive pattern between the child and his image: the specular image "reacts" in a most unexpected and "non-mirroring" way.

Brazelton et al. (1975) documented reactions of concern in 5-month-old babies when the object's behavior "violates the child's expectancy" of interaction; in an earlier investigation (1974), Brazelton et al. found reactions of concern, withdrawal, and

---

1. This reaction can be seen in R. Zazzo's film *A travers le miroir,* which was presented at a Symposium of the Scientific Psychological Association, Paris, 1973.

averting when the mothers did not practice normal *pausing* in their interactions with the children.

Mirror images simultaneously "imitate" the child's behavior, but such mimicry is a clear violation of the child's expectancy of interaction. It can also be argued that caretaker adults imitate a child's expressions and vocalizations as a characteristic pattern of interaction, but this imitation follows a certain rhythm and is not in perfect synchrony with the child. Therefore, the rhythm, if not the content, of the "interaction" is grossly violated by the mirror image's movement.

In this context it is important to clarify that the mirror's synchronic movement is not an example of "the control over the image" as has been suggested in the mirror literature; as with the human object, mastery is obtained through the realization of an expected *interactional* pattern. Interestingly, in a study of autistic children's reactions to their mirror images and to a deferred video-recorded image, Newman and Hill (1978) emphasize the autistic children's preference for a synchronic image; this result may be understood as the autistic child's utilization of a noninteractional rule; in this case the synchronic mirror image is more effectively affected by the child, who will thus prefer it to a less "controlled" image. On the other hand, Lewis and Brooks (1978) conclude that normal children show more withdrawal reactions to a synchronic self image than to a slightly delayed video image; in the latter case, the pattern of interaction probably is more like the normal pattern of a child being imitated by another person.

I would therefore propose that mirror anxiety reactions are related to the quality of synchronicity inherent in the images' movements. Observational studies support the premise that from the middle of the first year children become aware of the strangeness of this pattern of interaction. In view of the fact that both stranger-anxiety reactions and the mirror-image anxiety reactions among children who have never seen a mirror appear at around 8 months, I suggest that the two reactions are different aspects of the same underlying process of self-object differentiation.

Stranger anxiety is generally conceived as evidence of the child's having acquired object constancy (Bowlby, 1960), but the emergence of object constancy coincides with the emergence of self constancy, as has been pointed out by Solnit (1982) and Sandler (1977), who writes, "However, with self-object differentiation from the non-differentiated state, another constant object, an object with an equally enduring identity, also emerges for the child. This is *the child's own self*," which Sandler defines as "a mental representation which has both structural and experiental aspects, just as the object has, in the mind of the child" (p. 199).

While the concept of stranger anxiety refers mainly to the acquisition of object constancy, mirror-image anxiety is related to the constancy of the body image and its boundaries. This constancy refers mainly to the aspect of continuity in time, which is challenged by continuous changes and transformations occurring in the child's subjective experience; the mirror self-image is a special case of such a transformation: an exteriorization of the image of the body, a situation in which the child sees himself as others see him.

The relevance of the mirror image to the process of building a self representation and differentiating it from object representations has been emphasized by Mahler et al. (1975); for example, these authors interpret the comparisons that the 9-month-old child frequently makes between body parts and their reflection as a way of "clarifying for himself the relationship between himself and the 'image'" (p. 223). These deliberate movements also may be viewed as the kind of *dialogue* the child has with himself to which Sandler alluded when she postulated a process related to self-constancy in which "the child *constantly and automatically also scans and has a dialogue with his own self to get refuelling and affirmation, through the perception of cues, that his self is his old familiar self, that it is no stranger to him*" (p. 199). Yet, as already mentioned, something in this "dialogue" frightens the child.

The mirror image is confusing for the child not only because of its strange "interactive" pattern. Since this image's movement is synchronic with the child's kinesthetic sensations, it acquires a quality that only the child's own body has (i.e., hand movements are felt and simultaneously seen): this would mean that the child is receiving from the mirror rather bewildering me and nonme cues.

Freud (1919) referred to mirrors and the blurring of me-nonme boundaries in his study of "The Uncanny." Although Freud described the experiences of adults, the concept of the uncanny as developed by him is a very valuable theoretical model that allows a deeper understanding of the self-image anxiety reactions that I am discussing here. An essential aspect of Freud's concept of the uncanny is the coexistence of ideas that are different from each other; e.g., in something that is familiar there appear "occult" aspects; the unfamiliar that appears in the familiar provides the uncanny feeling. Freud defines the "unfamiliar" as a repressed content or way of thinking (e.g., animistic thought); hence, what is unfamiliar was previously familiar, and it is the process of repression that rendered it unfamiliar. The momentary lack of discrimination between reality and fantasy and between me and nonme produces the experience of the uncanny—a phenomenon that Bleger (1978) called "ambiguity." The reflected image poses to the child the problem of being *me* (since it moves in perfect synchrony with the kinesthetically perceived movements of the body) and *nonme* (because it is an external reality, outside the child's body boundaries).

In infancy the mirror image may thus acquire an uncanny quality every time it challenges the child's discrimination between reality and image and between me and nonme. This occurs when the child, because of the specific properties of the specular image, "sees" in it fused remainders of previously nondifferentiated aspects. I want to add here that, even from a purely cognitive point of view, the mirror image has an additional intrinsic incongruity because it does not have a path, as real objects do, and it appears out of, and disappears into, nowhere; at the same time this image offers an illusion of reality in view of its apparent tridimensionality.

The uncanny quality of the mirror image can also be gleaned in some cultural elaborations. In different social groups, self reflection in mirrors has elicited many magical, taboo-related, and frightening interpretations which are generally based on the belief that the reflected image has or may acquire an independent and *real* quality. According to my own observations, Israeli mothers of North African origin may be reluctant to show their children a mirror because they believe the child will see in it the image of a still unborn sibling. In the *Golden Bough,* Frazer (1911) describes cultures that forbid looking at a self reflection because it *is* the soul (Andamaneses and Mothumu in New Guinea) or because a wild animal may then attack the image (Zulu). We find here, again, in different cultural traditions and folklore, fears related to nondiscrimination between reality and fantasy, and between me and nonme that are provoked by reflected images.

The essential characteristics of the mirror image that produce a child's withdrawal and concern can be summarized as follows:

1. The mirror image behaves in a strange, nonmirroring way.

2. The mirror image presents the child with intermingled me-nonme cues.

3. The mirror image has ambiguous real-nonreal characteristics.

But if the mirror image indeed possesses these characteristics, how does the habitual familiarity with mirrors delay withdrawal reactions until almost the middle of the second year? Close observation of the child's "habitual familiarity" with mirrors immediately shows that it is a mutual experience between himself, his mother, and the mirror; the situation is usually a dialogue in which the mother interprets the image to the child, reducing its ambiguity to a level more tolerable for the child.

Habitual play with mirrors is in this sense a specific situation in which "holding" prevents excessive anxiety about body-image boundaries and me-nonme discrimination. The mirror situation, like the peekaboo game or play with the mother's body, all of which also are at their peak at around 8 months of age (Mahler et al., 1975), can be considered to reveal the problems the child confronts in this stage and some of the solutions he or she finds. The familiarization then relates not merely to "mirrors" but to looking into a mirror while being held (in Winnicott's sense) by the caretaker adult. And it is an essential property of the mirror that it simultaneously reflects child *and* mother.

Such experiences with mirrors (and the mother) disguise the anxiety-provoking characteristics of the self reflection. For this

92   *Beatrice Priel*

reason, I believe, withdrawal reactions were not reported before 15 to 18 months. Children familiar with mirrors display self-image anxiety somewhat earlier than they clearly recognize themselves in the mirror (according to the mark-manipulation criterion); that is why withdrawal reactions were, for a long time, considered a precursor of self recognition. On the basis of my hypothesis about self-image anxiety reactions, I conclude that as soon as the mirror image is identified precisely, its uncanniness is revealed. It is the undiscriminated that appears when the discrimination of the image emerges in its definite form. This explanation also holds true for the children unfamiliar with mirrors who showed withdrawal reactions as late as 26 months.

BIBLIOGRAPHY

AMSTERDAM, B. K. (1972). Mirror self-image reactions before age two. *Develpm. Psychobiol.*, 5:297–305.

———— & LEVITT, M. (1980). Consciousness of self and painful self-consciousness. *Psychoanal. Study Child*, 36:67–83.

BERTHENTAL, B. I. & FISHER, K. W. (1978). Development of self-recognition in the infant. *Develpm. Psychol.*, 14:1–44–50.

BLEGER, J. (1978). *Simbiosis y ambiguedad*, 4th ed. Buenos Aires: Editorial Paidos.

BOWLBY, J. (1960). Separation anxiety. *Int. J. Psychoanal.*, 41:83–113.

BRAZELTON, T. B., KOSLOWSKI, B., & MAIN, M. (1974). The origins of reciprocity. In *The Effect of the Infant on Its Caregiver*, ed. M. Lewis & L. A. Rosenblum. New York: Liley.

———— TRONICK, E., ADAMSON, L., ALS, H., & WEISS, S. (1975). Early mother-child reciprocity. In *Parent-Infant Interaction*. Ciba Foundation Symposium 33, Amsterdam: Elsevier.

BROOKS, J. & LEWIS, M. (1976). Visual self recognition in different representational forms. Paper presented at the 21st International Congress of Psychology, Paris.

DARWIN, C. R. (1877). A biographical sketch of an infant. *Mind*, 2:186–294.

DÉCARIE, T. G. (1983). Image speculaire et genese de la reconnaissance de soi. *Enfance*, 1–2:99–115.

DICKIE, J. R. & STRADER, W. H. (1974). Development of mirror image responses in infancy. *J. Psychol.*, 88:333–337.

DIXON, J. C. (1957). Development of self recognition. *J. Genet. Psychol.*, 91:251–256.

FRAZER, J. G. (1911). *The Golden Bough*. London: McMillan.

FREUD, S. (1919). The uncanny. *S.E.*, 17:217–256.

GALLUP, G. G. (1970). Chimpanzees. *Science*, 167:86–87.

—— (1977). Self recognition in primates. *Amer. Psychologist*, 32:328–338.

GESELL, A. & AMES, L. B. (1947). The infant's reaction to its mirror image. *J. Genet. Psychol.*, 70:141–154.

LEWIS, M. & BROOKS, J. (1975). Infants' social perception. In *Infant Perception*, ed. L. B. Cohen & P. Solapatek. New York: Academic Press.

—— (1978). Self-knowledge and emotional development. In *The Development of Affects*, ed. M. Lewis & L. A. Rosenblum. New York: Plenum Press, pp. 205–226.

MAHLER, M. S., PINE, F., & BERGMAN, A. (1975). *The Psychological Birth of the Human Infant*. New York: Basic Books.

NEWMAN, C. J. & HILL, S. D. (1978). Self recognition and stimulus preference in autistic children. *Develpm. Psychobiol.*, 11:571–578.

PAPOUSEK, H. & PAPOUSEK, M. (1974). Mirror images and self recognition in young human infants. *Develpm. Psychobiol.*, 7:149–157.

PREYER, W. T. (1881). *The Mind of the Child*. Paris: Alcan.

SANDLER, A.-M. (1977). Beyond eight-month anxiety. *Int. J. Psychoanal.*, 58:195–207.

SCHULMAN, A. H. & KAPLOWITZ, C. (1977). Mirror image responses during the first two years of life. *Develpm. Psychobiol.*, 10:133–142.

SOLNIT, A. J. (1982). Developmental perspectives on self and object constancy. *Psychoanal. Study Child*, 37:201–220.

WINNICOTT, D. W. (1967). Mirror-role of mother and family in child development. In *The Predicament of the Family*, ed. P. Lomas. London: Hogarth Press, pp. 26–33.

ZAZZO, R. (1975). La genèse de la conscience de soi. In *Psychologie de la conscience de soi*, ed. R. Angelergues et al. Paris: Presses Univ. de France.

—— (1981). Miroirs, espaces, images. In *La reconnaissance de son image chez l'enfant et l'animal*, ed. P. Mounoud & A. Vinter. Paris: Delachaux et Niestlé.

CLINICAL PAPERS

The Effect of Role Reversal on Delayed Marriage and Maternity

MARIA V. BERGMANN

IN RECENT YEARS, AN INCREASING NUMBER OF WOMEN HAVE COME to psychoanalytic treatment near the end of their fertility cycles. They are childless and afraid to remain so. They have postponed marriage and maternity in favor of professional opportunities and social and sexual freedom. As a rule, they have several college degrees, secure professional status, and a lifestyle that permits independence from men. They have had intense relationships, primarily with older or younger men—rarely with peers. In most cases the men did not want children—because they already were fathers.

Not infrequently these patients had previously been in treatment with attractive male therapists. Apparently, seductive aspects of the father-daughter relationship were repeated in an erotized transference (Blum, 1973) but ended in disappointment and remained unanalyzed.

The choice of the second analyst had been "researched." It had to be a woman who had accomplished combining marriage, maternity, and a profession. These patients disclosed various fears and anxieties: whether a woman can have both a child *and* the man she loves; whether she can have a child and yet retain her profession. A few women expressed a wish to have a child without a mate. Or there was anxiety about maternity as a "trap," or a "conviction" that a woman who has become professionally

Faculty, New York Freudian Society; Member, Division of Psychoanalysis (39), American Psychological Association.

successful will be regarded as "masculine" and no man will want her. The unconscious doubt in their capacity to produce a child had resulted in their "unintentionally" becoming pregnant: the majority of the patients studied had had one or several abortions prior to treatment. These women presented a characteristic picture with conflict derivatives from various stages of development. What stood out were incestuous feelings toward their fathers—feelings that had not been repressed following the oedipal period—and a deep yearning for closeness with their mothers.

Freud (1931) believed that becoming a wife and mother was a complementary process: the wish for a child stemmed from the earlier wish for a penis, and marriage and motherhood supplied a woman with her mature sexual identity and fulfillment. It is my impression, however, that the wish for the penis and the wish for a child are not as unified as Freud thought. Penis envy also can lead to a wish for a penis in heterosexual love but without integration of other adult goals.

Among my patients were women who enjoyed sex but whose unconscious conflicts prevented them from achieving motherhood; for others, maternity was decisive, but their sexual pleasures were inhibited. None of these patients had been able to unite the separate currents of maternity, sexuality, and professional activity. In terms of severity of psychopathology, these patients were no more disturbed than those who marry in order to have a child or stay in an unhappy marriage or settle for a lasting love relationship without children. They all suffered from essentially neurotic disturbances.

In this presentation I draw on the analyses of six women who differed in many respects, but who had a cluster of specific features in common: their difficulties began during their pre-oedipal period when their mothers failed to let the girls outgrow the symbiotic phase; there were narcissistic problems leading to a reversal of the role of mother and daughter; object relationships were disturbed early in life; and the fathers' seductive attitude toward the little girls was prominent.[1]

I suggest that this cluster of specific features constitutes a

1. For reasons of discretion, no individual case history can be given.

"central psychic constellation," which Silverman et al. (1975) define as "a psychic organization possessing sufficient cohesion and stability to maintain a significant impact upon the course of further development" (p. 155). These authors attempted to isolate phase-specific elements of character development related to the choice of defenses, affects, and the role of a given environment by the time a child is 3½ years old. The oedipus complex was viewed within a developmental continuum.

In this essay, data related to developmental lines (A. Freud, 1963) and to the central psychic constellation were obtained through reconstruction. Solnit (1982), Escoll (1983), and others have observed the reappearance of early object relationship themes in the transference and their significance for genetic reconstruction. In my patients, the central psychic constellation comprised a core of early psychic characteristics which became a predictable motivational system in adulthood and aided in the understanding of recurring problems related to marriage and maternity.

In this paper, the concept of the basic psychic constellation is used as a tool of reconstruction. In view of the similarity of some decisive specific data, it may become a tool of prediction within carefully specified limits in the treatment of adults who have certain related problems.

THE WISH FOR A SYMBIOTIC RELATIONSHIP

As these women approached the end of their fertility cycle, the wish for a child surfaced with particular urgency, reviving lifelong dormant wishes for closeness with mother. This yearning included symbiotic and later restitutional wishes in relation to the mother. Symbiotic wishes were preconscious: the patients hoped for an intimate relationship with their own wished-for infants—one that would provide this yearned-for feeling they themselves had lost too soon or never fully replaced by later intimate experiences with their mothers. Symbiotic wishes surfaced as transference fantasies early in treatment, or when a current love relationship had come to grief. Family romance fantasies sometimes disguised underlying symbiotic yearnings;

several patients expressed the wish to be the analyst's only child and exclusive love object.

The childless women had erected strong defenses against fears of reengulfment by their mothers (Mahler and Gosliner, 1955), and against fears of abandonment by either parent. These anxieties also appeared in the transference as strong ambivalent swings and difficulties in regulating closeness to and distance from another person. At the same time these women expressed yearnings for a father who would exclude the mother from father-daughter intimacies. During the preoedipal period, a need for exclusive dyadic object relationships had become firmly anchored (Mahler, 1971; Abelin, 1980). In adulthood, triadic relationships were tolerated only with inner conflicts and sometimes ended in divorce following the birth of a child.

As the childless women approached the end of the fertility cycle, their intense unfulfilled symbiotic wishes resurfaced with particular urgency. These wishes formed one of the strands in the central psychic constellation.

THE EMERGENCE OF "ROLE REVERSAL" AS A GENETIC TURNING POINT

In the course of normal development, most children reverse the roles of mother and child in both fantasy and play activities. In the women described here, however, the reversal of roles occurred in reality. The mothers' neediness forced these girls to alleviate the mothers' distress—by attempting to mother their mothers.

Every one of the patients was the oldest child in her family. She found herself mothering younger siblings as well as her mother. This was poignantly relived in the transference neurosis: when the analyst suffered from a minor visible injury, these patients became oversolicitous and competed in their caretaking fantasies with the analyst's family, particularly the husband. It became apparent from dreams and fantasies that in childhood (and to this very day), when the mothers had been ill, troubled, or unavailable, the little girls became helping caregivers in the family, a role encouraged by the fathers, who were frequently absent—actually, emotionally, or both. (In the generation now 40 years and over, most fathers had served in World War II.)

Each girl, perceiving her mother's neediness,[2] had become a mother to her own mother and siblings before she had had enough time to experience the protection, security, and pleasures enjoyed by children who had received adequate mothering. The mothers, in turn, had made these girls part of their narcissistic and anxiety-laden world by their demands on them. Memories of being the "child-mother" were relived with painful affects and vivid imagery.

In states of anxiety or stress, mothers had difficulties with impulse control. Discharge of stress temporarily led to a loss of personal communication with the child as a child, as if the mother had lost sight of the respective roles of each. The child in turn felt impelled to take care of the mother. In reliving early longings for the mother's emotional presence in the transference, the patients said they felt *unrecognized, ignored, overlooked;* one patient described her feeling as "emotionally disconfirmed."

Being unable to communicate rage reactions about being overlooked led to a structural regression with weakened self-esteem and a transitory loss of differentiation from the mother as caregiver. The withdrawal of the mother's object cathexis from the child "as a child" led to a disruption of self constancy, with an accompanying fantasy of *role reversal* shared by mother and child. This fantasy creates a temporary hiatus in the *real* relationship between them, and the child's self cathexis is temporarily weakened in the service of maintaining the tie to the object. This disturbance in the cohesiveness of the child's developing self representation and self constancy causes fragmentation of the child's developing self image. A diminished self cathexis will prevail until the child's inner representation of self corresponds again to the conscious experience of herself as a child or, seen from the object's point of view, until the mother regains her maternal role. Role reversal serves to prevent loss of

2. Freud (1923): "the ego is especially under the influence of perception, and . . . speaking broadly, perceptions may be said to have the same significance for the ego as instincts have for the id" (p. 40). See also Mahler (in Panel, 1958) and Spitz (1965).

relatedness between mother and child and thereby preserves some continuity within the child's self representation. Thus, in spite of its damaging effects, role reversal is a defensive operation in that it preserves the cohesiveness of the child's self. The child, rescued by a move toward lesser differentiation from the object but unsure of the object's "staying power," may, however, begin to experience separation anxiety and become phobia-prone.

In many instances, these girls exhibited a "quasi-parental precocity" which circumvented the emergence of sibling rivalry and characterologically gave way to precocious altruism and surrender toward those who were needier or younger (A. Freud, 1936). Reversal of the role of mother and child—both in reality and in fantasy—interfered with identification with the mother as a predictable, child-caring object.

A patient said, "When I remembered in my last hour that I saw my younger sister being nursed, I also remembered the first time my mother was home. It was after my sister was born. I had a nurse's outfit, and my doll was injured and bandaged all over and needed special attention. I thought that my mother had never been there for me *alone* because she didn't stay home until the younger children came. She taught me how to be a mother, how to take care of all the things she had to do and of the younger children. As long as I can remember, I tried to make life easier for her. Yet she feels a victim to this very day! I was always an adult and by the time I was grown up I had had it about being with children." This patient had picked lovers according to the model of serving helpless younger children. Her relationships had come to grief, however, because each time she had hoped in vain for reciprocity and protection from her mate as she originally had from her preoccupied mother.

When the mother experiences the child as a distant part of herself, "what is left out" of the relationship is never fully cathected, nor is it repressed (Burlingham, 1935). Thus, self perception, self constancy, internalization, and identification with the mother remain underdeveloped. Fear of abandonment assumes a central role (Brodey, 1965). *What is left out* will be left out again in the transference relationship, whether the analyst is in the role of parent or child. Instead, feelings of not being understood will be expressed (and often be correct), until words for "what was left out" have been found jointly by analyst and patient. In the transference, role-reversal fantasies appeared as fears of complete abandonment, if the patient would not comply by taking care of the analyst (mother) first (Fleming, 1975).

Patients remembered not being allowed to be rageful or needy. One patient said, "No wonder I don't want a baby. *She* is my baby. She is either a child or a queen." From early on, whenever the mother abdicated her role, the girl took care of her younger siblings. One patient commented, "I never understood that it took me so long to have wanted a child because I never felt I was allowed to be a child long enough myself." Another said, "I feel like a child or like a mother, but not as *me* with a continuing feeling of me." Or: "My mother loves me when I am her mother, but I want a mother too; I thought of you [the analyst] as my mother." This patient continued, "I feel so rejected when my mother can't cope, and at such moments I hate the idea of having a child."

I was struck by another feature that these women had in common—in all six cases there had been interferences with the girls' ability to engage in doll play. In normal development this activity provides opportunities for testing a variety of roles in fantasy— the child can play at being father or mother or sibling or baby. My patients, however, having actually been "little mother" to siblings and to their own mothers, showed significant disturbances in doll play. They recalled playing with the toys of siblings; of younger siblings being *their* "doll children," for whom they often created toys and games. They envied girls who had lovely dolls or children they visited whose mothers participated in doll play.

Almost without exception, memories predominated in which dolls were taken apart or destroyed. As younger siblings were their play objects, these girls had little emotional space for owning a doll on whom they could bestow love, about whom they could fantasy, and whom they could endow with unique features they did not have to share with anyone. I wondered whether this was a sign of disturbance in the mother-child intimacy which prevented these patients from experiencing first their mothers as unique, and later a man as unique and irreplaceable. The disturbance that resulted from the reversal of the roles of mother and child in reality seemed to have eliminated the desire to give fantasies free reign in doll play.

The disturbances in doll play had other repercussions. Doll play has been described as basic to the development of the female body image, including internal vaginal body cathexis (Kestenberg, 1968, 1971), and as crucial in overcoming fears of object loss, particularly in relation to the mother (Blum, in Panel, 1976). Hence the lack of doll play interfered with these developments.

While the parental attitudes had created difficulties, they also seemed to be responsible for specific strengths in these women. Both parents had considered their daughters special children and imbued them with high hopes for future achievements. These children became "exceptions" (Jacobson, 1959), and role reversal became a source of gratification for them. Yet, these girls felt helpless and weighed down by the emotional burdens placed upon them. They lost the sense of a carefree childhood too quickly: feeling both special and helpless created an oscillating self cathexis. Symbolically, by reversing roles these little girls became the mothers they never had had. Role reversal represented a defensive substitute for separation-individuation in the sense that the children acted precociously as "independent adult helpers," thereby creating a fantasied identity. But role reversal also defined these girls' place in the family: they could feel secure because they were needed.

These children grew up to become caregiving women, task-oriented, and responsible in their object relationships. The capacity "to take it" and the praise for being "special" promoted initiative, courage, and a sense of adventure. The ability to fight for something in spite of pain constituted a conscious motivational asset in solving inner conflict.

The disturbances of role reversal I described here constitute a specific variant on a theme of narcissistic pathology (Bergmann, 1980). As Brodey (1965) observed, if mothers have not resolved their earliest fear of abandonment, they are unable to cathect the child as a separate libidinal object. The child must "conform to expectation to prevent severe psychological decompensation in the parents" (p. 183).

Kernberg (1975) has described narcissistic patients who adopt a stance of coolness or self-preoccupied distance toward people they feel close to in order to control hostile feelings. This attitude enables them to maintain continuity of self cathexis and to avoid fragmentation of the self. These disturbances are also reminiscent of Bach's (1980) description of adults who cannot maintain subjective and objective self-awareness simultaneously, an incapacity that implies not accepting two children simultaneously: mothers who make a mother of the older child may then treat the younger child as a child.

What I have, for brevity's sake, labeled role reversal formed another, most important strand in these women's central psychic constellation, making them prone to subsequent disturbances in self and object constancy, namely, problems of internalization and identification with the mother's *maternal* aspects, and experiencing separation as total abandonment. Another strand of the central psychic constellation derived from a precociously sexualized father-daughter relationship.

THE FATHER'S ROLE

The threatening end of these women's childbearing capacity ushered in a turning point in the life cycle. Heightened incestuous guilt which emanated from the unmarried state and unconsciously affirmed the tie to the father surfaced at this time in life and added to inner pressures.

Inconsistent protectiveness by an emotionally unpredictable mother led to an intensification of the relationship between the little girl and her father.[3] In most cases, the patient had early memories of being close to her father whenever he was at home, probably earlier than the toddler's first discovery of him as a delightful companion following differentiation.

In these patients, the preoedipal tie to the father was characterized by a surge of wishes for security and protection from him, and he in turn took on a maternal role when the mother

---

3. Abelin (1980) described the father as "a second specific attachment object . . . [but] the toddler will most likely turn to *her mother for comfort*" (p. 155; my italics).

abdicated her functions. The intense mutual love between father and daughter and the aura of seductive fantasies which characterized their relationship from early on led to omnipotent feelings, created a sexual precocity, and made it difficult for the girl to delineate her realistic place in the family. Early love for the father along with increased ambivalence to the mother interfered with the resolution of the rapprochement crisis and intensified separation problems (Mahler, 1966, 1975; Abelin, 1980). Identification with the father was based on a need for security and nurture, which strengthened the incestuous tie to him and intensified a need for sustenance which sometimes assumed an addictive quality in adulthood. In analysis this need appeared concurrently with oral wishes, upon which penis envy was superimposed.

The sexualized tie to the father consolidated oedipal precocity and, in combination with role reversal, concretized the fantasy of having *had* babies with father; upon mother's withdrawal, externalization and role play assumed a concreteness and an aura of reality. Thus incestuous guilt became a permanent source of internal conflict, paid for by the childlessness. When identification with the maternal father produced the wish, "I want a child," it represented a bisexual and narcissistic wish for self-completion. In adulthood an independent wish for a baby increased separation anxiety and fears of abandonment. Identification with the mother did not include a wish for a baby, but identification with the maternal and oedipal father did.

The mother was recognized as being father's sexual mate, and the identification with her *sexual role* carried the girl into heterosexuality during adolescence. However, the mother also was devalued as "the child." At times of parental marital tensions these patients felt the need to protect their mothers, but secretly they sided with their fathers. This concretized and externalized the oedipal fantasy of being father's "other woman," a role that seemed much more desirable than that of the married mother, who was in danger of being abandoned. The mistress fantasy represented not only an oedipal victory over the mother but also a "preoedipal victory," that of remaining father's little girl at the same time.

Some of the women did not progress developmentally beyond

the "mistress phase" without analysis, much as they wanted to be married. They experienced sexual closeness with a mate and feelings of revenge and narcissistic triumph over their mothers. Oedipal feelings for the father were relived in analysis, sometimes with an unusual amount of pain that stemmed from the concreteness of the tie and from far-reaching disappointment in the childhood "love life" that ended by his becoming the girl's "lost lover." The father remained an idealized object of love and identification; there was much less ambivalence toward him than toward the mother. However, there frequently was a guilt-laden fantasy that professional prominence based on cognitive or intellectual capacities would make a woman "masculine" and cause infertility. The one-sided identification with mother and the depth of preference for father made it difficult to overcome bisexual wishes. In adulthood this led to anxiety about marital commitment.

The early sexualization of the relation to the father and the impaired capacity to separate from him formed another strand in the basic psychic constellation. The oedipal father fixation produced the fantasy that the little girl *had had* a baby with him and that she *had been* his "other woman." Unconscious themes of oedipal *and* maternal victory over the mother interfered with the postadolescent capacity for the transfer of love feelings and wishes for a baby to a man of her own who was a peer in adulthood.

THE NEGATIVE OEDIPAL CONSTELLATION

In these patients, the negative oedipal phase seemed short-circuited. As indicated, symbiotic wishes surfaced early in the treatment, either directly in fantasies or vigorously defended against, so that mother as the patient's "girl baby" was cared for lovingly or rejected with considerable frustration and rage.

The girl's identity formation was inhibited. Mahler (in Panel, 1958) describes two pivotal stages of identity formation: the separation-individuation phase and the phase of resolution of bisexual identification. The integration of body-image representations with pregenital concerns depends on successful identification with the parent of the same sex. In addition, "affirming emotional attitudes of both parents to the child's sexual identity" are of paramount importance for "distinct feelings of self-identity" and the solution of the oedipal conflict (p. 138).

Blos (1974) pointed out that the negative oedipal conflict survives in a repressed state until adolescence. My patients never fully experienced the negative oedipal conflict and therefore did not repress it in Blos's sense. It remained in a developmentally rudimentary form, amalgamated with revived symbiotic longings, seemingly from the time of its appearance until its reappearance in the transference.

I believe that normally the girl's hostility to her mother after the discovery of the sexual differences is mitigated and the love relationship with her safeguarded if the mother allows her little girl to be a "little woman" (and can accept her penis envy at the same time). The little girl allowed to apply her mother's cosmetics, strutting about in mother's high heels, and laughing with impish delight symbolizes phallic-exhibitionistic self-expression. Permission to express her need to show off her body, to perform, to be a tomboy without having to forfeit her simultaneous feminine development, and to play mother's role helps the girl to feel physically loved as a female child. This approval counteracts her lowered self-esteem due to penis envy and promotes oedipal in favor of pseudo-oedipal relationships with each parent. It helps her to accept her clitoris and vagina as adequate organs. When her feminine body image becomes anchored as lovable, the little girl feels able to reach the oedipal phase with mother's permission. She can then value her mother in spite of her "penislessness."

The mother's affirmation of the girl's femininity promotes identification with, and idealization of, the mother. The girl child needs this affirmation. The preoedipal as well as the oedipal girl needs mother-girl intimacy which grows out of sharing and loving "feminine things" and "women's concerns"; if a mother allows participation in her world and a girl can *play* being an adult woman, the girl feels she is permitted to remain a child. Insufficient consolidation of the love tie to the mother during the negative oedipal period will prevent repression of incestuous feelings toward the father during and following the oedipal phase and will continue into latency. A struggle to possess the mother exclusively will be avoided. Under more favorable conditions, the incest barrier is maintained because the oedipal mother belongs to the father. In my cases the incest barrier was not sufficiently affirmed: the mother always seemed too child-like to be experienced fully as a mother, and the father was too available as an incestuous love object, so that far-reaching characterological adaptation against threatening bisexual wishes and incestuous stirrings became urgent.

Many of these mothers preferred to share personal feelings with their daughters rather than their husbands, thereby exposing the fathers to the daughters' seductive wishes and behavior, which led to precocious oedipalized intimacies with the fathers. During the negative oedipal phase, the reemerging symbiotic wishes became sexualized, and wishes for separation from the mother failed once more.

Concrete wishes and fantasies directed toward the analyst became central early in the transference to fill a gap left open by disturbances of identification with the patient's mother. There was an unstated pressure on the analyst to help the patient overcome narcissistic self-devaluation stemming from her childless, unmarried state.

Thus, I see another trend forming the basic psychic constellation in the mother's lack of responsiveness to the girl's feminine and bisexual tendencies, which did not permit a sufficient flowering of the negative oedipal love tie and its subsequent repression. The sense of feminine identity was infirm and the girl was unprotected against sexualization and overstimulation in the oedipal father-girl relationship.

SPECIFIC PROBLEMS IN LATENCY AND ADOLESCENCE

Normal oedipal experiences strengthen the incest barrier and induce the growing child to differentiate identification from love. Internalization of the parents as oedipal objects promotes superego structuring and later oedipal mourning. Loewald (1973, p. 15) has observed that under favorable conditions oedipal relationships are transformed into internalized, intra-

psychic, depersonified relationships. Internalization as a completed process fosters emancipation from the original object.

In the women I have described this process did not take place.
The new objects, therefore, were experienced as incestuous.
Analysis had to bring out the extent to which both love and
idealization were still attached to the figure of the father. The
intrusiveness of both parents continued into latency and puberty, interfering with phase-specific needs for separation and
autonomy.

During adolescence, the fathers tended to supervise the girls'
attire—not, however, as one would expect, in the direction of
greater modesty but in ways which would enhance the girls'
seductiveness and sexual appeal. For instance, hairdos were discussed or sweaters that would make growing breasts protrude.
The mothers, on the other hand, tended to join the girls in the
excitement about their dates but were also most inquisitive. In
analysis we discovered that the excessive interest in the girls'
dates on the part of each parent confirmed once more the
strength of the tie and the fear of losing the daughter. This in
turn interfered with the girls' growing attempts to find a love
object who was a peer.

It is more difficult to describe the positive results of role reversal as they emerged in postadolescent sublimations since they
had not appeared as complaints. The patients assumed adult
responsibilities for their parents, particularly for the mother,
which consolidated in latency but became even more apparent in
adolescence. Characterologically this strong sense of responsibility disposed them toward a certain asceticism and fostered the
capacity from adolescence on to delay gratification and to yield
to others. These girls often became counselors or advisors to
other girls in love. They frequently became interested in the helping professions or in caring for other women's children. As
adults, for instance, they tended to become ideal mothers to
children of divorced boyfriends.

Jacobson (1964, p. 206f.) has pointed out how instability of the
superego interferes with identity formation and self constancy.
Although she does not use the term self constancy, she describes
persons whose sense of identity alters when the object relationships change from positive to negative affects and back

again—when they vacillate between love and hate. Object constancy and reality testing are interdependent, but the constant object implies a firm libidinal cathexis of the object representation, a realistic perception of the object, and a resultant capacity to sustain love (Bak, 1971).

In these patients, unfulfilled incestuous wishes surfaced again during adolescence and interfered with peer relationships and the choice of a mate. Their relations to men showed the imprint of the failure to resolve oedipal issues. Typically, initial idealization was followed by disappointment. This pattern became part of the character structure and resurfaced in their adult relationships to men. Alternating idealization and disillusionment also characterized the transference neurosis.

In masturbation fantasies, dreams, and in the transference, two topics predominated: primal scene fantasies in which the patient would replace the analyst's husband; and torture fantasies, attesting to the extensive sexual overstimulation during childhood. They were narrated with excruciating pain, an irrevocable sense of exclusion from the parental couple, and intense narcissistic injury.

ADULTHOOD AND MARRIAGE

When the core of the infantile neurosis has remained intact, there is only partial separation from the original objects in adulthood. Adult love relations can be sustained only as long as their unconscious connection to the original, ambivalently loved, oedipal objects is maintained and as long as revenge fantasies can remain dissociated or repressed.

As the unconscious incestuous tie to the father continued into adulthood, adult love relationships were playful, seductive, but not nourishing for the patient or her mate, except at the beginning. Before analysis, some of the women were frigid or could reach clitoral orgasm only by stimulation. The vagina remained excluded, sometimes unconsciously "saved" for father. There were typical fantasies that prevented orgasm: the women suspected the men to be primarily interested in themselves; at the same time, they felt obliged to satisfy their mates sexually, but often at the expense of their own sexual needs. This was another way in which role reversal in childhood interfered with orgasm in the adult woman.

It was as if in adult love relations, oedipal themes had become actualized, thereby burdening the adult love relations with incestuous guilt. On an unconscious level, these women had difficulties in differentiating lovers from their fathers, and their own sexual role or that of a mate from the relationship between mother and father.

The adult love relations repeated the pattern of the oedipal conflict. For a period, the adult love relationship drew its strength from the narcissistic triumph of circumventing the incest taboo. Initially, infantile grandiosity and narcissistic strivings found satisfaction in the love relationship. During the early phases of the relationship, parental idealizations were displaced upon the lover. A web of fantasy was spun around him, with unconscious hopes for assuaging childhood injuries and conscious wishes to realize adult life goals.

Unconsciously the lover needed to become the seductive parent, required to commit incest, which gave the love tie an addictive quality (Blum, 1973) and made it "very special." Uniqueness not experienced with mother early in life was thus temporarily found in some of the relationships via the unconscious incestuous fantasy that held the relationship together. The living out of incestuous oedipal wishes gave the relationship its special "magic." During the incestuous and narcissistically gratifying phase the woman remained the child, actively seeking good mothering but able to accept it only from a member of the opposite sex with whom she identified (Bergmann, 1982).

An intensive search for a husband took place ostensibly only and concealed a wish to find "the good mother of symbiosis" in the union with the lover. These women's love relationships lacked the depth of postoedipal commitment. The lovers alternately played the roles of parent and child, at times giving the analyst the impression that they were "playing house."

When parents have been prematurely disappointing, narcissistic gratification cannot be obtained later in life without the assistance of another person. The women therefore needed to keep their lovers in the role of a narcissistically gratifying parent; at the same time, the initial success in the adult relationship revived the conflict about losing the incestuous ties to each parent and led to overt anxiety. Separation from the mother seemed impossible: it implied not only forfeiting the symbiotic tie to her forever but also being saddled with feelings of guilt about leaving the mother who needed the daughter as a permanent caregiver. It was easier to have an adult relationship and divide commitment and love between father and adult lover.

For a time, these women succeeded in staving off separation anxiety and incestuous guilt, but the anxiety about separating from the *real* parents and the fear of making a commitment to marriage and maternity brought the unconscious conflict to the fore. In fact, analysis revealed time and again that the adult woman unconsciously still preferred her father to her lover or husband. As the woman unconsciously already "had had" her oedipal child with the father, the wish for a baby was pushed into the background.

In the second phase the idealizations gave way to disappointments because of unrequited childhood fantasies. Symbiotic and incestuous longings which had nurtured the love tie were transferred from the parents to the lover or husband only temporarily: disappointment brought the relationship to an end.

MARRIAGE

The achievement of marriage and maternity hinges on coming to terms with losses. Some women do not feel impelled to marry and have children; for a variety of reasons, they settle for an older or younger permanent mate—perhaps a series of them. My patients, however, wanted marriage and maternity, both of which were felt needs. Having been "special" and idealized children, they wanted to build a family of their own to experience and represent the parents as an ideal couple that truly cared for a child. Such deeply felt conscious ideals helped the analytic process.

Nevertheless, marriage was unconsciously equated with losing a part of the self that in fantasy represented a part of a parent as well. One patient dreamed: "I am marching down the aisle to get married and my future husband waits for me. I become frozen and cannot walk. I wake up." Unconsciously, the frozen stiffness represented the father's phallus and the patient could not marry lest she lose the nourishing tie to the father by not remaining his phallic extension. That the patient herself personified the paternal phallus by becoming frozen emerged as a reconstruction after an adolescent recollection made this connection clear to both the patient and myself (Lewin, 1933). Anxiety over object loss also may have caused the patient to awaken.

Another patient viewed marriage and motherhood as a "prison or trap." Her commitment to her lovers was tenuous and marred by overwhelming anxieties, while at the same time the tie to her parents remained a strong and active force. She commented that marriage was "the worst fear of my life."

As a rule it took several years of intensive analytic work for these women to relinquish incestuous, ambivalent ties to the parents, to feel free to fall in love with a peer, and to get married. Typically, after being sure of marriage, these patients proceeded to plan for a child. This demonstrated that they had at least partially forgiven their mothers.

MATERNITY

The repetition compulsion prevented these women from being able to tolerate triadic relationships without fears of abandonment, which in turn interfered with the wish to have a baby. Blos (1974) stresses that adult mothering is possible only if the young woman attains a postambivalent relationship to her mother.

It became apparent in analysis that just as the real and prospective mothers were not differentiated, the patient recalling her childhood could not differentiate herself from a fantasied prospective child. In both versions, mother and child were merged; the lover became the "good mother" (of symbiosis), while the "bad mother" image was displaced onto the real mother, her substitutes, such as the lover's wife, or a prospective child. The patients were fearful that the baby would replace them once again by being considered first. Unconsciously the prospective child was identified with a sibling or parental oedipal rival.

The child also represented the paternal phallus, and childbirth became linked to a castration fantasy and to early narcissistic disillusionments. Feelings of revenge for not having been permitted to remain the child were sometimes displaced in fantasy onto the would-be future child; moreover, these feelings sometimes merged with jealousy toward a sibling, particularly if he was male.

One patient said, "I can't have a baby because then I would have to lose my mother. To keep my child out of her life would kill her. It is as if I had kept her alive by letting *her* be my baby. If I had a real baby, I would have to give up my mother. I have such guilt toward her that I have to keep her alive." And another woman: "When I think of getting married, I have the image of a little girl holding the hand of a big man. I idealize someone I don't love as an adult woman. I obviously don't want to have a baby. It seems as though I had always been waiting for Daddy."

When contemplating having a child, many of these women demonstrated an incapacity to rely on the baby's father and to trust him. One patient said, "I have a fantasy of being alone; a cold wind is blowing, I am isolated and poor. I have no job and I am alone with a baby. If I get married and have a child, I shall be a wife and mother without a career and without money." This was a frequently recurring image. Another patient said, "I imagine having a baby and there's just nobody out there who cares. I have no parents and no husband—I am trapped! How am I going to rear this child alone and ever get back to my profession? Who is going to pay the bills? I feel all alone. It is a nightmare." Abandonment appeared to be a punishment for having abandoned the "child-mother."

Some of these women passed the child-bearing age without having achieved maternity. They then went through a period of intense mourning for not having been able to produce a child. The lost child represented the patient herself as well as the loss of a symbiotic union with her own mother.

SUMMARY

Role reversal is a phenomenon which appears not only in the interactions discussed here but in other types of relationships. Nor is it to be found only in this particular group of patients. When the wish for a child is too conflict-laden by fixation on the fantasy of a libidinally nourishing father and by the hope of finding the *real* mother, the establishment of an independent adult self is less likely.

The conflicts I focused on have previously been assigned to pregenital and incestuous oedipal fixations. Role reversal, if present, adds the dimension of narcissistic pathology, self constancy, and the development of object relations from childhood to adulthood.

The capacity to continue a profession, be a lover to a mate and mother to children initially necessitates—as does analytic work itself—the giving up of a considerable number of infantile gratifications. This process is encumbered by the weight of parental models who strove for infantile and narcissistic gratification themselves, not leaving enough room for the child to express and fulfill phase-specific infantile needs. Thus new identifications have to be created in adulthood.

In my patients, a central psychic constellation with role reversal as its most prominent feature remained active throughout the life cycle. They had intense symbiotic longings which propelled them toward a lifelong search to find the symbiotic mother in lover, husband, and baby. Only by achieving this could they forgive their own mothers for sporadically abandoning them emotionally.

The fantasy "once there was a baby no one would take care of" had its root in memories of childhood role reversal and in unconscious incestuous ties which did not permit separation from mother without superego punishment. The central experience of emotional abandonment led to impermanence of self and object constancy.

Reversing roles, the daughter became her mother's mother and identified with her father. A preference for dyadic over triadic relationships characterized unconscious conflicts. Role reversal lent conviction to the sense of having *had* a baby with father and being his "other woman," thereby intensifying an incestuous fixation.

The alternating currents of the oedipal conflict persisted in these women's adult love relationships in which they lived out an incestuous fantasy, sometimes addictive in character, but also consummated with heightened separation anxiety, whether the lover represented the patients' mother, father, or the self. Due to insufficient repression and superego structuring, these relationships could not become permanent.

These women could be described as "prisoners of childhood." Many of the clinical features they presented could be subsumed under "fate neurosis" (Deutsch, 1930). Psychoanalytic treatment enabled them to overcome some of the effects of role reversal. The giving up of erotized relationships via the analysis of the erotized transference (Freud, 1915a; Blum, 1973) was the most decisive step that led these women from being mistresses to independent womanhood.

BIBLIOGRAPHY

ABELIN, E. L. (1980). Triangulation. In *Rapprochement*, ed. R. Lax, S. Bach, & E. J. Burland. New York: Aronson, pp. 151–166.

BACH, S. (1980). Self-love and object-love. In *Rapprochement*, ed. R. Lax, S. Bach, & E. J. Burland. New York: Aronson, pp. 171–196.

BAK, R. C. (1971). Object-relationships in schizophrenia and perversion. *Int. J. Psychoanal.*, 52:235–242.

BERGMANN, M. V. (1980). On the genesis of narcissistic and phobic character formation in an adult patient. *Int. J. Psychoanal.*, 61:535–546.

——— (1982). The female oedipus complex. In *Early Female Development*, ed. D. Mendell. Jamaica, N.Y.: Spectrum, pp. 175–201.*

BLOS, P. (1974). The genealogy of the ego ideal. *Psychoanal. Study Child*, 29:43–86.

BLUM, H. P. (1973). The concept of erotized transference. *J. Amer. Psychoanal. Assn.*, 21:61–76.

——— (1977). The prototype of preoedipal reconstruction. *J. Amer. Psychoanal. Assn.*, 25:757–783.

BRODEY, W. M. (1965). On the dynamics of narcissism. *Psychoanal. Study Child*, 20:165–193.

BRUNSWICK, R. M. (1940). The preoedipal phase of the libido development. In *The Psychoanalytic Reader*, ed. R. Fliess. New York: Int. Univ. Press, 1948, pp. 261–284.

BURLINGHAM, D. T. (1935). Empathy between infant and mother. In *Psychoanalytic Studies of the Sighted and the Blind*. New York: Int. Univ. Press, 1972, pp. 52–70.

*I wish to thank Dr. Dale Mendell and Spectrum Publications for the permission to draw on some of my ideas first discussed in my article in this book.

DEUTSCH, H. (1930). Hysterical fate neurosis. In *Neuroses and Character Types*. New York: Int. Univ. Press, 1965, pp. 14–28.

EDGCUMBE, R. & BURGNER, M. (1975). The phallic-narcissistic phase. *Psychoanal. Study Child*, 30:161–179.

—— LUNDBERG, S., MARKOWITZ, R., & SALO, F. (1976). Some comments on the concept of the negative oedipal phase in girls. *Psychoanal. Study Child*, 31:35–59.

ESCOLL, P. (1983). The changing vistas of transference. *J. Amer. Psychoanal. Assn.*, 31:699–711.

FLEMING, J. (1975). Some observations on object constancy in the psychoanalysis of adults. *J. Amer. Psychoanal. Assn.*, 23:743–759.

FREUD, A. (1936). The ego and the mechanisms of defense. *W.*, 2.

—— (1963). The concept of developmental lines. *Psychoanal. Study Child*, 18:245–265.

—— (1965). Normality and pathology in childhood. *W.*, 6.

FREUD, S. (1915a). Observations on transference-love. *S.E.*, 12:157–171.

—— (1915b). Instincts and their vicissitudes. *S.E.*, 14:109–140.

—— (1917). On transformations of instinct as exemplified in anal erotism. *S.E.*, 17:125–133.

—— (1919). 'A child is being beaten.' *S.E.*, 17:175–204.

—— (1923). The ego and the id. *S.E.*, 19:3–66.

—— (1924). The dissolution of the oedipus complex. *S.E.*, 19:173–179.

—— (1931). Female sexuality. *S.E.*, 21:223–243.

GEDO, J. (1981). The oedipus complex in contemporary life. In *Advances in Clinical Psychoanalysis*. New York: Int. Univ. Press, pp. 349–366.

JACOBSON, E. (1959). The exceptions. *Psychoanal. Study Child*, 14:135–154.

—— (1964). *The Self and the Object World*. New York: Int. Univ. Press.

KERNBERG, O. F. (1975). Normal and pathological narcissism. In *Borderline Conditions and Pathological Narcissism*. New York: Aronson, pp. 37–45.

KESTENBERG, J. S. (1968). Outside and inside, male and female. *J. Amer. Psychoanal. Assn.*, 16:457–520.

—— (1971). From organ-object imagery to self and object representations. In *Separation-Individuation*, ed. J. B. McDevitt & C. G. Settlage. New York: Int. Univ. Press, pp. 75–99.

LEWIN, B. D. (1933). The body as phallus. *Psychoanal. Q.*, 1:22–47.

LOEWALD, H. W. (1973). On internalization. *Int. J. Psychoanal.*, 54:9–17.

—— (1979). The waning of the oedipus complex. *J. Amer. Psychoanal. Assn.*, 27:751–775.

MAHLER, M. S. (1966). Notes on the development of basic moods. In *Psychoanalysis—A General Psychology*, ed. R. M. Loewenstein, L. M. Newman, M. Schur, & A. J. Solnit. New York: Int. Univ. Press, pp. 152–168.

—— (1971). A study of the separation-individuation process. *Psychoanal. Study Child*, 26:403–424.

—— (1975). On the current status of the infantile neurosis. *J. Amer. Psychoanal. Assn.*, 23:323–333.

––––– & GOSLINER, B. J. (1955). On symbiotic child psychosis. *Psychoanal. Study Child*, 10:195–212.

NUNBERG, H. (1926). The will to recovery. In *Practice and Theory of Psychoanalysis*. New York: Int. Univ. Press, 1955, pp. 75–88.

PANEL (1958). Problems of identity. D. Rubinfine, reporter. *J. Amer. Psychoanal. Assn.*, 6:136–139.

––––– (1976). The psychology of women. E. Galenson, reporter. *J. Amer. Psychoanal. Assn.*, 24:105–108.

SILVERMAN, M. A., REES, K., & NEUBAUER, P. B. (1975). On a central psychic constellation. *Psychoanal. Study Child*, 30:127–157.

SOLNIT, A. J. (1982). Early psychic development as reflected in the psychoanalytic process. *Int. J. Psychoanal.*, 63:23–37.

SPITZ, R. A. (1965). *The First Year of Life*. New York: Int. Univ. Press.

Some Contributions of Adult Analysis to Child Analysis

CHARLES BRENNER, M.D.

THE CONTRIBUTIONS OF CHILD ANALYSIS TO ADULT ANALYSIS ARE familiar from long hearing and frequent repetition. There is little or nothing in the psychoanalytic literature, however, about what it is that adult analysis has contributed and has to contribute to child analysis. This paper, then, is like a voyage into unknown territory, a voyage of discovery. As such it can at best reveal the principal features and the broad outline of the terrain. To explore that terrain in more detail and to map it accurately are tasks which must await later visits. A first voyage can do no more than arouse interest and, hopefully, stimulate a desire to return at some time for a second and closer look.

One contribution of adult analysis to child analysis would seem at first glance to be merely a historical one. Adult analysis preceded child analysis and hence, in the historical sense, made it possible. There would have been no child analysis if analysis of adults had not shown the way, though once child analysis began, it developed on its own and is now a flourishing enterprise in its own right.

Still, one may wonder whether the facts of psychosexual development and functioning in childhood, which are so obvious to-

Lecturer in psychiatry, Yale University Medical School, clinical professor of psychiatry, State University of New York, and training and supervising analyst, New York Psychoanalytic Institute.

This paper was presented on November 3, 1984 at a symposium on the relation of child and adult analysis held by the Michigan Psychoanalytic Institute.

day and so easily accepted, could have been discerned by working with children alone. To attribute sexual longing and sexual
gratification to the mental lives of children without reference to
the data from analysis of adults would certainly have taken an
extraordinary degree of moral courage and independence of
thought. Could the early workers in the field of child analysis
have done it without being aware of what analysis of adults had
revealed of the importance of orality and of anality in adult
sexual life? Would it have been possible, had those early child
analysts been ignorant of the roles which are played by childhood memories and childhood fantasies in adult sexuality, roles
which could be demonstrated only by the psychoanalysis of adult
patients?

Little Hans, the first child analytic "patient," was of great importance to Freud as a confirmation of his ideas concerning the
sexual lives of adults and children. Here was an otherwise normal little boy who had incestuous and parricidal wishes and a
castration complex. The contribution of that analytic case to
work with adults was great, as far as confirmation of the validity
of reconstruction goes. At the same time one must be aware that
it was Freud's experience with adult patients that made possible
the therapy of the child. Freud himself made this quite clear in
his case report. Indeed, he concluded his discussion by saying
that the treatment of little Hans had demonstrated nothing to
him that he hadn't known already and at a few points in the
course of his presentation he made specific statements to that
effect. For example, he explained that he knew "by means of my
experiences with the analyses of grown-up people" what had
prompted Hans to say of his penis that "it's fixed in, of course"
(p. 35). Again, he "knew" (p. 48) the meaning of the game Hans
wanted to play with the loaded carts and he knew also what the
furniture vans symbolized to Hans. He also knew in advance
that, to Hans, stool = baby. In the last instance, in fact, he decided to say nothing about the equation of stool and baby to Hans's
father in order to allow the evidence for it to emerge without any
suggestion on the father's part. Thus one can see that, from the
very beginning, analytic work with children and analytic work
with adults have offered mutual support. Data from each con-
firms and/or disconfirms the findings of the other.

In 1975, at a meeting of the International Psycho-Analytical Association in London, Ann-Marie Sandler made the point that a knowledge of how a child—in her example, a 6-year-old—thinks is very useful when one is analyzing adults (Thiel and Treurniet, 1976). One can summarize her argument by saying that the child lives on in the adult with the result that what Sandler was analyzing was, in a very real sense, a 6-year-old in a grownup's mind and body. If you don't know how that 6-year-old thinks, you'll find it hard to understand what he's saying. The more you know about how such a child thinks, the better able you are to understand him when he tries to tell you something.

The correctness of this view seems indisputable. What I wish to add to it is that it works the other way around as well. The more experience one has in analyzing adults, the more one learns about how children think and about what is important to them—at any rate, what is of enduring importance to them in their mental lives.

One must not forget that it was data from the psychoanalysis of adults which have contributed most of what we know about the essential elements of psychic life and especially about psychic conflict. I have indicated already in my reference to the treatment of little Hans that the first child analysts learned about childhood sexuality from the data of adult analytic work. I suspect that there is also much to be learned from adult analysis about what features of childhood psychic life in general are of greatest importance or, at least, which ones have the greatest potential for pathogenesis.

Granting, then, that the data from child analysis and the data from adult analysis confirm and/or disconfirm the findings of the other and that each contributes to the other in these important ways, what can be said more specifically about the matter?

Let me begin by comparing some of the features of the situation in child analysis with the situation in adult analysis. As Anna Freud (1979) noted in her contribution to insight in psychoanalysis, children do not typically complain of and seek help for psychogenic difficulties. Typically a child is sent for treatment, he does not seek analysis. No doubt, as Anna Freud pointed out, this is related to the fact that children are less self-aware and self-observant than older persons are. In the field of mental illness as in that of physical illness, children are told, "You're sick. I'm going to take you to someone who will make you feel better." What an adult patient says on the basis of self-awareness, the parent of a child patient says to the child. Children are not as self-aware and self-observant as adults are, a fact which makes for differences in the analytic situation when one is working with a child, especially with a young child, from that of working with an adult.

Another difference between the analytic situation with a child patient and the situation with an adult patient is that children cannot be expected to obey the fundamental rule of analysis. You cannot say to a child, "Tell me everything that comes to mind, without exception," and expect a young child even to understand what you're telling him or her, let alone to comply.

Still another, well-known difference, which is closely related to the one just mentioned, is that children are up and about the room. You can't expect a child to lie on a couch and talk. Children interact with an analyst in all sorts of ways that are very different from what goes on between an adult patient and an analyst. The younger a child analysand, the more plentiful and the more important are behavioral data as analytic material and the less complete are verbal productions as compared with an adult analysand.

In sum, then, here are three obvious differences between the adult and the child analytic situation. Children can't use the couch; they can't follow the fundamental rule; and they haven't enough self-awareness to realize they're sick and that they need treatment. What consequences do these differences have? Do they put child analysis at a disadvantage when compared with adult analysis and in the position of having to depend upon it and learn from it?

I have heard the opinion expressed, though I have never seen it in print, that because a child cannot use the couch and cannot follow the fundamental rule, child analysis isn't really analysis. It is, in this view, a form of psychoanalytically oriented psychotherapy, something very interesting and worthwhile, but not really analysis. Anna Freud herself, in 1978, seemed to maintain that this is so and that it is, at least in part, an inevitable consequence of the fact that young children in particular are so little self-aware. They don't realize they're sick, they're satisfied with their symptoms, with their pathological compromise formations, so they have no desire or motive for revealing themselves to another person in words which will only give rise to unpleasure.

If one were to follow such ideas to their logical conclusion, one would have to say something like the following. By reason of their very immaturity children cannot reveal as fully and as clearly as adults can the nature of their pathogenic conflicts. One has to do more guessing with a child patient than with an adult one and, necessarily, the guessing one does with a child in analysis must rest, in part, on the firmer knowledge one has of these matters from analysis of adult patients. Child analysis would thus be, in this respect, an example of how psychoanalytically informed psychotherapy needs the findings of psychoanalysis to inform it. If it is really so that child analysis is not wholly comparable to adult analysis for the reasons mentioned, then child analysis must turn to the findings of adult analysis for some, at least, of its knowledge of the nature of pathogenic conflicts.

It seems to me, however, that this assessment of the relationship between child analysis and adult analysis is wrong on two counts. One has to do with the fundamental rule itself; the other, with a correct understanding of the psychoanalytic process and its therapeutic goal.

The fundamental rule was instituted as a substitute for hypnosis. Freud's original instruction to his patients was to remember what was happening when their symptom(s) first appeared. Their inability to do so was overcome at first by hypnotizing them, as Breuer had done. When he found hypnosis unsatisfactory for various reasons, Freud used suggestion. He told his patients to shut their eyes and assured them that when he pressed on their foreheads, a thought would occur to them which would either be the desired memory or would lead to it. From that, by what was truly a stroke of genius, he hit on the idea that if his patients would say every thought that came into their minds, without exception, whether they wanted to say it or not, the desired memories would be revealed. Thus, instead of overcoming his patients' resistance to remembering by means of hypnosis or suggestion, Freud tried to circumvent their resistance by having them agree to say whatever came to mind, whether they wanted to or not, whether it seemed apropos or not, whether it seemed sensible or foolish. To say everything without exception became the fundamental rule of psychoanalysis.

In time it became apparent that the rule had its limitations. For one thing, no patient abided by it strictly and without exception. Every patient withheld some thoughts sometimes. Moreover, there were patients, obsessional ones, whose very symptoms seemed to interfere. What to do with a patient who had two thoughts simultaneously and who couldn't decide which one to say first? Or with a patient who seemed to manufacture associations either to please or to frustrate the analyst? Such exceptions to the applicability of the fundamental rule led, in fact, to the paradoxical maxim that when a patient could really "free associate," it was a sign that analysis was finished, that the patient had been successfully analyzed.

In consequence of analysts' growing knowledge of the limitations of the applicability of the fundamental rule as it was first understood, the rule has come to be modified somewhat in practice. An adult patient today is less apt to be told to promise to report every thought without exception and is more likely to be advised to speak his or her thoughts as freely and with as little editing as possible and to be told that the more freely he or she can speak, the better. At any rate, this has been my own custom for many years with whichever patients do not already know enough about analysis to make such a recommendation superfluous. My experience has been that there is always time and occasion as analysis progresses to show a patient the advantages of not withholding any thoughts and of demonstrating the reasons why they sometimes do withhold. Moreover, every analyst uses as analytic material whatever behavior a patient manifests as well as what the patient says. A patient's expression, gait, tone of voice, position, movements on the couch, tears, and laughter are, as a matter of course, part of the analytic material. Thus the differences with respect to the fundamental rule between adult and child analysis are neither as extreme nor as absolute as they are often represented as being. Whether child or adult, a patient is encouraged to speak as freely as possible and, whether child or adult, a patient's behavior is no less analytic material than a patient's words. The contribution of adult analysis to child analysis is not a consequence of these differences between the two.

Such matters are, after all, but means to an end. The end is to learn from the analytic material what a patient's pathogenic conflicts are, to learn whence in childhood they came, and to interpret them to the patient at the proper time in an appropriate way. This is something which experience has shown can be satisfactorily accomplished by a competent analyst with a patient who is a child just as well as it can be with a patient who is an adult. The difficulties which arise to impede one's analytic understanding of a patient are due to other and more fundamentally important factors than the use of the couch or an ability to understand the fundamental rule and a conscious decision to adhere to it. Analyzability is fundamentally dependent on such factors as constitutional endowment, severity of conflict, and favorable or unfavorable external, environmental circumstances. A patient need not be adult or very sophisticated to be analyzable. I don't think, therefore, that the fact that adult patients are more self-aware than child patients, that they use the couch, and that they can understand the fundamental rule and consciously try to follow it make adult analysis so different from child analysis as to give it any great advantage over the latter. By and large a child's behavior tells as much and conceals as much about its inner conflicts as an adult's words do about its conflicts.

There is another difference between the situation in child analysis and the situation in adult analysis which has been much discussed and which might also be thought to give adult analysts a more profound and/or a more reliable knowledge of the nature of psychic conflict. This has to do with transference. The accepted view is that a true transference neurosis seldom, if ever, appears in the course of a child's analysis, while it is a *sine qua non* of adult analysis. Since the analysis of the transference neurosis is the most important source of knowledge concerning the nature and origin of pathogenic conflict, the argument goes, it follows that it is from analyzing an adult successfully that one learns most about such conflicts. Thus adult analysis is allegedly the major source of our knowledge of psychopathology; it is the indispensable basis of metapsychology.

Here, again, I disagree. An intense transference reaction which can be successfully analyzed is, indeed, an indispensable source of analytic data in analyzing an adult. But think, for a moment, why this is so. It is so because it recreates the past. When an adult analytic patient develops such a transference reaction, the childhood origins of the patient's pathological compromise formations, i.e., of the patient's symptoms and pathological character traits, appear in a form which the analyst can better understand and which can be successfully interpreted to the patient. In short, the childhood pathogenic conflict appears in the patient's life in the transference in an analyzable form. What happened in a patient's mind many years or decades ago shows itself now in the transference as something to be analyzed in the present. It is because the past is so clearly recreated in the present in the transference reaction of an adult patient that it is such an indispensable source of knowledge about a patient's psychopathology and so essential to analyze. In the case of a child, however, the psychic past is neither so distant nor so little known, so inaccessible to scrutiny. The younger the child, the more recent are the origins of his pathogenic conflicts. Transference reactions are always significant, to be sure, and always valuable in child analysis as well as in adult analysis, but to a significant degree what must be recalled via transference in adult analysis is active in the here and now of psychic life in child analysis. Transferences are less from past to present and more from one current figure to another. They function more as displacements, less as revivals of the past, and for this reason, I believe, adult analysis has no more advantage over child analysis with respect to transference than it has with respect to those differentiating features mentioned earlier: adherence to the fundamental rule, use of the couch, etc. Those who say that the differences between transference reactions in child analysis and in adult analysis make the latter superior to the former as a source of information about pathogenic conflicts have yet to prove their assertion to be correct.

When one analyzes an adult patient, one deals first and foremost with the child that patient once was. The pathological compromise formations of later life which we identify as neurotic symptoms and as neurotic character traits in adults are all consequences of conflicts of childhood origin. These conflicts we understand result from childhood drive derivatives, i.e., from childhood wishes of instinctual origin, wishes which arouse in the child unpleasure in the form of anxiety and depressive affect. To minimize this unpleasure, defenses appear. They are the third component of psychic conflict. The fourth are the various manifestations of superego functioning. It is to the understanding of these conflicts and to their explication or interpretation that an analyst's efforts are directed. They are, in fact, a pathological residue of childhood which has lasted into adult life all but unchanged by the passage of time. The grown man or woman still longs for the childhood libidinal and aggressive wishes to be gratified; he still reacts to them with intense unpleasure, i.e., with anxiety and depressive affect whose ideational content is the familiar calamities of childhood: object loss, loss of love, and castration; he still seeks to minimize the unpleasure associated with his childhood wishes by defenses whose origins are no less childish than his wishes themselves; and he reacts as he did in childhood with various manifestations of superego functioning: with guilt, atonement, shame, self-abasement, self-injury, or, even, self-destruction. At every step in our analytic work, whether in dealing with drive derivatives, with defense, with anxiety and depressive affect, or with superego manifestations, we find ourselves confronted with a child. It is an elderly child, as children go, a child who is sometimes as old as we ourselves are, but it is nonetheless a child. Paradoxical as it may sound to say so, it is still true that every adult analysis is a child analysis.

I believe that the analysis of those 20-, 30-, or 40-year-old children whom we call adults has made a contribution to the analysis of younger children by virtue of their very age and experience. Those older children show us what the psychic residue of childhood is. They show us its lasting elements, its ineluctable essence. They give living proof of the indestructibility of childhood drive derivatives and of the conflicts associated with those drive derivatives. It is from adult analyses that child analysts have learned to distinguish clearly between an analytic attitude toward one's patients and a merely psychotherapeutic one (Anthony, 1982). The difference between the two is doubtless more often a subtle than a gross one, yet for all its subtlety it can have substantial consequences.

It is work with adult patients which convinces an analyst that the passage of time and the experience of growing up do not themselves necessarily result in a permanent amelioration in the consequences of psychic conflict. An adult patient may be quite satisfactorily mature in many ways and still suffer serious difficulties because of pathological compromise formations. The retrospective view which the analysis of such an old child affords is instructive to the analyst of young children. It shows that a young child may seem by all outward signs to have recovered from the ill effects of early psychic conflict and to have developed normally without in fact having done so. It reveals how important it is to analyze such conflicts when they give rise to pathological compromise formations if one is to have the best chance of avoiding trouble later on. Child analysts are skilled at the task of distinguishing between merely symptomatic improvement in a child and improvement which is a result of truly analytic work with the child. I suggest that this is a skill which at least originally was owing to experience with adult patients. One of the contributions which adult analysis has made to child analysis is, I believe, just this. By exploring the past of the child in the adult it has afforded to the child analyst a view of the future of the neurotically ill child who is in analysis now.

My final point is this. A parental attitude toward a child patient seems to be inescapable. It is built into the situation. One cannot, as an adult, honestly pretend to be a child's equal, to be on the same level as the child. One simply is not. Moreover, one stands *in loco parentis* by virtue of participating in a therapeutic situation with the child. What is essential, however, in doing child analysis is to carry that attitude no farther than is absolutely necessary. Being *in loco parentis* as a therapist is not the same as being like a parent in attitude and/or behavior. There are those who have thought otherwise, to be sure. I have heard an analyst—one who worked with adults, not with children—say, "What does being a good analyst mean? It means being a good parent, right?" My answer to this question, intended to be merely a rhetorical one, would be, "Wrong!" But if one's conscious aim is to be a good parent to adult patients, then all the more would one be moved to act the parent with a patient who is in physical fact still a child.

Child analysts today are well aware that it is not in the best interests of a child in analysis for the analyst to behave in parental fashion. To behave as an adult, yes, but not as a parent. Child analysts are well aware that there is no substitute for analysis in an analytic situation. All would agree that it is not a good idea for a parent to try to analyze his or her own children, however much the parent may know of analysis. No more should an analyst, however good a parent he or she is, assume the role of parent with a child in analysis. As much as possible an analyst must behave as an analyst. Exhortations to be human with one's patients are, or should be, unnecessary. It goes without saying that an analyst is a therapist, who is there to help another human being if help is possible. But an analyst helps best by being an analyst. If something else were therapeutically more effective than being an analyst, we should be doing that something else and not analyzing.

My reason for saying at length what is, or should be, so well known to all analysts is that it wasn't always so. One of the contributions of adult analysis to child analysis has been, I believe, to emphasize the importance of restricting the analyst's role as much as possible to analyzing. Time was when child analytic technique was much less analytic than it is today. It much more resembled what we would now think of as psychoanalytically informed psychotherapy. The same, be it noted, was true at that time of adult analytic technique as well.

It was not until relatively recently that it became the rule rather than the exception for analysts to analyze defenses and resistances rather than to try to overcome them in some other way. In this country the watershed was about 1950. Before that time most analysts really worked differently. As late as 1917 Freud himself wrote that a patient's resistances are finally to be overcome only with the help of the patient's positive transference to the analyst. This, he thought, was the legitimate role of suggestion in the psychoanalytic situation, a role which, he implied, is nevertheless a crucial one. Even two decades later those who were in the very forefront of psychoanalysis thought of character analysis as something rather different from symptom analysis. They were much influenced by W. Reich's (1928) notion that character traits are a kind of defensive armor plate which must be smashed through before one can analyze what is behind it.

The changes which resulted in psychoanalytic technique as we know it today were signaled by the publication of "Inhibitions, Symptoms and Anxiety" (1926) and were subsequently formulated by Fenichel (1941) and, most clearly, by Anna Freud (1936). In the years which followed it gradually became common knowledge that one analyzes every component of a psychic conflict which gives rise to a pathological compromise formation. One does not interpret only an instinctual wish, one interprets as well the anxiety and the depressive affect associated with it, the defenses, and the superego manifestations. Not just one, but all of them together give rise to whatever pathological compromise formations a patient may suffer from. Not just one, but all are to be dealt with analytically.

As this new understanding of conflict and pathological compromise formation became common knowledge, so did the changes in technique which were based upon it become common practice. What had been largely id analysis became ego and superego analysis as well.

There are many other aspects to this change in technique, but the one to which I especially wish to draw attention here is a certain change in analytic attitude. It used to be that an analyst had the attitude that a patient is divisible if not, like Gaul, into three parts, then at least into two. There was thought to be a normal, realistic, mature, adult part—the intact ego—and an infantile, neurotic, irrational part. In consequence, an analyst felt free to talk "nonanalytically" to a patient at times during analysis. Advice, usually wise advice, was often forthcoming from analyst to patient, as were observations on sundry subjects ranging from child rearing to politics and world affairs, art, literature, and life in general. Vestiges of this attitude certainly persist, but they are mere vestiges. Analysts today do not think of themselves as wise and knowing counselors, and they do not act as such to anything like the degree they used to. Analysts think of themselves as analysts, not as sages, and by and large they behave accordingly with their patients.

This change in the analytic situation is unquestionably a contribution which adult analysis has made to child analysis. The better understanding of conflict and compromise formation which had its beginning in 1926 with the publication of "Inhibitions, Symptoms and Anxiety" led to a significant change in the analytic situation of adult analysis, a change which was away from a previous tendency to combine a counseling attitude toward the patient with an analytic one. This in turn led analysts who analyzed children to change their attitude toward their patients in the same direction. Child analysts, too, have become less counselors, less preceptors, less substitute parents in their analytic work, and more just analysts than they used to be—not an inconsiderable contribution for adult analysis to have made to child analysis.

BIBLIOGRAPHY

ANTHONY, E. J. (1982). The comparable experience of a child and adult analyst. *Psychoanal. Study Child*, 37:339–366.

FENICHEL, O. (1941). *Problems of Psychoanalytic Technique*. Albany, N.Y.: Psychoanalytic Quarterly.

FREUD, A. (1936). *The Ego and the Mechanisms of Defense*. New York: Int. Univ. Press, 1946.

———— (1979). The role of insight in psychoanalysis and psychotherapy—introduction. In *Psychoanalytic Explorations of Technique,* ed. H. P. Blum. New York: Int. Univ. Press, 1980, pp. 3–7.

FREUD, S. (1909). Analysis of a phobia in a five-year-old boy. *S.E.*, 10:5–152.

———— (1917). Introductory lectures on psycho-analysis. *S.E.*, 16 & 17.

———— (1926). Inhibitions, symptoms and anxiety. *S.E.*, 20:75–174.

REICH, W. (1928). On character analysis. In *The Psychoanalytic Reader*, ed. R. Fliess. New York: Int. Univ. Press, 1948, pp. 129–147.

THIEL, J. H. & TREURNIET, N. (1976). Panel on 'The implications of recent advances in the knowledge of child development for the treatment of adults.' *Int. J. Psychoanal.*, 57:429–439.

On the Analytic Therapy of Homosexual Men

RICHARD A. ISAY, M.D.

MOST PSYCHOANALYSTS ASSUME THAT HOMOSEXUALITY REFLECTS an unfavorable unconscious solution to developmental conflicts, and that, consequently, the entire personality of the homosexual shows various disturbances. The number and kind of pathological deficits attributed to homosexuals are very large, and I have selected only a few for illustrative purposes. Bergler (1956) wrote of six traits: masochistic provocation and injustice collecting, defensive malice, flippancy, hypernarcissism, refusal to acknowledge accepted standards in nonsexual matters, and general unreliability. "The most interesting feature of this sextet of traits," he writes, "is its universality. Regardless of the level of intelligence, culture, background, or education, all homosexuals possess it" (p. 49). Homosexuals have been said to suffer from a large variety of ego defects (Panel, 1954, p. 344), including "primitive features of the ego" similar to those found in schizophrenia (Panel, 1960, p. 556) and sociopathy.[1] Glover (1932, p.

Clinical Associate Professor of Psychiatry, Cornell Medical College. Faculty, Columbia University Center for Psychoanalytic Training and Research.

A version of this paper was presented at the panel, "Toward a Further Understanding of Homosexual Men," American Psychoanalytic Association, December 18, 1983.

1. In the first Diagnostic and Statistical Manual of the American Psychiatric Association, DSM-I, homosexuality was listed in the category, "sociopathic personality disturbance." It was listed under "personality disorders and certain other nonpsychotic mental disorders" in DSM-II. The decision of

230) suggested that homosexuality and other perversions "help to patch over flaws in the development of reality-sense." Socarides (1968) wrote that approximately half of the patients who engage in homosexual practices have a "concomitant schizophrenia, paranoia, are latent or pseudoneurotic schizophrenics or are in the throes of a manic-depressive reaction. The other half, when neurotic, may be of the obsessional or, occasionally, of the phobic type" (p. 90). Most of the patients he labeled as schizophrenic would probably be classified in his later formulation (1978) as belonging to the class of Preoedipal Type #2, "Suffering from a transitional condition lying somewhere between the neuroses and psychoses" (p. 58).

Not all analysts subscribe to generalizations about the pathology of either homosexuals as a group or our homosexual patients. For example, Weiss remarked that many homosexuals he had known as patients and friends "did not reveal unrealistic, immature traits or neurotic symptoms, whereas many heterosexuals do reveal such traits" (Panel, 1960, p. 560). Rangell is quoted as stating: "one may end up as a borderline homosexual, or a well-integrated homosexual, or a borderline or narcissistic heterosexual or a well-functioning heterosexual" (Panel, 1977, p. 197). In a review, Person (1983) said, "It is particularly useful to be finished with some of the more pernicious stereotypes about homosexuality, and with the idea that homosexuality . . . must reflect a primitive level of ego integration" (p. 314). And, of course, Freud in his well-known "Letter to an American Mother," wrote on April 9, 1935: "Homosexuality is assuredly no advantage, but it is nothing to be ashamed of, no vice, no degradation, it cannot be classified as an illness; we consider it to be a variation of sexual function produced by a certain arrest of sexual development."

Because many psychoanalysts regard homosexuality as a pathological and a psychologically uneconomical solution to early conflict, we tend to believe that, whenever possible, it is in the best interest of the patient to change his sexual orientation. Presumably a homosexual man will then be able to live a hap-

the Board of Trustees of the American Psychiatric Association in 1973 and a subsequent vote of the membership removed homosexuality per se from DSM-III as a mental disorder.

pier life not only because he will be in less conflict with society, but because warring intrapsychic structures will be brought into greater harmony. He will be less inclined to act out "unacceptable impulses" as they become increasingly tolerated by a strengthened ego and successfully sublimated.

Freud was not sanguine about the possibility of changing a homosexual to a heterosexual or about its helpfulness. In the "Letter" quoted above, he continued:

> By asking me if I can help, you mean, I suppose, if I can abolish homosexuality and make normal heterosexuality take its place. The answer is, in a general way, we cannot promise to achieve it. In a certain number of cases we succeed in developing the blighted germs of heterosexual tendencies which are present in every homosexual, in the majority of cases it is no more possible. . . . What analysis can do for your son runs in a different line. If he is unhappy, torn by conflicts, inhibited in his social life, analysis may bring him harmony, peace of mind, full efficiency, whether he remains a homosexual or gets changed.

Why have analysts generally maintained the view of homosexuality as pathology, not only in contrast to what Freud wrote, but in the face of the evidence accumulated by nonanalytic studies? I shall briefly review these other approaches in order to give an idea of the nature of evidence and opinion that analysts have disregarded. The statistics cited by Kinsey et al. (1948) would appear to support a nonpathological view of homosexuality by force of the large numbers of homosexuals in the population at large: 4% of the adult white male population are exclusively homosexual throughout their lives after adolescence, and about 8% have been exclusively homosexual for at least 3 years between 16 and 55. In the postpubertal male population 37% have had at least one overt homosexual experience to the point of orgasm between the beginning of adolescence and old age, and this rises to 50% if one includes only men who do not marry before age 35 (p. 650f.).[2]

2. Although there are methodological and sampling problems in this study, a number of European surveys report a comparably high incidence of homosexuality and homosexual experiences. Marmor writes, "The psychiatrically intriguing question is how so substantial a number of men and wom-

Ford and Beach (1951) in their cross-cultural investigations
and studies of subhuman primates support the concept that homosexuality is not a disease. Their data show that

> . . . a biological tendency for inversion of sexual behavior is in-
> herent in most if not all mammals including the human spe-
> cies. . . . Some homosexual behavior occurs in a great many
> human societies. It tends to be more common in adolescence
> than in adulthood and appears to be practiced more frequently
> by men than women. This is also true of the other animal spe-
> cies—and particularly so in the infra-human primates. . . .
> Even in societies which severely restrict homosexual tenden-
> cies—some individuals do exhibit homosexual behavior. . . .
> Within the societies which, unlike our own, provide socially ac-
> ceptable homosexual roles, a number of individuals, predomi-
> nantly men, choose to exhibit some measure of homosexual
> behavior [p. 143].

Another source of data comes from psychology. The best
known study is Evelyn Hooker's (1957), which was designed to
determine the usefulness of projective psychological tests in di-
agnosing overt homosexual behavior and to assess whether or
not there are distinguishable personality characteristics in exclusively homosexual men. Summarizing the results, she wrote,
"the three judges agreed on two-thirds of the group as being
average to superior in adjustment. According to the judges,
some [homosexuals] may not be characterized by any demonstrable pathology" (see Marmor, 1965, p. 89). A number of
other investigators, using both projective and objective standardized tests, have also been unable to differentiate homosexual from heterosexual subjects and suggest that there is no
greater pathology among homosexuals than heterosexuals (see
the review by Riess, 1980).

The well-publicized Wolfenden Report (1957), which supported the decriminalization in England of homosexual acts between consenting adults in private, also was strongly critical of
the view that homosexuality was a disease. This report emphasized that no theories explaining the "perversion" were specific

---

en become preferentially motivated towards such behavior in spite of the
powerful cultural taboos against it" (see Freedman et al., 1975, p. 1512).

to it or conclusive of it, since the etiologic factors were found in other states. Karl Menninger in an introduction to the American edition (1963, p. 7) wrote in repudiation of that part of the report that refers to the nonpathological state of homosexuality: "homosexuality . . . constitutes evidence of immature sexuality and either arrested psychological development or regression. Whatever it be called by the public, there is no question in the minds of psychiatrists regarding the abnormality of such behavior" (quoted in Bayer, 1981, p. 39).

Finally, the fight against the American Psychiatric Association's decision in December 1973 to delete homosexuality as a mental disorder from DSM-III was to a large extent led by psychoanalysts and other dynamically oriented therapists who felt that such action would keep homosexuals from seeking and receiving the help we could offer them. Individual analysts as well as organized psychoanalysis, although not alone among mental health professionals and organizations, subsequently protested the decision and continue to do so (see Bayer, pp. 121f., 155–178).

The view of homosexuality as a disease has led many analysts to feel that it is in the best interest of their homosexual patients to help them to become heterosexual. Our literature is replete with recommendations in support of modifications of analytic technique that are deemed appropriate to the treatment of homosexual patients. Kolb and Johnson (1955) state that analytic neutrality may at times be misconstrued as permission for the patient to act out homosexual behavior, that the therapist should not encourage the patient's "self-destruction," and under some circumstances should terminate treatment if such behavior persists (p. 513). Serota expressed the belief that "the analyst who undertakes the treatment of a homosexual must have already consciously or unconsciously arrived at certain diagnostic conclusions regarding the existence of an intrapsychic conflict regarding homosexuality, a conviction that a heterosexual solution is possible, that the patient will attempt it at some point" (Panel, 1960, 566). Socarides (1968) is not alone in advocating under certain conditions the use of such nonanalytic techniques as suggesting to a homosexual patient that he seek out women or discussing with a patient how to engage in heterosexual sex (see Wiedeman, 1974, p. 676). Others would agree that a "flexible" analytic approach is indicated, such as encouraging the homosexual patient's turn to heterosexuality where phobic avoidance of women was involved (e.g., Bieber et al., 1962; Ovesey, 1965; Rado, 1949). In his literature review Wiedeman (1974) noted that "a purely analytic approach consisting only of interpretations, without any other elements of support, clarification, and confrontation with reality, hardly exists" (p. 676).

I am defining as homosexual a person who has a predominant erotic preference, usually for a long period of time, for others of the same sex. There are some heterosexuals who, for developmental reasons (adolescents) or opportunistic motives (some delinquents) or situational reasons (prison inmates) or as a defense against anxiety, may engage in homosexual behavior for varying periods of time and not be homosexual (Isay, 1986). Most homosexuals do engage in sexual activity, but one need not do so to be homosexual. There are individuals who may be homosexual and are unaware of it because of the repression or suppression of their fantasies.

I am emphasizing in this definition that it is the erotic preference as expressed in fantasy that defines the homosexual and not his behavior, since some homosexuals, like some heterosexuals, may be inhibited by social constraints from expressing their sexuality. I am taking into account that there is a relative preponderance, but not an exclusivity, of homoerotic fantasy. I am emphasizing the tenacity and longevity of the sexual orientation in adults, since the fantasy is usually recollected as being present from the latency years or early adolescence (Friedman and Stern, 1980, p. 431). This does not preclude its presence in childhood—in fact, many gay men do recollect strong homosexual fantasies and impulses from childhood—any more than the repression of childhood sexuality in heterosexuals precludes its presence in childhood. Considering a man to be homosexual because of the predominant erotic fantasy for others of the same sex, rather than one who necessarily expresses his sexuality in behavior, has implications for the assessment, understanding, and treatment of homosexual patients.

In my practice I have seen a number of homosexual men who have returned for further help after interrupting or completing treatment with other analysts, whose goal, either explicitly stated or implicitly guiding the treatment, had been to help the patient change his sexual orientation. My clinical material suggests that such efforts may cause symptomatic depression by contributing to an already diminished and injured self-esteem; and in some cases it may produce severe social problems in later life. My conclusion from listening to these patients is that the analyst's internalized social values interfere with the proper conduct of an analysis by causing the analyst to be unable to convey an appropriate positive regard for his patient or to maintain therapeutic neutrality. I shall illustrate this conclusion with two brief clinical examples.

A. was referred for further treatment after he had left his previous psychotherapist, an experienced analyst with a fine reputation. A. was 20 and a college junior when I started to see him. He complained of severe dysphoria; an inability to form any kind of satisfying, lasting relationship; a lackluster college performance; and having no goals in his life. He also complained about being gay. His parents wished he were straight. His mother badly wanted grandchildren, and he wanted to be able to please her. He had friendships with girls and on one occasion he had had intercourse; but his sexual fantasies from age 9 or 10 had been almost exclusively about other boys. He felt a complete lack of sexual interest in girls, although he enjoyed their friendship. He wanted most of all to be able to fall in love and have a boyfriend because he felt so lonely, but anytime someone liked him, he began to find the boy unattractive and lost interest. His previous three-times-weekly analytically oriented therapy came to a halt because of A.'s continued feeling that his therapist disapproved of him. Although he was never told explicitly not to be homosexual, whenever he cruised a bookstore or had sex, the therapist discouraged this behavior. Whenever he went out with another boy, his therapist wondered why he did not devote similar energy to a girl he had previously met and seemed to like. The therapist's interventions appeared to increase this patient's need for brief sexual encounters as he grew to feel that these comments and interpretations were basically motivated by the therapist's disapproval of his homosexuality and the way he was expressing it. A.'s feeling that his therapist disapproved of his behavior and did not like him was analyzed as projection. He felt increasingly depressed, defeated, and self-critical.

This patient's description of his previous therapeutic experience appeared to be more than distortions due to past or current transference phenomena. His narrative had a ring of truth and reality to it. Furthermore, the manner in which he presented his dissatisfaction with his sexuality evoked in me an initial impression that he could and should alter this long-established sexual orientation. It became clear after several weeks, however, that A.'s wish to please his ambivalently viewed mother and his introjection of hostile social values inimical to his sexual feelings were motivating his request for change. It also became clear that these factors had produced a ready transference to which his previous therapist had responded, not by attempting to understand the conflicts underlying the wish, but by complying with it. I shall return to the analyst's exploitation of transference in the service of attempting to change the patient's sexuality.

At some point in every intensive therapy, every gay patient expresses unhappiness and dissatisfaction with his homosexuality. With this patient, the despair over his being homosexual was an expression of transference, but it was also a displacement of anxiety, causing conflict that interfered with his being able to form close, meaningful relationships, to have gratifying sexual activity with other men, and a satisfying career. His unconscious or preconscious wish was that if the socially disadvantaged homosexuality were "cured," then his anxiety would disappear. In aligning himself with that wish, the previous therapist joined the patient in magical thinking and was eventually perceived as being unempathic and ignorant. In colluding with that manifestation of transference expressed as "I hate being gay," the therapist became a further expression and extension of the incorporated values of a society perceived as being critical and hostile. A.'s correct perception of his therapist's values caused him to interrupt treatment, but his identification with this trusted person's biased views of homosexuality further injured him. By challenging this important aspect of A.'s identity, the analyst unconsciously encouraged the self-denigration that contributed to his self-degrading and spiteful sexual behavior and depression.

Listening to this young man in what I believe to have been a manner that was both accepting of him and neutral in the sense of being nonjudgmental and curious established an atmosphere in which conflict, transference, defense, and resistance could be safely related and untangled. The early expressed wish to be heterosexual largely disappeared from the hours after the first weeks of analysis, as did his depression. The feelings of self-loathing from internalized social prejudice lessened in intensity as he experienced some measure of acceptance and regard from my attitude toward him. Frantic anonymous sex decreased in frequency, in part because of the AIDS scare, but in large measure because he no longer needed to act out angry, spiteful transference wishes in a masochistic way. Likewise, he became much more successful in his work, in part, for the same reason.

Another illustration is of a young man I saw in analysis for several years, who differed from the previous patient in the severity of his masochism and the manner in which he used it to evoke expressions of disgust, rejection, and attack.

B. had felt homosexual since childhood and had actively engaged in homosexual sex since early adolescence. He had neither heterosexual experience nor sexual interest in women. B. related to his previous therapist, along with other aspects of his history, many sexual incidents that he felt were sordid, and he portrayed them as such, along with his shame and disgust over being homosexual. He did this frequently, and on more than one occasion inquired if the therapist felt B. would be better if he gave up his homosexuality. His therapist's agreement and subsequent well-intended admonitions made the patient increasingly desperate, disillusioned, lonely, and enraged. He eventually left treatment and came to me wanting to become heterosexual, although skeptical of the possibility.

B.'s masochism was severe. It derived from early injury to his narcissism and the resulting self-directed, spiteful rage; from his identification with a hostile, masochistic mother; from the expression of passive sexual longings for an emotionally distant father; and, very importantly, from critical social attitudes perceived, identified with, and internalized when he was quite young. In the transference these wishes were expressed as a need to be humiliated, dominated, and rejected. I did not always succeed in my attempts to maintain an accepting and positive attitude toward him because his needs to disgust me and to evoke my rejection were so persistent. Nevertheless, my reciprocal responses to his transference were both manageable and useful to our understanding, and I believe I was generally successful not only in maintaining a neutral attitude but in conveying my acceptance and positive regard for him.

I do not view B.'s homosexuality as his problem. Because he had an exclusive, or nearly exclusive, homosexual fantasy life since childhood and because of his long-standing homosexual activity with little or no real heterosexual interest, I consider him to be gay. I do not believe, therefore, that there is any clinical justification for attempting to change his basic homosexual behavior, nor do I expect to be able to change his sexual orientation. This attitude has enabled us to analyze those aspects of his wish to be heterosexual that are related to the passive acquiescence to and acceptance of internalized critical social values, and it has made it possible for us to understand unrealistic projections of these social attitudes in the transference. We can now begin to have a less cluttered view of early conflict and other determinants of his masochism. Some of the angry, destructive, rebellious activity related to his response to social attitudes has diminished.

I am emphasizing the importance of an undeviatingly uncritical, accepting therapeutic stance in which thoughtfulness, caring, and regard for the patient are essential. By so doing I am not underestimating the value of the questioning, uncovering, and usual interpretive work of any analytic or dynamically oriented therapy. Nor am I advocating the unquestioning acceptance of the patient's views and values. Rather, I am attempting to demonstrate that an attitude of positive regard makes analytic work possible because it enables the patient to express and analyze negative transference distortions from both the past and present. This stance has therapeutic value because it is in part through his interaction with the analyst that any patient acquires a new, different, more positive, and more accepting image of himself (Loewald, 1960, p. 20). I believe that neither the positive attitude described nor the therapeutic action is different from that in any other analytic or psychotherapeutic work. Moreover, I want to emphasize the therapeutic danger of a position that is not neutral by virtue of the analyst's being oriented to changing the patient's sexuality. In my opinion, these cases illustrate what Schafer (1983) means when he writes: "The simplistic, partisan analyst, working in terms of . . . good and bad ways to live is failing to maintain the analytic attitude. In this failure, he or she can only be encouraging the analysand to fixate on some pattern of paranoid and depressive orientations, to persevere in sadomasochistic fantasizing and acting out, or to engage in wholesale repression of disturbing factors" (p. 5).

I now turn to those patients who have worked with well-intentioned, therapeutically zealous analysts who have managed to accomplish the mutually acceptable goal of curtailing homosexual behavior. Claims of achieving behavioral change in a highly motivated population of male and female homosexual patients have varied from about 20% to 50% with every variety of therapeutic modality (Marmor, 1980, p. 277). Bieber et al. (1962), who viewed homosexuality in terms of an underlying fear of heterosexuality, reported a 19% change of exclusive homosexuals to heterosexuality, using what was probably a modified psychoanalytic technique (p. 276). Socarides (1978) claims that of "forty-four overt homosexuals who had undergone psychoanalytic therapy, twenty patients, nearly 50 percent, developed full heterosexual functioning" (p. 406).

I intend to illustrate the emotional and social consequences of the attempted and seemingly successful change from homosexuality to heterosexuality for three patients whom I have seen in a long-term, psychoanalytically oriented psychotherapy beginning 10 to 15 years after the completion of their prior analyses. These three patients, according to the definition previously given, were homosexual when treated by their previous analysts. There appear to have been few of the "blighted germs of heterosexuality" in any of these men. In each case sexual behavior was temporarily modified, but the patients remained homosexual in that their sexual orientation, as expressed by the predominance of homosexual fantasy, remained unchanged. When I treated them, they either previously or currently had the additional difficult social and personal complication of a family.

When C. consulted me, he was 47 and the father of two adolescent girls. He had married in his late 20s shortly after the completion of a 5-year analysis. Before the analysis he had had an active homosexual life, including a relationship with a young man who he said was the only passion of his life. He had never enjoyed sex with women prior to his analysis and *learned* (patient's emphasis) to enjoy sex with them in his analysis. Although sex with men was not specifically prohibited, the love affair was proscribed and sex with women was prescribed. There had been no homosexual sex since his marriage. He sought therapeutic assistance because of persistent depression, no zest for living, low self-esteem, apathy in his work, and no sexual interest in his wife, with whom he had not had sexual relations since the birth of his last child. His masturbatory and other sexual fantasies were exclusively homosexual. He longed for the lost love of his youth.

This man was a devoted father and husband. His wife knew nothing of his past homosexual life. He had no regrets over the change in his sexual behavior, except that he felt something was missing in his life—he called it a "passion." C. was still homosexual: he had a conscious erotic preference for other men, still had an active homosexual fantasy life, and continued to long for the love of other men.

C. did not wish to resume analysis, but he did enter into analytically oriented therapy. He expressed a great deal of anger (which he had previously been unaware of) at his analyst for "manipulating" him. He grieved over having given up the passion that he spoke of so often. Over the course of 2 years of therapy his life felt less burdensome as his depression decreased. He became more tolerant of his homosexual fantasies and impulses and was able to think of himself as homosexual. He never resumed sex with his wife, nor did he resume his homosexual life because he felt it would disrupt his marriage.

C. always believed that his previous analysis had been successful. He had a wife and children from whom he gained enormous pleasure. He liked the conventionality, the relative lack of stress in his life, and his professional success. It became clear in our work, however, that the denial, repression, and unanalyzed acquiescence that had been necessary in order for him to achieve the renunciation of his homosexual behavior had affected his capacity to enjoy and achieve to the fullest extent possible, and that the failure to analyze these defenses and transference manifestations were in part responsible for the depression that motivated his return for further treatment. The question of whether or not he would have been happier living an active homosexual life is unanswerable. But it would appear that the analyst's "health" values (Hartmann, 1960) made it impossible for either the patient or the analyst to consider this other sexual and social option.

D. was in his late 30s, and had previously been in analysis for about 5 years, during which time he both married and separated. According to his recollection, he had felt homosexual since early adolescence and had engaged in homosexual sex since that time. He entered analysis in his 20s because of several unhappy relationships with other men, and because of depression and ambivalence about being homosexual. He met his wife during the analysis, and she was the first woman he had ever had sex with. Although his sexual relationship was not "great," he perceived it as adequate, and he gave up for a time all homosexual activity. Subsequently, however, his work became increasingly tedious, and he felt depressed, argumentative, and apathetic. He resumed occasional surreptitious homosexual sex; the relationship with his wife continued to deteriorate and finally ended in separation. He stopped his analysis at the time of the separation from his wife, ostensibly because he felt the analyst was unempathic and rigid. He sought consultation several years later because of continuing depression connected with low self-esteem.

When I saw this man, he had very little or no interest in women and not much more interest in having sex with other men, although he readily acknowledged he was homosexual. He wanted a stable relationship, which he felt was possible only in a conventional marriage. During 3 years of therapy, he mourned the loss of his wife and the probability that he would never have children, and he began to have an active sex life with other men. This patient's analyst had made essentially the same technical modifications as C.'s analyst: questioning homosexual behavior without actually prohibiting it, and encouraging dating and any heterosexual involvement. In both of these cases, the homosexual behavior was inhibited by the analyst's positively reinforcing the more acceptable heterosexual behavior and by his use of a probably unconscious, disapproving attitude that served as a negative reinforcement of homosexual behavior. Transference manifestations of wanting to be loved, the need to acquiesce, and the patients' passive longings were all used in the service of helping these patients to suppress their homosexual behavior.

The next patient, E., had had an analyst who, unlike the analysts of the two previous patients, gave the appearance of being noncoercive, nonjudgmental, and unmanipulative. Because the patient had not engaged in homosexual sex prior to or during his analysis, no apparent modifications in analytic technique or obvious violations of analytic neutrality were necessary to discourage such behavior. The observation afforded by E.'s subsequent long analysis suggested, however, that the analyst's social values had interfered with this patient's treatment. I want to illustrate with this case the ways in which the interpretation of homosexuality as a defense can convey the analyst's bias.

E. started his analysis when he was in his early 20s because of conflict about his homosexual fantasies and a lack of interest in girls. Homosexual masturbation fantasies and daydreams had persisted since before adolescence. When he entered this analysis he had never engaged in homosexual activity, except for very occasional adolescent sexual play that was clinically insignificant. Throughout the analysis the analyst consistently interpreted the homosexual fantasies as a defense against assuming aggressive male roles, which included having heterosexual sex. The analyst's view implicitly and comfortingly conveyed to the patient that he was not really homosexual and that what appeared to him to be homosexuality and what he feared was homosexuality could be analyzed and would disappear. He continued to have exclusively homosexual fantasies; but, because of a powerful positive transference, he did engage in occasional sex with girls, although he was frequently impotent. Shortly after the termination of the analysis, he married. Sexual interest in his wife rapidly waned and after several years of marriage, he began to have homosexual sex for the first time. When E. came to me in his late 30s, he was depressed, agitated, despairing, and confused. He was "wandering between two worlds" and wanted to find a way to bring them together.

The analyst's heterosexual bias was expressed largely and repeatedly in the interpretation of homosexual fantasy as defense against fears of heterosexuality and of competition; i.e., as the unsuccessful resolution of oedipal-stage conflict. When I began to treat E., it was clear that he had a need to feel enraged and to see his analyst as negligent and uncaring. Nevertheless, his perception of his former analyst's intolerance of homosexual behavior, expressed in the interpretation of E.'s homosexuality as a defense against heterosexuality, also appears to have been accurate. The analyst's inability to help the patient discover this aspect of his identity contributed to E.'s later symptoms and to the painful social situation he found himself in at the beginning of his subsequent treatment.[3]

In the three preceding illustrations each patient's transference wishes were unconsciously used by the analyst, because of the analyst's countertransference needs, to attempt to change his patient's sexual orientation. This, of course, made it impossible in these initial efforts for any of these patients to understand those essential conflicts which were expressed in the transference. For example, C. had acquiesced to what he perceived as his analyst's wish for him to behave heterosexually out of an attempt to be the good sibling. His brother had been the actively rebellious one. C. won his place by being acquiescent and agreeable. D. came to his subsequent therapy with an enormous unanalyzed rage connected with early narcissistic

3. Fantasies of a homosexual nature and homosexual behavior may, of course, be used at times defensively by some patients who are predominantly heterosexual. Homosexual men may use homosexual behavior, just as heterosexuals may use heterosexual behavior, to ward off intolerable affects. These issues are discussed in a forthcoming publication (Isay, 1986).

wounds. He had the feeling that he had been a replacement for a sibling killed in the war. As a child he had felt neither understood nor appreciated, perceiving that he had been treated as if he were his deceased older brother. He, of course, felt that his analyst had, like his parents, a need of his own in treating him as if he were "straight," and, feeling a similar lack of empathy in his analyst, believed he had again been misunderstood and unappreciated. E. had been rebellious as a child out of a longed-for love that he never received. His passivity and acquiescence expressed this deep longing for the love of both parents. Pleasing his analyst by attempting to be heterosexual, he could win a long-sought and always elusive love.

The exploitation of transference for hoped-for therapeutic gain is, of course, not new. Many of the gains of the brief analyses of the 1920s and the crisis-oriented and focal therapies today were and are in part based on such techniques. Those analysts who advocate, as mentioned earlier, the introduction of encouragement to overcome what they feel to be the homosexual's phobic avoidance of sex with women make conscious use of the transference for attempted therapeutic gain. My concern here, however, is with the analyst's unconscious exploitation of transference wishes as an expression of his value system and countertransference, which add a measure of insidious conviction to the patient's long-standing belief in his being intolerable or evil.

Not only had the understanding and exploration of conflict been limited in each of the previous therapies by the use of the patients' transference wishes in order to attempt to change their sexuality, but subsequent analytic exploration was made even more difficult by their ensuing marriages. In the cases of C. and E., the two men who remained married, it was more difficult to obtain a full understanding of underlying conflict because of the degree and extent of their defenses. In saying this, I am not questioning whether marriage and children were worthwhile compromises for these homosexual men, or for any homosexual man, nor if gay men can be happily married. I am only pointing out that the subsequent therapy was made more difficult by their social situation and by such factors as the denial, repression, reaction formation, and readiness to acquiesce which led them into marriage and, perhaps, to remain in their marriages (see also Person in Panel, 1977, p. 189). Furthermore, had there been a stronger bisexual orientation in any of these patients, the outcome of treatment might have been more successful.[4]

DISCUSSION

In emphasizing the problems that many analysts have in treating homosexual patients, I am not implying that psychoanalysis cannot help gay patients. On the contrary, I feel that both psychoanalysis and analytically oriented psychotherapy can be helpful to these patients in ways in which they are helpful to heterosexual patients and for the same spectrum and distribution of character problems, and symptomatic neurotic and psychotic reactions (see Bieber et al., 1962, p. 28). My experience suggests that the usual analytic attitude of positive regard and neutrality may be enormously, perhaps especially, helpful to any patient who has internalized the critical, deprecatory attitudes of a prejudiced society by helping him to acquire a more positive, accepting image of himself. It is at present, however, because of the "moral value irradiation" of our work, difficult to measure the true potential of psychoanalysis for the treatment of gay patients.

The difficulties that many analysts, as well as other therapists, have had in treating homosexual patients, I believe, derive from the confusion of "health ethics" with moral values, so that "empirically subjective values are posited as if they were 'objective' and accessible to empirical validation" (Hartmann, 1960, p. 67). These health ethics, interacting with countertransference, have skewed our data and interfered with our perception and comprehension of the many ways that homosexuality, like heterosexuality, can be expressed, some of which are healthy and some are not.

4. I believe it is likely that observations of the successful conversion of "homosexual" patients to heterosexuality over an indefinite or extended period of time are, in fact, due to the successful suppression of the homosexual component in men who have a strong bisexual orientation.

Freud implicitly recognized the problematic influence of social values when he responded to a letter by Ernest Jones of December 1, 1921, in which Jones asked for advice on the matter of accepting a homosexual applicant for psychoanalytic training: "The Dutch asked me some time ago about the propriety of accepting as member a doctor known to be manifestly homosexual. I advised against it, and now I hear from Van Emden that the man has been detected and committed to prison. Do you think this would be a safe general maxim to act on?"

In the Circular Letter of December 11, 1921, Otto Rank, in collaboration with Freud, officially responded from Vienna: "We would not want to answer your question, dear Ernest, concerning possible membership of homosexuals as you suggest; that is to say, we do not on principle want to exclude such persons because we also cannot condone their legal persecution. We believe that a decision in such cases should be reserved for an examination of the individual's other qualities."[5]

Psychoanalysts have also inadvertently contributed to social bias, as well as partaking of it. Psychoanalytic theory and practice have promulgated a theory of developmental aberration and illness that has been used by the neo-traditionalist theologians of all churches to reinforce the view that homosexuality is evil. This position is predicated on the idea that those acts are intrinsically evil that are perfectable and correctable. For example:

> . . . the evidence is still too fragmentary to unseat the prevailing scientific appraisal of homosexuality as the living-out of sick and stunted emotions. The odds are still high that the average individual who chooses homosexual behavior will be choosing a sick, immature way of life. The odds should determine the ethical decision, it seems to me, at least for the individual for whom professional analysis has confirmed his emotional sickness [Batcheler, 1980, p. 69].
> [Or:] What troubled people need—either singly or in com-

5. This letter was discovered by Dr. Hendrick Ruitenbeek, and can be found in the Rare Books and Manuscript Library of Columbia University. It was reprinted by Marmor (1980, p. 395). I want to thank Lottie M. Newman for reviewing the original letter and providing this translation.

bination—is to learn to take serious responsibility for their attitudes, behavior and circumstances . . . every failure to take a
possible maturational step has moral significance and falls under the rubric of original sin . . . we have also seen that this is
true even if the person's responsibility is mitigated by the process having taken place unconsciously. . . . It is impossible for
homosexuality not to be included in this category [p. 83].

[Or:] To the degree that they can hold the impulse in rein
and fail to do so, they are committing a sin, a violation of the
will of God or, in secular terms, an aberration from the norm
[p. 58].

The essential clinical issue for us as analysts and therapists is
the extent to which we can help our patients to be as free as
possible of those conflicts that interfere with their capacity to
live as gratifying and happy lives as it is within their grasp to
live. With gay patients, I believe that we must act to lessen the
burden of the instinctual sacrifices that society imposes on them
(Freud, 1927), and to help them resolve those conflicts that interfere with the most gratifying expression of their sexuality.
Again, to quote Hartmann (1960): "it would be absurd to expect that only what has survival value for the individual or species would actually be called 'good,' or that everything called
'evil' must have the opposite effect. . . . It is, however, particularly difficult to determine how far 'good' contributes to happiness—happiness being a highly complex psychological phenomenon, and the concept being ambiguous" (p. 66).

BIBLIOGRAPHY

BATCHELER, E., ed. (1980). *Homosexuality and Ethics*. New York: Pilgrim Press.
BAYER, R. (1981). *Homosexuality and American Psychiatry*. New York: Basic
Books.
BERGLER, E. (1956). *Homosexuality*. New York: Hill & Wang.
BIEBER, I. ET AL. (1962). *Homosexuality*. New York: Basic Books.
FORD, C. S. & BEACH, F. A. (1951). *Patterns of Sexual Behavior*. New York:
Harper.
FREEDMAN, A. M., KAPLAN, H. I., & SADOCK, B. J. (1975). *Comprehensive Text-
book of Psychiatry/II*. Baltimore: Williams & Wilkins.
FREUD, S. (1927). The future of an illusion. *S.E.*, 21:5–56.
———— (1935). Letter to an American Mother. In Bayer (1981), p. 27.

FRIEDMAN, R. C. & STERN, L. O. (1980). Juvenile aggressivity and sissiness in homosexual and heterosexual males. *J. Amer. Acad. Psychoanal.*, 8:427–440.

GLOVER, E. (1932). The relation of perversion formation to the development of reality-sense. In *On the Early Development of Mind.* New York: Int. Univ. Press, pp. 216–234.

HARTMANN, H. (1960). *Psychoanalysis and Moral Values.* New York: Int. Univ. Press.

HOOKER, E. (1957). The adjustment of the male overt homosexual. *J. Proj. Tech.*, 21:18–31.

ISAY, R. A. (1986). Homosexuality in homosexual and heterosexual men. In *The Psychology of Men*, ed., G. Fogel, F. Lane, & R. S. Liebert. New York: Basic Books (in press).

KINSEY, A. C., POMEROY, W. B., & MARTIN, C. E. (1948). *Sexual Behavior in the Human Male.* Philadelphia & London: Saunders.

KOLB, L. E. & JOHNSON, A. M. (1955). Etiology and therapy of overt homosexuality. *Psychoanal. Q.*, 24:506–515.

LOEWALD, H. W. (1960). On the therapeutic action of psychoanalysis. *Int. J. Psychoanal.*, 41:16–33.

MARMOR, J., ed. (1965). *Sexual Inversion.* New York: Basic Books.

—— (1980). *Homosexual Behavior.* New York: Basic Books.

OVESEY, L. (1965). Pseudohomosexuality and homosexuality in men. In Marmor (1965), pp. 211–233.

PANEL (1954). Perversion. Arlow, J. A., reporter. *J. Amer. Psychoanal. Assn.*, 2:336–345.

—— (1960). Theoretical and clinical aspects of male homosexuality. Socarides, C. W., reporter. *J. Amer. Psychoanal. Assn.*, 8:552–566.

—— (1977). The psychoanalytic treatment of male homosexuality. Payne, E. C., reporter. *J. Amer. Psychoanal. Assn.*, 25:183–199.

PERSON, E. (1983). Review of *Homosexualities*, by A. P. Bell & M. S. Weinberg. *J. Amer. Psychoanal. Assn.*, 31:306–314.

RADO, S. (1949). An adaptational view of sexual behavior. In *Psychosexual Development in Health and Disease*, ed. P. H. Hoch & J. Zubin. New York: Grune & Stratton, pp. 159–189.

RIESS, B. F. (1980). Psychological tests in homosexuality. In Marmor (1980), pp. 296–311.

SCHAFER, R. (1983). *The Analytic Attitude.* New York: Basic Books.

SOCARIDES, C. W. (1968). *The Overt Homosexual.* New York: Grune & Stratton.

—— (1978). *Homosexuality.* New York: Aronson.

WIEDEMAN, G. H. (1974). Homosexuality. *J. Amer. Psychoanal. Assn.*, 22:651–696.

WOLFENDEN REPORT (1957). Great Britain Committee on Homosexual Offenses and Prostitution. Authorized American edition (1963). New York: Stein & Day.

Growing up with a Handicapped Sibling

HANSI KENNEDY, Dip. Psych.

IT IS EVIDENT TO ALL WHO WORK WITH CHRONICALLY ILL OR HAND-
icapped children that their families are often threatened by
predicaments which cannot be resolved. A number of surveys
point to a high incidence of marital difficulties or breakdown in
such families and the adverse effects on siblings. Some studies
point to the unrealistic expectations which parents have of the
healthy child to compensate for their disappointment, guilt, or
feelings of failure in relation to the child who is handicapped.
Yet it would appear that the physically healthy children in these
families are rarely referred for treatment. Their problems may
seem less weighty in comparison with the difficulties facing their
ill or handicapped siblings; or recognition of their problems may
be precluded by the need of the parents to defend against their
own conflicts in relation to their damaged child.

Describing the reactions of parents to the birth of a defective
child, Solnit and Stark (1961) speak of the mother's mourning
reaction. She has to relinquish the image of an expected "perfect
baby," and has to adapt to the "sudden" birth of a threatening

Codirector, the Anna Freud Centre, which is at present supported by the
G. G. Bunzl Charitable Foundation, London; the Freud Centenary Fund,
London; the Anna Freud Foundation, New York; the John D. and Catherine
T. MacArthur Foundation, Chicago; the New-Land Foundation, Inc., New
York; the Leo Oppenheimer and Flora Oppenheimer Haas Trust, New York;
and a number of private supporters.
Presented as the Third Annual Marianne Kris Memorial Lecture at the
Meeting of the Association for Child Psychoanalysis, Chicago, March 1984.

handicapped child. In our Well-Baby Clinic (Model, 1984), we have recently had the opportunity to observe how a mother's capacity to relate appropriately to her second child was impaired by her preoccupation with her firstborn. This child, who was 3 years 4 months at the time, was born totally deaf.

When, at the age of 6 weeks, the new baby was first seen, Jenny K. was failing to thrive. Her muscle tone was impoverished; she showed postural delay; she had a high-pitched cry; was miserable and had gained little weight since birth. The mother breast-fed Jenny on demand and thought that her milk supply was adequate. In a test feeding it was discovered that the baby was not getting much milk despite her good ability to suck, and Mrs. K. was advised to complement her own feedings with the bottle.

Although Mrs. K. was not suffering from a recognizable depressive reaction, she could neither respond to her baby's needs nor follow suggestions given with the aim of improving Jenny's well-being. Mrs. K. was tense and showed a rather abstracted air: she asked many questions but hardly listened to the replies. She was evidently in the habit of reading while she gave the breast. She excused this behavior, saying, "I spend so much time feeding her, I must do something." The baby failed to gain adequate weight, and the staff learned that the mother's reluctance to introduce bottle feedings was based on her feelings of failure and inadequacy. She recalled that she had been able to feed Emily until she was 8 months. When she remarked that Jenny smiled and cooed, although "I don't talk to her very much," it was evident that she was equating Jenny with the deaf sister. When asked if she feared that Jenny too might be found to be deaf, Mrs. K. denied any anxiety and stressed that Jenny was so different from Emily and that she could tell that the child could hear. She was having difficulty, however, in meeting the needs of the two children, and she expressed her wish to be available to Emily on her return from nursery school.

Emily had a profound congenital deafness, thought to be genetic in origin. Various investigations for possible mental retardation were undertaken before her condition was diagnosed at the age of 8 months. It seems likely that Mrs. K. began to feel a failure as a mother when she could not experience early mutuality and responsiveness due to Emily's deafness. Mrs. K.'s distress over Emily's handicap led her to dedicate herself to the task of helping her overcome the effects of her deafness; and Mrs. K. had been successful in many ways. When Jenny's birth caused some withdrawal from Emily, she reacted with anger at home, with aggression at the nursery school, and with some resistance to her speech therapy program.

The revival of Mrs. K.'s mourning and preoccupation with Emily ensured that she could not cathect Jenny appropriately and respond to the child's physical condition. She was unable to enjoy her normal child. When Jenny was 10 weeks old, the mother's attitude changed: she seemed to become aware of Jenny's fragile condition and to begin to follow the pediatrician's advice. She took some photographs of Jenny to send to her own parents: in some of them Jenny was naked and the mother realized just how thin she was. She looked "like an advertisement for famine relief. I was shocked, I could not send on such photos."

Jenny's needs might have remained unmet for longer without the intensive support and help provided for Mrs. K. during these crucial weeks. Even today the child's future development is still at risk and further difficulties in relation to her deaf sister will arise and affect Jenny's negotiations of each and every developmental task.

In a paper written in 1979, Trevino discusses siblings of mentally retarded children. He observed that, initially, young children play with their disabled siblings on an equal basis. As they grow older, they have to redefine their role and begin to assume a superordinate position. Parental ambivalence toward the handicapped child who is often defensively overprotected and overindulged intensifies sibling rivalry. It often leads to the existence of two completely different sets of rules within the same family. Parents frequently demand that the normal child include the disabled child in peer group activities. Children close together in age often experience social discomfort when they have to deal with peer reactions and have to explain to their friends things they themselves often do not understand or cannot accept. Teasing and taunting about the handicapped child are not uncommon. While the normal child may become bitter over the extra favors and attention given to the afflicted child, the handicapped child may become intensely envious of the normality of his sibling. This affective interplay frequently results, in the siblings of the afflicted child, in feelings of guilt over their physical normality.

A number of studies consider the impact of chronic illnesses on healthy siblings (Bergmann and Wolfe, 1971; Binger, 1973; McKeever, 1983) and lay special stress on the resentment felt by healthy siblings vis-à-vis parental attention given to the sick child. They point to the healthy sibling's guilt which arises from having escaped the affliction—guilt further reinforced by the belief of somehow having brought it about. Bergmann and Wolfe observed and interviewed 25 siblings of their chronic patients at the orthopedic hospital in Cleveland. Just as the sick child wonders "Why did it happen to me?" the healthy sibling may wonder "Why did it *not* happen to me?" or "*When* will it happen to me?" The authors found that, as a means of coping with anxieties, defenses such as denial, repression, and reversal of affect were mobilized in the healthy children, in order to alleviate the stress of a constant awareness of the ill child's difficulties and/or deformity.

In an extensive survey of the psychoanalytic literature on siblings, Colonna and Newman (1983) draw particular attention to the dearth of in-depth studies of the reactions of healthy children to their physically ill or handicapped siblings.

At the Anna Freud Centre we have recently had a hemophilic twin and his brother in analysis. The parents first contacted us when the twins were 2 years old and expressed their concern over the healthy twin's temper tantrums. They wondered whether the necessary extra attention paid to his hemophilic brother might play some part (Lament and Wineman, 1984). The fact that these boys were twins clearly put additional strain on every member of the family, but the envy and rivalry between the children was without doubt increased by Timmy's illness. In comparing himself to his twin, Timmy felt deprived of a healthy body; while Max felt overlooked in relation to the special parental attention required for the care of his ill brother. The resultant narcissistic wounds dogged them from one developmental phase to the next, became involved with their conflicts and tasks, and greatly intensified the children's ambivalence toward their primary objects. Max's fear of injuring his afflicted twin, intensified by his death wishes, seemed to have figured largely in his passivity. For Timmy, a healthy twin was a great incentive for matching his brother's physical prowess, thereby promoting a more active role. While the healthy child's conflicts over aggression toward his twin appeared to contribute to the development of a harsh superego, Timmy's superego development was flawed by his anger, protest, and disinclination to please his parents. The twins are only just entering latency and it may be premature to make too many predictions about the future functioning of their superegos.

While there are several excellent psychoanalytic studies on children's reactions to death (especially Barnes, 1964; R. A. Furman, 1964a, 1964b; E. Furman, 1974), these focus mainly on the child's reactions to the loss of a parent. Children's reactions to the death of a sibling have not, to my knowledge, been a focus of psychoanalytic investigation, and few accounts of brief psychotherapeutic intervention have been published (Rosenblatt, 1969). Based on a study of 58 cases seen in psychiatric interviews or brief interventions, and followed up, Cain et al. (1964) demonstrate the limitations of the notion that the impact of a sibling's death primarily produces guilt reactions in the surviving children. The children they studied suffered from a range of disturbances. In 40 percent of cases there were either immediate, prolonged, or anniversary identifications of a hysterical kind with the dead sibling's prominent symptom. Many of the children developed what they called death phobias, where talion fears and identifications with the dead sibling were particularly striking. The children were often convinced not only that they would die, but that they would die at precisely the same age or from the same cause as the dead sibling. They had a heightened awareness and fear of death, feeling that it could strike any moment at themselves, their parents, or other siblings. The authors also emphasized overprotectiveness toward the remaining children as a typical and fearful parental response which often further reinforced the children's anxiety.

In another paper "On Replacing a Child," Cain and Cain (1964) describe how the dead child often lives on in a concrete day-to-day fashion. Photographs fill every room of the house, birthdays are celebrated, and his continued presence in the family is rationalized as "We all love him and like to think of him." The surviving or replacement children always seem to know and reverberate to illness and death.

The clinical pictures may reflect a prolonged mourning process. Bowlby (1963) describes, as characteristic of childhood mourning, the unconscious urge to recover the lost object and the denial that the object is permanently lost.

Pollock (1962) found that in a random sample of adult analytic patients a significant number had suffered parent or sibling loss in their childhood. The factors which determine a child's immediate and long-term reactions to the death of a sibling ultimately depend on various preconditions. These include the age and developmental level of the surviving sibling, the preexisting relationship to the sibling and the parents, the parents' reactions to the death, and their subsequent attitude to their remaining children. The child's fantasies about the illness and the death also are important. Combinations of these variables may lead to immediate disturbance or appear only in delayed and hidden conflictual reactions in adult life.

Many of the general features described in this brief review can be illustrated in the treatment material of my patient David D. He not only grew up with a handicapped sibling, but was also in some sense a "replacement child," who experienced at the age of 8 the death of the afflicted brother. My lack of familiarity with what others had already said gave me a double satisfaction. I first discovered with David the origin of his considerable suffering in relation to the life and death of his handicapped brother; and later I found our discoveries confirmed in the work of my colleagues.

David's analysis extended over almost 3 years, but I shall confine myself to those aspects of our work which have direct bearing on the subject under discussion.

David instigated his own referral for analysis when he told his parents that he needed help because he could not stop thinking about death. The parents had been aware of his anxiety in the preceding 6 months but had attributed this to difficulties occasioned by a move into a large secondary school at that time. He complained about bullies who lay in wait for him and attacked him in the playground. He said that some of the teachers hated him. In recent weeks he had used all sorts of ploys to stay away, feigning illness or exaggerating minor injuries. His sister called him a hypochondriac. On several occasions he persuaded the school nurse that he felt ill and needed to go home, especially on days when he was expected to take part in field games or sports. He was also sleeping badly, and his anxiety was manifest in restlessness and nonstop talking. After David told his parents that he could not stop thinking about death, they noticed that he sometimes flailed his arms about, in a manner reminiscent of his dead brother. They were puzzled by this behavior. It was 3½ years since Darren had died, and David appeared to have weathered his loss much better than the rest of the family.

David was the third child of parents whose potentially warm and harmonious family life was devastated by the illness and eventual death of their firstborn son, Darren. When Darren was 3 years old, he developed symptoms stemming from a degenerative neurological disorder. The parents were told that he could not be expected to live more than a year or 2. At the time their daughter Dora was only a few months old. The parents were heartbroken, sought all kinds of professional advice, and tried to cope as best they could. They decided that Darren should remain with the family and receive the best possible care. In the event he only died at the age of 14.

After Darren's terminal illness had been diagnosed, the parents were advised to have another child, and David was born 3 years later, a planned baby conceived to replace the ill and dying child. Mrs. D. had no recollection of anxiety about his birth, which was, in fact, straightforward. He was an easy and happy baby, and the mother breast-fed him for 5 months. There were no feeding or sleeping or toilet-training problems. He was described as an alert baby, advanced in his motor, speech, and social development. As a toddler, he would bang his head when he was angry; and the parents thought this linked with his need to curb his aggression on account of Darren's vulnerability. By the time David started walking, Darren was 7 years old, not particularly stunted in his growth but very unsteady in keeping his balance. He was always falling over, and the slightest push would knock him down and start him howling. On more than one occasion he broke a limb, and on many more it was feared that he had done so.

From the parents' account it seemed that the needs of each of their children had been carefully considered at every stage in their development. David was sent to nursery school at 3, but was always encouraged to have friends in to play so that he would not suffer from having a "handicapped brother." Both parents felt neither David nor Dora showed signs of stress or disturbance over Darren. They were kind and protective toward him, yet able to complain when he interfered with their activities. Although Darren was often restless and difficult to manage, he remained an integral member of the family until his death.

David was not quite 12 years old when he started analysis. He took full responsibility for his daily attendance in spite of a long and complicated journey. In periods of resistance he could develop sudden lapses of memory and go straight home after school, but he would then always telephone with profuse apologies and self-accusations, sometimes referring to himself as a "scatter-brained" boy. Most of the time the analytic work was facilitated by a genuine wish for help.

David impressed me at once as an attractive, intelligent, and articulate youngster. He was a little plump and looked more suited for intellectual pursuits than physical ones. He confirmed this impression right away when he told me sadly that some teachers and boys mockingly referred to him as "the great violin virtuoso." He felt utterly helpless vis-à-vis the bullies at school who teased him and attacked him physically. He also felt bullied by his sports master who sneered at his failures and who he felt forced him to participate even when he was feeling ill. His pleasure in learning was spoiled because he was always worrying about the next attack. In his first session he referred to his dead brother. His parents had taken him, together with his sister, to see a psychiatrist after Darren's death. He had enjoyed talking to the doctor, who had explained that it was natural to feel guilty about the death of a brother. But he did *not* feel guilty about Darren's death, only sorry and upset about losing him. He added, in a loving tone of voice, "Darren was such a good sport." My attempt to link this comment with his declaration that he himself was teased and humiliated for being bad at sports met with determined rejection. It alerted me straight away to the strength of his defensive repudiation of any criticism or hostility toward his dead brother.

Defenses against death wishes would seem to be an integral factor in the dynamics of the family containing a handicapped child. But with David this extended to a generalized condemnation of his own aggression which rendered him incapable of self-defense or even self-assertion. Although he expressed disapproval of the behavior of bullies, he could not express anger toward them. He even needed to mitigate his disapproval by finding excuses for his attackers. Morgan, the boy who tormented him most, "was probably so nasty because he had no one to give him affection. His mother had died a few months ago and he knew what it felt like when someone died."

David had strong reaction formations against sadism. He condemned any kind of violence, wars, revolutions, murders, and the death penalty. He was a staunch supporter of the "underdog," the victims and the weak; and his sympathy sounded quite genuine.

The dangers from the attacks David encountered in his daily life had to be rationalized and the anxiety blocked by denial or reversal. He usually arrived from school nursing some sort of injury. He sustained a bad thumb when a third-former jumped on his back, "but it was all done in fun and did not really hurt." He might, of course, have chipped a bone, but he did not really mind. Sometimes he introduced an account of his injuries by telling a joke. One of these concerned a man with false teeth which detached themselves when he ate toffees. Then he told me that a hard ball had hit his face and made his tooth bleed that day.

Long-distance running was particularly humiliating for David because he could never finish the course. His fear of straining his heart and dying made him drop down in exhaustion, hoping that an ambulance would come to his rescue. Instead he met further attacks in the form of scathing remarks by the sports master.

The analyst's office soon became a place where he gained temporary relief from these oppressing anxieties and where he could allow himself to regress. David cast me in the role of caregiver and provider and presented himself as the neglected, needy, and badly done-by child. He would arrive at the session looking a picture of misery, still dressed in sports gear, covered in mud, having "forgotten to shower and change at school and put on his coat." He would ask permission to warm himself by the radiator or wash his wounds and scratches. Sometimes he allowed himself to cry because he thought his ribs were broken in a fall and he did not want to appear a crybaby at school. He complained that he was starving and had not eaten since breakfast and needed a glass of water or preferably a hot drink. When he realized that I verbalized rather than gratified his longings to be fed and made more comfortable, he began to bring food and drink to the sessions and consume it with relish and exaggerated pleasure. Although he strongly denied my interpretation that this self-provision concealed his dissatisfaction and anger with me for not doing enough for him, the subsequent transference material confirmed my view. He began to linger on after sessions as though to invite me to throw him out in favor of others. He became intensely interested in and rivalrous with other patients. He wanted to hang up a "marvelous drawing" in the consulting room for everyone to admire. When he discovered that an older boy had a session after his, he asked me for a gun. He explained that he meant a toy gun, of course, and justified the demand by saying it was hard for him to ask for such things, but one had to be honest in analysis. While he could barely hide his anger with me for not providing the gun, he tried to strike up a friendship with the other patient rather than reveal his murderous impulses. One had to work painstakingly on his defenses—denial, reversal, and reaction formations—to demonstrate to David what he was covering up and why.

We learned that David's anger with his mother for depriving him of his fair share had early roots. It appeared to stem from a time when he felt envious of the attention and care his handicapped brother received from her. His initial identification with Darren, based on this envy, probably preceded his recognition of Darren's handicap. Later Darren's affliction, and certainly his death, mobilized fears that such misfortune could also strike him.

A pervasive preoccupation with illness, injury, and death was ever present in David. A boy in his school had died of leukemia and as a memorial the school made an appeal to parents to become blood donors. Of course, his mother volunteered, and took him to see a film about research into the illness. Another boy was killed in a road accident while riding a bicycle, and this tragedy was reported with complaints that his parents did not let him ride his bicycle in London. There was hardly a session in which he did not mention his dead brother in some context or another, and he began to remember some of Darren's accidents.

Occasionally he would wear a new shirt, pullover, or jacket and ostensibly display it, inviting my response. When I verbalized his wish that I notice his new clothes, he explained that it was not new and was really Darren's. When I wondered whether he minded the fact that his clothes were hand-me-downs, he assured me that he loved wearing garments that reminded him of Darren. He loved his brother and he hoped he would never forget him. In any case he could not possibly forget him because everyone at home was always talking about him anyway.

I gradually learned that David now slept in Darren's former room, which was still referred to by the family as Darren's room. Darren's toys had remained in the room and David had "inherited" them. There were many references to family celebrations when Darren was lovingly remembered. His birthday and death were always commemorated. When David reported that Darren and Dora shared a common birthday, he said, "I used to hate this when I was little because I felt left out. Now I hate it because I always have to think of Darren who might feel left out."

Darren had clearly remained a presence in the family, and the parents' mourning process still continued; but, for David, Darren seemed to live on in a very concrete way. He could be quite philosophical when discussing death. What was death? Life could not just end when the heart stopped beating or the brain stopped working. Darren's brain was damaged before his death. Even now, 3½ years later, he could not believe that Darren was no longer around. Sometimes when he walked about the house at night, he thought of meeting Darren behind a door. He believed firmly in life after death and he had seen two ghosts: the first ghost appeared when he slept in a hotel which was a converted eery old castle known to be haunted by an angry ancestor. The second ghost he saw at home, where he was particularly frightened because he was sure it was Darren coming to have a look around and see "what was going on." I reminded David that he had told me that he slept in Darren's room, wore his clothes, played with his toys, and that he well might feel that Darren would not like to see what was going on and might want to take his revenge. For once David readily agreed and added that this was exactly what he would do if he were in Darren's place and someone had stolen his things.

At this point David also began to wonder whether his tormentors at the school were attacking him because they felt envious of his being a bit more clever than they were. He spoke of being teased about getting good marks, knowing the answers in class, and talking in a posh accent. The teasing was no longer confined to his poor performance in sport. When these feelings were worked through in terms of his "survivor guilt," he experienced some relief—his level of anxiety decreased, and with it the excessively stringent control of any form of aggressive expression.

In the sessions David began to move about with increased freedom, displayed some pleasurable excitement, and permitted himself to make a token attack on me. He made and tested paper darts, and enjoyed it when they narrowly missed me. When eventually one hit me, he became anxious, apologized profusely, and almost at once slipped on the floor and knocked his arm against my desk. He rubbed his elbow as he examined my desk for any possible damage. This was one of many incidents in which he demonstrated his fear that phallic sexual/aggressive attacks would cause permanent damage or destroy the object, and therefore had to be inhibited or turned against himself. Indeed, these became habitual modes of defense.

His complaints about school now shifted away from bully boys. His music teacher, formerly much admired, was felt to be unfair in his criticism of David and in his failure to give him adequate recognition. Whereas, hitherto, active involvement in the music department had been relatively conflict-free and a sought-after refuge from the stresses encountered in the playground, David now spent his sessions working out schemes of revenge. He would not make sacrifices and give up free time to come to rehearsal; he would try to organize strike action of all orchestra members so that the teacher would beg him to play in the concert; he would write a protest about the undemocratic way the orchestra was run; and he would complain to the head of the school. It was quite clear that David provoked the teacher's hostility and criticism, but it took time to discover that David's resentment stemmed from a thwarted desire to lead the orchestra. It emerged that previously his teacher had been liberal in his praise and had told him that he had considerable musical talent. "And now," David blurted out, "he won't let me be leader of the orchestra because he wants his pet daughter instead." It was unfair and he resented it.

David began to talk about rows at home with his father. They had always had rows because his father lost his temper more easily than his mother and shouted at him. His father had always been strict and not always fair to him. When, as a small boy, he was naughty, his father spanked only him and not the others. Darren did not get spanked because he was handicapped and Dora escaped because she was a girl. Now his father teased David a lot and made him angry. Perhaps, he said pensively, he got angry more often than his father and he was the one who shouted. Usually he tried to leave the room to cool off but did not always make it. But his example was interesting. His father had been very nice recently, helping to build airplane models. They had fun working on a model together last Sunday. Soon afterwards his father walked behind him on the stairs and put his hands affectionately round his neck. David screamed in rage and swore at his father, who apologized for startling him. David felt awful and was ashamed to have tea with the family. I suggested that he screamed in fear rather than in rage—perhaps he feared his father might strangle him in retaliation for some of the things David sometimes wanted to do to him.

That night David had what he described as "a very painful dream." He was in a group of unknown people in a disused airfield. The people were hostile, ordered him about, and bullied him. When they chased him around, shouted at him, and finally locked him in a little hut, he felt angry rather than frightened. In the hut was a machine gun. He picked it up, stepped outside, and "mowed everyone down." He added, "and I didn't have a very nice feeling after I had done that." I said that feeling guilty was very painful even if these people in the dream had made him very angry so that he felt like killing them all. With a laugh, David added, "Like I feel at home when my Dad makes

me angry." The associations to the disused airfield led him to
talk about his wish to join the air cadets. He had obtained a leaflet
and shown it to his parents, but they said that the meeting times
clashed with his sessions and he would not be able to join. All his
life he had been interested in planes and now he wanted to learn
to fly. It was an interest he shared with his father who would have
become a pilot in his youth had he not failed his medical. But, he,
David, was fit and healthy and would not be put off joining the
air cadets for more than a term, whatever I or his parents said.

His masculine strivings showed in other ways as well. He
planned to build up his body: it was the only way to deal with
bullies. Once he was able to show that he could take them on in a
fight, he would gain the respect of the group. He put himself on
a diet, he walked to school to get exercise, and decided to spend
more time in the gymnasium and the swimming pool. At home
he started using a chest expander.

At about this time David saw the film *Jaws,* which mobilized his
sadistic fantasies as well as his castration anxiety. David's defenses against his sadistic wishes had so far only permitted their
emergence into consciousness in relatively tame and modulated
fantasies of revenge. Now he described *Jaws* in every gory detail
and proclaimed that it was the best film he ever saw. With a
considerable degree of anxious excitement he described the
"marvelous scene" where the sea was colored "bright red from
the blood with bits of the dead boy floating about." The scene he
found most enjoyable and exciting, however, was the one in
which the shark bit off a man's leg. He completely denied that
this film might have made him feel anxious as well as excited,
saying that he knew it was not real and that the sharks were only
expensive models constructed in film studios. But that night he
awoke from a dream so frightened that he dared not go to sleep
again. In the session that followed he looked pale and shaken,
and could not recall details of the dream until I had wondered
whether it had a connection with the previous day's material.

In the dream he was in a boat with an adult man. It was not
anyone he knew. Suddenly a shark knocked the boat over. They
fell in the water and the man disappeared. But he and a friend
were in the water and both boys were trying to get away from the
shark. The shark got hold of his friend and David failed in his

attempt to rescue him. He was reluctant to remember the rest of the dream and brushed it aside with a remark that it ended in a typical dream chase where one tries and tries but can't make the shore. He woke up, frightened and sweating, and didn't dare go to his parents' room. In his associations he was afraid his father might not be there; perhaps he had been the man who drowned in the dream.

David had more difficulty understanding the second part; he thought of Darren whom he once rescued when he fell over in the swimming pool. Even though it was in the shallow end, it was difficult to pull him out. His mother managed it, but Darren was winded and couldn't get his breath. David thought he was dead. Darren was the only dead person he ever saw. He died in the hospital, but he saw him in his coffin before the funeral. His parents did not want him to come along, but he insisted. He looked so pale and peaceful David could not forget the sight. It was like the ghost face he once saw in the house when he woke at night. Now he recalled the rest of the dream. "When we reached the shore it was more like a swimming pool with high walls and I couldn't pull myself up to get out of the water. When, in the end, I managed, it was too late, the shark had bitten off my leg too." He readily accepted my interpretation that both castration wishes toward father and fears of his own castration had been mobilized while watching the film. That was why he had pushed them out of his mind the day before; but they could not be kept away in the dream.

The thought of the swimming pool with high walls led to a memory of a time when he was 3 or 4 years old. His sister could swim already. This helped him to master his fear of going into the water. She could also pull herself up by the side of the pool and climb out that way, but he couldn't do so, and his swimming teacher made him swim all alone to the stairs in the deep end.

Up to this point in treatment he had described his older sister as kind, helpful, and motherly toward him. Now he reported that they had arguments over TV programs. When he did not give way, she attacked him. He recalled a fight they had had soon after Darren's death. She hit him really hard and sat on his chest so that he couldn't breathe. She was frightened when he went white in the face. His parents were very upset when he accused her of trying to kill him, and his mother started crying. We talked about the many other occasions on which Dora must have made him feel angry, inadequate, and helpless like in the dream when he couldn't manage to climb out and had to face the dangers of the deep water by himself. He smiled and said he always felt girls had all the privileges. They were spoiled, especially by their father; while boys were made to fetch and carry, give up the best seats, and get blamed and punished. To top it all, when it came to washing up, Dora believed in the equality of the sexes!

Yet, even such relatively mild expressions of anger and hostility toward his sister were followed by fears that she might suffer an accident or even meet with death. A few days later, David arrived at his session in a state of great anxiety. He was carrying a sealed letter for his mother. The school secretary had told him not to forget to give it to her right away. When I wondered what he thought the urgent message contained, he said that it might be a complaint about him, but it might also be a note to tell mother that Dora had met with an accident at school.

In this connection David recalled an accident he himself had had at junior school. He recalled that he had been quite a naughty child and was always fighting with other children at that time. Once he ran away from a boy whom he had hit in the playground, and slipped and damaged his front teeth. There was a lot of blood, he was rushed to the hospital, and now he had a crown on one front tooth. This accident was fraught with anxiety not only because it represented a symbolic castration in punishment for an aggressive attack, but also because his mother could not be reached. When he was rushed to the hospital, he felt unsupported in his ordeal.

The floodgates had been opened, and many childhood memories began to emerge. David experienced considerable relief. He became happier and more joyful every day, and better able to handle aggressive conflicts.

His enjoyment of all his activities gave opportunities for creative self-expression. Drama class was fun. The boys were paired off and asked to act a spontaneous funny scene. He and his friend chose one in which he was the doctor carrying out an operation on his patient. The patient asked, "Doctor, are you giving me gas or an anesthetic?" and David turned to an imaginary nurse and asked for a hammer. He added laughingly that he had the audience in fits as he pretended to knock his patient over the head with the hammer. Accidentally, he did, in fact, punch his patient during the so-called operation, but he just apologized in a whisper and no harm was done.

David recalled his enjoyment in fantasy games with his friends when he was little. In particular he recalled playing monster games with a special friend. They scared each other and then looked over their shoulder to check whether the monsters were chasing them. This led to the recollection that he did not like it when his friends asked questions about Darren who usually came with his mother to fetch him from school. His friend playfully called Darren a monster. He did not mind his friend saying that, but he protested when other children called Darren names and said he was mad.

Any such communication had to be followed by reassurances that Darren was really quite intelligent and if he made strange noises, it was because he was a handicapped boy and couldn't help it. Sometimes David got cross with children who teased Darren and that was why he had so many fights. It became clear that he used to be able to fight to defend Darren while he was alive, but later identified with the helpless brother when the bullies attacked him.

He recalled getting cross with Darren when friends visited him. He disrupted their games. When Darren was told to go away, he screamed, and his mother got cross with him for being unkind. Darren was unsteady on his feet and always fell over. He could not get up and one never knew how badly he was injured because he yelled so much. As David recalled these episodes, he said that he often felt sorry for Darren, but sometimes Darren made him very angry and upset and he sometimes wished that he would "hit the bucket."

It was only after we had worked for some time on his loving as well as his hostile feelings for Darren that David began to talk about his mother's sadness. He was once taken together with Darren to a children's concert and his mother became very upset when they had to leave because Darren behaved so badly. David did not much care for concerts then, but he minded when he saw his mother crying. He used to listen to his parents talking about

Darren and once heard his father say, "He is not like us, you can't expect it of him."

David's parents had been adamant that Darren's anticipated death had never been discussed with the children before he actually died. After a visit to a cousin, who was expecting her third baby, David reported that the parents did not really want another baby, but birth control did not always work. He thought most parents only wanted two children and that his parents had not really wanted him. It was a lot of work for his mother to look after a handicapped child as well as two others. When I carefully explored whether he thought he was born to replace his brother, he hotly denied this, saying no one knew that Darren was going to die, but they always worried about him. "And now I worry about who is going to die next in our family, that's why I was happy when I had my fourteenth birthday and nothing happened." David had not even mentioned this anxiety to me until the birthday had passed. The relief of having survived was liberating, however, and from that time on he began to talk about no longer needing analysis.

It seems to me that David's story illustrates very vividly the impact a handicapped child can have on his siblings' development. David was a potentially healthy and well-endowed child who grew up under the shadow of Darren's affliction—one which affected the whole family. He might have escaped the full impact of the fate of the "replacement child" because his parents' distress and anxiety were still focused on Darren. Nevertheless, in his early teens David complained bitterly about his parents' excessive concern about his safety, which he experienced as infantilizing and restricting.

Darren's handicap made David feel unable to express even age-appropriate aggression throughout his development. Even as a small toddler he appeared to have learned that knocking his own head was better than knocking Darren. This restriction on aggressive expression later led to strong reaction formations, talion fears, and a strict superego. In David's eyes, Darren received far more attention and much more indulgence from his mother; and his early longings to be in Darren's shoes formed a prototype for an identification with his rival for the mother's love. Later this identification must have mobilized considerable fears that he too would suffer Darren's fate. More positively it allowed him to empathize with his afflicted brother as well as to identify with his mother's protectiveness. From the analytic material it would seem that he never really understood the nature of Darren's affliction. The parents probably found it difficult to talk about it and preferred to use the umbrella term, "He is handicapped." This may have contributed to David's inability to come to terms with it and give his fantasies free reign.

David's intensified conflicts about death wishes and the expression of aggression must have increased the difficulty of negotiating the oedipal situation. His childhood recollections suggested, however, that he retained his ability to fight and defend himself and his brother against other children during the latency period.

Although, according to the parents, David coped better than the rest of the family with Darren's death, it heightened his anxieties and death became a formidable danger. Perhaps it was not so much the change of school which aroused his conflicts but the reinforced instinctual pressures of prepuberty which mobilized sexual and aggressive wishes and necessitated crippling defensive maneuvers.

It is, however, also possible to see some positive influences of this sibling relationship, even though the clinical material cited emphasized the negative ones. Indeed, it could be argued that these positive influences were of material help in the treatment process itself; and some of his character traits, capacity for concern, empathy, and insightfulness could, at appropriate points, be pressed into the service of the analysis.

It is, of course, impossible to predict the future of this child. Will he succumb to hypochondriacal symptoms or concerns? Will he be vulnerable to pervasive anxieties, especially those connected with illness or death? Will his relationships in his own future family be put in jeopardy and echo some of the miseries encountered in the past? Or will compassion and the character traits already well established lead to a medical career, the caring profession, a future defender of the needy or a crusader for the handicapped?

BIBLIOGRAPHY

BARNES, M. J. (1964). Reactions to the death of a mother. *Psychoanal. Study Child,* 19:334–357.

BERGMANN, T. & WOLFE, S. (1971). Observations of the reactions of healthy children to their chronically ill siblings. *Bull. Phila. Assn. Psychoanal.*, 21:145–161.

BINGER, C. M. (1973). Childhood leukemia—emotional impact on siblings. In *The Child in His Family*, ed. E. J. Anthony & C. Koupernik. New York: Wiley, 2:195–211.

BOWLBY, J. (1963). Pathological mourning and childhood mourning. *J. Amer. Psychoanal. Assn.*, 11:500–541.

CAIN, A. C. & CAIN, B. S. (1964). On replacing a child. *J. Amer. Acad. Child Psychiat.*, 3:443–456.

————— FAST, I., & ERICKSON, M. E. (1964). Children's disturbed reactions to the death of a sibling. *Amer. J. Orthopsychiat.*, 34:741–752.

COLONNA, A. B. & NEWMAN, L. M. (1983). The psychoanalytic literature on siblings. *Psychoanal. Study Child*, 38:285–310.

FURMAN, E. (1974). *A Child's Parent Dies*. New Haven & London: Yale Univ. Press.

FURMAN, R. A. (1964a). Death and the young child. *Psychoanal. Study Child*, 19:321–333.

————— (1964b). Death of a six-year-old's mother during his analysis. *Psychoanal. Study Child*, 19:377–397.

LAMENT, C. & WINEMAN, I. (1984). A psychoanalytic study of nonidentical twins. *Psychoanal. Study Child*, 39:331–370.

McKEEVER, P. (1983). Siblings of chronically ill children. *Amer. J. Orthopsychiat.*, 53:209–229.

MODEL, E. (1984). Failure to thrive. *Bull. Hampstead Clin.*, 7:127–132.

POLLOCK, G. H. (1962). Childhood parent and sibling loss in adult patients. *Arch. Gen. Psychiat.*, 7:295–305.

————— (1978). Childhood sibling loss and creativity. *Annu. Psychoanal.*, 6:443–481.

ROSENBLATT, B. (1969). A young boy's reaction to the death of his sister. *J. Amer. Acad. Child Psychiat.*, 8:321–335.

SOLNIT, A. J. & STARK, M. H. (1961). Mourning and the birth of a defective child. *Psychoanal. Study Child*, 16:523–537.

TREVINO, F. (1979). Siblings of handicapped children. *J. Contemp. Soc. Wk.*, 60:488–493.

WANN, E. (1978). The family and the handicapped child. In *The Child and His Family*, ed. E. J. Anthony & C. Chiland. New York: Wiley, 4:81–88.

Both Sides of the Barrier

Some Reflections on Childhood Fantasy

HANSI KENNEDY, Dip. Psych.,
GEORGE MORAN, M.A.,
STANLEY WISEBERG, M.B., B.S.,
F.R.C.Psych., D.P.M.,CLIFFORD YORKE,
M.R.C.S., L.R.C.P., F.R.C.Psych., D.P.M.

IN THE PSYCHOANALYTIC VIEW, FANTASY BRINGS TOGETHER DI-verse mental content, in the service of wish fulfillment, in constructions which do not correspond with either a past or a present reality. Fantasy is thereby distinguished from memories and percepts, although memories and percepts, distorted or not, may be used as material for fantasy formation. Indeed, affect, percept, and all other forms of mental content provide the psychic bricks with which fantasies are constructed, whether drawn together by primary-process ideation or variously disciplined by secondary-process thinking. Fantasy may relieve drive pressure and thereby have an economic function; in this respect, it is internally adaptive, although, if it arouses too much anxiety or interferes with certain aspects of ego functioning, it may jeopar-

From the Anna Freud Centre, London. This work is part of a continuing Study entitled "A Project to Study Variations of Normality and Pathology in Relation to Personality Development" funded by the John D. and Catherine T. MacArthur Foundation, Chicago.

In collaboration with P. Cohen, S. Marans, and P. Radford. This is a slightly amended version of a paper presented at the 5th Annual International Scientific Colloquium entitled "The Role of Fantasy in the Adaptive Process," the proceedings of which are published in the *Bulletin of the Hampstead Clinic*, 7:149–212, 1984.

dize adequate adaptations to the external world. We are, however, very familiar with many of the ways in which fantasy fosters adaptation to reality: Hartmann (1939) has laid particular stress on this aspect of fantasy functioning.

Two further points need to be added. First, in its wish-fulfilling function, fantasy is by no means exclusively a representative of the id. In its function as an internal regulator, fantasy may reconcile or bring into contiguity *conflicting* wishes. Second, the view that fantasy can fulfill manifold functions is linked with the concept of transmogrification—that is to say, the change in form and function over the course of development, sometimes in the most surprising manner. A brief vignette illustrates these points.

A woman whose childhood sexuality was characterized by beating fantasies experienced, in adulthood, masturbation fantasies in which she imagined the stages of her trial and sentence for a violent crime. She would mount the scaffold to be beheaded, and orgasm would occur with the fall of the executioner's sword. In addition to id derivatives, a fantasy of this kind includes a powerful superego component. This could not have been established when beating fantasies began, in early childhood, since it would have preceded the formation of the superego as a comparatively stable internal structure. From the standpoint of the topographical model, the beating fantasies existed *before* the repression barrier[1] was established, while the retributive elements in the execution fantasy were provided *after* it had been laid down. Stable internalization is crucial for the consolidation of the repression barrier and the supersession of infantile sexuality by infantile amnesia.

It is our intention to provide clinical illustrations relating to periods before and after the repression barrier is fully formed. We shall, however, concern ourselves with the *internal* rather than the *external* adaptive function of fantasy.

In the preverbal period of childhood, a wide range of activity

1. The term "repression barrier" is widely used at the Anna Freud Centre and bears the meaning allotted to it by a number of previous analysts, in particular Edward Glover (1949, pp. 53, 57, 71, 90, 126). We refer to the point at which the division between id and ego has become structuralized and sufficiently stable to play a major part in determining the onset of childhood amnesia and in facilitating the onset of latency.

organizes and expresses drives and conflicts in an action mode. Many of the play activities in the first and second year of life operate in the service of mastery and ego development and provide pleasure, though some would argue that these activities do not fully qualify as illustrations of fantasy. Examples include reversal of the feeding situation in the first year of life when a child attempts, with evident pleasure, to put a spoon or a biscuit into his mother's mouth, gives his unwanted food to the dog, or, somewhat later, prepares, eats, or serves "pretend food." Another typical sequence, in this case in the service of mastering separation, begins with peek-a-boo games, and proceeds to more complex activities in which the child leaves the mother and waves good-bye, plays games of hide-and-seek, or pretends to leave for the office or factory or to set out on a long journey. Defenses against feelings of helplessness and passive capitulation to mother's control, as well as a simple wish to be grown up, find expression in the wearing of mother's shoes, the carrying of father's briefcase or mother's shopping bag, and extend to more elaborate games involving dolls, props, and playing at mommies and daddies.

Such action-based behavior suspends, in some degree, reality appraisal. In the case of a 2-year-old, the dividing line between fantasy and reality is fluid and easily transcended, while in a 3-year-old reality appraisal is more firmly established and the distinction between current reality, past reality, and fantasy is more easily made. The boundaries will of course be repeatedly blurred and often be ill defined. Hand in hand with these developments, however, fantasy increases in complexity. In the example which follows, we see how fantasy copes with both impulse and defense in a way which serves internal adaptation, but which seeks the cooperation of the real world for its reinforcement.

Susie, a bright 3-year-old, was well aware of her mother's pregnancy and frequently spoke of "our baby" in either the mother's tummy or her own. Following the mother's miscarriage in the fifth month of pregnancy, Susie had difficulty in sleeping through the night without joining the parents in their room. She also began to insist that she was not Susie but "Katie," a 12-year-old "big girl." After battles with her mother, Katie would return to her, commiserate, and agree that Susie was "such a naughty girl." She would become very upset and protest when her parents did not address her as Katie. In her fantasy Susie did not go to nursery school but went to "big school" instead. She demanded that her classmates and nursery school teacher, as well as her parents, comply with her insistence that she was Katie. She introduced herself to strangers and friends as Katie and, when questioned about Susie's whereabouts, explained that Susie lived up the road or was buying flowers. Her father recalled that, just before he took Susie to visit her mother in the hospital, they had bought flowers "because Mommy was feeling sad." Katie confided to her parents that Susie's daddy had died, but the next day she reported that he was alive again.

Susie's death wishes were scarcely disguised. Although they were clearly conflictual, her development was not yet sufficiently advanced to make effective use of repression. Instead she tried to rid herself of the conflict by dividing herself into a "good" and a "bad" girl. While both remained in consciousness, she repudiated Susie's role, and gave herself the maturity, and hence the instinctual controls, of an older girl. This reflected her wish to avoid criticism and loss of love. We may even postulate that she had a primitive self-ideal and an emerging self-critical faculty. But the death wishes could not be repressed; and she probably knew that Katie was an invention.

Susie, then, attempted to deal with her death wishes and fears through a defensive fantasy. The threatened arrival of a new baby had fostered the need to be more grown up; and the strength of her destructive wishes demanded a greater degree of control than this little girl was able to mobilize. By changing her identity, she could also disown responsibility for Susie's actions, while at the same time continuing to express them. In this instance, the fantasy attempted to reconcile opposing wishes.

Some children of Susie's age are capable of expressing their anxieties and conflicts in more symbolic forms which do not require a comparable degree of manipulation of reality, of their objects, or of their self representation. James, a 3¾-year-old boy, was preoccupied with phallic competitive wishes toward his father and concomitant castration anxiety. On a visit to his aunt, he challenged his father for the attention of his hostess. He told his aunt about the film *Star Wars,* and drew her attention to a small stick. This, he said, was his "life force," like that of Luke Sky Walker and Darth Vader. James said that he was Luke and that he was only just learning how to use the life force, i.e., the stick. He put on a "pretend" helmet so that he could not see what he was doing while he learned to use his life force. This was necessary because otherwise he might touch his leg with his life force and cause it to fall off. He stood with his eyes tightly shut, slashing at the air and turning scarlet with the effort and excitement. He asked his aunt if she could see Darth Vader and if she could see whether his leg was all right. When he was reassured, he said that he would take off the helmet and announced: "I have learned how to do it. My leg will be all right as I won't touch it now that I can see. . . . Do you know the story of *Star Wars*? Darth Vader dies. Wasn't that sad? But Luke had the life force then." James at once became quite placating to his father, whose attention was suitably distracted from the aunt by these goings-on. The boy then reassuringly told his father to put the helmet on James/Luke again, because he had not quite learned how to use the life force and keep his leg safe.

James had reached a stage at which he revealed castration anxiety. He expressed this in a crude symbolization. A stick with a "life force" was not very far removed from the part of the body it represented. James utilized the ready-made fantasy of *Star Wars* which afforded him the protective omnipotence of its heroes. He compensated for his vulnerability through identification with a figure representing masculine prowess. For all his adopted strength and power, the fear of losing a part of his body remained in consciousness, even though he shut his eyes in a vain attempt to exclude it.

John, an articulate and intelligent boy of 6½, chose to express himself, both in analysis and at home, through dramatized play enactments. He was not much interested in formal learning but was very well aware of his surroundings and had a large fund of knowledge. Fantasy play gave him pleasure and served him defensively. Conflicting wishes were kept at a distance because he strenuously held on to the idea that he was *only* playing.

During the second year of analysis the content of his fantasy games focused on family romances and suggested attempts to resolve his oedipus complex which had featured prominently in the material. For example, he introduced a game in which two brothers, Fred and George, ran off to find a new home. In one variation, one brother was rescued by a nice man. (John had a male therapist.) In another, the boys heard their father coming; Fred told George that he hated his father, and the brothers ran off together. In another version, both parents went to the hospital, Fred and George ran away, became assistant managing directors of a supermarket, and lived with a nice shopkeeper.

John also created a wide range of royal family fantasies. He pretended that he and the therapist were artists living in poverty who were nevertheless invited to the palace and later became King and Queen. On another occasion he became Prince Charles and turned his therapist into Prince Andrew. In this he reversed his real relationship to his older sibling. Later, John played a "Prince game" in which the royalty bestowed on him tremendous privileges and authority and compensated for his lowly school performance. In this way he raised his self-esteem and gave the clear impression of one "born to be King." He knew that his father could trace kinship to Queen Victoria.

John utilized his store of knowledge to create stories which matched his conflictual wishes and sought to resolve them through dramatic transformations which were acceptable and even a source of pleasure, as long as he could insist that he was "only playing." The links with the oedipal constellation remained evident to the analyst, however, in spite of John's creative disguise. Attempts at interpretation were met with dismissive rebuttal and an urgent demand to continue the play. The royal robes were diaphanous, but John had no more than one foot across the repression barrier.

We set out from the long established position that repression proper can scarcely be said to operate before the establishment of the repression barrier and the onset of infantile amnesia with the resolution of the oedipus complex. Indeed, neither James nor Susie shows evidence of repression proper. Both children display their current conflicts, disguised rather than repressed, while John appears to be at the threshold of this developmental achievement.

The masturbation fantasies of children in the latency period are evidence of repression proper and are not nearly so transparent as the fantasies we have cited above. They also serve subsidiary aims of compensating for a large variety of frustrations, deprivations, and disappointments.

Lucy, who was 9 when she began analytic treatment, was very fond of horses. She said she did not ride because it was too expensive and "anyway there was no room in the front garden for a horse." For several months she had kept an imaginary horse called Black Beauty who lived in her bedroom and to whom she talked. The mother tolerated the child's fantasy companion, and regretted the fact that the family could not pay for riding lessons. Lucy claimed that her father was getting fed up with the horse, but "he should not be angry as it might upset Black Beauty."

At school, among her peer group, horse games provided an outlet for fantasy. It was after such a game that Lucy lost her voice. On this occasion her friend had designated Black Beauty's brother, Prince, as Lucy's horse. Although Lucy herself denied any angry feelings about this, she said she would have to leave her friend time to "simmer down." She needed this dominating friend, who was full of ideas, but resented her control. She eventually confided that although she outwardly complied with her friend's directive and called her horse Prince, she took secret pleasure in pretending that it was really *she* and not the friend who was the rider of Black Beauty. In the *shared* symbolic fantasy with the friend, she could accept the friend's domination; in the *private* fantasy, the situation was reversed in a secret triumph.

Black Beauty played an important part in the course of Lucy's treatment. She brought him to the Clinic and tied him up in the waiting room, and her references to him indicated the nature of her conflicts. If she was feeling tired and lazy and her mother had pressured her, she claimed she rode him on the way. She reported on the "naughty things" of which Black Beauty was capable, such as knocking over her mother's favorite vase and eating the flowers. Black Beauty could also be obstinate and, once dressed, he wouldn't open his mouth to eat his breakfast, and once fed, he wouldn't go out.

The unconscious conflicts behind Lucy's use of, and fantasies about, Black Beauty are more difficult to establish than in the three younger children. Psychoanalysts will infer a good deal from the material, but its meaning was much more effectively hidden from Lucy herself. The overall inference is that Lucy has an established repression barrier.

In the examples we have cited, we can see a healthy use of imagination to solve problems and ensure gratification in fantasy. This is not to say that fantasy cannot be indulged at the cost of object relationships and achievements. To some extent we have equated the young child's play with fantasy: indeed, action-play is the principal mode in which small children can express and communicate what goes on in their minds.

The development of the capacity to play is subject to a variety of influences from early infancy onward. As Winnicott (1971) has so well described, it is in the first instance rooted in the interaction of mother and child. In certain cases studied at the Clinic, playful interactions between mother and small child were absent. Explanations for this state of affairs varied. Sometimes a mother expected her young child to play with toys, by himself, and to stay quiet and occupied. Sometimes the mother failed to respect her child's pleasure and absorption in play activity, and intruded or interrupted him. Sometimes a child's play was directed by the mother to a point at which her own fantasies or externalizations were imposed on him, so that he was not allowed to express his own wishes in his own spontaneous way. Yet again, play was sometimes directly denigrated on account of its "childish" and unrealistic content. Such attitudes may interfere with the child's capacity to enjoy his or her fantasies-in-action and even lead to their total inhibition. Fantasy play then becomes a source of disapproval, danger, and shame.

We have tried to illustrate some of the ways in which fantasy undergoes change in the course of development, becomes subject to increasingly sophisticated defense activity and censorship, and thereby plays an important role in internal adaptation. It is well known that when the psychoanalyst attempts to undermine tenuous defenses, the very young child's only recourse may be to obliterate the therapist's voice by shouting or by covering his ears. In this way he seeks to keep at bay the words that threaten to call attention to unwanted or disowned mental content. Although the child increasingly builds up internal controls and defensive maneuvers against the eruption of primitive wishes, the repression barrier remains relatively permeable until super-ego structuralization, drive diminution, and the other changes which usher in latency have brought about its consolidation. Henceforth preconscious and unconscious systems compartmentalize the mind, but the degree of permeability remains of vital importance. Some measure of this capacity remains essential for imagination and creativity. Excessive impermeability leads to mental woodenness, inhibition, excessive personal constraint, and intolerance of id derivatives in self and others. The extent to which the individual can fantasize and control his fantasy depends, not only on the permeability of the various censorships, but also on the developmentally acquired characteristics of his ability to play and imagine.

BIBLIOGRAPHY

GLOVER, E. (1949). *Psycho-analysis.* London: Staples Press.
HARTMANN, H. (1939). *Ego Psychology and the Problem of Adaptation.* New York: Int. Univ. Press, 1958.
WINNICOTT, D. W. (1971). *Playing and Reality.* London: Tavistock Publications.

The Personal Myth

Points and Counterpoints
ANNA POTAMIANOU, Ph.D.

ERNST KRIS, WHO INTRODUCED THE CONCEPT OF THE PERSONAL myth into psychoanalytic writings (1956), connected it to an autobiographical set of memories that serve as a protective screen carefully constructed to cover significant omissions and distortions in the life history of the analysand. He thought that in some cases the personal myth covers specific periods of individual history, while in others it covers the total life history; in both instances it becomes the object of strong cathexes and takes its final form during puberty and adolescence.

The economic function of the personal myth is to help maintain repression through the strong counterinvestment of a specific set of autobiographical memories, thus preventing certain experiences and impulses from reaching consciousness. The countercathected set takes the place of a repressed fantasy from which it derives part of its investment and which represents variations on the theme of the family romance. The early fantasies, combined with early memories and elements of the family romance, are incorporated into the myth, which is the end product of the reinterpretation and reorganization of previous experiences. Concerning the developmental point of view, Kris follows closely Freud's (1909) line of thinking.

Bion (1963), on the other hand, as could be expected, is more

Training analyst, Paris Psychoanalytic Society; member, Greek Psychoanalytic Study Group; Scientific Director, Center for Mental Health, Athens. Presented at the First Delphi Conference, August 1984.

faithful to the Kleinian view, making of the private myth an essential part of the learning apparatus in the early stages of the child's development. Bion understands the fragmentation and dispersion of the private myth (i.e., of the preconception concerning the parental couple that exists in the infant's mind) as being the result of destructive attacks on the parents derived from envy, greed, and sadism. These destructive impulses and the associated fantasies burden the individual's intuitive faculty and capacity to learn from experience. As this faculty is an important piece of the ego's equipment for the discovery of psychic reality, it is evident that the impact of such an obstruction can considerably affect ego development.

Although the developmental aspect is an important issue, this presentation will focus on the dynamics and on the economic aspect of the personal myth, and also will present my personal view of the concept.

The first point I would like to stress is that Kris and many other analysts believe that the representations which have been repressed and covered by the personal myth can be unveiled during analysis; the patient's history is thus reconstructed and his autobiography is, in a sense, restored; his "truth" is revealed.

For many analysts there is no truth to be uncovered. The reality of events is constantly permeated by the subject's imagination; what we call the history of an individual can be no more than what has persisted in his or her memory of a past transformed by maturation and development, influenced by the frustrations that meet the individual's demands, and by the ways in which castration anxiety is experienced. Thus, lifting repression and working through a screen memory inevitably confront us with another screen memory, which invites analysis.

In this context, a certain type of defensive cleavage is irreducible, as Braunschweig (1971) said. Repressions succeed one another and the separation between psychic events corresponds to a necessity. If the tendency to reduce this type of cleavage to zero point were to prevail, the consequence would be a confusion between inner and outer reality as well as between subject and objects.

Thus, complete objectivity and consistency of knowledge recovered in psychoanalytic treatment are only ideal fictions, and as such cannot be the aim of the analyst. What analysis aims at is the knowledge and acceptance of the constant oscillation of the mental apparatus between the manifestations of movements of desire and resistance to those movements. In that sense, the analytic process itself, which is caught in this oscillation, constitutes for the analysand an experience par excellence of consecutive motions marking the return of the repressed, followed inevitably by new repression.

One can say that analysis is a myth-historical event that can never become a history *stricto sensu*. From the historical perspective, it absorbs certain elements from concrete events that happened at a specific time and place and involved specific interrelational occurrences as well as the reliving of this past in another specific historical moment, that of the analysis. From the myth it retains the personal elaboration of these elements in the light of the subject's fantasies. In the psychoanalytic treatment the elements are supposed to be reported in words, not through acting or somatic manifestations.

It is true that myth was originally related to a sacred act, and there was a time, traces of which can be found in the *Odyssey,* when the term had the meaning of action as well as that of discourse.[1] Within the space of but a few lines, Homer ascribes to the word "myth" the meaning that has become familiar to us, that is the meaning of a narrative, but also an earlier meaning according to which myth is closely bound to action.

The evolution of language has given man possibilities other than discharge in action; the psychoanalytic process replicates this same itinerary: from action to logos. Through the interaction of the analytic relationship the analysand discovers that the things he says, the fictions, the myths he devises, go into the building of his history that develops in the light of his fantasies.

Aeschylus makes Prometheus say, "here are the facts, not words" (line 1080). In psychoanalytic terms, we could transcribe this as: "Here are facts as they emerge through the words," facts as they are shaped by each one of us through our mythicizing logos.

In psychoanalysis, the analysand feeds his own mythical cre-

1. In Book 21 of the *Odyssey,* line 71, it is said that Penelope tells the suitors (I translate freely): "the only justification you have been able to find for your actions is your ambition to make me your wife." "Myth" is used here for both "telling" and "actions."

ations into his analysis. His logos is mythical in the sense that
whatever he says and knows about himself, his past and his present, are products fashioned from fragments of perceptions and
events he has actually experienced, combined with elements that
do not correspond to any other reality but his own subjective
reality. These creations also are mythical in the sense that they
are verbalized, spoken, not enacted.

Psychoanalysis makes use of myth in two different ways: (1) as
a model-object that can absorb the needs, wishes, and conflicts of
Everyman (the oedipus myth, for instance); (2) as a vital synthesis (e.g., Aristoteles), a composition, through which the logos
of two subjects—analysand and analyst—deals with certain situations, events, and psychic productions.

There is, of course, still another thread which links analysis to
myth: and this is the question of origin. A myth, collective or
individual, relates how things started (for instance, how a series
of events was initiated). Consequently, it refers to origins in time
and to the idea of origin in general, i.e., the *arché*, which is
outside time. But the question of origins is also central to
analysis.

Following this thread, we are introduced to the core of the
personal myth. If we consider all the material an analysand
brings to his analysis as a myth-historeme, there is a central core
for which I propose to reserve the term of "personal myth."

This kernel consists of a representational constellation that
binds together elements of the three so-called primal fantasies:
i.e., the primal scene, the scene of seduction, and the scene of
castration. I would say that the personal myth is the thread that
runs through these three fantasies, weaving a conscious representational morpheme that infiltrates the individual's self perception and understanding of events and which molds the
screen memories. Its sources remain unconscious.

The place each person makes for himself in the interplay
between these fantasies and his perception of the outside
world—i.e., the stimuli of his environment—organizes the set of
conscious representations which go into building the myth. Autobiographical data are arranged in ways that can fit in with the
mythical conceptions of each person. As A. de Mijolla (1981)
said, we keep telling ourselves stories that correspond to our own
personal truth (p. 221).

When the child is faced with the subjective experience of the loss of the object, or with the object's inadequacies, what becomes unbearable for the child is the dependence on this object. The realization that this dependence is rooted in the biological reality of the differences of generations and in the existence of parental sexuality gets interwoven with the pain of realizing that the difference of ages also implies irreducible differences in capacities for control and for pleasure. This is a narcissistic traumatic experience, to which the perception of the differences of sexes that channels desires toward the two parents adds one more factor of considerable sexual stimulation and disappointment.

The response to these disappointments and losses and the attempt to correct them are autoactivities resulting in the emergence of the three schemas, called primal fantasies. Their mode of formation and their influence on psychic life seem to depend more on the personality structure of the individual than on their having been experienced in reality or in imagination. At least, this is what clinical facts indicate.

Personality structure also influences the organization of the personal myth. When projection holds the scene, the personal myth appears as if it were structured by, and enacted in, the external world. With the schizophrenic, the myth seems inscribed in the psyche of the subject through the experience of the all-invading objects. For the psychosomatic patient, one can say that the physical body becomes the holder of a myth which cannot be elaborated on the mental level. Depressive emptiness is often covered by the maniclike use of mythical productions developing around self-hatred and self-debasement. In all cases, beyond circumscribed neuroses, the myth is not constituted as a coherent psychic production.

In all cases the analyst comes across a central mythical core, around which remembrances, perceptions, and representations are arranged.

A patient of mine, Mr. A., a good-looking man in his 30s, had successfully finished his university studies and was now working in the field he had trained for. He came to see me because of a general malaise and difficulties in his relationships and work. He felt incapable of handling the demands of life. He complained of the fact that his interests always seemed to be split in two directions—between professional and artistic concerns; between two professional fields (actually he had chosen one, but was still thinking about the other); between women and men.

He thought he liked men; he had had many homosexual relations, but could not find real pleasure in the relationships. He considered his homosexuality as a debasement and a danger to his professional life. Much anxiety was attached to homosexual representations; he felt frustrated and guilty. But his relations with women did not bring him any satisfaction either; they were clearly colored by strong sadomasochistic tendencies and by the fear of closer contact. He was equally dissatisfied with his general relations to friends because he was conscious of being extremely aggressive in his dealings with them after an initial phase in which he left himself "too open," as he said, to the relationship.

The patient's discourse was vivid, full of interesting images; he was clearly a well-educated person. We decided to work together in spite of some factors which could raise questions concerning analyzability. Those factors were: the extreme sensitivity to separations, a way of thinking pervaded with magic, the massiveness of his investments, and the tendency to maintain a split between the somatic illnesses he referred to and psychic pain.

The first two years of analysis were by no means easy. Mr. A. insisted on his incapacity throughout his life to deal with his problems. His history, as presented, as well as his functioning, revealed the evidence of his inadequacies and of his fragility. He emphasized the overprotectiveness of his mother, her never failing care, but also her demands for total obedience, her violence when he misbehaved or refused to comply with orders, and her intrusive behavior. The mother was ever-present, the father was distant, left out of the mother-son loving couple, often ill, undemanding, uninteresting, and certainly not able to present his son with the model of a capable or strong man.

In the transference, especially during the first period, Mr. A. was most eager to please me, always in agreement with what I had to say. He meticulously cleaned his shoes before entering my office, keeping a slightly bent posture. Little by little a terrifying image of analysis emerged: It was a trap in which he was caught, while I, a magician, a surgeon with long sharp nails, or a midwife who would let him die (as he thought his mother had been responsible for the deaths of his two brothers), looked upon his suffering unmoved. I also was the anal-sadistic mother who tried to take away from him his thoughts as his own mother had wanted to take from him his worm-infested feces when he had been a small child.

He went through moments of depersonalization and phases when he experienced fragmentation and feelings of bursting. Often, especially during the first year, various physical illnesses were in the foreground; these ranged from serious ones to fevers and other unimportant ailments. Through them my patient solicited my attention and care, while offering proof of the frailty of his mental and physical defensive organization.

One day the patient told me that by now he was convinced that he was a desperate case: but how could it be otherwise, since he was as weak as his father had been? He then went on to tell me of his conviction of the correctness of a theory he said he once heard, that a child always took the sex of the weaker of the two parents. In his case it was the father who had been worn out by his mother in marriage. His father had lost all the joys and pleasures of life prior to his marriage (women; going out on a binge with male friends; drinking, party-going, singing, etc.). He had become a quiet, morose man, of no use to his wife or son.

Long ago Mr. A. had told me of his father's frequent injunctions to his wife, "Do not walk around the house half-naked in front of the child; send away the servant girl; the boy has grown up and we should not have her around." He also had spoken of the fury in his father's eyes when, as a very young boy, the patient had put on some tulle strips and tried to dance in front of his father and one of his friends. At that point I said, "He was of no use, except for interdictions."

The patient was amazed. He had never realized the importance or weight of this aspect of his father's role. Various new remembrances emerged, enabling him to see material already discussed in a new light: he saw himself playing, lonely and depressed in a room next to the parent's room; one day he had opened the door and seen his father caressing his mother's breasts. His mother had an air of abandonment and great pleasure. When he was very young, he had wished his mother could be kept in a tin box until he grew old enough to marry her. In his fantasy his father was put away in a dark storeroom and left

there lying in the dirt. The patient also recalled having grown
very fond of a young woman teacher, who, he thought, had eyes
only for his father.

Mr. A. began to understand the meaning of some of his
fears—those of corpses and of ghosts when he was young, and
his actual reluctance to visit his father's grave. He also became
aware of the reason he could not touch a woman's breasts, something he had up to now associated with breast feeding. (He had
been weaned early, because his mother's milk "hadn't been good
enough.") He could also work out the reasons for his homosexual attempts and their failure; why he was unable to have a
satisfying relationship with a woman; and whence came his need
to maintain a terrifying maternal imago. He remembered that
he had been very afraid of having to undergo an appendectomy,
as a young friend of his had, because the surgeon might
eventually discover something like ovaries in his belly. "Woman
and man," he said, "I wanted to have it both ways. That was what
the myth was about—the child getting the sex of the weak parent. If my father was disgustingly weak and ill, he could not be a
man giving pleasure to my mother; and if I was like him, I could
have mother's constant love and care, without incurring my father's hostility. I could also be the seductive, sweet, gentle woman for other men, but no pleasure was possible there either, as
my father did not accept me in that role." At this point he spoke
of a complementary aspect of his personal myth: the moment a
child is born (the child taking the sex of the weaker of the two
parents), an adult person is dying. This is, he thought, how the
world manages not to get overcrowded by people. This is—I
would add—how parental sexuality gets related to death and
castration.

I will end this case report here to discuss what I consider
important in the economy of the personal myth.

DISCUSSION

The economic function of the personal myth is to serve repression. But I think it fulfills yet another important role, which has
to do with the differentiation between inner and outer world.
The mythical constructions of an individual constitute what one

could consider as the most personal mode of shaping his or her own reality; they contribute to the structuring and maintenance of the individual's unique inner world.

Analysis is concerned with the intrapersonal, but on the intrapersonal keyboard desires and defenses mingle with the contributions of the outer world. Psychoanalysis, then, as already said, has the dimensions of a myth-historical event and the analyst has to accept the double allegiance of the analytic process to the stream of the myth and to the stream of the individual's history.

The mythical stream irrigates analysis with the flow of desires and with the individual's modes of treating those desires. It presents the analyst with the vicissitudes of representations animated by fantasies. The historical stream provides information that concerns the unfolding of the relational spectrum. What the patient brings to the analysis is a discourse, marked by gaps in its historical continuity and its signifying cohesion. The analyst's contribution to the process of analysis is his availability to listen, so that he may eventually introduce a different order in the way the patient apprehends and comprehends himself.

If the patient feeds into his analysis the mythical creations relating to his history, as perceived in the light of his fantasies, the analyst, on the other hand, remains oriented toward the analysand's associations, which he will use to link the myth to the history, in the very process of disconnecting them. By pinpointing the products of the fundamental structures in each patient's psychic world and their actual mode of expression (symptoms, dreams, character traits, acting out, somatization) which go beyond, but at the same time preserve the past, while transforming it, the analyst will succeed in making explicit their functioning, while following their development.

At this point a question arises to which analysts have given different answers. Many analysts believe that the personal myth has to be erased or diluted as repression is lifted so that the patient's history can be reconstructed. Others adopt the inverse position, claiming that it is the patient's myth, or the mythology, that should be reconstructed on the trail of the patient's history. The analyst's function should aim at restoring the symbolic value of these core fantasies (Nicolaïdis, 1971).

In my view, the problem in analysis is not to erase the myth in order to reconstruct history or to give priority to the symbolic function of the myth, but rather to help the patient assume the fact that his ego can never acquire complete control over the primary processes and that secondary processes will always be subject to the incursion of movements of desire. Finally, the only truth to be uncovered is the one pertaining to the existence and the power of the unconscious with the ensuing division in the psychic apparatus. This is valid for the analysand as well as for the analyst in the myth-historical event of their encounter.

Once we have acknowledged the dynamism of the creation of our myths, what role can we tolerate them to assume in our psychic economy?

They can certainly be viewed as a constellation of ideas, of representations, that emerge in order to fill the void left by repression. When the object escapes the subject's grasp, frustration and distress are the sources of an inner evocation of images and forms. What is unbearable for the ego, i.e., the evocative representations, is repressed, but repression leaves gaps in perception and memory which allow for omissions in the historical continuity of the subject's life. The gaps are filled by the mythical morphemes that shape the self-image and influence the perception and understanding of the surrounding world. Thus the mythical constellation of representations can be experienced by the analysand, and by the analyst, as a subjective creation arising from the break in continuity. But the same morphemes or representations can also be acknowledged as part of a creative process that ensures a participation in our own creation. Of course, this participation is quite different from the one encountered in the family romance construction, where the real parents are rejected. In the family romance, a fantasy of omnipotence usually shapes for the child a noble lineage that corresponds to an idealized image of the parents.

Here, the creation concerns the self-image and the molding of external events and of their perception into its matrix. Shreds of the individual's history and experiences—what Viderman (1977) called the little islands of the past—are bound together in a way that constitutes the fictions each person brings to his analysis; perceptual data and experiences are made to fit into the sketch traced by the thread running through the three primal fantasies, i.e., the personal myth. But the motivation in both instances—myth and family romance—is the same: defense against incestuous wishes; the desire to restore the traumatic experience related to parental sexuality by calling on infantile theories of sexuality; and the hope to recover, while reliving it in analysis, what has been lost or what has been experienced as insufficient. The patient's fiction is the only way he has to deal with the derivatives of his unconscious.

If to create is to see differently, to grasp the nature of things differently (Andreoli, 1972), and to produce one's own version of outer reality, the personal myth does just that, according to each person's capacity to weave pain and distress into a representative form. This is what Stein (1971) named the mythopoetic power of the individual. The myth reflects the individual's structure, and the structure shapes the myth.

This type of creation is, of course, not the end product of sublimation; it lacks the intention and the effort of artistic creation; it also lacks the deferment of pleasure and the delay of discharge orchestrated by thought, consciously oriented toward the artistic creation.

The play here is private; the stage and the auditorium are occupied by the same person. Nevertheless, I would say that the creator of a myth is a potential artist in the sense that the pleasure principle is the main motivating force in every creative process. The individual's self image and personal myth,[2] verbalized in the analysis, bring about the encounter of the individual with himself through the presentation of pieces of a text, introduced and reintroduced in the sessions according to a dynamically changing optic.

BIBLIOGRAPHY

ANDREOLI, A. (1972). Aux sources de l'expérience créative. In *Créativité ou Symptôme*, ed. N. Nicolaïdis & E. Schmid-Kitsikis. Paris: Coll. Psychopée, Clancier-Guernaud.

BION, W. (1963). *Elements of Psycho-Analysis*. London: Heinemann.

2. In the sense of the nonwritten word (Illiade, 1:443).

BRAUNSCHWEIG, D. (1971). Psychanalyse et réalité. *Rev. Franç. Psychanal.*, 35:655–794.

FREUD, S. (1895). Extracts from the Fliess papers. Letter 57. *S.E.*, 1:242–244.

———— (1909). Family romances. *S.E.*, 9:236–244.

GREENACRE, P. (1958). The family romance of the artist. In *Emotional Growth.* New York: Int. Univ. Press, 1971, 2:505–532.

KRIS, E. (1956). The personal myth. *J. Amer. Psychoanal. Assn.*, 4:653–681.

MIJOLLA, A. DE (1981). *Les visiteurs du Moi.* Paris: Belles Lettres.

NICOLAÏDIS, N. (1971). La réalité du mythe dans la cure psychanalytique. *Rev. Franç. Psychanal.*, 35:1011–1013.

STEIN, C. (1971). *L'enfant imaginaire.* Paris: Denoël.

VIDERMAN, S. (1977). *Le céleste et le sublunaire.* Paris: Presses Univ. de France.

Weeping during the Analysis of a Latency-Age Girl

MURIEL CHAVES WINESTINE, Ph.D.

I HAVE BEEN IMPRESSED WITH THE RELATIVE INFREQUENCY WITH which latency-age children weep during the course of an analysis. It was therefore of interest when such weeping occurred during my initial session with 7-year-old Jane. Although she was referred because of an "embryonic anorexia" which was encroaching upon her scholastic and social functioning, she offered her own reasons for wishing to see me. She explained that "a long time ago," when she was 4½, she accompanied her parents to a "classy" restaurant. While sipping from a fancy stemmed glass, it slipped from her fingers and the contents spilled all over herself and the tablecloth. At this point in her narration, she wept quietly and the tears flowed over her cheeks. She continued: she did not know why this accident troubled her so much since everyone, including the waiter, had been very nice to her. Maybe, she thought, she worried because it made her appear as a much younger child. Her parents later confirmed her account of this incident and were mildly amused that it continued to so impress their daughter.

Weeping frequently and inexplicably accompanied many of Jane's communications during analysis until one day she said to

Clinical Associate Professor, Department of Psychiatry, Cornell University Medical College; faculty, the Psychoanalytic Training Institute of the New York Freudian Society.

Earlier versions of this paper were read before the Cleveland Psychoanalytic Society on October 15, 1982, and the New York Psychoanalytic Society on October 11, 1983.

297

me, "I know now why I cry every time something reminds me of that accident in the restaurant; I knew then, after that happened, that I could never again be perfect." In this paper, I intend to use selected data from Jane's analysis to demonstrate the various meanings weeping had in this latency girl and how they became interrelated with other pathogenic components in this child's disturbance.

THE NATURE OF WEEPING

The shedding of tears furthers the homeostatic principle of regulating tension so well that it is a favorite mechanism of release during early childhood. However, the structure of latency ordinarily implies a striving for control along with a capacity to contain longings and drives and an ability to resolve conflicts within a fantasy system rather than through discharge phenomena such as weeping and crying.

For latency-age children, weeping and crying may represent evidence of loss of control over body, mind, and feelings (Bornstein, 1953), and may thus be looked upon with shame and embarrassment, as behavior which harkens back to prelatency days and which, if exposed, could earn them the label "crybabies."

In relation to superego conflicts typical of latency, Sarnoff (1976) described suppressed crying as a form of "crying inside," a phenomenon expressing sadness and guilt engendered by the child's ambivalence toward internal parental imagoes and the wish to do away with their psychic representations. Especially noteworthy is his observation that this suppressed crying is not only indicative of depressive affect but is often accompanied by psychosomatic symptoms such as vomiting, hives, rashes, stomachaches and headaches.

Although in common parlance weeping and crying are used synonymously, crying is characterized by vocalization and may or may not be accompanied by tears, whereas their presence is always a prominent feature in weeping, so that weeping may be defined as a shedding of tears elicited by an emotional stimulus.

That tears can be in the service of emotions and function to remove emotional as well as physical irritants is reflected in the dynamics of weeping in connection with the development of

object relations, unconscious symbolization, and concept formation. From a developmental point of view, Greenacre (1965) was
struck by the evidence that the capacity to shed tears is associated
with visual activity in humans. Although the lachrimal apparatus
is fully developed at birth and capable of secreting tears on
corneal irritation, tears do not accompany crying during the first
2 or 3 months of age. Indeed, the earliest emergence of tears in
emotional states (not dependent on physical stress) occurs at 4 to
6 months and corresponds to the early intrusion into the oneness
of the mother-infant relationship, as this is mediated through
vision. As vision develops, it extends the distance of contact between mother and child; particularly at about 6 months when
the child is able to sit up, vision greatly increases this range and
adds a more differentiated category of contact. It was Greenacre's impression that weeping then develops in conjunction
with the emotions evoked by seeing the stranger or missing the
familiar—and seeing may become the most sensitive axis to the
reaction to loss. It follows that vision becomes highly libidinized
with the eye as the site of trauma and potential conflict.

These propositions are consistent with the observations of
other psychoanalytic investigators who believe that the development of weeping is related to the development of self-nonself
differentiation. The development of tears may actually be a link
between the original reflex cry of the infant, conditioned to
purposive behavior as a call for help, and the development of
object relations leading to separation anxiety and grief reactions.
The ability to weep, then, might be related to the line of development that leads to the ultimate ability to conceptualize objects
internally. If weeping functions to expel painful affects from the
body, it also might function to expel the bad internalized object
(Sadoff, 1966).

While weeping occurs in a state of affective distress, it may
bring about a change of psychic attitude in which hostile aggression is neutralized and energy can also be utilized in a positive,
nondestructive manner (Haugsgjerd, 1980). Weeping can thus
have a central function in the working through of experiences of
loss, as in mourning. However, the relation between weeping
and hostile aggression is complicated (Greenacre, 1965). The
show of tears is under some control by the weeper. The tear-

fulness, which is part of the feeling of helplessness and resignation in a situation about which one can no longer expect to do
much actively, may secondarily take on further aggressive significance. It may express reproach against another person as
though to say, "See what you have done to me." This communicative function of weeping, aside from the soothing, reparative function, can be exploited for secondary purposes, especially exhibitionism serving sadomasochistic ends.

Furthermore, the analysis of weeping may reveal a frustrating
event which can be traced to deeply hidden narcissistic injuries.
It is within this framework that Greenacre's two classic clinical
papers (1945a, 1945b) may be viewed. Noting the developmental reciprocity between weeping and urination as tension-dis-
charge processes, Greenacre related weeping to childhood disturbances of urination and hypothesized that weeping represents a displaced wish to urinate. Clinical evidence derived
from women analysands provided clues pointing to its over-
determination: it represented resignation over not possessing a
penis; it symbolized the fantasy of an illusory penis, with weeping substituting for male urination; and it served aggressive demands for the male organ accompanied by fantasies of its possession. Greenacre described exhibitionism, a visual fascination
focused on male urination, and a body-phallus identification as
common in these women.

My data from a child analysis, while verifying Greenacre's
findings, further suggest that oral and anal elements may remain concealed and obscured by cathexes displaced onto later
phallic narcissistic traumas. I will also offer some speculations on
whether an anal trauma connected with an out-of-phase development contributed to my patient's unusual propensity for
weeping in the expression of symptoms and resolution of her
conflicts.

CASE PRESENTATION

BACKGROUND

An only child, Jane S. was very small for her age, and her doll-
like appearance and manner seemed at odds with her depressed
demeanor and taut body posture. Her speech had a mild sibilan-

cy, and there was an occasional slurring of words. Her parents sought treatment only after she had ceased to comply with their efforts to talk her out of her problems, when her eating constrictions threatened her school and social adjustment, and when her pediatrician assured them that her increasing physical complaints, i.e., upper respiratory ailments, rashes, stomachaches and headaches, were not organic in origin.

Disinterested in food since infancy, Jane was otherwise described as intelligent, delightful, obedient, agreeable, entertaining, and especially well-liked by adults. Other problems were denied or rationalized, although gradually a cluster of symptoms involving compulsions and fears emerged. The onset of her difficulties was attributed to an incident that occurred the previous year: on a visit to a friend's house, the child's mother forced Jane to eat her lunch after which Jane gagged and vomited. Thereafter, to allay Jane's spreading anxiety, Mrs. S. collaborated in countless maneuvers to assure Jane that she would not be forced or even asked to eat—to no avail. Jane's anxiety at school so mounted in anticipation of the lunch hour, that her teacher finally insisted that help be obtained.

It is significant that Jane was born with an anal stricture which was treated for the first 6 months by frequent digital dilations. This failed to ameliorate the condition and in order to reduce pain, a procedure of digital extraction of feces was followed by mother and nursemaid. At 3 years, a barium enema indicated that there were no abnormal bowel conditions. Eventually a new stool softener was effective in forming slippery and slimy stool, thus alleviating the condition. The stool softener was discontinued when Jane was approximately 4 years, and aside from occasional constipation, elimination proceeded uneventfully. Bladder training was started at 2½ years by providing Jane with a potty seat and continued uncoercively with Jane training herself and proudly showing off the urine in the potty.

From infancy, Jane showed little interest in either sucking or eating. This became more fixed around 3 years when she displayed a marked disinterest in sweets. Her pediatrician's findings were unremarkable, and he attributed her small stature to her genetic endowment. He was encouraging when told that an analysis was underway.

Soon after birth, Jane was reared by a succession of live-in nursemaids and housekeepers. Although they were carefully chosen, there was the inevitable history of loss and change. Mrs. S. worked long hours, often not seeing Jane during weekday evenings. In good conscience, she tried to compensate during weekends. Mr. S., although sporadically more available to Jane during the week, was often away on business.

Mr. and Mrs. S. presented themselves as a tight family unit, who spent weekends and holidays together, who loved each other and their child, and who were devoted to providing her with whatever she needed. With this background of support Jane began her analysis.

TREATMENT

In identification with her parents' denial of her emotional problems, Jane initially sought to keep busy during the sessions, expressing the wish to "keep my mind off my troubles." Nevertheless, she showed warmth and a rich capacity for relatedness. She soon revealed her longings when early in treatment she said to me, "I like you and wish I could stay here." Transference wishes established me as an analyst-mother whose office and residence were adjacent. In doll play Jane created a similarly combined school and residence where the pupil-daughter was never separated from the teacher-mother. These preoccupations prompted passive aggressive demands upon her actual mother in the form of an incipient school phobia: Mrs. S. usually dropped Jane off at school each morning before she rushed off to work. Previously, Jane had not objected, but shortly after she began analysis, as they approached the school, Jane complained of nausea, vomited several times, and pleaded with her mother not to go to work, insisting that she needed her *now*. Distressed, Mrs. S. was conflicted over this rapid decline in Jane's compliance. In the course of discussions with me, Mrs. S. reluctantly came to her own conclusion that she must spend more time with Jane during midweek evenings. Although genuinely concerned, Mrs. S. resented this encroachment on her time, but when I explained the imminence of a school phobia, she complied with her own recommendation. Upon being promised by her mother that she would make more time available during the evenings, Jane quickly relinquished her hold on her mother during the mornings.

Sometime later in my waiting room, I found Jane sitting on her nursemaid's lap quietly weeping. Still weeping in my office, she explained that she usually saw a patient's coat in the waiting room closet; this served as a hint that I was in my office, even though she could neither see nor hear me beyond the closed doors. Today, the coat was missing and it felt as though I was missing as well. "It felt as though no one was there." Jane's associations led to the frustration she felt when she made frequent telephone calls to her mother's office and could not reach her, though she often knew that her mother would not be available. The worst feeling was when she called at the end of the day and not even the secretary answered because the switchboard was "cut off." I told Jane that her weeping suggested that when she missed her mother, it made her feel not only sad and lonely but also helplessly cut off and angry. I added that she felt the same way about me today when she could not see me as soon as she arrived. When the session was over, Jane empathically but also diplomatically explained to her nursemaid (who was offended) that her weeping had nothing to do with her, but that "I have feelings about my mommy that get carried over to Dr. Winestine."

Jane recalled other feelings of being "cut off" through associating my needlework with her maternal grandmother, whom she had not seen "in a very, very long time." To my further surprise, she added, "And did you know that my grandfather never saw me and he *never* saw my mother!" I wondered how this was possible and she exclaimed, "Because he is blind." Weeping accompanied this explanation and I asked whether she thought that her blind grandfather could weep for her since her own weeping now seemed to be a possible identification with his blindness in connection with the nonseen, lost object. Jane had accepted her mother's explanation that she no longer saw her grandparents because they lived too far away—though it confused her, as it did me, since I knew that they actually lived nearby in an adjacent state. Although Mrs. S. had not mentioned this during our exploratory meeting despite my usual questions about grandparents, she now confirmed that her father has been blind since his sixteenth year and she denied any psychological effects by attesting to his immense financial and professional success. Mrs. S. did complain that her parents were insufferably controlling, hostile, and intrusive. Her mother, especially, was hateful toward Mr. S. and tried to exclude him from family visits. Finally, over some petty disagreement concerning Jane's fifth birthday party, Mrs. S. terminated all contact, declaring that she never again intended to see her parents. In response to Jane's probing, Mrs. S. eventually told her the truth about why she no longer saw her grandparents. Jane's longings for and am- bivalence to her grandmother had implications for her rela- tionship with her own parents as well as for the transference.

In answer to my question, Jane explained that it was unusual for her to weep in front of anyone. At home, though, she often curled up like a baby into a small space in her closet and wept in solitude. During sessions, she began to play out her fantasies about unborn babies, especially how they move up and down inside the mother's stomach the way an elevator goes up and down its shaft. "Ooh," she said, "maybe that has something to do with why I'm afraid of elevators." The fantasy represented a regressive wish to be in utero, a state in which she and mother were inseparable and to which Jane humorously added, "There was always room service." But she feared that the elevator would crash, or go out of control, or that the gates would jam, and she would never get out.[1] She associated the elevator gates with the sliding sides of her crib: she recalled that after she could climb over the sides of the crib, she would do so and sneak into her parents' bedroom and try to hide underneath her mother's long dressing gown. Initially, her mother had laughed, but subse- quently she exploded with anger. It was much safer to gratify her fantasies in the closet, where her tears made her nice and warm and everything was under her own control. We worked on

1. These fears, centered on the "up and down elevator," seemed to me to be graphic expressions of Jane's early sensations and feelings when mother and nursemaid had digitally probed and removed stools. These concerns surfaced more directly in Jane's subsequent material and could then be in- terpreted. On the other hand, her apparent wish for and fear of a sibling (in her fantasies about unborn babies) never became clear.

her conflictual feelings: that she displaced onto the elevator her feelings of helplessness but also her fear of rage (her own as well as her mother's) going out of control.

Baby games appeared in the transference as she snuggled and hid under a table while calling out to make sure I was there. At home, however, she surreptitiously bit her mother and was heard to murmur under her breath, "I hate you." Quickly, the oral aggression was somatized: her throat felt sore and she was anxious lest she choke on her phlegm; the stuff was so disgusting that she neither wanted to keep it in nor to let it out, and she did not know what to do. She was further agitated because the school nurse, feeling provoked by Jane's incessant complaints, said something about a tonsillectomy. Jane's associations to "disgusting stuff" related to times in the past when she felt the same way about her BM—she did not want to keep it in, but it hurt too much to let it out; it felt "too dangerous." I suggested that perhaps she now worried about letting anything disgusting leave her mouth so soon after she had dared to express angry feelings at her mother by biting and whispering hatred. I said I knew it had hurt her, in the past, to let go of the contents of her bowels. The pain may have become connected with thoughts and fears of abandonment whenever she released not only her loving and agreeable feelings but also the feelings that were hateful and bad. Was it possible that she experienced the nurse's insensitive comment about the tonsillectomy as punitive, as she had felt about the pain connected with the bad BM? (There was no evidence at this time of any recall of the barium enema.)

In her second year of analysis resistances related to the developmental and conflictual nature of Jane's compliance and efforts at control became increasingly evident. One day she sat in the middle of the floor, exposed, vulnerable, and weeping. She objected to her mother's intrusion while she had played with a friend. She added that mother had instructed her that "analysis is a place to get things out." Jane protested helplessly that she had "nothing" to let out—no words, no answers, no feelings; no thoughts popped into her head, and she felt like a "dope." This time I experienced Jane's weeping as a reproach now cast in the anal mode. I said that along with her mother's intrusiveness, she might also resent me; I was being intrusive by asking her to tell me her thoughts—that is, to comply with the analytic rule; she might fear that I, too, would not want to be with her unless she complied. I added that her weeping might express her conflicts over wishes not to comply and to make me feel bad and guilty.

In this context two other aspects of Jane's communications were significant. First, during this phase her talking was often interspersed with yawning. When I finally asked why she thought she yawned so much, she responded, "I wish you could know what I mean without my having to tell you, without my using words."[2] Second, I observed an onrush of speech, characterized by compulsive detail which obscured rather than clarified meaning; it was as though her determination to leave nothing out concealed her wish to reveal nothing. Accordingly, her thoughts seemed ill-formed and diffuse, in contrast to the brightness with which she repeated and replicated her mother's opinions. Furthermore, her confused thoughts seemed to be indicative of her confused body schema as demonstrated in her drawings, bodily awkwardness in sports, and extremely poor block building. The yawning may have attested to preverbal regressive wishes for merger and new possibilities of internalization through breathing. But it also seemed likely, in view of the passivity with which she experienced the anal phase, that a sense of mastery and autonomy in regard to motoric development and speech normally negotiated during the rapprochement stage of separation-individuation was incomplete. Apparently, Jane did not experience words and thoughts, particularly when they conveyed aggressive impulses, as her own productions. I interpreted that perhaps her yawning now appeared as a transference wish that I remove undesirable words from her mouth as her mother had removed the BM from her anus. Following this work, Jane dared to tell me that in her mind, all along, she had wanted to call *me* a "dope."

Immediately thereafter Jane reported her first dream: "I was

2. Near the end of Jane's analysis, the yawning was superseded by a type of gasping between sentences, which, according to Jane, represented abortive breathing; she feared that if she took the time to breathe fully, another student in class might interrupt and intrude upon her answer with still another question, thus depriving Jane of an opportunity to complete her own thoughts and answers.

in the park with my class and a man came along and chose me *first* to go with him. Then he began to roll me down the hill and tumbled on top of me. I was frightened." Although the over-determined meaning of "to be first" unraveled throughout the analysis, Jane's initial associations were that to be first meant to be ahead of the others, i.e., the smartest, the most perfect, who never made a mistake. But it also meant to be "first in line," i.e., the smallest. To be small was to be perfect as long as she was perceived as a cute, smart, little 4-year-old rather than as a grotesque "midget" (a reference to her own small stature). "I'm not big on eating" was the way Jane put it, implying her wish to exert control over her body as well as over her environment. To be perfect also meant to have a perfect body; it was in connection with this idea that a profound bisexual fantasy and identification emerged: "Sometimes I wish I were a boy who could always turn back to being a girl. When I pee, I pretend I'm a boy and I do it like a boy. In school, I play only with the boys. But the ones willing to play with me are not the ones popular with the other boys." She believed that boys exerted admirable control over their urine, in contrast to girls who "have to go all the time." Jane told me that her mother urinated excessively and was even teased at work because of this. Jane's eyes filled with tears which rolled down her cheeks as she expressed displeasure over being constantly reminded by her mother to urinate, whereas actually Jane identified with her father and deliberately withheld and controlled her urine. I learned that she saw her father urinate since they performed their morning ablutions together. She acknowledged that they used to bathe together on weekends until she was told she was "too big." It also emerged that Jane dealt with her excitement by compulsive masturbation which stopped only because her "pebble" (clitoris) became sore. She described the soothing quality of the masturbation, acknowledging that she missed it as an aid in falling asleep.

Soon thereafter, Jane developed a "snout" tic. She described a wish to thrust her tongue against the fleshy inside of her upper lip. There was an itch and it felt as though something was stuck inside the flesh that could neither be reached nor removed. She considered it less disgusting to use her tongue than her thumb, which would have exposed her wish to suck. A drawing of this ideation represented a bizarre mouth-anus with prominent teeth. Jane likened the pleasure of sucking the flesh to "landing on a soft quilt." (Her transitional object had been a soft quilt which her father discarded when she was 5 years old.) I interpreted the sucking as a replacement for the relinquished masturbation, indicating that it had the same soothing qualities as the lost quilt, the lost "pebble." Derivatives of oral components of the tic were expressed through further drawings and play and revealed fantasies that her throat was like a "grinding machine that turned food into BM" as well as oral-incorporative wishes for a penis. Eating inhibitions and constrictions could now be interpreted as also representing her wish to exert control over what went into her body, in contrast to the lack of control she had felt over what came out.

Jane's conflicts over being a girl, exemplified by her weeping and emulation of male urination, were in part an identification with her father as the aggressor. She related how aggressively and sadistically he had reacted to her eating and food difficulties, particularly when she stuffed food into her cheeks and failed to swallow. Once, he poured a bowl of oatmeal over her head. And on her fifth birthday, he pushed her face into the birthday cake after she had poked her finger into the icing. I interpreted how her oral impulses were thus drawn into a sadomasochistic relationship with her father. She recalled that in restaurants, after going to the bathroom, she often walked back to the table very slowly and exhibitionistically, provoking her father's impatience and enjoying this control over him. Subsequent associations referred again to her anger at the friend's mother who had forced her to eat. "I could have murdered her," Jane said. I could then interpret the defensive function of her fixation on this woman and that the phobia connected with her eating served to screen out her fear and rage and retaliative wishes related to her father.

After this hour, Jane baked brownies at home and ceremoniously arranged for us to eat them during a session. She went out to "trick or treat" on Halloween, ate and hoarded huge amounts of candy. She began to eat volumes of food and gradually the symptoms related to eating disappeared, facilitating extensive socializing. Ironically, Mr. S. objected when she gained weight. In discussion with me he revealed his perfectionistic ideal for Jane which was connected with his original desire for a boy child—but not one resembling himself, considered homely, but one who would better serve his narcissism.

In the middle of the second year of her analysis, Jane entered a phase during which she appeared for sessions in her favorite afterschool apparel, a silver space suit, to which she incongruously added elaborate hairdos. She drew overadorned girls carrying balloons, flowers, and Yo-Yos in their hands and wearing high fancy hats. Other drawings demonstrated the relationship between her bisexual fantasies and her ambivalence and hostility toward each parent: her mother was alternately depicted as a "cloud lady" subject to cloudbursts and as a beautiful but foolish woman who did not even know that one of her long earrings had fallen off and was missing; her father was hanged in effigy and ridiculed in front of his colleagues. She proposed playing a trick on her mother to cause her to lose bladder control. But mostly Jane proceeded to admire herself in the floor-length mirror on a bathroom door adjacent to my office while complaining that her mother spent so much time applying her makeup and looking at *herself* in the mirror.[3] Jane poignantly added, "What I like about it here is that you have no one to look at but me." Thus she became accessible to the interpretation that much of the phallic embellishments in her drawing were also in the service of healing her narcissistic injuries.

Dwelling on phallic themes, Jane spent many sessions playing with a favorite toy, a self-fashioned slingshot. Concomitantly, a neck tic appeared in which she stretched her head to the side. In response to my question whether the stretching was related to the stretched rubber band in the slingshot, she explained that there was a pain in her neck and she wished there was a "hole in the back of my neck to let out the pain." She recalled being told that when her mother was a child, she had a slingshot and once shot at the neck of a boy who sat in front of her. Jane then performed tricks with her double-jointed thumb. She told me that she also exhibited this trick thumb to the boys at school and

3. The mother's excessive use of the mirror might reflect a developmental lack of mirroring of her femininity as a consequence of her father's blindness.

confessed that she felt delighted when they ran away from her in disgust. I interpreted her wish to show boys that she, too, had something with which to disgust and attack but also excite them, helping her to understand its phallic equivalence.

I suggested to Jane that the pain in her neck seemed reminiscent of the pain in her anus, but at this time might also represent her identification with the attacker (since she had agreed that she was being a "pain in the neck," i.e., a pest, as far as the boys in school were concerned). In this context I reconstructed some of the feelings she may have experienced during the barium enema. When she returned for her next session, she reported that after checking with her parents about the barium enema, she learned something she had forgotten: because she had been struggling and crying, the doctor had requested that her father hold her down during the entire procedure. Jane then recalled her first dream about the man tumbling on top of her and said that now she thought that the man in that dream represented her father. Eventually, she expressed anxiety that the vagina, like the anus, had to be stretched to accommodate the big penis, the one she saw when she used to bathe with her Daddy.

Jane then wept, stating that it was "not proper to talk about such things." She told me that her mother was currently on jury duty and could send people to jail (presumably Jane and her father). Superego admonishments derived from the image of mother as jailor gave rise to further resistance during ensuing sessions.

At this point her weeping could be interpreted as being related to her own frightening, forbidden, sexual feelings, her crying and fright when she was given the barium enema, and her excitement when she took baths together with her father.

This interpretation was followed by a series of dreams dealing with oedipal themes in which superego conflicts were resolved by defensive splitting of self and object representations into preoedipal and oedipal objects. The preoedipal concerns were illustrated by a dream about a relationship with an older sister (the analyst) who cooked and played with her and who sometimes shared the father, though at other times he was absent. Her frank oedipal rivalry for her father's attention was illustrated by the following dream: "I was riding alone in a convertible car, one without a top." An exciting event of the previous evening provided the day residue: Jane's mother had inserted her finger into a hole in her husband's undershirt and playfully torn it to shreds. Jane joined in the fun until her father was without a shirt, "topless," and Jane admired his hairy chest. She had no trouble recognizing that her father was represented in the dream as the topless convertible; she realized that being alone with him was similar to the first dream, when she was chosen "first," which she now understood to mean being chosen ahead of or instead of mother. A more benign superego was evidenced when she expressed relief that she now found it less scary to be "first." Moreover, the convertible might also apply to herself; and she denied that she still wanted to go back and forth, i.e., convert, between being a girl and a boy. As a matter of fact, at present she played only with the girls.

Although Jane's oedipal competitiveness had become overt, her ambitions remained characterized by urethral and phallic elements. She wept over her athletic incompetence and awkwardness and felt frustrated in her aspirations to perform gymnastics like an "Olympic champion." She developed a transitory body tic in connection with her identification of her body as a fecal phallus. She stiffened prior to falling asleep and likened this stiffening to the strain she experienced during defecation. She told me that a long time ago, when her mother used to remove the BMs with her fingers, Jane thought that the other half of the BM remained inside of her. She corrected my comment that it might have represented a wish for a baby, and said, "No, I think that I thought it was like a penis inside me." Soon thereafter, she was fascinated with pictures of dolphins in one of my books and recalled, from her recent trip to Florida, how graceful and slippery they had appeared as they flopped about in the water doing somersaults. I ventured a reconstruction: I suggested that admiring the slippery and graceful dolphins revived a past memory of her own slippery BMs; they had fallen out of her body following the use of a stool softener. While the stool softener relieved her pain and helped to form the slippery BMs, they fell out of her into the water, thereby eliminating her control over them or an opportunity to integrate the experience into her body image. Instead, it may have represented a loss connected with her belief that one half of the BM had remained within her and was like a penis. Jane wept in response, and I recalled that the accident when the glass slipped out of her fingers had happened soon after the loss of the illusory "feces-penis" and may have so humiliated her because it had reminded her once again of her sense of loss and being out of control.

In the next session, as though she had figured it out all by herself, Jane said, "I know now why I cried every time something reminded me of that accident. I knew that after it happened, I could never again be perfect." Working through a major feature of the restaurant screen memory, namely, the collapse in her capacity to deny her sense of body imperfection and the public display of her shame, led to greater insight into the nature of her depressive affect as one of the sources of her weeping. Following this work, in the third year of analysis, she proceeded gradually to master the Yo-Yo, demonstrated better and more logical block building, and, with the aid of a coach, improved her gymnastic skills.

One day during this phase, Jane came to her session with a bloody nose and most reluctantly told me the following: a few weeks ago, while her parents were reorganizing her room, she was jumping on her bed and inadvertently spilled a glass of juice over the floor. Since her father had already warned her to stop jumping, he became angry and smacked her across her face causing a nosebleed. At the time, Jane became frightened and docile. Telling me about this incident in her session, she ventured a fantasy: she wished that blood would fall all over her homework and when the teacher asked why this happened, Jane would blame her father. I interpreted the self-destructive aims in her conflict. The price she paid for wishing to punish her father also involved punishing herself in the form of exhibiting this messy homework. I further suggested that the revival of feelings connected with the accident in the restaurant might have prompted her to act it out again; the spilling of the juice on the floor may have repeated the spilling from the stemmed glass, in both of which losing control was equated with making a mess. This time, however, she succeeded in provoking Daddy to attack her for messing, as she may have felt he was doing during the barium enema.

Jane wept profusely. It made her feel sad to have such bad thoughts about her father and she was glad that he was on a business trip to a faraway city and thus could not know of her thoughts. This regression to magical thinking was implemented by references to witches. She watched the television show, "Bewitched," in which women gang up on a man. Finally, I said that I, too, might seem like a witch, one who still made her have bad thoughts about her father. This made me castrating like her grandmother who she knew hated her father and who had wished to eliminate him. Jane also wept when she said that she never liked to have bad thoughts about me. We analyzed how she wished to repudiate any bad or ambivalent feelings toward me because of her wish to maintain me as the loving grandmother, the one for whom she longed and whom she missed and who gave her animal crackers and napped with her. She told me that she had also missed me during a recent vacation trip with her parents during which she had had the following dream: "You called me by a special and favorite nickname, which only my mommy uses." Jane's association was that her mother would feel angry if anyone else knew this secret name. I interpreted her fear that her mother might withdraw her love if she knew of Jane's attachment to me and how in the transference I could then be viewed as the grandmother who was the intruder. Jane might even worry that her mother would stop her seeing me as she had stopped the visits to her grandmother. At this point Jane's weeping could also be interpreted as the expression of her wish to expel the bad introjects—her own intrusive and bossy mother, and her sadistic father—but she feared the consequences of never seeing them again and of losing their love. This had been her mother's actual fate. My assumption that Jane struggled to resolve this conflict by remaining preoedipally attached to her mother was derived from her currently expressing envy of her aged dog whose feces were being removed digitally by Mrs. S.

The theme of nosebleeds stimulated associations to menstruation, a topic that was then being discussed in Jane's school. We continued working through the displaced libidinal and aggressive meanings of the body products and secretions—stool, urine, blood, and tears. Jane excused herself for the first time during a session in order to urinate in the bathroom. She said that she no longer held back her urine and while she knew she was too young, she frequently checked whether she was menstruating. She looked forward to it, even though she was not completely clear what it had to do with having a baby. She spent several sessions looking at books about the body, and sought clarification about the differences and functions of the male and female organs. Her drawings reflected greater sophistication and differentiation.

Her parents too were gratified by the progress Jane made during her analysis. Her father proudly reported a noteworthy incident to me: he had told her that she was tired and ordered her to bed early, whereupon she said, "How do you know if I'm tired, it's not your body, it's mine." He also told me of a successful family ski holiday during which Jane had separated from them to attend ski classes and learned how to ski. She also enjoyed a school trip of a week's duration. She then arranged with her best friend to attend sleep-away camp and no longer felt criticized by her friends for being too conforming and proper.

At the end of her 3-year analysis, she was able to separate comfortably from her parents, function well at school, participate in sports, and enjoy age-appropriate activities with peers of the same sex.

DISCUSSION

Overt, profuse, and frequent weeping is rarely seen during the analysis of latency-aged children. It is therefore not surprising to find that, in Jane's case, weeping was an overdetermined behavior that served a variety of functions: it was a mode of tension release, a means of expressing affects, and a symptom—a compromise formation of impulse and defense.[4]

4. After the completion of this paper, a related article on weeping (Wood and Wood, 1984) was published. While distinguishing between weeping and tearfulness, the authors suggest that the tearful feeling state during an analytic session is occasioned by the ego temporarily threatened with being inundated by complex memories and affects for which the ego cannot provide appropriate satisfying and integrated verbal expression.

While the preceding analytic material provides clear examples of each of these functions, it is less obvious how and why weeping, rather than another form of behavior, assumed such prominence and significance. I would speculate that the reasons are to be sought in the anal trauma. In Jane's case, the out-of-phase, excessive stimulation of her anus may have prematurely activated the libidinization of the anal zone and interfered with the natural dominance of the oral phase, thereby upsetting the orderly sequence and timetable of libidinal and aggressive organization so crucial to drive and ego development. While self-nonself differentiation and the establishment of an intact body image normally aided by the proper sequencing of phases were thus thwarted, a significant degree of differentiation did occur as attested to by Jane's relatively intact capacity for object relations. That her eyes became a site of conflict was particularly exemplified by weeping as her primary, somatized response to her perception of loss. It was as though "the disappointed eye, failing to find the lost object, behaves very much like the physically irritated or traumatized eye which defends itself with soothing tear lotion" (Greenacre, 1965, p. 213).

Freud (1917), in discussing the transformation of instincts, stressed that one part of the body may become unconsciously analogous to another part and that an organic correspondence reappears in the psychic sphere as an unconscious identity. There was evidence that Jane had a fused mental representation of mouth and anus which she graphically depicted in her early drawings. The anal manipulations during the oral phase led to a distorted libidinal development. It may be of even greater importance, however, that Jane did not experience the "supercharged moment" of the anal phase (Pine, 1980), the control over bowel movement. The whole experience of giving up excrement was incompletely perceived and blurred. Consequently, Jane may have remained on guard about soiling and wetting and formed a substratum of anxiety, as though she had actually been subject to toilet accidents. Indeed, the fear of a soiling accident may have been the primary experience defended by the screen memory of the accident in the restaurant. On the other hand, a sense of control, pride, and mastery in connection with her urination, and her capacity to interrupt and resume it, contributed to a sense of an integrated and well-functioning self. The lack of control over her bowels may have led to a compensatory use of urethral control and an exacerbated fantasy of an illusory penis and bisexual identification in her quest for perfection.

It is possible that the functions of her mouth—eating, breathing, yawning, and talking—were symbolically tied to those of the anus and as such felt to be too aggressive and subject to external control and intrusion. Paradoxically, while weeping is ordinarily experienced as a loss of control by latency children, in Jane weeping inherited the compensatory functions of urination. Moreover, the free flow of tears was in sharp contrast to her early inability to let go of the contents of her bowels.

The analysis of weeping revealed a traumatizing event which was also linked to more deeply hidden narcissistic injuries—the loss of her imagined penis following the expulsion of the feces. The illusory penis, derivatives of which were expressed during the analysis, was maintained as a psychic reality to protect her against narcissistic depletion (Grossman and Stewart, 1976). The fantasy of absorbing the highly valued penis into her body is typical for the girl during the anal phase, during which possession of phallic power is represented in the imagination as an anal incorporation of the father's penis. In Jane's case, visual and oral incorporation continued in response to the additional stimulation provided by her father's exposure. It might be argued that for Jane there was a suffusion of the entire organism with stimulation—which was further burdened by the sexual and aggressive experiences connected with her father. This may have led, on the one hand, to her readiness to develop somatic symptoms in response to all kinds of stress (Galenson and Roiphe, 1971). On the other hand, this suffusion led to a relative lack of specificity of discharge which was later reproduced when one response too readily and inappropriately substituted for another, e.g., when the urinary urge was transformed into weeping. This factor also gave rise, during Jane's analysis, to a variety of autoerotic discharges and defensive activities, of which Jane's tics, masturbation, and even weeping may be examples. When the veneer of her compensated behavior broke down under stress, it revealed these polymorphous perverse drives very close to the surface.

SUMMARY

Prior to analysis, Jane's depressed demeanor and somatization were suggestive of suppressed crying. Overt weeping came to the fore only in the treatment. The analysis disclosed the over-determination of this symptom and the variety of functions it served. In addition to being a mode of tension release and a means of expressing affects, it was involved in conflicts. Weeping also represented a wish for contact coupled with a desire to attack, both of which were defended against. From a developmental and genetic point of view, her weeping may be perceived as symptomatic of the narcissistic vulnerability that inevitably follows an out-of-phase overstimulation and its influence on the interrelated drive and ego formation. From a dynamic point of view, weeping was used in the service of intrapsychic conflicts derived from all phases of development.

BIBLIOGRAPHY

BORNSTEIN, B. (1953). Masturbation in the latency period. *Psychoanal. Study Child*, 8:65–78.
FREUD, S. (1917). On transformations of instinct, as exemplified in anal erotism. *S.E.*, 17:125–133.
GALENSON, E. & ROIPHE, H. (1971). The impact of early sexual discovery on mood, defensive organization, and symbolization. *Psychoanal. Study Child*, 26:195–216.
GREENACRE, P. (1945a). Urination and weeping. In *Trauma, Growth, and Personality*. New York: Int. Univ. Press, 1952, pp. 106–119.
_____ (1945b). Pathological weeping. *Ibid.*, pp. 120–131.
_____ (1952). Some factors producing different types of genital and pregenital organization. *Ibid.*, pp. 293–302.
_____ (1953). Penis awe and its relation to penis envy. In *Drives, Affects, Behavior*, ed. R. M. Loewenstein. New York: Int. Univ. Press, pp. 176–190.
_____ (1965). On the development and function of tears. *Psychoanal. Study Child*, 20:209–219.
_____ (1973). The primal scene and the sense of reality. *Psychoanal. Q.*, 42:10–41.

318   *Muriel Chaves Winestine*

GROSSMAN, W. I. & STEWART, W. A. (1976). Penis envy. *J. Amer. Psychoanal. Assn.*, 24:193–212.
HAUGSGJERD, T. L. (1980). The release of tears. *Int. Rev. Psychoanal.*, 7:299–308.
HEILBRUN, G. (1955). On weeping. *Psychoanal. Q.*, 24:245–255.
LACOMBE, P. (1958). A special mechanism of pathological weeping. *Psychoanal. Q.*, 27:246–251.
LÖFGREN, L. B. (1966). On weeping. *Int. J. Psychoanal.*, 47:375–381.
MAHLER, M. S. (1963). Thoughts about development and individuation. *Psychoanal. Study Child*, 18:307–324.
PINE, F. (1980). In the beginning. Read at the New York Psychoanalytic Society, May 27.
SADOFF, R. L. (1966). On the nature of crying and weeping. *Psychiat. Q.*, 40:490–503.
SARNOFF, C. (1976). *Latency.* New York: Aronson.
WOOD, E. C. & WOOD, C. D. (1984). Tearfulness. *J. Amer. Psychoanal. Assn.*, 32:117–136.

Fantasy and the Body-Mind Problem

Some Preliminary Observations

CLIFFORD YORKE, M.R.C.S., L.R.C.P., F.R.C.Psych., D.P.M.

THE TOPIC CHOSEN FOR THIS COLLOQUIUM AFFORDS A GREAT DEAL of latitude. It allows us to discuss fantasy in relation to what is loosely referred to as the "body-mind problem." The initial enthusiasm with which the suggestion was met was, however, quickly tempered by the realization that traps for the unwary littered the road ahead. We had already reached some accord on a working definition of fantasy (Kennedy et al., 1985); but what did we mean by the "body-mind" problem? Were we concerned with the way in which the body representation developed and the part it played in the self representation as a whole? Was our interest in the way in which the somatic pathways, through which excitation was discharged, increasingly gave way to mental channels of release? Was our interest primarily in the ways in which

Codirector, the Anna Freud Centre, Hampstead, London, which is at present supported by the G. G. Bunzl Charitable Foundation, London; the Freud Centenary Fund, London; the Anna Freud Foundation, New York; the John D. and Catherine T. MacArthur Foundation, Chicago; the New-Land Foundation, Inc., New York; the Leo Oppenheimer and Flora Oppenheimer Haas Trust, New York; and a number of private supporters.

Presented at the 6th International Scientific Colloquium entitled "Fantasy and Body Representation in Physical Disturbances," held at the Centre on October 26 and 27, 1984.

The author wishes to thank Rose Edgcumbe, George Moran, Hansi Kennedy, and Stanley Wiseberg for their helpful comments and suggestions.

psychogenetic disturbance expressed itself somatically? Were we mainly concerned with the psychological management of physical diseases or disability? Or did we wish to emphasize the unity of body and mind rather than any polarization between them? These matters, and a good many others, arose in the course of discussion, and it became clear that the term "body-mind problem" could be used to accommodate almost anything in which any given person had an interest, as long as both mind and body were in it somewhere.

Nevertheless, it occurred to some of us that it might be helpful, at the very start of our deliberations, to remind ourselves, with the assistance of one or two vignettes taken from clinical practice, of some of the ways in which fantasy became involved in disturbances whose presentation was physical but whose origin was psychic—and perhaps vice versa. It was decided to allot some 15 to 20 minutes to a brief and succinct review of some of these issues and to find a suitable victim to carry out these preliminary rites.

Before proceeding further, I invite you to consider the following:

In the course of analysis a woman develops a headache. It is relieved when a specific fantasy is brought to light—namely, that her head is inside the analyst's bottom, and is being tightly squeezed by it. Since the fantasy is initially a childhood one, it is a small head in a rather frighteningly large bottom—originally the mother's. Another patient, this time a man (though the gender is unimportant), develops a pain in his head, although in this instance the pain has a rapidly intermittent quality and, in this respect, is different from the experience of sustained pressure by a tight band. The symptom disappears when the analyst helps the patient to verbalize the memory of a time at which his father used to beat him about the head in an attempt to force him to eat up the remains of the food on his plate.

In the first of these simple examples, fantasy is expressed via somatic sensations. In the second, we have a rather striking instance of "somatic remembering" in which the somatic memory is rendered redundant when it gives way to verbal recall (Yorke, 1978). But consider again: a patient has a thumping sensation in the head which accompanies sweating, a pounding of the heart, and a raised pulse rate. We would be justified in suspecting that we were dealing with rather pronounced somatic concomitants of severe anxiety, even though the source of the anxiety may as yet be unknown to either patient or analyst. There would not, in this example, necessarily be any somatic representation of the mental content, although it is striking that the physiological concomitants of anxiety vary in their expression from patient to patient, so that in some, for example, the hair stands on end, while others have more powerful urges to empty the bladder.

Consider again: a patient complains that her head throbs and aches, and that she cannot hold it upright because her neck is stiff. A careful anamnesis and diagnostic formulation suggest that a wish to possess the father's penis has achieved a bodily, though symbolized and distorted, representation, while the need to disown the wish finds expression in the inability to hold the head erect, in spite of the erotization suggested by the throbbing sensations. We thus have a rather simplified example of a somatic dramatization of a conflict, even though, for present purposes, we have not attempted to trace the psychic precipitants, the regressive instinctual shifts, the reinforcement of instinctual pressures at key fixation points, and the threatened return of the repressed that leads to the symptom compromise.

We would want to distinguish a symptom formation of this kind from that displayed by a patient who invariably develops a pain in her head whenever she gets excessively excited, unduly angry, or is threatened by mounting sexual or aggressive drive pressures. If, furthermore, the history declares a susceptibility to headaches at times of excitation for as long as the patient can remember, we shall suspect that her headaches are of an altogether different character. We would ask ourselves whether, in this instance, fairly specific *somatic* pathways remain open for the discharge of *mental* excitation, irrespective of its character. The excitation and its expression are not restricted to anxiety and its physiological concomitants. But, as in the latter, fantasy—or, indeed, psychic content of any specific kind—has no part to play in its genesis. No doubt the symptom will be subject to psychic elaboration of a secondary kind, and perhaps become a focus for subsequent organized, fantastic expression.

Consider yet again: a patient presents with an intense and

burning headache which he claims is totally unrelieved by any medication, never lets up, and, in spite of all medical examinations, investigations, and assurances to the contrary, must be the expression of serious disease—perhaps, in this instance, a tumor of the brain. The analyst tries to talk to the patient, to discuss his relationships and family affairs, and to take some kind of history, but finds he is quite unable to hold the patient's attention for more than moments at a time. In this example, there is little possibility of determining the way in which important aspects of psychogenesis have found expression in a delusional and hypochondriacal disturbance. The fantasy content—if such there be—of the disturbance cannot be known beyond the patient's conscious declaration of malignancy at work.

It is at this point that the complexity of the subject under discussion becomes so abundantly clear that we are compelled to recognize that any attempt to do it justice in a brief presentation is bound to come to grief. Nevertheless, the exercise may not have been wasted if it has managed to make its point. In recognizing the daunting nature of the whole enterprise, a small group at the Centre came to the conclusion that something simpler was called for. For all the dangers of reductive thinking, we hope that too much violence will not be done to clinical phenomena if we look at fantasy in relation to three principal categories of bodily disturbance.

1. There are those conditions, already briefly exemplified, in which the somatic disturbance is *initiated* by the psyche. I have referred, for example, to the somatic concomitants, or better, the physiological correlates, of psychic anxiety and to the possibility of further fantastic psychic elaboration. In the case of more complex conditions, such as conversion hysteria, fantasy would play a part in the somatic dramatization of the conflicts involved, but would undergo considerable distortion in the process.

2. There are somatic disturbances which have important psychological sequelae. In such instances, we are moving from the somatic to the psychic and not, as in our earlier discussions, from the psychic to the somatic. In these cases, we may be dealing with fantasy *exacerbated* by the physical disturbance or initiated, at least in part, by the physical distress.

3. We have to consider somatic disturbances, the *management* or *treatment* of which has important psychological consequences, including the initiation or exacerbation of fantasy.

When we examined these groupings and tried to illustrate them, a number of clinical vignettes engaged our attention and fostered further discussion. They were drawn from everyday life as well as treatment situations and ranged from the very simple and easily categorized to the more complex and problematic. One concerned a 4-year-old boy who was watching a video recording of President Kennedy's assassination. He suddenly complained of a headache and instantly fell asleep. He was carried to bed without waking and slept, undisturbed, throughout the night. The psychogenesis of the episode—which had, incidentally, no further consequence—was not in doubt. The group thought it likely that the experience involved a fantasied identification with the President/father.

This brief but dramatic occurrence is therefore easily assigned to the first of our three categories; but it tells us absolutely nothing about what it is that makes the fantasied identification with the murdered man take such a striking physical form. We do not often raise this kind of question in the case of young children, perhaps because we are used to the frequency with which children deal with their conflicts through some kind of somatic expression. The question, nevertheless, will not go away. Indeed, it is part of a larger question with important implications. We are all aware, for example, that many people use their physicality, whether pathological or within the normative range, to give expression to drives, affects, mental attitudes, and character, in relation to self or objects. And, at the opposite end of the scale, there are many who make but limited use of the body in these respects, and accord it little significance, tending to relate to others on the basis of intellective and cognitive style, even though drives and drive derivatives play an important part in activation, motivation, and intention. Questions of this kind serve as a rather severe reminder that turning one's back on complexities in the interests of order and convenience may simplify tasks, but does little to solve problems.

Although the following vignette reveals the arbitrary nature of our categorization, it is not included only on that account. A

girl of 14 was admitted to an oncology unit with an osteosar-
coma, for which almost immediate amputation of the left leg was
arranged. After the operation, cytotoxic drugs were administered with consequent loss of hair. The girl was reluctant to wear
a wig or to use a prosthesis. Although she was not in analysis, she
was in regular psychotherapeutic contact, both on the ward and
as an outpatient, with a member of our staff.

Seen postoperatively, the girl showed some nocturnal anxiety
and sleeplessness. These symptoms persisted and may have been
exacerbated by the revival, through the amputation, of old prohibitions against masturbation and concomitant fears of punishment. At any rate, she developed the habit of repeatedly rubbing
her left eye. A stye shortly developed in her eyelid and was
followed by a series of others. Her concern about the eye condition seemed quite excessive in the light of the recent amputation.
Although the styes were undoubtedly due to infection, it is possible that the eye-rubbing involved a masturbatory displacement.
Incidentally, the importance of the stye to the patient was indicated by a drawing in which it was conspicuously represented. It
is notable that this drawing depicts a girl with normal hair and
two legs showing through transparent clothing. In this way compensatory fantasy restores to the body its preillness state, while
retaining the minor blemish of the stye.

This sad story raises some very searching questions. As psychoanalysts, we are all familiar with the way in which a minor
ailment can be exploited by neurotic anxieties and become a
focus for the expression of disturbing psychological conflicts.
We are also familiar with patients who have suffered major physical damage or catastrophe and have become reconciled to their
disability in a way which both surprises and impresses. In such
instances, we often assume—or, indeed, discover—that the disability has drawn upon itself preexisting conflictual disturbances
and, by catering, for example, to masochistic trends and pathological guilt, affords a greater measure of tranquillity than
would otherwise be expected. In the case just described, we may
reach a different conclusion. Are not the life-threatening nature
of the girl's illness and the catastrophe of her disability so great
that a psychic danger, derived from the past and elaborated in
fantasy, is preferable to the recognition of the predicament in

which she really finds herself? Does the displacement of her anxieties to the comparatively trivial matter of the stye have a defensive and, in the circumstances, adaptive function?

It may be that the real danger is so devastating that fantasied dangers, arising from the childhood conflicts, organize themselves around the stye. If, as the therapist suspected, these childhood conflicts included a fear of punishment for castration wishes against a younger brother, the stye may again be of special significance. For this younger brother had developed, some years earlier, a malignant tumor of the left eye. Was, then, the stye unconsciously experienced as a retaliation, taking an eye for an eye? Even if this were the case, it may arguably have seemed preferable to structure the anxieties around a minor infection than to structure them around major bodily damage and mutilation.

In all this, the choice of the left eye is striking: it was, after all, the left leg which was amputated, and the left eye that was extirpated in treating the brother's tumor. If the girl's anxieties shifted from the stye to a fear of going blind, as seems possible in the light of all the information available, then this raises a further question. Can an unconscious equation of blindness with death represent the child's apprehension of death as the ultimate disaster? The boy who was watching the video recording could afford to die a symbolic death. For the girl, reality went beyond any symbol.

In making a rough and ready grouping of fantasy in relation to bodily disturbances, we made provision for those cases in which continuing medical treatment and management initiate, exacerbate, or maintain fantasy. It would be hard to find a better example than juvenile (type 1) diabetes, as George Moran (1984a) has illustrated. He gave some indications of the complexities of the matter—the difficulties encountered in disentangling the effect on fantasy of the management of the illness from the effects of the illness itself (see also Moran, 1984b).

My last illustration, too, involves features deriving from physical illness as well as its treatment.

In the fifth week after birth, a little girl who had been easy to mother became increasingly fretful and distressed. It was almost impossible to comfort her, and she could be fed only with difficulty. A relationship of relative harmony had given way to one of mutual and inexplicable misery; and the mother was at her wits' end to know what to do. It was not until the fourth month that the child's failure to thrive led to hospital admission. A diagnosis was made of infantile cortical hyperosteosis, or Caffey's disease—a rare illness occurring in early childhood, characterized by lesions under the periosteum of the long bones, ribs, and skull, and giving rise to pain and localized tenderness.

The *physical* illness subsided, as it usually does, within 18 months; but not before serious consequences could be avoided. From the very nature of the malady, attempts to comfort the child by holding and cuddling had intensified the pain of which she sought to be rid, and the mother's instinctive efforts to soothe her had a dire and paradoxical result. This was not, however, the only circumstance which had important consequences for the child's subsequent development. Once the diagnosis was established, treatment was instituted, first with cortisone and later by injections of ACTH. The side effects of the treatment, as a result of which the child became obese and relatively immobile, added to the difficulty of management and further interfered with both physical and psychological development. Unable to crawl, she could not approach, follow, or leave her mother; and when treatment was discontinued at the age of 2 years, she started to walk almost immediately. She had, in effect, bypassed an important stage in her development.

The child did not, however, come to our attention until she was 10 years old, when she was referred for assessment and possible treatment. A detailed account of the disturbance and the child's analysis has been given by Melzak (1982); but for our present illustrative purposes a very few points will suffice. Although a school report described the girl as "mature and sensible" and said that "she mixes well with other children," the relationship with the parents, and particularly the mother, was intensely fraught and difficult. Indeed, although the mother appeared to have tried hard to understand the child's needs from the time of her physical illness onward, she became, over the years, increasingly exhausted and angered by the child's demands. Mother and child were repeatedly precipitated into clashes which sometimes led to physical as well as verbal violence.

The girl's explosive assaults and fits of screaming usually began with an outraged refusal to do whatever her parents wanted her to do. The sadomasochistic relationship with her mother was intense, while she got along rather better, but by no means well, with the father. The relationship with her mother was repeated with the analyst. Two kinds of attack on the object could be distinguished. In the first, the assaults were spontaneous and occurred whenever the child felt humiliated or feared intrusive—and physical—attacks upon her body. She sometimes tried to anticipate and forestall these "threats" by listing, in the most disconcerting way, the therapist's physical movements and gestures, including the involuntary ones. The second type of aggressive act was premeditated, and its torturing and malevolent quality was unmistakably pleasurable and intent on inflicting suffering. While this behavior might again have included significant defensive functions, these were less in evidence than in the first type of maneuver.

In a case of this kind, we are struck by the fact that, in early infancy, the balance between pain and pleasure becomes decidedly weighted in favor of the former; but this is by no means all. Where the pain not only precedes, but continues through, the early stages of self-object differentiation, the experiences of that pain become inextricably associated with both self and object. The object is pain-inflicting and the self, too, maintains its painful nexus. No doubt these experiences are compounded when diagnostic investigations and, later, treatment by injection are undertaken. But a further step is taken in the second year of life when, even for children whose development is within the normative range, the object is experienced as cruel. For this particular child, this experience of cruelty was enormously reinforced. It could perhaps be said, without too much exaggeration, that, in a very large measure, care became cruelty and cruelty, paradoxically, was in some respects care. This must have had a decisive influence on the child's sadomasochistic relationship with her mother and have conferred a comparable stamp on her treatment relationship with the therapist. The side effects of the cortisone and the ACTH compounded the problem since, for some time, they restricted the child's ability to move from, or toward, the pain-inflicting—and later cruel—object.

Perhaps it is as well that these attempts to illustrate our three categories of bodily disturbance in relation to fantasy are less than clear-cut. We would be suspicious were it otherwise. In the end, someone will have to elaborate the issues in some detail, and to use a nosographical framework firmly based on psycho-analytic psychology. Meanwhile, it was never intended that this presentation do more than remind ourselves of the difficulties of the subject, and raise a few questions for discussion.

BIBLIOGRAPHY

KENNEDY, H., MORAN, G. S., WISEBERG, S., & YORKE, C. (1985). Both sides of the barrier. *Psychoanal. Study Child,* 40:275–283.

MELZAK, S. (1982). A child who was hard to mother. Read at the Anna Freud Centre, London.

MORAN, G. S. (1984a). Psychoanalytic treatment of diabetic children. *Psychoanal. Study Child,* 39:407–447.

―――― (1984b). On the interaction between psychological disturbance and childhood diabetes. *Bull. Hampstead Clin.,* 8 (in press).

YORKE, C. (1978). Notes on the developmental point of view in the diagnostic assessment of adults and children. *Bull. Hampstead Clin.,* 1:163–180.

APPLIED ANALYSIS

Sublimation and Its Limitations in Charles Dickens

E. C. M. FRIJLING-SCHREUDER, M.D.

IN THE EXTENSIVE LITERATURE ON DICKENS, ONE THEME IS OFTEN dominant: in the course of his life, his novels became increasingly gloomy. In all of his work his preoccupation with social abuse is strong, but there is an enormous difference between *Nicholas Nickleby* and *Oliver Twist* and the sinister atmosphere in *Edwin Drood.* I see this development not only as a result of his disappointment in life but far more as a result of a progressive neurosis. It is this topic which I shall use to show where sublimations become autonomous and where they remain vulnerable. Why Dickens? In the first place, because he had such an enormous capacity for sublimation. In the second place, I have been acquainted with him through his novels for some 60 years, which is longer than I have known any of my patients. His biography was written shortly after his death by his friend John Forster (1872–74), and what the delicacy of the friend omitted was later supplied, e.g., by Pope-Hennessy (1946) and Angus Wilson (1970), to name only two of the very numerous writers about Dickens.

Dickens wrote only about what he had seen himself. He also wrote a great deal about himself in his letters to Forster. In this way we can often recognize the link between his own experiences and specific figures in his novels. For example, he wrote to a friend, "Mrs. Nickleby herself, sitting bodily before me in a solid

Emeritus Professor of Child Psychiatry, Amsterdam University; Training analyst, Dutch Psychoanalytic Society.

chair, once asked me if I really believed there ever was such a woman?" (Pope-Hennessy, p. 143). I shall return to this theme, but first a few facts about Dickens's life.

Dickens was born in Portsea in 1812; a brother born after him died soon after his birth; and a sister, 6 years younger, also died in childhood. His father was a naval clerk who was frequently transferred: from Portsea to Portsmouth to London to Chatham. All these moves took place before Dickens was 5 years old. The years in Chatham from 5 to 9 were the happiest of his childhood. His father took him for long walks.

As Dickens described his youth, he was a sickly, not very well cared-for child, who could not take part in the boisterous activities of his peers. He made up for this, however, by storytelling and organizing fantasy play.

When the family moved to London in 1821, Charles was left behind in Chatham for a few months, after which he traveled to London by coach, sitting alone in the wet straw. He wrote, "I consumed my sandwiches in solitude and dreariness and it rained hard all the way and I thought life sloppier than I expected to find it" (Forster, p. 11). In London, the family fortunes rapidly went downhill. Charles was left to his fate. Nobody thought about finding a school for him. He went around distributing pamphlets about "The Institute for Young Ladies," which his mother was trying to start but which never saw one young lady enter. He took all the household goods to the pawnbroker. In the end, his mother's nephew, Lament, found a job for him in a blacking warehouse belonging to her nephew's family. Charles had to clean and label the bottles which contained the blacking material. He felt neglected and rejected. The situation was so painful to him that, though it lasted less than a year, it completely changed his view of life.

For 25 years this episode remained a carefully guarded, shameful secret. Then, in the course of a walk, Forster mentioned that a friend of Dickens had seen Dickens as a boy at work in a warehouse near the Strand. Dickens broke off the conversation, but subsequently wrote to Forster about his life during the blacking warehouse period. Only thereafter was Dickens able to talk about it. In _David Copperfield_ he described the episode, but he changed the blacking warehouse into the wine merchant's establishment of David's terrible stepfather. Moreover, he depicted David's own parents as dead, relieved of their responsibility for the horrible episode as well as punished by the writer with early death. Writing to Forster, Dickens described this episode:

> It is wonderful to me how I could have been so easily cast away at such an age. It is wonderful to me that, even after my descent into the poor little drudge I had been since we came to London, no one had compassion enough on me—a child of singular abilities: quick, eager, delicate, and soon hurt, bodily or mentally—to suggest that something might have been spared, as certainly it might have been, to place me at any common school. Our friends, I take it, were tired out. No one made any sign. My father and mother were quite satisfied. They could hardly have been more so, if I had been twenty years of age, distinguished at a grammar-school and going to Cambridge.
>
> The blacking warehouse . . . was a crazy, tumble-down old house, abutting of course on the river, and literally overrun with rats. Its wainscotted rooms and its rotten floors and staircase, and the old grey rats swarming down in the cellars, and the sound of their squeaking and scuffling coming up the stairs at all times, and the dirt and the decay of the place, rise up vividly before me, as if I were there again [Forster, 1:21].
>
> My whole nature was so penetrated with the grief and humiliation . . . that even now, famous and caressed and happy, I often forget in my dreams that I have a dear wife and children; even that I am a man; and wander desolately back to that time of my life [1:23].

These events must have been even more humiliating in comparison to what happened to his sister Fanny. She obtained a place as a pupil at the Royal Academy of Music and even received an award. Charles was present: "I could not bear to think of myself—beyond the reach of all such honourable emulation and success. The tears ran down my face. I felt as if my heart were rent. I prayed, when I went to bed that night, to be lifted out of the humiliation and neglect in which I was. I never had suffered so much before. There was no envy in this" (Forster, 1:31).

On his twelfth birthday, Charles started at the blacking warehouse. Two weeks later, his father was sent to the debtor's prison, the Marshalsea. A few months later he was released when he was able to pay his debt after the death of grandmother Dickens, who, having been in service all her life, left some money. Dickens lovingly painted her portrait in Mrs. Rouncewell in *Bleak House*.

But even then Charles "never heard a word of being taken away, or being otherwise than quite provided for" (Forster, 1:32). In the end, his father quarreled with his employer and this led to Charles's dismissal. The quarrel was made up again, but his father decided that Charles would go to school. His mother wanted him to stay on his job. Dickens said, "I never afterwards forgot, I never shall forget, I never can forget, that my mother was warm for my being sent back" (Forster, 1:32).

From 1824 to 1826 Dickens went to a boarding school, after which he clerked for an attorney for 2 years and then became a reporter. When he was about 17 years old, he fell in love with the daughter of a banker, Maria Beadnell. He was still very poor and she was unattainable. When he tried to accompany Maria and her mother on their morning walk, Mrs. Beadnell turned into a shop, saying, "And now, Mr. Dicken, we wish *you* good morning," accentuating her disdain by the mispronounciation of his name (Wilson, p. 101). In the end Maria was sent to Paris. This episode made a deep impression on Dickens. After describing this love in relation to Dora in *David Copperfield,* he wrote to Forster, who thought Dickens had exaggerated his feelings: "It excluded every other idea from my mind for four years . . . nothing can exaggerate that and so I suffered and so worked . . . that to see the mere cause of it all, now, loosens my hold upon myself" (1:47). This episode of his boyhood love gave rise, 25 years later, to the description of a quite different comic figure in Flora in *Little Dorritt.* De Levita (1967) wrote about this type of persisting unhappy love in adolescence as a phenomenon in children who have missed contact with the peer group in latency. We have seen the dramatic interruption of latency in Dickens's youth.

At 24, Dickens married the 20-year-old daughter of his editor at the *Morning Chronicle.* Catherine Hogarth's father not only was Dickens's editor, he also had been a Scottish Writer to the Signet and friend and legal advisor to Walter Scott, then just deceased, whom Dickens revered. The marriage lasted 20 years, and from the beginning Catherine's sisters played important roles in it, first Maria and later Georgina Hogarth. Catherine and Charles had 10 children, 7 sons all named after famous writers. The first year of the marriage was a very joyous and happy one. The young couple lived in cramped quarters with Dickens's brother Fred and Mary Hogarth, who loved her charming and successful brother-in-law until her sudden death in 1837 at the age of 17. As Wilson said, "his feelings for Mary Hogarth, like his feelings for Maria Beadnell, were to get out of hand, once again to dominate and distort his attitude to women, especially in his fiction, because, as with his relationship with Maria, he was not given time to resolve his relationship with Mary into his overall scheme of life" (p. 110). Dickens was desperate and could not get over it. For the only time until the last decade of his life he failed to produce the monthly issues of his serials. He explained this to his readers in a short note. A year later he wrote to his wife that he heard Mary's voice every night in his dreams. In 1841 when her brother died just as suddenly, Dickens had to make funeral arrangements. He had his wife's brother buried in the same grave as Mary, a place Dickens had reserved for himself. He wrote: "The desire to be buried next her is as strong upon me now, as it was five years ago; and I *know* (I don't think there ever was a love like that I bear her) that it will never diminish" (Wilson, p. 114).

Their deaths left Dickens bereaved and depressed, feelings which he referred to only much later in *David Copperfield* (1849–50). After the deaths of David's child-wife Dora (Maria Beadnell and Mary Hogarth) and his friend Steerforth, David traveled aimlessly through Europe for 3 years. Describing David's mood, Dickens wrote, "From the accumulated sadness into which I fell, I had at length no hope of ever issuing again, I roamed from place to place, carrying my burden with me everywhere. I felt its whole weight now; and I dropped beneath it, and I said in my heart that it could never be lightened. When this despondency was at its worst, I believed that I should die. Sometimes, I thought that I would like to die at home; and actually turned back on my road that I might get there soon. At other times, I passed on farther away, from city to city, seeking I know not what, and trying to leave I know not what behind" (p. 789). Here he described not only his long-lasting sadness but also the restlessness which played so large a part in his later life. Very soon he became quite famous and rich, counting a large circle of painters and writers as his friends. He was an excellent host, a generous father to the 10 children he begot in 15 years, and there always was at least one extra Hogarth under his roof.

Dickens was not active in politics. His days as a parliamentary reporter left him with an abhorrence of the politics of his time. But he was a staunch champion of many causes: better working conditions; prison and law reforms; abolishment of public executions, the death penalty, and imprisonment for debt. His social radicalism was a predominant feature of his journalistic essays and all his novels. While Dickens painted the faces of the poor and the oppressed in bold strokes, he always depicted them as respectable human beings whose individual characteristics never disappeared as a result of their fate. Chesterton (1906) felt very strongly that Dickens's sympathy for the poor came from within himself. Dickens arouses our indignation about their circumstances while at the same time showing us their joy.

Dickens traveled extensively through England, France, Italy, and America. His travels may in part have been occasioned by the fact that his parents, brothers, sisters, and in-laws eagerly exploited his new position. He had to advertise that he would no longer pay his father's debts, though he had been paying the rent for his parents since early in his career. Later he broke off relations with his brother Fred for the same reason.

Apart from his endless roamings through London in his sleepless nights, when he suffered from fatigue, dark moods, and depression, his hobby was acting. He gave charity performances, visited by royalty. In 1857, Mrs. Dickens took Hans Christian Andersen to a private performance of *Frozen Deep*, which was also attended by the Queen, Prince Albert, and the King of the Belgians (Pope-Hennessy, pp. 362, 366). After the performance the guests were served oysters and champagne. In the *Frozen Deep*, Dickens played the hero who saves the rival and then dies at the feet of the woman they both love. In the same year, he decided to perform for a large audience in Manchester. Since his own daughters were unable to act, a manager found a family of professional actresses, Mrs. Ternan and her two daughters Maria and Ellen for him. Maria was the girl at whose feet he died, but he became violently enamored of Ellen. After the success of the play a deep despondency set in. He traveled with his friend, Wilkie Collins, but remained deeply depressed. He increasingly became convinced that his marriage had never been satisfactory. His wife reacted to this crisis with tears, but she did not oppose him. She agreed to a separation and lived on an annuity in a small house with her eldest son. Dickens kept all the other children and Gadshill and continued his life there with his sister-in-law Georgina, who had been living with them for many years. Ellen obtained an apartment where Dickens visited regularly. This infatuation was not strange, but the circumstances of his separation and the masochistic exhibitionism and hypocrisy with which he wrote about it on the front page of *Household Words* were unexpected, especially in view of the protest of all his friends. He broke off with everyone who had any contact with his wife or her family and so lost many of his friends. Only Miss Coutts, who took an active part in his charities, remained a friend of both.

While he had previously begun the public readings from his work, after the break with his wife he constantly sought reaffirmation of his popularity in the enormous applause he received following these readings. He surrounded himself with more and more famous people and sycophantic youngsters. His restlessness increased as his health deteriorated. He dragged himself from performance to performance until he succumbed in 1870.

Discussion

As many analytic writers have pointed out, Freud's usage of sublimation (1905, 1914, 1923) was not consistent and subject to many changes (e.g., Kris, 1952, 1955; Hartmann, 1955). Nor has the distinction between sublimation and neutralization proposed by these authors to account for the vicissitudes of both sexual and aggressive drives been generally accepted (e.g., Eissler, 1963). There also is disagreement on whether sublimation is a nondefensive ego activity or, as Anna Freud (1936) viewed it, a mechanism of defense. In general, however, sublimation refers to a shift in the aims of the drives from a socially unacceptable goal to an acceptable one. Usually it also implies a transformation of the energy discharged. The accompanying change in the quality of satisfaction, however, is not always the same. As Kuiper (1980) points out, different sublimations have a different degree of stability. He believes that it makes a great difference whether sublimation occurs from inner abundance or in an effort to solve a persistent unconscious conflict. We find sublimation from abundance when there is reasonable satisfaction of instinctual impulses, a satisfactory sexual life, or, as Kuiper says, at least the inner readiness for it. The exercise of personal gifts and the resultant pleasure in functioning motivate a person's performance, which in turn increases his satisfaction.

Dickens showed these characteristics in his delight in observing and in his contacts with all kinds of people. He enjoyed thinking out plots, writing about and creating the endless variety of figures in his novels. This pleasure remained constant during his entire life. The full use of observation, fantasy, and language was always available to him. These functions were autonomous and resistant to conflict involvement throughout his life and were still evident in his last uncompleted novel.

In other respects, however, it is difficult to say whether Dickens's capacity to draw on his own life experiences, especially the pain he suffered as a child, represented a true sublimation—a drive discharge in a modified form—or a variety of defensive measures. It seems to me that these are best understood in terms of a whole range of more or less successful efforts at sublimation that needed to be repeated as they became increasingly involved in conflict and Dickens's progressive neurosis. It might even be assumed that the latter became progressively evident as sublimations failed in stability and especially aggression could no longer be contained.

For example, Dickens's pleasure in functioning as a writer and the great success he attained certainly enabled him to conquer many of the adverse circumstances of his early childhood. So did his sense of humor. He was able to see the comic side of the most horrible situations, thereby also rendering the reforms for which he pleaded more acceptable to his readers.

On the other hand, he never seemed to have fully overcome his bitterness in relation to his parents and his jealousy of his sister Fanny, whether these feelings were conscious or not, as well as the narcissistic hurt engendered by the Maria Beadnell episode. He seemed to have been impelled to deal with these in his novels over and over again, in different ways, many times humorously, but with steadily more apparent gloom and depression.

Dickens drew the portrait of his mother first in Mrs. Nickleby and later in Mrs. Micawber, who, like Mrs. John Dickens, came from a slightly higher social level than her husband and never loses an opportunity to inform everyone of this fact. Quite unrealistically she continually expects people to find new and more profitable jobs for her husband. She is full of illusions about him and nearly as flighty and as careless as he is. Mrs. Nickleby is superficial and a bit of a flirt and susceptible to any flattery. She is very proud of her "sound common sense." I give an example of her thought processes in a dialogue with her sensible daughter:

> "Kate, my dear," said Mrs. Nickleby; "I don't know how it is, but a fine warm summer day like this, with the birds singing in every direction, always puts me in mind of roast pig, with sage and onion sauce and made gravy."
>
> "That's a curious association of ideas, is it not, mama?"
>
> "Upon my word, my dear, I don't know," replied Mrs. Nickleby. "Roast pig—let me see. On the day five weeks after you were christened, we had a roast—no that couldn't have been a pig, either, because I recollect there were a pair of them to carve, and your poor papa and I could never have thought of sitting down to two pigs—they must have been partridges. Roast pig! I hardly think we ever could have had one, now I come to remember, for your papa could never bear the sight of them in the shops, and used to say that they always put him in mind of very little babies, only the pigs had much fairer complexions . . . [p. 524].

Dickens published this caricature in 1839, but 10 years later, in *David Copperfield,* he drew a double portrait of his mother

and father in Mrs. and Mr. Micawber. They accompany David
(a self-portrait) from his entry into Murdstone and Grimby's
warehouse until the happy unmasking of the villain, Heep,
when David is a widower. Mr. Micawber, like John Dickens, is
always in financial difficulties and always expects other people
to provide for him. He is unreliable, changeable, and pompous.
For example, after spending a very jovial evening with Mr. and
Mrs. Micawber, David receives the following grandiloquent letter from him next morning (p. 256):

> My dear young friend,
> The die is cast—all is over. Hiding the ravages of care with a
> sickly mask of mirth, I have not informed you, this evening,
> that there is no hope of the remittance! Under these circum-
> stances, alike humiliating to endure, I have discharged the pe-
> cuniary liability contracted at this establishment, by giving a
> note of hand, made payable fourteen days after date, at my
> residence, Pentonvill, London. When it becomes due, it will not
> be taken up. The result is destruction. The bolt is impending,
> and the tree must fall.
> Let the wretched man who now addresses you, my dear Cop-
> perfield, be a beacon to you through life. He writes with that
> intention, and in that hope. If he could think himself of so
> much use, one gleam of day might, by possibility, penetrate
> into the cheerless dungeon of his remaining existence—
> though his longevity is at present (to say the least of it) ex-
> tremely problematical.
> This is the last communication, my dear Copperfield, you
> will ever receive
>   From
>   The
>   Beggared Outcast
>   Wilkins Micawber

It is clear that Dickens took revenge for the many occasions
when he paid his father's debts. Dickens gives his resentment
against his parents a form which for him and for his readers
changes the suffering into pleasure—a feat indicative of a wide
range of defensive measures. But these are only partially successful: the rancor comes through in the description of these
characters and is not solved by it. We see the continuing and

increasing bitterness not only in Dickens's own life but also in the fate Dickens assigns to the characters in his novels. In *Nicholas Nickleby*, the father of the hero has died before the book starts (as has David's father in *David Copperfield*), but Mrs. Nickleby in all her silliness is the mother of the excellent hero and heroine, Nicholas and Kate.

In *David Copperfield*, Mr. and Mrs. Micawber are secondary figures in no way related to the hero. The young David is their lodger for a short time during which he makes many visits to the pawnbroker, as did the young Charles, but now David does that to help his host and not his own family. Mr. Micawber, for all his carelessness and his constant borrowing, even from persons who can in no way afford to lend, is still a sympathetic figure who in the end unmasks the villain of the book.

How different this is in the later novel *Little Dorritt*. Old Mr. Dorritt has been in the debtor's prison for more than 20 years. He speaks in the same pretentious way as Mr. Micawber, but Dickens uses him to describe the deformation of character by prison life. Mr. Dorritt is a hypocrite. His daughter is helping him by going out as a seamstress, but he continues to beg from the other poor prisoners and their visitors in the same hypocritical manner. Fanny, Dickens's older sister, is little Dorritt's older sister in the book, but she does not study at the Royal Academy of Music but performs with her uncle in cheap third-rate music halls. When Mr. Dorritt leaves jail, he does not lose the shadow of the prison. He is always afraid that someone will know about it and that he will not get due respect in his new high position.

The anger is not ameliorated by the pleasure in writing. Aggression and humor are at war in the descriptions. Compensation for earlier humiliations which Dickens achieves brilliantly by writing succeeds only partially where the conflict is imprisoned by repression. The hostility against his parents could not be neutralized. The neurosis grew worse. It seems to me that the first years of Dickens's life, with the death of a little brother, the many moves, the birth of the siblings, the repression of his jealousy toward Fanny and of the rage against his mother prepared the neurotic development. Dickens's continuous preoccupation with death could be seen in this context, though it is certainly also a frequent literary theme as well as a common experience of his period. He was a loving father, but sometimes he reproached his wife for the many children, as though she alone had been responsible for their coming into the world, as a child reproaches his mother for the arrival of a sibling. The contrast between the quality of his books, which rises steadily until the end of his life, and the increasingly grim and sad mood in his novels is part of the same theme.

Dickens's anger against Maria Beadnell followed the same pattern. He first painted her portrait in Dora in *David Copperfield* as a charming, gentle, but extremely silly little child-wife. Whereas Maria's father was a well-to-do banker, Dora's father dies and leaves nothing. Dora herself dies very young, after having a still-born child.

Maria Beadnell, then Mrs. Winter, sought contact again with the now famous Dickens. Obviously she regretted not having recognized the future genius in the young Dickens. Mr. and Mrs. Dickens received Mr. and Mrs. Winter. It was a great disappointment, but Dickens used Maria's efforts to reawaken past feelings in *Little Dorritt,* where he drew a sharp caricature of her in the figure of Flora Finching. Flora is the daughter of one of Dickens's most abject figures, the slum exploiter Casby. The middle-aged Flora tries to return to the romantic secrecy of her infatuation when she was 17. However, she is too fond of port and pastry and accompanies her mad aunt who gives Dickens occasion to vent more drollery.

Dora is the adored child-wife. Flora is a ridiculous, but cordial and well-meaning woman. In the third portrait in this series, Estella, in *Great Expectations* (1821), however, Dickens's rancor triumphs. We find Estella in the weird atmosphere of Miss Havisham—the jilted bride—who lives in her moldering bridal finery in a darkened room. Estella is educated to take vengeance on men for the insult to her adopted parent. Pip, the book's hero, passes through the years in unrequited love for her, but love is not a word that has any meaning for her. When Pip reproaches her for marrying a dissipated man, she feels so little for Pip that she asks him: "Do you want me then to deceive and entrap you?" (p. 291). Gradually, by hints and half-sentences, we learn that she was born in prison as the daughter of a murderess and a galley prisoner. The sense of doom pervades a large part of the book, though there is no lovelier picture of adolescence than that of Pip and Herbert. In the original version, Dickens made Pip live his whole life in solitude, but his literary friend Bulwer Lytton found that too sad. A later version ends with a new meeting between Pip and a widowed and profoundly changed Estella.

It is not difficult to recognize in these plots what Freud (1909) described as the family romance. Kate Friedlander (1941) characterized these fantasies as one of the ways in which the child loosens the tie to his parents. In 1941, *David Copperfield* was still the book most widely read by young people. Friedlander believed that this enormous appeal stemmed from the family romance. The continuous change between exact observation and family romance fantasies and Dickens's warm interest in all his figures often made the characters depicted in his novels more alive than the living. The changing degrees of neutralization make for autonomous observation in many instances, and in some for a preponderance of oedipal fantasy life; and his longing for the ideal woman betrays him into figures like little Nell in *The Old Curiosity Shop* (1840) or Agnes Wickham in *David Copperfield*.

My last point is not about the artist but about sublimation in general. The development of sublimation requires, according to Kuiper, the parents' love and respect for the child. In this the mutual pleasure experienced by parents and child in doing something together is especially important. Father Dickens and the very young Charles found great pleasure when his father put Charles on the table in the pub to recite a popular poem. I do not think that we should like to propagate this as an educational measure, but Dickens's contemporaries had a great reciter as a result.

BIBLIOGRAPHY

CHESTERTON, G. K. (1906). *Charles Dickens*. New York: Readers Club, 1942.
DICKENS, C. (1839). *Nicholas Nickleby*. New York: Signet Classics, 1982.
———— (1840). *The Old Curiosity Shop*. London: Everyman's Library, 1947.
———— (1849–50). *David Copperfield*. London: Everyman's Library, 1947.

_____ (1855–57). *Little Dorritt.* London: Everyman's Library, 1947.

_____ (1861). *Great Expectations.* London: Everyman's Library, 1947.

EISSLER, K. R. (1963). *Goethe.* Detroit: Wayne State Univ. Press, pp. 1406–37.

FORSTER, J. (1872–74). *The Life of Charles Dickens.* London: Everyman's Library.

FREUD, A. (1936). The ego and the mechanisms of defense. *W.*, 2.

FREUD, S. (1905). Three essays on the theory of sexuality. *S.E.*, 7:125–243.

_____ (1909). Family romances. *S.E.*, 9:235–241.

_____ (1914). On narcissism. *S.E.*, 14:67–102.

_____ (1923). The ego and the id. *S.E.*, 19:3–66.

FRIEDLANDER, K. (1941). Children's books and their function in latency and pre-puberty. *Amer. Imago*, 3:129–150, 1942.

KRIS, E. (1952). *Psychoanalytic Explorations in Art.* New York: Int. Univ. Press.

_____ (1955). Neutralization and sublimation. *Psychoanal. Study Child*, 10:30–46.

KUIPER, P. C. (1980). Enkele opmerkingen over sublimatie. In *Psychoanalytici aan het woord.* Deventer: van Loghum Slaterus, pp. 68–76.

HARTMANN, H. (1955). Notes on the theory of sublimation. *Psychoanal. Study Child*, 10:9–29.

LEVITA, D. J. DE (1967). Ongelukkige liefde in de adolescentie. In *Hoofdstukken uit de hedendaagse psychoanalyse.* Arnhem: van Loghum Slaterus, pp. 240–255.

POPE-HENNESSY, U. (1946). *Charles Dickens, 1812–1870.* Chatto & Windus.

WILSON, A. (1970). *The World of Charles Dickens.* New York: Viking Press.

Psychotherapy with Parent and Child in Failure-to-Thrive

Analogies to the Treatment of Severely Disturbed Adults

ELIZABETH L. LOEWALD, M.D.

INFANTS AND CHILDREN WITH FAILURE-TO-THRIVE HAVE A HEIGHT and weight below the third percentile of normal for their age and sex. On physical examination and laboratory investigation, doctors find no organic disease or genetic defect to account for the problem. The children commonly show developmental delays in areas of motoric, cognitive, language, and/or personal-social skills. Babies so affected are frequently rather uninterested in things and people; solemn or irritable. They may be inactive—or, instead, always restlessly on the go. They may refuse or regurgitate much of their food. Poor appetite and poor growth may be chronic—or may begin rather suddenly, tumbling them down the growth chart between two visits to the pediatrician.

In an outpatient project organized in 1978 at the Yale Child Study Center for the treatment of failure-to-thrive, it was the hypothesis of our therapy team that the central difficulty for each failure-to-thrive child lies in the impairment of a normal, mutually nourishing flow of communication and satisfactions between him and his primary caretaker. This had been described previously by several other clinicians. Some of our own clinical findings are described in the following pages. The giving

---

From the Yale Child Study Center, New Haven, Conn.

and receiving of food is in these cases a focal site of impairment. Whitten and his colleagues (1969) reported good evidence that growth failure in such cases is secondary to measurable under-eating by the child. The cause of the distressing dyssynchrony of mother and child may lie in defects in the child's ability to give and to receive emotionally, or in the parent's; or more often, in both. Failure-to-thrive is not a single disease, but a syndrome of common outcome. Thinking of its etiology as a spectrum seems to fit the clinical facts.

Toward one end of the spectrum we find children who have clear problems in communicating their needs age-appropriately; or in achieving reliable age-appropriate cycles of needs and satisfactions. Babies delayed by prematurity may enter this group; and hard-to-comfort, easily disrupted babies, with special sensitivities or vulnerabilities, or unusual social unresponsiveness. There are also "hard to love" babies—with disfiguring birth defects, or illnesses which render them hard to care for, unattractively delayed, or of dubious future potential. Even at this end of the spectrum, failure-to-thrive does not usually develop unless the attributes of the particular baby render him too difficult, too unlovable, for the particular person who parents him.

At the other end, we find children who were developmentally normal at birth and seem to have no innate blocks to progress, but who have mothers with clear problems in communicating with and finding satisfaction from their babies. Some, with chronic or acute depression, cannot be alert to the baby's signals or take pleasure in his care. Some, with psychosis or personality disorder, cannot decipher or respond to the baby's needs as separate and different from their own. Some are rejecting or overwhelmed by the baby's very existence. And we have observed this several times in parents who do not otherwise have any major psychiatric disorder. It can happen when a new mother has suffered a recent loss of her own much-needed parent; or a recent abandonment by the baby's father. It can arise when the urgent demands of the new baby remind her of hated younger siblings for whom she was prematurely responsible in the past. We do not know whether all, or just some, babies will respond by refusing food and wasting, in this impaired mother-child interaction. It is clear that many other factors enter in: the father's nurturing input, for example; stimulation from siblings; availability of grandparents.

In the intermediate range, the interaction of difficulties of parent and child is seen in all sorts of combinations. It is always the reciprocal capacity to make *each other* comfortable and satisfied which is impaired. We always find a child who does not eat enough and cannot enjoy his food and his surroundings robustly. We find a mother who is thwarted by the difficulties of nourishing this child, or by some particular inner conflict about doing it, or both. She is feeling starved herself of the nourishment and self-development she had expected from mothering.

As we encountered, in our treatment project, primitive defenses and intense, seemingly inappropriate reactions in many parents of failing children, we were reminded of experience with adult patients with psychotic, narcissistic, and borderline disorders. In working with such adults, we found it clinically useful to keep in mind the concept that different early stages of symbiosis and separation-individuation have been specially disturbed, in each of these diagnostic categories. Though it is never as neat as all that, it is helpful, for diagnosis and for ongoing management, to bear in mind the general points of fixation to which a patient characteristically regresses under stress.

Masterson (1981) views the schizophrenic person as having, chronically or acutely, fused self-object representations; as the baby does in the early symbiotic stage of psychic development. Ego boundaries are blurred. Reality testing is poor because of the indistinctness of the boundaries which make comparisons possible—and because massive projections confuse the field. The borderline person has progressed further psychologically, but has not been able to negotiate the full course of separation-individuation. He has some sense of separate self, and better reality testing than the schizophrenic person. But images of both self and others tend to be split: good and bad, perfect or rejected. He lives with a constant juggling of these images, and of personal relationships, in the urgent need to avoid the depression of abandonment. He uses primitive defenses—paranoid projections—feelings of depersonalization and unreality. Under stress, he may retreat further into transient psychoticlike episodes. The person with narcissistic personality disorder has predominantly firm ego boundaries, and good perception of reality. However, his self-object perception is fused, even more firmly than in the borderline patient; and around threats to his "self-object esteem," his perception of reality breaks down.

Among the 8 mothers with whom we worked in the project, only 2 would I now diagnose as "borderline" on the basis of life functioning before pregnancy with this particular child. And none were schizophrenic, or would be diagnosed as narcissistic personalities. However, it is interesting that the characteristics of thought mentioned in the categories above were rampant among them and were focused in relation to and about the child, sometimes reaching the point of near delusion about the child. This began to us to seem expectable—but often very hard to understand.

There were also analogies between particular mother-child pairs considered as a "unit," and some individual disordered adults. The failing baby often seemed to be perceived by the painfully conflicted mother as only a bad fragment of herself—like the hated parental figure, or the dangerous introject, or the identified "bad" body part, of a schizophrenic patient—having to be repudiated or sacrificed to preserve any sense of goodness or intactness for herself. Contrariwise, we saw a baby used as mother's "good" part. One mother of a sickly baby communed with him and seemed to worship him, all one Christmas Eve night, in a sort of ecstasy. She reported no sense that night of his actual infant needs for sleep or nourishment.

In saying this, we keep in mind that parenthood always involves ambiguity and times of fluid ego boundaries between parent and child. That is the necessity and the nature of it. But in these particular parents, there was often an impediment in the hydraulic flow, so to speak, from one ego state to another, from one affective state to another—from psychological fusion with the infant to adult ego competency in this regard. This is very like the disturbance of psychic homeostatic management in narcissistic disorders. In failure-to-thrive, there are vulnerabilities in parent and/or child, so that one partner is overtaxed by the efforts at homeostasis of the other. Sometimes it seems that the child's stoppage of growth and development is an emergency measure, however destructive, to keep equilibrium in this overstressed interpersonal situation. It is much like the schizophrenic's relapse into acute psychosis in the face of over-stress in the family system.

I will outline here just enough about our project to illuminate or suggest clinical experiences from which the thoughts of this paper come.

Ours was a small group of people interested in joining this part-time therapeutic venture. It included, at various times, two social workers, three pediatric nurses, a clinical psychologist, and myself. We informed local pediatricians and hospitals that we would like to work along with them in outpatient treatment of failure-to-thrive children, after the diagnosis was made. We would offer regular counseling and information to parents about the children or about themselves; periodic developmental testing of the child; play therapy for depressed or disturbed children; coordination of work with social and educational agencies for the family as needed; and regular consultation with the pediatrician, in whose hands the medical management of the child would remain.

I met with the pediatricians and the families as soon as possible after referral—most effectively while the child was still in the process of hospital diagnosis, and we could all make the treatment decision together. Then our team decided together on a treatment plan, with various of the members assigned as therapists according to their interests and skills. We saw parents and children together or in separate therapies, at home, or in our Child Development Unit. We met with parents and social service agencies, trying to relieve pressing housing or financial needs. We looked with parents for preschool activities for the child. We met weekly as a team to discuss all ongoing work. I supervised some team members individually in their therapy with parents or child. Some developmental testing and play sessions were video-taped, with parental consent. The team reviewed tapes together to pinpoint problems and assess progress. We also found them very useful for viewing with parents—to interest them in aspects of their child, and to make vivid for them the problems we saw.

Over 2 years, 15 referrals were made to our project. Of these, 8 families entered into treatment with us, for periods of a few weeks up to several years. The other 7 families refused treatment. That is a subject for inquiry in itself. Those 7 children were in trouble with growth and development equal to that of the other 8. Why was therapy refused? Sometimes the parents' particular distrust of doctors, or their especially strong denial of any problems in the child's failure-to-thrive, was involved. And we could not find a way to overcome that distrust. Sometimes the timing of our coming on the scene was too late for already angry and embattled parents. Or our mutual understanding of goals with the pediatrician was incomplete. Thus his sponsorship of us to the parents inspired too little confidence.

Our 8 children ranged in age from 4 months to 3 years. The group is too small for statistical analysis, but we note that they came from lower- and middle-class, from black and white families, and that the range of associated family problems was much what has been described by Leonard et al. (1966) and others. Single parenting, very youthful parenting, recent separations and losses for parents, depression, borderline ego defects in mothers, alcoholism, poverty, unemployment, severe marital conflicts—all of these difficulties were represented in our sample of families. The children also presented a variety of problems other than their poor growth. These included extreme prematurity with developmental lag; autistic behaviors; delays in speech development and other developmental areas; bulimia; psychophysiological symptoms in infants such as diarrhea and idiopathic rashes; tantrums and headbanging. Only 2 of the children had no demonstrable developmental delays. In some, we witnessed very clearly over time how developmental catching up and falling behind varied as parental problems waxed and waned.

We found no "typical case" of failure-to-thrive. I shall describe one child and his family, to illuminate some matters discussed further on.

We first saw Billy K. at age 16 months. His private pediatrician had referred him at the end of a diagnostic hospitalization. Billy had grown and developed well until age 9 months, when his height and weight fell rapidly from the 50th to the 15th percentile for age and sex. He had become anorectic, listless, quiet, and sad. He could not stand alone at 15 months, much less walk.

Billy's mother was a shy, plain, depressed woman, whose own mother had died when she was 12, and who had been overworked, demeaned, sexually abused, and neglected, by an alcoholic father. Billy's father had been physically and emotionally abused in childhood. He was a man of labile feelings, suspicious and sickly, with congenital heart disease, intelligent but unschooled. He worked sporadically at menial jobs. The family's diet and housing were marginal. The couple had no close friends or extended family with whom they were on good terms. The mother was constantly with Billy, her only child; but spoke with him little, and played with him less. They sat together by the TV much of the day. The father took a livelier but very sporadic interest in Billy. The onset of Billy's failure-to-thrive occurred when the father got another job after some months at home and was suddenly less available to Billy. Both parents tended to interpret Billy's disinterest in food, objects, and people as being "stubborn," or "he's mad at us." Hurt, they would retaliate by isolating or ignoring him. Though Mrs. K. could be warm and gentle with Billy, she could also be wholeheartedly or even sadistically rejecting. She was not worried by his poor appetite: she herself had only sporadic interest in food, and expected the same of him. But she did like and respect the pediatrician, and so agreed to Billy's diagnostic hospitalization. On finding no organic causes for Billy's decline, the doctor referred the family to us. The parents again respected his wishes, though they saw little reason for this. On developmental testing, we found Billy's language development only at the 9-month level. He was vocalizing very little. Personal-social and motoric skills were equally delayed. His play was lackluster and very limited in scope. Most of this did not concern the K.'s: "He'll catch up." But it did worry them that he was not walking; and they disliked his "tantrums".

Our treatment of Billy continued for 14 months. The much-valued pediatrician saw him regularly too during this time. For the first 6 months, a nurse member of our team saw Billy's parents twice a week in their apartment, observed and played with Billy there, and talked with the mother and often the father as well about Billy's developmental needs and about the family's financial and other problems. I did regular developmental testing of Billy at the Child Development Unit. This was an occasion for the parents to bring Billy to us; and sometimes to look at videotapes we had made of Billy's testing and play. The father particularly enjoyed this. In early months—though he did not sustain it—he often expressed interest in learning the reasons for his son's behavior. The parents seemed to value our work together and often sought our praise or advice. Meanwhile Billy learned to cruise, and walk, and vocalized somewhat more. His appetite and sleep and zest improved. However, during periods of special conflict between the parents—of which there were many—Billy always regressed on all fronts.

When our nurse team member left New Haven, the parents' treatment was taken over by one of our social workers. It took Mrs. K. many months to accept her and to keep the appointments. The father never actively worked with us again: the change of workers clearly meant our "not caring" to him. For the next 8 months, the format of therapy included weekly individual sessions for the mother, who had begun to want to talk over her past experiences and to consider the quality of her present life. Billy had weekly play sessions with me. Agency help was enlisted to look for better housing and a parent aide. During this time, Billy made more progress, though he never quite reached age-level in any developmental area. But next, as the parents were in more and more open conflict, Billy regressed to an almost nonverbal, nonplaying, anorectic state. Billy's father one day abruptly took Billy out of our care. He had decided to teach him himself: perhaps he never *would* cramp his freedom by sending him to school, he said. But the K.'s marriage soon dissolved. Mrs. K. had become pregnant— had a brief hospital stay for anxiety and depression—had the baby and released it for adoption. Meanwhile Billy was in a foster home, for the first time away from his mother, for several weeks. We saw him, with his foster mother, during this time. Though he was suddenly painfully shy with me, all reports were that he had made real strides recently in speech and social skills.

Billy returned to his mother; and she returned to regular meetings with her social worker. She also made a warm relationship to a parent aide, which continues as of this writing. Using this support, she has made a stable home for Billy. She has maintained the separation from her husband, done volunteer work, improved her appearance, and gotten more education. While maintaining her dislike of psychotherapy, she has acquired some reflectiveness and insight—and assertiveness too. Billy was referred to a rehabilitation center for speech therapy and stimulation of various skills, at age 3. Then he entered a city preschool special learning center, which he attended full time. He makes gradual developmental progress. Though somewhat odd and crotchety in manner, he can now make real contact with adults and peers. His appetite, weight, and height are no longer concerns. He and his mother visit us or chat with us on the street, now and then. The contact is a warm one.

We cannot say for sure that Billy's development would have been normal in a more supportive environment. But it *was* clear that his curve of good development was interrupted at 9 months, along with his onset of failure-to-thrive. The sudden loss of his father's presence—in a setting of parental conflict, inadequate and erratic stimulation, and symbiotic attachment to a depressed mother—appears to have been the major precipitant. (The loss of father may have affected Billy indirectly as well, through the sadness and anger it engendered in the mother.) From then on, we observed many times how good family functioning enabled Billy to grow and develop; and how family depression and discontent resulted in Billy's regression.

With this background, I now return to our question: can we understand something more about failure-to-thrive by making comparisons between the two clinical groups of my title? Here, first, is a list of clinical features found both in work with failure-to-thrive families and with certain severely disturbed adults.

1. Factors contributing to the pathology are frequently multiple and on many levels. A crucial impasse presents to us, in

which a baby is doing very badly—or a disturbed adult is de-compensating. But there is usually, on investigation, a back-drop of past and present familial psychological problems or other health problems, divorce, death, poverty, substance abuse, etc., which loads the present impasse with ominous meanings. For reasons of history, the adults of both groups come to their crisis lacking role models and compensatory sup-ports. They are weighed down by many varieties of negative experience. What degree of psychic developmental damage they themselves have suffered remains to be discovered.

2. Diagnosis is often not easy. Even though the growth failure of the child—or, for example, the impending divorce, or the work failure, or the suicidal thoughts of the borderline pa-tient—are emergencies to be dealt with, the roots of the prob-lems may reveal themselves only slowly.

3. The psychological problems prove pervasive and invasive in both groups. That is not to say that prognosis is always gloomy, nor the time needed for improvement always long. But the symptoms—the growth failure of the baby, or the outbreak of psychosis in the adult—indicate conflict at the deepest, ear-liest psychological levels.

We have understood for some time, for example, that the acute schizophrenic breakdown of a young college student stressed by leaving home, exposure to homosexual temptations, etc., indicates a massive failure of ego homeostasis. An imper-fectly individuated ego, under developmental stress, has tem-porarily lost its holding structure. Primitive infantile de-fenses—dissociations, hallucinations, projective identifications, defective reality testing—have resurfaced in this crisis to main-tain *some* structure. But such regression, in our student, may be quite temporary. It may vanish quickly, with medication, with reduction of life stress, with reinforced denial, or availability of new supports. Nevertheless, the patient has suffered a cata-clysm of the ego, however briefly.

In the same way, in our failure-to-thrive mother-infant pair, the baby's wasting is a temporary "solution" to deep conflict between elements of their psychological "unit." We have, early on, clinical glimpses of the conflict raging. The mother some-times fondles and beseeches her baby; sometimes puts him or her roughly in the crib and walks away. She talks, weeping, about her own loving mother of the past, but is fiercely angry at her too. The baby seems equally conflicted. He reaches for food hungrily, then spits it out and clamps his jaws. Or, though he has many developmental urges, he only lies apathetic and anorectic in his mother's arms. His mother, like the college student described, talks to us about the baby with surprising projections, distortions of reality, or at times true delusion.

When the impasse between mother and child begins to lessen, these extremes of thought and behavior often melt away quite soon. But they are, however briefly and circumscribed, psychotic extremes.

4. As a consequence of this intense conflict, work with both groups arouses strong countertransferences in therapists. We defend against contagion from the patient's helplessness or rage by using *our* more primitive defenses. I will mention this important finding further on.

5. With both groups, the course of therapy is usually, though not always, a long one. It may be interminable. The disturbed adult patient may regain functional sanity; and the failing baby may begin to thrive. But in both cases, a rise in family stresses may cause repeated relapses. Monitoring and support must often continue over years. In considering the hurdles and cycles of our parent work in the failure-to-thrive project, we found that as with borderline and schizophrenic adult patients, periods of angry withdrawal and then further useful work often alternated. The mother's psychological separateness from the baby emerged in parallel with, or in antiphony with, her individuation from the therapist, in interesting ways. We understood the cause of this to be the defect or fragility of her capacity to form and maintain object relationships.

6. The goals of therapy must be individually tailored and retailored, for both groups. Questions of the developmental potential of the participants, and the modes and time frames for maximizing the potential, are involved, as I will try to spell out a little more.

I have described our effort to tailor a treatment approach to each failure-to-thrive case. If the small child in question needed stimulation and practice of his evolving skills, or an ongoing relationship with a therapist because of atypicality or early depression, we tried to provide this. If parents were unable to nurture the child adequately for reasons of their own draining life crises, or strong negative meanings which the child held for them, we wanted to address this in their own counseling. In some of our cases, both things could be done; as well as valuable meetings with child and parents and siblings all together. But we met many difficulties. For a long time with some families, the best interests of one member seemed to run counter to the needs of another. There are recognizable phases of the work, with characteristic therapeutic problems in each.

For example: often we began treatment faced by parents' initial negative transference to us as "critical depriving parents." Sometimes focus with mother on the child's needs had to be postponed some weeks, while she ventilated her feelings and perceptions of the baby. Gradually, building on this, we could carefully direct our inquiries, to open up some of the major difficulties between them.

There was a middle phase of treatment in which, though the first phase had brought relief and progress, the parents were reluctant to stay. Missed appointments, or outright bolting, might occur just as the mother began to indicate some feeling of closeness with her therapist, and some stirrings of desire to change aspects of her life. The experience of an alliance was new and frightening to some mothers. And also, a resumption of separation-individuation in the mother's development was sometimes occurring in treatment. In Mahler's words, the mother seemed to enact with us a "practicing subphase." She needed to leave therapy and return; to be angry and to repair. But sometimes this resulted in a premature rupture of therapy which was harmful to the child.

The child therapist's growing closeness to their child was threatening to some mothers. So was the sharing of a therapist *with* the child. Balance of the therapist's "giving" to mother and father was frequently a tender issue. In the case of Billy, our regular work with mother and child ended abruptly for a whole year, when Billy's father decided that *he* could help Billy best, and he would not brook "outside influence" on his wife. We had been unable to find means of giving to this father in ways he experienced as meant for him. His wife's gradual psychological growth, in her therapy, he felt as abandonment and exclusion.

During this middle phase, issues around food, for baby *and* mother's nourishment, were no longer denied but were highly charged. What to feed the baby, whether he should eat what parents eat, was a focus for gratifications and deprivings. And often, the therapist was now struggling to convince the mother to eat enough herself. This battle too seemed to be part of the mother's own individuation.

These, then, were some of the circumstances we met in treatment. Very often, interactions were complicated by mother's ambivalence, splitting, projective identifications, strong jealousies, and needs. The treatment turmoil was like that with borderline and psychotic adults. We treated a mother who used to call one or another of us urgently on the phone—then say, "Wait a minute," and leave her end of the phone indefinitely. Asked about it another day, she could not recall having phoned. Although many of these parents had ordinarily functioned at a less regressed level in their personal and work relationships, in this particular relationship to and about a particular child, they were indeed regressed. As we came to know their histories more fully, we learned also about how many wider psychosocial connections were broken, or in conflict, for these mothers and babies. The complexes, mother-father-child; grandparent-parent-child; and even community-nuclear family, had all been disturbed. (This we usually learn gradually, too, in our work with borderline and psychotic patients.)

The failure-to-thrive work raises our consciousness about the normal lively interplay of a mother and a baby on many psychological levels. They share equally and unequally a symbiotic oneness, at different times. Mother uses baby too as a transitional object, as he uses her. He is a carrier of her relationship to her past. He is, increasingly, a real object to whom she relates. Meanwhile he is responding and growing in all these modes himself.

In many of our 8 cases, the child had his own reasons for difficulties with response and growth. In *every* case, we felt an impoverishment of the play of levels on which mother and baby could be together. In terms of psychological differentiation, there was a shift, for both, toward less differentiated levels of interacting. And transitions *between* levels were harder for these mothers and children to negotiate. Shifts were sudden, unpredictable, abrasive, for one or both partners. One example of this concerns Billy. When he was 4, Mrs. K. was pregnant with another child; her marriage had ended and she had no other reliable family ties; she became symptomatically depressed and needed psychiatric hospitalization for the first time. Billy was separated from her for the first time, sent to a foster home. Mrs. K. was puzzling what to do next. Overall, this proved to be a watershed period for her move toward independence. And there were real later benefits for Billy. But it was chilling to us to hear the *way* she puzzled. She seemed to have withdrawn all emotional investment from Billy. She talked about giving up the baby and keeping Billy (as she later did); or giving up Billy and keeping the baby, to "start over." Her affect about all this was entirely cold. It was as though *we* remembered her 4 years of daily life with Billy, and she had quite forgotten. Nor did she ever mention *his* feelings in all this.

In the treatment phase we did witness mothers experiencing their children as schizophrenic patients sometimes experience an "offending" part of their own bodies. (These are things we witness less often now in adults, since antipsychotic medication is in wide use. I am thinking, for example, of the psychotic person who gouges out his eye because his "seeing" is evil.) One of our mothers—a sane and conscientious woman—was almost intolerably revolted by the greed for food of the 3-year-old South American orphan child the family had adopted. In the adoptive house, the child responded strongly to this: stopped gaining and growing.

Certainly, we often saw the child patient treated by the mother not as a separate human being, but as only a symbol—a hope or fear, a tormentor, and a part object. The mother who used to call us and leave us on the telephone was the same who worshipped her infant son all one Christmas night. She had perhaps the most fragile ego functioning of all our mothers. We saw in our joint sessions how the child's signals of hunger, fatigue, earache, passed her by—though it was her dream and intention to live for this boy, and she felt she had not enough time left to eat for herself.

Therapists learn about much current self-abuse and abuse of others by disturbed patients. In treating failure-to-thrive children and their parents, as in treating severely borderline or psychotic adults, there are decisions to make about calling police, hospitalizing, or separating children from parents. In treating failure-to-thrive, we are trying to clear the way for the child to eat and grow, and not to suffer irreversible gross developmental damage. We try to judge the possibilities for needed changes in parenting and the probable speed of this, as well as the crucial developmental needs of the child at that moment. Can the child change to be more lovable and less straining for these parents? Are there other people at home to nurture him when his mother can't? Where is he developmentally, as to object constancy, if one is considering his removal from parents?

I have mentioned our calling Protective Services when Billy's father threw him across the room. There was another decision to make when Billy was 3. He was living alone now with his mother, who was working nights, and sleeping days, and doing little else. We discovered on a house call that Mrs. K. was keeping Billy in his crib all day, beside her as she dozed; and in his crib with a friend babysitting all night. He was grossly deprived of cognitive and social and motor stimulation for weeks. She was skipping most of our appointments. But we did not call Protective Services—rightly or wrongly—because of our estimates of the relative gains and losses of our separating the two just then. Also, from our work with Mrs. K., we found it probable that she would keep her alliance with us and with her pediatrician, and work on attending to Billy's needs along with her own, within a reasonable time frame.

Treating patients in the two groups under discussion, our countertransference can be intense. (I am using the word here to denote the strong feelings stirred in us by the intense neediness, manipulativeness, criticism, and suspicion of these patients with ourselves and with their babies.) Our clinical skills are taxed. Transferences to us are immediate and strong; often negative. For our part, we often identify strongly with the needy child. Or we wish intensely to give the parent the parenting she has never had. But meanwhile we are frequently anxious and helpless to effect change—not the good doctors *we* need to be. That feeling is familiar to therapists of borderline patients. Moreover, we may be cut off from our colleagues by our own angry, competitive feelings—because the parents find another person so very helpful, and ourselves so useless. On pediatric wards where diagnostic studies of failure-to-thrive are often conducted, the effects of these countertransferences on staff morale are familiar. In our team treatment effort, we found each other's support and observations indispensable. In inpatient treatment of psychotic and severely borderline patients, that situation is the same.

I bring this up because the degree of transference, and the need to use it in diagnosis and treatment, seemed to us one of our most important findings. Perhaps this has not yet been prominent enough in the literature. In a paper addressed to pediatricians we suggested that early self-awareness of his helpless, angry feelings is a diagnostic signal to the doctor that a mother-child dysfunction of this type is operating.

Our team approach to treatment helped us use our countertransference. For one example: our social worker treated a mother and father; and I their 3-year-old son, who was very small for his age and had severe lags in language and in personal-social development. I used to return Jeffry to the social worker's room at the end of play sessions. There, a few weeks into the treatment, I began feeling strangely embattled and angry with Jeffry's mother in our few minutes together. I began to dread those minutes—though our conversation seemed bland enough. When I talked with the social worker about it, she listened attentively, but was surprised and puzzled at my vehemence that this mother was somehow "against" her son's treatment. Sorting this out—beginning with where it had bothered *me* into such competitiveness and anger—we began to understand more about the real degree of this mother's uncertainty and defensiveness about her mothering. The social worker was then better able to open up this issue; to the eventual relief of mother, myself, and indeed Jeffry. It had been well hidden, in the counseling alone, with these compliant, intellectualizing, and quite emotion-shy parents.

Therapists of borderline adult patients must deal with many of their own strong counteremotions. They can use them—as in our case just cited—to locate important hidden themes and defenses of their patients. Also, in a long-term therapy, the doctor's occasional clear acknowledgment of a strong counter-reaction (which the patient has certainly noticed) often gives the latter a quite fresh view on his own behavior. Honest dialogue between them about reciprocal feelings can be one instigator of change. To put it another way: primary process begins to be raised to secondary process.

However, in our experience, such dialogue rarely seemed appropriate with our failure-to-thrive parents. Thus, we did not speak to Jeffry's mother about my feelings in response to her attitude. We tried only to use the insight we had gained to foster her awareness of her actual dreads of Jeffry. Or with Billy's father, we did not find it possible to look *with him* at the meaning of our misunderstandings. These parent therapies were of course often shorter and less personally focused than treatment which is sought out individually by an adult. But even beyond that difference—our patient-therapist issues were more commonly acted out than mutually discussed. There was in this way a similarity to early stages of treatment of psychotic adults. Perhaps this speaks to the level of regression—of dedifferentiation—to which these parents have been forced by the parent-infant impasse. The need to preserve fragile self-esteem and to deny painful negative feelings toward the child leaves the parent little room for self-scrutiny. Nor do parent and therapist feel "separate" enough, for awhile, to compare feelings. There is more primary than secondary process, much of the time.

I will end with some comparisons of treatment goals in our two groups: failure-to-thrive families and severely disturbed individual adults. The crucial question for both is: how far can development be resumed? Can the life situation of the psychotic person, in his isolation, or his enmeshment in his family of origin, be changed? If it is, has he the coping skills and the still-available psychic energy to grow? If that is lacking, should we think primarily of his comfort and safety, and not hope for growth? And the failure-to-thrive children: are they and their parents capable of more range and mobility in their emotional life together—enough to allow for the child's growth? And in this case we add the worry: will change come fast enough to allow the child to make developmental progressions in the order and time frame which Nature has decreed. (I think here of language development; or of the early prerequisites for a later ability to be intimate.) Should mother and child be separated, for the child's sake? Does the child find just *this* mother essential to his psychic development at this time, or does he not? And who else is available for his parenting?

We never know many of these answers. Yet we try to devise treatment modes and time frames. Of course, the patients help devise them. In the adult group, there are, for example, young people who are overstressed by first leaving home, who become acutely psychotic. Some of these regain psychic control and can cope again after a brief hospital stay. Some do not. Similarly in our project, we dealt with depressed mothers and failing infants, who responded to treatment rapidly, slowly, or not at all. For a more chronic adult psychotic patient, we choose among individual or group or milieu therapy, medication or none, halfway house, work and socialization support—or even several years inside a hospital. We choose along with the patient, and according to what is available. I think the nature of the choices, if not the scale and expression of them, is similar in our failure-to-thrive work. Thus it is very right for the pediatric medical center to offer as many referral options as possible. And in locations where the pediatrician has no team available to join him in this therapy, his psychological preparedness for a wide range of new developments, as the treatment unfolds, will be helpful to him.

In both groups considered, I believe the attention in treatment to infantile needs—the disturbed adult's, the baby's, the parents'—is a primary agent of healing. Searles (1961) has seen his therapy of schizophrenic patients as having to reach a point of real emotional symbiosis, felt by both parties. The patient's individuation and recovery begin from there. Since the time of his earlier writings, many more treatment facets have been understood and devised for that patient group—not the least of which is antipsychotic medication. But I agree that there sometimes comes a period, in therapy, of peace, effortless reciprocity and "match" between doctor and patient, which presages the chance of progress. And I think this is what Pruett and Leonard (1973) were saying in their paper, "The Screaming Baby." They suggest that in certain miserable mother-child impasses, the doctor should try to make something good happen as soon as possible. While there are many reasons for that advice, Pruett and Leonard seem to me to suggest that we begin our positive alliance with the mother by locating and attending to *her* misery. Her discomfort, in the interrupted symbiosis with her baby, is very much like the child's, and needs an attuned response.

With adult patients and adult parents we counsel, we are trying to meet them on many psychic levels, to work toward change. That is true too in therapy of the young child. But there, because of his vigorous developmental energies, only waiting to be unleashed, we sometimes feel we just get on and ride. With adults it is slower, muted, more partial. But in failure-to-thrive work there is something to ride on. That is the developmental push of parenthood, in new mothers and fathers. In our project, we could feel that in all parents we worked with, however disturbed they were.

So treatment is a matter of balancing, on many moving vectors, for therapist and patient. That is so, probably, in all psychotherapy—but we see it more dramatically with the two groups I have been discussing.

BIBLIOGRAPHY

LEONARD, M. F., RHYMES, J., & SOLNIT, A. J. (1966). Failure to thrive in infants. *Amer. J. Dis. Child.*, 111:600–612.

LOEWALD, E. L. & ROTNEM, D. (1984). Failure to thrive in pediatric practice. Submitted for publication.

MAHLER, M. S. (1972). On the first three subphases of the separation-individuation process. In *Selected Papers of Margaret S. Mahler*. New York: Aronson, 1979.

MASTERSON, J. F. (1981). *The Narcissistic and Borderline Disorders*. New York: Brunner/Mazel.

PRUETT, K. D. & LEONARD, M. F. (1973). The screaming baby. *J. Amer. Acad. Child Psychiat.*, 17:289–293.

ROTNEM, D. & LOEWALD, E. L. (1984). Therapeutic considerations in a clinic-based failure-to-thrive intervention. Submitted for publication.

SEARLES, H. F. (1961). Phases of patient-therapist interaction in the psychotherapy of chronic schizophrenia. In *Collected Papers on Schizophrenia and Related Subjects*. New York: Int. Univ. Press, 1965, pp. 521–559.

WHITTEN, C. F., PETTIT, M. G., & FISCHOFF, J. (1969). Evidence that growth failure from maternal deprivation is secondary to undereating. *J. Amer. Med. Assn.*, 209:1675–1682.

Losses in Adoption

The Need for Dialogue
STEVEN L. NICKMAN, M.D.

ADOPTION IS ACKNOWLEDGED AS A VITALLY IMPORTANT INSTITU-
tion in our society; nevertheless, growing up as an adopted child
involves losses, risks, and deprivations which affect the development of personality. One type of loss is the disruption of existing
attachments, which might be called "overt loss." This risk is
clearly present for children placed after 6 months, but may be a
factor even in the earliest weeks. A second type of risk is "status
loss" which arises from having a different appearance from that
of the adopters, or otherwise having it known by others that one
is "different." A third, complex class of risk arises from social
and intrapsychic factors which I group under the heading of
"covert losses"; the knowledge of having been relinquished, with
concomitant effects upon self-esteem; lack of knowledge about
one's original parents; and various kinds of stigmatizing experience which cause adoptees to feel that their status in our society
is ambiguous and their rights compromised. I will refer to all
three types, but will emphasize the effects of covert losses on
individual development, and ways in which parents can be
helped to minimize such effects.

Around 1970, American couples who sought to adopt healthy

Clinical Instructor in Psychiatry, Harvard Medical School; Assistant in Psychiatry, Massachusetts General Hospital; Medical Director, New Bedford
(Mass.) Area Center for Human Services, Inc.; Candidate, Boston Psychoanalytic Institute.

The generous help of several colleagues is acknowledged, and in particular
that of Stephen B. Bernstein, M.D., and Ana Maria Rizzuto, M.D.

white infants began to encounter difficulty. Agency waiting lists grew longer and longer, and couples were asked whether they would accept a toddler or older child, a child of mixed race, or an infant with medical problems. The "baby famine" has been attributed to increased availability of oral contraceptives and abortion, and greater social acceptance of unwed motherhood. It has also been claimed that the total number of available infants remained the same, but that adoption itself had grown in popularity as a way of creating a family. Whatever the demographic reasons, adoption is more diverse and confusing in 1985 than it was 30 years ago. A principal argument of this paper will be that the new diversity allows new vantage points from which to examine old issues. That adoptees are at increased risk is now generally accepted; there is no unanimity, however, on the old question of "when and how to tell."

This question acquires new dimensions when one considers what the corresponding dilemmas might be in the case of adoptees placed in latency or adolescence. The timing question, if broadened to accommodate the variety of contemporary adoptive practice, leads to the definition of a more general need in adoptive families—the need for dialogue.

The literature of psychiatry, psychoanalysis, and social work over the last 40 years attests that there are differences between the life experience of adopted persons and that of other people, and that these differences are often manifested as some form of psychopathology. Most authors agree that adoptees are vulnerable and that the existing structure of adoption is in need of reforms (Sorosky et al., 1979; Kirk, 1981). Schechter (1960), in an often-cited paper, refers to the disproportionate number of adoptees in his private practice. Subsequently other authors responded to this finding; a majority agreed that adoptees were at risk, and tried in various ways to account for it.

Kirk (1964) emphasized the interaction of the adoptive family and the outside world. His surveys led to the formulation of a "theory of adoption and mental health." He identified a covert bias against adoption in the general populations he sampled. He also described two contrasting ways in which adoptive parents approach adoption: "acknowledgment of difference" and "denial of difference" between adoptive and biological bonds. Parents who acknowledge difference are said to be in a better position to prepare their children for life. He recommended that adoptive parents utilize introspection to recognize that their role as adopters is regarded as deviant in our society, and that they use their awareness of "deviance from the norm" to help their adopted children achieve comfort with their own status.

McWhinnie (1967), Triseliotis (1973), and Raynor (1980) interviewed populations of adult adoptees. These studies had different structures and goals, but each identified a range of outcomes in terms of overall psychological adjustment. Of note is McWhinnie's finding: while children wanted to be told the circumstances of their adoption, they did not bring the matter up, and "this whole question of discussing adoption within the adoptive family showed a lack of communication between the world of adults and that of children" (p. 265). The children "emerged as being much more logical and having more understanding than their adoptive parents assumed, and resented parental attitudes which implied that they could not understand adoption and that details about this were no concern of theirs" (ibid).

Triseliotis found that of those adoptees who had poor relationships with their adoptive families, most blamed this on insensitive handling of the fact of adoption by their adoptive parents. Learning of adoption during adolescence or adult life led to bitterness. The preferred age for disclosure, from these adoptees' point of view, was between 4 and 8 years. All three authors stress the great importance of an open, communicative atmosphere and the availability of some specific information about the birth parents.

Goffman (1963) describes the dilemmas of individuals who are stigmatized with respect to conventional social values, and various ways they find to "manage" this information. His description is relevant to adoptees, since both the status of being adopted and the common circumstance among adoptees of illegitimate birth are stigmatizing in our society.

Numerous authors have described familial factors which affect the development of adopted children. Prominent among these observations are "genealogical bewilderment" (Wellisch, 1952; Sants, 1964), the harmful effects of family secrets (Tridon et al., 1981), the harsh treatment encountered by adoptees in

juvenile court (Lewis et al., 1975), and the unconscious equation
made by some mothers between an adopted child and foreign
matter or feces (Reeves, 1971).

Wieder (1977a, 1978a) and participants of a Panel (1967) emphasize that the traditional prescription is to "tell" between the
ages of 2 and 4, at the time when the child is negotiating self-
esteem issues and attempting to find his or her place in the
family. They regard learning about adoption at that age as potentially damaging for healthy development. Residual concerns
from the anal stage would predispose the child toward experiencing himself as a piece of unwanted foreign matter; working
through of the oedipal conflict is complicated by the introduction of a set of phantom parents, and the child experiences
difficulty in reaching a clear identification with the role and
values of the adoptive parent of the same sex. Superego formation is interfered with, and representations of the biological and
adoptive parents tend to remain separate; now one set and now
the other carries the valence of "good parents." This persistent
influence toward splitting implies that either set of parents may
also be seen as the "bad ones" who do not care about the child.

Peller (1961, 1963) argues that what a toddler needs to know is
that he or she is a beloved member of the family, and that there is
no corresponding need to know that one is adopted. Wieder
(1977a, 1978a) and Schechter et al. (1964) emphasize that adoptive disclosure should be carefully timed according to the child's
readiness to hear. Schechter (1970) describes common problems
and conflicts of adoptive parents; Blum (1983) emphasizes the
importance of adoptive parents' relationships with their own
parents as an influence on the success of adoption.

Brinich (1980) offers a classification of adoptive traumas in
terms of developmental stages, emphasizing those aspects of a
child's experience which influence his self and object representations. He states that the child's ability to develop healthy self-
regard depends on the parents' capacity to accept the child's
good and bad self as parts of one person, rather than as "our
good child" and the "bad child" of the biological parents. He
further says, "the treatment of an adoptive child will necessarily
include analysis of transference manifestations deriving from
both the adoptive parent and the (unknown) biological parents,"

about whom the child will have constructed elaborate fantasies "in order to make sense of his adoption. Adopted children can be compared to children who have experienced real losses or traumas which reinforce their neurotic conflicts. All the psychoanalytic . . . assistance in the world cannot undo the fact that the adopted child has been rejected or abandoned. This is one reason why adopted children present a particularly difficult therapeutic challenge" (p. 126).

Bourgeois (1975) reviews the history of adoption and contrasts the situation in the Western world with that in areas of Polynesia, where infants are freely given by one couple to another as an expected aspect of the local culture, and where there is no question of secrecy since the child and the biological parents are encouraged to maintain their ties. Writing of adoption in the West he cites Lebovici and Soulé: "It is much more difficult to be adopting parents than to be adopted children" (p. 82; my tr.). He supports the idea of guidance for adopting parents, and states that there are two types of psychopathology in adopted children. One is due to deprivation of relationships: multiple placements, brutal changes, periods in more or less pathogenic group homes, early frustrations, with all the resulting sequelae for the personality; the second arises in relation to the "artificial" (cultural) situation of being adopted. He believes that problems of the first type are very frequent, while those of the second are less well understood. In those rare cases in which factors of early loss can be effectively ruled out, the result "depends . . . on the attitude of the adoptive parents" (p. 84).

The importance of verbal interaction with parents for a child's personality development has been well studied (Spitz, 1957; Mahler et al., 1975; Arlow, 1976). Most of the existing literature is concerned with the infant and toddler when the exchanges are primarily affective and regulatory. Little has been written on the topic of parent-child dialogues involving specific content, occurring in the school years and later. The work of Furman (1974) provides an application of this concept to help the child with a specific crisis—in this instance, bereavement. Such dialogues play an essential part in normal developmental crises; without a sense of being understood and helped to understand and accept one's own feelings, a child labors under a handicap.

A recent contribution has come from cognitive-developmental theory. Brodzinsky et al. (1984a, 1984b, 1985) studied adopted children and controls with respect to their understanding of the adoption process over time. They demonstrated that, contrary to earlier ideas, a child's understanding of adoption does not grow by gradual accretion beginning in the earliest years; rather, children commonly display an apparent early acceptance and understanding of the situation; this "understanding" shifts between 6 and 8 to a more complex attitude characterized by worry and questioning, in accordance with the cognitive growth which has occurred during the intervening years. Parents have been observed to wonder what had gone wrong, or to blame themselves for mishandling the "telling" process. Brodzinsky et al. suggest, instead, that adoptive parents often make the mistaken assumption that "telling" automatically leads to "understanding" on the part of the child; they emphasize that such understanding develops within the child as a result of both information acquired from outside and the internal development of cognitive capacities.

The present literature on adoption is confusing. Some papers emphasize pathology in the family, others stress inherent traumas in adoption itself, while yet others describe societal pressures on adoptive families. Useful guidelines for adoptive parents are in short supply, while the adoption process itself has become more diverse.

I will present several observations based on my clinical experience with more than 100 adoptees and their families over the course of 15 years. Of these approximately a third were seen for brief evaluations (1 to 3 visits); another third for extended evaluations, brief therapy, or case management; and the remainder for psychotherapy (20 to 200 or more visits). About half were adolescents; the remainder was about evenly divided between adults and children 12 years of age or younger. All but 5 were unrelated by blood to their adopters, but this small group overlapped with the nonrelated adoptees because of shared issues involving secrecy, self-esteem, and identity. (Other instances of adoption by relatives and stepparents, concurrently seen in my practice, did not figure significantly in the development of my thoughts, although there is substantial overlap between the two populations in important respects.)

The circumstances of being adopted are a special case of universal human dilemmas. By reconsidering those dilemmas, non-adopted individuals (particularly parents and professionals) can mobilize an ability to empathize with the adoptee and understand certain of his behaviors. We all wonder where we came from and how we will meet our end; these are the primary questions from which religion and philosophy spring. How do we contemplate a past in which we played no part and a future which will proceed without us? Blood ties attenuate the pain of these questions for most people; adoptees, however, are brought closer to a sense of basic anxiety about their place in the world. Modes of coping with stress vary among adoptees, as they do among other people. There are, however, tendencies which are common enough to merit attention.

Frequent among these are the adjustment to life as a stigmatized, depressed individual (see case 3 below) or as a rebel (see case 4); these have in common the experience of being adopted as painful, shameful, secret, and indicative of diminished personal worth. By contrast, many adoptees will follow a life path which is unconventional, though not explicitly pathological. The idea of the quest, pilgrimage, or crusade, which has had perennial appeal in history and mythology, has special meaning for many adoptees. In the sense of Winnicott's "transitional area of experience" (1971b), it is likely that the search constitutes a preferred mode of life for many people, and that adopted persons are particularly likely to gravitate toward it.

Bill B., age 14, wrote a story in which he identified himself with the protagonist, a king who assembles a large army to conquer evil spirits and ogres, helped by a wizard. Asked about the particular significance of evil in the story, he said, "If you can see it from an adopted kid's point of view, you're trying to find your parents. Evil is what keeps you from finding them. Once the battle's over, you settle down and live a quiet life."

"The search" finds its most explicit form in an adopted person's deliberate search for a birth parent. As a characterological mode in people in general, it is connected with oedipal curiosity, greed, and scoptophilia. For the adoptee, however, his personal history provides the analogy for the "somatic compliance" described by Freud (1905) in his account of symptom choice. For anyone who chooses this mode, unconventional behavior may be prominent at certain times of life.

A predilection for "the search" can look to a concerned parent like floundering, goallessness, or outright rebellion. Adoptive parents have the difficult but important task of respecting their child's need to be in some sense lost, until such time as his internal economy allows him to "find" himself. These experiences, as Brinich (1980) notes, can be extremely difficult for parents. Adoptees are particularly prone to rebel against parental standards and pressures; the knowledge of separate origins contributes to the need for, or the sense of entitlement to, autonomous self-definition. Simply stated, an adopted son or daughter cannot be expected to be a conformist. If he is, he may be inhibiting an important part of himself for the sake of basic security, or out of a sense of guilt or responsibility toward his adopters.

The devotion of many adoptees and birth parents to the cause of open birth records is a complex social phenomenon. It embodies the passion and longings of individuals who believe that present law and customs are responsible for some part of their difficulties. It also carries the support of some adoption workers, mental health professionals, and legislators, who are convinced that specific mental health issues or civil rights issues are involved, analogous to the repressions which women, blacks, and homosexuals have fought against in recent years. And to the extent that any cause will attract its share of people who live their lives in a questing mode, the movement to liberalize adoption-record legislation can be said to be another embodiment of "the search" in its characterological aspect. (To be sure, proposed adoption reforms are not limited to the open records issue. At least three other major changes are taking place. One, the establishment of adoption registries to help adoptees and birth parents find each other, is closely allied to the open records issue. The others include an increase in the types of children considered adoptable and the controversial movement toward "open adoption" in which a biological parent retains some right to be in contact with the child.)

DISCLOSURE OF ADOPTION AND THE CHILD'S FANTASY LIFE

There is a causal relationship between the disclosure of adoption, the nature of a child's subsequent fantasy life, and the eventual development of personality, including characteristic ego attributes and defensive patterns.

Fantasy allows the entrance into consciousness of powerful affects and drives, in tolerable doses which can be mastered by available ego resources. The ability to fantasize during latency is one of the major avenues leading to sublimation (Sarnoff, 1976); it is both an alternative and a precursor to repression. Fantasy can also be put at the service of processing strong affective experiences such as grief, shame, and loneliness. (An example is Tom Sawyer's recourse to a mock-medieval battle in the forest, after Becky spurns his friendly advances.) Such affects are frequent at those moments when adoptees are trying to come to terms with their status. Fantasizing by adopted children, however, is subject to particular constraints, and it is likely that the disclosure of adoption to a young child introduces an ongoing interference with the ability to distinguish between reality and fantasy.

The natural tendency to construct family romance fantasy leads adopted children, like others, to speculate about imaginary parents. The elaboration of fantasy meets an obstacle in these children, however. For those who remember previous homes, the actual past loss of objects intrudes painfully, and the act of fantasizing may become a depressive reverie. For those who were placed at a very young age, the potentially painful knowledge of their adopted status may rob the fantasy of the playful quality which it needs in order to serve the child as a healthy mechanism for obtaining a sense of personal autonomy and a tolerable emotional distance from the parents (Rizzuto, 1982). The imagined "other" parents are not imaginary, but are instead inexplicably absent, and the attribution to them of good or bad qualities may be closer to an attempt at reality testing than it is to true fantasizing. In either case, fantasy about one's origins becomes tinged with unpleasant affect; and since fantasizing about origins is a major part of a child's imaginative life, he or she may continue to have difficulty in making use of fantasy as a conflict-free mental process, whether as defensive or creative activity.

Every reference to a fairy godmother in children's stories, every exposure to myths or news items about parents and children taking leave of one another, every arrival of a new sibling, every separation from the parents takes on special meaning for adopted children. In addition, their contacts with adults outside the family circle are tinged by their sense of having an unknown origin. Schoolteachers, family friends, celebrities (both famous and infamous) are suspected of being the true progenitors; peers close in age are suspected of being lost biological siblings. "A few adoptees . . . developed a firm belief that a particular person who had formerly shown them kindness or given them presents or persistently looked at them, was possibly an original parent" (Triseliotis, 1973, p. 35).

The investment of a child's casual contacts with this sense of mystery may be inevitable to some degree when a child is adopted. But early and frequent "telling" may predispose toward greater difficulty in this regard by interfering with the normal repression of abandonment fears and of unacceptable oedipal wishes. It may interfere in a continuing way with the ability to invest energy in love objects or work, and also with the ability to enjoy a playful sense of mystery and fantasy when that mode of experience is available. The blurring of this distinction is described by many adoptees; some speak of walking down the street scanning the faces of passersby for traces of resemblance to themselves.

Amy A., age 6, had begun to object to going off to school in the morning. Her first grade teacher, Mrs. Y., was middle-aged and brisk, unlike last year's young teacher, Miss Z., whose gentle manner had made school a wonderful experience for Amy. Mrs. A. was taken aback when Amy confided, "I'm afraid Mrs. Y. will steal me from you the way you stole me from my real mother."

In treatment Amy demonstrated via puppet play her preoccupation with mother-child relationships and specifically her concern with abandonment. Eventually she made it clear that her fantasy went a step further: the kind, gentle Miss Z. was her original mother, and the changeover to the more work-oriented, demanding first grade teacher had been experienced as a reliving of her fantasy of the transition from biological to adoptive family—a version which could be called "paradise lost."

The 14-year-old Bill B. (mentioned above) was referred by his residential school because he had formed a pact with another adopted boy. The two of them rubbed each other's knuckles with sandpaper until they bled; this was a repetitive, symbolic enactment of their "blood-brotherhood." They were convinced that they were biological siblings because they were both adopted and had similar interests. Such sadomasochistic alliances have previously been described in residentially placed adolescent groups (Bettelheim, 1954); of note here is the blurring of the fantasy-reality distinction, contributed to by the impossibility of definitely disconfirming the boys' hypothesis about a biological relationship between them.

If the ability to fantasize freely is impeded by factors related to the very knowledge of adoption (i.e., if fantasy is less available because there is interference with the ability to distinguish between fantasy and fact, or because the act of fantasizing has acquired painful associations), the child will be at a disadvantage. He may fantasize privately about both sets of parents, at times casting one set in a good role and the other in a pejorative one, and at other times reversing the positions. Such fantasizing is likely to remain internal and thus untested in any explicit way in the outside world, either because it is experienced as painful or because the child believes that expression of it would be poorly tolerated by parents. Since such fantasy does not link up with other developing ego strengths, the child is more likely to carry forward past conflicts and sources of depressive affect unmodified into adolescence. This constitutes a heavy loading of what Blos (1968) has called "residual trauma" to be dealt with by the growth processes of adolescence.

THE IMPORTANCE OF FAMILY DIALOGUE FOR A CHILD'S NECESSARY MOURNING PROCESS

The adopted child typically undergoes at least two kinds of loss, both of which he needs to mourn. For this purpose he requires a continuing dialogue with his parents. The child's awareness that he or she was not kept by the progenitors[1] is the major such loss, and in spite of attempts to detoxify this knowledge for infant adoptees by early, carefully dosed "telling," there is evidence (Brodzinsky et al., 1984a, 1984b) that its full emotional impact comes in midlatency when the necessary cognitive stages have been reached.

All adoptees experience a discontinuity in time in relation to knowledge of their family status. For infant adoptees who were told early, the disclosure may or may not cause difficulty at the time, but realistic understanding of adoption will occur later, during latency, often with grieving responses. For adoptees placed early but told later, major new information is presented at a specific point in time, and the process of assimilating it begins. Children placed later must deal with several kinds of burden: in addition to the effects of deprivation or abuse in the original environment, and of prolonged states in limbo and belonging to no one, they are asked to adjust to a new family and new relationships while still trying to sort out past memories and loyalties.

Children adopted as toddlers also constitute a special case. They may retain memories of their previous home. The operation of defense mechanisms, however, will render most of these children similar to the first group mentioned, in the sense that latency can be expected to bring with it a new evaluation of the self as an adopted person, no matter how the adoptive parents may have dealt with the child about his past.

All of these factors may be considered together under the heading of *not having been kept by one's original parents*. (There is good reason to call this the primary loss in adoption: the fact that the child did not come into the world as a wanted person, into the arms of a man and woman who together could eagerly and lovingly assume his care.) This knowledge often leads to subsequent experience of the self as a devalued person.

1. Some adoptees and adoptive parents object to the use of the word "parents" when applied to individuals who may never have fulfilled any parental role toward the child except for conception and parturition. Needless to say, birth mothers (who have now formed their own organizations for mutual support) are inclined to insist on their status as parents, even in absentia.

Disclosure of adoption may be experienced by both parents and child as a kind of abandonment, comparable to the child's feeling or experience of abandonment by original parents. For the parents who must disclose, the act may feel like a betrayal of the child and may reawaken old feelings of their own defectiveness (in the case of infertile couples) or guilty fantasies of having stolen another couple's child; such feelings must be defended against, and at times the emotional climate of disclosure, or the subsequent failure to establish a satisfactory dialogue about adoption (Blum, 1983), can be traced to such unresolved parental feelings.

The motives for disclosure of adoption to a child may be mixed. In most cases it is done because the placing agency prescribed it, and the parents respect the agency's wisdom and may fear its power. Parents generally believe that it is in the child's best interest. Occasionally, however, the timing or wording of the revelation betrays a latent motive of anger or sadism toward the child (Solnit, in Panel, 1967).

Some children may feel that the people they know as parents are, by "telling," abdicating a part of their parental role and function. This part is not now fulfilled, however, by the "true" parents whose existence has been disclosed; instead, these "true" progenitors remain enigmas whose unveiling begins to serve as a seed crystal for the formation of fantasies, but whose existence as living, developing beings remains hidden. Under these circumstances many a thoughtful child will wonder why his parents felt it necessary to diminish themselves in the child's own eyes and to arouse a hope for new relationships which never materalize. This process may adversely affect the adopted child's experience of his parents as persons who love and care for him.

Another consequence of this new knowledge is its effects on the young child's cognitive and emotional development and the links between them. A child in the oedipal period, who has not acquired the capacity to abstract, may hear the statement that he has "another mother" as an assault on the cognitive structure of his world. The word "mother" may lose some of its powerful affective valence as a tangible transitional phenomenon which links him to the specific individual he knows as his mother. "Mother" (or "parents") may now undergo a change in semantic status for the child, becoming more abstract and denoting some ill-defined qualities shared by his own "mother" and an unknown person. The child's ability to negotiate such a hurdle without suffering a significant break in the continuity of experience (Winnicott, 1956, 1971a) will depend on how well he has mastered the symbolizing function of language independently of its affective content.

The major intervention which can help a child grieve these various losses (not having been kept, confusion about his adoptive parents and his role in their family, as well as social stigma and semantic ambiguity which still exist for adoptees in our society) is *dialogue or discourse about adoption* which begins at an appropriate age and continues intermittently throughout the various stages of development.

(A couple in their 60s learned of the engagement of their son, in training for what promised to be a prestigious professional career. He shared with them his mixed feelings about telling his fiancee that he had been adopted; they advised him strongly to overcome his hesitation, stressing that there was nothing shameful about being adopted and that if the young woman had feelings about it, it would be best to find out now. Though aware of these things intellectually, the young man needed his parents' guidance under stress.)

Furman (1974), describing necessary preconditions for a child to mourn the loss of a parent, stresses the importance of a trusted, loved adult who can help the child to grieve. The losses of bereaved children are severe and complex, but those of adoptees can be more subtle and more confusing. Parents who cannot "connect" with their children about adoption—those who "deny difference," in Kirk's terminology (1964)—fail to help in important ways and thereby add another dimension of loss to the child's experience.

Dialogue established by the parents can help to detoxify the disturbing aspects of adoption so that they may become integrated into the child's conscious image of himself and his world. What needs to be conveyed will depend upon the child's age at the time of placement, and known facts about the biological parents and their circumstances. The dialogue should be open-ended, and not terminated at some arbitrary point when parents, uncomfortable with the subject, decide that their job is done. Many parents have "given" their children knowledge of adoption, but failed to help them know what to do with this knowledge or what attitude to take toward it. At the other extreme, some parents lay undue emphasis on the child's adopted status. The first course leads to residual confusion; the latter, to painful self-consciousness. Attainment of a fruitful dialogue depends upon a nondefensive stance on the parents' part as well as on sensitivity to how much a child or adolescent wishes, or needs, to confront the facts of adoption at a given moment.

If inner development and the nurturant environment have helped the adoptee to *work through his losses in a conscious mode* so that they are in tolerable harmony with conscious ego contents, chances are good for a normal development. If, however, the facts and feelings connected with adoption remain largely painful and unspeakable, the fantasies it engenders may be acted out unconsciously, and the adopted person may repeatedly endanger his position in his family or the outside world, by performing actions which represent his unconscious identification with progenitors conceived of as bad or unworthy.

CLINICAL EXAMPLES

Four cases will illustrate various degrees to which adopted-related trauma can be integrated into conscious life by means of useful dialogue with parents. The extent and nature of such dialogue may strongly influence the integrity and resilience of adopted persons. Although it would have been desirable to demonstrate a differential outcome based solely on "age of telling," a vast majority of early-placed adoptees seen by clinicians were first told prior to age 5, and this held true for my practice as well. The most crucial variable, however, is the quality of "adoptive dialogue" within a home, and this did not prove difficult to assess.

Case 1. Miss C., a mental health worker in her late 30s, had "always known" that she was adopted. She had been able to discuss this fact with her parents, who responded nondefensively to her questions, and occasionally suggested that some reaction of hers might be related to adoption; she experienced these remarks as helpful rather than intrusive. She did well in school and was popular with peers.

While in graduate school, Miss C. initiated a search for her birth mother, receiving help from an adoptees' organization. She began the search without her parents' knowledge, feeling a need to do this alone, but later shared its results with them. She did not succeed in meeting this mother, who had died previously; she did, however, meet other relatives. She felt that this outcome was probably for the best, since from what she learned about "the woman," she thought it likely that her birth mother might have become dependent upon her in a way Miss C. would not have welcomed.

She said it was only in the past few years that she had been able to discuss adoption and her search with equanimity. She believed no one should search until adulthood, because of the possibility of severe disappointment for a vulnerable young person. She functioned fairly well in her work, which involved placing acting-out adolescents in foster homes; she had encountered some difficulties, however, which she attributed to "burn-out." She felt drained by her efforts, and sought to change to a more administrative type of job.

She was liked by co-workers and had an active social life. She shared the above information with me, knowing of my interest in adoption. What emerged most prominently in her account was the openness of her parents to her concerns about adoption. Though they had told her early of her adopted status, they were not preoccupied by it.

Miss C. was not free of adoption-related problems, but had reached a high level of functioning. She had received support from her parents, retroactively, for having made her search, which she accomplished in spite of practical and emotional difficulty; she had since maintained a good relationship with them. Her character was autonomous, and she had considerable spontaneity; yet she said of herself, "I still have trouble with commitment and separation, and I think it has to do with original rejection."

Case 2. Dan D., the adopted son of a professional family, was referred to his second therapist at 13. In early childhood he was doted on, partly because of a previous family tragedy; the parents were somewhat isolated and vulnerable to depression. Dan's welcome arrival validated them as parents, and they were delighted with his appearance, though they could never quite forget how different his features and coloration were from theirs. Mr. and Mrs. D. followed the agency prescription to "tell early," but for reasons related to their own lowered self-esteem, they laid undue stress on the topic. Occasionally they referred to differences between Dan's appearance and their own, in what they felt was a very positive way.

The word adoption was introduced before Dan's second birthday. Two major events had occurred shortly before: the death of his maternal grandfather, and the family's relocation to a different part of the country. He suffered from psychogenic diarrhea which subsided as the family became acclimated to their new home. Affectionate interchanges were marked at times by the use of the word "adopted." The parents rationalized this as a gradual desensitization and a reassurance of their love, "which he might doubt since he already knows he's adopted."

Dan's temperament was cheerful, determined, and willful. He had good relationships with both parents, but his mother was put off by his stubbornness. Following the birth of a "biological" brother when Dan was 5, he showed a depressed mood and became aggressive toward the brother within a year. Soon thereafter, he began making remarks denigrating his own value and intelligence and hinting that his parents might not want to keep him. It was clear to the parents that Dan had concerns about adoption. The first trial at therapy focused upon his self-depreciation and the frequent conflicts he was now having with his parents, but little change was seen and treatment was terminated by the parents after 18 months.

When I saw Dan several years later, I inquired early about his feelings as an adopted person. He was a bright, verbal, attractive adolescent who showed sadness when talking about adoption and felt guilt toward his parents because of the scenes which he frequently created. In spite of his initial openness, I could not engage him on a deep level, and at times it appeared there was a collusion between the boy and his parents to use adoption as a convenient rationalization for his difficulties within and outside the family.

Dan told me that he had long rebuffed his father's attempts to get closer to him. He gave as his reason the fantasy that "They're coming in a helicopter. It could be any day. They'll take me with them, and why get closer to Dad if I'm going to lose him?" On one occasion his parents were critical of his low level of effort and his poor grades. He wept, the parents reported, and said, "I want to be a fuck-up. I want to show them how they fucked me up by leaving me."

I was unable to elicit specific fantasies about the original parents; instead Dan intellectualized, repeating the few details provided by the adoption agency. At home, however, he once expressed the fantasy that his first mother was "living alone in a poor apartment somewhere." He often erupted in rages and continued to underachieve in school. He commented on his dilemma in therapy: "The part of me that wants to go with my parents' values is separate from the part that wants to screw up. Sometimes I really get mad at them, but I realize later it wasn't their fault. If I can get them to fight with me, then I have those two parts of myself together; they both come together to fight my parents off. And that way when I leave I'll still have all of myself."

Dan was a likable boy who had some successes in academics, music, and contact sports. He played outdoors with his brother and the brother's friends, but used these romps to regress and avoid his own work. His choice of reading material, films, and television programs reflected a preoccupation with aggression. He showed no difficulties with reality testing during interviews, but projective testing indicated the presence of disturbing, primitive fantasies. The testing did not suggest any feelings of being insufficiently loved or nurtured at home, however, nor were any preoccupations identified which could be specifically related to adoption.

Dan had friends, but often felt lonely. On entering high school he chose companions less bright than he who admired him but were also nonachievers. His failure to develop areas of solid success and his absorption in passive pursuits suggested that passivity might be present as a characterological response to the knowledge of having been passively transferred from one set of parents to another—though more specific rebellion against the adoptive parents was of course present as well.

Dan chose to end his therapy during tenth grade. Subsequently he went to boarding school in an adjoining state where he had to repeat a year; there he improved his work habits markedly. Though his ideas about his future were still vague, he was active in sports and dramatics, and was now eager to please his parents by academic success. His visits home were tranquil, and the parents reported their greatly increased hopes for him.

Dan D. required a physical distancing from his parents in order to experience his activities as being for himself. He then began to differentiate his adoptive parents' wishes for him from his own wishes for himself. He was predisposed to his difficulty by his parents' emotional vulnerability in his early years, which had led them to overstress adoption, and by the birth of a brother, which exacerbated his concerns about his place in the family.

In therapy Dan was able to articulate an intrapsychic conflict: a struggle between two types of ego ideal, one derived from his internalization of the adoptive parents' values, and the other from a poorly articulated fantasy of the biological parents. The difference between the two was most marked with respect to the management of aggression, and the ability to delay gratification. Dan struggled against this pain by trying to force the environment to reunite these separate parts of the self. It is clear from this example that an adoptee's family romance fantasy may exert a powerful influence even when available to consciousness, and that therapy alone may not suffice to resolve the conflict between opposing loyalties.

Although dialogue existed between Dan and his parents about adoption, and he was able to trust them with his feelings and fantasies at times, the dialogue was less helpful than it might have been because Dan identified it as something his parents wanted to engage in with him. From their standpoint it was a way of keeping in contact with a son who seemed increasingly distant from them, but from his point of view it felt depressing and was experienced at times as a capitulation.

Case 3. Mrs. E., a 36-year-old married woman, brought her son Evan for treatment. She worried that he was not masculine enough and that his school was unsympathetic to his special needs. Due to medical problems in the parents, Evan, age 10, was an only child, though the Es. would have preferred a larger family. He was a sturdy, gentle boy who was mildly anxious in social situations, but fully masculine in bearing. He had slight learning problems and had been placed in a prestigious private school which laid more emphasis on competition than Evan could be comfortable with.

After Evan's evalution, Mrs. E. confided, "Evan is doing fine, but I'm very unhappy and tense. In my dreams I am adrift." Evan, in fact, no longer needed my attention, and I began to see his mother in psychotherapy for her depression.

Mrs. E. had "always" known she was adopted. Her father was a professional man and the family enjoyed comfortable circumstances, but tension existed between her parents; her father suffered professional difficulties, and an older sister was retarded and institutionalized. The subject of adoption was never discussed.

She had married a man of means and carried on a busy schedule. Burdened by her obligations, she felt unable to shed any of them. Her major complaints were that she always felt guilty of some failure in her duties toward her son, her husband, or her aging parents; and a sense that she was left out of all decisions. Their house was in her husband's name only, because a psychiatrist she had consulted had told him she was unstable. She frequently entertained her husband's guests on short notice, but was not consciously aware of feeling victimized; instead she felt unworthy.

In her treatment, a connection was established between her feelings about her adoption and her acquiescent, depressed, self-punitive character structure. She conveyed the message, "Since I had nothing to say about my fate in the beginning, I must be someone who cannot act, but can only be acted upon. Since I owe my life to people who had no obligation to me, I must spend it fulfilling obligations."

With reference to adoption, she said, "Birthdays are hard for me. I keep thinking there must be some poor soul out there wondering what became of me." Yet she would not allow herself to act on her barely acknowledged curiosity about her original parents, maintaining that her adoptive parents would learn of it and be terribly hurt: "I could never do that to them."

When Mrs. E. was satisfied that her son was continuing to progress, she gradually discontinued her own treatment, saying that things were better now; she was setting more limits, but the "visits" felt like an additional burden in her round of activities. She was never able to experience her therapy as being fully for herself—rather, it was to help her be a better wife and mother.

As a child and adolescent, Mrs. E. had not been given permission to think about adoption as an important aspect of her life. Paradoxically, however, she had developed a strong conscious belief that she owed her very existence to this event. Its primary representation in her mental life was a strong unconscious identification as an abandoned, helpless child who had no choices. She had early turned her hostile feelings against herself, but her masochistic, depressive stance also maintained a persistent accusation against the very people toward whom she consciously felt loyal and indebted. As a biological mother, she carried her difficulties with self-esteem into her relationship with her son, whom she pushed to perform in every sphere. (He once retorted, perhaps picking up on a strong family theme, "It's not my fault if I'm an only child!")

Case 4. Frank F. was placed with the F. family at 15 months with his biological brother George, 3 years older. Their mother had a psychiatric disorder. Both children had been taken from her when Frank was 6 weeks old; they remained together in one foster home until placement with the Fs.

The family had three older "home-made" children when Frank and George arrived. One year later they asked that George be removed because of his stealing. Frank remained in the home; during that year his biological mother died and the Fs., moved by pity, adopted him in response to the placing agency's request. During that same year a fourth biological child was born.

The youngest child developed a life-threatening illness when she was 7, and the hospital social worker assigned to help the family began hearing of their difficulties with Frank's behavior. He had stolen from family members, broken into a neighbor's house, and exhibited himself to two women. The parents were at a loss to understand how he could be so inconsiderate at such a painful time; they had only one method of punishment, which was to restrict him to his room or to the house, but admitted that this was not working. (The family had had counseling elsewhere for Frank's problem during the previous year. Psychological testing was done and conjoint family treatment begun, but the family withdrew dissatisfied after five sessions.)

The social worker then referred Frank to me. Mr. and Mrs. F., in their 50s, looked depressed and resigned. They were bewildered by Frank's "smart-ass" attitude and acting-out behavior; they said he had been getting into trouble since fourth grade and that they could no longer trust him. Asked about their knowledge of his original parents, they hesitated and looked more depressed. Their only certain knowledge was that his mother was dead and his father had served time in prison for an offense involving armed robbery and drugs. Mrs. F. directly expressed the fear that Frank might have inherited his bad behavior. George by now had been living in an adoptive home in a distant state for some years; the Fs. had agreed to an approach by the other adoptive family, suggesting that they bring George to meet Frank. They admitted that the week-long visit had been exciting to Frank, but were not eager to repeat the contact since "they weren't exactly our kind of people." Mr. and Mrs. F. had avoided talking with Frank about his origins and early memories, for fear of activating his bad heredity, and they never referred to his adoption except when the subject of George was raised.

Frank was a nice-looking young adolescent, now 13½, neatly dressed, of bright-average intelligence consistent with his past testing. He readily admitted that his present situation was terrible both at home and in school. He always seemed to do things that got adults angry at him, but could express no ideas of his own about why this was so. He thought he was well liked by peers, and was proud that girls seemed to find him attractive. He had no particular interests or skills beyond listening to rock music, nor any career aspirations except for a vague interest in joining the army. His range of affect was narrow and although he was able to laugh at appropriate times, he appeared chronically, moderately depressed. His eyes filled twice in the first interview: when he talked about feeling unjustly punished by his parents, and when he described what it was like to say good-bye to George at the end of his visit the previous year.

I saw Frank in therapy over a period of 13 months. The topic of adoption was virtually impossible for him to discuss. He said at first that he rarely thought about it. Asked what he knew of his original parents, he said that his mother was dead, and his father had been in jail; he thought his father "must be an asshole." I said he must feel sad that he had never known his first parents and rarely saw his brother, and commented on the long-standing discomfort between Frank and his adoptive family. He listened intently and occasionally appeared close to tears, but he found little to say in response. Once during a drawing game he identified a primitive, wild-looking face as "my biological father." New crises would develop in the family around Frank's misconduct at home or in school; Mr. F. would insist on seeing me first, or would brief me on the new development in Frank's presence. Frank would become tearful when this happened, but my attempts to set a limit on Mr. F.'s intrusive behavior met with no success.

A stay at an overnight camp was arranged; Frank was asked to leave early because of theft and minor vandalism. The family responded by restricting him to the house indefinitely, outside of school hours. The parents discontinued therapy, feeling it had done no good, and initiated contact with a public agency for temporary placement. They remained ambivalently involved with Frank for some time after this request, but eventually asked that he be moved.

A foster home was found to which he initially adjusted well. A few months later, however, he was involved in an escapade featuring alcohol and exhibitionism in front of younger children. Although the foster parents liked him, they could not withstand community pressure and he had to leave. Placement in a group living situation was required. Mr. and Mrs. F. told social workers that they might take Frank back at some future time "if he were straightened out." They seemed unable to recognize any contribution of their own to the difficulty.

Frank occupies a fourth position on the continuum. His adoption by the Fs., motivated largely by a sense of social responsibility, was marked by their inability to relax with the boy and trust him, because of their knowledge of his origins. They could not tolerate his brother's testing behavior and terminated early with him, but they believed a younger child would be more malleable. They were unable to talk with him about the process of his adoption and the reasons for it.

Frank developed fantasies about his father which were entirely negative, and his fixed sadness about his unknown mother's death resembled an unresolved grief reaction. The inability of Mr. and Mrs. F. to enter into a dialogue with Frank about his transition to their family resulted in his failure to identify with them and their values, and ultimately contributed to disruption of the adoption. It is unclear whether he will have further contact with the Fs.; what seems clear enough is that they viewed him, when he was bad, not as their son with both good and bad potential, but as the bad son of the original parents (Brinich, 1980). His future adjustment as an adult does not appear promising.

HELPING ADOPTIVE PARENTS

An infant has no past, and a young toddler scarcely any; adoptive parents, at least, have been encouraged to believe this and to view the child as "all theirs"—or, to be more precise, to believe that all the important experience the child would have would occur in the adoptive home. They were advised to regard adopting as a joyful experience scarcely different from procreating a child. The only catch was that one had to "tell," preferably before school age. Many parents viewed this task with mixed feelings.

By the late 1950s several reports had appeared which suggested that knowledge of adopted status may be disturbing to a young child. In addition, personal accounts were published which vehemently attacked certain common practices in the "telling" process, such as the "white lie" that the child's parents had been killed in a car accident.

The great majority of adoptive parents, in this era, had adopted infants or young toddlers, and had not been prepared for the possibility that these children might be at risk in any way. The professional community, including pediatricians and many child mental health workers, generally either did not recognize this possibility or had such a vague awareness of it that they were not able to translate their clinical impressions into useful recommendations for parents.

To develop in health, adoptees must learn to forgive their abandoners. The dilemma must be formulated and eventually resolved. And because adoption is still a foreign body in our society, adoptees and their families are at risk; even the posing of the problem goes against the grain for many who would believe that adopting a child is no different from "having one's own."

Blum (1983) cogently described the psychological forces which operate to limit or enhance an adopting couple's comfort with the process of adoption. He emphasized the threat posed by infertility to an individual's identity and to a marriage and the importance of emotional support by the grandparents who may feel threatened by adoption. Kirk (1964, 1981) also concerned himself with adoptive parents' needs. The concepts of "generational continuity" and "shared fate" elaborated by these two authors are primarily addressed to parents adopting infants, however.

The best methods of adoptive practice for infant placements were still under study when adoption diversified in the 1970s. The questions most often asked prior to that time were when and how to tell, and how to deal with adolescents' rebellion and expressed desire to find their birth parents. Recent changes in the patterns of adoption offer the opportunity to find a more informed stance on these old questions.

As in Roman and Babylonian times, as in certain contemporary non-Western societies, and even as in the United States a hundred years ago, adoption in North America and Western Europe now includes types of family formation which were foreign to midcentury practitioners of adoption. Parents cannot pretend that a child placed during latency or adolescence had no life before adoption. Are these special situations, to be considered separately from the handling of infant adoption? Or do these forms represent opposite ends of a continuum, on which the adoption of older infants and toddlers occupies a more central position?

The latter is a more useful viewpoint and can serve as a theoretical base from which to provide guidance to parents who adopt children at various ages. At whatever age they joined their families, these children will continue to require guidance and communication with respect to their adoptive status as they proceed to negotiate their individual growth and development. The question of "telling," and the closely allied idea of dialogue with a child about adoption, can be viewed from several standpoints.

1. One might first ask, *why tell at all?* Current arguments for telling can be summarized briefly: (a) It would be traumatic for the child to learn about his adoption from another source. (b) It is best to be honest, and as long as there is love, the fact of adoption need not figure greatly in the child's life. (c) The child's birth mother might seek him out later. (d) In the case of a racially different child, he or she needs some explanation. (e) When a child is adopted past early infancy but before continuity of memory is established, the persistence of memory traces or of fragmentary conscious memories makes it necessary to bring these into harmony with the child's present existence. I am aware of only one argument against telling: the belief that an adoptee can never fully recover from the impact of knowing that he did not originate with the parents he knows.

2. The question of *age for telling* arises in pure form with children placed in the first 18 to 24 months of life, who can be presumed to retain few if any memories of prior caretakers. In the case of a child adopted at 9 or 10 years, however, adopters ignore his preadoptive life at the child's peril and their own. The question of "telling" does not arise here; instead what is required is to help the child gradually to integrate memories of his previous life and caretakers with his present existence. (Even people adopting children of early school age or older have been known to change their first names, modify their bodies by circumcision or other cosmetic operations soon after placement, or in other ways violate the child's existence as an individual human being before he has had the time to throw in his lot emotionally with the family.)

When a child is placed between infancy and the latency period there is a continuum with respect to conscious and unconscious memory of life with previous parents or foster parents: the older the child, the more in consciousness or accessible to conscious memory. With children placed between 2 and 4, parents should be especially alert to the emergence of memory traces, in order to help the child experience disclosure as coming partly from within himself.

3. One dimension of "telling" relates to internal and externally conditioned *needs of the adopter*. Internal needs arise from the adopter's discomfort with what he or she has brought about:

feelings of guilt at having "stolen" a child, need for approval for what he experiences as a deviant act, need to have the child "understand" so the adopter may be free of the guilt he feels for having destroyed a potential family unit. Externally conditioned need arises from observable physical differences between the child and his adopters, or from other circumstances which make it impossible for the adopters to deny the fact of adoption to their community. The most obvious is the lack of a pregnancy; in addition, there are darker-skinned children, and those who are obviously no longer newborns. Parents feel the need to "tell" the community in these cases (often mainly to gain the community's approval) long before a need would arise to tell the child. In such situations, parents may experience the need to tell the child as stemming directly from the fact that the community already knows.

4. Another influence on "telling" is the *quality of early bonding* between child and adopters. While unsuccessful outcomes arise more commonly in the case of later placed children, many occur with those placed in the earliest weeks. Of these families, a majority present the history that from early on the child was felt to be alien, rejecting, "not what we wanted," or of questionable heredity. As children in these families grow older, "telling" is embedded in a negatively tinged preoccupation with the entire adoptive process (see case 4 above). Most cases of traumatic disclosure occur in such situations; for example, when a child watching a television program on adoption "casually" turns to his mother and asks if he himself is adopted, and receives the answer then and there that he is, though the subject has never been broached before. Or when a parent, in a fit of anger at a latency or adolescent child, will first come out with the information by comparing the adoptee's behavior with some negative piece of information about the biological parents.

With respect to "early" or "late" disclosure, arguments can be summarized as follows:

Early disclosure (before age 5) accustoms the child to the word "adopted," which he hears in a loving context; later he will gradually come to understand its meaning, but this process will be less traumatic because of prior exposure to the word. If told in latency or subsequently, a child will resent his parents' having known an important fact about him which was not shared—or he may hear it from another source if the parents wait too long.

Arguments which favor later telling (Peller, 1961, 1963; Schechter, 1964) are based on psychoanalytic developmental theory or on cognitive studies of children's development (Brodzinsky et al., 1984a, 1984b, 1985). It is argued, and case material has shown, that a child's ability to resolve the oedipal conflict and identify with the parent of the same sex is interfered with by presenting him with the knowledge of adoption during the oedipal years. On the one hand, he is attempting to establish his place within the family; simultaneously, he is being told that in an important sense he does not belong to it.

How is one to proceed? What advice should be given to the parents of an infant, a toddler, a school-age or older child who inquire about the present state about when and how to tell or talk about adoption? The following guidelines attempt to combine the idea of *disclosure* per se with those of *ongoing dialogue* following disclosure, and *initiating dialogue* with a later-placed child.

1. The possibility of not telling at all is rarely discussed these days, but it deserves careful examination by clinicians and parents. Our society is not accustomed to sustain this kind of secrecy, and it is known that such secrecy at times breeds pathology. Probably most situations in which this alternative was tried would turn out badly. Yet adopters may look with brief fascination at this alternative and wish it were possible to "get away with it." For many, rejecting the idea of not telling is a stage in the process of accepting the status of adoptive parenthood.

2. There seems little reason to tell a child below the age of 5 that he or she is adopted if the placement occurred prior to 18-24 months and the child is of the same racial group as the parents.

3. A child placed after age 18 months may retain memories which become stimulated by sensory impressions and which are accessible via spoken language. Parents of such a child ought to remain alert to changes in mood or other signs that earlier circumstances are being recalled. They might suggest, "Maybe you're remembering something." If the child responds with deepened affect or specific content, the importance of this event should be recognized by the parents. It should be recorded for

future conversations, and the emergence of other such memories or memory traces should be anticipated and welcomed even if the affect is sad or agitated. The *fact of adoption* need not be brought up explicitly as soon as this sort of thing emerges, but if another caretaker is specifically recalled or asked about by the child, a simple disclosure should occur: "Yes, another woman used to take care of you." Further elaboration on what adoption means may or may not be demanded by such a preschool child, but if pressed for, should be given.

4. In the case of preschool children who are identifiably different in appearance from their adopters, parents should be watchful, in addition, for signs that the child has become aware of this difference (either by his own observation or because someone has called his attention to it). Again, the first sign of such awareness is not an immediate signal for "telling." Parents need to learn what a child is experiencing before they can respond helpfully. At certain times a child may merely be looking for reassurance that the parents love him and intend to keep him; at others, more thorough disclosure of adoption may be called for. If, in addition to specific concerns, early memories have also emerged, the case is stronger for disclosure to a preschool child whose appearance differs from that of his adopters.

5. If placement occurred after age 2, and the child is intellectually normal, a large variety of experiences will have been encoded in verbal memory before placement in the adoptive home. When adopters choose not to learn about, record, or perpetuate such memories, they will exacerbate the discontinuity experienced by the child. In such situations the existence of previous caretakers should be acknowledged from the beginning. If they are not mentioned by the child, parents should work to safeguard the continuity of the child's experience by reminding him or her of the previous living situation from time to time, still bearing in mind that too frequent reminders might arouse fears of losing his present home.

When children in this group ask questions about their origins, it is not necessarily the procreative aspect which is on their minds, and they may not need information about it at this stage. Once the child is aware that a transition has occurred, however, he will want reassurance that the old and new parents were acquainted and respected one another (as is the case with all children who maintain allegiances to different adults: parents and teachers, divorced parents; the fact that these examples are of simultaneous allegiances, while adoption has to do with sequential allegiances, is of no consequence). If such is not the case, parents and professionals need to bear in mind that the child needs to know it regardless.

This often becomes a dilemma, particularly when children are placed after abuse or neglect. Adoptive parents must remember that the child needs to know he started off in good hands, and was transferred willingly, for good reasons, to other good hands. If this does not correspond to objective reality or their perception of it, adopters may need to be reminded that the child will have plenty of chances later on to learn more about his early circumstances, when his own self-concept is more fully formed and he can tolerate the introduction of unpleasant facts. Later disillusionment is less damaging to the personality than having started out with serious threats to self-esteem.

6. In other early placements the ideal time for disclosure would appear to be between 6 and 8. Before age 6, two major obstacles stand in the way of a child's assimilating the knowledge of adoption. The first, described by Wieder (1977a, 1977b, 1978a, 1978b), Peller (1961, 1963), and Schechter (1960, 1964) relates to the child's need to feel firmly established in his home (i.e., to have arrived at a temporary closure on oedipal dilemmas) before he is challenged with information of such importance. Not only oedipal concerns are at issue, but also those belonging to prior stages of development. Fear of loss of the object, and later, fear of loss of the object's love, are still present to some degree in 2- to 4-year-olds, the age at which agencies still routinely advise parents that disclosure should occur.

The other obstacle is a cognitive one (Brodzinsky et al., 1984a, 1984b; Shapiro and Perry, 1976). It is questionable whether a prelatency child can comprehend the meaning of relinquishment and an adoptive connection in a useful way—a way, that is, which mobilizes the affect that must eventually follow on such disclosure. Disclosure during the preschool period presents the risk that a child will be given emotionally threatening information at a time when he can neither fully comprehend it, nor work through the losses implied by the information.

What can one do in the interim, if the decision is made to wait until 6 or later? *Foreshadowing* is an important preparatory process. By this term I refer to exposure of the child to a wide range of family situations. Divorce, remarriage, bereavement, stepfamilies, stepparent adoption, and nonrelative adoption are familiar to most children through their own or their parents' social contacts. The parents of a young adopted child can refer to these various but normal circumstances in a natural way when the occasion arises, and explain them in a way which will allow the child to experience himself as less deviant, when he subsequently learns of his adoption, than he otherwise might.

Implicit in this recommendation to tell at 6 to 8 years is the belief that following initial disclosure, the postoedipal child will in most cases go through a period of active grieving and preoccupation with origins and self-worth, which may last a year or 2 in a fairly intense form and then gradually recede. If such is the case, as my clinical experience leads me to believe, then this period ought to occur, insofar as possible, at a point in a child's life when it is least likely to interfere with ongoing development. As mentioned above, the years prior to 6 do not seem best. Disclosure during adolescence can be devastating to a child's self-esteem and to his faith in his parents. One is left with early latency (6 to 8), late latency (8 to 10), and preadolescence (10 to 12).

The most desirable timing is in early latency, prior to age 8; the ensuing period of preoccupation and mourning will be largely completed some time in later latency, and this period will occur simultaneously with the pleasures of increased competence and joining the peer group, which present substantial compensations for depressed mood in a child. It will most likely have run its course before the beginning of preadolescence, when a child needs to focus on detail both in school and in organized peer activities.

CONCLUSIONS

Growing up as an adopted person differs in several respects from growing up as the biological child of one's parents. There is often a predisposition toward a questing or rebellious style of behavior. The disclosure of adoption has effects on the nature of a growing child's fantasy life and, at times, on his cognitive style. Adoptees have a need to mourn several kinds of loss: overt or object losses, status losses, and covert losses such as the assault on self-esteem which arises from the knowledge of not having remained with one's original parents.

The parents' most important task is not so much to "find the moment to tell," but rather to be alert through their son's or daughter's lifetime to moments when the multifarious meanings of being adopted (emotional, fantasied, and practical) impinge on the child's life and require explanation, clarification, support, or direction. They often need the help of professionals in order to carry out this aspect of their parental function. Parent support groups may be of great help, especially to parents who have adopted older, handicapped, or disturbed children; but some of these parents' comments are telling. They often remark that "the psychiatrist didn't understand; the people in the group were the only ones who did." The need for dialogue and the still-troublesome question of when to tell are both touched on by one mother's comment to me: "He's never really been *told,* because he always *knew.* If you told them later, you'd really talk about it."

The diversification of adoption reflects that of our society; it reflects, also, society's increasing commitment to the rights of the child. New types of adoption present special problems, but it can only be viewed as salutary that now it is much harder to maintain the stance that the "old adoption" was problem-free. Adoption of infants, toddlers, and older children forms a continuum. To the extent that professionals can help parents mobilize empathy and carry on appropriate dialogue with their adopted children, these children can be expected to enter adult life with the capacity to behave as citizens and to live fulfilled lives.

BIBLIOGRAPHY

ARLOW, J. A. (1976). Communication and character. *Psychoanal. Study Child,* 31:139–163.

BETTELHEIM, B. (1954). *Symbolic Wounds.* New York: Free Press.

BLOS, P. (1968). Character formation in adolescence. *Psychoanal. Study Child,* 23:245–263.

BLUM, H. P. (1983). Adoptive parents. *Psychoanal. Study Child,* 38:141–163.

BOURGEOIS, M. (1975). L'adoption et ses aspects psychiatriques. *Ann. medico-psychol.,* 133:73–103.

Brinich, P. M. (1980). Some potential effects of adoption on self and object representations. *Psychoanal. Study Child*, 35:107–133.

Brodzinsky, D. M., Schechter, D. E., & Braff, A. M. (1985). Children's knowledge of adoption. In *Thinking about the family*, ed. R. Ashmore & D. M. Brodzinsky. Hillsdale, N.J.: Erlbaum (in press).

—— —— —— & Singer, L. M. (1984a). Psychological and academic adjustment in adopted children. *J. Consult. Clin. Psychol.*, 52:582–590.

—— Singer, L. M., & Braff, A. M. (1984b). Children's understanding of adoption. *Child Developm.*, 55:869–878.

Freud, S. (1905). Fragment of an analysis of a case of hysteria. *S.E.*, 7:3–122.

—— (1917). Mourning and melancholia. *S.E.*, 14:243–256.

Furman, E. (1974). *A Child's Parent Dies.* New Haven & London: Yale Univ. Press.

Goffman, E. (1963). *Stigma.* Englewood Cliffs, N.J.: Prentice-Hall.

Goldstein, J., Freud, A., & Solnit, A. J. (1973). *Beyond the Best Interests of the Child.* New York: Free Press.

—— —— —— (1979). *Before the Best Interests of the Child.* New York: Free Press.

Kirk, H. D. (1964). *Shared Fate.* New York: Free Press.

—— (1981). *Adoptive Kinship.* Toronto: Butterworths.

Lebovici, S. & Soulé, M. (1970). *La connaissance de l'enfant par la psychanalyse.* Paris: Presses Univ. de France, pp. 526–571.

Lewis, D. O., Balla, D., Lewis, M., & Gore, R. (1975). The treatment of adopted versus neglected children in the court. *Amer. J. Psychiat.*, 132:142–145.

McWhinnie, A. M. (1967). *Adopted Children and How They Grow Up.* London: Routledge and Kegan Paul.

Mahler, M. S., Pine, F., & Bergman, A. (1975). *The Psychological Birth of the Human Infant.* New York: Basic Books.

Offord, D. R., Aponte, J. R., & Cross, L. A. (1969). Presenting symptomatology of adopted children. *Arch. Gen. Psychiat.*, 20:110–116.

Panel (1967). Psychoanalytic theory as it relates to adoption. M. D. Schechter, reporter. *J. Amer. Psychoanal. Assn.*, 15:695–708.

Peller, L. E. (1961). About telling the child about his adoption. *Bull. Phila. Assn. Psychoanal.*, 11:145–154.

—— (1963). Further comments on adoption. *Bull. Phila. Assn. Psychoanal.*, 13:1–14.

Raynor, L. (1980). *The Adopted Child Comes of Age.* London: George Allen & Unwin.

Reeves, A. C. (1971). Children with surrogate parents. *Brit. J. Med. Psychol.*, 44:155–171.

Rizzuto, A. M. (1982). Personal communication.

Sants, J. H. (1964). Genealogical bewilderment in children with substitute parents. *Brit. J. Med. Psychol.*, 37:133–141.

Sarnoff, C. (1976). *Latency.* New York: Aronson.

Schechter, M. D. (1960). Observations on adopted children. *Arch. Gen. Psychiat.*, 3:21–32.

_____ (1970). About adoptive parents. In *Parenthood*, ed. E. J. Anthony & T. Benedek. Boston: Little, Brown, pp. 353–371.

_____ CARLSON, P., SIMMONS, J. Q., & WORK, H. (1964). Emotional problems in the adoptee. *Arch. Gen. Psychiat.*, 10:109–118.

SHAPIRO, T. & PERRY, R. (1976). Latency revisited. *Psychoanal. Study Child*, 31:79–105.

SOROSKY, A. D., BARAN, A., & PANNOR, R. (1979). *The Adoption Triangle*. Garden City, N.J.: Doubleday.

SPITZ, R. A. (1957). *No and Yes*. New York: Int. Univ. Press.

TRIDON, P., VIDAILHET, C., & EDELSON, V. (1981). Le non-dit chez l'enfant. *Ann. Pediat.*, 28:91–96.

TRISELIOTIS, J. (1973). *In Search of Origins*. London: Routledge & Kegan Paul.

WEILLISCH, E. (1952). Children without genealogy. *Ment. Hlth.*, 13:41–42.

WIEDER, H. (1977a). On being told of adoption. *Psychoanal. Q.*, 46:1–22.

_____ (1977b). The family romance fantasies of adopted children. *Psychoanal. Q.*, 46:185–200.

_____ (1978a). On when and whether to disclose about adoption. *J. Amer. Psychoanal. Assn.*, 26:793–811.

_____ (1978b). Special problems in the psychoanalysis of adopted children. In *Child Analysis and Therapy*, ed. J. Glenn. New York: Aronson, pp. 557–577.

WINNICOTT, D. W. (1956). The antisocial tendency. In *Collected Papers*. New York: Basic Books, 1958, pp. 306–315.

_____ (1971a). *Therapeutic Consultations in Child Psychiatry*. New York: Basic Books.

_____ (1971b). *Playing and Reality*. New York: Basic Books.

Michelangelo's *Ignudi*, Hermaphrodism, and Creativity

JEROME D. OREMLAND, M.D.

MICHELANGELO IS THE UNSURPASSED MASTER OF PORTRAYING THE
male body. Most surprising, at times, is Michelangelo's artful,
interesting, and beautiful feminization of men, e.g., the *Bacchus*
(ca. 1497), the *Dying Slave* (ca. 1514), and the *Apollo David* (ca.
1530).[1] Michelangelo truly recreated, in various forms, Hermaphroditus, the beautiful son of Hermes and Aphrodite who
became united in a single body with the nymph Salmacis. The
recreation of Hermaphroditus, perhaps, reaches its apogee in
some of Michelangelo's *ignudi* (fig. 1), those 20 nude adolescents
who with celestial abandonment frame the *Histories* (fig. 2), the 9
grand narratives that constitute the spine of his decoration of the
Sistine Ceiling.

Chief of Psychiatry, San Francisco Children's Hospital and Adult Medical
Center; Clinical Professor of Psychiatry, University of California, San Francisco; Faculty, San Francisco Psychoanalytic Institute; and Director, San Francisco Postgraduate Institute for Psychotherapy.

This paper was awarded the 1984 Fritz Schmidl Memorial Prize by the
Seattle Psychoanalytic Society.

1. Space constraint makes it impossible to present illustrations of all the
Michelangelo art referred to in the text. The reader is referred to Liebert
(1982) and Hibbard (1974) for, among other things, their completeness and
accuracy of presentation of the Michelangelo *oeuvres*.

Although Michelangelo could draw, paint, and sculpt beautiful and feminine women, e.g., *Mary* in the St. Peter's *Pietá* (ca. 1498), *Libica, Delphica*, and
the young woman in God's arm in the *Awakening of Adam*, all in the Sistine
Ceiling, his artful masculinization of women is also impressive, e.g., the *Night*
(ca. 1527) in the Medici Chapel, and the *Cumaea* in the Ceiling.

Figure 1. *Ignudo,* Altar Wall Group

A great deal has been written and even more omitted about Michelangelo's homosexuality (Clements, 1966). Ample evidence can be found in the letters, the artistic depictions, and the poems that Michelangelo had intense sexual feelings toward young men (Clements, 1966; Oremland, 1980; Liebert, 1982a). Although analytic interpreters differ regarding the overtness of homosexual consummation in these relationships, the corre-

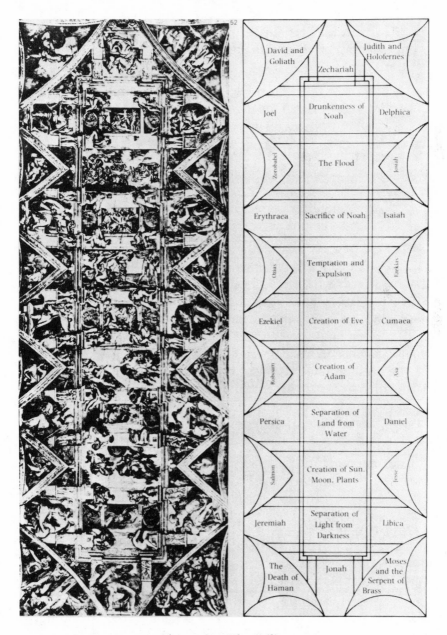

52

David and Goliath		Judith and Holofernes
	Zechariah	
Joel	Drunkenness of Noah	Delphica
Zorobabel	The Flood	Josiah
Erythraea	Sacrifice of Noah	Isaiah
Ozias	Temptation and Expulsion	Ezekias
Ezekiel	Creation of Eve	Cumaea
Roboam	Creation of Adam	Asa
Persica	Separation of Land from Water	Daniel
Salmon	Creation of Sun, Moon, Plants	Jesse
Jeremiah	Separation of Light from Darkness	Libica
The Death of Haman	Jonah	Moses and the Serpent of Brass

Figure 2. *The Ceiling*

spondence and poetry suggest that this was more than a homoerotic orientation; that Michelangelo had a series of homosexual
relationships (Clements, 1966; Oremland, 1980).

Poem for Tommaso
What from thee I long for and learn to
    know deep within me
Cannot be well understood by outward
    acts and signs.
[Clements, 1966, p. 207].

Poem for the dead Cecchino
Do yet attest for him how gracious I was in bed
When he embraced, and in what the soul doth live.
[Clements, 1966, p. 147].

More specifically, the Michelangelo poetry, when studied with
the sculptured works, drawings, and letters, suggests that certain
of these relationships were characterized by sexualized adoration, adoption, and subjugation to the young man.

To understand psychodynamically these relationships and
their relevance to his art, we need to review, albeit briefly, some
of the well-established facts regarding the circumstances of
Michelangelo's early life.

MICHELANGELO AND HIS MOTHER

The sparse biographical material available about Michelangelo,
particularly of his earlier years, has been detailed by many modern biographical and psychoanalytic authors (Sterba and Sterba,
1956; Tolnay, 1967; Hibbard, 1974; Liebert, 1982a; Oremland,
1978, 1980). Psychoanalytic writers place importance on Michelangelo's having been given, shortly after his birth, to a wet nurse,
the daughter and wife of stonecutters in Settignano, a small
village near Florence. Even though this custom was frequent in
Renaissance Tuscany, Michelangelo's placement had special significance in that it was probably necessitated by his mother's
illness and was intensified by his being returned, probably shortly after weaning (a second loss, the loss of the wet nurse) to his
almost constantly pregnant, probably chronically ill mother
(Ross, 1974; Oremland, 1980). The effect of these early mater-

nal disruptions was fatefully intensified by the mother's death in 1481 when Michelangelo was 6.

In the Michelangelo correspondence, only two references to his mother exist in all the information we have from Michelangelo. In a frequently quoted letter to Vasari, Michelangelo wrote,

> If I possess anything of good in my mental constitution, it comes from my having been born in your clear climate of Arezzo . . . I drew the chisel and the mallet upon which I carve statues in together with my nurse's milk [Symonds, 1892, p. 26].

The quote suggests the importance of the wet nurse in Settignano, and the association in his mind of that early nurturing relationship with a sense of well-being with the objects for sculpting: stone, the chisel, and the mallet (Liebert, 1982a).

The other reference to the mother is in a late letter to his nephew Leonardo. Michelangelo's interest in Leonardo's children, Michelangelo's only heirs, was considerable.[2] With each pregnancy of Leonardo's wife, Michelangelo suggested names, usually that of one of his brothers. No mention was made of what should be done if the baby were a girl. Yet, in a letter dated June 27, 1562, 2 years before Michelangelo's death, when writing regarding a pregnancy, he suggested if the baby were a girl, perhaps she could be named Francesca, his mother's name (Condivi, 1553; Ramsden, 1963; Oremland, 1978).

MICHELANGELO AND HIS FATHER

Although psychoanalytic interest has largely been in the relationship of certain of Michelangelo's depictions, particularly the *madonnas* and the *pietás*, to the early loss of the mother, considerable speculation has been advanced regarding the effect of his complicated relation with his father on his life and art (Sterba and Sterba, 1956; Frank, 1966; Oremland, 1978, 1980; Liebert,

2. Leonardo was the eldest child of Buonarroto, Michelangelo's next youngest and favorite brother. Of Michelangelo's four brothers, only Buonarroto married. The eldest, Leonardo, became a monk and the two youngest were essentially ne'er-do-wells.

1982a). It is well documented that Michelangelo's father, Lodovico, and Michelangelo's uncle were violent men prone to harsh and severe physical punishment of the young Buonarroti boys. The known information suggests that the father attempted to discourage Michelangelo's artistic pursuits, fearing they would not lead to a financially remunerative life. His concern was partly for Michelangelo, but probably more so for his own welfare. Lodovico's negotiations with the painter Domenico Ghirlandaio and later with Lorenzo the Magnificent regarding Michelangelo's apprenticeship and education seem heavily tinged with self-serving motives and his inclination to exploit his son's abilities.

It is known that Michelangelo's older brother, Leonardo, became a Dominican monk and a follower of Savonarola when Michelangelo was 16. Functionally, Michelangelo early became the eldest son and the head of the family, even to the point of disciplining the younger brothers. It is likely that Michelangelo's father remarried when Michelangelo was about 10 years old, and there may even have been a stepbrother, Matteo. However, neither the stepmother nor stepbrother is mentioned in the correspondence or in Michelangelo's reminiscences.

Lodovico was in no way successful and always in debt. In fact, his employment consisted of minor political appointments dependent on low-level patronage. As early as 1497, his indebtedness to his brother-in-law had grown to the extent that his brother-in-law wanted to have him arrested. Later, a sister-in-law sued him for indebtedness. In both situations, the father implored Michelangelo to help him with money and influence. One view explains Lodovico's irresponsible and reproachable behavior as the result of his inability to reconcile himself to the change in the family fortune. (Although his father's bank had failed many years before, Lodovico persistently attempted to live the life of a gentleman on the meager proceeds of his farm lands.) This charitable view obscures that Lodovico was a pretentious, prideful, ineffectual, suspicious man who harbored the family's misfortune to justify and explain away his own repeated failures.

Much of Michelangelo's existing correspondence, particularly during the early periods in Rome, was to his father. The correspondence seems peculiarly banal. As early as 1500, the letters largely involved Michelangelo's attempts to help his father and his brothers with money and influence. Their requests for help often came at times when he was barely finding his own way. For example, the correspondence during his stay in Bologna, 1506–08, when he was living under extreme hardship with the threat of plague and struggling with the bronze casting of the statue of Julius II, seems particularly illustrative of his family's insensitivity. Their steady stream of requests of a petty sort and their detailing of their financial difficulties are strangely devoid of concern for his welfare. It is rare indeed to come across a passage in which they express any concern for him, or in which any help is offered to him. In general, Michelangelo's responses to the father and the brothers were consistently helpful. Though frequently irritated with the father and chiding the brothers, Michelangelo repeatedly offered money, loans, gifts, advice, and concern. For example, we know that in 1511, while Michelangelo was laboring horrendously with the Ceiling, the father took some money from Michelangelo's account without permission. It was only by direct confrontation that the matter was clarified. Michelangelo later forgave part of it as a gift. In 1512 Michelangelo purchased a farm and a shop for the father and brothers. In 1513, shortly after the completion of the Ceiling, Michelangelo forgave the father's and brothers' indebtedness to him and essentially agreed to support them all. During this period, there were many letters in which friends cautioned Michelangelo about giving the father or the brothers money or property directly because of concern about their judgment and intentions.

Particularly revealing of this complex relationship are the salutations of the letters to the father. In accord with the time, they are highly reverential, most often beginning "dearest father" or "most revered father." Strikingly, in corresponding with friends and brothers, even as early as his mid-20s, Michelangelo almost invariably refers to his father by his first name, Lodovico. For example, in a letter to his brother Buonarroto dated February 1, 1507, warning about a difficulty with some helpers, he writes: "I write you this, not because I care anything about them, since they are not worth three coppers between them, but so that *Lodovico* won't be astonished if they come to talk to him" (Linscott, 1963,

p. 195; italics added). The referring to his father by his first name suggests how early, perhaps ambivalently, Michelangelo realized he was the father to his father and his brothers.

It is true that when Lodovico was near death, he sought reconciliation with Michelangelo. At that time in ways atypical for him, Lodovico acknowledged his gratitude to Michelangelo. Michelangelo's seemingly incomplete poem written on the death of his father in 1531 is, indeed, ambivalent, complex, and touching. The poem must be read keeping in mind that Michelangelo's favorite brother, Buonarroto, had died but 3 years before.

> Though earlier my heart as pressed me so . . .
> My great sorrow though my weeping woe.
>
> Between the son dying first and you, thereafter,
> of whom I'm speaking, tongue, pen, and lament.
>
> One was brother to me, you were our father;
> Love strains toward him, to you my obligation,
> I don't know which hurt strains or irks me further.
>
> My brother's painted in my recollection,
> And it carves you alive inside my heart,
> For face and heart more strain and more affliction.
>
> And yet, as for the debit, it gives me quiet
> My brother paid it green, and you mature;
> Death in old age makes others feel less hurt.
>
> And if the best of love in Heaven increases
> Between father and son, as virtues all grow . . .
>
> [Linscott, 1963, p. 61f.].

The poem clearly shows a complex response to the father's death; as Liebert (1982) sensitively noted, "And it [departure] carves you alive inside my heart" is particularly telling for it fully reveals Michelangelo's lack of capacity to mourn the father toward whom there was such ambivalence.

Generally, the correspondence with the father and the brothers marks Michelangelo, though irascible, as a man of devotion and integrity who seemed unable to recognize and free himself from burdens. This proclivity toward being victimized and subjugated, perhaps a repetitive reenactment of his early relationship with the father and uncle, continued as a central thread throughout his life, giving him a near paranoid quality, especially later in his life (Liebert, 1982a). As an artistic theme, subjugation appeared early in his art. In the *Victory* (ca. 1529), the victim bent under the knee of the handsome young man is seen by many as a self-portrait (Clements, 1968; Oremland, 1980).

ADORATION, ADOPTION, AND SUBJUGATION

Being victimized, often with humiliating and painful consequences, had a curious specificity regarding beautiful young men. This tendency markedly increased in his 50s and 60s with the sexualized adoration, adoption, and submission to Gherardo Perini, Febo di Poggio, Tommaso de' Cavalieri, and particularly Francisco Bracci, called Cecchino.

The nature of the relationship with Gherardo Perini is least clear. Though directly named in the satirist Pietro Aretino's widely quoted slurs regarding Michelangelo's homosexuality, Perini, only 5 years younger than Michelangelo, is never alluded to in any of the existing poetry, nor are there any known drawings made for him. Yet, the extent of submissive yearning for Perini cannot be dismissed in light of a note penned on a sketch (ca. 1522-30), "I beg you not to make me draw this evening since Perino's not here" (Clements, 1966, p. 145).

The letters to Febo di Poggio, a model and homosexual prostitute, attest to the extent Michelangelo overtly exposed himself to being exploited. Michelangelo's pathetic pleadings as Febo connived to obtain money and drawings from him are only somewhat understandable in terms of Michelangelo's fear of blackmail. The letters tell us much of how helpless Michelangelo made himself in his attempt to extricate himself from obvious victimization.

Tommaso de' Cavalieri, widely regarded as an unusually handsome nobleman, came into Michelangelo's life in 1532 when Tommaso was but 23. Tommaso married in 1538 and had two children. The intensity of Michelangelo's feelings for Tommaso as evidenced in many love poems and the various "presentation" drawings is remarkable.

My mind expression finds in thee alone.
Thus like the moonlight's silver ray I shine.
We only see her beams on the far sky.
When the sun's fiery rays are o'er her thrown.
[Clements, 1966, p. 187].

In the *Rape of Ganymede* drawing (ca. 1532) (fig. 3) for Tommaso, a copy of which survives, the intensity of the desire to be possessed and possess with its oral-incorporative, anal-penetrative, and bisexual (the genital ambiguity, the pretty boy face) components are graphically portrayed. The *Tityus* (ca. 1532) drawing, also for Tommaso, vividly portrays the desired sexualized submission that is clearly evident in the love poetry (Clements, 1968):

With thee, my groveling thought I heavenward raise.
Borne upward by thy bold, aspiring wing.
I follow where thou wilt—a helpless thing.
Cold in the sun and warm in winter days.
My will, my friend, rest only upon thine;
[Clements, 1966, p. 187].

Therefore because I cannot shun the blow
I rather seek, say who must rule my breast,
Gliding between his gladness and his woe?
If only chains and bands can make me blest,
No marvel if alone and bare I go
An armed Cavalieri's captive and slave confessed
["Cavalieri" is a pun on Tommaso's surname, Cavalieri].
[Clements, 1966, p. 110].

It seems less certain that a sexual physical relationship actualized between Michelangelo and Tommaso. In fact, the entire nature of the relationship seems different from that with the other young men. Tommaso, it seems, never exploited Michelangelo's masochistic tendencies, although Michelangelo offered him ample opportunity.

If vanquished and imprisoned, I am to be blest,
It is no marvel if nude and alone,
I remain the prisoner of an armed Cavalier.
[Clements, 1966, p. 211].

Tommaso remained Michelangelo's loyal, helpful, and young friend until Michelangelo's death. Of great importance is that

Figure 3. *Ganymede* (ca. 1532)

this relationship evidences that Michelangelo could tolerate being loved (Liebert, 1982a).

The relationship between Michelangelo and the 13-year-old Cecchino is endlessly fascinating. Cecchino came into Michelangelo's life probably in 1542 when Cecchino's father, a Florentine exile, moved to Rome. Cecchino soon passed into the custody of his admiring uncle, the poet Luigi del Riccio, a close friend of Michelangelo. Cecchino was lionized for his beauty by a collection of Roman artistic savants, and it seems was the sexual companion to most of them including Michelangelo.

Michelangelo's adoration of Cecchino was one of those remarkable situations in which a great man is captivated by a young boy—Thomas Mann's *Knabenliebe*. Like the fictitious Gustave Aschenbach to Tadizo, Leonardo to Salai (little Satan), and Julius III and the monkey boy, the degree of excitement about and the intensity of feelings with which Michelangelo endowed this lad are almost of mythical proportions.

Cecchino's death at age 15 in 1544 added a romantic quality to his brief life. The poetic eulogizing of him, including Michelangelo's 50 poems, although somewhat forced by Luigi, are truly remarkable examples of the idealization of a youth by older men. As Michelangelo wrote,

> Buried here is that Braccio with those face
> God wished to correct Nature.
> But because that wealth is lost of which men
> take not care,
> He showed him to the world and quickly took
> him back to Himself.
> [Clements, 1966, p. 143].

> Or
> I was born Bracci; after the first wail
> My eyes saw sunlight only a short space.
> I am here forever, nor would wish it less,
> In him who loved me greatly living still.
> [Linscott, 1963, p. 122].

It is nearly unbelievable that this gamin would end in a tomb designed by Michelangelo with a bust executed by one of

Michelangelo's more talented assistants, Urbano, in one of the most important churches on Rome's Capitol Hill, the Santa Maria d'Aracoeli.

Psychoanalytically, the degree of idealization with which these men, including Michelangelo, endowed this lad, perhaps as an attempt to recapture their own youth and unfulfilled aspirations, is a study in its own right of a particular kind of narcissism and of a certain kind of homosexuality. It may have been of a special significance for Michelangelo that "Cecchino" is the double diminutive of Francesco, the masculine equivalent of Francesca, Michelangelo's mother's name. Michelangelo's adoration and adoption of "little" Francesco may have been an undoing of his having been abandoned by his mother, Francesca (Oremland, 1980).

In summary, Michelangelo's wish to be subjugated was a repetitive, erotized, sadomasochistic reenactment of the way he had been treated by his father (and uncle). Further, the proclivity toward being victimized and subjugated was Michelangelo's expiation of conscious and unconscious guilt, his self-hate, over the death of the mother, guilt for anger at the mother for dying and at the father for being the instrument of her death (the repeated pregnancies). More profoundly, it seems, as Liebert (1982b) has argued persuasively, that "throughout [Michelangelo's] life, the controlling fantasy and unconscious conflict that determined the artistic resolution in form and content of many of his works involve the yearning for eternal union with an idealized powerful paternal transformation of early maternal figures which were lost in childhood" (p. 9ff.).

Yet, at base, I hold that Michelangelo was for these young men the "mother" he wished he had had and the adoration, a protection against the early loss. Michelangelo essentially wished to have been so adored by his mother that he could never have been left. Dynamically, it is suggested that what was tragically enacted as adoring subjugation to beautiful young men was self-other fusion experiences related to mastery attempts of early maternal loss. The intensity of the tendency toward fusion of self and other is clearly articulated by Michelangelo in the *Two Dialogues* published by Donato Giannotti in 1540:

Whenever I see someone who possesses some virtue, who shows
some quickness of genius, who can do more, say something
more fittingly than others, I am constrained to fall in love with
him, and I give myself to him as booty, for I am no longer my
own, by all this . . . I . . . [am] quite diminished and lost; for
many days after I should not know in which world I was
[Clements, 1968, p. 152].

In short, what manifested itself as Michelangelo's homo-
erotism is a complex mixture of repetitions and reparations at
various levels reflecting specifics of his early experience; yet,
profoundly and fundamentally, it was a specific mastery repetition as Michelangelo attempted to be the wished-for adopting
mother. This mastery repetition with its corresponding presex-
ual continuance of earlier fusion experiences is vividly portrayed in Michelangelo's first *madonna* sculpture, *The Madonna of
the Stairs* (ca. 1491), in which the Herculean Infant seems to be
reentering the mother's body, and in his last major work, the
Rondanini *Pietá* (ca. 1556–64), in which there is overt fusion of
the adult son into the body of the mother (Frank, 1966;
Oremland, 1978).

Linking such ideas regarding Michelangelo's personal dynamics to universal themes, I am tempted to position the Jesus
and the thematically related Ganymede myths as compelling
organizing themes in his life personally and artistically.
Throughout his life, Michelangelo's strong internalization
(more precisely, incorporation) of Jesus is clear in his poetry and
art. This is particularly evident in the mystical poetry following
the death of Vittoria Colonna in 1547 that increased until his
death in 1564. Artistically, the internalization of Jesus reached
its clearest expression in the only sculptural pieces Michelangelo
executed solely for himself, the Florentine *Pietá* (ca. 1547–55),
in which the centrally placed Nicodemus, embodying Michelangelo's self-portrait, tenderly returns the dead Jesus to His mother, and the Rondanini *Pietá* (ca. 1556–64), both of which were
intended for his tomb and neither of which could he complete.

As an aside, one cannot but be impressed by the fact that
Michelangelo received the commission for the Sistine Ceiling
when he was 33, the age when Jesus was crucified. It is tempting
to consider the possible symbolic significance for Michelangelo

of the numerological tie between Jesus' age at the end of His corporeal and the beginning of His spiritual ministry and Michelangelo's being "called" to create the Ceiling. Perhaps, it was this coinciding that "strengthened" Michelangelo and accounted for his having been able to depart from the *Genesis* text in the Ceiling's decoration as he concurrently developed new artistic styles in a medium essentially alien to him, frescos painting (Tolnay, 1969). Perhaps, as the Crucifixion marked the beginning of Jesus' most untethered ministry, being "called" to do and the ordeal of doing the Ceiling marked Michelangelo's artistically becoming less tethered and monumentally expressive—his personal transcendence.

On a personal level, much of this "transcendence" can be understood in terms of a reworking of the ambivalence toward the violent, weak, and disappointing father in the relationship with the violent, powerful, and disappointing Julius II, who were the same age.[3] Significantly it was during the time of creating the Ceiling that Michelangelo overtly became "father" to his father and brothers, fully and openly taking financial responsibility for them.

The Jesus and Ganymede myths, when considered from both sides (son to father and father to son), allow us to see the wish to be adopted and the need to adopt with potential homoerotic love and homoerotic destruction by powerful fathers who effect their wishes in strange ways. Yet, on a deeper level, the Jesus myth contains a basic emphasis on preoedipal attachment to an auto-inseminated mother that I feel is crucial to understanding

---

3. It is of some interest that Julius, when he first "sought out" Michelangelo, was about the same age as Michelangelo was when Michelangelo began the relationship with Febo di Poggio. Although there were previous similar relationships with some young men, the amount of abuse that we know Michelangelo received from Febo and the amount of adoration Michelangelo bestowed on him mark this relationship as being, perhaps, a special repetition. The repetition suggests that Michelangelo's adoration of Febo was Michelangelo's doing for Febo what he wished his father (and the Pope) had done for him. Michelangelo provided the all-loving, all-accepting, and all-protecting father he wished he had had. Michelangelo's taking the abuse in such a blind, erotized way suggests his unconscious need for punishment for the hostility he felt toward his father. In effect, Michelangelo allowed Febo to do to him what he would have liked to have done to the father (and the Pope).

Michelangelo. In short, on various levels underlying Michelangelo's manifested homoeroticism is primal biunity.

I hold that these considerations of personal dynamics, when taken together with varying emphases, help us understand Michelangelo's self-hate, self-torment, relationships, and "homosexuality." In combination they also help us understand his relations with the series of young men who came into his life in the second half of his long life. Yet, whatever ideas we gather regarding Michelangelo as man and his relationships and how he needlessly and painfully suffered, our task here is directed toward what his "hermaphroditic" artistic expressions, in particular the *ignudi,* tell us about his creativity and creativity in general.

HERMAPHRODISM AND BIUNITY

I propose that particularly in creative individuals a shifting, at times, confused sense of maleness and femaleness, often loosely termed homosexuality, should not be considered along the conventional ideas suggested by the gender-defining words "masculine" and "feminine." I suggest that the subjective sense of shifting maleness and femaleness in the creative is closely related to elemental qualities concerning continuing developmentally early, in that way primitive, fantasies of hermaphrodism, autoinsemination, and autogestation. Such primitive fantasies, a kind of *primal biunity,* have long been closely associated with creativity in literature, mythology, and psychoanalytic theory.

Before looking at the complex gender representations pictorialized in the *ignudi,* I shall illustrate this hypothesis by studying Michelangelo's provocative, enigmatic, unfortunately now lost *Leda and the Swan* (ca. 1529) (fig. 4). If the Bos rendition is accurate, as most Michelangelo scholars believe, the complex Leda image contains an autoerotic, hermaphroditic autoinsemination infrastructure to its latently homoerotic theme. I hold that the central figure, the Leda, not only is a phallicized and masculinized female with the specific developmental and defensive implications Liebert (1982a) described, but limns self-fellatio and oral self-insemination—essential hermaphrodism.

Figure 4. *Leda and the Swan* (ca. 1529)

The image represents primal oneness, a primitive biunity. The fertilized egg—if we continue this line of thought—symbolizes the parthenogenic self-conception; for the artist, it is the art object itself.[4]

It is of particular interest that the *ignudi* tend to be more clearly gender-defined as we look from altar to entrance wall. In general, the adolescents toward the altar wall, those close to primal creation, are more meditative, pensive, and feminized (fig. 1).[5] The boys nearer the entrance are more reactive and, like Noah and his family, more gender-defined (fig. 5). The *ignudi's* progression altar to entrance wall becomes a visual evolution. It is not a smooth evolution for the middle group (fig. 6) is filled with turmoil and terror.

Generally, art historians, such as Esther Dotson (1979) and Howard Hibbard (1974), ignoring the feminization of some of the adolescents, link the *ignudi* to the neo-Platonic idealization of the nude body. Liebert's (1982a) excellent psychoanalytic biography of Michelangelo emphasizes that the *ignudi* are beautiful portrayals of Michelangelo's interest in and fascination with the male body "represent[ing] an extraordinary achievement in the creative sublimation of homosexual longings" (p. 153). Liebert suggests that Michelangelo's extraordinary ability to depict the male nude is a "sublimation of homosexual longings" with an implication of conflict, defense, and "energy" transformation. In contrast, I am exploring how these portrayals help us understand creativity.[6]

---

4. The twinships in the *Leda*, again using the Bos rendition, have relevance to this thesis. Identical twins symbolize unity in individuality and individuality in unity, a kind of narcissistic homosexuality, as can be read easily into the Castor and Pollux part of the Leda myth. Considering a variety of narcissistic infrastructures adds a deeper understanding to the dynamics of homosexual behaviors.

5. It must be kept in mind that many adolescent boys are, for a period of time, rather hermaphroditic, particularly regarding breast development and underdeveloped genitalia, sometimes partially hidden under pubescent fat folds (Stolz and Stolz, 1951). The *ignudi* vividly show Michelangelo's ability to observe and use all aspects of nature for his expressive purposes.

6. From the standpoint of "sublimation" in the traditional sense, such images as the collections of *glans penises* that pass for "Rovere" acorns in the

To explore the *ignudi* further, we must consider one of the multitude of themes that constitute the Ceiling (fig. 2), a masterpiece of near unsizable complexity. The sanctuary itself is a remarkably simple structure. Essentially a rectangular prism, the entrance wall faces the altar wall across the long axis of the prism. The upper walls of the prism end in a major architectural cornice above which is the clerestory with its rectangular windows arched by semicircular extensions framed by the lunettes. These lunettes develop an architectural complexity as dormers form spandrels piercing the major horizontal surface, the rectangular, shallow-arched ceiling.

Within the Ceiling's thematic progressions, artistically enhanced through use of the very architecture of the Chapel, is an artistic "structure." Conventionally the decoration is regarded as a series of tiers. Spatially the tiers become visual metaphor—lower, corporeal, and specific; higher, spiritual (sublimation in its true meaning), and generic. There is also an interrelated corresponding longitudinal metaphoric progression—entrance (secular) to altar (spiritual).

Thematically, occupying the lunettes and spandrels, the lowest tier of Michelangelo's decoration, the level surrounding the semicircular upper portion of the clerestory windows, is a ring of frescos, the *mortals* (fig. 2). The *mortals*, reflecting the progression within the fourteenth-century frescoes below—a series depicting historical-spiritual events in the lives of Moses and Jesus—are paintings of the families of the Kings of Israel, the ancestors of Christ. The ring sets the theme of human continuity and becoming. Intertwined and positionally somewhat higher are the *bronzed nudes* (fig. 7), dark male forms encased by and struggling with the very architecture of the Ceiling artistically enhanced by Michelangelo. These *bronzed nudes* are truly transitional figures thematically and stylistically linking the mortals below and the immortals above.

Immediately above the *mortals* on elegant thrones are 7 Old Testament prophets and 5 sibyls spatially and thematically inter-

---

ignudi's cornucopia might be examples; although, if we consider Michelangelo's anger at Julius II and the task and his wry sense of humor, this visual double entendre could well have been intentional.

Figure 5. *Ignudo,* Entrance Wall Group

Figure 6. *Ignudo,* Middle Group

Figure 7. *Bronzed Nude* (example)

relating the lowest level with the frescos of the highest level, the *Histories* (fig. 2), the longitudinal band of the Ceiling. The 7 prophets know God and in their dialogue with God define Him. Their complement, the 5 sibyls, bring intuitive knowledge of mankind foretelling his fate. Spatially intertwined, the prophets and sibyls, the *Seers*, become a complemental composite of male and female (Wind, 1965). The *Seers* are a philosophic extension of the thematically and artistically complex 4 Old Testament accounts of heroic men and women (Moses, David, Esther, and Judith) doing God's work that occupy the 4 corners of the Chapel, the *pendentives* (fig. 2).

The *Histories* are depictions of selected verses from *Genesis*. Michelangelo surrounded his 9 grand panels that longitudinally cross the Ceiling of the Sistine Chapel with 20 nude adolescents, the *ignudi*. Although fully human in form, they truly are "angels" without wings. It is in the *Histories* that Michelangelo limns the transformation of the Divine into mankind. At this highest level directly above the altar, the breasted androgynic God (*Separation of Light from Darkness*, fig. 8) transmutes altar to entrance wall into the highly gender-defined and procreative Noah's family worshipping Him (*The Sacrifice of Noah*, fig. 2). Before our eyes, primal creativity transmutes into human generativity. As living frames for the central narrative panels, the *ignudi* on a corporeal level concomitantly transform altar to entrance from hermaphroditic biunity to gender-defined masculinity. As God becomes gender-defined humankind, His creativity is transformed into human generativity underscored by the corresponding lessening of the epicene quality in the *ignudi*.

Through the idiom of selected verses from *Genesis* and other Old Testament accounts, among the many interrelated topical and universal themes that constitute the Ceiling, Michelangelo portrays in a fundamental way humankind's progression (fig. 2).[7] God becoming man and woman is his metaphor for a living creature becoming a human being. Pictorially, Michelangelo transmutes the Divine into humankind, a pictorial explication of

7. This study of the *ignudi* is part of a larger psychoanalytic exegesis of the Ceiling that regrettably can only touch on the thematic and formal complexity of Michelangelo's decoration.

Figure 8. *Separation of Light from Darkness*

the neo-Platonic consciousness of the essential divinity of mankind (Tolnay, 1969). Man and God become a dialectic tenderly
portrayed in the ineffably beautiful *Awakening of Adam*; neither
exists without the other. In Michelangelo's hands the Bible's
account of the descent of man becomes the "ascent" of humankind.[8] In the "ascent," primal creativity becomes human
generativity.

As a subtheme of the transmutation of the human creature
into the human being, Michelangelo suggests that as gender
differentiation prevails, generativity becomes the primary, for
most, the sole continuation of primal creativity. Each, creativity
and generativity, is divine but on vastly different levels. From
this view, in a way more explicit only in Hindu sculpture, Michelangelo's androgynous forms in the Ceiling (the breasted God
and the hermaphroditic *ignudi*) portray the biunity of the male
and female principles inherent in creativity. The most noteworthy example in the Hindu idiom is the overtly hermaphroditic
form of Shiva, the *Ardhanarishvara* (fig. 9). As the "lord who is
half-female," this manifestation is closely associated with "creating, the embodiment of the ultimate source from which unfolds
the observable world *out of his own substance*" (Kramrisch, 1981, p.
27; italics added).

It is our achievement of a differentiated, integrated sense of
gender that allows us to respond to these artistic representations
not only as feminized males but more basically as depictions of
the essential biunity that Michelangelo knew to be a part of,
specifically, the creative component in every human being. Who,
more than Michelangelo, knew, to quote Erikson (1954):

All in all, the creative individual's typical cycle of moods and
attitudes . . . probably permits him, at the height of consummation, to identify with father, mother, and newborn child all in
one; to represent, in equal measure, his father's potency, his
mother's fertility, and his own reborn ideal identity. It is ob-

8. The original consecration of the Chapel was to the Assumption of the
Virgin Mary, and the primary altarpiece was a painting of the Assumption by
Perugino. In the Ceiling Michelangelo takes the doctrinal *Assumption* unveiling its humanistic meaning: even the simplest of beings (Mary), when touched
by God (the humanistic spirit), is deified.

Figure 9. *Ardhanarishvara*

vious, then, why mankind participates, with pity and terror, with ambivalent admiration and ill-concealed abhorrence in the hybris of creative men, and why such hybris, in these men themselves, can call forth all the sinister forces of . . . conflict [p. 49].

I suggest that what Michelangelo expressed in his hermaphroditic images is the shifting sense of maleness and femaleness with at times fusion that he experienced within himself, and what he at times tragically, crudely, and grotesquely enacted in his "homosexual" relationships. I suggest that such subjective fluidities are behavioral and ideational manifestations closely related to hypotheses regarding extraordinary, shifting, intrapsychic capacities in creative individuals (Kris, 1952). In short, Michelangelo portrays in his hermaphroditic images the biunity, perhaps, even the nascent creativity, that we can find in our primal selves. This is why his hermaphroditic images transcend culture and epoch and are endlessly interesting, at times disturbing, to countless tens of thousands.

Can we understand such dynamics developmentally?

CREATIVITY, OBJECT RELATIONS, AND PERPETUITY

I suggest that Michelangelo, through the *ignudi,* portrays increasing gender definition as a metaphor for being self-defined on many levels. With self-definition there are gain and loss. Michelangelo proclaims, perhaps protests, that the defining into male and female and the concomitant domestication are at the expense of generic creativity. Begetting children and sowing seed (Noah above the entrance wall in the *Drunkenness of Noah* tilling his field fulfilling the fate of the condemned Adam), though derived from and distantly related to primal creativity (God in a frenzied dance of creation), are at great expense (fig. 2). The theme is vividly repeated vertically in the contrast between the *ignudi* and the *bronzed nudes* (fig. 7). The *bronzed nudes* are men clearly sexually defined but encased by their situation with an overwhelming quality of despair. The *bronzed nudes* truly represent the expense of being defined. They embody the transition from the energy-filled "angels" above, the *ignudi,* to the bleakness of domestication below, the *mortals* (fig. 2). As we

ponder the *mortals,* we must remind ourselves that these hud-
dled triads are the families of kings! Their preoccupation with
shelter, sustenance, and begetting seems light years away from
the electrifying events above. Their creativity has been subsumed by continuance.

DEVELOPMENTAL ORIGINS OF CREATIVITY

It seems that in the *ignudi* Michelangelo portrays a fascinating
paradox—creating and procreating are one, yet on vastly different levels. In it, perhaps, is a personal revelation. Michelangelo
repeatedly, as do many creative individuals, referred to his art as
his love, at times as his wife, and to his works as his children. As
he wrote his student and eventual biographer, Giorgio Vasari, "I
have too much of a wife and [that is] this art, which has already
given me tribulations, and my children will be the work I leave
behind"(Clements, 1968, p. 192). Perhaps, his self-revelation
heightens the distinction between the psychoanalytic understanding of that which is the creative object and the psychoanalytic understanding of creativity.

Psychoanalysis has made major contributions to understanding artistic contents by demonstrating that forms and themes are
often manifested enactments of various mastery and compromise formations. Yet, that *genre* of psychoanalytic study, when it
comes to understanding the origins and genesis of creativity—
and in this psychoanalysis is in good company—has yet to contribute greatly. However, some beginnings do exist, particularly
Winnicott's (1953) explorations of the "part me and part not me"
aspect of the personality. In this metaphoric "transitional
space," Winnicott locates—to use his term—play, the dream,
and creativity.

In Winnicott's speculations regarding the development of object relatedness, he noted a "transitional phase" in which the
young child endows a connotative thing in the external world
with psychological significance, the transitional object, traditionally a blanket. This endowing of a connotative thing becomes
part of a process by which the early external presences—the
composite of mothering functions and figures in the infant's
life—become differentiated, integrated, and internalized as a

concept, the mother, the primal other. Viewed this way, the transitional object is the primal other one step removed as it is being internalized in the process of differentiation and separation of self from nonself—in metapsychological terms, differentiation of self from object; in interpersonal terms, separation of self from other.

The transitional period bridges two monumental developmental epochs. The transitional period comprises the early experiencing of all that is external as part of the self-nonself matrix as it is transformed into differentiated, integrated concepts of self and object. The transitional phase is the beginning of separateness; to use Winnicott's poetic language, it is "continuity becoming contiguity." Contiguity demands communication and communication is symbolization. The transitional phase coforms the separate object (an external event), the intrapsychic object representation (an internal event), and symbolization. (This transitional process in reverse can be seen in the very development of the art object. The sculptor as he inhales, eats, and is covered by the dust physically, as well as psychologically, becomes one with the stone as it becomes sculpture; similarly with paint and painter, as the paint becomes the painting.)

Winnicott's emphasis on the developmental importance of connotative *things* endowed with meaning and its relation to activating symbol formation introduced developmental events into the study of creativity. His experiential object-related consideration represents a substantial shift in the psychoanalytic exploration of creativity complementing Kris's (1952) emphasis on intrapsychic fluidity and Greenacre's (1957) near physiological emphasis on innate, extraordinary sensorimotoric, conceptual endowment. All three add valuably to the traditional psychoanalytic emphasis on mastery and resolution of conflict in motivating creativity (Freud, 1900, 1910, 1914; Oremland, 1981, 1984).

Winnicott's object-related view allows for speculation regarding the state and significance of the "transitional space" as it is influenced by developmental vicissitudes in the life of each individual. Developmentally, creative people seem to be those singular few individuals who maintain an extraordinary kinship to, or in fact maintain developmental continuances of, transitional phenomena.[9] As perpetuators of transitional phenomena, creative people maintain the ongoing capacity to explore anew the external and the internal and to invent, enact, and play with symbols akin to the initial discovering we all experienced as differentiation of self from nonself progressed. Such perpetuators are the truly creative people whom we cherish, sometimes treat badly, for through them we can, at times, vicariously reexperience the precious early excitement of initial discovery and the precious early excitement of forming novel and ever-varying symbols.

This emphasis on transitional experiencing enlarges our understanding of the subjective sense of creativity as "happening" somewhere out there and yet within and the peculiar communicating nature of creativity. It helps us understand the developmental origin of the "unseen audience," the "that" out there and yet inside that is being communicated within creativity. The "that" of creativity, like the transitional object, is a transformation of the primal other. In fact, the "that" is a "who," in essence a protective presence, a veritable matrix upon which higher order enactment activities, including mastery enactments, are played out. This view parallels Lewin's (1953) schematic concept of the dream "upon" the dream screen, and Erikson's understanding of child's "play" (1954, 1977).

The creative object, like the early "that," is part self and part other, and part of and yet separate from both. The process of the development of the creative object recapitulates primary biunity emerging into differentiation.[10] Creating when viewed this way

9. From this view, the transitional object and its institutional and psychopathological counterpart, the amulet and the fetish, are keystone developmental concepts for understanding the art object. Winnicott's emphasis on connotative things endowed with meaning closely parallels Emile Durkheim's (1915) description of the fundamental element of all religions, primitive and sophisticated alike. The transitional object links the art object and religious object to the beginning of relatedness, a compelling parallel to the historical linkage between art and religion. Just as a historical commonality exists between the idol maker and the artist, a developmental commonality seems to exist among the child playing, the primitive idol maker, and the artist.

10. It is creativity's intimacy with this threshold that differentiates it from mystical experience. The mystical "state" attempts to establish the "oceanic"

is a form of object relating (Winnicott, 1967; Oremland, 1984). Like object relatedness, creativity at base is a reestablishing of primal biunity with the primal object out of which a new object comes into being. Like object relatedness, creativity seeks a version of the primal object out of which evolves the creation of a new object that is a version of the primal object and the self.

Stated another way, creativity is a "parthenogenic" version of object relatedness. Both are intensely motivated by object seeking and both potentially provide personal perpetuity through issue. The *oeuvre* of the artist is as crucial to his continuance as is the child for the artist's "object-related" cohort. The art object, like the child, is simultaneously the past (the primal object), the present (the self), and the future (an amalgam of both). Creativity, like generativity, potentially assures continuities. Both can provide psychological immortality.

I suggest that this awesome, sometimes terrifying sense of parthenogenetic biunity at times informed Michelangelo's art in compelling and wondrous ways. His hermaphroditic images allow us specifically to reexperience primal unity with its miraculous sense of creative omnipotence. Perhaps, an even more abstract artistic expression of this awesome sense of parthenogenetic capacity is the fascinating triptychal form, interlocking circles with his initial contained in one, that was Michelangelo's self-styled logo (fig. 10). The logo is a pictorial expression of Michelangelo's special ability to become one with other and to produce something that is part him and part not him. In the emblem, we can see a complex self-concept: the self (the circle containing the "M") merged with other with a "that" emerging from and yet merged with the merged two. Michelan-

---

feeling, perhaps paralleling the earliest developmental periods. Creativity parallels the transitional period, the emerging differentiation of self and nonself with the formation of communication. Yet, when studied closely, creativity encompasses both for the "moments" of inspiration seem subjectively close to the mystical "state." Viewed this way, the creative process can be thought of as a developmental recapitulation begun by regressive dedifferentiation that progresses into transitional functioning. But creativity requires a third step. The transitional experiencing must give way to a different tertiary process as the object on a more cognitive level is worked on, over, and with until it becomes the art piece. Developmentally, creativity is a progression and intermixing of infantile, childlike, and adult functioning.

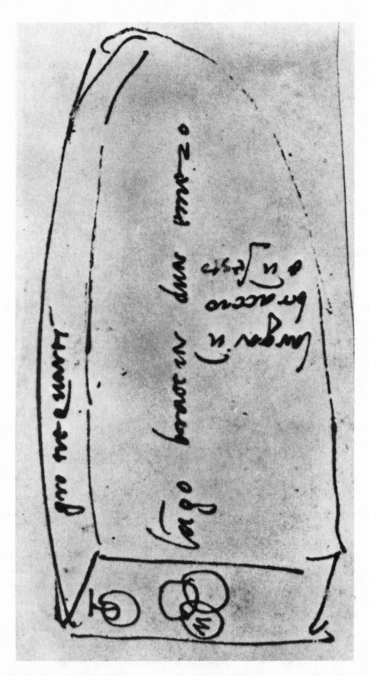

Figure 10. Logo

gelo's logo seems an extraordinary, economic, visual depiction of his ability to continue the transitional state, a pictorial expression of the artist's ability to reestablish a oneness with the primal other, a primal biunity, and to reemerge via the creation of a "that."

SUMMARY

My thesis is that what manifested itself as Michelangelo's "homosexuality" is multileveled reenactments and enactments. On the surface is a reenactment of the sadomasochistic qualities that characterized his relationship with his father. Beneath this sadomasochism reenactment is a shifting sense and unclarity of maleness and femaleness related to defensive "phallicizing" of females and "maternalizing" of males in his vain hope of regaining the mother(s) lost early in his childhood. More profoundly enacted was a complex mastery undoing of those early maternal losses by his becoming the "adopting" mother rather than being the abandoned child. These dynamics, I hold, in varying combinations and with varying emphasis, help us understand Michelangelo's relationships and his suffering that informed his art formally and thematically.

With regard to identifying the developmental contribution to Michelangelo's creativity, I place emphasis on the deeper level of mastery of maternal loss through fusion with her—described, enacted, and pictorialized by him—and continuing, intensified, transitional functioning. Through fusion and reemerging via all important connotative things endowed with meaning and fashioned toward that end—the very stuff of art—Michelangelo repeatedly "found" her, himself, and the world anew. I suggest that with awesome precision, his hermaphroditic images depict the subjective primal fusion experience that underlies creativity. It is the epicene quality of creativity limned as the progression in gender definition of the *ignudi* and brought to vivid profile in certain of the *ignudi* (fig. 1) that makes these 20 youths of the Sistine Chapel an endless wonderment to countless tens of thousands for nearly half a millennium.

BIBLIOGRAPHY

CLEMENTS, R. J. (1966). *The Poetry of Michelangelo*. New York: New York Univ. Press.

——— (1968). *Michelangelo*. New York: New York Univ. Press.

CONDIVI, A. (1553). *The Life of Michelangelo*, tr. A. S. Wohl. Baton Rouge: Louisiana State Univ. Press, 1976.

DOTSON, E. G. (1979). An Augustinian interpretation of Michelangelo's Sistine Ceiling. *Art Bull.*, 61:223–256; 405–429.

DURKHEIM, E. (1915). *The Elementary Forms of the Religious Life*. New York: Free Press, 1965.

ERIKSON, E. H. (1954). The dream specimen of psychoanalysis. *J. Amer. Psychoanal. Assn.*, 2:5–56.

——— (1977). *Toys and Reason*. New York: Norton.

FRANK, G. (1966). The enigma of Michelangelo's *Pietá* Rondanini. *Amer. Imago*, 23:287–315.

FREUD, S. (1900). The interpretation of dreams. *S.E.*, 4 & 5.

——— (1910). Leonardo da Vinci and a memory of his childhood. *S.E.*, 11:59–137.

——— (1914). Remembering, repeating and working-through. *S.E.*, 12:145–156.

GREENACRE, P. (1957). The childhood of the artist. *Psychoanal. Study Child*, 12:47–72.

HIBBARD, H. (1974). *Michelangelo*. New York: Harper & Row.

KRAMRISCH, S. (1981). *Manifestations of Shiva*. Philadelphia: Museum of Art.

KRIS, E. (1952). *Psychoanalytic Explorations in Art*. New York: Int. Univ. Press.

LEWIN, B. D. (1953). Reconsideration of the dream screen. *Psychoanal. Q.* 22:174–199.

LIEBERT, R. S. (1982a). *Michelangelo*. New Haven: Yale Univ. Press.

——— (1982b). Michelangelo's lost painting of *Leda and the Swan*. Read at the American Psychoanalytic Association meetings, New York, December, 1982.

LINSCOTT, R. N., ed. (1963). *Complete Poems and Selected Letters of Michelangelo*, tr. C. Gilbert. New York: Random House.

OREMLAND, J. D. (1978). Michelangelo's *Pietá*. *Psychoanal. Study Child*, 33:563–591.

——— (1980). Mourning and its effect on Michelangelo's art. *Annu. Psychoanal.*, 8:317–351.

——— (1981). The wide scope of psychoanalytic investigations of art. *Dialogue*, 5:3–13.

——— (1984). The role of empathy in the capacity to appreciate art (in press).

RAMSDEN, E. H. (1963). *The Letters of Michelangelo*. Stanford: Stanford Univ. Press.

ROSS, J. B. (1974). The middle-class child in urban Italy. In *The History of Childhood*, ed. L. de Mause. New York: Harper & Row, pp. 183–229.

STERBA, R. & STERBA, E. (1956). The anxieties of Michelangelo Buonarroti. *Int. J. Psychoanal.*, 37:325–330.

STOLZ, H. R. & STOLZ, L. M. (1951).*Somatic Development of Adolescent Boys.* New York: Macmillan, pp. 367–394.

SYMONDS, J. A. (1892). *The Life of Michelangelo Buonarroti.* New York: Modern Library.

TOLNAY, C. DE (1967). *The Youth of Michelangelo.* Princeton: Princeton Univ. Press.

———— (1969). *The Sistine Ceiling.* Princeton: Princeton Univ. Press.

WIND, E. (1965). Michelangelo's prophets and sibyls. *Proc. Brit. Acad.,* 51:45–84.

WINNICOTT, D. W. (1953). Transitional objects and transitional phenomena. *Int. J. Psychoanal.,* 34:89–97.

———— (1967). The location of cultural experience. *Int. J. Psychoanal.,* 48:368–372.

Oedipal Configurations in Young Father-Raised Children

KYLE DEAN PRUETT, M.D.

> Only when I became a father did I begin to notice my
> own father's tender and intimate nurturing qualities.
> His lingering glances, his abiding soft strength, his
> wish to feed which stopped short at suckling, his end-
> less jokes about my mother's belly, his unfailing memo-
> ry about my infancy. For the first time in my life, I
> understood the meaning of the word generation. A
> lost secret of our language is that it is really a verb,
> masquerading as a noun.
> —Attributed to DOSTOEVSKY

THIS COMMUNICATION OFFERS SOME THOUGHTS AND QUESTIONS
conceived during an ongoing longitudinal study of the natural
history of a natural experiment. I describe a group of families
that find and create for themselves a classic reversal of the most
seminal occupation of our species, that of parenting. In these
families the father raises the babies and the mother wins the
bread. I have previously reported on the early development of
infants and toddlers raised in these circumstances (Pruett, 1983,
1985). Here I report the first observations gleaned of the 4-year
follow-up of these families, with special emphasis on a pivotal
event in the lives of these 4- to 6-year-olds, the maturation of
sexual identity. What actually happens to the development of a
child's sense of himself or herself as male or female when the
primary nurturing figure is an adult male? Anything different,

Associate Clinical Professor of Psychiatry, Child Study Center, Yale University, New Haven, Connecticut.

435

worrisome, useful? More specifically, how goes the passage through the oedipal years when the father is the primary caretaker and presumably the main source of identity, and the mother is the more remote breadwinner who comes and goes, and brings society, the external world, and its accoutrements into the intimacy of the family circle?

I shall leave to the discussion, the questions which inevitably surface as this material is reviewed. Are these children different? And, if they are different, do the differences matter? Or are they subtly irrelevant? What *are* their primary identifications, their primary sexual identifications, and their primary conflicts?

To assist in correcting the myopia of our deficiencies in clinical research on the father-infant bond, I began 4 years ago to focus on a group of special interest to me—the primary nurturing father, his infant, and his spouse. From an initial focus on the development of these infants and toddlers, we are now well into the era of the beginning development of sense of self, mature awareness of sexual difference, and, finally, into the oedipal thicket. It is to this most recent process that we turn our scrutiny to see what we see.

It may be helpful first to review what usually occurs during this period of life. Anna Freud (1947) reminds us that (in the traditional family) on the road to the development of object love, aided by the growth of intelligence and perception, children eventually cease to live in the intimate emotional partnership with the mother only, and enter into the larger family group, consisting of siblings, and typically the father. Envy and jealousy are part and parcel of the transition. The relationship to the father becomes increasingly complex, the closer one gets to the fourth year and the expected arrival of the phallic phase. Traditional fathers typically seem to children to possess unlimited quantities of power, strength, and mystery. Although he is clearly loved and admired, he is also feared by the child. Most problematic, however, is the hatred the child feels for the father in his role as a rival for the mother's love. Although such ambivalence appears in the second and third years, it is full-blown by the time the child reaches the stage of phallic evolution. Again, according to Freud (1925), only then do male and female children begin to proceed along differing paths. The boy identifies increasingly with his father, imitating him in many ways. Concomitantly, and often abruptly, the boy ceases to be mother's dependent baby, turning into " a young dude," who often acts condescendingly toward her at the same time as he demands her attention, striving endlessly to impress (instead of *need*) her through his repeated acts of derring-do, aimed at holding onto first place in her heart. His sexual curiosity is directed toward his mother's intimate *interaction* with the father rather than mother as sexual object herself. Often he will wait for just the right moment to pounce into bed as father departs for work or morning shower.

The female child, according to Freudian theory, has grown out of her total attachment to her mother and begins, instead, to copy and imitate her mother in myriad ways. As part of the imitation process, she turns her affection and love more in the direction of her father and seeks his appreciation and adoration, usually at her mother's expense.

> Both sexes in this manner have their first experience of being in love, with all the turmoil of feelings, hopes and wishes, disappointments and frustrations, joy and sorrow, anger, jealousy, and despondency which this state involves. Their love for the parent of the opposite sex creates, or in the case of the boy intensifies, the already existing rivalry with the parent of the same sex. The boy thus loves the mother, attaches his instinctual desires to her, and wishes for the death of the father who stands in his way; the girl loves the father and, in the service of the wish to have first place with him, fantasies doing away with the mother. It is this family constellation of the young child for which, in comparison with the Greek myth, the term *oedipus complex* has been introduced [A. Freud, 1947, p. 468f.].

Finally, through the punishing, unremitting clarity and assistance of reality, the children recognize the futility of their oedipal wishes. The resulting discouragement and sadness are often profound and acute.

It would certainly be naïve, in the face of ongoing psychoanalytic research, to assume that this is the only transaction occurring during the fourth and fifth years of life. Yet, the child's sexual research certainly does occupy much waking and sleeping time. Fantasies about the act of procreation as a normal extension of the discovery of sexual difference are also important.

With the advance in ego psychology, analysts have become significantly more appreciative of and interested in the child's active efforts at mastery in all areas of psychic drive and energy. Historically this has led to an increasing acceptance of Freud's earlier postulates of bisexual elements being active in *both* sexes in the yearning for a baby. Jacobson (1950) and Boehm (1930) have helped us move further away from Freud's early "chauvinistic position," by suggesting that older boys may regress to the feminine phase, but, in fear of emasculation, "hide their desire for woman's maternal resources, womb and breasts, behind the façade of male chauvinism and misogyny" (Boehm, 1930, p. 466).

Jacobson postulated unstintingly about the power of generativity in the male, reflecting what she believed are the boy's frustrated strivings to assume generative and generational authority. To describe the presence of phallic strivings fused with generative and reproductive strivings, Ross (1982) has added to the psychoanalytic lexicon the concept of ambisexuality which he assumes is present in both male and female children. The special circumstances of these study children provide us with a unique opportunity to look at the existence and sequelae of such bisexual, ambisexual, or androgynous identifications.

It is widely known that the 3- to 3½-year-old male child frequently expresses a strong wish to give birth to babies. At the least complex level, the 3-year-old child may interest himself in raising or nursing babies. Others explore the physiologic possiblities and mysteries. Most commonly, childbirth fantasies become almost instantaneously problematic for boys the moment they reach consciousness. Such appearances may be as, or more, problematic for the environment in which they appear. It is this divergence—where the prototypical boy experiences only short-lived maternal strivings consciously, and the prototypical girl experiences longer and more conflict-free maternal strivings and ambitions—which has such far-reaching sequelae for gender and role determination and constriction in eventual paternal behavior or choice.

Whatever visage they present, the boy's preoedipal strivings toward productivity and generativity, along with the broad strokes of maternal identification, eventually become subjugated to the paternal identification, which climaxes the oedipal-crisis opportunity and eventually galvanizes the young boy's sexuality. It is this assumption of a some-day paternity which in Ross's words (1982) promises to "atone best for deficits inherent in being of only one sex, and which thereby helps resolve inescapable conflicts in the boy's overall sexual, as well as his more delimited, gender identity" (p. 203).

We see in these more contemporary and refined derivations of Freud's initial theory of the "bedrock" of bisexuality (1937) the theoretical conceptualization of the opportunity for the oedipal child's identification with motherly mothers and fatherly fathers, but also fatherly mothers and motherly fathers.

DESCRIPTION OF THE STUDY

I shall briefly describe the ongoing research population. A small group of 17 families was recruited primarily from general pediatric practices in the Greater New Haven area to study: (1) the development of infants from 2 to 24 months; (2) the psychodynamic characteristics of these fathers; (3) their nurturing patterns; and (4) their relationships to the infants' mothers. Although the parenting might be shared with the mothers, the fathers had to bear the major responsibility for, and the commitment to, parenting. The arrangement need not be considered permanent, but whatever the arrangement, the infant's primary affectional tie was to the father. Though not by original design, most of the infants were firstborn. The families ranged across the socioeconomic spectrum from welfare through blue- and white-collar workers to professional; there were 8 male and 9 female infants. The parents ranged in age from 19 to 36, with the mean age of 24 for fathers and 25 for mothers.

Within the format of this paper, I can offer only the most schematic review of the initial findings. (1) Children raised primarily by men can be vigorous, competent, and thriving infants who may be especially comfortable with and interested in stimulation from the external environment. In fact many of the infants functioned well above the expected norms on the standardized test of development. The youngest group of infants (2 to 12 months) performed problem-solving tasks on a level of babies who are often 4 to 12 months their seniors; social skills were 2 to 10 months ahead of schedule. The older babies in the group (12 to 22 months) performed as impressively. (2) These men are capable of forming the intense, reciprocal, nurturing attachment so critical in the early life of the thriving human organism. (3) The choice and style of caretaking were drawn from deep within the father's own adaptive narcissistic wish to nurture and be nurtured; moreover, their nurturing style was not merely that of a mother's substitute, "wife-mirror" or *in loco matris*. (4) The father's nurturing style is a distillate of selected identifications and disidentifications with the important objects in his own life. Therefore such nurturing capacities do not seem wholly determined by genetic endowment or gender identity.

Interestingly, the manner and time sequence in which these families decided on this caretaking system had little impact on how well the children developed. The family's decisions could be roughly bunched into thirds: the first third deciding *prior* to the pregnancy; the second, *during* the pregnancy; and the third, in the neonatal period. The latter group was usually pressed into the choice for economic reasons, i.e., father lost his job, mother didn't. The *timing* of the decision could not be correlated, positively or negatively, with how well the infants did on developmental examination.

Using retrospective psychoanalytically oriented interviewing techniques, I first interviewed the fathers at home while they were caring for their infants. Extensive histories were taken and naturalistic observations were recorded of the father-infant dyad in the process of typical "male care." After the initial interview, I examined the babies in a laboratory setting at the Child Development Unit of the Yale Child Study Center, using the Yale Developmental Schedules to assess in detail their developmental competence in gross and fine motor performance, adaptive problem-solving, language skills, and personal-social function. A final interview was then conducted, again preferably at home, and usually the most extensive, with both mother and father to take a marital history and to record further naturalistic observations about the family triad.

The focus of ʰis paper, however, is the special privilege of the longitudinal view: 2 years and 4 years after entering the study, all the original families (save one which had left the area and could not be contacted) were studied again with the original investigation method.

Some of the children within this narrowly circumscribed study population are now old enough to show us in their play their own attempts to achieve oedipal resolution and comfort. Seven of the original study population are now over the age of 4. Of those children, 3 are still in the care of their fathers as primary nurturing figures. One child is in the custody of his father, who separated from his wife. The other 3 children in this older age group are now primarily in the care of their mothers (all of these with siblings). I have chosen two children, one male and one female, to describe at some length because their own diagnostic play material articulates some of the resolutions these children achieve and/or attempt.

First, a word about the psychoanalytically oriented diagnostic play interview adopted in my research. The assessment of cognitive and developmental functions is conducted quite separately from the semi-structured, diagnostic play interview. In the latter the skilled clinician's primary responsibility is to stay out of the children's way as they reveal, step by step, at their own pace and in their own words or actions, the quality, content, and character of their experiential world, both inner and outer. I have found Greenspan's (1981) framework for the systematic observation of the child in diagnostic play interviews helpful in thinking about this clinical material. Seven categories for observation are used for both the descriptive and the age-appropriateness of functional play. The categories used to organize the diagnostic play interviews are as follows:

1. the physical integrity of the child
2. the emotional tone of the child during the assessment
3. how the child relates to the clinician as a human being
4. the specific affects and anxieties that become elaborated during the interview
5. the way the child uses the environment of the playroom, the waiting room, or even the parking lot
6. thematic development; the way the child develops themes in terms of richness, organization, depth, and, probably most important, sequence

7. the subjective feelings of the clinician, i.e., his reaction to the child or the impact that the child has on the diagnostician.

CASE MATERIAL

CASE 1

Helen H., just 6, greeted me with a somewhat overfamiliar "Hi" in the waiting room as her father shook my hand to renew our biannual acquaintance of 4 years' duration. Helen looked momentarily shy and beamed warmly, but did not speak as we walked to the playroom. She came easily and quickly without a backward glance at her father. She was perky, strongly built, apparently well coordinated, and she walked in a confident, almost cocky, manner into the playroom. She was dressed in a pink sweat suit, which was a bit short at the midriff, and a pair of work boots. She walked up to the large two-way mirror, and preened and groomed momentarily. There was a slightly infantile, lispy quality to her speech, which gradually diminished completely as the session progressed. She seemed almost too comfortable and sought no permission to explore the room. After a few moments of somehow both feigning coyness and familiarity, she began to set the play table with dishes, pots and pans, announcing that we should have something to eat. She chatted comfortably about her present life situation, describing how her father had been away from home on weekdays for almost 3 months in a nearby town, returning home on the weekends, as his computer firm had required that he do some consultation out of town. Her mother continued to work out of the home full-time, and her younger sister had just begun to attend nursery school and Helen's daycare center. Her father also cared for her younger sister while he was at home, given her mother's work schedule. Helen reacted unequivocally to her father's attentions to her sibling, often complaining that he was "too nice," and physically intruding in his routine care of her baby sister. Although her father was now working part-time, his computer terminal was at home and he still served as primary caretaker for her. Her chitchat also revealed, as we were both eating our "chicken soup," that she liked to eat fast and "to be sloppy," inviting me to appreciate her silliness and interest in regression. "Being sloppy" often led to her mother putting her in her room when her mother was home in the evenings. She reported that her mother needed to discipline her while she was still in her business dress "good clothes," a fact which seemed to amuse her. Helen seemed to enjoy the contrast between her sloppiness and well-dressed, well-organized "businesswoman mommies."

Bringing our luncheon to an abrupt close, she turned toward a collection of animals, which had clearly been interesting her for some time. As though she could not hold herself away any longer, she gathered the animals up into her arms and announced that she wanted to organize a farm, turning a playhouse into a barn. Having obviously taken charge of the play session, she had become increasingly relaxed and was clearly enjoying herself. She organized the space competently by using blocks as fences, separating the good animals from the "sloppy animals." She became momentarily fascinated with the bodies of the farming family life dolls, especially the "4-year-old boy," who "seemed to have something loose inside," as she shook it around to try to discover the exact nature of the boy's "inside things." During this investigation, she was absentmindedly rubbing her hand tenderly across her exposed belly, her sweatshirt having worked its way up over her navel.

She next organized a "sneak attack" on this pleasant little farm scene by the lion and bear, who managed to sneak up in a competently deceptive way, but were finally chased away by the police guard, the father and the mother. She assembled a revenge party led by the bull, who sneaked in an equally competent fashion around the back side of the lion's lair. When I complimented her on what a "super sneaker" she was, she reported that she enjoyed getting up in the middle of the night, sneaking into the kitchen, and getting a slice of cake without anybody in her family knowing. She smiled at me with a kind of complicity and pleasure. She then introduced yet another sequence of the family being in danger by telling me, "This is going to be exciting," as though she wanted to rivet my attention for the next sequence. She quite purposefully isolated the mother in one corner of the barn, and gathered the father, the 2-year-old, the 4-year-old, and the 7-year-old into the other corner of the barn. The following dialogue then occurred:

H: The whole family is inside. . . . The little baby has to be near the father. . . . The little baby likes to be near the father.

KP: What makes the little baby want to be near the father?

H: Because the father has to take care and make sure he doesn't wander off and get in trouble with the big guys.

KP: Mommies don't do that?

H: The big fathers do that . . . because they know how to do it good.

KP: How about big mothers?

H: Only the really *big, big, big, big* mothers can do it. [It appears that mother must be larger than life to perform this function.]

Helen then orchestrated several other major offensives led by the bull, who cut and stabbed the lion with his mighty horns, all with excited, animated giggling and laughing. The grateful little pig thanked the bull for protecting him. The following dialogue ensued:

KP [animating the little pig]: Thank you, Bull, for protecting us from the lion and bear. You are so powerful!

H: I'm going out there to get that lion and bear and bring them back for dinner. . . . I'm going to bring them back here, and we can cook them and eat them for dinner.

KP: How is the bear meat?

H: It's really good if you cook it good.

KP: Who cooks the dinner?

H [designating the father doll]: Him, of course, what did you think? [The "Dummy" designation is implied but well-manneredly deleted.]

The play sequence was brought to a perfunctory close when the baby calf was brought in, stood next to its mother, and Helen announced, "That's the end of the story, and they lived happily ever after." I asked, "Is there a lesson to that story?" After a long pause, Helen replied, "Yes, the little baby pig should never, never go out because it's too dangerous out there."

Helen then turned her attention to an examination of the doctor's kit. She conducted a very competent examination of her own chest and abdomen, giving humorously accurate representations of heart sounds and borborygmies, all the while coyly exposing her belly. She turned to examine a pair of baby dolls and announced that the first one was suffering from an "affection of the neck and of the bottom," and proceeded to inject medicine into both loci. She abruptly assigned me the role of the doctor, and assumed for herself the role of mother, taking care of one of the sick babies.

H: My baby is sick, and she's crying all the time. She has a problem with her heart beating very slow.

KP: Oh, my, that is quite a serious problem. I think we'd better see if we can help her.

H: She has a very funny feeling in her head, and she's been dreaming about something funny.

KP: My, you certainly do know a lot about your baby.

H: I am a good mommy. I am a *real* good mommy.

KP: I have a special tool that lets us look at dreams. Shall we use it to see if we can see what dreams are bothering your baby? [I appropriate a plastic microscope for the purpose.]

H: Yes, let's look right now. . . . [She looks excitedly.] I see a hundred animals . . . [long pause] fighting.

KP: What are they fighting about?

H: There isn't enough food!

KP: And that's what bothers your baby?

H: Yes, that's it, yes, that's right. All we need is more food, more food! Then she won't cry.

At this point, she introduced the baby's father into the story of the office visit for the first time. The father held the baby, and a brief dialogue with the doctor ensued in which the father was informed of the diagnosis of the baby's problem. The baby miraculously was cured of his hunger, and the family celebrated by going to a wedding. Helen was remarkably detailed in her representation of the wedding, including a respectable rendering of a few bars from *Lohengrin.* The baby was part of the wedding ceremony and managed to become extremely excited whenever the baby came in contact with the father, repeatedly saying, "Da-do, Da-do, Da-do." After being informed that the session was about to end, Helen took her final tour of the playroom and discovered a pair of guns which she had not yet used. She handed the smaller gun to me, kept the larger one for herself, and announced that she would be the sheriff, and I was to be a "cowboy, a bad cowboy, who comes to take all the money." Initially she appeared to be quite competent managing the guns and their mechanics, but she became silent and somewhat distant as she sat in a chair, looking off into space while she held the gun tightly in her hands. I commented that she seemed to be thinking about something. She said, "Yes, my daddy doesn't like his yucky job." Though she had momentarily lost her interest in the gun play, she quickly recovered by introducing a classic Western confrontation between the cowboy and sheriff. She sprang instantly back to life, and action-played a robust sheriff, who then challenged the bad cowboy to a shoot-out. The shoot-out, however, was postponed "for tomorrow" when the cowboy accepted the challenge. The shoot-out occurred as planned the next day over a bag of gold. The sheriff, however, suggested that the combatants lay down their arms and put up their fists. Helen then proceeded to shadowbox with me with great pleasure and vigor, being careful not to make physical contact with my hands or body. She ended the story with a surprising turn. She announced that she was going to give the money to the robber, who had now sworn to be good for the rest of his days, "Or else. . . . "

Summary. This typically rich play sequence raises many questions about Helen's use of play as metaphor. The levels of representational and symbolic thinking are sophisticated. She demonstrates a broad range of affect, humor, moralizing, and appropriate relatedness to the interviewer. The thematic material is rich, rapidly moving, and appropriately modulated. Although it is clear that the thematic content in her play is age-appropriate and the themes are logically connected from the beginning to the end of the interview, some of the subtle movements in and around typically male and feminine identifications are interesting. While her repertoire of defensive and coping strategies is appropriate and extensive, and in keeping with expectations for female development, there is a kind of unconflicted phallic tinge to it, what with sneak attacks, bulls, gunslingers, combined with interest in body contents, and preoccupations with inner spaces. Aggressive themes, reproductive curiosity, feeding and nurturing occupations, and superego explorations, especially with mother, are all richly displayed. There are also markers of some acute effects of the father's recent absences. Mother seems rather absent in the play, and her major affective connection, as might be expected, is reserved for the father as the dinner cooker, protector, nurturing figure, and "big bull." Yet for Helen's own sense of self, the ambisexual nurturing-phallic mosaic seems richly intact.

CASE 2

One of the younger children in the study, Alan A., had just turned 4 the week prior to our interview. When I first saw him, he was lying comfortably with his back against his father's chest while devouring a Doctor Seuss *I-Can-Read* book for his father's admiration. Upon my approach, he scrambled down from his father's lap, put the book away, and took a tour through the clothes closet of the waiting room, emerging from the far end with a "bet-you-can't-get-me" laugh. When I explained that he would be coming to my play office with me while his father waited in the waiting room, he sobered rather quickly but agreed to go. From this cue, I invited the father to come to tour the playroom with us. As soon as the choreography was clear to Alan, he animatedly suggested, "Let's go, Doc. We've got playing to do." He closed the door on his father, albeit counterphobically, and then took a rather rapid "hot-potato tour" of the playroom.

Alan was somewhat small for his age, well dressed in designer bib overall jeans, sneakers, and a Yale sweatshirt. His curiosity kept pace with his anxiety about being separated from his father and in the presence of this semistrange man through a variety of competencies. His first play consisted of giving me a small bear hand puppet while he donned the goose hand puppet as he admired the "bird head's big mouth." The bird head immediately informed the bear that he meant "business."

A: I am a bird head with a *big, big, big* beaker.
KP: What do you like to do with your big beak?
A: I like to bite noses.
KP: Oh, dear, and I have such a nice, fine nose!
A: No, I like to bite *people's* noses.

Alan then proceeded to turn away from the bear, and instead

systematically bit the noses of all the people in the human puppet family. He saved the father puppet until last and took special pleasure in biting the father puppet's nose; eventually the whole head found its way into the goose's mouth. This led to a play disruption, but it also served to bind a good deal of his initial separation anxiety, and his play became increasingly sophisticated and well organized.

Alan next named all of the barnyard animals as he collected them into a pile in the middle of the floor. He arranged a landscape around the pile of animals consisting of a house, a family, two trucks, and a pair of guns. He excitedly clapped his hands together, looked at me, and announced, "We're going to have a city, right here." Throughout these opening moves, Alan's speech became gradually more articulate and less immature. Finally, the opening gambits seemed to come to a comfortable conclusion when he clutched the small gun in both hands, sprayed the entire room with imaginary bullets of his phallic competence, and settled into play.

Alan turned to the doctor's kit and began a sequence of examinations, first of his own chest and belly, extending then to my chest, and then eventually to a baby and a father. The father apparently had been laid low by a "piece of meat in his blood." The father was restored to health by repeated injections to the stomach and crotch, carefully administered by this admiring, but somewhat overeager 4-year-old physician. The father suddenly jumped to his feet and announced that he was "all better." Alan then rushed excitedly to the far side of the playroom, grabbed his guns again, and began blasting away indiscriminately. This was the first of what was to be possibly a dozen rather brief, somewhat unique play "disruptions." They were not disruptions in the classic sense, because the story line was always continuous and coherent. Instead, it was as though Alan found himself suddenly overstimulated by the thematic content, responded with a brief flurry of semidistracted and excited discharge, and was then able to return to his state of previous regulation, thereby preventing the loss of pleasure in his play.

After the father had been restored to health, Alan decided to organize the family and run a zoo. He delineated the animals carefully as to who was nice and who was not nice and built a series of fences and pens for his zoo animals.

KP: Now, who goes where?
A: All the animals that don't bite get to be together. The lion and the bear have to be in their own caves [cages].
KP: How did the good animals get so good?
A: They took swimming lessons.
KP: And that made them good?
A: You bet!

Alan placed a mother in charge of the animals as a zoo keeper. She was originally placed in the cages with the good animals, but then was brought back outside the gates, "where she won't get so yuckied up. She's not scared. She is a *mommy!*" He momentarily considered whether to give the mother a companion, but his plan foundered when he could not decide which sex to assign to a somewhat unisex doll. The doll was first called a "little boy," but then the physiognomy did not seem to match. Alan then changed it to a "bad little girl," and then back to a boy, and then finally discarded the idea altogether. He found a milk bottle and poured the imaginary contents of the bottle all over the good animals. He then handed me the bottle and instructed me to pour the imaginary contents over the lion. The "milk" turned the lion into a statue, clearly neutralizing his aggressive potential.

Suddenly, it began to "rain," and the family retreated to the house, where Alan discovered that the father had "a problem." "He cannot stand up." He decided to take the father to the doctor, who then examined him and found "carrots in his blood." I introduced a small male child doll, who came to express some concern about the father's well-being. Doctor Alan announced that the father would have to stay in the hospital for seven days. The little boy reported that he could not stay at home alone because his mother and father no longer lived together. (This was indeed the situation facing Alan for the last 10 months of his life.) Alan would have none of my entrees to talk about the parallel in his own life, and instead plied the young boy with promises of going to the zoo, and even having his own zoo. When I asked about the absence of the mother in the trip to the zoo, Alan replied, "Mommy doesn't come to the zoo."

KP: How come the Mommy does not come to the zoo?

A: She doesn't come because she is at work.

KP: What does Mommy do at her work?

A: She does important things. She gets money and gives it to Dad . . . and she spends a lot of time at work. . . . That's why she can never come to the zoo.

Alan said this with palpable sadness and sat back on his heels, his body slumped momentarily like a balloon with a slow leak. Suddenly the boy and the father got in the truck and drove recklessly to the zoo, on the way encountering a policeman, who arrested them for speeding and "driving crazy." Father and son together joined forces to throw the policeman into the lion's den. The boy then, at Alan's direction, jumped fearlessly into the lion's den and kicked the lion out of the zoo. The father, at my direction, came to admire the son for his strength and fearlessness. Alan then suggested that the boy and the father lie down together to take a rest. The rest, however, was disrupted almost immediately by Alan's taking up arms to go kill a tiger who had been hiding in the closet—discovered only during the close of the play sequence.

After this brief disruption, Alan returned to the theme of the trip to the zoo. Now, however, the trip to the zoo involved increasing numbers of fellow travelers. All available zoo and farm animals, puppets, and life dolls were invited into an increasingly stimulating, upward spiral of visits to the zoo, camping trips, boat rides, and going out to dinner at "fancy restaurants." Two of the cows were briefly examined and announced to be pregnant. As I commented on the increasing excitement and noted everybody's clamoring for what they wanted to do first, Alan quickly changed his tune from that of cruise director to that of conflict resolver, working skillfully to settle conflicts over who got to do "what they want *first*." Finally, it was agreed upon that everyone would go for a boat ride out in the *deepest* part of the water, "where the whales are." Alan invited everyone to the boat and then gave a description of how to use a gun safely so that "you don't have to have it scare you so much." Eventually guns turned out to be an important part of the outing on the water. This final play sequence was quite a remarkable one thematically. Alan walked to the top of the three-step stair in the playroom and instructed me to bring all of the animals and life dolls and puppets to him so that they could all get ready to go swimming together.

A [in the style of an ever-enthusiastic camp counselor]: Does everybody know how to swim?

KP: No, the pig and the lion don't know how.

A [angrily]: Yes, everybody knows how to swim. Come on, let's go. I'm going to shoot some fishes with this gun.

KP: OK, who's going to go first?

A: All right. The pig doesn't know how, but I'm going to teach the pig. Now look, Pig, you hold your breath, and you don't swallow the water, and you kick your legs and you pull your hands through the water like gloves. OK, now, are you ready? In you go. [He throws the pig in the water and makes a struggling sound but then allows the pig its success.] OK, Dad, you're next. You know how to swim very, very, very, *very* well, don't you? I'm going to let you go in the deep part. Watch. You can take off like a bullet!

KP: He really *is* a good swimmer.

A: Yes, he is the best! [The remainder of the collection of dolls and animals is thrown, one by one, into the "deep water."] Did everyone have a good time?

KP: Yeah, yeah, yeah!

A: [notices at this point that the bull has been overlooked. He leans over to pick the bull up and asks the bull if it wants to go swimming.]

KP: [animating the bull]: No, I don't want to go swimming. I'm so big and strong I don't have to go near the water if I don't want to.

A: Oh, no, you're just being a big shot because you're scared. Here, I'll help you learn how to swim. Do you need a gun? Here, use this gun. You need a gun to help you learn how to swim. Just put it between your legs and be sure to use it. Don't let it drop out!

Alan then completed this play sequence by throwing himself headlong onto the floor and making swimming motions from one end of the playroom to the other. He rescued the goose with which he began the play session and which mysteriously had forgotten how to swim. He placed the gun in the goose's mouth and told the goose to hold onto the gun and then he would be able to swim. He instructed, "Be sure to shoot the gun off; don't just let it sit there. And then you'll learn how to swim really fast."

At the end of the session, he assisted in cleaning up and asked to go show his father the guns, which he did with great flourish.

Summary. Alan was a physically intact child with clear and articulate speech, also highly animated and personable, as well as warm and curious. He demonstrated a rich range of age-appropriate affect and an almost precocious capacity to move comfortably between modulated and overstimulating interchanges in his play. His energies are also being devoted to coping with castration anxiety. Strains of object loss are also heard as he struggles to deal with his parents' separation. His defensive and adaptive repertoire, being at the younger end of the phallic-oedipal sequence of development, was not quite as varied as Helen's, but was nonetheless quite rich. Identification with this aggressor, superego formation, reproductive curiosity, interest in body contents were all present, as were certain powerful affects. Longing for intimacy with his father and sadness over his mother's distance were obvious throughout. Some beginning reaction formation and an abiding commitment to phallic competence and exhibitionism, though strong, did not eclipse his strong nurturing reproductive wishes and identifications. I felt comfortable about his masculinity, as I did about Helen's femininity, but Alan's phallic style had a nurturing tinge to it.

DISCUSSION

Having followed these children over a period of 4 years, I had the clear impression that there were no signs of overt pathology, either cognitively or emotionally. It is difficult, however, to disentangle the effects of parental separation, chronically for Alan, or more acutely for Helen as she tries to cope with the recent weekday absences of her father. Furthermore, development itself is much more complex as a process now than at the time these children entered the study (Pruett, 1983). The family constellations continue to evolve as well.

The absence of severe psychological distresses or obvious mental illnesses in this group of children suggests that men as primary nurturing caregivers can do a creditable, adequate job of parenting. If these children are not troubled, are they different in some way? The answer which most adequately represents this material is both yes and no. In the psychosexual levels of maturation, varieties of available affect, quality of object relationships, and defensive profiles measured so far (this is still an incomplete sampling of the original population at 4 years), there are no gross personality markers that reliably distinguish these children from their more traditionally nurtured peers. Dependency vs. nurturance, robust pleasure orientations, assertiveness, vigorous drives for mastery, anger/protest—all are clearly present. There seems to be no significant lack of character flexibility in any of these children, nor could one call them remotely character-constricted. If anything, we are seeing rudimentary signs that these children, secure in their gender identities, may be, in fact, more characterologically flexible, particularly around the ease with which they move back and forth between identifications with maternal and paternal activities and attributes.

If these children have any unique, nuclear, organizing fantasies, they may center around the father as a procreative and nurturing force at a kind of pregender level. This may give, particularly for the male children, a special tinge to their negative oedipal feelings. When Alan wants to take a rest with his father after a particularly successful phallic outing, we are seeing a positive phallic identification, but also one of many prevalent examples of thematic material centering around the unfortunately named "negative oedipal complex" (Freud's designation for the young boy's erotic interest in his father).

Although there seems to be nothing especially unique about the way these children deal with most of the thematic material affectively, it has become clear that fathers and mothers are not very interchangeable in their roles. All children must disengage from the primary love object while integrating many of the object's modulating and ameliorating functions. But the experience remains quite different for boys and girls. All three of the boys who have reached the phallic/oedipal phase in their psychosexual development—and Alan is typical of them—have manifested some sadness around the issue of yielding their mothers to their fathers. The little girl, on the other hand, does not have to give up a father who is her primary nurturing parent. There are some hints that some of the boys are doing a bit worse affectively than the girls during the fourth and fifth years, even without the parental separation seen in Alan's family. Is this attributable to the fact that the girls may still *have* their mothers as rivals, whereas boys must be rivalrous with the primary nurturing figure in their lives? If typically raised girls appear more depressed for that reason, these boys seem to be suffering the same fate.

Interestingly, although it is not the focus of this paper, some of the precocious development reported during the second year of life seems to have slackened somewhat in these children, although the data are not fully analyzed. Nevertheless, I think we can answer one question now: for these older children, it appears that the precocious development seen early in the study was not secondary to increased anxiety over early maternal deprivation, as might have been posited at the time of the initial data collection. In fact, it may be an artifact of some infant assessment in general that there is a favoring or loading of father-released functioning and behavior. There does seem to be some clinically empirical evidence to strengthen an initial speculation that having a father as a primary nurturing figure may well stimulate more curiosity and interest in father as a procreator than is true of more traditionally raised children. Helen's interest in the loose particle inside the male doll, and Alan's fascination with the meat and carrots inside the father who could not walk, raise the specter that these may be much more active issues for these children than they are for their more typically raised peers. (Alan had, in fact, suffered transient fecal retention at 3 years, 4 months, when his father's sister spent a Christmas with them, during the 8th month of her pregnancy.)

Possibly more interesting than the questions raised and addressed by this focus on sexual identity are some broader questions of style. It is well known that fathers handle their babies differently than mothers in subtle but distinct ways. Both Helen and Alan played in ways which were remarkably similar to the descriptions of father-infant play delineated by Yogman (1982) and Parke (1979). The expectation that time together will be full, complete, fun, stimulating and jocular, if a bit chaotic and disorganized, seemed to pervade much of their play. Is it possible that we are seeing the history and sequelae of that particular handling style in these children as a central focus of their affective organizational system?

In closing, a note of gratitude to these children for reminding us again of the overriding complexities and fascinations of early experience, but also a note of caution. As the most accurate view of human experience comes over the *life cycle*, these stories are hardly finished. Yet, such stories do help us, like the birth of Dostoevsky's child, see beneath the constrictions of gender and role. I close with the final couplet of an eighteenth-century Anglican hymn that attempts the same vision theologically, from a more heavenly perspective, of male nurturing capacities:

> Milk of the breast that cannot cloy,
> He like a nurse will bring;
> And when we see His promise nigh
> Oh, how we'll suck and sing![1]

BIBLIOGRAPHY

BOEHM, F. (1930). The femininity complex in men. *Int. J. Psychoanal.*, 11:444–469.

FREUD, A. (1947). Emotional and instinctual development. *W.*, 4:458–488.

———— (1965). Normality and pathology in childhood. *W.*, 6.

FREUD, S. (1925). Some psychical consequences of the anatomical distinction between the sexes. *S.E.*, 19:241–258.

———— (1937). Analysis terminable and interminable. *S.E.*, 23:209–253.

GREENSPAN, S. (1981). *The Clinical Interview of the Child.* New York: McGraw-Hill.

JACOBSON, E. (1950). Development of the wish for a child in boys. *Psychoanal. Study Child*, 5:139–152.

LYTTLETON/HART-DAVIS (1979). *Letters.* London: John Murray, 1982, 2:7.

PARKE, R. (1979). Perspectives on father-infant interaction. In *Handbook of Infant Development*, ed. J. Osofsky. New York: Wiley, pp. 549–590.

1. Thanks to my colleague, Robert Evans, M.D., for bringing this couplet to my attention.

PRUETT, K. D. (1983). Infants of primary nurturing fathers. *Psychoanal. Study Child*, 38:257–277.

———— (1985). Children of the father-mothers. In *Frontiers of Infant Psychiatry*, ed. J. Hall, E. Galenson, & R. Tyson. New York: Basic Books (in press).

Ross, J. (1982). From mother to father. In *Father and Child*, ed. S. Cath, A. Gurwitt, & J. Ross. Boston: Little, Brown, pp. 189–203.

YOGMAN, M. (1982). Development of the father-infant relationship. In *Theory and Research in Behavioral Pediatrics*, ed. G. Fitzgerald, F. Lester, & M. Yogman. New York: Plenum, pp. 221–279.

On "Happiness"

ISIDOR SILBERMANN, M.D., F.A.C.P.

"HAPPINESS," AS IT IS GENERALLY CONCEIVED—AS A CONTINUOUS or long-lasting state, and as the ultimate fulfillment of deep-seated longings, starting with childhood wishes and fantasies—is an illusion. It cannot be reached, not even with extreme effort and sophisticated guidelines. On the other hand, man is fortunate if he occasionally experiences subjective, very personal, and relatively brief "feelings of happiness" with extraordinarily heightened pleasure and harmonious contentment.

The quest for happiness must have begun when the sojourn of Adam and Eve in Paradise was ended. They were evicted forever, their return prevented by two seraphim guarding the entrance with flaming swords. They had to leave their abode of heavenly bliss because knowledge had grown in their minds and had made them see reality in the nakedness of its manifold aspects. Paradoxically, great thinkers through the years have developed various ingenious ideas concerning ways in which man might find his way back to the Garden of Eden with the help of knowledge. However, all their efforts could neither remove the flaming barriers nor open the gates to the felicity of Paradise.

Inspired by their belief that the gods dwelled in the heavens, the ancients tried to build the Tower of Babel. Totally disregarding reality, they expected that it would enable them to ascend to the celestial abode. They failed. Confused by the multitude and variety of their languages, they misunderstood one another. Discords tore them apart, and erroneous concepts destroyed their labors. Philosophers of all times went astray in the same way.

Faculty, New York Psychoanalytic Institute.

The quest for happiness on earth prevented men from asking the fundamental question: "Can a long-lasting state of happiness be reached and maintained?" Led by their belief that heaven could be brought to earth, the seekers became entangled in an endless labyrinth.

In our day, a varied but similar scenario is offered to us. Brilliant astronomers, preoccupied with the question of extraterrestrial life, search one star after another, as if they hoped to ascend the astral Jacob's ladder to the seat of Olympian bliss.

Some approaches of the philosophers in their search for happiness may be found in the instructive book, *The Idea of Happiness* (McGill, 1967), where we find guidelines reaching back to antiquity. These include the following: by developing practical and moral virtues, becoming honorable and just; by rational thinking and the development of propitious human relationships; by cultivating love and goodness, exercising autonomy of will and purposeful intelligent behavior; by engaging in creative activity; by stoic fulfillment, limitation, or elimination of desires; by avoidance of painful affects, wishes, and aspirations; by mystical union with the Supreme Being; by self-realization, self-actualization, self-expansion; by developing to the whole and ideal man; by striving for the chief good.

The quest for happiness seems to be universal. In our Declaration of Independence, for instance, we find the statement that it is man's inalienable "right to pursue happiness." However, the wise founding fathers omitted to recommend how this "right" could be realized and the lofty goal attained.

Plato said, "Happiness is desired by all, although it is difficult to say just *what it is*" (p. 505; my italics). Many philosophers tried to find the answer to that question. Happiness, they stated, is: maximum pleasure, the highest attainable good for men, the fulfillment of personal wishes, the experience of a mystical encounter with God, the fulfillment of the potentialities of both the irrational and the rational sides of human nature, etc. Very few great thinkers declared that happiness is unattainable in life—particularly those who believed happiness to be a supernatural phenomenon.

Webster (1952) defines happiness as "a state of well-being characterized by relative permanence, by dominantly agreeable emotion ranging in value from mere contentment to positive felicity, and by a natural desire for its continuation. Mental and moral health and freedom from irksome cares are its normal conditions."

The English language has two distinct words, "luck" and "happiness," for the German term *Glück*. The readers of Goethe's conversations with Eckermann must make this distinction, and the translations indicate that Goethe agreed with the general opinion that he was lucky, but felt that happiness had escaped him. He said, "Basically my life has been nothing but effort and work and I can say that during my last 75 years I have not felt comfortable, not even for 4 weeks. My real happiness was my poetic creativity, which, however, was hindered and disturbed by my public position and activity" (p. 63; my tr.).

Fine (1977) mentioned Hegel as having once observed that "Happiness is to be found in the empty pages of history" (p. 18). Fine believed that "Man seeks happiness, yet for the most part he finds unhappiness" (p. 25). And Herman Hesse (1974) in his enchanting essay *Glück* stated:

Many experienced it only once, many only a few times [p. 49].

Only late in my life have I come to this all-embracing and sanctified meaning of the word happiness. Whether for hours or only for minutes, I experienced happiness only for short moments. Even now in my old age I have come close to it only at very rare instances [p. 52; my tr.].

Freud referred to happiness on several occasions. Early in his career, in a letter dated January 16, 1898, he wrote to Fliess: "Happiness is the deferred fulfilment of a prehistoric wish. That is why wealth brings so little happiness; money is not an infantile wish" (p. 244). Late in his life, he devoted an entire chapter to happiness in his *Civilization and Its Discontents* (1930). He introduced this book by responding to a letter from Romain Rolland, who had described his purely subjective religious feelings as limitless or "oceanic": "I cannot discover this 'oceanic' feeling in myself. . . . From my own experience I could not convince myself of the primary nature of such a feeling. But this gives me no right to deny that it does in fact occur in other people" (p. 65).

Contrasting *Glücksgefühle*, or "feelings of happiness" (p. 79), and a permanent state of felicity, he wrote:

. . . . the intention that man should be 'happy' is not included in the plan of 'Creation' [p. 76]. The programme of becoming happy . . . *cannot* be fulfilled; yet we must not—indeed, we cannot—give up our effort to bring it *nearer* to fulfilment by some means or other [p. 83].

At the height of being in love the boundary between ego and object threatens to melt away. Against all the evidence of his senses, a man who is in love declares that 'I' and 'you' are one, and is prepared to behave as if it were a fact! [p. 66].

What do they [men] demand of life and wish to achieve in it? . . . They strive after happiness; they want to become happy and remain so. This endeavour has two sides, a positive and a negative aim. It aims, on the one hand, at an absence of pain and unpleasure, and, on the other, at the experiencing of strong feelings of pleasure. In its narrower sense the word 'happiness' only relates to the last. . . . What we call happiness in the strictest sense comes from the (preferably *sudden*) satisfaction of needs which have been dammed up to a high degree, and it is from its nature *only possible as an episodic phenomenon* [p. 76].

The feeling of happiness derived from the satisfaction of a *wild* instinctual impulse untamed by the ego is incomparably more intense than that derived from sating an instinct that has been tamed. The irresistibility of perverse instincts, and perhaps the attraction in general of forbidden things, find an economic explanation here [p. 79].

There are . . . many paths which *may* [Freud's italics] lead to such happiness as is attainable by men; but there is none which does so for certain [p. 85].

One gains the most if one can sufficiently heighten the yield of pleasure from the sources of psychical and intellectual work . . . such satisfactions seem 'finer and higher' [p. 79].

People who are receptive to the influence of art cannot set too high a value on it as a source of pleasure and consolation in life. Nevertheless the mild narcosis induced in us by art can do no more than bring about a *transient withdrawal from the pressure of vital needs; and it is not strong enough to make us forget real misery* [p. 81].

. . . the programme of the pleasure principle . . . consists in finding the satisfaction of happiness. . . . Integration in, or adaptation to, a human community appears as a scarcely avoidable condition which must be fulfilled before this aim of happiness can be achieved. . . . The development of the individual seems to us to be a product of the interaction between two urges, the urge towards happiness, which we usually call 'egoistic', and the urge towards union with others in the community, which we call 'altruistic' [p. 140; my italics].

Freud's remark that much misunderstanding has been created by the careless way in which language uses the word love is very pertinent (p. 102). The same holds true, I might add, for happiness. The careless usage of that term can be seen in such expressions as partial happiness, general and personal happiness, perfect and imperfect happiness, natural and altruistic, supernatural, sexual, egotistic, narcissistic, and community happiness. It contributes little to say that happiness will be attained through knowledge, morality, riches, social activity, or withdrawal, indulgence, or asceticism, the gratification of suppressed childhood wishes, or of wild untamed instinctual impulses. It would seem more appropriate to say that all those factors might, under certain circumstances, contribute to the emergence of what we call "feelings of happiness."

In this context I wish to raise two questions: Could we use happiness for the gratification of the deep longings of an adult who, having experienced a mother's severe rejection, is now permitted to drink at the breast of a nursing woman? Can we use happiness for the sexual gratifications of a compulsive masturbator or promiscuous homosexual? It seems incorrect to say that the feeling of happiness derived from the satisfaction of a wild instinctual impulse, untamed by the ego, is incomparably more intense than that derived from sating an instinct that has been tamed. Are we to assume that pathological or perverted sexual experiences or wild unlimited narcissistic indulgences are free of feelings of guilt, do not mobilize the superego, do not evoke depressive emotions and anxieties? Do our clinical observations prove that perversions create happiness or a continuous state of felicity? Have we not learned that these orgastic pleasures, although perhaps more intense, are less fulfilling? Can we not assume that the compulsion to repeat is an indication that the patient has never been happy? The perverted as well as the addicted would like to live in a state of unlimited narcissistic indulgence, to drift in a vast orgastic ocean, disregarding reality and decrying its limitations. Can we call the feeling they experience happiness? The wild sexual acts of a homosexual man, for instance, lacking among other essential ingredients the experience of identification, of melting together with the partner of the other or even the same sex—can we call the resulting feeling happiness? One out of many possible examples might illuminate this point.

A young depressed homosexual man became vaguely aware that his life had brought him close to the gutter and self-destruction. On entering therapy, he described his existence: "Either I sleep, totally exhausted, during the day, or I cruise around in various avenues during the night, pick up or am picked up by another guy. We do not exchange a word, we do not get acquainted, I do not know his name. Neither does he know mine. Silently we go to some place, undress silently and hastily, perform our act wildly and leave, as two strangers, each going his own way. A short time later I am gripped again by a savage desire. During one night I might have five or six identical encounters. Each time two total strangers driven by passion meet and part as strangers, momentarily satiated like gluttons who greedily stuffed themselves. The pleasure is shortlived, wild but empty, the aftertaste is bad and stale; until the urge for another of the same drives me into the repeated intoxicating and frightening experience. Exhausted, I drag myself home, and drained of all feelings, thoughts, and energies, I fall into deep sleep until that consuming sexual hunger awakens me, and then the cycle starts again."

When asked whether this kind of life brought him fulfilling happiness, he looked astonished and answered, "For moments I imagine I am happy, that is, during the lonely orgasm; but really even those short moments are without flavor. They are insipid, and leave me with an empty depressing feeling. My life has offered me nothing but the physical satisfaction of my sexual hunger; and that is not enough to make me happy. Happiness has not come my way at all. I am a self-destructive, misery-haunted person."

Another question must be asked: What is the relationship of aggression to happiness? That the one is in opposition to the other was explicitly stated by Freud (1930):

> It is clearly not easy for man to give up the satisfaction of this

inclination to aggression. . . . It is always possible to bind together a considerable number of people in love, so long as there
are other people left over to receive the manifestations of their
aggressiveness [p. 114].

   . . . civilization is a process in the service of Eros, whose purpose is to combine single human individuals, and after that
families, then races, peoples and nations, into one great unity,
the unity of mankind. . . . But man's natural aggressive instinct,
the hostility of each against all and of all against each, opposes
this programme of civilization [p. 122].

Accepting that truth to be self-evident, we find it confirmed by
daily events all over the world. One is bound to wonder how such
a polarity as love and aggression could possibly enable individual
human beings and all of humanity to live in a state of happiness.
The aggressive drive fragments, tears the strivings of Eros
asunder; its destructive power makes it nearly impossible to
maintain—except for short moments—a stable propitious balance, the basic element in feelings of happiness. If we turn again
to the beginning of Creation, we learn that it was not love which
made it possible for Adam and Eve to remain in the Garden of
Eden, but that it was aggression which banned them forever and
posted the flaming swords at its gate.

How can happiness become a continuous common good, particularly when its tender roots are destroyed as soon as they start
to sprout? *There are only occasional and short-lived feelings of happiness,* and these appear only when the opposing drives are in
harmony, which enables the ego to unfold to its maximum
capacity.

When Freud raised the question how it happened that certain
animals have arrived at a kind of perpetual peace and cooperation which is essential to happiness, he said, "it may be that a
temporary balance has been reached between the influences of
their environment and the mutually contending instincts within
them" (p. 123). One is tempted to add that mankind must consider itself fortunate that it is far from ever reaching such constant happiness, for it would result, to use Freud's words, in the
"cessation of development" (p. 123). Thus one must conclude
that civilization and continuous happiness are mutually ex-

clusive since there cannot be development without frustration, without challenges, without distress and conflict.

Happiness cannot be manufactured by the various recipes offered to us. Happiness, says Freud, "is something essentially subjective" (p. 89). It grows on personal soil, its roots deep in the individual mind. Feelings of happiness are the masterful achievement of the "ego at its best" when its functions work in harmonious cooperation and coordination and its capacity unfolds at a given time to its possible maximum.

It is understandable that men have always sought to recapture that state of primordial felicity—that panacea which would free them from misery, despair, hopeless isolation, and helplessness; which would bring them liberty, justice, and equality, freedom from pain and hunger; and which would create conditions where love would nullify aggression, where swords would be melted into ploughshares, and the lamb would lie down peacefully with the lion.

The efforts of the philosophers to find the key to the gates of Olympian bliss have found support in social reformers—preachers, gurus, leaders of various cults, and also a few psychotherapists. One such therapist, Fine (1977), writes, "Psychoanalysis may be said to be related to philosophy in one or more of three ways: One of them is as a means of reaching happiness by means of the analytic ideal. Man can find happiness if he loves rather than hates, has pleasure, sexual gratification, has a feeling life, a sense of identity, works, is creative, has a role in the social order, is able to communicate and is reasonably free from psychiatric symptoms" (p. 19). However, Fine did not believe that this big order is easily achievable: "Although man seeks happiness yet for the most part he finds unhappiness" (p. 25); "There can be little doubt that the analytic ideal is reached by only a small minority in either our or other cultures" (p. 20). Another of his statements deserves our attention, i.e., that psychotherapy aims at creating mental health, "which is close to what we have been discussing under the name of happiness" (p. 42).

Freud's (1937) succinct description of the aim of psychoanalysis cannot be surpassed: "The business of the analysis is to secure the best possible psychological conditions for the functions of the ego; with that it has discharged its task" (p. 250). According to Freud, to achieve all-embracing happiness is not the aim of psychoanalysis. Following Hartmann (1939), one must raise another question in connection with the general concept of happiness, which means freedom from cares, suffering, pain, distress, and an abundance of gratifications. Hartmann reminds us that a healthy person must have the capacity to suffer and to be depressed. He further states that total rationality is not to be conceived as the hallmark of mental health.

Happiness, as generally conceived, is not identical with mental health or improved welfare conditions. It cannot be reached by changed social structures, advancement of technology, "love-cultures," altered beliefs or altered civilizations, more constructive human relationships, increased wealth, comfort, or the so-called perfect life, whatever that means. Even if a new social order and new regulations were to provide a more comfortable life, eliminate hunger and frustrations, improve people's social standing and freedom, heighten enjoyment, and bring more justice to them, happiness would not grow out of that hotbed of palatable existence. History has confirmed that general happiness is not an article that can be sold and bought in the marketplace, nor can it be acquired by *external* means. Happiness, as the attribute of Paradise, evaporated when Adam and Eve became ordinary people. Only occasionally a vestigial infinitesimal drop seems to condense and briefly suffuse those who have *developed in themselves* the capacity to experience the feeling of Elysian harmonies.

Since it is obvious from what has been said thus far that general happiness is out of human reach, I shall concern myself with the purely personal, subjective, and rather rare feelings of happiness. Most of us are aware of the great difficulties we face when we try to describe emotions—to put them into words and coherent sentences. Often we hope that symbols, metaphors, images might help us capture their tone and color. How shall we express their depth and intensity? Are their rapid mutations suddenly graspable? Do they just as quickly grow dim and remote? How shall we evaluate their strong impact or soothing impression, their whispering announcement and their grave aftereffects? It is with some misgivings that I attempt a description of personal feelings of happiness. We might experience them at one time or another, but for limited moments only, with a kind of inner smile and radiancy. For each of us, the specific conditions leading to the experience of happiness are unique.

When such feelings of happiness overwhelm us, we find ourselves close to the recapture of the narcissistic bliss of early childhood, now combined with the wisdom of maturity. With silent breath one experiences oneself as a firm part of this world, grounded without being chained to it. Reality is seen in focus and at the same time in varying distances; time and timelessness exist together; here and now are present as well as absent. We feel as if we had come close to the ideal fulfillment of deep longings. There is an embracing feeling of harmony, jubilant elation, and simultaneous calmness. Stormy desires and painful frustrations have become nebulous and remote. There is a contemplative looking into the center of one's inner self, a listening with introspection to the melodious flow of one's ideas in concord with one's feeling. Although the rational mind is astute, it leaves unlimited room for fantasy. Libido and aggression seem to be in balance; denials are not at work, suffering and frustrations are not negated but utilized as necessary stimuli. The ego shows maximum plasticity and mobility, swinging freely between past and present and fearlessly looking into the future. There is a deep sense of mastery, of achievement with minimal tension and maximal contentment and heightened pleasure— pleasure of an unusual illuminating quality. Those feelings oscillate with inner vibrations. Since pressure and fear have lost their gravity, one feels suspended in an atmosphere of weightlessness and oneness; of having broken through barriers, and of having stepped out of limiting confinement into a wide open space. These feelings of happiness, although very personal and subjective, are not self-centered or constricted in narrow ego boundaries, but expansive, beyond one's transitional spheres (Silbermann, 1979). One looks at the world with sharpened but also dreamy eyes. These feelings of happiness, fed by the strength of one's inner fire, are experienced by an ego with maximum equipoise.

I return to Herman Hesse who in his masterfully poetic essay on *Glück* spoke about his feelings of happiness. He denies as

banal that happiness means a good marriage, an enriching career, or the acquisition of the graspable goods of life; happiness
is more than wisdom and having all that brings joy, "happiness is
the wholeness, the eternal melodies of the universe, and the
harmony of the spheres. This limitless music in glittering eter-
nity is pure and perfect presence, and knows no time, no history.
Joining in the singing of the choir of the spheres, joining in the
round and round dance of the world, joining in the eternal
laughter of God, and feeling of being one with the universe, that
is our participation in happiness" (p. 48f.; my tr.).

Mircea Eliade (1959) interprets the feelings of happiness as
those moments when man transcends the Profane and reaches
the Sacred; when he becomes reconnected with the cosmos and
for a short time ascends to transhuman life, transcends the ordinary worldly reality which is full of misery, slime, and nettles.
The word happiness as a symbolic expression—"symbols are
pregnant with messages" (p. 137)—indicates the all-pervading
wish for sharing "in the most high" (p. 118). One might add that
feelings of happiness have a mystical character. They are expressions of the highest level of human existence, and they are
characterized by harmony and tranquillity. The loss of Paradise
is replaced during these transcendent subjective experiences by
the loss of chaos and anxiety. It is the experience of having been
permitted, as it were, to glance for a brief moment through the
guarded gate into Paradise, to breathe a whiff of its inspiring
and invigorating air.

Let us now return to Freud's statement about the aim of psychoanalysis: "The business of analysis is to secure the best possible psychological conditions for the functions of the ego; with
that it has discharged its task."

Psychoanalysis through work on pathological defenses helps
the ego to look at the unconscious and to allow its content to
move slowly into the ego, the drives to become transformed and
utilized for new stimuli. By constant weighing and scrutinizing
the various stimuli, the ego is enabled to bring about balance, to
work proficiently, and to respond with greater resilience to the
different tension-vacillations without experiencing intolerable
anxiety. Analytic therapy helps the ego functions to become
better aligned and more coherent, to be less scattered, to replace

Isidor Silbermann

disorder with order, and to enable "synthesis and fragmentation at their best" to work (Silbermann, 1961, 1981). This in turn nurtures the function of differentiation. A well-integrated ego recognizes the "right" of the sexual and aggressive drives, will look for and find their acceptable gratifications, steering the appropriate passage between the two. Psychoanalysis, if successful, will enable man to take life's pitfalls, move across its many thresholds essentially undisturbed, and remain unshaken by anxieties. The cured patient will adapt to frustrations and pain and, becoming adjusted to the inner and outer demands, will not be derailed by swings of mood in either direction. Psychoanalysis strives to make people *contented* and adjusted to life. Once that goal has been reached, no attempt is made to reach the lofty and illusory goal of perpetual happiness.

However, one might wonder how this concurs with the previously quoted statement by Freud: "Yet we must not—indeed, we cannot—give up our efforts to bring it [happiness] *nearer* to fulfilment by some means or other" (my italics). I suggest that he referred to "the essentially subjective and personal feelings of happiness," which arise in some people on some relatively rare occasions as vestigial reappearances of early experiences of man in his historical and personal childhood.

When man and woman in tender love and intense identifications melt together in sexual embrace and flow together in orgastic fulfillment, they have reached that sphere where conflicts and their personal boundaries seem to have dissolved; they have recaptured the primeval unity of *illum tempus*. Those moments are filled with feelings of happiness and heightened contentment, reflected also in their peacefully smiling faces and their enchanted relaxation. When a woman in love with her husband creates a child, she carries her baby with heartfelt expectation. When she delivers the child with anxiety and pain, she also experiences a radiant sense of lightness, newness, peace, and feelings of happiness.

When the artist or scientist struggling with his work achieves his goal and has mastered the various conflicts, he might feel that harmony, peace, and contentment—far too short, alas—which are basic to the feeling of happiness. During psychoanalytic therapy it sometimes happens that the patient suddenly feels a calm elation when associations and interpretations have helped him to throw light into the dark corners of his unconscious and have opened up new vistas. When he senses that he has reached a salient point and insight, he is moved by some feelings of happiness.

When the lover of the arts feels both united with and a part of the *objet d'art,* he is moved to deep affective identification. Calm feelings of happiness might be his. These sacred moments are remote from his profane everyday life. Think of someone standing in the temple of Poseidon in Sounion, surrounded by splendid unaccustomed light. As the sounds of the sea reach his dreamy ears, he finds himself removed from the ground into utter purity and breathtaking sublimity. For radiant moments he has lost conflicts, and is filled with heightened contentment. Standing on earth, he feels suspended, free of the pressures of time or space, and conscious only of inner peace and devotion. When one stands in deep admiration before the Charioteer in Delphi or creations like Michelangelo's Moses in Rome, or in the Chapel of the Medici in Florence, or in front of paintings by Leonardo da Vinci, Monet, El Greco, and van Gogh, feelings of happiness may flow silently through his being. In that brief time he seems to have left gravity behind and transcended to a different sphere where misery is gone and glory reigns.

While observing patients undergoing insulin-shock treatment in England (1940), I was struck by a sudden change in their expressions—from pain and despair to a soothing smile when they returned to consciousness. When they regained the power of speech, still very weak, some said, "I feel happy; I have crossed the bridge between death and life." They felt reborn. They had escaped from a confused, malfunctioning, scattered ego into a more composed ego state, where, within certain limits, the various functions seemed to have reached at least temporary harmony and coordination, where an improved balance prevented the arousal of anxiety and terror. They felt that a crucial battle had been won, that they had accomplished a major task, had recaptured ground. A previously derailed life seemed to have lost its dark shadows, delusive misconceptions had been altered into a new confidence, and contentment seemed to have grown stronger roots.

When narcissistic positions are replaced by altruistic cooperation, aggression harmonizes with libido, self-destruction
changes into constructive activity, the ego is converted from a
battlefield with frequent defeats into a workshop where the various functions can unfold their capabilities, and, with never-end-
ing balancing, produce coordinated forward movement. When
the ego has gained strength and gathered economic advantage
from the reduction of pathological defenses, it can mature and
develop more freely. This somewhat restored ego will be able to
lend its uncloaked ear, as it were, to the demands of the id and
the unconscious. It can grant them formerly prohibited gratifications. Patients then experience their "rebirth" with the temporary effervescence of feelings of happiness.

When Freud (1930) referred to these feelings of happiness, he
said,

> . . . to put it more correctly, originally the ego includes every-
> thing, later it separates off an external world from itself. Our
> present ego-feeling is, therefore, only a shrunken residue of a
> much more inclusive—indeed, an all-embracing—feeling
> which corresponded to a more intimate bond between the ego
> and the world about it. If we may assume that there are many
> people in whose mental life this primary ego-feeling has per-
> sisted to a greater or less degree, it would exist in them side by
> side with the narrower and more sharply demarcated ego-feel-
> ing of maturity, like a counterpart of it. In that case, the idea-
> tional contents appropriate to it would be precisely those of
> limitlessness and of a bond with the universe—the same ideas
> with which my friend [Romain Rolland] elucidated the 'oceanic'
> feeling [p. 68].

In rare moments when harmony and *near*-optimal balance are
achieved, the ego experiences the elevating feelings of happiness. On the other end of the spectrum, when grave disequi-
librium occurs, the ego experiences anxiety and even terror (Silbermann, 1983). Due to the loss of coherence and strength, it
may also experience degrees of depression.

The feelings of happiness are not accidental events. They are
the outgrowth of constant introspection, scrutiny, and the effort
to understand oneself. They come from striving for harmony;
for the solution of ever-present conflicts; for the achievement of

a propitious relationship between body and mind, the unconscious and the conscious, yielding and restraint, the superego demands and the ego, fantasy and reality, emotions and thoughts. They cannot develop without an appropriate relationship to the world around, or without the adequate blending of libido and aggression, or without an acceptance of regressions in the service of the ego, of frustrations, struggle, hardship, disappointments, even defeats, and further without the ability to differentiate, to distinguish between past and present. In brief, the search for mastery in a perplexing multitude of activities is essential for the ascendance of feelings of happiness. If the ego has reached a state where its conflict-free sphere can expand, its transitional sphere can extend, its several functions remain in harmonious coordination; and if its strength is not sapped by pathological defenses; if it is unscarred by traumatic memories and unshaken by mounting tensions, with resulting anxieties—then we may assume that such an ego will experience a kind of well-being and contentment.

People born with a well-endowed ego nucleus and transitional spheres, when favored with a propitious caring environment, have a greater chance to mature and develop properly, to adapt and adjust, to be less anxious and frustrated than those whose endowments, maturation, and development were impeded. The latter will find life a dim dwelling place of frequent pain and misery and agitation. The first type lives in a way that permits the ego to expand to a state of enhanced functioning. Such an ego will enable its owner to experience the illuminating emotions we call feelings of happiness. In these *ephemeral* moments, sublimations have been at work, mingled with the awareness that adequate utilization and indulgence of libido and aggression have also been enjoyed. When near harmony is established and heightened contentment is joined by inner tranquillity, a radiant and silent pleasure and a kind of breathtaking reverence are experienced. Such an experience may explain why Mircea Eliade speaks of moving from the "profane to the sacred."

Psychoanalysis aims at making the ego a well-functioning system able to adapt, to adjust, and to accept frustrations. When it succeeds, it has readied the soil from which transient feelings of happiness can grow.

BIBLIOGRAPHY

ECKERMANN, J. P. (1836–48). *Gespräche mit Goethe.* Berlin: Knaur, 1964.

ELIADE, M. (1959). *The Sacred and the Profane.* New York: Harcourt, Brace, & World.

FINE, R. (1977). Psychoanalysis as a philosophical system. *J. Psychohist.*, 5:1–59.

FREUD, S. (1898). Letter 82. In *The Origins of Psychoanalysis.* New York: Basic Books, 1954, pp. 243–244.

———— (1930). Civilization and its discontents. *S.E.*, 21:59–145.

———— (1937). Analysis terminable and interminable. *S.E.*, 23:209–253.

HARTMANN, H. (1939). Psychoanalysis and the concept of health. In *Essays on Ego Psychology.* New York: Int. Univ. Press, 1964, pp. 1–18.

HESSE, H. (1974). *Glück.* Berlin: Suhrkamp.

MCGILL, V. J. (1967). *The Idea of Happiness.* New York: Praeger.

PLATO. *The Republic.* Penguin Books, 1955.

SILBERMANN, I. (1940). The psychical experiences during shocks in shock-therapy. *Int. J. Psychoanal.*, 21:3–22.

———— (1961). Synthesis and fragmentation. *Psychoanal. Study Child*, 16:90–117.

———— (1979). Mental transitional spheres. *Psychoanal. Q.*, 48:85–106.

———— (1981). Balance and anxiety. *Psychoanal. Study Child*, 36:365–378.

———— (1983). Anxiety and terror. *Psychoanal. Study Child*, 38:569–574.

The Joke in "The Moses of Michelangelo"

Imagination and Creativity
VANN SPRUIELL, M.D.

A SET OF PARTICULAR ACTS OF IMAGINATION BY FREUD WERE gathered in the paper, "The Moses of Michelangelo" (1914a), an example of Freud's remarkable creativity. But the sources of data about "creativity" are problematic, and the limitations of psychoanalysis applied to the biographies of great creators, or to the minds of unusually gifted patients, are well known. Still, keeping sources and limitations in mind, psychoanalysts do study the reaches of individual human minds in disciplined ways. The collectivity of psychoanalytic knowledge allows for certain generalizations. When works on creativity and imaginativeness *lack* foundations made out of disciplined studies of individuals in depth, the superstructures are flawed. *The Act of Creation,* by Arthur Koestler (1964), and *Imagination,* by Harold Rugg (1963), bear witness. Koestler and Rugg, nonanalysts, present valuable ideas when borrowed or derived from psychoanalysis (especially in the case of Koestler, with spare or sneering acknowledgment—if any at all). But what is not borrowed in each is trivial.

Practicing analysts are daily privy to the secret imaginations of

Training and supervising analyst, New Orleans Psychoanalytic Institute.

Presented at the Hampstead International Colloquium on "The Role of Fantasy in the Adaptive Process," October, 1983.

I am grateful to Drs. Leonard Shengold, Edward Weinshel, and others, for their helpful criticisms of earlier versions of this paper.

473

people who are usually at least intelligent, often talented, sometimes gifted, and occasionally genuinely creative—in reparative and evolutionary, if not revolutionary ways. Out of the fecund psychic swamps in which we live, we pay—we *should* pay—close attention to our own imaginations. Psychoanalysts often measure up to their patients: they are usually at least intelligent, often talented, sometimes gifted, and occasionally even creative—in those evolutionary, reparative ways suggested above. It pleases me to believe that most analysts are more or less imaginative—unless they set up inner walls against that imaginativeness. After all, psychoanalysts work simultaneously stimulated and deprived; they are denied immediate gratifications but posed unending emotional puzzles. Rosen (1958) began to examine the subject from this direction.

But it is hard to examine the workings of ordinary imagination, and harder to study the unusual imaginations of radical innovators (Spruiell, 1977). Unfortunately, *revolutionary* geniuses rarely seek analysis. Even if they did, little or nothing could be communicated publicly about them by their analysts. Nor do would-be or actual heroes knowingly volunteer their most interesting secrets to biographers, nor write them down in their own autobiographies. Public writings are made as much to conceal as reveal.

Freud, more than other geniuses, opened some of his soul to the world, partly against his inclinations, but necessarily because of his quests. I have chosen "The Moses of Michelangelo" to explore Freud's extraordinary imagination at work, for several reasons which will become clear below. Among them is the paper's exquisite condensation of private meanings with public purposes. The exploration will come upon several apparently disparate topics. The first of these has to do with jokes; the second, the strange fascination the statue of Moses had for Freud—a fascination that was itself fascinating; finally, a discussion of what generalizations, if any, can be made about imaginative activities and the limitations of these generalizations.

JOKES

Picasso once said that every good work of art is a kind of joke. Diego Rivera, the revolutionary Mexican muralist, agreed.

Every piece of worthwhile art, properly understood, is not only like a joke, it is shocking. It must connect its elements in a new way; the world comes to be seen in a new way. A punch line of a joke may get a laugh, or perhaps only a smile. A first view of a great work of art *may* make one smile, more likely not. But it will be shocking, often without the viewer knowing quite why. "So art may not *be* a joke," Rivera said, "but it is always like one."[1]

Freud completed his paper, "The Moses of Michelangelo," on New Year's Day, 1914. He had been thinking about it for at least 13 years, struggling with it, talking to his colleagues about it. His thoughts reached a pitch of intensity in 1912 and 1913. But once the paper was completed, he still did not want to publish it. Jones, Ferenczi, Abraham, Rank, and Sachs were dismayed. Freud told them he had more doubts about its conclusions than usual; he worried that it might seem amateurish. The paper meant something more to him than other papers had. Finally, he gave in to his friends' good advice, but he still insisted that it be published anonymously! Why? "It is only a joke," he wrote Jones, "but perhaps not a bad one." To Abraham, he also wrote, "It is only a joke" (Jones, 1955, p. 366).

Not for 10 years would Freud publicly admit authorship. Nineteen years after its completion, he wrote Edoardo Weiss: "My feeling for this piece of work is rather like that towards a love-child. For three lonely September weeks in 1913 I stood every day in the church in front of the statue, studied it, measured it, sketched it, until I captured the understanding for it which I ventured to express in the essay only anonymously. Only much later did I legitimatize this non-analytical child" (Jones, 1955, p. 367).

Every day by himself before a piece of marble for three weeks? Love-child? This after 11 years of regular visits to the object of his fascination? And then he was unwilling to put his name to the paper. Freud had had similar uncharacteristic reactions to "Totem and Taboo" and later would to "Moses and Monotheism," two other works he was inclined to publish anonymously. "The Moses of Michelangelo" was more than a demon-

1. Reported to me by his daughter, Ruth Rivera, in a series of interviews in 1970.

stration of the application of the psychoanalytic way of thinking, more than a scholarly exercise. It was a work of art itself, thus a personal statement. But was Freud being self-deprecatory and trivializing when he called it a joke? One would not think so, in view of the letter to Edoardo Weiss about his "love-child."

Before examining another great work of his, the much neglected *Jokes and Their Relation to the Unconscious*, where we find similarities between jokes and works of art, it would be worthwhile to draw a sketch of the "love-child." That child was the product of breaking the rules which purport to separate science from art, rules which would dictate conformity and submission to authority rather than revolution, and rules which call for conventional solutions to oedipal dilemmas.

THE MOSES OF MICHELANGELO

The essay begins with a *kind* of a joke. Its title has a footnote attached, supposedly supplied by the editors but obviously by Freud himself. An apology is made for the unconventionality of the contribution, but the explanation is offered that the anonymous author's "mode of thought has in point of fact a certain resemblance to the methodology of psycho-analysis" (1914a, p. 211). Confessing himself to be a layman in the field of art or its history, Freud explains that he puzzles over the power of a work of art to so grip an admirer. It can only have to do with the *intention* of the artist. Mere intellectual understanding cannot suffice the diviner; what the artist "aims at is to awaken in us the same emotional attitude, the same mental constellation as that which in him produced the impetus to create" (p. 212). To understand a work of art like the statue of Moses, it is necessary to *interpret* it. That is the only way to discover the intentions and emotional activities of the artist.

Freud tells of his peculiar fascination for Michelangelo's statue in the Church of San Pietro in Vincoli, originally designed to be one of the two central figures of the grand tomb to be built for Pope Julius II. Although Freud could not allow himself to visit the statue until September 5, 1901, he almost certainly had seen copies of the work in Vienna and in the Louvre. In the Louvre, also, were the originals of the famous Heroic and Dying Captives, which Michelangelo had intended for the tomb (Liebert, 1983).

The conventional assumption has been that the Moses represents the prophet in startled rage at the blasphemy of his followers—an instant before he smashes the Tablets. "How often have I mounted the steep steps from the unlovely Corso Cavour to the lonely piazza where the deserted church stands, and have essayed to support the angry scorn of the hero's glance! Sometimes I have crept cautiously out of the half-gloom of the interior as though I myself belonged to the mob upon whom his eye is turned—the mob which can hold fast no conviction, which has neither faith nor patience, and which rejoices when it has regained its illusory idols" (p. 213).

But the interpretations offered by nonpsychoanalytic scholars of other aspects of the great statue are consistent only in their contradictions. Certain peculiarities are interpreted as having various meanings—or no meaning at all. "Has then," Freud asks (p. 215), "the master-hand indeed traced such a vague or ambiguous script in the stone, that so many different readings of it are possible?"

The master-hand had not. Freud develops, and argues for, his own daring thesis, a thesis well known to all psychoanalysts. Michelangelo had *not* depicted the Biblical Moses about to rise up in wrath and cast down the tablets. Moses had *started* to his feet, but felt the tablets slipping from under his arm. Then, contrary to the Bible, but according to Michelangelo, he *controlled* himself, sank back into a sitting position, and *saved* the tablets: "Michelangelo must have had the presumption to emend the sacred text and to falsify the character of that holy man" (p. 230). He converts Moses "so that the giant frame with its tremendous physical power becomes only a concrete expression of *the highest mental achievement that is possible in a man, that of struggling successfully against an inward passion for the sake of a cause to which he has devoted himself*" (p. 233; my italics).

Why would Michelangelo do such a thing for the central figure which was to identify Moses with Julius II himself? Freud stresses the intensity of the attachment between Julius and Michelangelo, the similarities between these passionate and violent men, and the similar grandness in their designs—the one in terms of the reformation and reestablishment of the Papal supremacy, the other in terms of art the likes of which had not been seen before. Freud speculates that Michelangelo, as the more introspective of the two, was reproaching both, "thus, in self-criticism, rising superior to his own nature" (p. 234.).

Freud understood the sources of his insights. He was a great admirer of great men and had a pantheon of heroes with whom he identified. The most important was probably Moses. But he was identified with Michelangelo too, and likely with the great Julius II. He also identified Julius with one of the most important of his infantile objects.[2] The struggle envisioned in the paper had a general meaning, "the highest mental achievement that is possible in a man." It also had personal meanings having to do with three spheres: (1) Freud's feelings about—one might say transferences to—his own great creation, the concepts of psychoanalysis. His own "highest mental achievement" was then endangered by the defections of Jung and Adler. (2) The necessities of his outside professional life: to retain his leadership and control his own passions for the sake of a higher cause. (3) The resolution of specific conflicts which had arisen during infancy, which had manifested themselves repeatedly in his adult life—particularly before periods of great creativity. The resolution was manifest in Freud's subsequent life: after the break with Breuer, the death of his own father, the rupture with Fliess, and the loss of Jung, there were to be no more fathers acknowledged in that life.[3]

"JOKES AND THEIR RELATION TO THE UNCONSCIOUS" IN CONTEXT

Freud's works, especially those written during his several phases of great productivity, should not be read singly; they should be read in blocks. Different as individual papers from the same timeframes may seem on the surface, they are all related. For

2. Shengold's (1972) paper suggests the same identification.
3. Even though, as Shengold (1972) convincingly infers, the repressed cravings and conflicts found denial and disguised expression in his ambivalent relations with his follower Abraham, and in his grief after Abraham's premature death.

example, after the preparatory monographs on Leonardo (1910) and *Totem and Taboo* (1913), he published in 1914, besides three technical papers, the "Moses," an artistic statement, "On the History of the Psycho-analytic Movement," a professional statement; and two important theoretical statements, one major and the other minor, "On Narcissism" and "Reflections on Schoolboy Psychology."

Similarly, in 1905 he published the "Fragment of an Analysis of a Case of Hysteria," *Three Essays on the Theory of Sexuality,* and *Jokes and Their Relation to the Unconscious*—and two minor papers as well. In fact, Freud wrote the books on jokes and sexuality *side by side.* That is, he kept the manuscripts by each other, and worked on one or the other as it pleased him. Among their common attributes is the view they give of Freud's imagination operating at different levels simultaneously. The two books, seemingly so different, are integrally related. During the next three years, he followed up certain of the motifs in these works with psychoanalytic applications to the fields of drama, literature, religion, sexual morality, and character.

The themes in these works began, of course, in the dream book (1900). They were continued in *The Psychopathology of Everyday Life* (1901).[4] Of the major and subsidiary themes contained in all these works are two more which I wish to emphasize here, even though they may seem extraneous: Freud delineated a model of the mind which would contain mundane states of ordinary, "normal" consciousness; everyday and necessary alterations of rationality encompassed in wit, jest, humor, jokes— and, it must be stressed, art; the ubiquitous "slips" of the mind in daily life; the strange nightly states of dream life; and finally, psychopathology. Freud thought in 1900 in terms of *junctures* of chains of associations as "nodal points," and he believed that the

4. The first indication known to us of Freud's interest in the subject of this book is in a letter to Fliess on August 26, 1898 (Freud, 1950, p. 261). Freud described his inability to recall the name of *Julius Mosen,* a well-known poet. His self analysis showed that he had "personal reasons" for repressing the name Mosen, that infantile material determined the repressions, and that the substitute names that did occur to him were, like neurotic symptoms, compromise formations. This was the first recorded conjunction by Freud of the names, Julius and Mosen.

contents of dreams came from them. He later came to believe that the final forms of *all* conscious psychic acts, not just dreams, came about from these nodal points. Freud wanted one model for the psychic apparatus, in which differences could be accounted for in terms of *quantitative* rather than qualitative distinctions. Freud was developing the economic point of view of his metapsychology.

The other major theme had to do with the understanding of the motivational role of conscious and unconscious sexuality, arising from diverse origins in earliest childhood, finally organized and synthesized during adolescence as genitality. Freud was able to elucidate the role of the sexual drive in *all* of mental life, from the most primitive to the most advanced, from the most ordinary to the most exalted. Freud was honing his concepts of drives as motivational forces, countered by opposing transforming and altering forces: along with the economic, he was developing dynamic, genetic, and structural (Ucs.-Pcs.-Cs.) points of view.

In summary, he was consolidating and fleshing out the contributions of *The Interpretation of Dreams.* Having begun with the study of pathology—the study of pathological states supposedly in one kind of human being, the patient, by another kind of human being, the doctor—Freud moved to the view of their possessing psychic apparatuses which were qualitatively identical. Many differences among individuals which were apparently qualitative in nature were actually quantitative differences. Doctor, patient, dreamer, joker, creator, and scoundrel have fundamentally similar minds. Lewin (1955) claims that Freud admitted that he had "forgotten" that the structure of a symptom and the structure of the analytic situation resemble the structure of the dream and the activities of the dreamer. He "forgot" when he developed his theories of narcissism, when the dream became equivalent to psychotic operations. But—so this essay argues— he "remembered" his earlier discovery in a disguised way in the same year, 1914, in the form of the Moses paper. He "remembered" again, consciously, in "Analysis Terminable and Interminable" (1937).

Jokes and Their Relation to the Unconscious (1905) was stimulated, according to Jones (1955, p. 335), by complaints by Fliess that

Freud relayed so many bad jokes, and was so intrigued by plays on words. (It is to be noted that "Three Contributions. . . " was also stimulated by Fliess—who, however, protested that Freud "forgot" that the concept of universal bisexuality was his own. A bitter controversy ensued, and the relationship was destroyed.)

The Joke book, one of Freud's most important, has been neglected in English for several reasons. Jokes are even harder to translate than poems. Freud did not revise this book, as he repeatedly revised the ones on dreams and sexuality. Further, there has been a general coarsening of taste in the Western World. Many jokes that would have been adjudged daring, funny, or risque in 1905 have become "bad jokes" today. Finally, *Der Witz* does not have quite the meaning of either "joke" in English, which has a wider meaning, or "wit," which has a narrower meaning. Nevertheless, it is a pity that the work is so ignored. The Joke book bubbles with ideas, many not further elaborated to this day. And it is both ground to figure, and figure to ground to its companion, *Three Essays on the Theory of Sexuality.*

Freud wanted to explain the pleasure obtained from jokes. He thought it depended on their *techniques* as well as their *tendencies.* Techniques involve condensation, displacement, indirect presentation by means of allusion, plays on words, the breaking of ordinary burdensome rules of logic, and *the establishment of unexpected connections between disparate ideas.* It is this latter that Koestler (1964) calls "bisociation," the coming together of lines of thought from different levels of the mind. The same process was depicted by Freud in 1900 in his "nodal points" of crossing lines of associations. These techniques are like those that operate in *sexual foreplay.* Foreplay derives from the diverse infantile roots of sexuality, the "component instincts." In "harmless" jokes, the pleasure is like the "harmless" play with words in childhood. In "tendentious" jokes, which always have to do with more genitally organized erotic and aggressive sources, there is a sudden organization of the pregenital components into foreplay, with a surprising, even shocking, climax, an orgasticlike discharge. Such jokes allow access to ordinarily suppressed unconscious fantasies, and combine them with preconscious fantasies on other levels. The result is a discharge and a saving of energy equivalent, Freud thought, to the forces ordinarily maintaining the repression. "Harmless jokes," according to Freud, resemble the nonorgastic play of children more directly.

What dreams, fantasies, humor, wit, symptoms, creative acts—what psychic acts have in common is that all emanate from a psychic structure shared in qualitative essentials by almost all human beings. Following Waelder (1930), we would say that *every* psychic act obeys the principle of multiple determination and function. More specifically, what creative acts and jokes, and to a lesser extent, dreams, share is the sudden, shocking, joining, by the viewer or listener, of previously buried sexual and aggressive fantasies with fantasies more closely related to everyday, conscious perception.

But who makes up jokes? What impels them to do it? What are the dynamics of the creation of a work of art? Freud did not know, nor do we. In 1930, he remarked: "Even the best and fullest of them [biographies of great men] could not answer the two questions which alone seem worth knowing about. It would not throw any light on the riddle of the miraculous gift that makes an artist, and it could not help us to comprehend any better the value and effect of his works" (p. 211). However, we do understand more about the riddles of two internal, intrapsychic creations: the relative resolution of the oedipus complex and the reorganization of libidinal development in adolescence. Both resemble works of art: they bring together new conscious and unconscious possibilities in tangible forms. Both synthesize, organize, gratify, stabilize, serve adaptive purposes. Both involve the creation of new structures, the superego proper at the end of the oedipal period, and a new, adultlike ego ideal in mid-adolescence. The latter allows and combines genital orgasms and genital love, while repressing perverse fantasies or subsuming them under what we classify as foreplay.

FREUD'S IMAGINATION

Freud created a work of art with several characters in it: the Biblical Moses transmuted into the Moses of the statue, the sculptor, Michelangelo, and the Pope, Julius II. But there are always other characters existing implicitly in a dream, a play, or a work of art. The most important of these shadowy or even invisible figures is the dreamer, the playwright, the artist. "The Moses of Michelangelo" has to do with Freud himself. If that is acknowledged, other figures relevant to his present and past—all the way to infantile times—help set the context. Some even appear in disguise. Some do not appear at all, but are nevertheless there. If we imagined a play about the girlhood of the Empress Josephine, we would have to think of Napoleon, whether his name were mentioned or not. Just as the examination of a dream would force us to think about what relevant players had been left out, so it is profitable to think about those relevant players not mentioned in Freud's paper. They can be approached through mention of certain historical and mythological facts about Moses, Michelangelo, Julius II, and Freud himself. All or most of these facts were known to Freud. Looked at in this way, a number of common themes emerge which can be inferred to be contents of Freud's mind. The possession of certain historical and mythological facts was the raw material, and the insights into motivational themes were the tools in the workroom of Freud's imagination. The *use* of the materials and tools is another matter, one which is much more mysterious.

The Biblical account of the birth of *Moses,* his abandonment during infancy, rescue, and subsequent career as hero, conforms to Rank's *Myth of the Birth of a Hero* (1959). Only two comments need be offered here. One has to do with the 3-years older brother of Moses, *Aaron.* Freud does not mention him in this particular paper, but he is nonetheless crucial to it: Aaron was the traditional founder and head of the Jewish priesthood. Earlier, he had served as the "mouth" of Moses when the two were seeking the release of the Jews from Egypt. His magic rod also helped impress the Pharaoh, who acceded to the Exodus. After serving with Moses, Aaron later betrayed him. It was *he* who made the golden calf; it was the sight of that icon that caused Moses to cast down the tablets in rage. The other seemingly extraneous comment to be made here is the reminder of the existence of a large literature concerning the importance of Freud's identification with Moses (Shengold, 1972).

It has been mentioned that the *statue* of Moses was planned as one of the two central figures of the tomb of Julius II, a tomb that was to be the greatest monument in the Western world. The statue of Moses was to represent Julius, whose ambitions were to emulate not only the prophet but St. Paul as well. In one of the great variety of plans for this tomb, dragged out over the years, was a proposed statue of St. Paul to match the one of Moses. The theme of this monumental stone drama: Julius was to revolutionize his people and his church, temporally and religiously. It has been mentioned that Freud believed that Michelangelo had the temerity to alter the actions of the Biblical Moses, alter them in such a way that the statue represented someone more like Julius, and more, we have the right to presume, like himself. Clearly, Julius was to be Paul's equal, even superior—perhaps superior to Moses!

But the great crown itself, the tomb, finally emerged only as a pathetic travesty of Michelangelo's vision. He died believing his life to have been a failure for not having been allowed to make that tomb. Completion would have confirmed the artist's hubris: he, Michelangelo, would have been greatest of them all!

Michelangelo Buonarroti was the oldest son born to a mother who died when he was 6—after producing 4 more little brothers. He seems hardly to have known her, as he was left with a family to nurse him in the village of Settignano, where most of the people worked as stonecutters. He was reclaimed by his father when he was put in school in Florence. After an apprenticeship to a sculptor, his talent was noticed by Lorenzo Magnifico, who took him into the Medici household.[5] During his subsequent adolescence, Michelangelo was exposed daily, intimately, to the greatest minds of that part of the Renaissance, the philosopher Ficino, the poet Politan, Lorenzo himself, and others making up the members of the "Humanistic Academy" of the Medicis. Michelangelo not only became the genius we know as sculptor and painter, he became an accomplished poet as well. He was academically better educated than his future patron, Julius II. It is sometimes forgotten that it was the complex intelligence embodied in the art that appealed to the Pope. Along with his

5. Ironically, Lorenzo's younger brother, Giuliano, had been the victim of a famous murder plotted by the Cardinal Riario della Rovere, the cousin and fraternal rival of Julius (who may or may not have taken part in the plot) to destroy both of the Medicis. It can be safely presumed that Freud knew these facts. Whether he connected them or not will probably never be known to us.

successful intentions to reunite the Papal states, he aimed to further a humanistic religious revolution which would prefigure the Reformation and Counter-Reformation.

Michelangelo never married, and as far as is known was never involved in any way with women (with the exception of an autumnal, Platonic friendship with the elderly Vittoria Colonna). He was, however, devoted to his father and brothers, and, when not directly supporting them, led them, lectured them, and lent to them. It is known that he had passionate attachments to other men, especially if they were young and handsome. The general assumption has been that he was homosexual, and that is relevant to this essay—although his actual sexual behavior is not.

Biographical material on *Pope Julius* is scant. He came from a family that Faulkner would have regarded Snopesian. His uncle was ruthlessly ambitious, not only for himself, but to raise the status of his family. The uncle rose from a low position to become Pope Sixtus IV in 1471. He was not an effective Pope, but was a master of simony and nepotism. However, he did patronize the arts, and he built the Sistine Chapel. After his election, the new Pope made his wastrel nephew, Riario, then 25, a Cardinal; he had raised Riario himself, taken him from his sister as a child, brought him up as a spoiled son. He also made a Cardinal the future Julius, his impoverished brother's son, Giuliano della Rovere, 2 years older than Riario. After the abortive attempt to assassinate the brothers, Lorenzo and Giuliano de Medici, Cardinal Riario died, or was murdered. Although Sixtus IV was aware of the plot, it is not known if his nephew Giuliano had any hand in it. After Cardinal Riario's death, Sixtus IV not only excommunicated the Medicis, but grieved in a fashion gossips called "unseemly." But then he turned his attentions to his brother's son, the future Julius II. Julius, too, profited by the death of a favored "brother."

Giuliano della Rovere, like his rival, Cardinal Riario, was a man of the world. He acknowledged three daughters as his own. He became Pope in 1503, as his uncle Sixtus IV had, by the liberal use of simony. However, after he was elected Pope, he became a reformer, and tried to rid the Church of both simony and nepotism. But, sorrily, he needed money for his enterprises and, if anything, intensified the practice of selling indulgences.

The steady increases in the price needed to buy special fates for the souls of the dead, stimulated by Julius and the two Medici Popes who followed, had much to do with the Protestant Reformation.

Freud was born on May 6, 1856, in a small town in what is now Czechoslovakia. He was the first child of a young woman of 21 and a much older father. The family was Jewish, middle-class, and included, at least living nearby, a married half-brother about the same age as his mother, a nephew who was a little older, a niece a little younger, and a Catholic Nanny. When he was 11 months old, a brother was born. Eight months later, in December, 1857, when Sigmund was a toddler of 19 months, the younger brother died. A year later, on December 31, 1858, a sister, Anna, was born.[6] Four more daughters and one son were to follow in quick succession. With the birth of Anna, the Nanny was dismissed for reasons which mystified the child. When Freud was 3, economic necessity made for relocations of the families; they must have been important to the young boy. His immediate family moved to Vienna. The half-brothers, Emanuel and Philipp, with the nephew John and the niece, Pauline, moved to England.

Jones (1953, p. 4f.) relates perceived omens contributing to the family myths from infancy that a hero had been born. Whatever post-hoc omens are found for heroes, there is no doubt that Sigmund was a gifted, adored, oldest son. Every effort was made to stimulate the child and to find opportunities for him. But if we judge from what is known about the effects of personal losses during infancy and early childhood, Freud's multiple losses cannot be ignored. *Freud* certainly did not ignore them. He revealed more about his unconscious conflicts in his public and private writings than any famous man in history.

It will be remembered that Freud lost his place at the breast at 11 months to his infant brother—*Julius*.[7] Julius was the name

6. It cannot escape the attention of the psychoanalyst that Freud was completing "The Moses of Michelangelo" during the anniversary of his infant brother's death, and completed it just after the anniversary of his sister's birth 56 years before.

7. Shengold (1972) follows Jones (1953) in emphasizing the importance of the name Julius for Freud—and, indeed, names of important people in general, particularly fathers.

that supplied the infantile component of Freud's parapraxis when he was unable to remember the name of the poet, Julius Mosen. In a letter to Fliess on October 3, 1897, Freud alluded to the impact that the fulfillment of his death wishes toward little Julius had had—a tendency that remained ever after (Freud, 1950, p. 219).[8] There is no mention of the shattering effect the death of Julius must have had on the family, particularly his mother.[9]

Freud also lost his Nanny at the same time Anna was born. Later, he lost his uncle, nephew, niece, and family home. With the consolidation of his oedipal conflicts, the boy undoubtedly condensed and reworked *all* of these losses. No other inference is reasonable. According to Freud's fantasies during his unending self analysis, his repetitive needs to attach himself to other men—the most famous of whom were Breuer, Fliess, and Jung—and then to break with them were connected with murderous oedipal conflicts with his father and, at the same time, *tied to his fantasies about Julius* (Jones, 1955, p. 146). Fliess, a man younger than Freud by 2 years, and thus in a similar position to him as Julius, was to be the Great Man. Freud unconsciously had to restore Julius. Later, Jung was to be the Joshua, destined to enter the Promised Land, while he, Freud, could have no more than a view from Mt. Pisgah. Freud's famous fainting spells, each in a context of murderous feelings between father and son, each referring to Freud's myth about Julius, each preceding an agonizing break, first with Fliess, then with Jung, were symptoms of the struggle, before its effective mastery, of oedipal fantasies regressively expressed in terms of preoedipal object losses.

8. In the same letter, he revealed presumably screen memories of seeing his mother "*nudam*" when he was between the ages of 2 and 2½, with the consequence that his "libido had been aroused." There, too, he told the fantasy that his original seducer had been the Nanny, that his "companion in (sexual) crime" had been his nephew John, and that the two little boys had treated his little niece "shockingly." It is to be noted that if the dating of the memory of seeing his mother nude were correct—and it probably was, because the date of the train trip when the incident occurred is known—his mother would have been in the latter stages of her pregnancy with Anna.

9. Another radical innovator who had a similar loss was Diego Rivera, whose identical twin died when he was 18 months old. Rivera (1960) describes the psychotic grief of his mother, necessitating his removal from the home for several years.

After 1914, Freud's search for a father, for restitution, for being murdered like Abel, for being like Ishmael banished into the wilderness in favor of a brother, for giving away his birthright for a mess of pottage like Esau, for betraying his brother like Aaron, for being expelled by his brothers like Joseph,[10] all seemed to end. With the ending, Freud *became* the father. He identified further with his own ego ideal, in part transubstantiated as "The Moses of Michelangelo." Psychoanalysis could be revolutionized once more: put it in the basic form we know today.

Michelangelo's Moses was for Freud—at once—Moses, an altered Moses, Michelangelo, Julius II, Michelangelo himself, Freud's Julius-brother-father, and Freud himself. All in relation to early separations; all in relation to brothers and fathers; to fratricides and patricides. Freud's paper proposed solutions to riddles: an artistic riddle; a riddle having to do with the mastery of passions in favor of civilization; a riddle about the threatened fragmentation of psychoanalysis; a deeper, personal riddle having to do with Freud's inner conflicts about mastering oedipal guilt, and his reluctance to acknowledge his own fatherhood.

THE INFLUENCE OF PSYCHOANALYSIS ON ART HISTORY

Did Freud's imaginative solution to the strange posture of Michelangelo's Moses stir the world of art history? It did not. Most art histories either treat his thesis as a joke, in the pejorative sense, or make no mention of it. Even the psychoanalyst best known for his interest in Michelangelo, Liebert (1983), discounts its plausibility. Has Freud's imaginative reconstruction of Michelangelo's intentions about the statue, the meanings of his relationship with his alterego Julius II, the ambitions to make the greatest tomb known in Western history, or Freud's allusions to their complex urges to revolutionize and humanize the Church—have any of these made any difference to colleagues in history, biography, and Renaissance studies? Apparently not. Of

10. The references to Abel, Ishmael, Esau, Aaron, and Joseph are from my thoughts. While I have no idea whether Freud would have connected them in this way, there is no doubt that he was thoroughly familiar with these Biblical heroes.

course, scholars have known that Michelangelo was a gifted poet who had a complex and educated mind, partly as a result of his adolescent experiences in the palace of Lorenzo Magnifico. They have known that both Michelangelo and Julius II had quite complex religious conceptions—in keeping with the spasms that were taking place in the beliefs of Western man. Although Julius appreciated art, the important quality of his collaboration with Michelangelo was religious and philosophical in nature. Julius meant to build a St. Peter's, reunite the Papal states, and establish a new Church in the religious sense. But there is little mention of the *meanings* of the art he coaxed, goaded, and cajoled Michelangelo and Raphael to express. These were new meanings that came before Luther, before the Reformation, before the Counter-Reformation.

And *was* Michelangelo capable of presuming to rewrite the sacred texts? It is not hard to believe. One only needs to think of him as a ferocious old genius, grieving that his life had been a failure because he could not build the Tomb. The struggle over the ferocity shows in the Moses, controlling a towering passion. Yet, one thinks also of the statues the older Michelangelo made, with their almost unbearable poignancy. One thinks of his chalk portrait of the great Pope: an older, sadder Julius, then near death. It was a portrait that rivaled Raphael's masterpiece, also in the Uffizi. One thinks of Michelangelo's passion still alive in his 80s, when he furiously hacked away with his mallet at the Pieta now in the Duomo—he could not get one of Christ's legs right. For me, that work, scarred by its creator, is the greatest of all. Michelangelo, like Julius, like Freud—like all great geniuses—was unbelievably audacious. Those who would be geniuses, but fail, are called grandiose.

Was Freud "right" in his interpretations of Michelangelo's intentions? I don't know—who could know what was in the sculptor's mind? But I think Freud was as "right" as we can expect anyone to be, if only for the fact that no other plausible explanation exists for the statue's peculiarities. I certainly think Freud was being "right" about his own struggles to maintain and even institute another revolution in his own psychoanalysis, struggling to control his own passion for the sake of a higher cause, unsure that he would prevail. "At the moment," he wrote

Ferenczi 10½ months after completing the paper, "the situation in Vienna makes me feel more like the historical Moses than the Michelangelo one" (Jones, 1955, p. 367).

If it is reasonable to assume that Freud's "The Moses of Michelangelo" had meanings in terms of his attachment to a "collective alternate," psychoanalysis, and had meanings in terms of his outside professional and personal life, is it reasonable to assume that it had to do with continuing unconscious fantasies whose pasts extended all the way back to Freud's infancy? There is no alternative to assuming that about *any* creator and his creation. We do have some intriguing details pertaining to Freud's early life and to the expression of derivatives of infantile conflicts later. Most of these details came from letters to Fliess, as Freud was conducting his self analysis. Others come from reliable observations made by those closest to him. Information hitherto unavailable will doubtlessly add to, and correct present information. Leaving aside documentary details, some of the unquestionable facts about Freud's life have been mentioned, along with some of the memories and reconstructions *which he himself made* and relayed to others. I believe Freud was essentially "right" about his own interpretations about his past, even if at the time he did not have the sophistication about infantile development now available.

THE JOKE

How was "The Moses of Michelangelo" a joke for Freud? It was a private joke, not to be shared. My guess is that despite the worry and pain, he finally prevailed and *saw into* his fascination: once more he had been doing and undoing the murder of little Julius—a magical infantile fratricide which fronted for fantasies of two others, the crimes of patricide and filicide. Freud must have felt a shock in once more finding a repeatedly lost insight, and he must have felt something that goes along with once more undoing the repression of a familiar fantasy: wry humor—an awareness of the personal comedy which cohabits with personal tragedy. Freud, by then doomed with cancer, expressed this mixture in "Humour" (1927). In times of peril, a kindly superego reassures the frightened childlike ego that things can't be quite as bad as they might seem—or as they might in fact be. It is possible that there was another private joke, but one that was less important: Freud wrote a paper touching upon the most profound issues of psychoanalysis—passion, redolent with derivatives of sexuality and aggression—without once mentioning either word!

The "Moses of Michelangelo" was analogous to a good interpretation. It imaginatively brought together elements of transference, "outside" life, and infantile past. This time the interpretation apparently finally "took." The sequence of finding and losing an idealized man was not to be repeated in Freud's lifetime. The paper is also a work of art. It allows admirers to share the artist's imagination, his method, and the personal truth which can go beyond it to become collective truth.

The Sandlers (1983) have argued that the "second censorship," that between consciousness and preconsciousness, should be reconsidered. Freud's work of art then demonstrates his marvelous *access* to different levels of preconscious fantasy, and his even more marvelous capacity to relate or *synthesize* the levels "closer to the unconscious," and the levels closer to the reaches of rational and moral thought.

SUMMARY

In this paper I have tried to demonstrate (but not account for) the intricacies of the creation by Freud of a paper that had a special personal meaning. "The Moses of Michelangelo" was the product of the imaginative processes of a genius. Freud was first fascinated with the statue, then fascinated with his own fascination. Over 13 years, he spent many, many hours standing before the statue, brooding about its meaning. The final work of art— and that is what the paper turned out to be—came as a result of insights that were simultaneously derived from unresolved conflicts out of Freud's infantile past, unresolved conflicts in his contemporary external world, and unresolved conflicts of a transference nature toward his own creation, psychoanalysis. The paper represented an actualization of a complex synthesis Freud made: it was at once a work of art which could be shared

with others, an intimate (and highly "mutative") interpretation
made to himself, and a joke that he enjoyed privately.

BIBLIOGRAPHY

FREUD, S. (1900). The interpretation of dreams. *S.E.*, 4 & 5.
_____ (1901). The psychopathology of everyday life. *S.E.*, 6.
_____ (1905a). Fragment of an analysis of a case of hysteria. *S.E.*, 7:7–122.
_____ (1905b). Three essays on the theory of sexuality. *S.E.*, 7:130–243.
_____ (1905c). Jokes and their relation to the unconscious. *S.E.*, 8:9–236.
_____ (1910). Leonardo da Vinci and a memory of his childhood. *S.E.*, 11:63–137.
_____ (1913). Totem and taboo. *S.E.*, 13:1–161.
_____ (1914a). The Moses of Michelangelo. *S.E.*, 13:211–238.
_____ (1914b). On the history of the psycho-analytic movement. *S.E.*, 14:7–66.
_____ (1914c). On narcissism. *S.E.*, 14:73–102.
_____ (1914d). Some reflections on schoolboy psychology. *S.E.*, 13:241–244.
_____ (1927). Humour. *S.E.*, 21:161–166.
_____ (1930). The Goethe prize. *S.E.*, 21:207–212.
_____ (1950). *The Origins of Psycho-Analysis.* New York: Basic Books, 1954.
GREENACRE, P. (1957). The childhood of the artist. *Psychoanal. Study Child,* 12:47–72.
JONES, E. (1953–57). *The Life and Work of Sigmund Freud,* 3 vols. New York: Basic Books.
KOESTLER, A. (1964). *The Act of Creation.* New York: Macmillan.
LEWIN, B. D. (1955). Dream psychology and the analytic situation. *Psychoanal. Q.,* 24:169–199.
LIEBERT, R. S. (1983). *Michelangelo.* New Haven & London: Yale Univ. Press.
RANK, O. (1959). *The Myth of the Birth of the Hero,* ed. P. Freund. New York: Knopf.
RIVERA, D. (1960). *My Art, My Life.* New York: Citadel Press.
ROSEN, V. H. (1958). Abstract thinking and object relations. *J. Amer. Psychoanal. Assn.,* 6:653–671.
RUGG, H. (1963). *Imagination.* New York: Harper & Row.
SANDLER, J. & SANDLER, A.-M. (1983). The 'second censorship', the 'three box model' and some technical implications. *Int. J. Psychoanal.,* 64:413–425.
SHENGOLD, L. (1972). A parapraxis of Freud's in relation to Karl Abraham. *Amer. Imago,* 29:123–159.
SPRUIELL, V. (1977). Creativity. In *International Encyclopedia of Psychiatry, Psychology, Psychoanalysis and Neurology,* ed. B. Wolman. New York: Aesculapius Press, 3:437–440.
WAELDER, R. (1930). The principle of multiple function. *Psychoanal. Q.,* 5:45–62.

Remembered Images and Trauma

A Psychology of the Supernatural
LENORE CAGEN TERR, M.D.

> From ghoulies and ghosties and long-leggity
> beasties
> And things that go bump in the night, Good
> Lord, deliver us!
> —A Cornish Prayer

EVER SINCE I WAS A SMALL CHILD WHO LISTENED AVIDLY TO A weekly Sunday afternoon radio show in which supernatural mysteries were solved in a most sensible manner—of course, only following 20 minutes of terror and 8 minutes of commercials—my ears have twitched expectantly to the tones of a ghost story. For years in practice, I did not hear any creepy intimations from my patients, but in the early 1970s just shortly before I embarked on the Chowchilla kidnapping field studies, I began to notice that a few of the persons who had come to me for evaluation of individual psychic traumas said that they had experienced bizarre occurrences, strange coincidences, or unusual visions. For the first few years, my ears tweaked, but my brain seemed not to respond. As time went on and my "collection" of individually traumatized patients grew, I could not help notice several posttraumatic mental effects which accounted for such

Clinical Professor of Psychiatry, University of California San Francisco School of Medicine.

The library assistance of Esther Raiken is gratefully acknowledged.

eerie phenomena as omens, presentiments, predictive dreams, and the sense of no future (for some explanations, see Terr, 1984). The Chowchilla studies (Terr, 1979, 1983a) brought several of these rather strange mental effects to light, but I discovered others—at least in the ordinary psychological sense—from the statements of individually traumatized patients or from young children who had suffered traumas within small groups (Terr, 1985).

Although posttraumatic perceptual distortions were one of the most immediate and dramatic findings at Chowchilla (6 children immediately misperceived and 3 hallucinated), I diverted my attention a while from the feels, smells, sights, and sounds accompanying trauma and concentrated instead on the kinds of time distortion which come along with shocks, emphasizing their presentations as weird experiences (Terr, 1983b, 1984). In the summer of 1983, however, 2 child patients, Duane and Winifred H.,[1] experienced the "ghosts" of their sister, Holly, who had also been my patient before she died, and it was Holly's "ghost" who brought me back sharply to the world of posttraumatic "visions" and hallucination. Could immediate problems with perception and later distorted memories of perception accompanying severe frights bring on the "ghoulies, ghosties, and long-leggity beasties"? I decided to look back through the spontaneous musings of 56 traumatized children and 32 overwhelmed adults which I had inscribed into my records over the years to see if I could find the "supernatural" there. Obviously I had not asked my patients directly about clouds, specters, apparitions, possessions, or visits from the Devil—the question had only come to mind in 1984, and the data were collected beginning in 1974. Bearing in mind that prevalence certainly could not be checked in this way, I sought to find the posttraumatic sensory phenomena related to ghosts and hauntings, to look at the mental mechanisms involved, and to postulate how these phenomena might be reflected in our cultural and literary heritage.

Few psychoanalytic or child psychiatric researchers have written about ghosts and such. Shapiro et al. (1980) conducted an

---

1. All names used in this paper are fictitious. First names and last initials correspond to those used in all my other publications.

interview study of normal 3- and 4-year-olds' conceptions of ghosts; they concluded that very young children's ideas about ghosts depended upon cultural input as well as upon early remembered images of night-visiting parents. M. Katan (1962, 1966), examining *The Turn of the Screw,* proposed that because the very young Henry James had presumably witnessed his parents having intercourse, he was impelled to write his profoundly disturbing ghost story. In my opinion, however, the best psychoanalytic works on the subject of ghosts and "ghoulies" are Freud's "Delusions and Dreams in Jensen's 'Gradiva'" (1907) and "The Uncanny" (1919).

In his analysis of the uncanny, or the bizarre and spooky in literature and human experience, Freud makes the consistent point that the return of repressed internal conflict (usually of elements of the oedipus complex) lies beneath the surface of the occult. Freud's reasoning holds up very well. Emerging internal anxieties certainly do show up in such ghost stories as the traditional Spanish children's tale, "The Tinker and the Ghost," in which a dead person comes back entirely in cut-up parts, or in Arthur Conan Doyle's short story for adults, "The Brown Hand," in which a ghost returns in order to reclaim his severed hand from the pathologist who had been keeping it in a specimen jar. World literature holds enough mutilated brothers of the "Headless Horseman" to demand that when we consider specters and apparitions, the return of repressed castration fears be given a prominent place.

Freud (1919) recognized, however, that he had not exhausted the subject of rare, unnatural experience. He says, "we must be prepared to admit that there are other elements besides those which we have so far laid down as determining the production of uncanny feelings" (p. 247). Even though Freud goes on to say in the same paragraph that "what remains probably calls for an *aesthetic* [my italics] enquiry," in this paper I attempt a psychological and, I hope, not a strictly literary, investigation of the supernatural.

The return of the repressed, Freud's most important explanation for "uncanniness," is an important underlying theme in some of my examples—and rightly so. My intention is not to supplant repressed internal conflict as a possible causality for weird human experience, but to *add* externally precipitated psychic trauma to the very short list of underlying reasons for the "uncanny."

When the ego is unexpectedly overwhelmed by external events, everything outside the person may begin to look spooky, eerie, and overdetermined. Much of this supernatural effect may be due to the traumatized individual's restitutive efforts at finding explanations for the unexplainable, trying to think through the unthinkable, and in planning for the unanticipatable. As a character in Ingmar Bergman's *Fanny and Alexander* comments months after the sudden, unexpected death of her adult son, "Reality is shattered."

Both trauma and the return of the repressed account for supernatural phenomena. If those interested in the psychology of the paranormal look back with a fresh eye at Freud's "The Uncanny," they will find psychic trauma in many of Freud's examples, just as they will undoubtedly find oedipal rivalries and castration anxiety in mine.

I have singled out five aspects of posttraumatic mental functioning in adults and children, which may account for some supernatural experience: (1) Intensely vivid and repeated memories of perceptions and sensory impressions of a traumatic event lead to a sense of being "haunted." (2) Subsequently elaborated and distorted remembrances of perceptions account for "seeing what one had never actually seen," and/or for a sense of being hounded by aggressors. (3) Posttraumatic hallucinations create "ghosts." (4) Intrusions of whole images after traumatic events appear as "possessions," and extrusions of images make for "alteregos." (5) The contagious nature of posttraumatic symptoms and their accompanying anxiety disseminates these supernatural phenomena into the group at large.

In this paper I present each of these five trauma-related origins for supernatural experience; mention film, folklore, or literary examples of each; and present clinical cases of both children and adults to illustrate them. Some of the waking hallucinations described by my patients will possibly sound like fantasies or nightmares and some of the night dreams, like real experiences. Although I designate what each child and adult thought his experience was, these blurred boundaries between fantasy, dream, and reality are not atypical, because in psychic trauma these elements often reflect and repeat one another in a confusing way. It is important to note that despite the very obvious differences in developmental phases among the patients who serve as clinical examples in this report, their uncanny or supernatural experiences are quite similar. I have observed this rather surprising "sameness" among trauma victims in regard to other types of posttraumatic symptomatology as well (Terr, 1979). Finally, I believe that this and my 1984 paper can be taken as two parts of one theme—psychic trauma causes paranormal experience. A connection between externally generated terror and the occult is demonstrable in clinical practice and in society at large.

REPETITIVE MEMORIES OF TRAUMATIC PERCEPTIONS

Each of us bears his own Hell.
—VIRGIL, *Aeneid* 6

The posttraumatic memory—a mental image which has the intensity of a current perception and does not decay over time—turns up again and again in repeated dreams, the hallmark symptom of the old "traumatic neurosis" or the more currently designated "posttraumatic stress disorder." These exact repetitions of scenes originally felt, watched, smelled, heard, and registered in the brain are even more bothersome in waking life than in sleep. They can be experienced as flashbacks by older teenagers and adults or as daydreams by victims of all ages (Terr, 1979). Most of us accept our night dreams because we dream frequently from birth on. But adults and older teenagers do not tolerate daytime visions so well because they can be far more bothersome and intrusive. (Children are more accustomed to daydreaming than are adults.) Waking-state traumatic images, when repeatedly encountered in an intrusive and invasive fashion, may come to be seen as a "haunting."

Gwendolyn G., for instance, "saw" her little brother's bleeding face for 2 years after an automobile accident which killed both her older and her younger brothers and which scarred her. The

15-year-old spoke of "daydreams" that she had experienced since her accident at age 13. They were worse than her sleeping dreams, she thought. "I remember waking in the ambulance," she told me, "and I saw my little brother. I saw blood all over his face. I couldn't see his features. I looked away. . . . All along [since the accident] I've had a continual daydream of my brother's face—especially when I see other little kids. I dreamed his face [at night] two times a week for a year. But now I have different [night] dreams of my younger brother—I see him at home or at a distance. These are not terrifying, but comforting." Gwendolyn had found some solace in her recent dreams, which included wished-for reunions, but she felt only pain from her daytime visions, which never veered away from their horrible and literal depictions.

The visual remnants of a horrible event occupied many waking hours of another auto accident victim, Solomon W. The late adolescent repeatedly pictured a gruesome detail from the death of his friend, Joe, who was sitting in the passenger seat of Solomon's car when it was hit from the rear and exploded: "Joe made no sound. I saw the outline of his body burning." Ten months after Joe's death, Solomon said, "I'm not having nightmares lately, but when I'm awake I see the picture of Joe burning over and over. I watched him burn up." The 17-year-old Solomon looked a little surprised to think that he had ever seen such a horrible sight. "I'm daydreaming every day. I still see it. The daydreams are terrible."

The word "haunting" comes directly from a victim, a survivor of the 1977 Tenerife air crash which took 503 lives. Sue W. and her sister Lana L. both survived the disaster, but their mother died. This is what the 21-year-old Mrs. W. said 1½ years after the crash: "I have the image every once in a while of Mom below me [in a burning hole] with her arms out—stitches of clothes on. She wanted to come to me. She was calling for me. I was afraid of her because of how she looked. Just for a second. Then I remember trying to get out of the plane. . . . I always remember that image of my mother. That's what I'd like to forget. . . . Many times I see the fire. *The picture haunts me.* . . . I can't hang photos of my mother or go to her grave. Sometimes I forget she's dead. Still sometimes I can't believe it. I say to myself, 'Mom's not working today' when I see her car. That's pretty weird."

As Horowitz (1976) points out, after a traumatic experience, denial of external reality often alternates with intrusive images. In Sue W.'s case, the intrusive "pictures" would not go away, not only because of her defensive denial but also because of her guilt. The young woman's conscience could not release its grip. She was indeed "haunted" both by a real image from the past and by a continual, internally generated reprimand.

Lana L. was, in her own way, more "haunted" than her sister Sue, although Lana did not choose that wording. The older sister, at 27, was repeatedly bedeviled by three perceptual remembrances, each from a different sensory mode. It was Lana who had "let go" as their mother fell into the burning hole in the exploding aircraft. She told me 1½ years after the crash, "I had a hold on her—her hands. She was screaming, 'Help me, Lana.' I panicked. I started to climb up. I thought, 'I have to go for help.' I remember letting go. She had a strong grip. I remember letting go as she clutched at me. As I let go, she slipped away. I don't know what happened to her. They never found her body. Now I wake up smelling fire when there *is* none. I hear 'Help me, Help me' when I'm awake. I can't judge how often. Sometimes every day."

In folklore and in literature, hauntings tend to be related to houses, not people. The Greek, Pliny, wrote his friend Sura in the first century A.D. to tell him about a haunted house in Athens; and the modern Argentinian writer, Cortázar, relates in his short story, "House Taken Over," how a brother and a sister must abandon their home to seemingly motivationless, noisy, space-occupying, and invisible poltergeists. In posttraumatic situations, however, it appears to be the victim himself, not the house, that is "haunted." Perhaps houses offer a site upon which the flashback-seeing, scream-hearing, and fire-smelling survivor can displace some of his unbearable anxiety. Once that survivor leaves the house or dies, his home becomes the town's generally acknowledged repository for the still-lingering traumatic anxiety which has been transmitted to the neighbors, friends, and younger family members who knew the victim. As long as the displacement of anxiety rests with the original house, everyone else may rest comfortably in his own house.

MEMORY ELABORATIONS AND DISTORTIONS

> They who dream by day are cognizant of many things
> which escape those who dream only by night.
> —POE, "Eleonora" (1841)

Memories of perceptual impressions that become modified and changed in some way account for the "weird" experiences of some trauma patients. I have observed two types of elaborations: (1) transfer of an impression from one sensory modality to another; and (2) distortion of perceptual impressions.

Transfer of Perceptual Impressions. When a sensory impression connected with trauma is originally taken in mainly through one perceptual modality and then is modified in the brain to appear to have emanated from a different perceptual organ, the sufferer is left with the bizarre, "uncanny" sense of having seen what he had never actually seen, or of having been in two places at once. I do not know why and how the brain accomplishes this transfer of sensations, but it appears to do precisely that, usually by transforming nonvisual memories into visual ones. Night-dreaming may be the prototype for this brainwork, since many of our conflicts and instinctual needs are translated by the brain into visual symbols during dreaming (Freud, 1900). Certainly metaphor-making is another way of changing an emotional sense into a linguistic visual picture.

Curt P., 16 years, came to my office 2 months after his friend Charlie pulled him out of a burning car. The automobile exploded just seconds after Charlie's heroic rescue. Curt had been briefly unconscious from the impact, and upon coming to found himself trapped inside surrounded with suffocating black smoke and fire. He said to me, "I *saw* Death, so whatever comes, it's no big deal." Curt may have been employing a strong metaphor. It is more likely, however, that he had felt the heat and smelled the smoke and subsequently converted these sensations into a "vision" of Death. Folklore and literature are full of such visual sightings. My favorite is a very, very short story by Jean Cocteau, "Death and the Gardener," in which a laborer meets Death as he works in his prince's garden, thinks that he sees the

Black Lord make a "menacing gesture," and thereupon begs his employer, the prince, to give him his swiftest horse so that he can escape to Ispahan. Later the prince himself meets Death in the garden and asks him to explain his gesture. "Your gardener misunderstood," says Death. "My signal was not menace—it was surprise. I recognized the man and knew that tonight I must pick him up far away in Ispahan." More classic personifications of Death may be found in the myth of the tricks played against Thanatos by Sisyphus, the story of how Heracles saved Alcestes by wrestling with Death, and in "Erlkönig," a German folk ballad about a child who sees Death coming after him, which was set by Franz Schubert into an unforgettably scary song.

Henry H., a 25-year-old Olympic-class boxer, sought my help because he had never recovered from the shock of the gunshot suicide of his teenage brother who had been very close to him. In his first session 5 years after Willy's death, Mr. H. talked about how he had spontaneously shifted an originally tactile perception to the visual mode. He had noticed many things at his brother's funeral with his eyes, but his hands conveyed to his brain the most shocking data of all:

> At Willy's funeral there was an open casket. The morticians didn't do it too well. I looked at him and I felt on the side of his head there was a blue area kind of covered over. Before he was buried I wanted to hold him. I didn't even think about it. I held his head to my chest and I felt the back of his head. There wasn't much there! I see it! I *see* no back of the head. . . . My memory has become visual. . . .
>
> My dreams usually have to do with my head. I see my head broken open. Like once, a man—half-man, half-animal—was eating my head. I'm more terrified because I'm seeing it. It stays with me in the day. I get headaches [he had in fact been losing the hair in spots from the back of his head for a few years]. . . .
>
> I used to doodle my fantasies. After Willy died, I drew shootings and demonic faces. My girlfriend looked at them and was shocked.

Mr. H.'s touch sensations had become visual memories. He was seeing what he originally had touched with his hands. He was dreaming it and drawing pictures of it. In many ways he was living inside a bad dream. From *Alice in Wonderland* to *The Wizard of Oz* we have numerous literary examples of such waking nightmares.

Probably the most arresting transfer of impressions which I recorded from a patient came from Betsy T., a 9-year-old, whom I interviewed for the first time just a week after her grandmother was murdered. Betsy and her grandmother had both been afraid of Betsy's mother's current boyfriend who they knew was "wanted" in another state for a robbery. To ensure Betsy's "safety," Mrs. T. sent Betsy to stay a few days with Grandma. One morning the boyfriend rang the grandmother's doorbell and proceeded to insist upon driving Grandma and Betsy to the child's school. He then came back to Grandma's apartment where he robbed and strangled the old woman. Upon her return from school Betsy was spared the sight of her grandmother's body, but the child felt intensely guilty for failing to protect her grandmother, and she was horrified that her worst fears had indeed come true. In treatment 8 months after the terrible events, I found that Betsy had begun to experience as a visual memory what she had originally heard in words from her family and from the police. "Sometimes—once—I thought about Grandma's death," she told me, "after my mother called me on the phone. I could just *see* it happening when Grandma was killed. In slow motion."

When one reasons out what Betsy's visualizations imply, it seems that the young girl had put herself in two places at once— at school where she had actually been on the day of the killing, and in her grandmother's apartment which she now clearly could "see." This is, of course, physically impossible though psychologically common. A recent movie contains two examples of the same sort of "supernatural" phenomenon, although the first of these may be the "negative" to my young patient's experience. Ingmar Bergman's *Fanny and Alexander* shows us a brother and a sister who are cowering on the floor of a locked upstairs room in their stepfather's house at the very same time as they are being carried out of the miserably unhappy place concealed in a trunk. Perhaps this is simply a theatrical trick, the viewer thinks, but minutes later Alexander, safe in his Uncle Isak's home, simultaneously sees himself impassively watching his stepfather, the Bishop, die a most hideous death. Alexander again is in two places at once—at Uncle Isak's house and in the Bishop's burning mansion.

Bergman's semi-autobiographical *Fanny and Alexander* depicts considerable psychic trauma, and it is this overwhelmingly upsetting state of affairs that gives rise to the creepy double perceptions of being in two places at once. When Alexander, safe in Uncle Isak's house, "watches" his stepfather's gruesome death, Alexander is quite like my patient Betsy, who, although actually safe at school, could later visualize her grandmother's murder. On the other hand, Bergman more literally shows us a fright from his own childhood when he films young Alexander locked in a room upstairs while being carried outside simultaneously in a trunk; this scene represents a real terror in the writer-director's life with its accompanying denial in fantasy. Bergman's biographer Cowie (1982) tells that Ingmar, as a preschooler, was inadvertantly locked in an upstairs closet. While his grandmother desperately searched for the keys, the frantic child bit through the hem of his mother's dress. Bergman re-created this closet "scene" twice before *Fanny and Alexander:* in *Hour of the Wolf,* a man describes to his wife such a childhood incident and its accompanying hallucinations; and in Bergman's 1973 stage production of Strindberg's *A Dream Play,* the director arranged for the old man to die offstage locked in a closet—a terrifying and entirely personal interpretation of a scene for which Strindberg himself had left no such staging directions. Bergman's "locked upstairs" portion of *Fanny and Alexander,* thus, has the ring of personal posttraumatic reenactment. A wished-for rescue, Bergman's internal fantasy related to his closet ordeal, serves as one of the writer-director's two simultaneous perceptions.

From these examples, we see that traumatically derived double perceptions may arise from positions of safety (conjuring up past horrors), from positions of peril (conjuring up imagined escapes), or from traumatic observations which are simply shifted from one perceptual mode to another. The splittings, reversals, denials in fantasy, distancings, and intrusions of trauma-related imagery required to service posttraumatic wishes to repair, to undo, or even to accept responsibility for uncontrollable events indicate how deep a terrified person must dip into his

"packet" of defenses. Failures of repression which so characteristically occur in psychic trauma (Terr, 1979) probably account for some of this drastic mental maneuvering. Stimulus
overload of the brain, as yet entirely hypothetical, probably also
plays a role in the cognitive and perceptual "misfirings" which
accompany trauma.

Distortion of Perceptual Impressions. During and following a psychically traumatic event, perceptions, especially visual ones, may
go awry, particularly when the victim is mentally registering the
characteristics of his tormentors. Although a witness may remember, detail for detail, the happenings during a traumatic
event, he may grossly misperceive his assailants.

After the traumatic event is over, misperceptions tend to continue and to extend themselves (Terr, 1983a). Two months
after she was raped in a distant city by two young black strangers, Jeanette C.'s continuing misperceptions were fairly typical
of this kind of posttraumatic mistake. "I never want to be prejudiced," the 23-year-old Oriental stewardess told me at that
time. "I don't want to develop something like that. About a
week after it happened I went to Portland with my boyfriend. I
thought I saw the guy [one of the rapists] in a 7-11 Store, and I
grabbed Bill and we left. Sometimes I see black people and they
remind me of him. . . . Both guys who attacked me smelled like
sour milk. That smell may be common among black people, but
I didn't smell it before. I smell it now. Only on men. Not wom-
en. . . . Last night I stopped at a gas station to get something—a
black guy was helping me, and I smelled the smell again. I was
just aware—aware of it."

These continually changing and augmenting memories of
perceptions could cast a strange light upon life in society for the
already frightened victim. Inanimate objects might seem ani-
mate and familiar people unfamiliar. The latter was the case for
5-year-old Frances C., the victim of two attempts by her father, a
professional spy, to snatch her. Several men climbed the little
girl's roof, opened her window, and called her to come out.
Frances screamed. Her mother rushed in and slammed the window on a spy's hands. The next day Mr. C. grabbed Frances at a
friend's house, where she had been playing. She cried out, wet
her pants, and the friend's father rescued her.

Frances began to misperceive her own father, familiar as he

previously had been. Although the kindergartner had not said much before to her mother about Oriental people, Frances began to think that her caucasian father was "different"—Chinese, perhaps. "I get scared of my father at night," she told me when I first met her at age 6. "I worry he's here. Sometimes I think I see him. Some people look Chinese. My father looks Chinese or Japanese. My father has black greasy hair. He wouldn't give back his mustache. He cut it off. We didn't like it cut off." I met Frances's mother again 3 years after the father's frightening kidnapping attempts. Mrs. C. told me that Frances was still firmly resisting visitations with her father who was, by then (quite ironically), stationed in Asia.

In literature and in lore, the metamorphosing villain is a particularly spooky, supernatural character. This changeable person-monster may depict what the trauma victim "sees" when he so habitually remembers with distortion the originally ordinary-looking object of his fright. In Oscar Wilde's *The Portrait of Dorian Gray,* a handsome but terribly destructive man keeps a truer depiction of himself—a painting, ugly and marred—in his private apartments. Vampire stories and human-beast changeling tales (Barry Malzberg's 1975 "Transfer," for instance) tell in pungent detail all about this kind of frightening metamorphosis. At the movie theater, such evolutions from beauty to beast can be actually shown to the viewer. These terrifying perceptual tricks may bring vicarious posttraumatic nightmares to more than one child in the audience.

Rather than metamorphosing, the monster, ghost, or returning villain may simply be "seen" by his victim in his original form—only at unexpected or even impossible times and/or places. A 45-year-old woman, raped 2 years previously by a man of Middle-Eastern origins, told me, "When I walk by someone with the same skin coloring, they remind me of him. I believe he's in jail." (He *was* still in jail.) A 16-year-old, raped and severely injured by a stranger when she was age 8, said, "I think I see the man—about once a year." Charlene L.'s parents had told her that "the man" had been deported to another country, but Charlene did not, could not believe them. She believed, instead, what she "saw" with her own "eyes."

In his 1907 paper on Jensen's *Gradiva* Freud relates the same kind of story that my trauma sufferers tell in the preceding paragraphs. He states that he knew a physician whose hyperthyroid patient, a young woman, had died, perhaps, the physician thought, in part, because of a thoughtlessly written prescription the doctor had released to her. Although Freud does not say this, the physician probably was highly upset and dismayed at his patient's death. A trauma? Not by Freud's 1920 definition, but perhaps a shock and a sense of loss of personal control for this doctor. Years later a young woman came to visit the physician, who, usually "obtuse" to uncanny things (Freud, 1919, p. 220), for an instant believed that he was seeing the very same patient who had died. It took him moments to realize that the visiting young woman now before him was not a returning dead person, but rather her sister who was hyperthyroid herself and looked quite like her dead sibling. Freud then confesses that he himself was the doctor in this example, but Freud does not explain *why* he misperceived so "uncannily." I think he did so because of an old, shocking, external event well beyond his control—the death of his young patient. This death was accompanied by a retrospectively acute sense of guilt for some possible carelessness and a lingering tendency to misperceive any possible avenger—in this case, the dead patient herself.

When an inanimate "aggressor" is given animation by a misperceiving trauma victim, we have the attribution of human characteristics to an entirely inhuman item—a spooky state of affairs, indeed. Nathaniel Hawthorne (1868) had proposed to himself in a sketch for a story that he never wrote, "a steam engine in a factory is supposed to possess a malignant spirit." More than 100 years later Stephen King published *Christine* (1983), the story of a supernatural car.

I found an interesting clinical example of this animation of the inanimate in the case of a 12-year-old recent Russian immigrant who had been knocked down in a crosswalk by a careless driver. Natasha D. happened to see a run-amok car movie, perhaps *Christine* or *The Car,* a few months after her accident. She took the film very seriously indeed. Natasha told me,

> The car that hit me looked like a shark. Big Toyotas and American cars look like the shark. I was on the bus Friday. I hadn't wanted to go to school. I got on at 25th Street and I saw THE CAR! I was amazed—I did not expect that. Then the bus took off, and I got off two blocks later and walked home. [Natasha did not return to school that day.]

My brother loves movies about cars hitting people. I turn around and do not look. I saw a movie with my parents. I always want to be with them if they're watching movies. It was about a 50s car going around killing people with the devil in the car. My mother was grabbing me. I left after a half hour, but I should have seen the ending [because some suspense might have been relieved]. I was sitting shaking,

I still think the man who hit me was Japanese. I couldn't accept that he was something else. [The police report stated he was "white."] My parents used to tell me a man—a gypsy— would come and take you away in a bag. It was like a joke.

Natasha's comments are filled with perceptual distortions—a sharklike car, a Japanese driver, and a self-motivated automobile returning to the scene of the crime, 25th Street. Natasha's comments further reflect how some of our cultural heritage and our prejudices may be derived from the aftereffects of traumatic events. Movies about demon cars on the loose and European parents' warnings about gypsies who steal young children are too close to the realm of posttraumatic misperception to deserve compartmentalization from their originating mental conditions—the posttraumatic stress disorders.

HALLUCINATIONS

Alas, how is't with you,
That you do bend your eye on vacancy,
And with th' incorporal air do hold discourse?
                    —SHAKESPEARE, *Hamlet*, 3:4

After traumatic events that contribute to the death of someone close, a survivor may "see" or "feel" his dead friend or family member. I became very aware of a newly emerging "ghost" when Holly H., a 7-year-old whom I had been treating for over a year for sequelae of her evisceration at 5 in a freak swimming pool accident, died suddenly during surgery. Within a month or two of Holly's death, her 4-year-old sister, Winifred, and her brother, Duane, by then 7, began experiencing "visits" from Holly. Neither surviving sibling (there was a third—Cindy, 9, who never felt a "visit") referred to Holly's sensed presence as a "ghost," but their posttraumatic misperceptions were the stuff of which ghost stories are made.

Two months after Holly died, Winifred told me, "My sister lives in a children's cemetery and she plays every day with the other children buried there. . . . She comes to me in my sleep *and* with my eyes open. . . . She wants to play with me. I'm frightened. I don't want to play." A few months later Winifred said, "Holly's the angel on my Christmas tree" and "Mousie [Holly's favorite toy in my office] is in a tree; and only me, Grandma and Grandpa can see her. The others cannot. I lost a balloon and Grandma told me that Holly would catch it above the clouds. . . . Mousie is watching everything." I worked therapeutically with Winifred, talking with her and playing about her presleep hallucinations of Holly, her dreams of Holly's invitations to play, and her sense (inspired by Grandma) that Holly was still watching her. About 6 months after Holly's death, Winifred seemed to have stopped "seeing" her dead sister. Several months later Winifred's mother wrote me that Winnie no longer was bothered by "visits" from Holly.

Duane never thought that he could "see" Holly; he "felt" her instead. For Duane, Holly's ghost was a "poltergeist," although the youngster did not use this word. Seven months after Holly died, Duane told his mother that he was hoping the weather would be nice for a weekend family trip to Disneyland, but "Holly plays tricks. It would be just like her to make it rain at Disneyland." He went on to elaborate. "She makes the doors close behind me when I don't want them closed." Duane and Holly had been born only 10 months apart and were more like twins than siblings. They shared a secret language and committed frequent pranks during Holly's short lifetime. The close relationship itself and the traumatic circumstances surrounding Holly's injury and death set up Duane's sense that his sister was still with him. Grandma's comments about heaven may further have magnified this tendency.

Duane's family spent 8 months in England, returning to the U.S. about 14 months after Holly's death. By this time Duane believed that his ghost-prankster sister controlled much of the world's weather. "All the time we were in England," he told me upon his return, "it didn't rain at all in California. But did rain in London. Now we've returned and it's raining again in California!" I pointed out to Duane that he had left at the beginning of California's dry season and had come back in time for the October rains. But in this regard, the youngster would hear of no realities. He had, he felt, one additional piece of telling evidence for me. "Mommy goes to the cemetery to visit Holly," he said, "and it *always* rains there—no matter how nice it was before."

In some ways the type of learning which occurs during a traumatic event resembles imprinting more than it does conditioning. Even though the traumatized victim can be of any age (a specific age, according to the experimental psychologists, is an absolute necessity for imprinting), the mental effects of trauma linger in the same uncannily tenacious way as does imprinting learning. It is hard, well-nigh impossible, to unlearn a traumatic event, once experienced. The visual images and feeling impressions associated with the actual moments of the ordeal return to a trauma sufferer with a regularity which would bedevil the sanest among us. No wonder ghosts seem never to give up even after the ghosts' hosts have grown up.

Consider Marcia H., for instance. She was 6 years old in postwar Bavaria when she contracted pneumonia and nearly died. The last rites of the Catholic Church were administered. And then, just as Marcia realized that she was going to live after all, a hospital nurse told Marcia that her guardian, her grandmother, had decided to give her up for adoption to some villagers. It was Christmastime. On the way to a hospital party, the nurse and Marcia stopped off at a room for which the nurse appeared to be responsible. A man lay dead on a bed. A younger man with trenchcoat and hat was visiting. The nurse put cotton in the dead man's mouth, wrapped part of his face with gauze, and took Marcia to the party. Just before the horrified, staring child could flee the room, she "saw" a huge black cat standing on the corpse's chest.

Marcia's mother, whom Marcia had barely known, came back to Germany from the U.S. to rescue the hapless 6-year-old before any adoption could take place. Marcia H. never received any psychotherapy until she was 38. She came to me then because of visual, tactile, and auditory hallucinations. It was Christmastime, and she was about to lose a good job. Furthermore, her one-year marriage was in serious trouble. Mrs. H. did not drink, use drugs, or harbor any serious physical diseases, yet she believed that she was about to die. She was being "visited" by characters from the late 1940s, who in her mind were Death's messengers. One was a man in a trenchcoat and saddle shoes. Another was a woman with shoulder pads and deep decolletage. Each visitor was an agent of Death, and each would motion her to come along. The terrified woman would sit in her chair or on her bed motionless. She dared not indicate any willingness to die, or she *would* die, she believed. "Once recently," Mrs. H. told me, "a cloud came into my bedroom and centered in a chair. I lay in the bed, sat up, and moved to the middle of the bed. The cloud sat down in a chair and said, 'Come with me.' I replied, 'No. I need a little more time.' I felt the cloud was a 'he.' He slowly got up and walked out the door. Sometimes I sense a black panther in my room or a very large black cat. . . . I've felt a presence many times. I'm used to it. I always feel it will be around Christmas."

Marcia H. showed no evidence—other than her hallucinations—of psychosis. A neurologist saw Mrs. H. in consultation and diagnosed migraine auras. She did have headaches, but these were not necessarily associated with her visions. Another neurologist suggested "hypnagogic phenomena." Any of these diagnoses might have been correct, but there were some strong psychological reasons, too, for Mrs. H.'s apparitions. She was under extreme work and marriage stress—probably the most stressful period in her life since age 6. It was Christmas, again, and Mrs. H. herself knew that the Christmas holidays exacerbated her old fears and visions. All indications suggested that she was traumatized at age 6 by the gruesome witnessing of a dead man's in-hospital preparation for embalming, an event which she endured at the hospital very shortly after nearly dying herself and being shockingly abandoned by her grandmother, her only real "mother." The sign that a psychic trauma had most likely occurred in the Bavarian hospital room was the young Marcia's visual hallucination of the huge cat—an incongruity even for a small village hospital in postwar Germany. In the process of losing control of her life as an adult—just as she originally had lost control as a child—Mrs. H. began to hallucinate fully fleshed people from the era of the first traumatic event in the late 1940s, along with a cloud and a large black cat. What Marcia H. saw as "ghosts," I saw as posttraumatic hallucinations. We never had the time to agree or disagree fully, however. Her husband insisted she quit her floundering job and leave psychotherapy "for financial reasons." I wonder if Mrs. H. still sees her "ghosts."

There is no question from my 88 individually traumatized patients that the majority of posttraumatic hallucinations are visual. This is odd, because visual hallucinations have been so often otherwise associated with drugged states or organic mental conditions. Psychic trauma appears to be entirely emotional.

When people die in a traumatic fashion, their loved ones often dream that they visit. But there is a vast difference between the wished-for reunions of night dreams and the fear-provoking visitations of the wakeful state. (As a matter of fact, the 1983 *Encyclopedia Americana* catalogues two kinds of ghosts—harmful or vengeful ones, and souls of beloved people who may be helpful to the living. The first type of ghost initiates contact himself, but in the instance of type 2, the living person must seek out the contact.) Parkes (1970), in a study of London widows, noted that some women sensed their husbands' presences during the first year of mourning. On the other hand, Parkes did not connect this phenomenon to psychic trauma, nor did he differentiate which widows had experienced the shocking, unexpected deaths of their husbands. As far as I know, this differentiation has not yet been made or correlated with "presences."[2] Anna Freud, too (1967), discusses the "appearance" of comforting or menacing apparitions after personal losses, but she does not bring up psychic trauma in this context. Trauma probably is a factor in the phenomenon of "presences," but further studies will be necessary before this idea can be validated.

The traumatic death of a husband *did* precipitate apparitions for one Tenerife air disaster widow whom I briefly treated. Evelyn E., 69 years, lost her husband, Mack, in the conflagration. She was on the plane with him, and she broke her hip and back jumping off the wing of the exploding 747. Mack's ghost, like Marcia H.'s visitors, was fully colored, flesh-toned, and dressed in ordinary street clothes.[3] Mrs. E. was a bright, verbal,

2. See Chapter 5 of *Bereavement* (1984) for an up-to-date review of the literature on childhood grief and mourning. No "presences" are mentioned in this work.

3. In *Fanny and Alexander*, the ghost of 10-year-old Alexander's father, a man who died traumatically and unexpectedly, also is flesh-toned. He wears a white suit, but a dark tie and shoes, and is visible only to Alexander. The boy

and particularly visual person, an extremely successful artist. She could not believe that she was really "seeing" a ghost, and so she thought of her experiences as hallucinations. Here are her words 1½ years after the disaster:

> Something had cut Mack's head from above . . . his head split open and he was bleeding copiously. He wiped his face—he had been a brigadier general—and he looked forward and saw the hole in the plane and said, "Ev—go through that hole." He was strong, healthy, 9 years older than me. I looked into his eyes. That's all. I'm still trying to recognize what he was saying to me. We were very close. The whole picture is there in my head. No human should ever be exposed to anything that bad.
>
> My husband loved red cashmere sweaters. He had white hair and was tall and handsome. He would stand in the doorway with his red sweater and I'd lie down on the bed and he'd put his hands on the transom and say he was happy. *I see him like that.* I saw that daily at first.
>
> He had the sweater on in the accident. He had an old one which I found 3 months ago. I picked it up and smelled him—it still smelled like him. I put it back.

Human "ghosts" can be substantial, fleshy, and fully formed, or they may be wispy and transparent, as were the classical ghosts of Odysseus' visit to the mouth of Hades. Henry H., 25 years, often saw a "specter" of his dead brother, Willy, particularly at shopping centers, where they used to "hang out" together and at holiday times when they often had spent many hours together. Marcia H.'s "cloud" was a "he," although I never learned "who." He, too, was a vapor.

Shapiro et al. (1980) showed normal nursery school children a number of ghost drawings (many of which, I think, looked a great deal like a popular cartoon character) and asked them to pick the one that was most like a ghost. The investigators found that the youngsters considered ghosts to be floating and begowned, usually legless, or at least with hidden legs. To my patients who experienced "visions," "specters," or "tricksters" connected with an ordeal, the forms of their ghosts appeared so

---

had shrunk away horrified from his father's last rasping breaths, and the death scene was evidently a traumatic one, as it was depicted by Bergman.

variable that one could not escape the conclusion that these personally derived ghosts are far less stereotypical than the "Caspers" or the besheeted little figures who scurry about at dusk on Halloween.

The "ghost" may turn out to be a fairly common finding when psychic trauma is connected with a shocking death. In most ghost stories, the "ghost" wanders about because something is unresolved from his sudden and premature death. In my opinion, this lack of resolution is an internal problem for the ghost storyteller, not a problem for the ghost at all. Ghosts depend upon a victim's posttraumatic misperception and hallucination for their very existence. When I used to think of "ghosts," I usually imagined the typical, fully draped, whitish, floating figure which Freud (1900) had said stemmed from an infantile awareness of the mother's nocturnal visits to the child. On the other hand, from what I now understand from the "ghost" sightings of traumatized patients, specters may look, feel, or sound like anything at all. Each ghost's characteristics are drawn from the patient's inner life as well as the external traumatic event, so that each ghost is unique. Such, too, is the individuality of literary ghosts, ranging from the ragtag gaggle of skeletons of M. R. James's "Wailing Well," to the invisible, letter-writing, first wife of Edith Wharton's "Pomegranate Seed," to the ghost of the very solid footprints—albeit with an amputated toe—of Ambrose Bierce's "The Middle Toe of the Right Foot."

The animal ghost occasionally represents a child's image of a traumatizing aggressor. A bloodthirsty, ravaging beast, symbolizing the child's terror and peril at the moment of his loss of control, the animal ghost may arise from an animating misperception of the inanimate (similar to Natasha's shark-car); he may represent a mental condensation, or he may be "born" as a displacement from an originally human aggressor (see Shelby S.'s ghost on p. 527). Usually, though, the animal ghost is simply the very same creature who had attacked the child in the first place—only the child has been told, of course, that the critter was destroyed.

There are numbers of animal ghosts in literature, including the werewolves of middle European folklore and the *Wolfen* style beasts of the movies. Some are highly individual; for instance, the bulldog ghost who looked just like his dead human forebear in Le Fanu's "Squire Toby's Will," or the black cat who extracted a terrible final revenge from the man who had injured both her and her dead namesake, an Apache woman, in Bram Stoker's "The Squaw." Horrible as they may seem, literary animal phantoms cannot compete, however, with the hideous ghost-beasts which pursue real children.

Carolyn C., 8 years, for instance, was unexpectedly attacked by a neighborhood dog, Bowser, who severed her trachea, permanently scarred her chest, and very nearly killed her. Four years later Carolyn began treatment with me because she played "dog" compulsively, barked part of her evenings away, bit her parents' legs under the table, and felt continually fearful, self-conscious, and on guard. Bowser was very real to Carolyn, even though she knew consciously that he had been "put to sleep" following his rampage. To establish how real Bowser had remained to Carolyn 5 years after the attack, I include a nightmare that Carolyn told me when she was 13:

> I was coming home and I walk into the house. And—like—I can see my parents. I walk over a little more and I can see my brothers and sisters. These two dogs, and more and more dogs that look like Bowser all have blood on them in the same area Bowser had blood at my accident. My Mom and Dad and my brothers and sisters and *my* two dogs are dead. All of them. And then Bowser comes walking out, and it's like all the dogs lined up in a circle, and then Bowser is the only one with a white face without blood on it. It's like he saved me for himself. And then Bowser starts attacking me and everything. I'm sitting there fighting—trying to fight him off. All of a sudden all the fighting, barking, growling, and screaming stops. I can't hear anything. And there is this floating sensation. I can see my body— and the rest of the bodies—and the dogs and everything. And everything's still quiet and I get this floating sensation. Then I wake up.

At 8, Carolyn had accepted her own death when Bowser knocked her down and began attacking her: "I felt like I was dying—sort of like I was dying. Like I was just accepting it." She repeated this acceptance and surrender to Death time and again in her vivid nightmares. In her waking life Carolyn felt terrified, not death-accepting in the least. Especially before falling asleep, Carolyn compulsively avoided Bowser's "attacks." She said at age 12, "I'm afraid Bowser could rush through the dog door into my room. I *know* Bowser is dead, but at night I believe he is rushing in. I cover myself up with blankets to avoid an attack by Bowser. I feel safer sleeping next to people. I check the dog door each night myself. I'm not sure someone has closed it." If Carolyn knew that Bowser was dead, who could be rushing through the dog door?

As Shapiro et al. (1980) demonstrated, normal, untraumatized, middle-class 3- and 4-year-olds think that they know what ghosts are, but I shall present here quite a unique ghost which was "seen" by a little girl before she reached age 4. From Carla T.'s example, we can see how very specific is a post-traumatic ghost, as opposed to the rather uniform phantoms described by Shapiro's Manhattan preschoolers. Carla was attacked at age 3 years by a Doberman pinscher, Gumbo, owned by two teenaged horsewomen renting Carla's grandparents' corral. When Carla tried to enter the riding area of the ranch, Gumbo knocked her down and ripped open her scalp and face.

For the first 3 months after the attack Carla sang a song: "There Was a Doberman That Bit Me and Now He's Dead." Then in October Carla's grandmother, who had lived on the ranch, died suddenly. The song stopped. The next June, Carla told a "joke": "Why does a man sit on a chair? Because he is dead." She asked her mother, "If you smoke, Mommy, will you die?" At this juncture, her mother brought her to me for psychiatric evaluation. Mrs. T. told me, "Since Carla was bitten by the dog, she plays Monster and comes up and growls with her hands up. If I ask her to stop doing something, she keeps doing it. 'It's not me, Mommy, it's the ghost.'" Carla was cute and very winning despite a few deep facial scars. She confided to me:

> When I grow up, I have to walk to kindergarten. But I'll take a wrong turn and tell my mother, "*You* have to drive me." I want her to drive me to kindergarten, too. Mom has to come with me. I want her to be with me. I get scared if she's not with me. If anybody's not with me and the lights are turned off, I'll be scared.
> I'm scared of ghosts. They're like this [she panted like a dog

and put out clawed hands]. Ghosts come from animals—dead animals—I know dead animals. *All* animals come dead. I know a dog, Gumbo, that came dead. . . . The ghost I'm scared of is a dead dog.

There was a dog who hurt me. One time I had a dog bite and I went to the hospital. . . . I was in Grandma and Grandpa's farm to say hello to a horse, when a dog came and bited me. I wasn't playing with the dog. I was going to go through the gate to the horse, and he just came. I thought I was going to die when the dog was on me. I knew what dying was. Suddenly he jumped on me, attacked me, and I was starting to cry. [Her language is interesting here. Carla probably could not get her crying started because she was too frightened and too shocked to cry.] He was biting on my head [note the detailed, moment-for-moment recall in a child 38 months old at the time of the attack]. I ground me [she means: she clung to the earth] and I didn't do anything to him. . . . I couldn't see his face. I couldn't see nothing. He bled my hands and feet. I got a surprise for you [she showed me some scribbled paper which she said was a puppet]. I was sneaking in the farm. *That's* why he attacked me. That is wrong [to sneak]. . . . I felt I did the wrong thing and the dog did the right thing. It was the dog's farm and the dog's gate. The dog died because he bounded. "Bounded" is a Spanish word. And that's the way he acted. He died by himself.

I think ghosts are dead animals. The ghost I'm scared of is a dead dog. [She was repeating herself here, almost like reciting a litany.] I'm scared of monsters, too, but they're something different. They're *not* dead animals. They scare people and they touch them. I used to have a wonderful Grandma [she continued without pause]. She died. Nothing happened to her. I was sad when she died. I can remember her.

This less than 4-year-old child was able to distinguish natural death from death caused by attack. Carla never *was* bothered by Grandma's "ghost." She had not condensed her mental imagery of the two upsetting events, even though they had come only 2 months apart.

Before giving up the animal ghost for good, I wish to introduce just one more supernatural creature who does, I think, represent a very young child's condensation. Marlys Y. was 3 years, 4 months when her noncustodial parent, the father, "stole" her and hid her in Colorado for 3 months. She was returned by the Colorado police to her mother following their arrest of her father and her overnight confinement in foster care.

In her first visit to my office at age 3 years, 9 months, Marlys played games which indicated that she was terrified of policemen and freeways. She told me that Daddy had warned her to stay away from cops ("they're bad") and to tell him whenever she saw a police car on a freeway ("they get you and take you away"). She repeated the story of her father's arrest several times. Her mother was unable to bring Marlys for treatment more than once every 6 weeks. At the beginning of the child's fifth visit Mrs. Y. mentioned that the 4-year-old Marlys was drinking her milk more willingly lately. I had not known that the little girl had been rejecting milk ever since her return from Colorado, and so, when Marlys was alone with me, I asked her to tell me about it. The 4½-year-old child answered:

> I like milk a lot now. I want to see my Mommy. I used to be scared of milk. I think there are ghostess in it. There really isn't such thing as ghostess. I don't want to stay here all day long! I saw a ghost in California when [after] I went to Colorado. I don't like talking about ghostess. It's an animal and a machine.
>
> Edna—no Ida—no Edna had a dog [in Colorado. Edna apparently was a friend of Dad's]. Edna's dog bit my elbow. My Dad put a bandaid on it and the blood dripped on the floor.
>
> [We had known nothing before about this dog bite. I asked Marlys if her Mom could come into the office so Marlys could tell her what happened. The child agreed.]
>
> Mom, are there ghostess? [Marlys did not mention the dog bite first, but rather the ghost.] Ghostess scare people. [Her mother said there were none.] My ghost—a dog—he scratches me. He's black. My animal ghost is black. [Marlys was negating the whiteness of her ghost, which she had associated with milk. She knew her colors.]

For me, this youngster's dog ghost was entirely unexpected. No deaths had taken place in Colorado, nor had anyone in California known about the dog bite, which in and of itself was probably not very serious. In this instance, the tremendous stress of a 3-month period "on the lam" with her father, separated from mother, raided by police, and put into foster care was condensed by this preschooler into the one piece of mental imagery—a "ghostess," a dog the color and fluidity of milk. Like Ernst Kris's (1956) Dorothy, Marlys had condensed separate elements of a rather long, stressful period into one image. Condensations do not occur after trauma in *all* very young children—certainly Carla had not condensed various perceptions into her animal ghost—but some 2-, 3-, and 4-year-olds affix one internally derived symbol onto their memories of an overwhelming external event (Terr, 1985) and others pull together several well-separated events into a formless, timeless amalgam (Terr, 1984, p. 645f.). It appears that posttraumatic condensations more commonly occur in 2- and 3-year-old victims than they do at any other time in childhood, and even at *that* age, they are not universal.

From the "ghost stories" I have told in this section, there appear to be three types of waking-state posttraumatic phantoms: (1) images of dead or lost companions, who, although terribly scary, simultaneously offer wished-for reunions with prematurely cut-off survivors; (2) phantoms of long-gone bystanders or hallucinatory animal-images which had been actually present or present only in a child's mind at the time of a relatively early trauma; and (3) ghosts which repeat their originally real, wildly aggressive, out-of-control rage, sexuality, or sheer animalism. Ghosts can be men, beasts, or even inanimate objects like cars. They may never be "seen," but rather are felt, heard, or insinuated. Ghosts may literally re-create an actual attacker. They may also represent condensations or defensive displacements, partly removed from the real-life aggressor.

INTRUSIONS AND EXTRUSIONS OF IMAGERY

who's in, who's out;
—SHAKESPEARE, *King Lear*, 5:3

Occasionally a traumatized patient will take in whole the image of his assailant or the image of another victim with whom he strongly identifies. Or he may project the picture of the victim onto another real person or onto a totally imaginary "person." Internalization of imagery leads to the supernatural sense of being taken over by another human being or a force—either through "reincarnation" or through "possession." Externalization of imagery leads to the belief in reincarnation of a victim into another person outside of the self or the construction of an alterego. The use of these very maladaptive defensive operations indicates how wounded the psyche may become following one overwhelmingly frightening experience. In the past the few traumatized persons who experienced these "delusions" would probably have been considered "psychotic" or "religious fanatics."

Internalization. Introjection of whole images after a trauma can be accompanied by the sense of a personal receipt of a reincarnation or of being "possessed." It is relatively uncommon (2 adults and 1 child exhibited massive internalization in this group of 88).

Serena B., 10½ years, was playing in the woods with her best friend and cousin, Lois, and a stray cat. Serena went off to buy cat food and came back to find her cousin gone (although she later thought that she had heard "a little moan"). Lois's body was soon discovered in the very spot where the two girls had been playing. Lois had been raped and strangled. The murderer was never apprehended. Serena was spared the sight of Lois's body, but her mother told me, "She had a morbid curiosity. She wanted to go see Lois. She wanted to know how she looked and what had been done to her."

Serena told me the first time I met her 5 days after the murder, "My aunt said, 'Bring me back to the exact place you left Lois,' and they found her. My aunt found her. They wouldn't let me see her. I *wanted* to see her. I wanted to see what was the matter with her. I wanted to see my cousin. *That's* the whole story." Although Serena protested that "that was all," she went on shortly afterward to talk about her identification with the murder victim. "In private," she said, "I think of how awful it was. I picture myself in her place. And I think of how she felt—what she did—if she tried to struggle. One of those." (This is, of course, the phenomenon, "being in two places at once" as described on p. 501f.)

A year and a half later I asked Mrs. B. to bring the young girl back for a follow-up appointment. The 12-year-old was still compulsively raking through her dead cousin's feelings and behaviors just before she had died. "I lie in bed and think. . . . I was trying to think why they wanted to kill her. . . . I lay in bed thinking. Just thinking. Just thinking what it must have been like." Mrs. B. commented in her own separate session, "She screams in her sleep, 'No, don't do that,' or 'Stop that' or 'Mommy!'" The child herself reported many repeated dreams in which "a whole bunch of snakes squirm all over me. They go all over my hands. They're little and squirmy. Ugh! Don't squeeze!" To me Serena's dream sounds like a horror story from Edgar Allan Poe—a premature burial and an attack by the worms of the grave. But whether the death and helplessness of the dream or the sexual symbolism strike one from the first, the post-traumatic introjection of the victim remains the most obvious terror-striking note in this repeated nightmare. And it is this intense identification which may lead some sufferers of severe fright to an uncanny sense of being different, of being taken over, after an overwhelming event.

Serena's musings never progressed so far as to give her a sense of harboring Lois's reincarnated self or of being possessed, but the next example takes us a little further along the road to this type of posttraumatic "spiritual" takeover. Mrs. Francine S., 32 years, came to me for treatment 18 months after her husband was seriously brain-injured in an automobile accident. Mrs. S. was awakened from sleep at 6 A.M. by the shocking phone call, "met" her comatose husband in the emergency room, and launched into a living nightmare which let up very little in the following 1½ years.

Mrs. S. was bothered, she said, by an early thought she had related to the accident. "I wondered [during the first shocking moments] if I'd end up like my Gramma. She was a widow, young, with four children. I loved my Gramma. I have been told that I am just like her. And I wonder about that. I wondered if history was repeating itself kind of like."

Mrs. S. had introjected remembered, old images of her long-suffering grandmother at the first moments of her overwhelming ordeal. From that time on, the internalized image of Gramma had stuck. There was the element of "reincarnation" here, although the educated young woman said she did not believe in such things. "But still," she said, "it feels weird."

The next example takes us much further toward a personal

"takeover"—a surrender of the ego. Twenty-three-year-old Mathew R.'s introjection of a remembered image of the trolley car driver who had hit him from the rear 6 months earlier led him to a sense of being "possessed." Just before he was struck off his motorcycle and dragged beneath the trolley, the young Mexican-American man had looked behind him at the driver. "He got close," Mr. R. remembered, "and a shiver ran up my spine. He looked like a zombie. Lifeless. . . . I turned around and looked . . . he was wearing dark sunglasses. A caucasian. Lifeless. Around 30. He had no emotion. Like a mannequin. . . . Mannequinlike people scare me. I dream of dummies."

Mr. R. went directly to a description of his "possession," clearly indicating that he was quite aware of his identification with the trolley driver: "I try to put myself in the position of the driver. *When he enters me,* I feel weird and I don't like it. I try to think of something else. I pray then. I say 'Our Father' or 'Hail Mary' or I talk in prayer. It feels like I start getting into a trance. I don't like that!"

What had happened on occasion to Mr. R. since his accident was a sense of "possession." The driver had penetrated Mr. R.— much in the same way as the original event had penetrated the young man's mind, despite his attempts to cope and defend himself. After the accident when Mr. R. was repeatedly "taken over" by his identification with the driver, he felt himself slip into a "trance." He himself became dummylike at those moments—a mannequin. To combat this, he groped for childhood prayers— the old automatic ones, like "Our Father in heaven, hallowed be Thy name" or "Hail Mary full of grace." Mr. R.'s "possession" thus carried its own inbuilt "cures"—the same ones with which over the centuries countless country priests have tried to exorcise the possessing devils out from the innocents who were harboring them.

"Possession" is not that common in our society—even given such horror films as *The Exorcist.* At least in the one instance of Mathew R., however, we can see that possession can be a direct aftereffect of psychic trauma.

Externalization. When I looked for extrusion or projection of traumatic images, I found that 3 children and no adults utilized this rather uncommon mechanism. An 8-year-old boy, who at 3 had been kidnapped at gunpoint from his very prominent family, developed an alterego at 5, the same age so many normal youngsters tentatively "find" imaginary playmates. And 2 boys, a 7-year-old and a 17-year-old, both from impoverished black families, thought that they had perceived "reborn" victims in their younger siblings.

Posttraumatically projected "reincarnations" are different, I think, from the type of introjected personal takeovers described above. Solomon W., the 17-year-old boy described on p. 498, witnessed his best friend Joe's death in the passenger seat of Solomon's car. Two months after the trauma, Solomon had partly incorporated some aspects of Joe. ("I put myself in Joe's place trying to think what he's thinking now wherever he is. Sometimes I think he is in heaven trying to help me do what I want to do. Other times I think he's in hell trying to get me.") But, more persistently, Solomon projected Joe's image onto his own toddler-aged brother. Six months after Joe's death, Solomon told me, "Sometimes I feel my little brother has received my friend's reincarnation. It's in his eyes. He looks at me funny without smiling. I wonder, 'Could it be?' You never know."

Much in the same fashion, Douglas S., a 7½-year-old witness to the fatal beating of his toddler brother, Little Andy, by his stepfather, Big Andy, began to believe in "reincarnation," although he had never acquired this word in his urban ghetto-derived vocabulary. One week after the killing, Douglas and I had the following conversation:

> I got nuthin' to worry about. Mama is pregnant anyway. Another baby would be maybe jus' like Lil' Andy. I don't know.
> Each baby is different, Doug. Each one is made new by a mother and a father.
> I'm not so sure about *that.*
> You know your Mama had a baby inside her *before* Lil' Andy died. Remember how big her belly looked?
> Uh huh. [Douglas nodded affirmatively.]
> So how could Little Andy get inside of her instead of the new baby that was already growing there?
> [Douglas looked puzzled.] I don't know. But I think Lil' Andy might be able to get inside anyway.

Luckily for Douglas, Mama gave birth to a girl. But Douglas

still dreamed at night about Little Andy. At about the time that Grandmother, the court-appointed custodian, stopped bringing Douglas to see me, Doug was struggling with sleeping imagery of a grown-up Lil' Andy and a younger, perhaps regressed, self. "I dream about him," Douglas said in his last session. "I dreamed he was growed up. He had him a motorcycle. I was jus' 5 years old. I said, 'Andy.' And he say, 'What?' I say, 'Would you give me a ride?' He say, 'Yes.' He was goin' real fast too. I had me a ride. I tried to stop thinking about it. Grandma told me that. The [dream] jus' comes a lot of times—every time I take a nap. When I wake up [Grandma says] I can't [i.e., "I'm not supposed to"] think about it the rest of the day."

An extruded trauma-related image of the self may end up in the form of an alterego. At 3 years of age Alan J. was kidnapped at home from his mother by a gun-toting young man, who demanded a sizable ransom for the child's return. The terrified Alan was held for about a day by his abductor until the F.B.I. arranged for payment, release of the boy, and the surprise capture of the kidnapper. Alan, who lives far from San Francisco, was brought to me at age 8 by his parents. They had recently heard about my work with the Chowchilla kidnap victims, and they wondered if any remaining effects from Alan's kidnapping still could be detected. The young lad had been quiet for some time about his experience and was an excellent student, a friendly, well-behaved boy. I asked 8-year-old Alan, who participated very eagerly in the sessions, if he had ever played pretend games. He answered:

I don't have any games of imagination. Wait. Oh yeah. I do. A long time ago—I guess I was 5—I had a fake person I made up. I would say he would die some day. And he had a funeral. I called him Dill. I named him for dill pickles. I made him up a couple years ago when I was 5, and I still have him in my mind. He never speaks. [Alan was silent during his kidnapping.] I pretend he's dead. I look up at the sky and I see his face. Dill was just my age. He had white hair, a purple face, and yellow eyes. I made him up because I picked up a rotten dill pickle. I picked up my doll—a boy doll—and I said, "You're rotten too." Then I saw Dill. He looked like my doll, but my doll didn't have a purple face and yellow eyes.

When I was 6 on my birthday, Dill died. He was going outside
and he had a heart attack. I called the hospital and they said they
were all filled up. Then I didn't know *what* to do. Then Dill just
died. [Note the traumatic way Dill dies. Alan loses all control of
the situation.]

I pretend I had a coffin. I put Dill in. Then I pretend my Mom
called the funeral service and the funeral service was the next
day. . . . Dill is in space now. I see his face at nighttime. He's
floating around in his coffin [this is a waking hallucination,
much as the "ghosts" previously described are hallucinations].
Now E.T. is on top of him with his little finger glowing. They're
just floating up there. It doesn't bother me. It's not comforting,
either. It just makes me sad 'cause Dill's not back. . . . I *knew* Dill
was going to die. I just knew it. I knew about 5 days before. It was
just after my birthday party. I always thought Dill would have to
die. . . . I feel Dill keeps me safe. I don't expect another disaster
except another kidnapping. I'd use my fire escape. I have an
escape route. I think I can predict another kidnapping. I just
guessed there'd be another kidnapping *soon* and there *was*. He
[a recent kidnap-murderer of another 3-year-old in the same
city where Alan was kidnapped] got the idea off me. I think I
caused that kidnapping. I think I can predict other things like
"Hawaii will have a volcano"; "there's going to be an earthquake
somewhere in California"; "my friend Troy *will* grow up. He
wants to be a rock star, but he won't. He's going to work in a
business like his father." I think I will cause it to happen by
thinking it. But now I think I'm magic. Ever since I was
kidnapped.

Because I did not have the opportunity to follow Alan for the 5
years after his kidnapping, I could only retrospectively reconstruct the mental events which occurred in Alan after his traumatic experience. I knew that the child had been terrified and
helpless at the time he was taken. He did not speak to the kidnapper ("I was a crier, not a talker. I didn't talk to the kidnapper. I
didn't cry, though, when I was kidnapped, and I don't know
why"). Alan's parents had decided to "downplay" the whole
thing upon the child's return, to treat him "normally," and to
avoid any psychotherapy. When they brought Alan to me at 8,
Alan remembered his three biggest worries during the kidnapping: "I had no pants on. I felt embarrassed. . . . I was afraid he

[the kidnapper] would injure my arm. He got close to my arm at his apartment. He touched it—pulled it—because he wanted me to go to sleep. . . . I was scared I wouldn't see my mother again." The child had thus feared permanent separation and injury during his ordeal. He had been paralytically unable to take action—even to speak. He had been traumatized.

Much of Alan's helplessness and fear was "expelled," or projected, at age 5 onto an alterego, Dill. Dill could die traumatically, pass into a silent state of remembrance and visualization, and thus carry for Alan much of his hated sense of utter helplessness. Alan, on the other hand, could begin to feel magically in control, "safe"—of course, ultimately responsible for all of the murder-kidnappings, for each of the earthquakes in California or the volcanic eruptions in Hawaii, but at the same time hyperalert to disasters and able to fend off overwhelming surprises. The splitting into a vulnerable dead being (Dill) and a healthy boy (Alan) had brought on a tentative and highly compromised sense of well-being for the young lad. Of course, the in-control real child, Alan, had to accept enormous guilty responsibility for worldwide and small-scale disasters, which he now felt he could predict psychically. But this accomplishment of general well-being had taken place only with the "help" of a weird, supernatural-seeming alterego, Dill, who would now take much of the punishment.

A doppelgänger is "a ghostly counterpart and companion of a person; especially a ghostly double of a live person that haunts him through life and is usually visible only to himself" (Webster's *Third International Dictionary*). How like a doppelgänger was Alan's Dill—and how like Alan's story is Henry James's "The Jolly Corner," a tale of a late middle-aged man who returns from England where he spent his entire adulthood and meets, in his old house in New York, the ghost of himself as he would have been had he stayed there. In both Alan's true story and James's fictional one, the protagonist *cannot* recognize that his ghostly double *is* himself.

In religion, one hears of special saints who have suffered for our particular sins, guardian angels, and the like. Perhaps these were derived, in part, as posttraumatic alteregos. Obviously far more than old psychic trauma goes into religious imagery, but the hapless Dill and the martyred Jesus have some qualities in common. One can see how a projected, unwanted image of the hurt self can be extruded outward onto imageries of holy fathers and mothers or sainted agemates.

CONTAGION OF POSTTRAUMATIC IMAGERY

'Tis now the very witching time of night,
When churchyards yawn and hell itself breathes out
Contagion to this world.
                              —SHAKESPEARE, *Hamlet*, 3:2

In previous writings (1981, 1983c), I have emphasized how contagious posttraumatic play can be among children. Other posttraumatic effects such as time distortions, fears, and misperceptions can be "caught" in the same way. Because traumatic anxiety is so intense, so intrusive, and so omnipresent for the victim, his friends and family begin to respond to this horrible undertone of emotion. Eventually those people who exist at some distance from the victim may also be affected, and the traumatic anxiety with its accompanying play, rumors, or stories may actually be transmitted into new generations. It was in this way that "Ring around the Rosie," a children's game from the Middle Ages, was eventually brought into the twentieth-century American nursery school.

My daughter used to refuse to play "Ring around the Rosie" at preschool. "It scares me a little," she would say. "I *don't* like that game." She perceived entirely on her own the tremendous anxiety which had appended itself to this frequently played children's ditty. I learned 15 years after her persistent refusals to join in the nursery school circle that "Ring around the Rosie" had originated in the terrors of the Black Plague. This posttraumatic game has been infecting new generations of normal children for the past 600 years or so.

It is indeed difficult to "trap" posttraumatic contagion directly in clinical practice, yet I had the unique chance to evaluate one such case. A mother asked me to interview her 9-year-old girl, Hilary M., because she was afraid the youngster, a bright and able 4th-grader, was being affected by the rape of her friend

Shelby S. Mrs. M. told me that Shelby had been attacked by a male stranger in the park 18 months earlier, and that since that time a group of Shelby's girlfriends always played "a strange game" on the school playground. When Mrs. M. had volunteered for schoolyard duty the previous month, she had become concerned about the girls' wild cackling, their screams of excitement, and their endless repetitions of the sometimes violent play. Mrs. M. knew that Shelby had told Hilary about the rape when it occurred, but, as far as she knew, the girls had not talked about it subsequently.

Hilary came to my office only once. We discussed the playground game which Hilary admitted made her feel quite nervous. "We play rabbits—a little animallike," Hilary said. "Behind the tree is an invisible wolf. 'He' pretends to catch us and he keeps us in a cage. We are all trapped until only one is left. And then they free us and the wolf dies. Sometimes the school bell rings and nothing [in the play] ends. The wolf is invisible. Maybe he's invisible because nobody wants to *be* 'wolf.' We used to play animals last year, too. It was a group game. I can't think of who started it."

The children's invisible wolf may have been one of those horrifying posttraumatic ghost-aggressors which I have described in the section on animal ghosts—this time, not an exact depiction but a displacement to a beast from a human aggressor, Shelby's rapist. In this instance the animal phantom was being spread about from child to child. The catchiness did not come through rumor or even through storytelling—instead it happened through the simple but compelling medium of a recess game on the school playground. A mother had observed the invisible wolf's out-of-control effect on her youngster, and she had come to my office with a question. We might be able, perhaps, to stop the invasion of Shelby's girl-ravishing wolf into Hilary's psyche, but the wolf imagery was demanding expression in several other youngsters as well. Would Mrs. M. return to the school for Hilary's 8th-grade graduation to find a new group of 9-year-olds playing "Rabbit and Wolf" out there on the playground? Most likely, we would not be afforded the opportunity to find out. Once at Chowchilla I did have such an opportunity, however, and to my amazement I discovered that a posttraumatic game had indeed been transmitted to a new generation of youngsters (Terr, 1981, p. 750f.).

Some ghost "ideas" are transmitted by anecdotal tale, rumor, and gossip. Some "ghosts" may be spread entirely nonverbally, as Shelby's wolf-ghost was passed around, sneaking into the minds of children the way a ghost sneaks under the cracks in a door as "he" enters a room. But the most "supernatural" thing about posttraumatic anxiety is its longevity, its failure to die. A trauma victim may go off to live in Brazil, but the victim's games or the gossip or the rumors which fly about him take on lives of their own. Traumatic anxiety *is* a ghost! It moves through the generations with the stealth and the cunning of a most skilled specter. It tricks us into letting it into our homes and then it turns around and haunts us with bad dreams and upsetting images.

DISCUSSION

As I travel into the world of psychic trauma, I begin to perceive more and more universal, societal, cultural, and individual effects which have originated in overwhelming external events. Many ideas which we have long taken for granted derive from terrible frights and from traumas. "Normal" adults and children have incorporated these mental effects into their thinking, whether or not they themselves were traumatized. Although the scientifically sophisticated person may "pooh-pooh" concepts like omens, telepathy, future prediction, living day to day, hauntings, seeing what could not actually have been seen, ghosts, poltergeists, reincarnations, possessions, alteregos, and doppelgängers, the ordinary member of society hears about these ideas, wonders, and transmits them (believed or unbelieved) to others. There is something impelling about weird experience. It tempts even the most solidly grounded among us.

In 1981 I interviewed 25 normal small-town schoolchildren who were randomly selected and then age-, ethnic-, and sex-matched to the kidnapped children of Chowchilla (Terr, 1983d). This "control study" was done mainly to check in a "normal" population two findings from my 4- to 5-year follow-up at Chowchilla (Terr, 1983a)—dreams of personal death and the sense of a severely limited future. To my surprise—and at first glance, to my dismay—I found that 8 of these "normal" children dreamed repeated terror dreams, 8 had died in a dream, and 5 youngsters did not believe that they would live a full 70-year life-span. Using these findings along with the youngsters' answers to questions about past frights, fears, play, and weird behaviors, I found that 10 of the 25 "normal" McFarland and Porterville youngsters had been severely frightened by external events in the past; 5 of these children described enough confirmatory symptoms (fears, posttraumatic play, reenactment) to lead me to conclude that they had been psychically traumatized.

The discovery of 10 severely frightened youngsters among 25 "normals" suggests that sharply affecting outside events and their psychological aftermaths are much more common than might have been anticipated. Psychic trauma may not quite be the all-or-nothing affair which Freud's 1920 definition, "a breach in the stimulus barrier," would imply. If trauma consisted of a spectrum of conditions ranging from extreme fright to posttraumatic stress disorder depending upon the type and number of ego functions compromised by the external shock, then it might be easier to conceive how our culture becomes so filled with trauma-related aftereffects.

One reason, therefore, that we are so culturally burdened with anxiety-provoking ghost stories and hauntings is that all of us, at least as very small children, have probably been severely frightened by actual events, perhaps even traumatized. The psychodynamics of the posttraumatic stress disorders probably are part of normal development as well because severe externally generated fright is such a common experience in childhood.

The second reason that so many "uncanny" tales catch on among us is the power of posttraumatic "contagion." Because we can easily fantasize overwhelming helplessness, whether or not we have ever experienced an out-and-out trauma, we can easily empathize with the traumatized person. We transmit his games without pausing much to consider. We tell his stories about time-warps, risings up of the dead, reincarnations, and dream predictions without evaluating. And we experience small chills of transmitted traumatic anxiety every time we play such games or pass along such stories. The chill of traumatic affect is a little different from the anticipatory tension of signal anxiety—it is weird; it is strange; and it feels entirely "uncanny."

SUMMARY

In this paper I have described five kinds of posttraumatic imagery along with the types of hauntings and houndings which emanate from these vivid memories. The inquiry I have made is meant as a very preliminary effort. Certainly, if psychiatry and psychoanalysis become interested in these weird phenomena, more controlled studies, more specific research protocols, and more direct field work will be needed before we will be able fully to understand the "ununderstandable."

That spooky Sunday afternoon radio show which I used to adore (I can't begin to remember its name) provided a full explanation at the end of each episode. At the conclusion of this essay, I regret that I cannot give a correspondingly full naturalistic explanation for all the supernatural phenomena that psychic trauma sufferers have related to me. So instead, I will conclude with the beginnings of another ghost story. This tale is a true one. Its setting is exotic—much like that Sunday afternoon radio program I loved, as a matter of fact—and its wording is a bit slangy. But what comes through from this ghost story is a horror, to me far more hair-raising than any of the "Cujos," the "Omens" or the "Halloweens" that my young patients feel impelled to tell me about. I think that from what I have presented, it will be obvious what Margot M. endured in her last year of living in Rabat. I am confident that everyone can pick up the supernatural significances which her traumatically heightened perceptions brought to this grisly scene. Margot told me her "story" in a session 6 months after the traumatic occurrence she relates.

A Midnight Ride to Marrakesh

My old landlady, the Haja, wanted me to come back from Rabat to Marrakesh to throw out some Moroccan tenants living in the flat that I used to rent from her. So she showed up at my job on the last day of Ramaddan—a weird time in Morocco anyway, because nobody eats all day and they get into foul moods and do crazy things. She wanted me to come right back with her, and we set right off for Marrakesh on the 10 P.M. train to Casablanca.

We traded trains at midnight. There were no seats on the Rabat-Casablanca run. We were standing there. A man in black with a beard—he looked like the Devil—he was with us. He looked at us—at the Haja—the train was still moving. We were trying to catch another train to Marrakesh. There was a mad rush to catch the other train.

The man in black hopped off. I hopped off. Haja, 60 or 62 years old, decided to hop off too. She grabbed the bar getting off. The train was moving. Her djellabah got caught and she got sucked under the train. And she was killed. *And I didn't do anything.* . . .

The man was this dark force and he was leading us to destruction. He disappeared. I didn't see him anymore. . . . I couldn't look. I knew the train ran over Haja's head. All kinds of people gathered around me—around the train, but the man in black seemed gone for good. The midnight train pulled out of the station, and I stayed.

I see it in flashbacks. Always. When I'm talking about it. Sometimes at night. Sometimes at odd times. When I'm not talking about it, it comes unbidden. I saw the train pull her in. She made this weird sound —ahhllll—and then a guttural throaty sound. I can hear it right now. I always see it—the part of losing balance, getting sucked under. I want to put my hand out to get her. *But I could not move. I just didn't.* . . .

There are a lot of negative forces in Morocco. Witches make spells on people. I went to the Huafa [a witch] once in Tamara in August after the Haja was killed, and I asked her what she saw my life doing. Funny, she said I'd stay in Morocco and marry a Moroccan guy—but here I am now in the U.S., and I think I'm finished with Morocco. But Morocco just won't finish with me. I hate it. I wish it would all go away.

I think sometimes, "I wonder why the man in black didn't come back?"

BIBLIOGRAPHY

ANONYMOUS. The tinker and the ghost. In *Three Golden Oranges,* ed. R. Boggs & M. Davis. New York: Montauk Books, 1967, pp. 97–108.

BIERCE, A. (approx. 1910). The middle toe of the right foot. In Pronzini et al. (1981), pp. 168–176.

COCTEAU, J. (1923). Death and the gardener. In Manguel (1983), p. 249.

CORTÁZAR, J. (1963). House taken over. In Manguel (1983), pp. 1-6.

COWIE, P. (1982). *Ingmar Bergman.* New York: Charles Scribner.

DOYLE, A. C. (1899). The brown hand. In *The Best Supernatural Tales of Arthur Conan Doyle,* sel. E. F. Bleiler. New York: Dover, 1979, pp. 43–59.

FREUD, A. (1967). About losing and being lost. *Psychoanal. Study Child,* 22:9–19.

FREUD, S. (1900). The interpretation of dreams. *S.E.,* 4 & 5.

——— (1907). Delusions and dreams in Jensen's 'Gradiva.' *S.E.,* 9:1–95.

——— (1919). The 'uncanny.' *S.E.,* 17:217–256.

——— (1920). Beyond the pleasure principle. *S.E.,* 18:3–64.

HAWTHORNE, N. (1868). From the 'American Notebooks.' In Manguel (1983), pp. 950–951.

HOROWITZ, M. (1976). *Stress Response Syndromes.* New York: Aronson.

JAMES, M. R. (1904). Wailing well. In *The Collected Ghost Stories of M. R. James.* London: Edward Arnold, 1934, pp. 626–642.

KATAN, M. (1962). A causerie on Henry James's *The Turn of the Screw. Psychoanal. Study Child,* 17:473–493.

——— (1966). The origin of *The Turn of the Screw. Psychoanal. Study Child,* 21:583–635.

KING, S. (1983). *Christine.* New York: Viking.

KRIS, E. (1956). The recovery of childhood memories in psychoanalysis. *Psychoanal. Study Child,* 11:54–88.

LE FANU, J. S. (1923). Squire Toby's will. In Pronzini et al. (1981), pp. 62–90.

MALZBERG, B. N. (1975). Transfer. In Pronzini et al. (1981), pp. 507–513.

MANGUEL, A., ed. (1983). *Black Water.* New York: Clarkson N. Potter.

OSTERWEIS, M., SOLOMON, F., & GREEN, M., eds. (1984). *Bereavement.* Washington, D.C.: National Academy of Science.

PARKES, C. (1970). The first year of bereavement. *Psychiatry,* 33:444–467.

PLINY THE YOUNGER (62–113 A.D.). Letter to Sura. In *Harvard Classics,* ed. C. W. Eliot. New York: Collier, 1937, 9:311–314.

PRONZINI, B., MALZBERG, B., & GREENBERG, M., eds. (1981). *The Arbor House Treasury of Horror and the Supernatural.* New York: Arbor House.

SHAPIRO, T., SHERMAN, M., & OSOWSKY, I. (1980). Preschool children's conception of ghosts. *J. Amer. Acad. Child Psychiat.,* 19:41–55.

STOKER, B. (1914). The squaw. In Pronzini et al. (1981), pp. 91–102.

TERR, L. C. (1979). Children of Chowchilla. *Psychoanal. Study Child,* 34:547–623.

——— (1981). 'Forbidden games.' *J. Amer. Acad. Child Psychiat.,* 20:741–760.

——— (1983a). Chowchilla revisited. *Amer. J. Psychiat.,* 140:1543–1550.

——— (1983b). Time sense following psychic trauma. *Amer. J. Orthopsychiat.,* 53:244–261.

——— (1983c). Play therapy and psychic trauma. In *Handbook of Play Therapy,* ed. C. Schaefer & K. O'Connor. New York: Wiley-Interscience, pp. 308–319.

——— (1983d). Life attitudes, dreams, and psychic trauma in a group of "normal" children. *J. Amer. Acad. Child Psychiat.,* 22:221–230.

———— (1984). Time and trauma. *Psychoanal. Study Child,* 39:633–666.

———— (1985). Children traumatized in small groups. In *Posttraumatic Stress Disorder in Children,* ed. S. Eth & R. Pynoos. Washington, D.C.: American Psychiatric Association.

WHARTON, E. (1931). Pomegranate seed. In Manguel (1983), pp. 62–91.

WILDE, O. (1890). *The Portrait of Dorian Gray.* New York: Oxford Univ. Press, 1982.

Psychoanalysis and Biography

ELISABETH YOUNG-BRUEHL, Ph.D.

SINCE WORLD WAR II MANY REFLECTIONS ON THE NATURE AND method of biography have been published. As a glance at a library card catalogue will reveal, most of these treat biography "as a literary form." But recently it has also been considered as a type of history-writing, or even of social science, as a type of psychology-writing. These last two characterizations appear together in reflections on what is known as "psychobiography," a subspecies of psychohistory and also a branch of "applied psychoanalysis."

The literature on psychobiography—by historians, psychoanalysts, and general biographical practitioners—is mainly methodological. Commentators focus on how psychological—predominantly psychoanalytic—theory has been and ought to be applied to the data and documents, memories and memorabilia from which a biography can be constructed. This focus is, of course, not detachable from the question of which theory is to be applied. And so it has been the case that methodological discussion of psychobiography has generally followed the course of theoretical discussion of psychoanalysis: the first period of psychobiographical writing, through the 1920s, was dominated by early Freudian theory, while the postwar period has been dominated by various ego psychologies.

Regardless of whether or not they advocate a particular theory, methodological commentators have generally agreed about

Associate Professor of Letters in the College of Letters, Wesleyan University.

Presented to the Kanzer Seminar on Psychiatry and the Humanities, October 18, 1984 at Yale University.

what kind of psychobiographical practice they find unacceptable. A psychobiographer must not indulge in "wild psychoanalysis," that is, must not set a simplified theory down upon the data and read off the result. When this is done, the result is something as misleading as Binion's announcement (1968) at the very beginning of his study of Lou Andreas Salomé that she had "a craving for her father excited by excretion and attended by darkling visions of reentering his bowel-womb to repossess his penis" (p. 6). Good practice is, not surprisingly, more difficult to describe, and the number of psychobiographers that any commentator is willing to hold up as exemplary is very small. But most writers do agree that theory or theories should be used flexibly for "listening with the third ear" (in Reik's much-quoted phrase) to biographical materials and then used cautiously in interpretation, with due and frank regard being given to all interpretive difficulties.

Among the interpretive difficulties are those associated with and consequent to the differences between therapeutic practice and biography-writing—difficulties which are obvious but not always obviously taken into account. At the least, there are three areas of difference, which I should indicate telegraphically:

1. The biographical subject is not an analysand: there is no analytic transference to be analyzed, and no possibility of confirmation of an analyst's construction; further, the type and quantity of materials to be analyzed are not comparable in the two activities, and there is no free association ordering the biographical materials.

2. The biographer is not functioning as an analyst (even if he or she is one by training), and there is thus only an analogue to "countertransference."

3. A biography is not a case history: the subject's life must be narrated, not told in theoretical categories, and it must be set in the world, among other people (whose stories must also be narrated), and in relation to intellectual, social, economic, and political institutions and events.

Commentators on psychobiography have developed, in complement to these differences, typologies of psychobiology. In 1960, for example, Heinz Kohut, noting that most psychobiographies to that date were focused on "creative minds and their creations," distinguished three types according to their aims: (1) biographies supported by psychoanalysis and designed to illuminate the personalities of significant individuals; (2) psychoanalytic pathographies designed primarily to expand psychoanalytic knowledge or to apply existing knowledge; and (3) biographies focused on creativity or disturbances of creativity and designed to explore the development of ego functions involved in creativity. (The line between case study and biography in the last two categories is not always clear.) To these types should be added a fourth: biographies of "the great man in history" designed to illuminate both a personality and his context, of the relation between life history and history.

Methodological reflections of the three kinds I have sketched have helped to bring recent psychobiographical writing to a sophistication not observable in its first enthusiastic period, when bad practice was little more than *biographie de la boudoir* or debunking of exalted reputations, and even good practice tended toward what might be called "applied oedipus complex."[1] And the milieu in which psychobiography is practiced has changed. Hardly a recent biography is now unsupported by at least acquaintance with psychoanalysis, and few readers are astonished to find biographical subjects no longer—to use Eric Havelock's characterization—*bien coiffe* and cut off at the chest like Victorian portrait busts. Nonetheless, there is little evidence in the methodological literature that the development of psychobiography since Freud has been important for psychoanalytic theory, or that the relation between psychoanalysis and biography can be reciprocal.

In what follows, I am going to take two paths, which will eventually come together. On the methodological level, my questions will be: (1) whether and how psychobiography can take into account the traditional aim of biography-writing, that is, moral pedagogy or the presentation of exemplary lives; and (2) why methodological commentary on psychobiography has

1. That early psychoanalytic biographies were "case studies" designed primarily to extend generalizations about the oedipus complex from pathological to normal or exceptional individuals is apparent in *The Minutes of the Vienna Psychoanalytic Society* (1962), particularly for meetings 32 and 33, p. 265ff.

ignored the fact that there are so few psychobiographies of women by women and only a few more of women by men. These two tracks will show, I think, how ahistorical methodological reflections on psychobiography have been, but such a demonstration is not my main purpose.

The literature of psychobiography, oriented as it is toward "how to" methodological questions about application of theory, does not touch, it seems to me, the motivational level, the question: why do people write biographies? About this question, the literature itself has not been supported by psychoanalysis, illuminating for psychoanalysis or psychoanalytically concerned with creativity—to use Kohut's categories.[2] By focusing my attention on two of the most imaginative modern biographies—Freud's 1910 "pathography" of Leonardo da Vinci and Virginia Woolf's 1928 novel called *Orlando: A Biography* I shall sketch out a direction for inquiry into this motivational question, not a general answer to it. I have chosen two works that are incomparable in many respects—certainly in their relationship to psychoanalytic theory—for reasons which I shall develop.

I

Works on biography as a literary form, histories of biography-writing, and psychoanalytic retrospectives on the developments leading to psychobiography have all contributed to what might be called the Standard History of Biography. This Standard History acknowledges Greek and Roman founding fathers, sets Christian hagiography out of its bounds, notes the correlation between concern for individuals and new forms of biography and autobiography in the Renaissance, and really begins in earnest with the eighteenth century and the most discussed and praised biography in English, Boswell's *Life of Johnson*. The Standard History then goes on to lament and variously explain the low estate of nineteenth-century mammoth hero-worshipping or minutiae-assembling eulogistic biographies. The twentieth century is presented as the century of both artistic and scientific

2. An extensive annotated bibliography on the methodological literature has been compiled by William Gilmore (1976).

overcoming. Between them, Freud and Lytton Strachey ushered in the modern biography, and it became a widely shared hope that the genre would be relatively free of sins of omission like idealizing falsehoods and suppression of evidence, and sins of commission like lack of scientificity or objectivity and lack of candor about once forbidden topics. Whether truth-scientific or truth-artistic, the goal is truth.

The Standard History applauds the disappearance of purposes like the one stated by Plutarch, who admitted that he had set out to write his *Lives* for the instruction of others but eventually came to find himself "proceeding and attaching myself [to the writing] for my own; the virtues of these great men serving me as a sort of looking-glass, in which I see how to adjust and adorn my own life" (p. 293). Plutarch's conviction that these great Greeks and Romans should be presented with all their shortcomings of virtue in order that their greatness be all the more instructive was shared by most biography writers of the High Period, the eighteenth century. As Samuel Johnson said: "We must confess the faults of our favorite to gain credit for the praise of his excellences." Mallet's preface to his life of Bacon (1740) was typical: "Whoever undertakes to write the life of any person . . . ought to look upon this law as prescribed to him: He is fairly to record the faults as well as the good qualities, the failings as well as the perfections, of the Dead; with this great view: to warn and improve the Living" (p. vii).

For Mallet's law, but against the moralism of Mallet's view, Lytton Strachey's *Eminent Victorians* (1918) took up arms. Strachey held that biography should be for biographical art's sake; all moral "ulterior motives" were to be removed with the purgative "acid and ice" of irony. Since Freud, psychobiographers of any of the three types Heinz Kohut distinguished have also followed Mallet's law—with more emphasis on theoretical explanation, rather than simple recording, of failing and perfections—but rejected his goal of warning and improving the living, including the living biographer. Impartial truth, like biographical art, is supposed to be its own recommendation and is not to serve personal or social moral ends.

The *locus classicus* for the psychobiographical truth-aim is a passage in Freud's essay on Leonardo da Vinci, which the Standard History notes as the strongest rap upon the knuckles ever given to moral didacticism in biography-writing. In the final section of that essay Freud wrote:

> . . . biographers are fixated on their heroes in a quite special way. In most cases they have chosen their hero as the subject of their studies because—for reasons of their own personal and emotional life—they have felt a special affection for him from the very first. They then devote their energies to a task of idealization, aimed at enrolling the great man among the class of their infantile models—at reviving in him, perhaps, the child's idea of his father. To gratify this wish they obliterate the individual features of their subject's physiognomy; they smooth over the traces of his life's struggles with internal and external resistances, and they tolerate in him no vestige of human weakness or imperfection [p. 130].

This passage, aimed broadly and nonspecifically at biographers in general, set the terms for modern psychobiographical revisionism; it can be heard, for example, in Jones's biography (1953) of Freud as he deals with Freud's "psychoneurotic period" and his relationship with Fliess by suggesting that hero worship should not obscure Freud's struggle. The passage that follows in Freud's text is, however, seldom quoted: Biographers "present us with what is in fact a cold, strange, ideal figure, instead of a human being to whom we might feel ourselves distantly related." Freud does not say what this "distant relation" is to be—but I shall take the phrase as a clue to the complexity of his study.

Methodological commentators on Freud's essay focus on his critique of biographers' transferences to and fixations on their subjects, but, in fact, this critique is only a part of the general theme of the essay, which is the connection between creativity and paternal authority. Although he noted that Leonardo had tried to outdo his father in the elegance of his personal manners and that he had sought a father substitute in one of his patrons, Freud concluded that Leonardo's achievements as a natural scientist depended upon his freedom from authority, ultimately, paternal authority:

> [Leonardo] dared to utter the bold assertion which contains

within itself the justification for all independent research: '*He who appeals to authority when there is a difference of opinion works with his memory rather than with his reason.*' Thus he became the first modern natural scientist . . . [p. 222].

Freud then went on to explain psychoanalytically Leonardo's conviction that the study of nature is the source of all truth:

> . . . we see that the 'ancients' and authority simply correspond to his father, and nature once more becomes the tender and kindly mother who had nourished him. In most other human beings— no less to-day than in primaeval times—the need for support from an authority of some sort is so compelling that their world begins to totter if that authority is threatened. Only Leonardo could dispense with that support; he would not have been able to do so had he not learnt in the first years of his life to do without his father. His later scientific research, with all its boldness and independence, presupposed the existence of in- fantile sexual researches uninhibited by his father, and was a prolongation of them with the sexual element excluded [p. 122f.].

The phrase "with the sexual element excluded" refers the read- er back to an earlier discussion of types of sublimation and their relation to infantile sexual researches, children's sexual curi- osity. Freud noted that this infant drive undergoes repression along with repression of libido, with three possible results in later life: first, severe inhibition of intellectual activity; second, "compulsive brooding" (p. 80), or the sexualization of intellec- tual activity; and, finally, the model type, maintenance of suc- cessful early sublimation in continued research: "the libido evades the fate of repression by being sublimated from the very beginning into curiosity" (p. 80). Leonardo was a person of the third type, and he paid the price typical of successful sublima- tion, that is: "Sexual repression, which has made the instinct [or *Trieb*, for research] so strong through the addition to it of subli- mated libido, is still taken into account by the instinct, in that it avoids any concern with sexual themes" (p. 80).

In this discussion, Freud, by implication, raised a question about what factors allow sublimation that does not repress and thus exclude the sexual element, that is, sublimation that could result in independent research of the sort a psychoanalyst or

psychobiographer undertakes—research concerned with sexual
themes. Even though he noted several times Leonardo's lack of
interest in psychology, however, Freud eagerly enrolled Leonardo's cooperation in the project of his study: "Leonardo himself,
with his love of truth and his thirst for knowledge, would not
have discouraged an attempt to take the trivial peculiarities and
riddles in his nature as a starting-point, for discovering what
determined his mental and intellectual development. We do
homage to him by learning from him" (p. 130f.). And then, as
though he had not written his critique of biographers' special
affections for their subjects, Freud candidly admitted his own
affection for Leonardo: "Like others I have succumbed to the
attraction of this great and mysterious man, in whose nature one
seems to detect powerful instinctual passions which can nevertheless only express themselves in so remarkably subdued a
manner" (p. 134).

Freud found in his Leonardo a predecessor and a comrade in
research, a fellow searcher after truth, and "succumbed" to his
attraction. He also described the stages and struggles of Leonardo's quest for truth, as well as the inhibitions of his sexual life, his
sublimated or "ideal homosexual" affection for young men to
whom he could give his own version of the maternal nourishment he had received as an infant. With these remarks, Freud
offered his first theoretical elaboration of the concept of narcissism, and a gesture toward the reflections on ego and sexual
ideals he made in the 1914 essay "On Narcissism."

In the discussion of Leonardo's sublimations, Freud also ges-
tured toward another concept that was to be crucial for his later
work: Eros, the life instinct. Both of these theoretical elaborations spoke to the limits Freud set around his study of Leonardo:
"Instincts [*Triebe*] and their transformations are at the limit of
what is discernible by psycho-analysis," he wrote. Specifically:
"two characteristics of Leonardo . . . are inexplicable by the
efforts of psycho-analysis: his quite special tendency towards
instinctual repressions, and his extraordinary capacity for sub-
limating the primitive instincts" (p. 136). The concept of narcissism and the late dual instinct theory, the theory of Eros and
the death instinct, were directed at these borders. And a third
reverberation of the Leonardo essay, Freud's discussion of the

origin of religion in *Totem and Taboo* (1913), with its theory of primal patricide and the formation of a fraternal group, connected the specific study of Leonardo's creativity with a vast vein of cultural speculation. Freud himself said of this direction in his thought that it took him beyond his recognition (gained in self-analysis) of his own hostility toward his father and on toward analysis of his murderous wishes—a direction he did not attribute to Leonardo.

Freud's essay is an example of Kohut's second type of psychobiography: a pathography designed primarily to expand psychoanalytic knowledge or to apply existing knowledge. But this characterization certainly does not touch upon the complex motivations apparent in the essay, and it also obscures how closely related, at the level of motivation, this type of psychobiography is to one designed to illuminate personality and one designed to explore creativity.

Freud had had a long-standing interest in Leonardo. He referred to him in his correspondence with Fliess in conjunction with Fliess's speculations (interestingly enough, not mentioned in the psychopathography) about left-handedness. He noted in other correspondences that his interest was renewed by a patient who had similar character traits without similar genius (presumably, this was the Rat Man, on whose case Freud had based his 1909 study of obsessional neurosis). His decision to write the Leonardo study came as he returned from his journey to America and prepared for the March, 1910 Nuremberg conference, that is, at a moment of great confidence in the success of psychoanalysis but also a moment when attacks—personal and theoretical—came from many directions. Freud's expectations for Jung's contributions to "the cause" were still high, but edges of doubt had begun to form because of Jung's tendency to "exclude the sexual element" from psychoanalytic theory.

Leonardo had the advantage, as a comrade in independent research, of being quite beyond the fray of discussion and dissension with which Freud was contending: he was a timeless, constant partner. He also served well as an example of how creativity can be rechanneled and renewed, and inhibitions about bringing work to completion addressed with shifts from artistic to scientific work and back—that is, with different processes of sublimation. As a figure both of Freud's imagination and like it, Leonardo gave Freud the opportunity both to move beyond the recent summations of psychoanalysis that he had written—to open new paths of research—and to do so in a mode of artistic sublimation. Freud called his Leonardo study "the only pretty thing I have ever written"[3] and felt the need to defend himself, in the text against the anticipated charge that he had produced a "psychoanalytic novel" (p. 134). These roles that Leonardo seems to have served are summed up in a letter Freud wrote to Ferenczi 6 months after he finished the essay. In this letter he both acknowledged that he no longer needed to continue his self-analysis in his earlier manner and made explicit the concern with his own homosexual cathexis that is implicit generally in the Leonardo study and particularly inferable from the essay's silence over Fliess's special interest, Leonardo's left-handedness:

> You not only noticed, but also understood, that I no longer have any need to uncover my personality completely, and you correctly traced this back to the traumatic reason for it. Since Fliess's case, with the overcoming of which you recently saw me occupied, that need has been extinguished. A part of the homosexual cathexis has been withdrawn and made use of to enlarge my own ego. I have succeeded where the paranoiac fails [see Schur, 1972, p. 256].

The Leonardo study was followed, then, by the case study of Schreber's paranoid psychosis (1911)—a mode of unsuccessful sublimation of sexual curiosity (and homosexual cathexis) that Freud had not listed in the Leonardo essay.

Freud's Leonardo essay is itself an "essay" (in the original sense of the term) of sublimation: it presents the identifications and idealizations of "independent research," but also of withdrawal and redeployment of cathexis for the formation of what Freud (1914) called an ego ideal. Theoretically, the Leonardo study demonstrated, rather than discussed, a preliminary answer to Freud's implicit question about sublimation that does not

---

3. I have been unable to trace this remark, and thus cite it from Gerard Lauzun's biographical study of Freud (1965), p. 62.

exclude the sexual element: a narcissistic identification or an internalization resulting in an enhancing enlargement of the ego is the opposite of regressive relinquishment of libido and curiosity to authority—originally paternal authority. The corollary to Freud's critique of Victorian biographer's idealizations based on infantile models—father figures—is his construction of ego-enhancing idealization that is not a father figure but an androgynous figure. In other words, Freud's practice contains the theoretical implication that nonrepressive sublimation is tied to (perhaps even requires) the formation of an ego ideal incorporating—to adapt Freud's own description of Leonardo—Mother Nature and Father stripped of his inhibiting authority. Such an ideal sanctions redeployment of libido (including homosexual strivings) without repression.

Until World War II, Freud's Leonardo study was taken as the touchstone for the theory and practice of psychobiography. Later theorists found it too preoccupied with instinctual drives and childhood events, too little concerned with ego functions, too focused on intrapsychic conflict, and not enough concerned with external conflicts and historical setting. Psychobiographical practice has also moved away from study of creative individuals toward study of (in Erikson's often-cited phrase) "the great man in history." The scope of psychobiography has enlarged, case studies giving way to life studies, and its aims have become more strictly scientific and historical. But Freud's criticisms of biographical father-figure idealization have continued to be taken very seriously. His practice, his own quite different mode of what might be called androgynizing idealization, however, has been neither explored nor questioned for its theoretical or its methodological implications.

Mack (1971) observed, "Whereas before 1955, psychoanalytic biographical interest centered predominantly on artists and writers (those concerned with the inner life and its vicissitudes), since that time, the interest seems to have shifted to the study of figures who have their impact in the public sphere, or, more dramatically stated, upon history itself" (p. 151). Mack noted the theoretical reasons for this shift by citing developments within psychoanalysis, but he claimed that the main nontheoretical reason was one of "historical urgency": "We have become increasingly anxious about the men who lead us" (p. 157). This development has taken psychoanalytically informed biography-writing far from biography's traditional aims—self-reflexive adjusting and adorning of the writer's life or pedagogical warning and improving of the living. It has also, ironically, taken (male) biography-writing back to concern with father figures—in a negative key: destruction of bad father figures goes forth without Freud's insights into the ego enhancement permitted by constraining paternal authority in androgynizing idealization. To this generalization, I would like to note a great exception—Erikson's *Gandhi* (1969)—a biographical model much less imitated than his *Luther* (1958), which is no exception.

The region of psychoanalytically supported biography-writing where concern with individuals in contexts—life histories in histories—has not been disconnected from concern with the traditional aims of biography-writing or from Freud's concern with ego enhancement is a region for which there is no map—so my turn to it now will result in only a sketch.

II

Biographies of and by women hardly have a place in the Standard History, which simply records that three Englishwomen wrote biographies of their husbands in the late seventeenth century, that during the High Period of the eighteenth century no women attained prominence as biographers, that Mrs. Gaskell published her *Life of Charlotte Brontë* in 1857, and that Virginia Woolf wrote reviews of and manifestoes about biography-writing in the 1920s. The rich tradition of minor biographies written from the late eighteenth century through the decade of the "new biography" announced by Virginia Woolf is ignored—with Woolf's sanction. To date, there exists no history of women's biographies or of women in biographies, and no comment within the literature on psychobiography about studies of women. There has also been almost no comment on the most obvious historical pattern in women's biographical writing: namely, that in periods of feminist activity there have always been upsurges of interest in exemplary women's lives told biographically. This pattern is clearest in biographies of feminist writers—the late nineteenth- and early twentieth-century feminist movements each received biographies of Mary Wollstonecraft, for just one example—but it holds for biographies of women writers in general. Further, and correlatively, there has been, until very recently, no comment on the most obvious aim of women's biographies: namely, the traditional aim of moral improvement or the creating of looking glasses for the adornment and adjustment of women's lives.

In essays like "Women and Fiction" (1929) and *A Room of One's Own*, Virginia Woolf helped usher in modern critical concern for women's writing and for the conditions under which women have written. In her essays on biography-writing, in which she analyzed and praised biographies by Lytton Strachey and Harold Nicolson, she contributed to the repudiation of Victorian biographical conventions. In her critical work, however, she brought these two concerns together only to remark that women's biography had not been born. She put its possibility into the future as she contemplated the changes she hoped would come in women's educational, political, and social opportunities:

> Women's gift will be trained and strengthened. The novel will cease to be the dumping ground for personal emotions. It will become, more than at present, a work of art like any other, and its resources and limitations will be explored.
>
> From this it is a short step to the practice of the sophisticated arts, hitherto so little practiced by women—to the writing of essays and criticism, history and biography [1929, p. 84].

While she slighted the tradition of female biography—even though she had drawn on it to construct probing portraits of women writers, including Mary Wollstonecraft—Virginia Woolf did, at least, acknowledge that this tradition had always been limited by the very historical conditions that had limited both its subjects and writers. Woolf did eventually contribute a biography that was like any other of the "new biographies" written by her Bloomsbury colleagues, a study of Roger Fry. But the real fruit of her reflections was a novel she wrote in 1928 and called *Orlando: A Biography*. With this book, Woolf invented both the subject of her biography and biographical form in which a character called "the biographer" is in the text not only writing

the biography but offering a running commentary on biographical conventions. Her inspiration or model was a "real life" subject, her lover Vita Sackville-West, wife of the biographer
Harold Nicolson, whose son Nigel (1973) made of Woolf's portrait of his mother the often-quoted remark that it is "the most
charming love letter in literature" (p. 201). But Orlando is a
biographical novelty: a subject that is an impressionistic history
of English literature and biography from 1586 to 1928.

The young Orlando grows up in Elizabethan England as a
male, educated, very wealthy, close to the Court, and then progresses into adulthood as an ambassador to Constantinople.
During his ambassadorship, at the age of 30, Orlando falls into a
trance and on the seventh day of his creative slumber emerges as
a woman. After some proto-Romantic adventures among gypsy
tribespeople, the female Orlando returns to Queen Anne's England in time to hobnob with the Restoration literary luminaries;
that is, she is born again (so to speak) at the moment when
women writers emerged onto the English literary scene. Orlando's biographer reflects on what her change of costume and
gender means for Orlando's life and letters:

> The difference between the sexes is, happily, one of great pro-
> fundity. Clothes are but a symbol of something hid deep be-
> neath. It was a change in Orlando herself that dictated her
> choice of a woman's dress and of a woman's sex. And perhaps in
> this she was only expressing rather more openly than usual—
> openness indeed was the soul of her nature—something that
> happens to most people without being thus plainly expressed.
> For here again, we come to a dilemma. Different though the
> sexes are, they intermix. In every human being a vacillation
> from one sex to the other takes place, and often it is only the
> clothes that keep the male or female likeness, while underneath
> the sex is the very opposite of what is above [p. 188].

In the middle of Victoria's reign, Orlando, behaving like a
Hegelian, succumbs to the damp and chilly "spirit of the age"
and marries. Her husband, however, is as androgynous as she
and quite undominating, as he spends most of the time of their
marriage on a seafaring expedition to Cape Horn. Their son,
somehow conceived and gestated, is born in such a magical way

that Orlando feels him not at all and is completely undistracted by his presence from her usual pursuits, including her literary project, a poem called "The Oak Tree," begun in her youth and finally finished, published, and awarded a prize as King Edward reigns. Orlando has 360 rooms of her own and a fortune much in excess of the 500 pounds annually that Virginia Woolf had stipulated as the necessary sum for a female writer's independence.

Orlando may be the only female subject of a woman's biography and the only heroine in a modern English novel who transcends—albeit after fantasy fashion—the restrictions that are the thematic foci of women's writing in both genres. *Orlando* is a mock biography, a parody of the styles and conventions of the entire modern Standard History of Biography. The work is also something of a caprice or joke—and thus worth taking seriously for what it is: a way to make all too real constraints disappear, to overcome inhibitions—in life and in letters, in family context and in history. Because Orlando did not exist, it was necessary for Virginia Woolf to invent her/him.

But it is significant, I think, that Woolf's idealizing fantasy was broadly historical—as none of her previous novels had been. Her ideal androgyne could be imagined emerging as a writer only in an idealized moment. This is an exaggerated example of what might be called the female historicity complex. Unlike Freud, who could write of Leonardo as though he had lived at any time, as though he were timeless, set in a "family romance" not a period, Woolf imagined a biography that recapitulates a sociohistorical development. Orlando, like so many heroes and heroines of nineteenth-century fiction, is presented as parentless. Orlando's in-the-text biographer, like children who imagine themselves adopted or express their hostility toward their parents by replacing them with real or imagined ones of more exalted status or accomplishment, gives Orlando neither mother nor father; or, more accurately, presents him as coming from a vaguely conjured male warrior line, but without any mother to speak of. Orlando first appears not as a child, but as a youth— maternally loved by no one less than Queen Elizabeth I. He is a creature of his historical setting. And Orlando the female writer is, after nearly two centuries of inability to complete her poem, finally granted, at the end of Victoria's reign, the perfect moment to be the creature of:

> Orlando had so ordered it that she was in an extremely happy position; she needed neither fight her age nor submit to it; she was of it, yet remained herself. Now, therefore, she could write, and write she did. She wrote. She wrote. She wrote [p. 266].

For her biographer (now genderless in the text, not "he" as at the beginning of the book), Orlando is, so to speak, a literary-sexual ideal: a sexual ideal who, when loved, cures by love not just incapacity for love but incapacity for writing. She played this role for Woolf but also for "the biographer," whose biography is saved from "extinction" by Orlando's great literary outburst. The in-the-text biographer does not describe the poem called "The Oak Tree," but simply presents Orlando "thinking and imagining"—that is, neither killing like a warrior male nor loving like women are expected to do ("Love is slipping off one's petticoat and—But we all know what love is" [p. 269])—and then leaves Orlando at her desk to take a rhapsodic two-page-long nature walk while Orlando completes the poem. The form of sublimation signaled here is quite complex: Woolf fashions an ego ideal, the androgynous biographer, whose writing is redeemed by the literary-sexual ideal, the biographical subject Orlando. The redeployment of Woolf's libido (including her homosexual drives) is mediated by the biographer in the text who is allowed to assume the task of writing that does not exclude the sexual element.

Few women's biographies present so dramatically their writer's constructions of ego and sexual ideals (or lend themselves to questioning how those ideals may relate to homosexual cathexis), but the transposition of a family romance into a historical-contextual romance that is so exaggerated and so amusing in Woolf's fantasy-biography is typical of many women's biographies. In recent biographical writing the transposition takes a quite different and quite serious form. There is a great emphasis on placing subjects in their historical periods and empathetically feeling with them their fight or their submission. There is also a strong impulse to rescue women from the standard histories that neglect them, devalue or overlook their achievements as those achievements relate to the possibilities of the times. But such acts of rescue often have the motivation—for the biographers—of self-rescues, and this is what they share with Woolf's work. Thus Bell Chevigny (1983), author of a biography of Margaret Fuller, and one of the few recent biographers to have reflected in psychoanalytic terms (hers are borrowed from Melanie Klein) on her writing experience, notes:

> Whether our foremothers are famous or their histories neglected, the act of daughters writing about them is likely to be, on some level, an act of retrieval which is experienced as a rescue. When the work is most intensely experienced as rescue, the fantasy of reciprocal reparations is likely to become an underlying impulse in it. That is, in the rescue—the reparative interpretation and re-creation—of a woman who was neglected or misunderstood, we may be seeking indirectly the reparative rescue of ourselves, in the sense of coming to understand and accept ourselves better [p. 89].

The view here is of daughters rescuing mothers, but the dynamic described seems also to run in the opposite generational direction: the biographer, who re-creates the subject, has an almost parental narcissistic love for her—a love that seeks to redeem her from the historical misunderstandings and distortions in which she has been entangled, as parents may seek to fulfill their own ideals by redeeming a child from sufferings the parents once endured. Although Chevigny, like many contemporary feminists, emphasizes only relations between women, her use of the word "re-creation" implies that both parents (not just the mother) are joined or rejoined in a projected biography-ideal. But in such an androgynized biographical "position," paternal authority does not inhibit maternal rescue of the daughter-subject, or the feeling that the subject is rescuing when rescued.

The delineation of a family romance in historical terms is also apparent in recent biographical writing marked by strong disappointment in "foremothers" and compensatory androgynizing visions. Carolyn Heilbrun's *Reinventing Womanhood* (1979) is quite candid on the topic. After telling autobiographically of her disappointment in her own mother, whose lack of autonomy she pitied, and of her admiration for her father, Heilbrun criticizes women's fiction for "failure of imagination," that is, for failure to supply the kind of autonomous female figures women need as "role models."

> With remarkably few exceptions, women writers do not imagine women characters with even the autonomy they themselves achieved. . . . Woman's persistent problem has been to discover for herself an identity not limited by custom or defined by attachment to some man. Remarkably, her search for identity has been less successful within the world of fiction than outside it. [Women writers] when they wish to create an individual fulfilling more than a symbiotic role, projected the ideal of autonomy onto a male character [p. 71ff.].

Thus far, there is little disagreement between Heilbrun and Virginia Woolf, but Heilbrun goes further. Lacking suitable role models from the past, real or invented, women ought to adopt, she suggests, male role models—but critically, cautiously, and in a feminist spirit. In a series of biographical vignettes, Heilbrun offers "how not to" examples of male-identified women; these are presented as cautionary tales about the "paranoid style" with respect to feminism of male-identified women and they carry the message that paternal authority is not to be assimilated with the male models. "Reinventing womanhood" is a project for overcoming the family romance historicized; it is a consciously projected futureward idealization, "toward a new androgyny," for the writer and for succeeding generations to "live up to" and write out in fictions.

The idealizing in women's biographies takes many different forms—many more than I have suggested with the foregoing examples. But these forms have in common a conscious impulse for historical overcoming, or, to put the matter another way, for invention of ideal figures—role models, in social terms, ego ideals in psychodynamic terms—who are historically redemptive by virtue of having been redeemed from patriarchally defined feminine existences. The biographical search is close to fiction, both in the sense that it is closely related to similar searches in fiction and in the sense that it involves a type of fictionalization: the conscious impulse in ego-ideal formation creates a character (so to speak) for unconscious projections to inhabit and vivify.

To consider this fictionalization further, it would be illuminat-

ing to compare with Freud's Leonardo study a female psychoanalyst's study of a female subject—but there is not one to turn
to.[4] The culturist or historicist critique of Freudian psychoanalysis, and particularly of Freud's theorizing about female
development, was largely initiated, as is well known, by women
analysts. Freud himself had made it clear that he felt that women
analysts would be able to correct his own male theoretical bias
and particularly to explore the mother-child, preoedipal relations of both sexes. But it is interesting to note that these critics—
Karen Horney and Clara Thompson in America, for example—
did not write psychobiographically about women of creative accomplishment. Similarly, the wide-ranging attention given by
American ego psychologists and British object relations theorists
to the conditions and modalities of artistic creativity has seldom
extended to women. One might claim that psychoanalytic theory
of female development must be criticized and reformulated—
purified of its Victorian or patriarchal or phallocentric biases—
before it is applied to women of accomplishment; but this does
not explain why psychobiographical study had not been part of
such a critical reformulation, as Freud's study of Leonardo was
part of the reformulation of his early theory. I think that what is
involved here is historical restriction upon idealizing: as
Heilbrun suggested in her literary context, female ego ideals or
referents for the construction of ego ideals are missing for historical reasons—to which the phallocentrism of psychoanalysis
has contributed even while its radical critique of civilized discontents has done so much to challenge historical restrictions. Cross-
cultural anthropological studies have, thus, presented themselves to analytic writers as more illuminating than biographical
studies, for in societies not so, or not in the same ways, patriarchal as our own, other possibilities for female development
can be discovered and inherited theories—with their patriarchal
authority—more effectively criticized. "Anthropologized" fictions, like those of Monique Wittig (*Les Guérillères*), also go in this
direction.

To these kinds of reflections, which are cultural, a specifically

4. For instances of female psychoanalysts concerned with female creativity,
see Deutsch (1928) and Greenacre (1960).

psychodynamic dimension ought to be added. Freud's reflections on the formation of ego and sexual ideals and the processes of sublimation were confined to males—as his own demonstration in the Leonardo essay was. In his later work on female development (1931), Freud claimed that the reproachful hostility a female child feels toward her mother when she discovers her lack of a penis remains with her, and may combine in different ways and degrees with reproaches over prohibitions on sexual activity, insufficient feedings, or divisions of attention among siblings. This formulation has been both elaborated and revised along with the concept of the castration complex that is central to it, but this work has not extended to the relationship between a female child's attitude toward her mother and her modes of idealization or ego-ideal formation (or, in Freud's later theory, superego development). Similarly, Freud's discussions of the ways in which "infantile sexual researches" can be either repressed, converted into sexualized thinking, or—rarely—successfully sublimated into other forms of research or "pursuit of truth," and his later discussion of the relations among these ways of sublimation, narcissism, and ego-ideal formation, were developed only for males. He took it for granted that only a woman with a strong "masculinity complex" would make artistic or scientific contributions, but he did not—even given this assumption—ask what modes of sublimation would be involved or consider the capacity of female analysts not to "exclude the sexual element" from their research. Freud's proposition that freedom from or repudiation of paternal authority is the condition of independent research was also made only with regard for male development.

In feminist biographies of women, the complexity of a double burden is quite apparent—no matter what specific mode of idealization is involved: paternal authority in its historical manifestations is questioned by the writer—with regard to herself and her subject—in the process of an ego-ideal formation that is problematic precisely because of that paternal authority as it is reflected in the family romance and in social conventions. Virginia Woolf's psychically ingenious double idealization—her projection of an ego ideal in-the-text biographer who is redeemed, allowed to write, by an androgynous sexual ideal, Orlando—is both a reflection of the double burden and a means of overcoming it. Freud's androgynizing idealization was—could be—simpler, both because it was ahistorical and because he was male.

III

Focusing attention on the motivations of biographers as I have here could be interpreted as a contribution to the denigration of biography—a way of claiming that biography cannot be truthful and objective, cannot be properly historical, a way of claiming that idealizing Victorian biography really triumphed over its critics. I have tried to indicate, however, that there is a great difference between idealization as Freud criticized it in the Victorian biographers and idealization as Freud practiced it in his Leonardo essay. The difference is between repression and sublimation—in Freud's terms. In Virginia Woolf's "biography," the form of the sublimation is also keyed to the personal and historical inhibitions to be overcome, as it is in feminist biographies of the nonfictional, scholarly sort. I have tried to suggest that the sublimation process I have connected with androgynizing idealization is one that allows concern with "the sexual element" in scientific and artistic research by virtue of its critical relation to paternal authority and received ideas. Further, biography that results in the adjustment and adornment of the life— and perhaps also the theory—of the biographer has its own truth. This is not "objective" truth—but, then, what is objective truth?

Even when the methods of modern historical and psychological research are used in them, biographies are portraits of relationships. Virginia Woolf was recognizing this when she placed "the biographer" in the text of her biography—and used this figure in the text both to sabotage biographical conventions and to record and reflect Orlando's life. Freud was recognizing his relationship with Leonardo when he confessed that he had succumbed to "this great and mysterious man," and when he invoked Leonardo's sanction for a study that repudiated the biographical conventions of Freud's own time. Feminist theory and psychoanalytic theory also have in common a more general recognition: namely, that "subjectivity" cannot be eliminated from historical or scientific inquiry—an effort to do this is an effort to conform to another type of idealization, the idealization named "objectivity." Freud's distinction between repression and sublimation ought to be remembered at this methodological level as well. But that is another story.

BIBLIOGRAPHY

BINION, R. (1968). *Frau Lou.* Princeton: Princeton Univ. Press.
CHEVIGNY, B. (1983). Daughters writing. *Feminist Studies,* 9:79–100.
DEUTSCH, H. (1928). George Sand. *Imago,* 14 (also excerpted in *Psychology of Women.* New York: Grune & Stratton, 1944, 1:297ff.).
ERIKSON, E. H. (1958). *Young Man Luther.* New York: W. W. Norton.
_____ (1969). *Gandhi's Truth.* New York: W. W. Norton.
FREUD, S. (1909). Notes upon a case of obsessional neurosis. *S.E.,* 9:153–251.
_____ (1910). Leonardo da Vinci and a memory of his childhood. *S.E.,* 10:59–137.
_____ (1911). [The Case of Schreber]. *S.E.,* 12:3–80.
_____ (1913). Totem and taboo. *S.E.,* 13:1–162.
_____ (1914). On narcissism. *S.E.,* 14:67–102.
_____ (1931). Female sexuality. *S.E.,* 21:223–246.
GILMORE, W. (1976). The methodology of psychohistory. *Psychohist. Rev.,* 5:(2)4–33.
GREENACRE, P. (1960). Woman as artist. *Psychoanal. Q.,* 9:208–226.
HEILBRUN, C. (1979). *Reinventing Womanhood.* New York: W. W. Norton.
JONES, E. (1953). *The Life and Work of Sigmund Freud.* New York: Basic Books.
KOHUT, H. (1960). Beyond the bounds of the basic rule. *J. Amer. Psychoanal. Assn.,* 8:567–586.
LAUZUN, G. (1965). *Sigmund Freud.* Greenwich, Ct.: Fawcett Publications.
MACK, J. (1971). Psychoanalysis and historical biography. *J. Amer. Psychoanal. Assn.,* 19:143–179.
MALLET, D. (1740). *The Life of Francis Bacon.* London: A. Millar.
NICOLSON, N. (1972). *Portrait of A Marriage.* New York: Atheneum.
NUNBERG, H. AND FEDERN, E., ed. (1962). *Minutes of the Vienna Psychoanalytic Society, Vol. I, 1906–1908.* New York: Int. Univ. Press.
PLUTARCH (n.d.). Timoleon. *Plutarch's Lives.* New York: Modern Library.
SCHUR, M. (1972). *Freud.* New York: Int. Univ. Press.
STRACHEY, L. (1918). *Eminent Victorians.* New York: Putnam.
WOOLF, V. (1928). *Orlando.* New York: Harcourt, Brace, Jovanovich, 1956.
_____ (1929). Women and fiction. *Granite and Rainbow.* New York: Harcourt, Brace, 1958.

Index